SECOND EDITION

Statistical Methods for the Social Sciences

SECOND EDITION

Statistical Methods for the Social Sciences

Alan Agresti
Department of Statistics
University of Florida

Barbara Finlay
Department of Sociology
Texas A & M University

Dellen Publishing Company
San Francisco

Collier Macmillan Publishers
London

divisions of Macmillan, Inc.

On the cover: The cover, *Floating World*, was executed by San Francisco artist Gregg Renfrow in 1984. The work is on polymer plexiglass and measures $67\frac{1}{4}'' \times 53''$.

Chapter opening pages: The chapter opening pages present a series of drawings by Sam Richardson. The drawings refer to the wedge shape as a vehicle for surface textures and sculptural elements such as pries and ropes.

Permissions: Dellen Publishing Company
                400 Pacific Avenue
                San Francisco, California 94133

Orders: Dellen Publishing Company
           % Macmillan Publishing Company
           Front and Brown Streets
           Riverside, New Jersey 08075

Collier Macmillan Canada, Inc.

Library of Congress Cataloging-in-Publication Data

Agresti, Alan.
  Statistical methods for the social sciences.

  Includes bibliographies and index.
  1. Statistics.   2. Social sciences—Statistical
methods.   I. Finlay, Barbara.   II. Title.
QA276.12.A34   1986   519.5'024'301   85–16031

Printing   8 9   Year   1

ISBN 0-02-301120-3

To our parents

Louis J. Agresti and Marjorie H. Agresti

Grace Finlay and the memory of James Finlay, Jr.

CONTENTS

Chapter 14

Comparison of Several Groups While Controlling for a Covariate   441

Chapter 15

Models for Categorical Variables   481

Chapter 16

An Introduction to Advanced Methodology   509

Tables   525

PREFACE

This book is designed as a text for introductory courses in statistics at the undergraduate or beginning graduate level. It is intended especially for students in social science disciplines. The social science orientation determined both the choice of techniques to be discussed and the selection of examples and problems. The many examples and problems included in the book are based on research studies in sociology, political science, education, geography, anthropology, psychology, history, journalism, and speech. A small amount of elementary algebra is the only mathematical prerequisite for understanding the material presented and working the problems.

The book is suited for use in either a single-term or a two-term sequence. Chapters 1–9 form a basis for a one-term introductory course. If the instructor has only one term and wishes to go further than Chapter 9 or wishes to cover some material in greater depth, some sections could easily be omitted without disturbing the continuity of presentation. We suggest, for example, the following sections for possible omission: 6.5, 6.7, 7.3, 7.4, 8.3–8.5, 9.4, and 9.5. Also, Chapters 7–9 and Sections 13.1–13.2 are self-contained, and the instructor could move directly into any of these after covering the fundamentals in Chapters 1–6. Four possible paths for a one-term course are as follows:

1. Chapters 1–9 (possibly omitting sections noted above): Standard cross-section of methods, including basic descriptive and inferential statistics, two-sample procedures, categorical data, and linear regression

2. Chapters 1–6, 9–12: Emphasis on bivariate and multiple regression

3. Chapters 1–7, 13: Emphasis on group comparisons and analysis of variance

4. Chapters 1–8, 10, 15: Emphasis on nonparametrics and categorical data

Chapters 10–16 are primarily concerned with regression modeling, and they could be used as the basis of a second course. These chapters can also be naturally linked to an introduction to a computer package such as SPSS^X, the SAS System, BMDP, or OSIRIS, using data sets and printouts provided in the text.

This edition contains some changes and additions in content, compared to the first edition. The technical level has been lowered somewhat in the first nine chapters, to make the book more easily accessible to undergraduate students. The chapters on categorical data have been reorganized, with a separate chapter given to the important concepts of multivariate relationships and the use of statistical control. A new chapter (15) has been added on advanced methods for categorical data, with emphasis on logistic regression and loglinear models—methods that have recently become very popular in social science research. Many homework problems have been added to each chapter, with particular emphasis on elementary problems.

The book is organized first by type of procedure (e.g., comparing two groups in Chapter 7, bivariate association in Chapters 8–9). For each type of procedure, the sections and chapters are also classified according to the levels of measurement of the variables analyzed. Throughout the book, we have attempted to provide under-standing through intuition and example, rather than through mathematical deri-vations. We believe it is of primary importance that the student develop an understanding of the purposes of the various procedures and their interpretations. We feel that this is best accomplished by exposure to realistic but simple examples and to numerous homework problems. Thus, many problems appear at the end of each chapter.

In view of the increasing reliance of users of statistics on sophisticated pocket calculators, home computers, and computer software packages, we have omitted many traditional shortcut computational formulas and formulas for coded and grouped data. In later chapters, computationally complex procedures such as multi-ple regression and analysis of variance are taught by explaining how to interpret output from a computer package program. Since it is unlikely that students will ever do such analyses by hand, the matrix-based formulas for obtaining parameter esti-mates, sums of squares, and standard errors have been omitted from this book.

Unlike many other statistics textbooks, we have integrated the presentation of descriptive and inferential methods from a very early point. We believe that artificially dividing these topics into separate presentations leads to confusion for many stu-dents. Hence, we present the foundations of inference early in the text (Chapters 5 and 6). In later chapters, we present new descriptive measures together with the corresponding inferential procedures so that the student becomes familiar with a unified process of describing and making inferences for a wide variety of problems.

Some material appears in the text in end-of-chapter Notes or in paragraphs or subsections marked by asterisks. This material is optional, being of lesser impor-tance to beginning students, although it often provides a broader coverage of topics for the interested student. Likewise, nearly every chapter contains a number of optional problems identified by asterisks. These problems either refer to the optional text material, introduce additional material related to the chapter, or pose questions of a more difficult or theoretical nature than the unstarred ones.

Finally, we have not attempted to provide a catalog of every technique for every situation. This text is meant to be primarily a teaching tool, not an encyclopedic cookbook. We do feel that we have covered the most important procedures for social science research, however, and we have included some methods that are not usually described in introductory statistics books, which are useful to social scien-tists, for example:

1. Procedures that are more powerful than chi-square when categories in a cross-classification table are ordered
2. Controlling for variables, and testing for causal relationships
3. Models for nonlinear relationships and for statistical interaction
4. Analysis of variance and covariance using dummy variables
5. Loglinear and logit models for categorical data
6. Introductions to path analysis, factor analysis, and LISREL

We hope that the combination of our respective fields of expertise has led to a book that is statistically sound as well as relevant to social science problems. We believe that the student who works through this book successfully will have acquired a good foundation in statistical methodology.

Acknowledgments

We are grateful to the Literary Executor of the late Sir Ronald A. Fisher, F.R.S., to Dr. Frank Yates, F.R.S., and to Longman Group Ltd., London, for permission to reprint Tables IV and V from their book *Statistical Tables for Biological, Agricultural and Medical Research*, 6th ed., 1974.

Many people who read the first edition or earlier versions of this manuscript made suggestions that led to improvements. We would like to give special thanks to Susan Reiland, Maureen Hallinan, Shirley Scritchfield, Sonja Wright, and Douglas Zahn for their help with the first edition, and Jeff Witmer, E. Jacquelin Dietz, Dorothy K. Davidson, and Mary Sue Younger for their comments that helped in the preparation of the second edition. Other individuals who provided helpful advice include John Henretta, Michael Radelet, and Andrew Rosalsky.

Our gratitude extends to many other individuals who helped this book to reach fruition. Our publisher, Don Dellen, was a source of much encouragement and support, and we especially appreciate the free rein he gave us in decisions about the book content and style. Excellent editorial services were provided by Susan Reiland. Brenda Wise, Ruth Byrne, and Edna Larrick worked patiently and conscientiously in typing the manuscript. Finally, we would like to give special thanks to Gerald Leslie and William Mendenhall, who, as former chairmen of the Departments of Sociology and Statistics, respectively, are responsible for the cooperation between these departments at the University of Florida which led to the courses from which this textbook was developed.

SECOND EDITION

Statistical Methods for the Social Sciences

PART I

INTRODUCTION TO UNIVARIATE STATISTICAL ANALYSIS

CHAPTER 1

Introduction

Contents

1.1 Introduction to Statistical Methodology

Within the past 20 to 30 years, almost all social science disciplines have seen a rapid increase in the use of statistics. The increase is evident in the changes in the content of articles published in major journals, in the styles of textbooks, and in the increasingly common requirement of academic departments that their majors take courses in statistics. A quick glance through recent issues of *American Political Science Review*, *American Sociological Review*, *Social Forces*, or other leading social science journals is enough to convince one of the central place of statistics in social science research. Job advertisements for social scientists commonly list a knowledge of statistics as an important work tool. Almost any student preparing for a career as a social scientist must become familiar with basic statistical methodology.

The study of statistics is also useful to those who do not expect to become professional social scientists. In fact, statistics is an important part of a general education for living in today's world. Almost daily we are confronted with advertising, news reporting, political campaigning, and other communications containing statistical arguments. The study of statistics helps us to understand and evaluate these arguments.

Science and Observation

Much of science involves collecting and organizing information about the world around us. Although different sciences have different subject matters and therefore different methods, all sciences engage in some form of information-gathering through observation. The social sciences use a wide variety of information-gathering techniques. Among these are questionnaire surveys, telephone surveys, content analysis of literary materials, planned experiments, and direct observation of behavior in natural settings. In addition, social scientists often utilize information already observed and recorded for other purposes, such as police records, census materials, and hospital files. The information gathered through such processes is collectively called *data*. These data consist of measurements taken on the various characteristics being observed. The measurements are obtained by classifying observations according to specific rules. Thus, we can measure sex by classifying individuals according to gender; we can measure age by classifying people according to the number of years since birth; and we can measure the populations of cities by obtaining census counts for their numbers of residents.

What Is Statistics?

The general field of statistics involves methods for (a) designing and carrying out research studies; (b) describing collected data; and (c) making decisions, predictions, or inferences about phenomena represented by the data. In this book, we deal primarily with the latter two aspects. This is not to imply that the other aspects of the research process are unimportant. If a study is poorly designed or if the data are improperly collected or recorded, then the conclusions may be worthless or misleading, no matter how good a statistical analysis is performed. Methods for designing and carrying out research studies are covered in detail in textbooks on research methods (e.g., Bailey, 1982).

The descriptive aspect of statistics allows researchers to summarize large quantities of data using measures that are easily understood by an observer. It would always be possible, of course, simply to present a long list of measurements for each characteristic being observed. In a study of ages at first marriage, for example, we might just present the reader with a listing of the ages of all persons marrying for the first time within the past year in a particular county. This kind of detail, however, is not easy to assess—the reader simply gets bogged down in numbers. Instead of presenting *all* observations, we could use one of several statistical measures that would summarize the *typical* age at marriage in the collection of data. This would be much more meaningful to most people than the complete listing.

The other aspect of statistics that we will study is making decisions or inferences about characteristics by interpreting data patterns. This process often takes the form of noting whether an *expected* or *predicted* pattern of data values is actually found in the observations. We might expect, for example, that Catholics would be more likely to believe in life after death than would Unitarians. In order to decide whether this expectation is true, we might survey a number of Catholics and Unitarians, questioning them about their views concerning an afterlife. We could then use the statistical methodology described in this textbook to make comparisons between the two groups and to make a decision about whether the prediction is true for Catholics and Unitarians in general. In addition, we could estimate how great the difference is between the beliefs of the two groups.

Inherent in both the descriptive and decision-making aspects of statistics is the development of explanations for complex social processes. Much of social science research deals with sorting out relationships among such factors as political party preference, income, degree of education, religion, race, sex, and so forth. *Statistical models*, mathematical representations of such relationships, provide a mechanism for doing so. We shall see that many relatively simple statistical procedures are based on the assumption of a particular model for a real-world situation.

1.2 Description and Inference

A statistical procedure is usually classified as *descriptive* or *inferential*. In order to see the distinction between these purposes, it is necessary to understand the terms *population* and *sample*.

Population and Sample

The *population* is the total set of individual objects or persons of interest in a study.

A *sample* is a subset of the population that is actually observed.

Although research is directed toward learning about populations, it is often necessary to study only samples from those populations. For example, the Gallup and

Harris polling organizations typically select samples of about 1,000–1,500 Americans to get information about political and social beliefs and voting preferences of the population of all Americans. Similarly, the Environmental Protection Agency samples automobiles of various kinds to obtain data on gasoline mileage performance, although the population of interest to them is the collection of all such automobiles. Characteristics of such populations can usually be determined quite well by selecting samples that are small relative to the size of the population, if proper sampling schemes are used.

Descriptive Statistics

Descriptive statistical methods consist of graphical and numerical techniques for summarizing the information in a collection of data.

Descriptive statistics are used to summarize certain characteristics of a sample. We might want to describe the typical age of a group of individuals by computing the *average* age of the group, for example. Graphs, tables, and descriptive numbers such as averages and percentages are easier to comprehend and interpret than long listings of data. In effect, the main purpose of descriptive statistical methods is to reduce the whole collection of data to simpler and more understandable terms without distorting or losing much of the available information. Descriptive statistics can be defined for a sample, and corresponding measures can be defined for the entire population.

Inferential Statistics

Inferential statistical methods consist of procedures for making generalizations about characteristics of a population, based on information contained in a sample taken from that population.

Example 1.1 illustrates a situation in which an inferential statistical method would be useful.

Example 1.1   A representative in a state legislature must decide whether to vote for or against ratification of a proposed constitutional amendment that bans abortions except when the mother's life is in danger. After hearing many arguments pro and con, he decides to vote for it if he can be convinced that a majority of his voting-age constituents support it. Thus, the population of interest to him is the collection of some 100,000 voting-age residents in his district. Since it is impossible to discuss the issue with everyone, his staff samples 200 residents and records their opinions on the ratification of the amendment. Based on the results of this poll, he must make an *inference* about whether a majority of the entire population of his constituents favors ratification of the amendment.

Suppose that the data are obtained for the sample of 200 constituents and that 40% indicate support for the passage of the amendment. Using this information, the legislator could use an inferential statistical procedure to help him make some conclusion about the percentage of the *entire population* who favor the amendment. He might then decide between the following conclusions:

1. A majority of his entire constituency favors the amendment.
2. A minority favors the amendment.
3. There is insufficient evidence to make a prediction without considerable risk of being incorrect. ■

Parameters and
Statistics

Parameters and Statistics

The characteristics of the population about which we make inferences using the sample data are called *parameters*. The corresponding characteristics of the sample data, upon which we base our inferences about the parameters, are called *statistics*.

To illustrate, in Example 1.1, the legislator must make a decision about the percentage of his 100,000 constituents who support the constitutional amendment banning abortion—namely, whether it exceeds 50%. The parameter of interest is the true, but unknown, population percentage in favor of the amendment. The inference about this parameter is based on a statistic—the percentage of the 200 constituents in the *sample* who favor the amendment. Once the sample is obtained, the sample statistic is known—40% in this case. Since this number *describes* a particular characteristic of the sample, it is an example of a descriptive statistic. The parameter about which the inference is made, on the other hand, is unknown. In summary, known sample statistics are used in making inferences about unknown population parameters.

It is the parameters of the population that are of primary concern in most studies, not the statistics calculated from just the particular sample selected. The sample and the statistics describing it are important only insofar as they provide information about the unknown parameters of interest. A very important aspect of statistical inference involves obtaining a measure of the accuracy of the sample statistic that is used to *estimate* or *predict* the value of a population parameter. The legislator needs an indication of how sure he can be about whether a majority of his constituents favor passage of the amendment. An inferential statistical method gives him a way to predict how close the *sample* value of 40% is likely to be to the true (unknown) percentage of the *population* of constituents favoring the amendment.

When an entire population is studied, there is no need to use inferential statistical methods, since the parameters of interest in that population can be exactly calculated. For example, many characteristics (e.g., age and home ownership) are observed for virtually all Americans during census years. When the population of interest is small, as in a study of the voting records of members of the U.S. Senate on bills concerning defense appropriations, we would probably want to study the records of the entire population instead of only a sample. In most social science research, however, it is impossible to study the entire population due to practical considerations. We shall observe that it is usually unnecessary to do so, even if it is theoretically possible, since very good precision can be obtained by making inferences about population characteristics from relatively small samples (e.g., 1,500 individuals out of the entire American populace).

Defining Populations Whenever inferential statistical procedures are used, it is important to specify clearly the population to which the inferences apply. In some cases, there is a clearly defined set of individuals or objects that constitutes the population. In Example 1.1, it was the collection of voting-age residents of the representative's district. Often, however, the population to which the generalizations refer is a *conceptual* one. For example, a team of researchers may decide to test a new drug designed to relieve severe depression. They wish to use the results for a sample of patients suffering from depression to make inferences about the conceptual population of all individuals who might suffer depressive symptoms now or sometime in the future. Or, a consumer organization may evaluate a new model of an automobile by observing the average number of breakdowns in ten sample autos during a standardized 5,000-mile drive. Inferences would then relate the performance on this drive to the conceptual population of all autos of this model that could be manufactured.

A caution is due here. The researcher would often like to make generalizations to a broader population than the one to which the sample results can be statistically extended. A psychologist may conduct an experiment using a sample of students in an introductory psychology course. Statistical inference may be used to generalize the sample results to the population of all the students in the class. For the research to be of wider interest, however, the psychologist might claim that the conclusions can be generalized to *all* college students, to *all* young adults, or even to a more heterogeneous group. These generalizations may well be wrong, since it is not known whether the sample really represents those populations. Most likely, it does not. The reader should be careful to ascertain the scope of the conclusions that are made in research articles, political and government pronouncements, advertisements, and the mass media. The basis for the conclusions should be evaluated critically by noting the characteristics of the actual sample upon which the inferences are built. Some desirable and undesirable types of samples will be discussed in the next chapter.

Over the last couple of decades, social scientists have increasingly recognized the power of inferential statistical methods. Hence, a discussion of statistical inference occupies a large portion of this textbook. The basic inferential procedures of estimation and hypothesis testing are explained in Chapters 5 and 6. In the remaining chapters, whenever a new sample descriptive statistic is introduced, we show how these basic inferential procedures may be used for making conclusions about the corresponding population parameter.

1.3
The Role of
Computers in
Statistics

Computer Program
Packages

Within the past decade, the computer industry has expanded very rapidly, both in the capacity and efficiency of its machines and in its accessibility to persons who are not technically trained. An important aspect of this expansion has been the development of *canned* or *packaged* programs. These packages consist of sets of computer programs for a variety of techniques. The programs are stored in the memory of the computer, and a user can *call* any one of them by supplying a few relatively simple commands, according to the requirements of the particular package. Thus, a person who has no knowledge of programming languages such as FORTRAN, COBOL, PL-1, or Basic, can do very complex computer analyses by using the packaged programs.

Many of these packages are primarily statistical in nature. They contain a wide variety of data-editing capabilities and statistical procedures, any of which can be applied to the user's data by a few standard commands. Some of the commonly used packages on university campuses are the Statistical Package for the Social Sciences (SPSS and SPSS^X), the SAS System,* OSIRIS, Minitab, and Biomedical Computer Programs (BMDP). These packages have made many statistical procedures much more feasible for research purposes, and have greatly reduced the time necessary to perform the procedures. In addition, the accuracy of such computations is greatly improved, since calculations done by hand often result in mistakes or crude answers, especially when the number of observations is large. With the availability of computers and packaged programs, the statistical analysis of relatively large data sets is technically as easy as that of small ones, which is desirable since larger samples usually provide more information than smaller samples.

Later in this book, some statistical procedures will be presented by using examples of the output of such packaged programs. In Chapters 9–16 especially, our presentation places very little emphasis on hand calculation of the statistical measures. The reason for this is that these procedures would almost always be done by computer in real situations, since the amount of hand computation time would be prohibitive. One purpose of this textbook is to teach the student what to look for in a computer printout and how to interpret the information obtained. However, knowledge of computer programming is not necessary for reading these chapters.

Uses and Misuses

A word of caution should be inserted at this point. The easy accessibility of very complex and powerful statistical procedures by means of packaged programs and even hand calculators has its dangers as well as its benefits. It is quite simple, for example, for the user to apply inappropriate procedures to the data. A computer will perform the analysis requested whether or not the assumptions required for its use are satisfied. Thus, many incorrect analyses have been made by researchers because insufficient time was taken to understand the nature of a statistical procedure, the assumptions underlying its use, or its application to the specific problem. It is of utmost importance to understand a statistical procedure before applying it to col-

*SAS is the registered trademark of SAS Institute, Inc., Cary, North Carolina, U.S.A.

lected data. Even when we read about similar research projects that used the same type of analysis, we should not assume that they were correct without understanding the reasons. It may well be that another procedure is more appropriate for the purpose at hand.

Just knowing how to run a statistical package program, then, does not imply that a proper analysis will be done. A good background in statistics is necessary in order to know which packaged program to run, which options to choose in that program, and how to make valid conclusions based on the program's output. The main purpose of this text is to help provide such a background. Nevertheless, consulting a trained statistician is often a good way to clarify one's own ideas as well as to get advice about the most appropriate methods to use for the problem at hand.

Summary

The discipline of statistics includes methods for designing research projects, collecting and organizing data, and analyzing and interpreting collections of data. Statistical procedures are often applied to measurements made on a *sample* selected from the *population* of interest. These procedures include *descriptive methods* for summarizing particular aspects of the sample and population. Samples are described by *statistics*, while populations are described by *parameters*. Statistical procedures also include *inferential methods* for making decisions or predictions about the population parameters using the sample statistics. Many of the complex statistical procedures that are important in the social sciences can be easily applied using computer program packages.

Problems

1. Distinguish between *description* and *inference* as two purposes for using statistical methods.

2. Give an example of a situation in which inferential statistical methods would not be needed.

3.
a. Distinguish between a *statistic* and a *parameter*.
b. In an article in a weekly news magazine, it is reported that 60% of graduating college seniors have tried marijuana. Would you expect this value to be a statistic or a parameter? Why?

4. The student government at the University of Wisconsin decides to conduct a study about alcohol abuse among students. One hundred of the 40,000 students are sampled and asked to complete a questionnaire. One of the questions asked is "On how many days in the past week did you consume at least one alcoholic drink?"
a. Describe the population of interest.
b. For the 40,000 students, suppose that one parameter of interest is the most common response to the question given above. What sample statistic could be used to make an inference about this parameter?

5. A sociologist is interested in estimating the average age at marriage for women in New England in the early eighteenth century. She finds within her state archives reasonably complete marriage records for a large Puritan village for the years 1700–1730. She then takes a sample of those marriage records, noting the age of the bride for each. The average age of the brides in the sample is computed to be 24.1 years. The sociologist then estimates the average age at marriage for the population to be between 23.5 and 24.7 years, based on a statistical procedure we will study in Chapter 5.

a. What is the population to which this generalization can be made?
b. What part of this example is descriptive?
c. What part of this example is inferential?
d. What can the researcher say about marriage ages in New England during the years studied?

6. On an election night broadcast, a television network reports that 53% of the first 1,000 votes cast in Massachusetts in the presidential contest are for the Democratic candidate.

a. Describe the population of interest.
b. About what population parameter do we wish to make an inference?
c. What sample statistic could be used in making this inference?
d. Does the sample statistic in part **c** necessarily need to be close in value to the population parameter in part **b**? Why?

7. Look at a few recent issues of a major journal in your field, such as *American Sociological Review*, *American Political Science Review*, or the *Annals of the American Association of Geographers*. What proportion of the articles use statistics? Find some examples of both descriptive and inferential statistics.

8. Find out what computer packages are available on your campus. Which are commonly used in social science research?

Bibliography   Bailey, D. (1982). *Methods of Social Research*, 2nd ed. New York: The Free Press.
Fisher, R. A. (1970). *Statistical Methods for Research Workers*, 14th ed. New York: Hafner.

CHAPTER 2

The Measurement Process

Contents

The ultimate goals of social science research are to understand, explain, and make predictions about social phenomena. We have seen in Chapter 1 that, for inferential purposes, samples are selected from populations. So in order to make inferences, we must decide which members of the population to sample. In addition, our ideas about these phenomena must be converted into actual data through measurement. The process of *operationalizing* (developing ways to measure) abstract concepts such as prejudice, love, intelligence, and status is one of the most difficult problems of social research. This process is not, strictly speaking, statistical in nature, but the problems related to finding valid and reliable measures of concepts have important consequences for the statistical analysis of the data obtained. Invalid or unreliable data-gathering instruments render the statistical manipulations of the data meaningless. In addition, the way in which observations are measured has important consequences for the kinds of statistical procedures that may be appropriately applied.

The first section of this chapter deals with some of the important statistical aspects of measurement. In the second and third sections, we consider some of the principal methods for selecting the sample upon which the measurements are to be taken.

2.1 Variables and Their Measurement

The characteristics that are measured for each of the members of a sample are usually referred to as *variables*.

Variables

Variable
A *variable* is a characteristic that can take on more than one value among members of a sample or population.

At any time, each member of a population or sample has one particular value on a variable, but different members may possess different values. Examples of commonly used variables in social research are sex (with values male and female); age at last birthday (with values 0, 1, 2, 3, and so on); religious affiliation (Baptist, Methodist, Roman Catholic, Unitarian, and so forth); social status (upper class, middle class, and lower class); and yearly income (perhaps measured in units of thousands of dollars).

In some studies, statistical methods are used for analyzing data on a single variable. These analyses are called *univariate*, since they involve only one variable at a time. We might wish, for example, to describe the murder rates in U.S. cities or the yearly incomes of migrant workers in California. Most social science investigations utilize statistical methods that enable us to study simultaneously a number of variables. Studies that deal with the relationship of two variables are called *bivariate*, while those focusing on more than two are called *multivariate* analyses. Bivariate and multivariate procedures can be used, for example, to study the effect on city murder rates of such variables as the size of the police force, the percentage of unemployed residents, the average family income, the inequality of income among residents, the degree of racial heterogeneity, and the conviction rate in murder trials. The statistical analysis would enable us to answer such questions as "To what extent is unemployment related to the murder rate?" and "Do cities with high conviction rates in murder trials tend to have relatively low murder rates?" We will study the fundamental statistical procedures for univariate analyses in Chapters 3–6, for bivariate analyses in Chapters 7–9, and for multivariate analyses in Chapters 10–16.

The particular statistical technique that is appropriate for analyzing a set of variables depends on the way in which those variables are measured. In the remainder of this section, we introduce two schemes for classifying variables. The first uses a set of levels of measurement relating to the nature of the possible values for the variable. The second scheme refers to the number of different possible values that the variable can assume.

Levels of Measurement

We will refer to three distinct *levels of measurement*; these differ in the extent to which observations can be compared. From lowest to highest in the degree to which comparisons can be made, the levels are *nominal*, *ordinal*, and *interval*.

A *nominal* scale of measurement is a set of categories that vary in some quality but not in magnitude. Each observation can be classified into one and only one of the categories, which often represent different types of some phenomenon. For example, marriage form would be classified on a nominal scale, with levels such as monogamy, polygyny, and polyandry. State of residence would have the levels Alabama, Alaska, and so on. Other common variables measured with nominal scales are religious affiliation, sex, race, occupation, method of teaching, and political party preference. Variables measured on nominal scales are referred to as *nominal variables*. Nominal variables are often called *qualitative*, since two distinct values for such a variable differ in quality, not in quantity. Although the different categories of nominal scales are often referred to as the *levels* of the scale, no level can be interpreted as being greater than, higher than, or smaller than any other level. Names or labels can be used to identify the categories of a nominal variable, but those names do not represent different magnitudes of the variable.

When the possible values of a variable can be compared in magnitude, with different values representing different quantities, the variable is called *quantitative*. Each possible value of a quantitative variable is *greater than* or *less than* any other possible value. The quantitative variables that are the most crude in measurement level are measured on an *ordinal* scale, and are called *ordinal variables*. There is a natural ordering of the values on an ordinal scale, but the distances between the values do not have a precise numerical meaning. Some ordinal scales give each observation a separate rank (first, second, third, and so on). Examples would be rank in high school graduating class, place in a race, or rank of one's score on an examination. For each of these variables, we can compare two observations by indicating which is greater (higher in rank) on the variable.

More often in social science research, ordinal scales consist of a collection of naturally ordered categories. To illustrate, social class may be classified into upper, middle, and lower; political philosophy may be measured as liberal, moderate, or conservative; attitudes toward busing to achieve racial integration in schools may be classified as very favorable, favorable, neutral, unfavorable, or very unfavorable.

These types of variables are referred to as **ordinal categorical**. For all ordinal measured variables, there is a clear ordering of the categories or observations, but the absolute distances between them are unknown. For example, we can conclude that a person categorized as moderate is *more* liberal than a person categorized as conservative, but we cannot give a numerical value for *how much more* liberal that person is.

Interval scales, in addition to incorporating orderings, have the property that there is a specific numerical distance between each pair of levels.* Hence, we can compare values not only in terms of which is *larger* or *older* (for example), but also in terms of *how much larger* or *how much older*. In interval scales, the distances between all adjacent levels are equal.

Examples of interval variables are the age of an individual, the birth rate of a nation, the population size of a city, the number of years of education one has completed, and the amount of federal income tax one has paid during the past year. In each case, we can compare two values by identifying the following properties:

1. Whether they are different (the nominal property)
2. Which one possesses the greater magnitude (the ordinal property)
3. The distance between them (the interval property)

For example, we can say that a 60-year-old individual has a *different* age than a 20-year-old individual (nominally, they are labeled differently according to age); that one is *older* (an ordinal comparison); and that one is *40 years older* (an interval comparison).

Table 2.1 summarizes the types of comparisons that can be made for the three levels of measurement. It is important to understand the distinctions among them, because each level has a set of statistical methods that are most appropriate for that level.

Table 2.1 Ways of Comparing Observations by Measurement Level of the Variable

	MEASUREMENT LEVEL	WAYS OF COMPARING TWO OBSERVATIONS ON THE VARIABLE	EXAMPLE
QUANTITATIVE	Interval	Are they different? Which is larger? How much larger?	Age
	Ordinal	Are they different? Which is larger?	Social class
QUALITATIVE	Nominal	Are they different?	Religious affiliation

*Those interval scales for which it is also possible to compare values using ratios are called *ratio scales*. In reality, nearly all social science variables that can be measured on an interval scale can also be measured on a ratio scale. In addition, there are few statistical procedures that are designed for ratio variables but not for interval variables. Thus, we make no distinction between the two in this text, and we use the terminology *interval variable* to refer to a variable measurable on *at least* an interval scale, i.e., on an interval or ratio scale.

Statistical Procedures and Levels of Measurement

The measurement levels may be viewed as forming a hierarchy. From the least to the most quantitative, they can be ordered as nominal, ordinal, and interval. It is always possible to move downward in the hierarchy with respect to a specific measurement. In other words, any variable measured at the interval level may be treated as if it were ordinal or nominal, and an ordinal variable may be treated as a nominal variable. For example, age is an interval variable. Since the various ages are also ordered, age could be treated as an ordinal variable, using ordered categories such as under 20, 21–35, 36–55, and over 55. We could even treat it as a nominal variable, with levels such as working age and nonworking age.

This fact is important because it implies that statistical procedures designed for variables measured at a certain level can also be used for variables measured at a higher level. A statistical procedure developed for ordinal variables, for example, can be used with interval variables as well, by using just the order characteristics of the numerical measurements. Normally, we would want to apply the statistical technique specifically appropriate for the actual scale of measurement (e.g., interval level techniques for interval variables), since we then utilize the characteristics of the data to the fullest. However, we shall see that some techniques appropriate for interval level data also require other assumptions about those variables. Sometimes, techniques developed for ordinal level data are used with interval variables because they require fewer and less stringent assumptions.

It is not possible to move in the other direction in the measurement hierarchy. If a variable is measured only on a nominal scale, it is not possible to treat it on the ordinal level, since there is no natural ordering of the categories. Hence, it is not correct to apply statistical procedures based on ordinal level measurement to variables measured on nominal scales; similarly, it is not strictly appropriate to apply statistical procedures designed for interval level measurement to variables measured on ordinal or nominal scales. In general, it is important to try to measure variables at as high a level as possible, because more powerful statistical techniques can be used with higher-level variables.

One should be aware that the various levels of measurement refer to the way in which the researcher conceptualizes and measures social phenomena and not to the phenomena themselves. *Place of residence* may be used to indicate the geographic place name of one's residence (nominal), the distance of that residence from a point on the globe (interval), the size of one's community (interval or ordinal), or other kinds of sociological variables.

Discrete and Continuous Variables

Another way in which quantitative variables are classified has to do with the number of possible values that the variables can theoretically assume.

Discrete and Continuous Variables

A variable is *discrete* if it can take on an enumerable set of values, and *continuous* if it can take on a continuum of possible values.

This classification is also used in some situations to determine which statistical method is most appropriate.

Examples of discrete variables are the number of children in a family, the population size of a city, yearly income (in dollars, say), and the number of visits to a physician in a year. Any variable that can be phrased as "the number of . . . " is discrete, since the possible values {0, 1, 2, 3, 4, . . . } for the variable can be enumerated. Examples of continuous variables are height, weight, age, the amount of time it takes to read a passage of a book, and the amount of electricity used in a month. It is impossible to enumerate or to give a rule for counting all the distinct potential values of a continuous variable. The amount of time needed to read a book, for example, could take on the value 8.6294473 . . . hours.

With discrete variables, we cannot subdivide the basic unit of measurement. For example, 2.5 is not a possible value for the number of children in a family. On the other hand, a collection of values for a continuous variable can always be refined; that is, between any two possible values, there is always another possible value. For example, an individual does not age in discrete jumps. Between 20 and 21 years of age, there is 20.5 years (among other values); between 20.5 and 21, there is 20.7. At some well-defined point during the year in which a person ages from 20 to 21, that person is 20.3275 years old, and similarly for every other real number between 20 and 21. There is a continuous, infinite collection of age values between 20 and 21 alone.

The distinction between discrete and continuous variables is often somewhat blurry in practice, because of the way variables are actually measured. Since most continuous variables must be rounded when measured, we often treat continuous variables as though they are discrete. We usually say that an individual is 20 years old whenever that person's age is somewhere between 20 and 21. Other variables of this type are prejudice, intelligence, anomie, achievement motivation, and other internalized attitudes or orientations toward some object. Such variables are assumed to vary continuously, but our measurements of them describe, at best, only crudely defined sections of the underlying continuous distributions. Thus, a scale of prejudice may vary in discrete units from 0 to 20, but each discrete value is assumed to include all the values within a certain continuous range of the degree of prejudice.

On the other hand, some variables, though discrete, may take on a very large number of different values. In measuring annual family income, the potential values might be $0.00, $0.01, $0.02, $0.03, . . . , up to some reasonable upper bound ($10 million, say). Statistical methods for continuous variables are often simpler to apply than the corresponding methods for discrete variables. Thus, we shall often find it useful to treat a discrete variable that may take on many different values as if it were continuous. For example, we shall treat variables such as income and college entrance examination score as continuous variables. In summary, we believe that the discrete–continuous classification is less important than the nominal–ordinal–interval measurement scale classification in affecting the choice of statistical analysis.

2.2
Types of
Sampling
Procedures

Since inferential statistics involves making conclusions about population parameters from sample statistics, the quality of the inferences depends crucially on how well the sample represents the population. In this section, we briefly summarize some sampling procedures that tend to have good statistical properties. The remainder of the text is then concerned with methods for analyzing the data obtained.

Random Sampling

The formulas presented in this book for inferential statistical procedures are based on the assumption that the sample was obtained by *simple random sampling*.

Simple Random Sample

A *simple random sample* of n members of a population is one in which each possible sample of size n has the same chance of being selected.

In this definition, n denotes the sample size being considered. To illustrate the notion of simple random sampling, suppose that a survey interviewer needs to administer a questionnaire to one randomly selected adult member of each of several separate households. If a particular household contains four adults (say, mother, father, aunt, and uncle, identified as M, F, A, and U, respectively), then a random sample of n = 1 of the adults is one in which each of the four is equally likely to be interviewed. The selection might be obtained, for example, by placing the four names on four identical ballots and selecting one blindly from a hat. A random sample of n = 2 of the adults would be one in which each of the possible samples of size 2 is equally likely to be selected. There are six such potential samples: (M, F), (M, A), (M, U), (F, A), (F, U), and (A, U). To obtain a random sample of size 2, we could blindly select two of the ballots from the hat.

Depending on the type of population considered, the members of a sample could be individuals, families, schools, houses, cities, state legislatures, records of reported crimes, books listed in the card catalog, and so on. In practical applications, random samples are usually chosen *without replacement*, meaning that at each selection, each member of the population *yet unchosen* is equally likely to be selected. In other words, each member appears at most once in a particular random sample.

We need a list of all the members in the population in order to select a random sample. This list is sometimes referred to as the *sampling frame*. The most common method for selecting a random sample from a population involves the use of a *random number table* to ensure for each member an equal chance of being chosen at each step.

Random Number Table

A *random number table* is a table containing a sequence of numbers that is generated according to a scheme whereby each digit is equally likely to be any of the integers 0, 1, 2, . . . , 9.

Table 2.2 is a section of a random number table. Now, suppose that we wanted to select a random sample of size *n* from a population of size *N*. Using a random number table, we would proceed as follows:

1. Assign the numbers 1 to *N* to the members in the sampling frame.
2. Choose numbers from the random number table until *n* distinct numbers between 1 and *N* are obtained.
3. Include in the sample the members with assigned numbers corresponding to the random numbers selected.

Suppose, for example, that we wished to choose a random sample of *n* = 100 students from a student body of size *N* = 27,000 in a university. If a list of these students were available (such as a student directory), we could assign numbers 00001 to 27000 to the students, using 00001 for the first student in the list, 00002 for the second student in the list, and so on. Then 100 random five-digit numbers with values between 00001 and 27000 are selected from Table 2.2. For example, if we used the first column of five-digit numbers in Table 2.2, the first three random numbers are 10480, 22368, and 24130; thus, the first three students selected would be those numbered 10480, 22368, and 24130 in the listing.

In selecting the 100 five-digit numbers, we would skip numbers greater than 27000 (such as the next nine five-digit numbers in Table 2.2), since there is no student in the sampling frame with an assigned number that large. After using the first column of five-digit numbers, we would move to the next column of numbers and continue. If the population size were between 1,000 and 9,999, we would use only four digits at a time. The column (or row) from which we begin obtaining the numbers does not matter, as long as it is not chosen so that a particular member will be included in the sample.

The importance of this sampling method is that it allows statistical inferential procedures to be easily derived. However, in practice, it is often more feasible to use some other sampling procedure that still incorporates some form of randomization.

Systematic Sampling

A sampling procedure that is sometimes easier to implement than the simple random sample, but is usually equally as good for inference-making, is *systematic random sampling*.

Systematic Random Sample

Let *k* denote the ratio given by *k* = *N*/*n*; that is, *k* is the population size divided by the desired sample size. Then, a ***systematic random sample*** is one in which **(a)** a member is chosen at random out of the first *k* names in the sampling frame, and **(b)** every *k*th member listed after that one is selected. We refer to the number *k* as the ***skip number***.

To illustrate, suppose that we decided to obtain a systematic sample of 100 students out of a total of 27,000 students listed in a campus directory. Then *N* = 27,000, *n* = 100, and *k* = 27,000/100 = 270. We would choose one student at

Table 2.2 Random Numbers

LINE/COL.	(1)	(2)	(3)	(4)	(5)	(6)	(7)	(8)	(9)	(10)	(11)	(12)	(13)	(14)
1	10480	15011	01536	02011	81647	91646	69179	14194	62590	36207	20969	99570	91291	90700
2	22368	46573	25595	85393	30995	89198	27982	53402	93965	34095	52666	19174	39615	99505
3	24130	48360	22527	97265	76393	64809	15179	24830	49340	32081	30680	19655	63348	58629
4	42167	93093	06243	61680	07856	16376	39440	53537	71341	57004	00849	74917	97758	16379
5	37570	39975	81837	16656	06121	91782	60468	81305	49684	60672	14110	06927	01263	54613
6	77921	06907	11008	42751	27756	53498	18602	70659	90655	15053	21916	81825	44394	42880
7	99562	72905	56420	69994	98872	31016	71194	18738	44013	48840	63213	21069	10634	12952
8	96301	91977	05463	07972	18876	20922	94595	56869	69014	60045	18425	84903	42508	32307
9	89579	14342	63661	10281	17453	18103	57740	84378	25331	12566	58678	44947	05585	56941
10	85475	36857	53342	53988	53060	59533	38867	62300	08158	17983	16439	11458	18593	64952
11	28918	69578	88231	33276	70997	79936	56865	05859	90106	31595	01547	85590	91610	78188
12	63553	40961	48235	03427	49626	69445	18663	72695	52180	20847	12234	90511	33703	90322
13	09429	93969	52636	92737	88974	33488	36320	17617	30015	08272	84115	27156	30613	74952
14	10365	61129	87529	85689	48237	52267	67689	93394	01511	26358	85104	20285	29975	89868
15	07119	97336	71048	08178	77233	13916	47564	81056	97735	85977	29372	74461	28551	90707
16	51085	12765	51821	51259	77452	16308	60756	92144	49442	53900	70960	63990	75601	40719
17	02368	21382	52404	60268	89368	19885	55322	44819	01188	65255	64835	44919	05944	55157
18	01011	54092	33362	94904	31273	04146	18594	29852	71585	85030	51132	01915	92747	64951
19	52162	53916	46369	58586	23216	14513	83149	98736	23495	64350	94738	17752	35156	35749
20	07056	97628	33787	09998	42698	06691	76988	13602	51851	46104	88916	19509	25625	58104
21	48663	91245	85828	14346	09172	30168	90229	04734	59193	22178	30421	61666	99904	32812
22	54164	58492	22421	74103	47070	25306	76468	26384	58151	06646	21524	15227	96909	44592
23	32639	32363	05597	24200	13363	38005	94342	28728	35806	06912	17012	64161	18296	22851
24	29334	27001	87637	87308	58731	00256	45834	15398	46557	41135	10367	07684	36188	18510
25	02488	33062	28834	07351	19731	92420	60952	61280	50001	67658	32586	86679	50720	94953

Abridged from William H. Beyer, ed., *Handbook of Tables for Probability and Statistics*, 2nd ed., © The Chemical Rubber Co., 1968. Used by permission of the Chemical Rubber Co.

random (using a random number table) from the first 270 students listed in the directory, and then we would select every 270th student after the one selected randomly. If the random number selected were 52, then the numbers of the students selected would be 52, 52 + 270 = 322, 322 + 270 = 592, 592 + 270 = 862, 862 + 270 = 1,132, and so on. The 100th student selected for the sample will be listed in the last 270 names in the directory.

A systematic sample is often simpler to obtain than a random sample (since only one random number must be generated), yet it typically provides just as good a representation of the population. In fact, statistical formulas based on random sampling are also usually applicable to samples obtained by systematic sampling.

The main disadvantage of the systematic sample is that bias may be introduced if there is a regular cyclical fluctuation in the values of the variable throughout the sampling frame, with the period of the cycle equal to the skip number k. Suppose, for example, that as part of a content analysis of a daily newspaper, we are especially interested in the proportions of newspaper space devoted to foreign news, national news, state news, local news, sports, and advertising. The sampling frame might consist of the daily editions of the newspaper for the previous year. If we choose a systematic sample of these editions with k equal to 7 or a multiple of 7, only one day of the week would be sampled. This could lead to some bias in our interpretation of the amount of space devoted to each subject, since the format of the paper would tend to vary regularly with period 7; that is, all Sunday papers would be similar in format, all Monday papers would be similar, and so forth. If only Thursdays were sampled and if the newspaper carried special sections of advertisements for grocery stores and large department stores on that day, then clearly the results would be affected. Alphabetic listings (e.g., directories of names of individuals, counties, or cities) are usually irrelevant to most variables we would want to study, so systematic samples from a frame with alphabetically ordered sampling units are usually acceptable.

Stratified Sampling

Another sampling method sometimes used in social science research is the *stratified random sample*.

Stratified Random Sample

A *stratified random sample* is obtained by dividing the population into separate groups, called *strata*, and then taking a simple random sample from each stratum.

Stratified random samples are especially useful when we want to make comparisons among various strata on several variables. If we stratified according to race of individuals, for example, we might select a random sample of whites and another random sample of blacks from the population. The sampling is called *proportional* if the same proportions of the sample are chosen in the various strata as exist in the entire population. For example, if 90% of the population of interest is white and 10% is black, then the random sample taken of whites would be nine times larger than the random sample of blacks. The sampling is called *disproportional* if the sampled proportions chosen are different from the corresponding proportions in the population.

Disproportional stratified sampling is especially useful when we want to compare strata on some variable(s), but the size of at least one stratum is relatively small. A group that comprises a small proportion of the population may not have enough representation in a simple random sample to allow one to make precise inferences, especially if the total sample size is not very large. It is not possible to compare accurately American Indians to other Americans on the proportion favoring a constitutional amendment banning abortion, for example, if only three of the 1.000 people in the sample are American Indians. Disproportional stratified sampling, on the other hand, allows us to control the number of observations obtained from each stratum. This consideration becomes especially important when the strata are formed by combining levels of several variables. If we want to describe certain characteristics of the subset of the population who are female, black, under 30 years old, and heads of households, a random sample might yield too few observations from that subset.

One problem with any type of stratification is that, in order to carry out the procedure, we must know the stratum into which each member of the sampling frame belongs. Because of this, we are usually restricted in the kinds of variables that can be used for stratification (they must be easily identifiable) and in the populations to which this method can be applied. For example, it is fairly easy to get a stratified sample of a school population using grade level as the stratification variable. On the other hand, it is difficult to prepare an adequate sampling frame of city households stratified by income of household head.

Cluster Sampling   Random, systematic, and stratified sampling may be very expensive or even impossible to implement in many situations. For each of these methods, it is necessary to have access to a complete list of the members of the population. Such lists are relatively easy to obtain for sampling units such as colleges or cities; however, for sampling individuals or families, it is usually very difficult to get a complete list. If a telephone directory is used to obtain a sample of families, for example, there will be no representation of newcomers to the community, families with unlisted numbers, or families too poor to afford telephones. If these nonrepresented people differ from the rest of the population with respect to the characteristics being studied, the inferences that are made will be faulty. Also, if the measurement process requires personally interviewing the members of the sample and if the geographic area covered by the population is large, there is likely to be substantial travel time between interviews for samples obtained by any of these three methods.

The *cluster sampling* technique is useful for obtaining a sample when a complete listing of the population is not available, and for reducing sampling time and costs.

Cluster Sample

Suppose that the researcher divides the population into a large number of groups, called *clusters*, each of which consists of sampling units with some common (often geographic) property. Once the clusters are enumerated, a random sample of them is chosen. Then every sampling unit within the chosen clusters is selected. The resulting collection of sampling units is called a *cluster sample*.

If we plan to sample individuals or families in a city, we might use city blocks or city voting precincts as clusters. Since the sampling units within a cluster would be geographically close, travel time and expense are greatly reduced. For example, if we interview every individual or family living in a particular city block, we can obtain a large number of observations relatively quickly and with very little travel. As another example, in order to study patients in mental hospitals, we could first sample mental hospitals (the clusters) and then study individuals within those hospitals selected.

Stratified sampling is based on sampling from *within each* stratum; in cluster sampling, however, sampling is conducted *among* the clusters, and most clusters are not represented at all in the eventual sample. This fact is responsible for the main disadvantage in using a cluster sample—namely, we may need a larger sample in order to achieve as much accuracy in making inferences about population characteristics as would be obtained by using a random, stratified, or systematic sample. The reason for this is that observations obtained within a cluster often tend to be homogeneous. Several observations from a very homogeneous cluster may not provide much more information than a smaller number of observations. The homogeneity may be a result of the tendency of individuals living near one another to be similar on economic and demographic variables such as age, income, race, occupation, and opinion issues.

Multistage combinations of the sampling techniques described in this section are commonly used in social science research. If we plan to study various characteristics of the population of all adults in the United States, we could treat counties (or census tracts, say) as clusters and select a random sample of a certain number of them. Within each county selected, we could take a cluster sample of square-block regions. Within each region selected, we could take a systematic sample of every tenth house. Within each house selected, we could select one adult at random to serve as part of the sample.

For statistical inference procedures, stratified samples, cluster samples, and multistage samples such as the one just described require different formulas from the ones given in this book. These formulas can be quite complicated (or even unknown), even for relatively basic statistical methods. In short, for a fixed sample size, the results for stratified samples may be more precise than those stated in this textbook for simple random samples, whereas the results for cluster samples may be less precise. The reader should consult books specializing in sampling methodology for further details (Cochran, 1977; Kish, 1965; Mendenhall et al., 1971; Sudman, 1976). For a more complete discussion of important considerations for the design of a research project, the reader should consult books specializing in research methodology (Warwick and Lininger, 1975; Selltiz et al., 1976).

2.3 Sampling and Statistical Inference

Probability and Nonprobability Sampling

The four types of sampling techniques we have just discussed are known as *probability sampling techniques*. They enable us to specify the likelihood that any particular member of the population will be selected for the sample. It is this property that makes it possible to develop statistical inferential procedures based on the sample.

Nonprobability sampling techniques are those sampling procedures for which it is not possible to specify the likelihood of choosing a particular member of the population for the sample; hence, it is impossible to apply statistical inferential methods in a precise manner to data obtained by such a procedure. The population from which the sample has been drawn may be substantially different from the one of real interest.

One of the most common nonprobability sampling techniques is *quota sampling*. This is the method used when, for example, an interviewer is instructed to stand at a specific street corner and conduct interviews until 50 men and 50 women are in the sample. Severe biases may arise as a function of the time and location of the interview and the judgment of the interviewer. Working people, for example, might be underrepresented if the interviews are conducted on weekdays between 9:00 A.M. and 5:00 P.M.

Another example of a nonprobability sampling technique is *volunteer sampling*. Suppose a newspaper staff invites its readers to fill out and send in a coupon concerning their opinions on some issue. The readers who respond are not likely to be a representative cross section of the residents of the town in which the newspaper is published. The respondents will be those people who notice that coupon in that paper and who happen to feel strongly enough about the issue to write. Individuals possessing one specific opinion on that issue might be more likely to respond than individuals holding a different opinion.

Concept of Sampling Variability

The results of a study clearly depend on which sample is selected. If two researchers select different random samples from some population, there may be very little, if any, overlap between the two sample memberships. Hence, the values of the sample statistics will differ for the two samples, and the respective inferences based on these samples may differ. In order for the conclusions based on statistical methodology to be worthwhile, we need to be able to describe the extent to which the value of a particular statistic is likely to vary according to the sample chosen.

Sampling Error

The *sampling error* of a statistic refers to the error that is made when a statistic based on a sample is used to estimate or predict the value of a population parameter.

Probability sampling guards against having a systematic bias in the sampling error (e.g., a tendency to consistently underestimate the true values) and allows us to gauge its probable size. There is also variability in the values of sample statistics with nonprobability sampling, but that variability is not predictable as it is with probability samples. The concept of sampling variability will be discussed in greater detail in later chapters.

In Chapter 3, we will introduce some of the basic statistics used to describe samples. We also introduce the corresponding parameters for describing populations. Hence, our focus will be on the descriptive aspects of statistical methodology.

Summary

Statistics is concerned with the study of *variables*, both in isolation and in terms of the relationships among them. The particular statistical methods utilized depend on the levels of measurement of the variables—*nominal, ordinal,* or *interval*. Quantitative variables can also be classified as *discrete* or *continuous*. Inferential statistical procedures are appropriate only for *probability samples*, for which we have some control over the amount of possible *sampling error*. Examples of probability sampling include *simple random* sampling, *systematic* sampling, *stratified* sampling, *cluster* sampling, and *multistage* combinations of these. The formulas presented in this text refer to simple random sampling.

Problems

1. Explain the difference between the following:
a. Discrete variables and continuous variables
b. Simple random sample and systematic random sample

2. What is the scale of measurement that is most appropriate for each of the following variables?
a. Attitude toward legalization of marijuana (favor, neutral, oppose)
b. Sex (male, female)
c. Number of siblings (0, 1, 2, . . .)
d. Political party affiliation (Democrat, Republican, other)
e. Church affiliation (Roman Catholic, Baptist, Methodist, . . .)
f. Political philosophy (liberal, moderate, conservative)
g. Years of school completed (0, 1, 2, 3, . . .)
h. Highest degree obtained (high school, bachelor's, master's, doctorate)
i. College major (education, anthropology, physics, . . .)
j. Scholastic Aptitude Test score (200–800 range for scores)
k. Employment status (employed, unemployed)

3. Give the scale of measurement that is most appropriate for each of the following variables:
a. Occupation (plumber, teacher, etc.)
b. Occupational status (blue-collar, white-collar)

c. Social status (lower, middle, upper class)
d. Crime rate (50 per 1,000 population, etc.)
e. Population size (number of people)
f. Population growth rate (in percentages)
g. Community size (rural, small town, large town, small city, large city)
h. Annual income (in dollars per year)

4. Give the scale of measurement that is most appropriate for the variable "education completed" when it is measured as:
a. Number of years (0, 1, 2, 3, . . .)
b. (elementary school, middle school, high school, college, graduate school)
c. (public school, private school)

5. Give an example of a variable measured on a:
a. Nominal scale
b. Ordinal scale
c. Interval scale

6. A survey asks respondents to rank five issues according to their importance in determining the respondent's voting intention for U.S. senator (foreign policy, unemployment, inflation, the arms race, and civil rights), with the most important issue ranked 1 and the least important ranked 5. The rankings can be treated as five variables: "foreign policy ranking," "unemployment ranking," etc. These variables represent what level of measurement?

7. Which of the following variables are continuous when the measurements are as fine as possible?

Age
Number of children
Income
Population of cities
Latitude and longitude of a city
Distance of residence from place of employment

8. Which of the following variables could theoretically be measured on a continuous scale?

Method of contraception used
Length of residence in a state
Task completion time
Intelligence
Authoritarianism
Alienation

9. A class has twenty-five students. Use the column of the first two digits in the random number table (Table 2.2) to select a simple random sample of three students.

10. A *simple random sample* of size *n* is one in which (select the best response):

a. Every *n*th member is selected from the population.

b. Each possible sample of size *n* has the same chance of being selected.

c. Necessarily there is exactly the same proportion of women in the sample as there is in the population.

d. We keep sampling until we obtain a fixed number of people having various characteristics (e.g., males, females, or whites, blacks).

e. A particular minority-group member of the population is less likely to be chosen than a particular majority-group member.

f. All of the above

g. None of the above

11. In a local telephone directory, there are 300 pages with approximately 120 names per page.

a. Explain how you would choose a simple random sample of these names. Using the second and third columns of Table 2.2, select ten numbers that could be used in selecting such a sample.

b. How would you obtain a systematic sample of 200 names from the same directory?

c. Would cluster sampling be applicable in this situation? How could it be carried out and what would be the advantages and disadvantages?

12. Evaluate each of the following hypothetical situations, in terms of whether the method of selecting the sample is appropriate for obtaining information about the population of interest. How would you improve the sample design?

a. A principal in a large high school is interested in student attitudes toward a proposed general achievement test to determine which students should graduate. He lists all of the first-period classes, assigning a number to each. Then, using a random number table, he chooses a class at random and interviews every student in that class about the proposed test.

b. A congresswoman reports that letters to her office are running 3 to 1 in opposition to the passage of stricter gun control laws. She concludes that approximately 75% of her constituents oppose stricter gun control laws.

c. A new restaurant opened in January 1985. In June, after 6 months of operation, the owner applied for a loan to improve the building. On the loan application, an estimate of the yearly gross income of the business was requested. The owner has a record book that contains receipts for each day of operation since opening. It was decided to calculate the average daily receipt based on a sample of the daily records, and multiply that by the number of days of operation in a year. A systematic sample was taken, with *k* = 7, so every seventh record was sampled. The average daily receipt for this sample was then used to obtain an estimate of the yearly receipts.

d. An anthropology professor wanted to compare physical science majors with social science majors with respect to their attitudes toward premarital sex. She administered a questionnaire to her large class of Anthropology 437, Comparative Human Sexuality. She found no appreciable difference between her physical science and social science majors in their attitudes, so she concluded that the two student groups were about the same in their relative acceptance of premarital sex.

e. A questionnaire was mailed to a simple random sample of 500 household addresses in a city. Ten were returned as bad addresses, 63 were returned completed, and the rest were not returned. The researcher analyzed the 63 cases and reported that they represent a "random sample of city households."

13. I need to collect data on a sample of residents of registered nursing homes in my state. I obtain from the state a list of all nursing homes, which I number from 1 to 317. Beginning randomly, I choose every tenth home on the list, ending up with 31 homes. I then obtain lists of residents from those 31 homes, and I select a simple random sample from each list. What kinds of sampling have I used?

Bibliography   Cochran, W. G. (1977). *Sampling Techniques*, 2nd ed. New York: Wiley.

Kish, L. (1965). *Survey Sampling*. New York: Wiley.

Mendenhall, W., L. Ott, and R. L. Scheaffer (1971). *Elementary Survey Sampling*. Belmont, Calif.: Wadsworth.

Selltiz, C., L. Wrightsman, and S. W. Cook (1976). *Research Methods in Social Relations*, 3rd ed. New York: Holt, Rinehart and Winston.

Sudman, S. (1976). *Applied Sampling*, New York: Academic Press.

Warwick, D. and C. A. Lininger (1975). *The Sample Survey: Theory and Practice*. New York: McGraw-Hill.

CHAPTER 3

Descriptive Techniques

Contents

In Chapter 1 we observed that a primary reason for using statistics is to summarize and describe collections of data in order to make them more readily understandable. In this chapter we present some of the methods of data description that are frequently used. In the first section, we discuss statistical description through the use of simple tables and graphs. These tools help to provide an overall picture of the information contained in the data, and they are valuable as a first step in interpreting the data. They are also especially useful for presenting data to an audience that is mathematically unsophisticated. For inferential purposes, it is more useful to describe the data using numerical measures. Statistics that describe certain aspects of the *central location* of a collection of data are defined in Section 3.2. Statistics that describe the *dispersion* of the data about that central location are defined in Section 3.3. In the final section, we distinguish between a set of statistics for describing sample characteristics and the corresponding parameters for describing population characteristics.

To illustrate, suppose we plan to study the distribution of grade point averages (GPAs) at the University of Oregon. Our data might consist of the GPAs gathered from a random sample of student records at that university. We could summarize the data in a table or graph that portrays how many of the students have GPAs between 4.0 and 3.7, between 3.7 and 3.4, and so forth. We could, in addition, calculate a summary statistic that describes a typical GPA for that sample. We could also give a descriptive measure of the spread of the sample GPA values; that is, are most of them fairly close to the center of the scores, or are there many relatively small and large values as well? Finally, we would realize that the descriptive table, graph, and numerical statistics apply to that particular sample, and that there are corresponding characteristics for the population of all students at the University of Oregon.

3.1 Tabular and Graphical Description

Tables and graphs are often used to describe data and also to aid in checking whether the assumptions required for certain inferential statistical techniques are satisfied. In this section we consider some fundamental aspects of the use of these descriptive devices.

Example 3.1

Table 3.1 is a list of the fifty states with the number of members of the U.S. House of Representatives for each (based on 1980 census). If we were interested in presenting the information found in this table, we might want to summarize the data in some way, rather than simply to list all of the separate observations. A *frequency distribution* for the number of congressional representatives could be constructed for this purpose. ∎

Table 3.1

List of States with Number of Members in the House of Representatives

Alabama	7	Louisiana	8	Ohio	21
Alaska	1	Maine	2	Oklahoma	6
Arizona	5	Maryland	8	Oregon	5
Arkansas	4	Massachusetts	11	Pennsylvania	23
California	45	Michigan	18	Rhode Island	2
Colorado	6	Minnesota	8	South Carolina	6
Connecticut	6	Mississippi	5	South Dakota	1
Delaware	1	Missouri	9	Tennessee	9
Florida	19	Montana	2	Texas	27
Georgia	10	Nebraska	3	Utah	3
Hawaii	2	Nevada	2	Vermont	1
Idaho	2	New Hampshire	2	Virginia	10
Illinois	22	New Jersey	14	Washington	8
Indiana	10	New Mexico	3	West Virginia	4
Iowa	6	New York	34	Wisconsin	9
Kansas	5	North Carolina	11	Wyoming	1
Kentucky	7	North Dakota	1		

Frequency Distributions

In order to construct a frequency distribution, the values of the variable must be grouped into separate categories. Then the number (frequency) of observations in each category is counted.

Frequency Distribution

A *frequency distribution* is a listing of categories of possible values for a variable, together with a tabulation of the number of observations in each category.

For all continuous variables and for most interval variables that take on a large number of values, the categories consist of intervals of values rather than single discrete values of the variable. These intervals are usually of equal width and they should be *exhaustive*, that is, set up to include all possible values of the variable in question. In addition, they should be *mutually exclusive*; any possible value must fit into one and only one interval.

The width of the intervals in a frequency distribution depends both on the judgment of the researcher as to what makes sense and on the number of observations to be classified. Usually, the larger the number of observations, the greater the number of intervals that can be used. If too many intervals are used (say, more than 15), they are so narrow that the information presented is difficult to digest, and an overall pattern in the results may be obscured. If very few intervals are used, however, too much information may be lost through the pooling together of observations that may not be very similar. The researcher should follow this general guideline: The interval should not be so wide that two measurements included in it have a difference between them that is considered important. For example, if a difference of $2,000 in annual family income is not considered especially important but a difference of $3,000 is fairly important, we might choose the intervals 0–$1,999, $2,000–$3,999, $4,000–$5,999, and so forth.

Example 3.1 (continued)

To summarize the data in Table 3.1, we first need to decide on the appropriate interval width to use in describing delegation size. Suppose we use the intervals 0–4, 5–9, and so forth, up to 45–49, so that each interval contains five values. Then, counting the number of states within each interval of number of representatives, we would have the frequency distribution shown in Table 3.2. From looking at this frequency distribution, it is much more apparent than in the original listing that most of the states have fewer than ten representatives, for example. Of course, as with any summary method, some information has been lost as the cost of achieving clarity. It is no longer known from the frequency distribution which of the states have few or many representatives, nor are the exact numbers of representatives for the various states known.

Table 3.2
Frequency Distribution for the Number of Representatives to Congress for the 50 States

NUMBER OF REPRESENTATIVES	FREQUENCY
0–4	18
5–9	18
10–14	6
15–19	2
20–24	3
25–29	1
30–34	1
35–39	0
40–44	0
45–49	1
TOTAL	50

Relative Frequencies and Histograms

Frequency distributions are informative, but often they are not as useful in making comparisons among different groups as are distributions of *relative frequencies*.

Relative Frequency

The *relative frequency* for a category is the proportion of the total set of observations that is in that category.

In order to compute a relative frequency, we divide the number of observations in a category by the total number of observations in the entire distribution. The relative frequency is a proportion—a number between 0 and 1 that expresses the share of the total set of observations that is classified in that category. If we do this for each category of a frequency distribution, we obtain a *relative frequency distribution*.

These relative frequencies are multiplied by 100 to obtain *percentages*, which are more commonly used in the social sciences. The relative frequency distribution for the data on congressional representation presented in Table 3.2 would be constructed by dividing each frequency by 50, the total number of states. These relative frequencies are multiplied by 100 to get the percentages. For example, 18/50 = .36 is the relative frequency for the interval 0–4, and 100(.36) = 36 is the corresponding percentage. The entire relative frequency distribution is shown in Table 3.3, along with the corresponding percentage distribution.

Table 3.3
Relative Frequency Distribution and Percentages for Number of Congressional Representatives

NUMBER OF REPRESENTATIVES	FREQUENCY	RELATIVE FREQUENCY	PERCENTAGE
0–4	18	.36	36.0
5–9	18	.36	36.0
10–14	6	.12	12.0
15–19	2	.04	4.0
20–24	3	.06	6.0
25–29	1	.02	2.0
30–34	1	.02	2.0
35–39	0	.00	0.0
40–44	0	.00	0.0
45–49	1	.02	2.0
TOTAL	50	1.00	100.0

In many studies, we would like to compare two or more groups with respect to their distribution on some variable. Relative frequencies are especially useful for comparing the groups when their total sample sizes are different, since the division of the frequencies by the total sample size in effect standardizes or controls for such differences.

Example 3.2 Suppose we wanted to compare family incomes for students in a public high school and students in a private high school in a particular city. Both the frequency and relative frequency distributions for the two groups are shown in Table 3.4. Due to the large discrepancy in the sample sizes of the two groups, the differences in family income between the public school and the private school children are not as easily interpreted from the frequencies as from the relative frequencies. The frequency (106) of public school children with families earning over $45,000 annually is larger

Table 3.4
Relative Frequency Distributions of Income for Families of Children in Private and Public Schools

ANNUAL FAMILY INCOME	FREQUENCIES Private	Public	RELATIVE FREQUENCIES Private	Public
$45,000 and above	30	106	.221	.090
$30,000–$44,999	29	201	.213	.171
$15,000–$29,999	40	368	.294	.313
$0–$14,999	37	502	.272	.426
TOTAL	136	1,177	1.000	1.000

than the corresponding frequency (30) of private school children. In the relative frequency distributions, however, we see that relatively more families of children in the private school earn more than $45,000 annually; the public school tends to have relatively more children from low-income families. ■

Relative frequencies must always sum to 1.00 (and percentages to 100) if the categories or intervals are mutually exclusive and exhaustive.* When relative frequencies or percentages are presented in a table, the total number of cases upon which they are based should *always* be included. The statement that 60% of a random sample of 1,000 individuals favor a decrease in the national defense budget is much more striking than the same statement derived from a random sample of five individuals. Also, with small sample sizes, percentages and relative frequencies tend to be unstable. A chance fluctuation of one or two observations can make a relatively large change in the relative frequency distribution. For example, a change of two opinions out of five sampled could result in a change from 60% to 20% favoring a decrease in the defense budget.

A bar graph of the relative frequencies in the various categories for a variable is called a relative frequency *histogram*. In a histogram, the height of the bar over a particular category represents the relative number of observations in that category. Figure 3.1 is a relative frequency histogram for the distribution of congressional delegation size, using the intervals defined in Table 3.2.

Fig. 3.1 Relative Frequency Histogram for Congressional Delegation Sizes

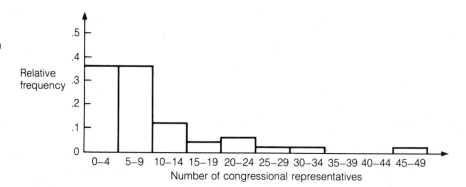

Although there are guidelines for drawing histograms (see Tufte, 1983), it is primarily a matter of common sense. As with frequency distributions, if too few intervals are used, too much information is lost or obscured. For example, Figure 3.2 is a histogram of congressional delegation size using the crude intervals 0–19, 20–39, and above 39. On the other hand, the histogram may be very irregular if too many intervals are used relative to the size of the data set.

Frequencies, relative frequencies, percentages, and histograms can be used to describe data of any measurement level. For nominal or ordinal variables, we usually take the levels of the variable to be the categories, instead of defining artificial categories.

*The process of rounding may lead to totals that are slightly above or below these figures.

Fig. 3.2 Relative Frequency Histogram for Congressional Delegation Sizes, Using Crude Intervals

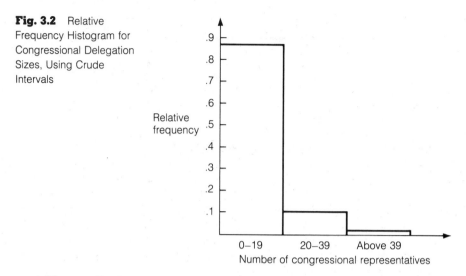

Example 3.3 Table 3.5 (page 38) gives frequencies and percentages of different types of family structure in the United States in 1981.* Figure 3.3 presents the same data in a histogram. Since family structure is a nominal variable, the order of the bars is not determined. By convention, though, they are usually ordered by frequency, except possibly for an "other" category, which is listed last. The order of presentation for an ordinal classification would be determined by the natural ordering of the levels of the variable. ∎

Fig. 3.3 Relative Frequency of Family Structure Types, U.S. Families, 1981

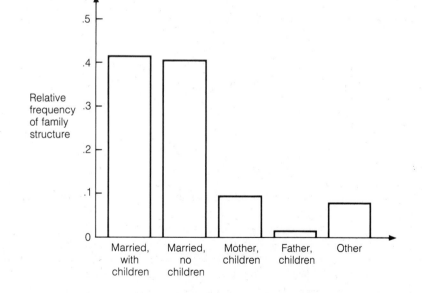

*It is actually sufficient in such a table to report just the percentages and the total sample size, since (apart from rounding) each frequency equals the corresponding percentage multiplied by the total sample size.

Table 3.5

Family Structure, U.S.
Families, 1981

TYPE OF FAMILY	NUMBER (THOUSANDS)	PERCENTAGE
Married couple with children	24,908	41.3
Married couple, no children	24,365	40.4
Single mother with children	5,609	9.3
Single father with children	663	1.1
Other families	4,704	7.8
TOTAL	60,249	99.9

Source: U.S. Bureau of the Census, *Current Population Reports*, Series P-20, No. 371 (May 1982).

Stem and Leaf Diagrams

Figure 3.4 shows an alternative representation of the data in Table 3.1. Each line in this diagram contains the observations that were summarized by a bar in the histogram in Figure 3.1. The *stem* is the first digit and the *leaf* is the second digit of each two-digit number. For instance, on the last line, the stem of 4 and the leaf of 5 represent the number 45. On the third line, the stem of 1 has three 0 leaves, corresponding to the three states that had 10 representatives. The stem of 0 in the first two lines is used for single-digit numbers; thus, for instance, 05 represents 5.

Fig. 3.4   Stem and Leaf
Diagram for Data in
Table 3.1

Stem	**Leaf**
0	1 1 1 1 1 1 2 2 2 2 2 2 2 3 3 3 4 4
0	5 5 5 5 6 6 6 6 6 7 7 8 8 8 8 9 9 9
1	0 0 0 1 1 4
1	8 9
2	1 2 3
2	7
3	4
3	
4	
4	5

Figure 3.4 is referred to as a *stem and leaf diagram*. When a data set is not very large, this is a useful way of displaying the data. A stem and leaf diagram conveys much of the same information as a histogram. If we turn it on its side, it portrays the same shape as the histogram. In fact, since the actual sample values can be recovered from the stem and leaf diagram, it stores information that is lost in drawing a histogram. For instance, from Figure 3.4 we see that the largest number of representatives for a state was 45 and the smallest number was 1 (for six states). For additional examples of stem and leaf diagrams and guidelines on their use, see Tukey (1977).

Sample and Population Distributions

Frequency distributions and histograms for a variable can be constructed both for the measurements in a population and for the measurements in a sample taken from that population. The first type is called the *population distribution* of the variable, and the second type is called a *sample distribution*. We can think of the sample distribution as being a blurry photograph of the population distribution. As the sample size increases and we obtain more information, the photograph gets clearer and the sample distribution looks more like the population distribution.

Another way of viewing the relationship between a sample distribution and the population distribution is as follows. Suppose a variable being measured is continuous, so that theoretically we could choose the intervals for a histogram as small as desired. Now, if the sample size could be indefinitely increased and the number of intervals simultaneously increased (so that their width narrows), we can imagine the shape of the histogram for the sample data converging to a smooth curve. For convenience in this text, we use such curves to represent the population distributions of variables. Figure 3.5 shows two sample histograms, one based on a sample of size 100 and the second based on a sample of size 500, and also a smooth curve representing the population distribution. Even if a variable is discrete, a smooth curve often provides a good approximation for the population distribution, especially when the collection of possible values of the variable is large (e.g., income).

Fig. 3.5 Histograms for a Continuous Variable

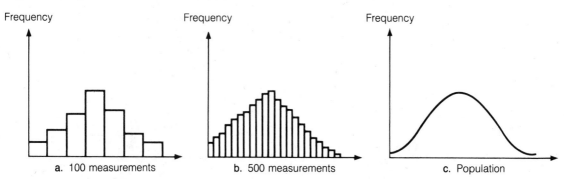

a. 100 measurements   b. 500 measurements   c. Population

The shape of the population distribution is often of interest. A population in which the distribution of a particular variable is bell-shaped is fundamentally different from a population in which the distribution of that variable is U-shaped. For example, a U-shaped distribution indicates a polarization on the variable between two segments of the population, whereas a bell-shaped distribution indicates that most of the population tends to be close to a central value (see Figure 3.6 on the next page). Also, we will see in later chapters that some inferential statistical procedures are based on certain assumptions about the form of the population distribution. Thus, it is often important for a researcher to construct a histogram of the sample distribution to get some information about the appearance of the corresponding population distribution.

Fig. 3.6 U-Shaped and
Bell-Shaped Frequency
Distributions

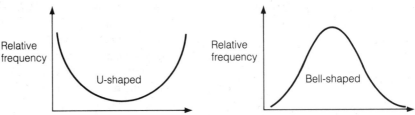

The relative frequency histogram for a sample of measurements may be considered to be an estimate of the corresponding population distribution of the variable. It is difficult, however, to make inferences in terms of such pictures, so we also must consider numerical descriptive measures. For example, if we had one relative frequency histogram representing age at first marriage for women in a Florida county and another representing age at first marriage for men, it might be difficult to compare the two histograms in words. By using numerical descriptive techniques, though, we could make comparisons such as, "On the average, the age at first marriage for men in the sample is 3 years older than the age for women in the sample." Inferences could then be made about the corresponding comparison for *all* men and women first married in that county. We now turn our attention to ways of making numerical descriptions of the data.

3.2 Measures of Central Tendency

In this section, we present some descriptive statistics that are used for characterizing the center of a frequency distribution. The statistics most commonly used for this purpose convey an impression of what the *typical* measurement in the sample is like, and all can be easily interpreted. These statistics are referred to as *measures of central tendency*.

The Mean

Probably the most well-known and frequently used measure of central tendency is the *mean*.

Sample Mean

The *sample mean* is the sum of the sample measurements divided by the sample size.

The term *average* is also used for this characteristic. We will use the following notation in stating a formula for the value of a mean calculated from sample observations.

Notation

The sample size is represented by n. The observations are denoted by Y_1, Y_2, . . . , Y_n. The symbol Σ (uppercase Greek letter sigma) means *the sum of*. The sample mean is denoted by $\bar{Y}$.

Throughout the text, we use n to denote the sample size. The n observations in the sample are symbolized by $Y_1, Y_2, \ldots, Y_n$, where Y_1 represents the first observation, Y_2 the second, and so forth up to Y_n, the last observation made. For example, if the sample size is $n = 200$, then the last observation is symbolized by Y_{200}. The symbol $\overline{Y}$, which we use to represent the sample mean, is read as "Y-bar." From the definition of the sample mean, we see that we can represent its calculation by the formula

$$\overline{Y} = \frac{Y_1 + Y_2 + \cdots + Y_n}{n}$$

The symbol $\displaystyle\sum_{i=1}^{n} Y_i$ may be used to represent the sum $Y_1 + Y_2 + \cdots + Y_n$. This symbol stands for the sum of the Y-values, where the index i (which identifies the observations) takes on all integer values from 1 to n. To illustrate, for a sample of size $n = 5$,

$$\sum_{i=1}^{5} Y_i = Y_1 + Y_2 + Y_3 + Y_4 + Y_5$$

Using this summation symbol, we have the shortened expression for the mean of a sample of n measurements,

$$\overline{Y} = \frac{\displaystyle\sum_{i=1}^{n} Y_i}{n}$$

The symbol Σ will often be used instead of $\Sigma_{i=1}^{n}$ when there is no confusion over the values of the index i. Example 3.4 illustrates the definition of the mean and the corresponding notation.

Example 3.4 A group of researchers in an alcoholism treatment center is interested in estimating the mean length of stay in the center for first-time patients. They randomly select ten records of individuals who had been institutionalized for alcoholism within the previous 2 years. The lengths of stay in the center, in days, for those ten individuals are as follows: 12, 7, 21, 10, 14, 5, 40, 14, 45, and 8.

For these data, the sample size is $n = 10$. We could identify Y_1 with 12, Y_2 with 7, and so forth, so that

$$\sum_{i=1}^{10} Y_i = 12 + 7 + 21 + 10 + 14 + 5 + 40 + 14 + 45 + 8 = 176$$

Thus, the mean length of stay in this treatment center for the sampled alcoholic patients equals

$$\overline{Y} = \frac{\Sigma Y_i}{n} = \frac{176}{10} = 17.6 \text{ days} \qquad \blacksquare$$

Before presenting additional examples, we consider some of the basic properties of the mean.

Properties of the Mean

1. The formula for the mean assumes the existence of numerical values $Y_1, Y_2, \ldots,$ Y_n for the observations, so that distances between pairs of observations are well defined and can be compared. Because of this, the mean is appropriate only for data measured on at least an interval scale. It would not make sense to find the mean of observations on an ordinal rating such as excellent, good, fair, and poor.* Nor would it be possible to compute the mean for observations on a nominal scale with categories such as Protestant, Catholic, Jewish, and other, even though these levels may sometimes be coded by numbers for convenience.

2. The mean may be interpreted as the point of balance on the number line when an equal weight is placed at each measurement point. For example, if an equal weight is centered at each of the observations given in Example 3.4, then the line balances if a fulcrum is placed at the point 17.6 (see Figure 3.7). The mean is therefore the *center of gravity* of the observations.†

Fig. 3.7 The Mean as the Center of Gravity

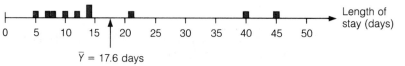

$\bar{Y} = 17.6$ days

3. Suppose that the sample means for two different sets of data based on sample sizes n_1 and n_2 are $\bar{Y}_1$ and $\bar{Y}_2$, respectively. Then the overall sample mean for the combined set of $(n_1 + n_2)$ measurements is the **weighted average**

$$\bar{Y} = \frac{n_1\bar{Y}_1 + n_2\bar{Y}_2}{n_1 + n_2} = \left(\frac{n_1}{n_1 + n_2}\right)\bar{Y}_1 + \left(\frac{n_2}{n_1 + n_2}\right)\bar{Y}_2$$

Each separate sample mean receives weight proportional to the number of observations on which it is based. The numerator $n_1\bar{Y}_1 + n_2\bar{Y}_2$ gives the total sum of all the measurements (since $n\bar{Y} = \Sigma\, Y$ for each set of measurements), and the denominator gives the total sample size. A similar formula can be given for combining *several* means to get one overall mean (see Problem 28 at the end of the chapter). Example 3.5 illustrates an application of the formula for combining two means.

Example 3.5　　Ten families are randomly selected in Florida and another ten families are randomly selected in Alabama. Instead of having data on the individual families, we have the summary information shown in Table 3.6. Four of the Florida families live in rural areas and have a mean income of $16,000, whereas the other six Florida families live in urban areas and have a mean income of $19,000. Eight of the Alabama families

---

*If we assigned numbers such as (4, 3, 2, 1) to the ordered levels (excellent, good, fair, poor) and then computed the mean, we would essentially be treating the levels as equidistant and, hence, as an interval scale.

†This property implies that the sum of the distances to the mean from the observations above the mean equals the sum of the distances to the mean from the observations below the mean.

live in rural areas and have a mean income of $17,000, and two of the Alabama families live in urban areas and have a mean income of $20,000. Which sample of size 10 has the larger mean income?

Table 3.6
Mean Family Income by
State and Residence

STATE	RURAL		URBAN	
	Mean	Sample size	Mean	Sample size
Florida	$16,000	4	$19,000	6
Alabama	$17,000	8	$20,000	2

For the two sets of observations from Alabama, $n_1 = 8$, $n_2 = 2$, $\bar{Y}_1 = \$17,000$, and $\bar{Y}_2 = \$20,000$. The overall mean income for the ten families in Alabama is

$$\bar{Y} = \frac{n_1\bar{Y}_1 + n_2\bar{Y}_2}{n_1 + n_2} = \frac{8(17,000) + 2(20,000)}{8 + 2} = \frac{176,000}{10} = \$17,600$$

The weighted average of $17,600 is four times closer to $17,000 (a distance of $600) than it is to $20,000 (a distance of $2,400). This is because there are four times as many observations with the mean of $17,000 ($n_1 = 8$) as there are with the mean of $20,000 ($n_2 = 2$).

The overall mean for the ten families in Florida is

$$\bar{Y} = \frac{4(16,000) + 6(19,000)}{4 + 6} = \$17,800$$

Within each residence category (urban, rural), the mean income is higher for the Alabama residents. However, the overall sample of ten families from Florida has a higher mean income than the overall sample of ten families from Alabama. The reason for this seeming paradox is that mean urban incomes are larger than mean rural incomes in both states, and the Florida sample has a higher proportion of urban residents than the Alabama sample. ∎

The mean is not always very typical of the measurements in the sample, in terms of being close in value to most of them. One example of this phenomenon occurs when the frequency distribution is U-shaped, in which case most of the observations are quite far from the mean in either direction. Another instance occurs when one or more of the measurements is much larger (smaller) than the others, as shown in Example 3.6.

Example 3.6 The owner of a small store reports that the mean annual income of employees in the business is $21,900. Upon closer inspection, we find that the actual yearly incomes of the seven employees are $8,200, $8,400, $8,700, $9,200, $9,300, $9,500, and $100,000. Further investigation reveals that the $100,000 income is the salary of one of the owner's sons, who happens to be an employee. ∎

The bell-shaped and U-shaped distributions in Figure 3.6 are *symmetric* about their means. Most distributions of variables studied in the social sciences, however, are not exactly symmetric. A nonsymmetric, single-peaked distribution is said to be *skewed to the right* or *skewed to the left*, according to the direction in which the longer tail of the distribution points (see Figure 3.8). The mean tends to be drawn in the direction of the tail of a skewed distribution, relative to the majority of the observations. In Example 3.6, the presence of the large observation $100,000 results in an extreme skewness to the right of the income distribution. Hence, the mean is drawn above most of the measurements (six of the seven). In general, the more highly skewed a frequency distribution is, the less representative of a typical observation the mean tends to be.

Fig. 3.8 Skewed Frequency Distributions

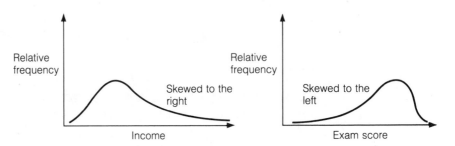

The Median   The *median* is a measure of central tendency that better describes a typical value when the sample distribution of measurements is highly skewed. The median is defined so that it splits the sample into two parts with equal numbers of observations, when the observations are arranged in order of magnitude.

Sample Median
The *sample median* is the measurement that falls in the middle when the sample measurements are ordered according to their magnitudes. If there is an odd number of observations, then the median is uniquely defined. If the sample size is even, then there are two middle measurements and the median is usually taken to be the mean of the two.

Example 3.7   The unemployment rates (in percent) for the five cities in New York State with populations of at least 175,000 are 6.2, 8.9, 6.3, 9.1, and 11.5. The ordered sample is 6.2, 6.3, 8.9, 9.1, 11.5. The middle measurement of the ordered sample is the third one, so the median is the third largest (also the third smallest) measurement, or 8.9%. ∎

Example 3.8   The ordered income measurements for the seven employees in the business described in Example 3.6 are 8,200, 8,400, 8,700, 9,200, 9,300, 9,500, and 100,000. The median is the fourth largest income, $9,200. In this case, the median provides a better description of the typical employee's income than does the mean. ∎

Example 3.9   For the data in Example 3.4, the ordered sample is 5, 7, 8, 10, 12, 14, 14, 21, 40, and 45. Since the sample size $n = 10$ is even, the median is the midpoint between the middle measurements 12 and 14, or $(12 + 14)/2 = 13$. The mean ($\bar{Y} = 17.6$) is larger than the median, due to the fact that two of the measurements are considerably larger than the others.   ■

When n is odd, the middle observation is the one with index $(n + 1)/2$. That is, the median is the value of the $(n + 1)/2$nd measurement, when they are ordered from smallest to largest.

Example 3.10   The job performance of a manager in an industrial plant is rated by twenty-one employees. The evaluations are summarized in Table 3.7. For $n = 21$ ordered scores, the middle score is the $(n + 1)/2 = (21 + 1)/2 = 11$th highest (ten are larger and ten are smaller), which falls in the good category. So the median rating of the manager's job performance is good.   ■

Table 3.7
Rating of the Manager by
21 Employees

RATING	FREQUENCY
Excellent	8
Good	4
Fair	6
Poor	3

Properties of the Median

1. The median is appropriate for data measured on at least an ordinal scale, since we need only the ordering of the data (and not the distances between the observations) to compute it. Example 3.10 is an illustration of its use for an ordinal scale.
2. For symmetric distributions, such as in Figure 3.6, the median and the mean are identical. To illustrate, the sample of measurements $Y_1 = 4$, $Y_2 = 5$, $Y_3 = 7$, $Y_4 = 9$, and $Y_5 = 10$ is symmetric about 7, which is both the median and the mean.
3. For skewed distributions, the mean lies toward the direction of skew (the longer tail) relative to the median (see Figure 3.9). Income distributions tend to be skewed to the right, though usually not as severely as in Example 3.6. The mean

Fig. 3.9 The Mean and the Median for Skewed Distributions

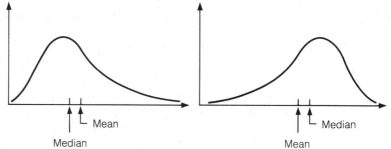

family income in the United States in 1981, for example, was about $2,500 higher than the median family income. The distribution of grades on an exam tends to be skewed to the left when there are some students who do considerably poorer than the others. In this case, the mean is less than the median.

4. The median is insensitive to the distances of the measurements from the middle measurement(s), since it is based only on the ordinal characteristics of the data. For example, the following sets of measurements all have medians of 10.

| 8, | 9, | 10, | 11, | 12 | | 8, | 9, | 10, | 11, | 100 |
| 0, | 9, | 10, | 10, | 10 | | 8, | 9, | 10, | 100, | 100 |

Thus, for interval variables, the median does not utilize all of the information available in the sample. Partly because of this, it is not as valuable as the mean for some inferential purposes.

However, the median does have certain advantages, compared to the mean. For instance, the median is usually more appropriate when the distribution is highly skewed (see Examples 3.6 and 3.8). The mean can be greatly affected by changes in extreme values (called *outliers*), whereas the median will be unaffected unless the value of the middle case also changes. The mean requires an interval scale, whereas the median can also be useful for ordinal scales (see Example 3.10).

The median is a special case of a more general set of measures of location called *percentiles*.

Percentile

The *pth percentile* is a number such that p% of the scores fall below it and $(100 - p)$% fall above it.

The median, in fact, is the $p = $ 50th percentile; that is, the median is larger than 50% of the measurements and smaller than the other 50%. Two other percentiles that are often listed in describing a frequency distribution are the *lower* and *upper quartiles*.

Lower and Upper Quartiles

The $p = $ 25th percentile is called the *lower quartile*.

The $p = $ 75th percentile is called the *upper quartile*.

The quartiles can be used with the median to split the distribution into four parts, each containing approximately one-fourth of the measurements (see Figure 3.10). The difference between the upper and lower quartiles is called the *interquartile range*. The middle half of the observations are within that range.

Fig. 3.10 The Quartiles and Interquartile Range

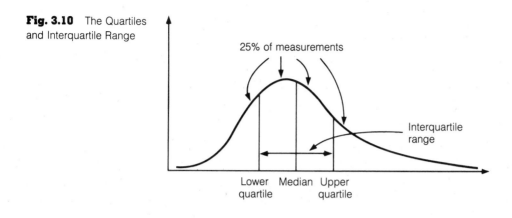

25% of measurements

Interquartile range

Lower quartile   Median   Upper quartile

Example 3.11   Public school expenditures per student are recorded for all the school districts in a particular state. The distribution of expenditures is described by the lower quartile of $1,250, the median of $1,400, and the upper quartile of $1,770. This means that a quarter of the school districts spent less than $1,250 per student on public education. Similarly, a quarter of the public school expenditures were between $1,250 and $1,400, between $1,400 and $1,770, and above $1,770. The interquartile range is $1,770 − $1,250 = $520, so the middle half of the public school expenditures fall within a range of $520.   ■

The Mode   Another measure that is occasionally used to describe a typical value for a sample is the *mode*.

Sample Mode

The *sample mode* is the value that occurs most frequently in the sample.

In Example 3.4, the mode is 14, which occurs twice. In Example 3.7, each value occurs just once, so there is no unique mode. The mode is more commonly used with categorical data or grouped frequency distributions than with ungrouped observations.

Modal Category

The *modal category* is the category or interval with the highest frequency.

In Example 3.10, the modal category is excellent, since the frequency of 8 for that rating is higher than the frequency for any other rating.

It should be noted that the mode need not be near the center of the distribution. In fact, it may be one of the most extreme values, as in Example 3.10. Thus, it may be somewhat inaccurate to call the mode a measure of central tendency. Many quantitative variables studied in the social sciences, though, tend to have distributions in which the mode is not near either extreme (as in bell-shaped distributions and in slightly skewed distributions such as those in Figures 3.9 and 3.10).

Properties of the Mode

1. The mode is appropriate for all levels of measurement. For example, we might be interested in which is the modal religion (nominal level) in some nation, which is the modal rating (ordinal level) given a teacher, or which is the modal number of years of education (interval level) completed by members of a certain ethnic group.

2. A frequency distribution is called *bimodal* (*trimodal, multimodal*) if there are two (three, many) values that occur with the greatest frequency. In practice, a distribution is usually referred to as bimodal if there are two distinct mounds in the distribution, even if they are not of exactly the same height (see Figure 3.11). Bimodal distributions often occur with attitudinal variables in which the response of an individual tends to be strongly in one direction or another, leading to polarization of the population. For example, a bimodal distribution might result from responses to the statement "It should be possible for a pregnant woman to obtain a legal abortion if she wants it for any reason," when the possible responses are strongly agree, agree, unsure, disagree, and strongly disagree.

Fig. 3.11 A Hypothetical Bimodal Distribution (Note Early Retirement with Benefits After 20 Years)

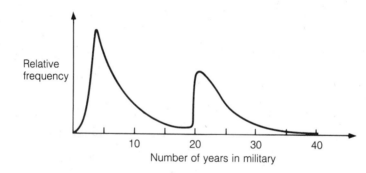

3. The mean, median, and mode are identical for a unimodal, symmetric distribution, such as a bell-shaped distribution (see Figure 3.6).

The mode is not used as often as the mean or median for describing a distribution of ungrouped measurements on an interval variable. Nevertheless, there are situations in which the mode may be a more appropriate measure to use than the mean or the median. For example, a company that makes unisex blue jeans may find the distribution of leg length of its potential customers to be bimodal, due to the mixture of men and women in the population of interest. Then it would not be in the best interest of the company to make most of its jeans to fit the mean or median leg length of its customers. The mode is most informative when we need a measure of the most frequently occurring level(s) of a variable.

The statistics described in this section should be viewed as complementary measures. You should not find it necessary to treat one of them as a better measure than the others, since they describe different aspects of the distribution of data. In any particular example, it may be beneficial to report some or all of their values. When we later consider inference procedures for variables measured on at least an interval scale, we will use primarily the mean. This is mainly due to the fact that, of these measures, the mean is the one that is used most often in practice.

Lastly, it should be kept in mind that these statistics are sometimes misused, as in Example 3.6. People who use statistical results sometimes choose the descriptive statistic that yields the impression they wish to convey. Other statistics that might lead to somewhat different interpretations are ignored. The educated reader should be on the lookout for misleading statistical analyses by considering the method of data presentation. Does the researcher justify the choice of measures?

3.3 Measures of Dispersion

A measure of central location alone is not adequate for numerically describing a frequency distribution, since it describes only a typical value of the distribution and not the spread of the measurements about that value. In order to illustrate this, let us consider the two distributions in Figure 3.12. The citizens of nation A and the citizens of nation B have the same mean yearly income ($10,000). However, the distributions of those incomes differ fundamentally, nation B being much more homogeneous. An income of $12,500 would be considered to be quite large for a resident of nation B, though not especially large relative to the incomes of the residents of nation A. In this section, we define some measures that can be used to quantify such differences for interval variables. These statistics describe the *variation* of the observations in a sample, and are referred to as **measures of dispersion**.

Fig. 3.12 Distributions with the Same Mean but Different Dispersions

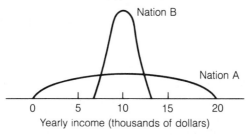

The Range

One very simple measure for expressing the dispersion in a sample is the *range* of the measurements.

Sample Range

The *sample range* is the difference between the largest and smallest measurements in a sample.

For nation A, as described by Figure 3.12, the range of income values is $20,000 − 0 = $20,000; for nation B, the range is $13,000 − $7,000 = $6,000. In this sense, nation A has a much greater dispersion of incomes than nation B. The interquartile range, defined in the previous section, is another type of range statistic. It would also be larger for nation A incomes than for nation B incomes.

However, the range is not sensitive to other characteristics of the dispersion of the data. The three distributions shown in Figure 3.13 all have the same mean (10,000) and range (20,000), yet they differ in dispersion about the center of the distribution. In terms of distances of the income measurements from their mean, nation A is the most disperse and nation B is the least disperse. That is, the incomes of the residents of nation A tend to be farthest from the mean of $10,000, and the incomes of the residents of nation B tend to be closest to that value.

Fig. 3.13 Distributions with the Same Mean and Range, but Different Dispersions About the Mean

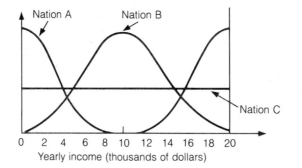

Yearly income (thousands of dollars)

Standard Deviation   Other measures of dispersion are based on the *deviations* of the measurements from some measure of central tendency, usually their mean.

Deviation

The *deviation* of the ith measurement from the sample mean is the quantity $(Y_i - \bar{Y})$, the difference between that observation and the sample mean.

For each observation, there is a corresponding deviation. A deviation is positive if the observation falls above the sample mean and negative if it falls below it. The interpretation of $\bar{Y}$ as the center of gravity of the data implies that the sum of the deviations about the mean, $\sum_{i=1}^{n} (Y_i - \bar{Y})$, equals 0 for any sample. Thus, to obtain a summary measure of dispersion, we need to consider either the absolute values or the squares of the deviations. The two measures we study incorporate the squares, which are easier to work with mathematically. The first of these measures is the *variance*.

Sample Variance

The *sample variance** of a set of n measurements $Y_1, \ldots, Y_n$ is

$$s^2 = \frac{\Sigma(Y_i - \bar{Y})^2}{n - 1} = \frac{(Y_1 - \bar{Y})^2 + (Y_2 - \bar{Y})^2 + \cdots + (Y_n - \bar{Y})^2}{n - 1}$$

---

*Some textbooks define the variance and standard deviation with n in the denominator rather than $(n - 1)$. See Note 7 at the end of this chapter.

The variance is approximately an average of the squared deviations. The units of measurements for the variance, though, are the squares of those for the original measurements, since it is based on *squared* deviations. This makes the variance difficult to interpret. It is customary to use the square root of the variance, called the *standard deviation*, for descriptive and interpretive purposes.

Sample Standard Deviation

The *sample standard deviation s* is the positive square root of the variance:

$$s = \sqrt{\frac{\Sigma(Y_i - \bar{Y})^2}{n - 1}}$$

From inspection of the formula for s, we see that the larger the deviations about the mean, the larger s tends to be.

Example 3.12

Each of the following sets of quiz scores in two small classes has a mean of 5 and a range of 10:

Class 1: 0, 4, 4, 5, 7, 10

Class 2: 0, 0, 1, 9, 10, 10

By inspection, it is clear that the scores in class 1 tend to be less disperse about the mean than those in class 2. For class 1,

$$s^2 = \frac{(0 - 5)^2 + (4 - 5)^2 + (4 - 5)^2 + (5 - 5)^2 + (7 - 5)^2 + (10 - 5)^2}{6 - 1}$$

$$= \frac{56}{5} = 11.2$$

so the standard deviation is $s = \sqrt{11.2} = 3.3$. Likewise, it can be verified that for class 2, $s^2 = 26.4$ and $s = 5.1$. Since $5.1 > 3.3$, the performances of students in class 2 are more variable than those in class 1, as expected. Similarly, if s_A, s_B, and s_C represent the standard deviations of the three distributions drawn in Figure 3.13, then we would have $s_B < s_C < s_A$.* ∎

It is important to understand that the expression $\Sigma (Y - \bar{Y})^2$ indicates that the deviations are squared and *then* added. If we added the deviations and then squared that sum, we would get 0.

Properties of the Standard Deviation

1. $s \geq 0$, with $s = 0$ only when all the observations have the same value, the situation corresponding to the minimum possible dispersion.

2. The greater the dispersion about the mean, the larger will be the value of s. An illustration of this property was given by Example 3.12.

*The notation $s_B < s_C < s_A$ means that s_B is less than s_C, which is less than s_A.

Example 3.13   As a way of comparing the difference in the forms of the family income distributions of a socialist and a capitalist nation, we could compare the standard deviations. If the two distributions have (or are adjusted to have) approximately the same mean, we would expect the standard deviation to be larger for the capitalist nation; that is, we would expect the capitalist nation to have a more heterogeneous income distribution.   ■

Note 4 at the end of this chapter presents two properties of standard deviations that refer to the effect of rescaling the data. We next discuss a property that helps us to understand the numerical value of s.

Interpreting the   Thus far, we do not have much of an intuitive feeling for the magnitude of the
Magnitude of s   standard deviation s other than in a comparative sense. A distribution with $s = 5.1$ is more disperse than one with $s = 3.3$, but how do we interpret *how large $s = 5.1$ is?* A precise answer to this question requires further knowledge of the exact mathematical form of a frequency distribution. We will see a detailed example of the role the standard deviation plays when we consider the *normal distribution* in Chapter 4. For the present, however, the approximation presented in the box provides a rough interpretation for the value of s for some data sets.

Empirical Rule

If the histogram of a collection of measurements is approximately bell-shaped, then:

1. About 68% of the measurements lie between $\bar{Y} - s$ and $\bar{Y} + s$.
2. About 95% of the measurements lie between $\bar{Y} - 2s$ and $\bar{Y} + 2s$.
3. All or nearly all of the measurements lie between $\bar{Y} - 3s$ and $\bar{Y} + 3s$.

The rule is referred to as the Empirical Rule because of the tendency of many distributions encountered in practice to be approximately bell-shaped. Figure 3.14 is a graphical portrayal of the rule.

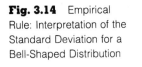

Fig. 3.14 Empirical Rule: Interpretation of the Standard Deviation for a Bell-Shaped Distribution

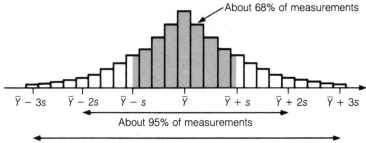

Example 3.14 The distribution of scores on the verbal portion of an aptitude test is approximately bell-shaped about the mean 500, with a standard deviation of 100 (see Figure 3.15). By the Empirical Rule, this implies that about 68% of the students scored between 400 and 600 on the test, since 400 and 600 are the numbers that are one standard deviation below and above the mean of 500. Similarly, about 95% of the students scored between 300 and 700. In other words, about 5% scored either below 300 or above 700. If the distribution is completely symmetric about 500, this implies that the top 2.5% of the scores were above 700 and the lowest 2.5% were below 300. ■

Fig. 3.15 A Bell-Shaped Distribution of Test Scores with Mean 500 and Standard Deviation 100

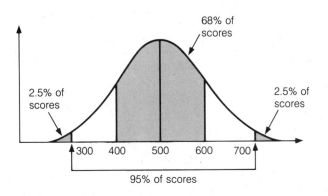

It should be emphasized that the percentages associated with the intervals about the mean in the Empirical Rule are approximate and refer only to distributions that are approximately bell-shaped. The exact percentages depend on the form of the distribution, as demonstrated in Example 3.15.

Example 3.15 A survey is conducted of 100 women who have been widowed for at least 1 year. One of the variables measured for the women is the number of illnesses requiring a visit to the hospital in the year following the death of the husband. The frequency distribution for these 100 women on this variable is given in Table 3.8 (next page). Rather than add the 100 separate measurements to obtain ΣY_i for the numerator of $\bar{Y}$, we can exploit the fact that most of the values occurred several times. To get the sum of the 100 observations, we multiply each possible value of the variable by the frequency of its occurrence, and then add; that is,

$$\Sigma Y_i = 55(0) + 25(1) + 7(2) + 4(3) + 3(4) + 3(5) + 0(6) + 2(7) + 1(8)$$
$$= 100$$

so that

$$\bar{Y} = \frac{\Sigma Y_i}{n} = 1.0$$

Table 3.8

Frequency Distribution of
the Number of Illnesses
Requiring a Hospital Visit

NUMBER OF HOSPITALIZATIONS	FREQUENCY
0	55
1	25
2	7
3	4
4	3
5	3
6	0
7	2
8	1
TOTAL	100

Similarly, multiplying each squared deviation by its frequency of occurrence, we calculate

$$\Sigma \, (Y_i - \bar{Y})^2 = 55(0 - 1)^2 + 25(1 - 1)^2 + \cdots + 1(8 - 1)^2 = 274$$

so that the standard deviation is

$$s = \sqrt{\frac{\Sigma(Y_i - \bar{Y})^2}{n - 1}} = \sqrt{\frac{274}{99}} = \sqrt{2.77} = 1.66$$

The values 0, 1, and 2 are all within one standard deviation of the mean. Now, 87 of the 100 observations occur at one of these three values, so 87% of the distribution falls within $\bar{Y} \pm s$. This is considerably larger than the 68% given in the Empirical Rule for bell-shaped distributions. Of course, the Empirical Rule does not apply to the frequency distribution in this example, since it is not even approximately bell-shaped. Instead, it is highly skewed to the right. We observe that the smallest value in the distribution (0) is less than one standard deviation below the mean; the largest value in the distribution (8), however, is more than four standard deviations above the mean. This is typical of what usually occurs with highly skewed distributions. As another example, suppose that we are informed that the scores on an exam are described by $\bar{Y} = 86$ and $s = 15$. Since the upper bound of 100 is less than one standard deviation above the mean, we might surmise that the distribution of scores is highly skewed to the left. ■

3.4 Sample Statistics and Population Parameters

We have used $\bar{Y}$ and s in this chapter as descriptions for measurements on a sample selected from a population. Since the values of $\bar{Y}$ and s depend on which elements of the population are sampled, a priori (before selecting the sample) they can be considered to be variables. Their values vary according to the particular sample selected and cannot be exactly predicted before the sample is chosen. Once the sample is obtained and they are computed, they become known sample statistics.

It is important at this stage to differentiate between the sample statistics and the corresponding measures that could be calculated for the entire population if we had the necessary information. In Section 1.2, we introduced the term *parameter* to represent a summary descriptive measure for the population. Thus, a statistic refers to a descriptive characteristic of a sample, while a parameter refers to a descriptive characteristic of the population from which the sample was taken. In this text, lowercase Greek letters will usually be used to denote parameters. Roman letters are usually used to denote the corresponding sample statistics.

Notation

Let μ (mu) and σ (sigma) denote the mean and standard deviation of the measurements Y_1, Y_2, . . . , Y_N on the variable for the entire population. The population size is denoted by N.

We refer to μ and σ as the *population mean* and *population standard deviation*, respectively. For instance, we can represent the value of the population mean by

$$\mu = \frac{\sum_{i=1}^{N} Y_i}{N}$$

This is the average of the population measurements. The population standard deviation is the square root of the average of the squared deviations of the population measurements about the population mean.

Whereas the statistics $\overline{Y}$ and s are variables whose values depend on the sample chosen, the parameters μ and σ are constants. This is because μ and σ refer to just one particular group of measurements—namely, the measurements taken on the entire population. Of course, the parameter values are usually unknown, which is the primary reason for sampling from populations and calculating sample statistics as estimates of their values. Much of the remainder of this text deals with methods of making inferences about unknown parameters (such as μ) by using sample statistics (such as $\overline{Y}$) as estimates of their values. Before considering these inferential procedures, though, we need to study some of the elements of probability that are basic to their formulation. The notions of the probability of an event and the probability distribution of a variable are the subjects of Chapter 4.

Summary

In this chapter, we have considered ways of *describing* the information in a sample. Data sets in social science research are often very large, and it is imperative to be able to describe in summary fashion the important characteristics of the information contained therein.

One route to describing the data involves the construction of a *frequency distribution* for the sample measurements. A *histogram* provides a picture of the frequency distribution. It consists of a graph of the relative frequencies for a particular collection of categories. We can tell from the histogram whether the distribution is approximately bell-shaped, U-shaped, highly skewed, or whatever. The *stem and leaf diagram* is a type of histogram that also presents the individual scores.

Measures of central tendency describe various aspects of the center of the collection of measurements. The *mean* is the sum of the measurements divided by the sample size. The *median* divides the ordered data set into two parts of equal numbers of observations. The *mode* is the most commonly occurring value.

Measures of dispersion describe the variability of the measurements. The *range* is the difference between the largest and smallest measurements. The *variance* describes the squared deviations about the mean. Its square root, the *standard deviation*, is easier to interpret. Most, if not all, of the measurements in a sample with a bell-shaped distribution fall within three standard deviations of the mean. These measures of central tendency and dispersion are summarized in Table 3.9.

A *statistic* is a summary measure of some aspect of a sample. A *parameter* is a summary measure of some aspect of a population and is usually of greater interest to the researcher than the particular value of the statistic, which depends on the sample chosen. *Statistical inference* is the use of statistics for making inferences about parameters.

Table 3.9   Measures of Central Tendency and Dispersion

	MEASURE	DEFINITION	APPROPRIATE SCALE OF MEASUREMENT
CENTRAL TENDENCY	Mean	$\bar{Y} = \dfrac{\Sigma Y_i}{n}$	Interval
	Median	Middle measurement of ordered sample	Ordinal, interval
	Mode	Most frequently occurring value	Nominal, ordinal, interval
DISPERSION	Variance	$s^2 = \dfrac{\Sigma(Y_i - \bar{Y})^2}{n-1}$	Interval
	Standard deviation	$s = \sqrt{\dfrac{\Sigma(Y_i - \bar{Y})^2}{n-1}}$	Interval
	Range	Difference between largest and smallest measurement	Interval

Notes

Section 3.2

1. The *least squares property* of the mean states that the sum of squares of deviations of a set of measurements about their mean is smaller than the sum of squares of deviations of those measurements about any other number. In other words, the data tend to fall closer to $\bar{Y}$ than to any other real number c, in the sense that $\Sigma(Y - \bar{Y})^2 < \Sigma(Y - c)^2$.

2. Unlike the situation with means, if we know the median for each of several sets of data, we cannot calculate the overall median for the combined set of measurements. We would need all the original observations in the various groups to determine the overall middle measurement. The observations would be pooled into one set, and then the median would be computed in the usual manner.

3. The quartiles of a distribution are often represented graphically using a *box and whiskers* plot. Suppose, for instance, that scores on an index of mental depression range in a particular sample from 2 to 75, with a lower quartile of 5, median of 10, and upper quartile of 20. The corresponding box and whiskers plot is as shown in Figure 3.16.

Fig. 3.16   Box and Whiskers Plot for Depression Index

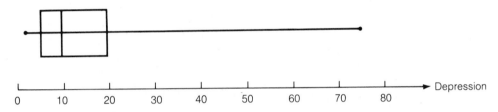

The *box* contains the central 50% of the distribution, from the lower quartile to the upper quartile. The median is marked by a line drawn vertically within the box. The *whiskers* extend from the quartiles to the minimum and maximum values. The box and whiskers plot given here indicates that the distribution of depression scores is skewed to the right (why?). For further discussion of these plots, see Tukey (1977).

Section 3.3

4. Another disadvantage of the range is that one very extreme score can have a large effect on its value, perhaps giving a misleading impression. In addition, a value of the range calculated from a sample of measurements will tend to underestimate the true population range; it cannot overestimate it. The reason for this is that the smallest and largest values in the sample cannot be more extreme than the smallest and largest values in the population, since the sample is a subset of the population. Thus, for inferential purposes, the sample range is inadequate (unless adjusted in some way) as an estimate of the population range. Nevertheless, the range has the advantages of being easily calculable and interpretable.

5. The mean and standard deviation of a sample may change if data are rescaled. The following properties give the effects of adding a constant or multiplying by a constant:

   a. If a fixed constant c is added to each measurement in a sample, then the new sample has mean $\bar{Y} + c$, and the standard deviation s is unchanged.

b. If each sample measurement is multiplied by a fixed constant c, then the new sample has mean $c\bar{Y}$ and standard deviation $|c|s$.

See Problems 3.23–3.25 for illustrations of these properties.

6. The sum of squares $\Sigma(Y - \bar{Y})^2$ is equivalent algebraically to $\Sigma Y^2 - n\bar{Y}^2$. The second expression can be simpler to use for hand calculation of s^2 and s. Since most basic statistics can be obtained directly using pocket calculators or computer packages, we do not emphasize these "shortcut" formulas in this text.

Section 3.4

7. The *population* variance or standard deviation is generally defined with the population size N, rather than $(N - 1)$, in the denominator. For instance, the population variance is $\Sigma(Y - \mu)^2/N$, the average squared deviation about the population mean. The sample formulas use $(n - 1)$ primarily because it is more convenient for the inferential statistical methods discussed later in the text.

Problems

1. The following set of fifty measurements represents the hypothetical percentages of individuals in the working force who are state, county, or city government employees for the fifty states.

15.19	16.69	22.15	5.98	11.70
11.60	20.31	8.99	25.51	27.94
21.08	17.83	18.62	16.04	14.45
13.76	13.40	15.59	27.19	8.12
16.43	15.58	10.64	19.45	24.09
20.92	23.30	14.91	8.77	14.58
7.56	26.88	22.87	19.96	15.17
25.11	14.76	20.83	22.80	17.99
18.40	12.17	11.14	18.71	22.67
11.01	10.02	12.80	10.35	16.25

a. Using the intervals .00%–3.00%, 3.01%–6.00%, 6.01%–9.00%, and so forth, tally the frequencies and construct a frequency distribution.
b. Find the relative frequencies for the intervals given in part a.
c. Sketch a relative frequency histogram, using the class intervals given in part a.
d. Identify the modal category.
e. Identify the class interval containing the median.

2. Refer to Table 3.1.
a. Construct a relative frequency distribution using the intervals 0–9, 10–19, 20–29, 30–39, and 40–49.

b. Draw the relative frequency histogram using the intervals of part **a**.

c. Construct a stem and leaf diagram using stems appropriate for these intervals.

3. The accompanying table gives the percentage distribution of married women in Japan using contraception, by method, for the year 1975. Draw a relative frequency histogram to display the data.

METHOD	PERCENTAGE
Pills	3
IUD	9
Sterilization	5
Condoms	50
Withdrawal	4
Other	29
TOTAL	100

Source: "Changing Contraceptive Patterns: A Global Perspective." *Population Bulletin, 32,* No. 3, Aug. 1977.

4. The table presents the 1960–1981 cumulative military expenditures (in billions of dollars) for the ten countries with the highest such expenditures for that period.

COUNTRY	EXPENDITURES
United States	1,820
Soviet Union	1,300
China	290
West Germany	239
France	224
United Kingdom	213
Saudi Arabia	93
Italy	82
Japan	77
Iran	60

Calculate each of the following:

a. Mean

b. Median

c. Range

d. Standard deviation

5. The table at the top of the next page lists the 1981 per capita gross national products (in U.S. dollars) for eight Central American countries. Calculate the mean, median, range, and standard deviation.

COUNTRY	PER CAPITA GNP
Belize	$1,030
Costa Rica	1,810
El Salvador	670
Guatemala	1,020
Honduras	530
Mexico	1,590
Nicaragua	660
Panama	1,350

6. Six newly elected representatives in a state legislature have ages 47, 63, 50, 58, 36, and 46. Find the mean, median, and standard deviation of the ages of the new representatives.

7. Why is the median sometimes preferred over the mean as a measure of central tendency? Give an example to illustrate your answer.

8. Give an example of a variable for which the mode could be calculated, but not the mean or median.

9. A group of high school students takes an exam. The mean score for the boys is 66, and the median is 74. Both the mean and the median score for the girls is 70. How can you explain the large difference between the two summary measures for the boys? Can you make a conclusion concerning which group did better? [*Hint:* How have you decided to define *better*?]

10.

a. If a distribution is highly skewed to the right, we expect the mean to be (select the best response):
   (i) Larger than the median
   (ii) Smaller than the median
   (iii) Equal to the median
b. For each of the following, would you expect the mean or the median to be greater? Explain why.
   (i) The selling price of new homes in 1984
   (ii) The number of children ever born per woman age 40 or over
   (iii) The score on an easy exam (mean = 88, standard deviation = 10)
   (iv) Age at death
   (v) The number of cars owned per family

11. For each of the following variables, indicate whether you would expect its relative frequency histogram to be bell-shaped, U-shaped, skewed to the right, or skewed to the left.

a. Exam score (scores fall between 0 and 100, with a mean of 90 and a standard deviation of 10)
b. IQ
c. Number of times arrested in past year
d. Time taken to complete difficult exam (maximum time is 1 hour)

e. Attitude toward legalization of abortion
f. Assessed value of home
g. Weekly church contribution (median is $5 and mean is $7.50)

12. Give examples of variables encountered in the social sciences having a distribution that you would expect to be:
a. Approximately symmetric
b. Skewed to the right
c. Skewed to the left
d. Bimodal
e. Skewed to the right, with a mode and median of 0 but a positive mean

13. The mean yearly income for the 200 police officers in a large city is $21,600, whereas the mean yearly income for the other 400 city employees is $19,500. Find the overall mean income for city employees.

14. A company conducts a study of the number of miles traveled using public transportation by its employees during a typical day. A random sample of ten employees yields the following values (in miles):

   0, 0, 4, 0, 0, 0, 10, 0, 6, 0

Calculate the mean, median, mode, range, variance, and standard deviation of these measurements.

15. Why is the standard deviation usually preferred over the range as a measure of dispersion?

16. For an exam given to a class, the students' scores ranged from 35 to 98, with a mean of 70. Which of the following is the most realistic value for the standard deviation: 1, 12, 60, or -10? Why?

17. In a large northern city, monthly payments to people on welfare last year were observed to have approximately a bell shape with mean $400 and standard deviation $80. Give a range of values within which all or nearly all the payments fell.

18. Suppose the distribution of the prices of new homes built in the United States in 1985 was approximately bell-shaped, with a mean of $82,000 and a standard deviation of $26,000. Describe the distribution using properties of the standard deviation. If your new house was priced half a standard deviation above the mean in 1985, how much did it cost?

19. The mean and standard deviation for the data in Problem 1 are $\bar{Y} = 16.77$ and $s = 5.60$. Calculate the exact percentage of sample observations falling in the following areas:
a. Within one standard deviation of the mean
b. Within two standard deviations of the mean
c. Within three standard deviations of the mean
d. More than one standard deviation above the mean
Compare these results to the approximations given in the Empirical Rule.

20. Grade point averages of graduating seniors at the University of Rochester are approximately bell-shaped in distribution, ranging from 2.0 to 4.0 with a mean of about 3.0. Using the fact that all or nearly all measurements for this form of distribution occur within three standard deviations of their mean, give an approximation for the value of the standard deviation.

21. As part of a study of college students' sexual behaviors, each student in a sample gives a response to the question, "With how many partners have you engaged in sexual intercourse?" The results are summarized by the descriptive statistics $\bar{Y} = 2.0$ and $s = 3.0$. Based on these values, do you expect the frequency distribution of this variable to be bell-shaped? Why?

22. What is the difference between the descriptive measures symbolized by the following?
a. $\bar{Y}$ and μ
b. s and σ

*23. The scores on a difficult exam have a mean of 52 and a standard deviation of 20. The teacher decides to boost each score by 25 points and then award an A for a score of 90 or above, a B for scores of 80–89, and so forth. In other words, the distribution has shifted in location by 25 units to the right, but the shape and spread of the distribution have not been affected. What are the mean and standard deviation of the shifted scores?

*24. Data on the proportion of residents who were victims of a crime in the previous 12 months are obtained for all metropolitan areas in the United States with populations exceeding 100,000. The mean and standard deviation are determined to be $\bar{Y} = .053$ and $s = .020$. For a public presentation, this variable is transformed to the related variable, number per 1,000 residents who were victims of a crime in the previous 12 months. In other words, each measurement in the original sample is multiplied by 1,000, so that the data may be displayed as integers instead of proportions. Find the mean and standard deviation for the newly defined variable.

*25. The results of the study described in Problem 14 are to be reported in a French newspaper. The ten measurements are converted to kilometer units for this purpose (1 mile = 1.6 kilometers). What are the mean and standard deviation of the converted measurements?

*26. Refer to Problem 1. Explain why the mean of these fifty measurements is not necessarily the same as the percentage, for the entire nation, of individuals in the working force who are government employees.

*27. The crude death rate is the number of deaths in a year, per size of the population, multiplied by 1,000. Mexico, in 1981, had a crude death rate of 8 (i.e., 8 deaths per 1,000 population), while the United States had a crude death rate of 9.

---

*Note: The problems in this text marked with an asterisk are of a more difficult or more theoretical nature than the others. Many of them are used to present additional material beyond that covered in the chapter discussions.

Using what you learned about weighted averages in Example 3.5, explain how this could happen even if the United States had a lower crude death rate for people of every age.

*28. Suppose that the sample means for k different sets of data based on sample sizes $n_1, n_2, \ldots, n_k$ are $\bar{Y}_1, \bar{Y}_2, \ldots, \bar{Y}_k$, respectively. Prove that the overall sample mean for the combined set of measurements is

$$\bar{Y} = \frac{n_1\bar{Y}_1 + n_2\bar{Y}_2 + \cdots + n_k\bar{Y}_k}{n_1 + n_2 + \cdots + n_k}$$

Interpret $\bar{Y}$ as a weighted average of $\bar{Y}_1, \bar{Y}_2, \ldots, \bar{Y}_k$.

*29. Show that $\sum_{i=1}^{n} (Y_i - \bar{Y})$ must equal 0 for any collection of measurements, $Y_1, Y_2, \ldots, Y_n$.

*30. A random sample of n individuals is selected for an experiment. Let X_i represent the measurement on the variable of interest for the ith individual, before the experiment is conducted. Let Y_i represent the measurement on that variable for the ith individual, after the experiment is finished. The difference in these measurements for the ith individual is $D_i = Y_i - X_i$.
   a. Letting $\bar{X}$, $\bar{Y}$, and $\bar{D}$ represent the means of these three sets of measurements, show that $\bar{D} = \bar{Y} - \bar{X}$.
   b. Is the median difference (i.e., the median of the D_i values) equal to the difference between the medians of the Y_i and X_i values? Show this is true, or give a counterexample to show that it is false.

*31. The Russian mathematician Tchebysheff proved that a proportion of no greater than $1/k^2$ of the measurements can lie more than k standard deviations from the mean. In this statement, k is any real number greater than 1. The upper bound of $1/k^2$ for the proportion of measurements that are more than k standard deviations from the mean holds for *any* distribution of numbers, not just bell-shaped ones.
   a. Find the upper bound for the proportion of measurements falling more than $k = 2$ standard deviations from the mean; more than $k = 3$ standard deviations from the mean; more than $k = 10$ standard deviations from the mean.
   b. Compare the upper bound for $k = 2$ to the approximate proportion of measurements falling more than two standard deviations from the mean in a bell-shaped distribution. Why is there a difference?

Bibliography   Huff, D. (1954). *How to Lie with Statistics*. New York: W. W. Norton.
Tufte, E. R. (1983). *The Visual Display of Quantitative Information*. Cheshire, Conn.: Graphics Press.
Tukey, J. W. (1977). *Exploratory Data Analysis*. Reading, Mass.: Addison-Wesley.

CHAPTER 4

Probability Distributions

Contents

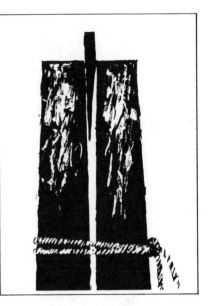

The study of probability has expanded in many directions since its early applications in seventeenth-century France as a means for evaluating gambling strategies in various games. Several courses could be devoted to a discussion of its philosophical foundations, theory, and application. In this chapter, we shall limit our consideration of probability to those aspects that form a foundation for basic statistical inference.

We first consider the notion of a probability distribution of a variable. A probability distribution provides a way of representing the chances of occurrence of the various possible values for the variable. We then introduce the normal distribution, the most important probability distribution for the methods discussed in this text. Next, we examine the concept of a sampling distribution, which is a probability distribution relating not to the specific measurements originally taken on the sample, but to some statistic calculated from those measurements (such as a sample mean or proportion). The importance of the normal distribution as a sampling distribution is illustrated in the last section, in a discussion of the Central Limit Theorem. This theorem, in itself a remarkable mathematical result, provides the mechanism for evaluating how close the mean $\bar{Y}$ of a set of sample observations is likely to be to the population mean μ.

Connection between Probability and Statistical Inference

In our study of probability in this chapter, we shall treat the parameter values as *known* numbers. This may seem artificial, since one of the main purposes of using statistical methods is to make inferences about *unknown* parameters using known sample statistics. However, we will see in the remaining chapters of the text that many inferential statistical procedures involve comparing observed sample statistics to *what we would expect to observe if the parameter values were particular numbers*. In order to illustrate the connection between statistical inference and probability reasoning using known parameter values, let us consider the following example.

Television networks often take a sample of voters on election day in order to make early predictions concerning the winners. Suppose that upon taking a poll of 1,000 voters in an election with two candidates, a network finds that 40% of the sampled individuals voted for Sam Stone and 60% voted for Betty McGee. In determining whether there is enough evidence to project the winner, the pollsters might consider the question, "If actually a majority of the entire population of voters prefers Stone, then what is the likelihood that in a sample of this size, only 40% or fewer of the *sampled* individuals would indicate a preference for Stone?" In other words, if Stone actually has enough support to win the election, then how likely would he be to obtain no more than 40% of the votes in a sample of size 1,000? If the likelihood is very small, it might be safe to predict that Stone will lose the election. In summary, the inference about the election outcome involves finding the probability of observing a certain sample result (40% or fewer of 1,000 voters favor Stone) under the supposition that the population percentage of voters preferring Stone (a parameter) actually exceeds 50%.

4.1 Probability Distributions for Discrete and Continuous Variables

There are several definitions and interpretations that have been given to the term *probability* over the last few centuries. In this book, we use the *relative frequency* conceptualization of this term; that is, we imagine a hypothetical sequence of repeated random observations on some phenomenon. Each observation may or may not result in some particular outcome. The *probability* of that outcome is defined to be the relative frequency of its occurrence *in the long run*.

Basic Concepts

Probability
The *probability* of a particular outcome in a random observation on a variable is the proportion of times that outcome would occur in the long run in repeated random sampling on the variable.

Being a relative frequency, a probability is a number between 0 and 1. For example, consider the possible outcome of a head landing up in flipping a balanced coin once. If the coin were repeatedly flipped, then it can be shown mathematically that the proportion of flips resulting in a head would tend toward .5 as the number of flips gets larger. Thus, we say that the probability of getting a head in any single flip of the coin equals .5. Similarly, in saying that the probability is .05 that a randomly selected adult in Philadelphia has been hospitalized for mental illness sometime in his or her lifetime, we mean that the proportion of *all* adults in Philadelphia who have been so hospitalized equals .05. If we repeatedly selected adults in Philadelphia at random, in the long run we would find 5% who have been hospitalized for mental problems.

Probability Distribution

When we consider the frequency distribution of a variable in a population, typically some values are represented more often than others. Thus, in sampling from that population, some values are more likely to occur than others. The *probability distribution* for a variable provides a listing of the probabilities of the various possible occurrences. The probability distribution of a *discrete* variable is such that a probability is assigned to each possible value of the variable. Each of the probabilities is a number between 0 and 1, and the sum of the probabilities of all possible values equals 1. If we let y represent a possible value of the variable Y and let $P(y)$ represent the probability of that value, then $0 \leq P(y) \leq 1$ and $\Sigma_{\text{all } y} P(y) = 1$. Example 4.1 illustrates a probability distribution for a discrete random variable.

Example 4.1

Five students, Jane Armstrong, Nancy Bolton, Robert Cash, Don Douglas, and Walter Edwards, are rated equal in terms of qualifications for admission to law school, ahead of other applicants. However, all but two of the positions have been filled for the entering class of students. Since only two more students may be admitted, the admissions committee decides to randomly choose two from the five top-rated candidates. In this strategy the committee is interested in the probability distribution of the variable Y = number of women admitted. Using the first letters of the last names to represent the students, the different combinations of students that could be admitted are (A, B), (A, C), (A, D), (A, E), (B, C), (B, D), (B, E), (C, D), (C, E), and (D, E). Each of these pairs is equally likely to be chosen, since the selection is to be made randomly. Since Y, the number of women admitted, equals 0 for three of the pairs, the probability of that occurrence is $P(0) = 3/10 = .3$. Similarly, $P(1) = .6$ and $P(2) = .1$, since there is only one pair for which both students are female. The probability distribution for Y is given in Table 4.1. We see that each probability is between 0 and 1 and that the sum of the probabilities is 1. ■

Table 4.1

Probability Distribution of Y = Number of Women Admitted

y	$P(y)$
0	.3
1	.6
2	.1
TOTAL	1.0

For a *continuous* variable, there is a continuum of possible values. The probability distribution of a continuous variable is one in which probabilities can be assigned to *intervals* of numbers. The probability that the variable falls in any particular interval is between 0 and 1, and the probability assigned to the interval containing all the possible values equals 1. The probability distribution of the continuous variable Y, distance student lives from his or her parents, would permit us to obtain, for example, $P(Y < 10)$, the probability that the distance is less than 10 miles. In the next section, we will give an illustration of a probability distribution for a continuous variable and show how to calculate such probabilities for any intervals.

What we referred to in Section 3.1 as the *population distribution* for a variable is, equivalently, the probability distribution for the value of an observation on that variable selected at random from that population. The relative frequency of some occurrence in the population is the probability of that occurrence when a single observation is selected randomly from that population. For example, if the relative frequency of individuals with a college education in a certain population is .30, then the probability that a randomly selected individual from that population has a college education is also .30.

Characterizing a Probability Distribution

Many useful probability distributions have mathematical formulas that can be used to calculate probabilities. In other situations, the probabilities are more easily obtained from tables or graphs of their values.

In a histogram of the probability distribution of a discrete variable, the *height* of the bar over a particular value represents the probability of that value. For example, Figure 4.1 is a histogram for the probability distribution of the number of women admitted as obtained in Example 4.1. In a graph of the probability distribution of a continuous variable, the *area* under the graph for a particular interval of values represents the probability that the variable occurs in that interval. For example, if the

Fig. 4.1 Histogram for the Probability Distribution of the Number of Women Admitted

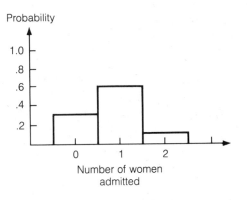

Number of women admitted

shaded area in Figure 4.2 equals one-tenth of the total area under the curve, then the probability is .1 that a student lives more than 2,000 miles from home. Those regions in which the graph is relatively high are the ones containing values most likely to be observed.

Fig. 4.2 Probability Distribution of Distance the Student Lives from Parents

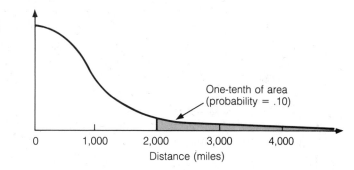

One-tenth of area (probability = .10)

Distance (miles)

As with a population distribution of measurements, a probability distribution can be characterized by parameters describing the central tendency and variability of the distribution. For example, if we repeatedly took random measurements on a variable having a particular probability distribution, then the mean of the measurements would converge to a number μ in the long run. This number serves as a measure of central tendency for a probability distribution and is called the *expected value* or *mean* of the distribution.* Similarly, the parameter σ (the standard deviation) can be used as a measure of variability for a probability distribution. Its square, the variance, measures the expected square of the deviation of an observation about the mean μ. The Empirical Rule (described in Section 3.3) can be used to interpret these descriptive measures. For example, if a probability distribution is approximately bell-shaped, then about 68% of the probability is concentrated between $\mu - \sigma$ and $\mu + \sigma$, whereas about 95% is between $\mu - 2\sigma$ and $\mu + 2\sigma$. We will not discuss formulas for computing these parameters in this text, since they are usually treated as unknown numbers. In Chapter 5, though, we will see how to estimate their values using sample data.

*If a probability distribution represents the population distribution of some variable, then μ is the mean of the variable in that population.

A *family* of probability distributions is a set of distributions with the same type of mathematical formula, but with their exact location and dispersion dependent on the values of one or more parameters. There are several families of probability distributions that are especially important in statistical analysis. Some of them are important because they give good approximations for the distributions of variables in the real world. Some are important because of their uses in statistical inference. In the next section, we study in some detail the family of normal probability distributions, which is important for both of these reasons.

4.2 The Normal Probability Distribution

A continuous variable with a probability distribution having a certain bell-shaped graph is said to be *normally distributed*. The family of normal probability distributions is the most important one in statistics. This family consists of a collection of bell-shaped curves with center and dispersion determined by the parameters μ and σ.*
The mathematical formula for this distribution is unimportant for our purposes, but we will need to develop a facility in using the tabulated probabilities associated with it.

The normal distribution is important partly because it serves as a good approximation for the distributions of many variables encountered in the application of statistics in the social sciences. In other words, histograms of sample data (representing continuous *or* discrete variables) often tend to be approximately bell-shaped. In such cases, we say that the variable is approximately normally distributed. In fact, we will see that some very fundamental statistical procedures are based on the assumption that the variables being analyzed are normally distributed in the population. Another important reason for the prominence of the normal distribution is its use in many inferential statistical methods. We shall see in Section 4.4, for example, that the normal distribution is used in determining how close one can expect a sample mean to be to the population mean.

We now present a more formal definition for the normal distribution and illustrate how to calculate probabilities associated with it.

Normal Distributions

The *family of normal distributions* is specified by a collection of symmetric, bell-shaped curves, each characterized by the value of the mean μ (any real number) and standard deviation σ (any positive number). The family has the property that for each fixed number z, the probability concentrated to the right of $\mu + z\sigma$ is the same for all normal distributions. These probabilities are listed in Table A at the end of the text.

Let us consider carefully the implications of this definition. First, the exact form of any particular normal distribution is determined by the mean μ and the standard deviation σ of that distribution. There is, for example, only one normal distribution

*Not all bell-shaped curves correspond to normal distributions, however—only the subset described by the formula in Note 1 at the end of the chapter.

centered around $\mu = 70.0$ with standard deviation $\sigma = 10.0$. Second, for particular values of μ and σ, the area under a normal curve beyond $\mu + z\sigma$ (i.e., the probability of an occurrence at least z standard deviations above the mean) depends only on the value of z. For example, we shall see that 2.28% of every normal distribution is concentrated beyond the number that is two standard deviations above the mean. Thus, if a variable has the normal distribution with mean 0 and standard deviation 1, then it has the probability .0228 of falling above $\mu + 2\sigma = 0 + 2(1) = 2$. Similarly, a normally distributed variable with mean 5 and standard deviation 3 has the probability .0228 of being larger than 11. In these two examples, we have taken the z-value to be $z = 2.00$ (see Figure 4.3).

Fig. 4.3 The Probability Above $\mu + 2\sigma$ for a Normal Distribution

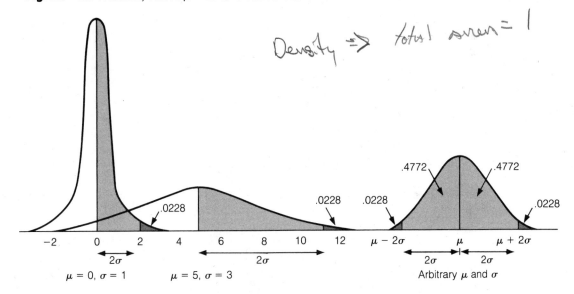

In the remaining chapters, we shall frequently have reason to make reference to a particular simplified normal distribution, called the *standard normal distribution*.

Standard Normal Distribution

The *standard normal distribution* is the normal distribution with parameter values $\mu = 0$ and $\sigma = 1$.

For this distribution, the number falling z standard deviations above the mean is $\mu + z\sigma = 0 + z(1) = z$. For instance, the score of 3 is three standard deviations above the mean. The standard normal distribution is portrayed at the top of Table A.

The *normal curve probabilities* associated with the collection of values that are at least z standard deviations above the mean are tabulated in Table A. The values for z

are listed to one decimal point in the left-hand column of the table, with the second decimal place listed above the separate columns. For example, if the second position to the right of the decimal point contains a 3, then use the fourth column in the body of the table. To illustrate, the tabulated probability corresponding to $z = 1.43$ is in the row labeled 1.4 and in the column labeled .03, and equals .0764. The entries in the main body of the table are the normal curve probabilities representing the areas under the right half of the normal distribution beyond $\mu + z\sigma$, and hence are numbers between 0 and .5. Example 4.2 illustrates the use of Table A and the connection between the normal distribution and the Empirical Rule.

Example 4.2   How much of the probability is concentrated within two standard deviations of the mean of a normal distribution?

The normal curve probability listed in Table A opposite $z = 2.00$ is .0228. Therefore the right-hand tail area above $\mu + 2\sigma$ equals .0228 for a normal distribution. The probability concentrated above μ equals .50, since the normal distribution is symmetric about μ. This implies that the area under the normal curve between μ and $\mu + 2\sigma$ equals $.5 - .0228 = .4772$ (see Figure 4.3). The area under the curve between $\mu - 2\sigma$ and μ also equals .4772, by symmetry. Thus, the total probability that a normally distributed variable is between $\mu - 2\sigma$ and $\mu + 2\sigma$ (i.e., within two standard deviations of the mean) is $2(.4772) = .9544$. It follows that if the distribution for some variable is approximately normal in shape, then about 95% of the measurements on that variable are within two standard deviations of the mean. So, we see that the approximate percentages given in the Empirical Rule in Section 3.3 are based on the exact percentages for the normal distribution. ■

Exercises   **1.** Using Table A, verify that the probability that a normally distributed variable is within one standard deviation of the mean equals .6826. [*Hint:* Let $z = 1.00$.]

2. Verify that the probability that a normally distributed variable is within three standard deviations of the mean equals .9973.

3. Verify that the probability that a normally distributed variable assumes a value between $\mu - 1.96\sigma$ and $\mu + 1.96\sigma$ equals .9500.

For some of the basic inferential procedures we will study in the next two chapters, we will need to find a z-value corresponding to a certain normal curve probability. This entails the reverse use of Table A from that of the previous example. We start out with the probability concentrated beyond some number, which would be listed in the body of Table A, and use it to find the z-value that expresses how many standard deviations that number is from the mean. In all such examples, it is helpful to sketch a normal curve to clarify the steps in obtaining the final solution.

Example 4.3   For a normal distribution, how many standard deviations from the mean is the 95th percentile? In other words, what is the value of z such that $\mu + z\sigma$ is above 95% of the distribution?

In order to find the z-value corresponding to the 95th percentile, we need to know the normal curve probability in the right-hand tail beyond the 95th percentile. Then, Table A can be used to find the z-value corresponding to that probability. Now, for $\mu + z\sigma$ to represent the 95th percentile, the probability below $\mu + z\sigma$ must equal .95, by the definition of a percentile. In other words, only 5% of the distribution is above the 95th percentile, so the right-hand tail probability equals .05 (see Figure 4.4). When we look up the normal curve probability of .0500 in Table A, we do not find it listed. Notice, though, that the probability .0505 corresponds to $z = 1.64$, and the probability .0495 corresponds to $z = 1.65$. By interpolation, the 95th percentile is about 1.645 standard deviations above the mean.* In other words, 5% of the normal distribution is located above $\mu + 1.645\sigma$, or more than 1.645 standard deviations above the mean.

Fig. 4.4 The 95th Percentile for a Normal Distribution

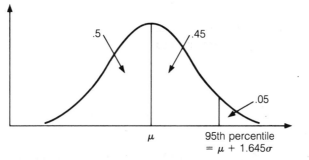

Let us consider the calculation of the 95th percentile for a particular normal distribution. Suppose that the ages of the representatives and senators in the U.S. Congress are approximately normally distributed, with a mean of 53 and a standard deviation of 11. Then, the 95th percentile equals

$$\mu + 1.645\sigma = 53 + 1.645(11) = 71$$

That is, about 5% of the members of Congress are over 71 years of age. By symmetry, about 5% of the members are aged under $\mu - 1.645\sigma = 35$ (the 5th percentile), and thus about 90% of the members of Congress are between 35 and 71 years old (i.e., within 1.645 standard deviations of the mean). ∎

Example 4.4   What is the z-value such that the probability is only .01 that a variable with a normal distribution falls more than z standard deviations from the mean (in either direction)?

In this example, it is necessary to find the z-value so that .01 is the probability that the variable is below $\mu - z\sigma$ or above $\mu + z\sigma$ (see Figure 4.5). Since the probability below $\mu - z\sigma$ equals the probability above $\mu + z\sigma$ by symmetry, the probability in just one tail is $.01/2 = .0050$. Now, the single-tail area of .0050 is the type of normal curve area that is tabulated in the body of Table A, so we look up .0050 in the table and notice that it corresponds to a z-value of about 2.58. Thus, the probability is .01

*In most places, we use z-values rounded off to two decimal places, so we will not discuss interpolation methods.

Fig. 4.5 Normal Curve Probabilities for Example 4.4

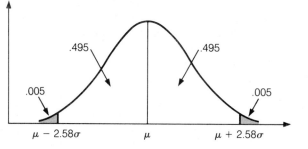

that a normally distributed variable falls more than 2.58 standard deviations from its mean. In other words, 99% of the measurements in a normal distribution are within 2.58 standard deviations of the mean.

Suppose, for example, that scores on an IQ test are scaled according to a normal distribution with mean $\mu = 100$ and standard deviation $\sigma = 16$. Then, about 99% of the scores fall between

$$\mu - 2.58\sigma = 100 - 2.58(16) = 58.7$$

and

$$\mu + 2.58\sigma = 100 + 2.58(16) = 141.3$$

z-Scores   We have used the symbol z in Table A in obtaining the probability of those values that are at least z standard deviations above the mean of a normal distribution. More generally, this symbol is used in statistics to express the distance between a number Y and the mean μ of a probability distribution, in terms of the number of standard deviations that Y is from μ.

---

z-Score

The **z-score** corresponding to Y is the number of standard deviations that Y is from μ.

Example 4.5   Suppose that scores on the verbal portion of the Scholastic Aptitude Test, a college entrance examination, are normally distributed with mean $\mu = 500$ and standard deviation $\sigma = 100$. Then, the z-score corresponding to the test score of $Y = 650$ is $z = 1.50$, since the score of 650 is 1.50 standard deviations above the mean. In other words, $Y = 650 = \mu + z\sigma$, where $z = 1.50$.

More generally, the distance between Y and μ equals $Y - \mu$, so that the z-score, which expresses this difference in units of standard deviations, is

$$z = \frac{Y - \mu}{\sigma}$$

To illustrate, when $\mu = 500$ and $\sigma = 100$, a measurement of $Y = 650$ corresponds to the z-score of

$$z = \frac{650 - 500}{100} = 1.50$$

Positive z-scores occur when the number Y falls above the mean μ, and negative z-scores occur when the number Y falls below the mean. The z-scores can be referred to Table A as was done in previous examples to obtain tail probabilities—right-hand tail probabilities for positive z-scores and left-hand tail probabilities for negative z-scores.

> To find the probability in the tail beyond a number Y for a normal distribution, notice that Y is $z = (Y - \mu)/\sigma$ standard deviations from μ. Thus, the probability is the area corresponding to that z-score in Table A.

Example 4.6 If $\mu = 500$ and $\sigma = 100$, then a value of 347 corresponds to a z-score of

$$z = \frac{Y - \mu}{\sigma} = \frac{347 - 500}{100} = -1.53$$

so the number 347 is 1.53 standard deviations below the mean. Looking up $z = 1.53$ in Table A,* we observe that the probability that a variable with this normal distribution takes on a value below 347 is .0630 (see Figure 4.6). ◼

Fig. 4.6 Normal Distribution for Example 4.6

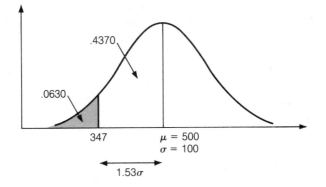

In succeeding chapters, it will often be helpful to have a shorthand notation for the z-value corresponding to a particular tail area under the normal curve.

> **Notation**
>
> Let the symbol z_a represent the z-score from Table A corresponding to the right-hand tail area of a (see Figure 4.7 at the top of the next page).

*Table A contains only positive z-values. Since the normal distribution is symmetric about the mean, the left-hand tail area below $-z$ equals the right-hand tail area above $+z$.

Fig. 4.7 Illustration of z_a Notation

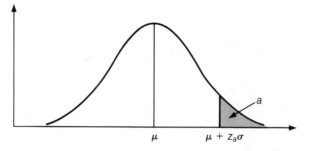

Example 4.7   Taking a = .025 in this notation, we have $z_{.025}$ = 1.96, since an area of .025 lies beyond $\mu + 1.96\sigma$. In other words, 1.96 is the z-score corresponding to a tail area of .025. Similarly, an area of .025 lies below $\mu - 1.96\sigma$, so that a total area of .05 lies more than 1.96σ from μ. ∎

Exercise   Verify that $z_{.10}$ = 1.28, $z_{.05}$ = 1.64, $z_{.01}$ = 2.33, and $z_{.005}$ = 2.58. Show that, since $z_{.01}$ = 2.33, 98% of a normal distribution is contained between $\mu - 2.33\sigma$ and $\mu + 2.33\sigma$.

For the standard normal distribution, $\mu = 0$ and $\sigma = 1$. Hence, $\mu + z_a\sigma = z_a$ is simply the number beyond which lies a tail area of a for the standard normal curve (see Figure 4.8). For example, the probability that a variable with the standard normal distribution falls above $z_{.025}$ = 1.96 simply equals .025, and the probability that it falls above 1.96 or below −1.96 equals .05. The main reason for studying this standardized distribution is that if the scores in a normal distribution are converted to z-scores (as is done in some inferential procedures), then those z-scores are centered around 0 and have a standard deviation of 1; that is, the z-scores have the standard normal distribution.

Fig. 4.8 The Standard Normal Distribution

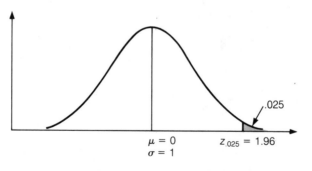

> If a variable has a normal distribution, and if its values are converted to z-scores by subtracting the mean and dividing by the standard deviation of the distribution, then the corresponding distribution of z-scores is the standard normal distribution.

Example 4.8   One of the findings of an energy study in a large metropolitan area is that the monthly use of electricity by households is normally distributed, with a mean of 700 and a standard deviation of 200 (kilowatt-hours). In order to see how many standard deviations from the mean each particular household is in electricity use, each observation is converted to a z-score. For example, a household using $Y = 600$ kilowatt-hours per month has a z-score of $z = (Y - \mu)/\sigma = (600 - 700)/200 = -.50$; a household using 900 kilowatt-hours per month has a z-score of $z = (900 - 700)/200 = 1.00$. Then, the distribution of z-scores for all the households in that area is the normal distribution with mean 0 and standard deviation 1—namely, the standard normal distribution. Each household with a z-score greater than 1.0 (i.e., electricity use more than one standard deviation above the mean) is sent a notice recommending a cutback in use, for conservation purposes. ■

We will be using z-scores and normal curve probabilities in many of the statistical procedures in coming chapters, so it is very important that you thoroughly understand the examples in this section and that you are able to do the related problems at the end of the chapter before proceeding to those chapters.

4.3
Sampling
Distributions

Basic Concepts

In the first two sections of this chapter, we have seen how a probability distribution describes the collection of possible values of a variable and their probabilities of occurrence. Unfortunately, exact descriptions of the distributions of most variables of interest in social science research are usually not available. Instead, we typically have access to sample data that can be used to estimate various characteristics of the distributions, such as the parameters μ and σ. For example, based on a sample of $n = 100$ migrant workers in California, we may obtain a value of the sample mean yearly income of $\bar{Y} = \$7,500$. We can then use $\bar{Y}$ as an estimate of μ, the actual mean yearly income of *all* California migrant workers.

When a sample statistic is used to estimate a population parameter, it is essential to attach to that estimate a measure of its goodness. The goodness of $\bar{Y}$ as an estimate of μ in the above example would depend on the answers to such questions as: How likely is it that the sample mean yearly income for 100 randomly sampled migrant workers is within \$1,000 of the population mean income μ? Within \$500? Within \$200? Now, just as the income of a California migrant worker is a variable, so is the mean income $\bar{Y}$ of $n = 100$ randomly selected California migrant workers. In other words, before the sample is obtained, the value of the sample mean is unknown (a variable). If several samples of size 100 each were selected, there would be a certain amount of *variation* in the $\bar{Y}$-values. There is a probability distribution that describes how much variation there would likely be if we repeatedly selected samples of a certain size n and formed a particular statistic. This distribution, which can be used to calculate probabilities of the possible values of the statistic based on observations in a *single* sample of size n, is called a *sampling distribution*.

Sampling Distribution

A *sampling distribution* is a probability distribution that specifies the probabilities of the possible values of a sample statistic.

Knowledge of the appropriate sampling distribution would allow us to calculate, for example, probabilities about:

1. The number of heads obtained in flipping a coin 12 times
2. The number of women obtained in selecting a random sample of 12 people for a jury
3. The mean family size for 50 families to be selected at random from some church membership list
4. The proportion of citizens who are registered Democrats, out of a random sample of 70 assembly-line employees

Before the samples are obtained, note that all of these are variables and have sampling distributions that describe the probabilities of their possible values. Thus, a sampling distribution is simply a particular type of probability distribution. Unlike the distributions considered in Section 4.1, a sampling distribution refers not to the probabilities associated with the separate measurements on the population, but to the probabilities associated with some statistic (i.e., some summary measure) to be computed from those measurements. The sampling distribution is especially important in inferential statistics because it gives us a mechanism for predicting how close a statistic will be to the parameter it is designed to estimate. For example, we can use it to determine the probability that the statistic falls within any given distance of that parameter.

One of the most important sampling distributions is that of the sample mean $\bar{Y}$. The actual form of this particular sampling distribution will be considered in the next section. Knowledge of it enables us to calculate, for example, probabilities concerning the value of the sample mean income of the 100 migrant workers. When we actually collect the sample and observe $\bar{Y}$, we do not actually know how close $\bar{Y}$ is to μ, since we do not know the value of μ. Based on the sampling distribution, though, we can make probabilistic statements about the error of estimation. For example, we might know from the sampling distribution that with very high probability (say, .99), $\bar{Y}$ will occur within at most \$350 of μ. Then, when we calculate $\bar{Y}$, we can be quite confident that μ is within \$350 of that value.

It may help in understanding the concept of a sampling distribution to consider a relative frequency interpretation. Suppose that several investigators each took separate random samples of 100 migrant workers, and each calculated a sample mean $\bar{Y}$ to use as an estimate of the population mean income μ. Certainly, we would not expect each sample of size 100 to yield the same sample mean, since the samples consist of different sets of people. There would be, however, some predictable amount of variability in the values of the sample means. After an extremely large number of samples of size 100 were collected, we could construct a histogram of the collection of $\bar{Y}$-values, thus empirically generating the sampling distribution of $\bar{Y}$. A sampling distribution of a statistic based on n measurements can, in general, be interpreted as the relative frequency distribution for that statistic that would be generated by repeatedly taking samples of size n, each time calculating the value of the statistic. It is not necessary to take several separate samples in practice, since the form of a sampling distribution can be derived theoretically using mathematical arguments. When we know the general form of the distribution, we can give probabilistic statements about the value of the sample statistic from one sample of measurements of some fixed size n.

The distribution given in Example 4.1 is an example of a sampling distribution—namely, the sampling distribution of the number of women admitted, when two students are randomly admitted from a group of five in which two are women. If we were *repeatedly* to select random samples of two of these five students, then in the long run, 30% of the pairs would have no women, 60% would include exactly one woman, and 10% would have two women (refer back to Table 4.1).

4.4 The Central Limit Theorem

We now consider an important result about the sampling distribution of the sample mean $\bar{Y}$. The theorem given below is important not only for the reasons discussed in the previous section, but also because statisticians have been able to prove very similar results about other basic statistics. This theorem is discussed in detail in this section so that you become more accustomed to the notion of a sampling distribution. Then, in the remainder of the text we describe more briefly the analogous results for the other statistics we study.

The Central Limit Theorem describes the shape of the sampling distribution of $\bar{Y}$ and gives the mean and standard deviation of that sampling distribution.

Notation
Let the symbol $\sigma_{\bar{Y}}$ denote the standard deviation of the sampling distribution of $\bar{Y}$. We refer to this measure as the *standard error* of the sampling distribution.

The standard error is a measure of the dispersion of the sampling distribution, and thus it can be used to describe how much variability there tends to be in the value of $\bar{Y}$ from sample to sample. We can interpret $\sigma_{\bar{Y}}$ as being the measure we would get if we repeatedly selected samples of size n from the population, calculated a $\bar{Y}$-value for each set of n measurements, and finally calculated the standard deviation of the $\bar{Y}$-values. Therefore, the standard error is basic to inferential procedures that predict how much error there could be in using $\bar{Y}$ to estimate μ. We use the symbol $\sigma_{\bar{Y}}$ (instead of σ) and the terminology *standard error* (instead of *standard deviation*) to distinguish this measure from the standard deviation σ of the population distribution of the variable.

Statement and Interpretation

We are now ready to state formally the Central Limit Theorem and make several comments about it.

Central Limit Theorem

Consider a random sample of n measurements from a population distribution having mean μ and standard deviation σ. Then, if n is sufficiently large, the sampling distribution of $\bar{Y}$ is approximately a normal distribution with mean μ and standard error $\sigma_{\bar{Y}} = \sigma/\sqrt{n}$.

Some implications and interpretations of the Central Limit Theorem follow.

1. Figure 4.9 displays a hypothetical population distribution for some variable and shows the corresponding sampling distributions of $\bar{Y}$ for the cases $n = 50$ and $n = 100$. As the sample size n increases, the standard error $\sigma_{\bar{Y}} = \sigma/\sqrt{n}$ decreases. The reason for this is that the denominator ($\sqrt{n}$) of the ratio increases, whereas the numerator is the population standard deviation (σ), which is a constant and is not dependent on the value of n. The interpretation of this fact is that $\bar{Y}$ tends to be closer to μ for larger values of n, since the sampling distribution becomes less disperse about μ. This is in agreement with our intuition that larger samples allow us to obtain more precise estimates of population characteristics. Thus, the error (referred to as *sampling error*) in estimating μ, which is due to the fact that we sampled only part of the population, tends to decrease as n increases.

2. The conclusion of the theorem about the sampling distribution being approximately normal in shape applies *no matter what the shape* of the population distribution. For large sample sizes, the sampling distribution of $\bar{Y}$ is approximately normal even if the population distribution is highly skewed or U-shaped. Figure 4.10 displays histograms of sampling distributions of $\bar{Y}$ for samples of sizes $n = 2$, 5, and 30, for four different shapes for the population distribution. Even if the population distribution itself is not normal, the sampling distribution

Fig. 4.9 A Population Distribution, and the Sampling Distributions of $\bar{Y}$ for $n = 50$ and $n = 100$.

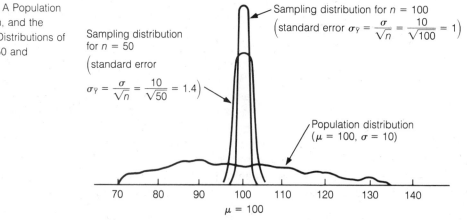

Sampling distribution for $n = 100$
$\left(\text{standard error } \sigma_{\bar{Y}} = \dfrac{\sigma}{\sqrt{n}} = \dfrac{10}{\sqrt{100}} = 1\right)$

Sampling distribution for $n = 50$
$\left(\text{standard error } \sigma_{\bar{Y}} = \dfrac{\sigma}{\sqrt{n}} = \dfrac{10}{\sqrt{50}} = 1.4\right)$

Population distribution
($\mu = 100$, $\sigma = 10$)

70   80   90   100   110   120   130   140

$\mu = 100$

Fig. 4.10 Four Different Population Distributions and the Corresponding Sampling Distributions of $\bar{Y}$

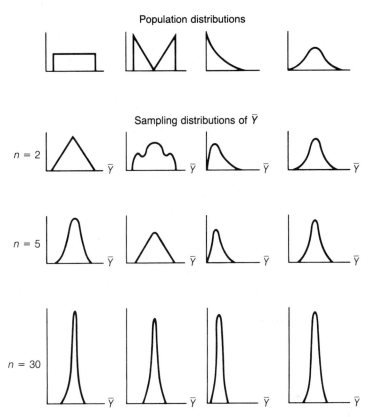

Population distributions

Sampling distributions of $\bar{Y}$

$n = 2$

$n = 5$

$n = 30$

has approximately a normal shape for n as small as 5, and the spread of the sampling distribution (characterized by $\sigma_{\bar{Y}}$) noticeably decreases as n increases.

3. The sampling distribution takes on a more normal shape as n increases. Although it is impossible to give a general statement about how large n must be before the sampling distribution achieves a shape close to normality (it largely depends on the skewness of the population distribution), a sample size of about 25 or 30 is usually sufficient to achieve a good approximation. If the *population* distribution is approximately bell-shaped, then the sampling distribution is well approximated by a normal curve for practically all sample sizes. Again, refer to Figure 4.10 for some examples.

4. The Central Limit Theorem can be proved theoretically using advanced mathematical arguments. We could also use the relative frequency interpretation to verify it empirically. Suppose that we repeatedly selected random samples of fixed size n from a distribution with mean μ and standard deviation σ, and that we calculated $\bar{Y}$ for each sample of n observations. Then, the histogram of the distribution of the $\bar{Y}$-values would be approximately a normal curve with standard error given by $\sigma/\sqrt{n}$, the population standard deviation divided by the square root of the sample size of each of the samples. The mean of the $\bar{Y}$-values would be approximately μ, the population mean.

5. Since the sampling distribution of $\bar{Y}$ is approximately normal about μ, with standard deviation $\sigma_{\bar{Y}}$, we can use Table A to calculate the probability that $\bar{Y}$ is within $z\sigma_{\bar{Y}}$ units of μ, for various values of z. To illustrate, $\bar{Y}$ will occur within $1.96\sigma_{\bar{Y}} = 1.96\sigma/\sqrt{n}$ units of μ with probability .95, since 95% of a normal distribution falls within 1.96 standard deviations of its mean. Reasoning of this nature is vital to the fundamental inferential statistical procedures that we will study in the next two chapters.

6. When we say that a sample size of about 25 or 30 or more is a sufficiently large sample, we are not implying that we have to choose only that size of a sample for precise statistical inference. In fact, depending on the precision desired, we may require a sample size of 30 or of several thousand. What we do mean is that if n is at least 30, then we can be very sure that the sampling distribution of $\bar{Y}$ is approximately normal in form, no matter what the form of the population distribution.

7. The sampling distribution of $\bar{Y}$ actually has mean μ and standard error $\sigma_{\bar{Y}} = \sigma/\sqrt{n}$ for *any* value of n. However, the shape of the sampling distribution of $\bar{Y}$ is normal for small n only if the population distribution is also normal (see the rightmost panel of Figure 4.10). The power of the Central Limit Theorem is based on the fact that, for *large n*, the sampling distribution of $\bar{Y}$ is approximately normal even if the population distribution is not.

Example 4.9 For the population of migrant workers in California, suppose that annual income is a variable having a distribution that is skewed to the right with a mean of $\mu = \$7,800$ and a standard deviation of $\sigma = \$1,500$. A researcher, unaware of these values, selects a random sample of 100 migrant workers and uses the sample mean annual income $\bar{Y}$ as an estimate of μ. Where is this sample mean likely to fall, relative to the population mean of $7,800?

We use the sampling distribution of $\bar{Y}$ to calculate probabilities about $\bar{Y}$. By the Central Limit Theorem, the sampling distribution of $\bar{Y}$ is approximately normal, even though the population distribution is skewed. The sampling distribution has the same mean as the population distribution—namely, $\mu = 7,800$. Its standard error is

$$\sigma_{\bar{Y}} = \frac{\sigma}{\sqrt{n}} = \frac{\$1,500}{\sqrt{100}} = \$150$$

Thus, the probability is about .68 that the researcher's sample mean falls within $150 of $\mu = \$7,800$, the probability is about .95 that $\bar{Y}$ falls within $300 of μ, and it is almost certain that $\bar{Y}$ falls within $450 (three standard errors) of μ. ∎

Example 4.10 The purpose of this example is to illustrate how the sampling distribution of $\bar{Y}$ can be used to calculate the probability that a sample mean will occur within a certain distance of the population mean μ, even if we do not know the value of μ. Suppose we plan to randomly sample 100 California migrant workers in order to estimate the mean annual income of all California migrant workers. We believe (based on a previous study) that the standard deviation of the population distribution on yearly income for this group is approximately $\sigma = \$1,500$. We shall calculate the probability that the sample mean income $\bar{Y}$ falls within \$200 of the true mean annual income μ for all California migrant workers.

Now, by the Central Limit Theorem, the sampling distribution of $\bar{Y}$ is approximately normal in shape and is centered about μ (whatever its value), with standard error

$$\sigma_{\bar{Y}} = \frac{\sigma}{\sqrt{n}} = \frac{\$1,500}{\sqrt{100}} = \$150$$

Hence, the probability that $\bar{Y}$ falls within \$200 of μ is the probability that a normally distributed variable falls within $200/150 = 1.33$ standard deviations of its mean. That is, the number of standard errors that $\mu + 200$ (or $\mu - 200$) is from μ is

$$z = [(\mu + 200) - \mu]/150 = 200/150 = 1.33 \qquad \text{(see Figure 4.11)}$$

From Table A, the probability that $\bar{Y}$ is *more than* 1.33 standard errors from μ (in either direction) is $2(.0918) = .1836$. It follows that the probability that $\bar{Y}$ is no more than \$200 from μ equals $1 - .1836 = .8164$. If, for the purposes of our survey, we require a higher probability that the sample mean $\bar{Y}$ falls no more than \$200 from the population annual mean income of California migrant workers, we could choose a larger sample so that the standard error is sufficiently small. ∎

Fig. 4.11 Sampling Distribution of $\bar{Y}$

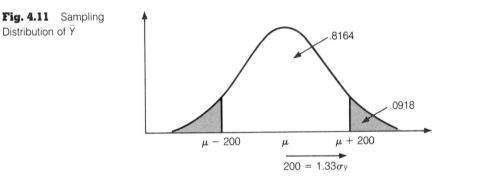

The Population, Sample, and Sampling Distributions

At this point, it may be instructive to review the three types of distributions among which it is necessary to distinguish in the remainder of this text—the *population* distribution, the distribution of the *sample*, and the *sampling* distribution.

1. The *population* distribution: This is the distribution from which we select the sample. This distribution is usually unknown in practice, so we formulate inferences about certain characteristics of it, such as the parameters μ and σ if the variable is at the interval level.

2. The distribution of the *sample*: This is the distribution of the measurements that we actually observe—that is, the sample observations $Y_1, Y_2, \ldots, Y_n$. The sample distribution may be graphically displayed in the form of a histogram of the observations, or numerically described by such sample statistics as $\bar{Y}$, the median, the sample standard deviation s, and so forth. The larger the sample size n, the closer this distribution should resemble the population distribution, and the closer the sample statistics (such as $\bar{Y}$) should be to the corresponding parameters of the population (such as μ).

3. The *sampling* distribution of a statistic: This is the probability distribution of some sample statistic, such as $\bar{Y}$. A sampling distribution describes how much variability there will tend to be in the value of a statistic among samples of a certain size.

Example 4.11 illustrates the distinctions among the sampling distribution, the population distribution, and the distribution of the sample.

Example 4.11   We consider the variable, age, as measured for the residents of a hypothetical community called Sunshine City. We suppose that Sunshine City was designed to attract retired individuals, and that its present population of 30,000 has a mean age $\mu = 60$ years, and a standard deviation $\sigma = 16$ years.

The population distribution of age in Sunshine City consists of $N = 30,000$ values on age. This distribution is described by the parameters $\mu = 60$ and $\sigma = 16$. Figure 4.12 displays a possible form for this distribution. The age values range from about 0 to 100, although most of them are between 40 and 90. The distribution is heavily skewed to the left, reflecting the predominance of older individuals in the community.

Fig. 4.12   The Population ($N = 30,000$) and Sample ($n = 100$) Distributions of Age for Residents of Sunshine City

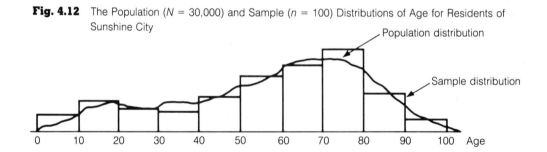

Suppose we selected a random sample of $n = 100$ residents of Sunshine City. We could construct a histogram of the 100 age values in the sample to get a sample distribution, and we could calculate sample statistics such as $\bar{Y}$ and s to describe this distribution. For example, we might get the histogram displayed in Figure 4.12, which is also skewed to the left with (perhaps) $\bar{Y} = 58.3$ and $s = 15.0$. The larger the sample size, the more this sample distribution is likely to resemble the population distribution, since the sample observations are a subset of the population values on age. If the entire population is sampled, then the two distributions are identical.

Before any sample of residents of Sunshine City is selected, we know from the Central Limit Theorem that, for large enough n, the sampling distribution of $\bar{Y}$ is approximately normal about $\mu = 60$ with a standard error of

$$\sigma_{\bar{Y}} = \frac{\sigma}{\sqrt{n}} = \frac{16}{\sqrt{n}}$$

For a random sample of size $n = 30$, the sampling distribution is approximately the normal distribution with mean 60 and standard error $\sigma_{\bar{Y}} = \sigma/\sqrt{n} = 16/\sqrt{30} = 2.92$. This sampling distribution is pictured in Figure 4.13, relative to the population distribution of age for residents of Sunshine City. Also shown in the figure is the sampling distribution of $\bar{Y}$ for $n = 100$, in which case the standard error is only $\sigma_{\bar{Y}} = 16/\sqrt{100} = 1.60$. Let us now review some of the remarks we made about the Central Limit Theorem for this particular example and these sampling distributions.

From Figure 4.13 and from the sizes of the standard errors, we see that the sampling distribution for $n = 100$ (for which $\sigma_{\bar{Y}} = 1.60$) is less disperse than the sampling distribution for $n = 30$ (for which $\sigma_{\bar{Y}} = 2.92$). The larger the sample size, in other words, the more likely it is that $\bar{Y}$ will be close to μ. As an illustration, for $n = 30$, the probability is .95 that $\bar{Y}$ occurs within $1.96\sigma_{\bar{Y}} = 1.96(2.92) = 5.72$ years of $\mu = 60$. When $n = 100$, though, the probability is .95 that $\bar{Y}$ occurs within $1.96\sigma_{\bar{Y}} = 1.96(1.60) = 3.14$ years of $\mu = 60$. So, when $n = 30$, $\bar{Y}$ is very likely to occur between about 54.3 (which is $60 - 5.7$) and 65.7 ($60 + 5.7$), whereas when $n = 100$, $\bar{Y}$ is very likely to occur between about 56.9 and 63.1. Both sampling distributions are much less disperse than the population distribution of age values, for which the standard deviation equals 16 and values occur anywhere from about 0 to 100.

We would not expect the *population* or *sample* distribution for a variable such as age to be normally distributed. In many societies, the distribution would not even be unimodal. It could be highly skewed to the right if the population is still growing and there is a predominance of younger people, or it could be highly skewed to the left, as in a community with a large proportion of older individuals, such as Sunshine City. Nevertheless, the *sampling* distribution of $\bar{Y}$ is approximately normal in any case whenever $n \geq 30$, because of the Central Limit Theorem.

Fig. 4.13 The Population Distribution and the Sampling Distributions of $\bar{Y}$ for $n = 30$ and $n = 100$

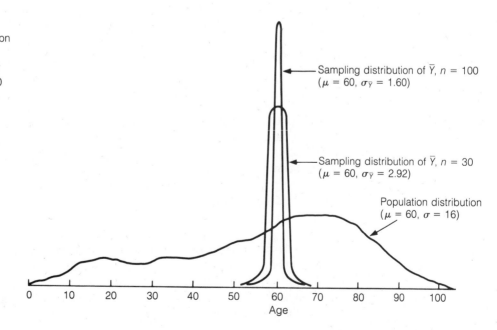

Sampling distribution of $\bar{Y}$, $n = 100$ ($\mu = 60$, $\sigma_{\bar{Y}} = 1.60$)

Sampling distribution of $\bar{Y}$, $n = 30$ ($\mu = 60$, $\sigma_{\bar{Y}} = 2.92$)

Population distribution ($\mu = 60$, $\sigma = 16$)

0   10   20   30   40   50   60   70   80   90   100

Age

The sampling distribution is more nearly normal in shape for larger values of n. For sampling only one observation, the sampling distribution of $\bar{Y} = Y_1$ is the probability distribution for one randomly selected measurement. This is simply the population distribution of the variable, which of course need not be the least bit normal. As n increases from 1 to 30, the sampling distribution assumes more of a bell shape. For $n \geq 30$, the sampling distribution of $\bar{Y}$ is well approximated by the normal distribution. As the sample size n approaches the population size N, the normal sampling distribution of $\bar{Y}$ converges to the single number μ. When the entire population is sampled, $\bar{Y} = \mu$ with probability 1 (i.e., the two measures are the same), reflecting the fact that the sampling distribution is concentrated at the point μ.

Suppose random samples of size $n = 30$ were repeatedly selected from Sunshine City, so that each of the 30,000 residents has an equal chance of being chosen for any one observation in each sample of size 30. Then the empirical sampling distribution of the $\bar{Y}$-values would cluster normally about $\mu = 60$ with a standard deviation of $\sigma_{\bar{Y}} = 2.92$. If random samples of size $n = 100$ were repeatedly selected, then the empirical sampling distribution of the $\bar{Y}$-values would cluster normally about $\mu = 60$ with a standard deviation of $\sigma_{\bar{Y}} = 1.60$.

We observed in Figure 4.13 a large difference in dispersion between the population distribution and the sampling distribution of $\bar{Y}$ (for $n = 30$ and $n = 100$). You should also be aware of the important distinction between the sample distribution (see Figure 4.12) of the measurements and the sampling distribution (see Figure 4.13) of the statistic $\bar{Y}$ calculated from these measurements. In particular, the sampling distribution can be theoretically stated (without observing the data) and is much less disperse. According to Figure 4.12, it would not be especially surprising to have some individuals of age under 40 in a sample of size 100, since many residents of Sunshine City are that young. However, according to the sampling distribution of $\bar{Y}$ for $n = 100$, it would be practically impossible to take a random sample of size 100 (or size 30) and obtain a sample mean age of $\bar{Y} \leq 40$. In fact, when $n = 100$, the standard error is $\sigma_{\bar{Y}} = 1.60$, and a value of $\bar{Y} = 40$ has a z-score of

$$z = \frac{40 - 60}{1.60} = -12.5$$

So, the $\bar{Y}$-value of 40 is more than 12 standard errors below the mean of the sampling distribution and is therefore an extremely unlikely event! Thus, although any particular individual sampled might have age anywhere between about 0 and 100, the sample mean $\bar{Y}$ calculated from a random sample of 100 measurements will almost certainly occur between about 55 and 65. That is, $\bar{Y}$ will very probably occur within about three standard errors (3×1.60) of the mean (60) of the sampling distribution.

■

Probability statements about $\bar{Y}$ are based on the Central Limit Theorem and (if σ is known) can be stated *before* observing the actual sample measurements. Of course, in practice, we typically do not know the values of parameters such as μ and σ. Nevertheless, in the next two chapters, we shall see how inferences about μ can also be based on this theorem.

Summary

We have interpreted the *probability* of an outcome as the proportion of times that the outcome would occur (in the long run) in repeated observations. A *probability distribution* for a variable provides a listing of the possible occurrences of the variable together with their probabilities. Probability distributions can be described by parameters, such as μ and σ.

The *normal distribution* is the most important probability distribution for statistical methodology. It is a symmetric bell-shaped curve with its functional form specified by the parameters μ and σ. The *z-score* for a number is a measure of how many standard deviations that number is from the mean of its distribution.

A *sampling distribution* is a probability distribution for a sample statistic. It provides a probabilistic description of the likely values of that statistic. The *Central Limit Theorem* gives the sampling distribution of the sample mean $\bar{Y}$. For sufficiently large sample sizes, that sampling distribution is approximately normal about μ, with standard error given by $\sigma/\sqrt{n}$, the population standard deviation divided by the square root of the sample size.

Notes

Section 4.2

1. The mathematical formula for a normal curve with mean μ and standard deviation σ is

$$f(y) = \frac{1}{\sqrt{2\pi}\,\sigma} \, e^{-(y-\mu)^2/(2\sigma^2)}$$

Section 4.4

2. The standard error formula given in the Central Limit Theorem is actually based on the assumption that the population size N is *infinitely* large relative to the sample size n. The exact formula for $\sigma_{\bar{Y}}$ for a *finite* population size N is

$$\sigma_{\bar{Y}} = \sqrt{\frac{N-n}{N-1}} \left(\frac{\sigma}{\sqrt{n}}\right)$$

The term $\sqrt{(N-n)/(N-1)}$ is called the *finite population correction*. It has very little influence as long as the sample size n is small relative to the population size N.

Example 4.12

A random sample of $n = 300$ students is selected out of a college student body of size $N = 30{,}000$. Then, the proportion of students sampled is only $n/N = 300/30{,}000 = .01$. The finite population correction equals

$$\sqrt{\frac{N-n}{N-1}} = \sqrt{\frac{30{,}000 - 300}{30{,}000 - 1}} = \sqrt{\frac{29{,}700}{29{,}999}} = \sqrt{.990} = .995$$

and hence $\sigma_{\bar{Y}} = .995\sigma/\sqrt{n}$, which is nearly identical to the formula $\sigma_{\bar{Y}} = \sigma/\sqrt{n}$ given in the theorem.

If $n = N$ (i.e., if we sample the entire population), then the finite population correction is $\sqrt{(N - n)/(N - 1)} = 0$, so that $\sigma_{\bar{Y}} = 0$. In other words, there is no sampling error since $\bar{Y} = \mu$. In practice, n/N is usually small, so in this text we give formulas only for standard errors of statistics based on an infinite population size. ∎

Problems

odd

1. Refer to Example 4.1. Construct the probability distribution of Y = number of *men* admitted, when two of the five students are randomly selected for admission.

2. Give the probability distribution for the outcome of selecting a single digit from a random number table.

3. For a normal distribution, find the probability that a measurement is:
a. More than one standard deviation above the mean
b. More than one standard deviation below the mean
c. More than .67 standard deviation above the mean
d. More than 1.64 standard deviations above the mean

4. Find the z-value for which the probability that a normal variable exceeds $\mu + z\sigma$ equals:
a. .01   **b.** .025   **c.** .05   **d.** .10   **e.** .25   **f.** .50

5. Find the z-values such that the interval from $\mu - z\sigma$ to $\mu + z\sigma$ contains 90%, 95%, 98%, and 99% of the probability for a normal distribution.

6. Find the z-values corresponding to the 90th, 95th, 98th, and 99th percentiles of a normal distribution.

7. A measurement is .64 standard deviation below the mean on some normally distributed variable. What proportion of the measurements are below that one? Above it?

8. What proportion of a normal distribution falls in the following ranges?
a. Above a z-score of 2.10
b. Below a z-score of -2.10
c. Above a z-score of -2.10

9. Find the z-score corresponding to the number that is less than 1% of the values for a normal distribution.

10. An IQ scale has approximately a normal distribution with a mean of 100 and a standard deviation of 16.
a. What proportion of people have an IQ of at least 120?
b. What proportion of people have an IQ of at least 84?
c. Find the IQ score such that only 1% of the population have IQ scores above that value.

11. Suppose that the weekly use of gasoline for motor travel for U.S. families is approximately normally distributed, with a mean of 16 gallons and a standard deviation of 5 gallons.
a. What proportion of families use more than 20 gallons per week?
b. What are the lower and upper quartiles?
c. Assuming that the standard deviation and the normal form would remain constant, to what level must the mean be reduced so that only 5% of the families use more than 20 gallons per week?

12. Suppose the distribution of murder rates for U.S. cities is normal, with a mean of 10.5 (per 100,000 residents) and a standard deviation of 3.8. Would you be surprised to find a city with a murder rate of 30? Why?

13. Monthly apartment rent payments in a large metropolitan area are approximately normal in distribution, with a mean of $350 and a standard deviation of $90. What proportion of the payments are at least $500 per month? What proportion are less than $250 per month?

14. Property taxes on homes in Oregon are approximately normal in distribution, with a mean of $1,000 and a standard deviation of $400. The property taxes for one particular home are $1,200.
a. What is the z-score corresponding to that value?
b. What proportion of the property taxes in the state exceed $1,200?

15. Suppose the distribution of yearly incomes of all migrant workers in California has a mean of $8,000 and a standard deviation of $3,200.
a. Assuming that the distribution is normal, what is the probability that a particular migrant worker has an income over $9,000?
b. If we plan on taking a random sample of 64 migrant workers, what is the sampling distribution of the sample mean income? Find the probability that the sample mean exceeds $9,000.

16. The population distribution of number of years of education for residents of a large city has a mean of 13.0 and a standard deviation of 3.0. Use the Central Limit Theorem to describe the sampling distribution of $\bar{Y}$ for a random sample of 36 residents.

17. The distribution of family size in a particular tribal society is skewed to the right, with $\mu = 5.2$ and $\sigma = 3.0$. These values are unknown to an anthropologist, who takes a sample of families in this society in order to estimate mean family size. Let $\bar{Y}$ denote the sample mean family size she obtains, based on a random sample of 36 families.
a. Describe the sampling distribution of $\bar{Y}$.
b. What is the probability that her sample mean is within .5 of the true mean?
c. Suppose she takes a random sample of size 100. Find the probability that the sample mean is within .5 of the true mean, and compare the answer to that obtained in part **b**.
d. Refer to part **c**. Would you be surprised if the anthropologist obtained $\bar{Y} = 4.0$? Why?

18. The scores on an anxiety index for adults in a large city are normally distributed, with a mean $\mu = 100$ and a standard deviation $\sigma = 15$. An individual is selected at random in this city.

a. Find the probability that the individual's anxiety score is at least 100.
b. Find the probability that the score exceeds 103.
c. Find the probability that the score is between 97 and 103.
d. Find the z-score corresponding to a score of 90 on the anxiety index. Would you be surprised to observe an index score of 90?
e. Suppose we converted all the scores on the index to z-scores; that is, for each adult in the city, subtract 100 from the score on the anxiety index and divide by 15. Then, what is the distribution of the z-scores?

19. Refer to Problem 18. A random sample of 225 adults in the city is to be chosen in a sample survey.

a. Describe the sampling distribution of the mean anxiety for a sample of size $n = 225$.
b. Find the probability that the mean exceeds 103.
c. Find the probability that the mean is between 97 and 103.
d. Find the z-score (for the sampling distribution) corresponding to a sample mean of $\bar{Y} = 90$, when the sample size is 225. Would you be surprised to observe a mean anxiety score of 90? Why?
e. Compare the results of parts a–d with those in Problem 18 and interpret the differences.
f. Repeat parts a–d for a random sample size of $n = 25$ and compare the results to those obtained for $n = 225$.

20. Refer to Problems 18 and 19.
a. Sketch the population distribution for the anxiety index.
b. Superimpose, on the sketch of part a, a sketch of the sampling distribution of the mean anxiety score for a random sample of 225 adults.
c. Superimpose, on the above sketches, a sketch of the sampling distribution of the mean anxiety score for a random sample of 25 adults.

21. An estimate is needed of the mean acreage of farms in Brazil. If we plan to take a random sample of 100 farms, then what is the probability that the sample mean acreage will be within 6 acres of the population mean acreage? Assume that 50 acres is a reasonable guess for the standard deviation of farm size.

22. An executive in a savings and loan association decided to estimate very precisely the mean amount of money that has been loaned to individuals for financing higher education in the past year. From past experience, he believes that $240 is a reasonable guess for the standard deviation of the distribution of loan amounts. He would like his estimate of the mean to be within $50 of the actual mean. What is the probability that the sample mean will be more than $50 from the actual mean for all such loans under the following conditions?
a. He takes a random sample of 36 loan records.
b. He takes a random sample of 64 loan records.
c. He takes a random sample of 144 loan records.

23. As part of a study investigating the relationship among voting patterns, political opinions, and age, a random sample of 100 individuals is chosen in what is considered to be a typical precinct.

a. What is the probability that the mean age of the individuals in the sample is within 2 years of the mean age for all individuals in the precinct? Assume that the standard deviation of the ages of all individuals in the precinct is $\sigma = 15$.

b. Would the probability be larger or smaller if $\sigma = 10$?

24. The Central Limit Theorem implies that (select the best response):

a. All variables have approximately bell-shaped sample distributions if we have at least 30 measurements in a random sample.

b. Population distributions are normal whenever the population size is large.

c. For large random samples, the sampling distribution of $\bar{Y}$ is approximately normal, regardless of the shape of the population distribution.

d. The sampling distribution looks more and more like the population distribution as we get more data.

e. All of the above

25. As the sample size increases, the standard error of the sampling distribution of $\bar{Y}$ (select the best response):

a. Increases

b. Decreases

c. Stays the same

26. Explain carefully the difference between a *distribution of sample measurements* and the *sampling distribution of $\bar{Y}$*.

*27. Show that for a discrete variable it would make sense to define the mean of its probability distribution as $\mu = \Sigma y P(y)$, where the sum is taken over all the possible values of the variable.

*28. Refer to Problem 27. Use the formula given there to find the mean of the probability distribution given in Example 4.1.

*29. The formula for the number of different combinations of n members that can be sampled from a group of N members is $N!/[n!(N - n)!]$, where $0! = 1$, $1! = 1$, $2! = 1 \cdot 2 = 2$, $3! = 1 \cdot 2 \cdot 3 = 6$, $4! = 1 \cdot 2 \cdot 3 \cdot 4 = 24$, and so forth. Using this formula, verify that the number of different combinations of two of the five students that could be admitted to law school in Example 4.1 equals 10.

*30. The population distribution associated with rolling a balanced die is the probability distribution in which each of the integers $\{1, 2, 3, 4, 5, 6\}$ has probability 1/6 of occurring. If the die were actually rolled n times, we could observe the relative frequencies of 1, 2, and so forth. These relative frequencies, which should be close to 1/6 if n is large, constitute the distribution of the sample. Suppose that we plan on rolling a die twice.

a. Enumerate the thirty-six possible pairs of numbers that you could get.

b. Treating these thirty-six pairs as equally likely, construct the sampling distribution for the average of the two numbers rolled.

c. What is the shape of the population distribution? What is the shape of the sampling distribution of the mean for $n = 2$?

*31. (*Class exercise*) The accompanying table represents the ages of all fifty heads of households in a small Nova Scotian village. The population distribution of all these ages is characterized by the parameters $\mu = 47.18$ and $\sigma = 14.74$.

NAME	AGE	NAME	AGE	NAME	AGE	NAME	AGE
Allison	50	Hanley	66	Moseley	49	Stewart	33
Arnold	45	Hohn	51	Moulton	30	Stoddard	36
Bashley	23	Isley	57	Munley	28	Stuart	25
Bentley	28	Janeway	40	Nance	31	Thames	29
Bold	67	Johnson	36	Neider	45	Thomas	57
Cash	62	Kirsch	38	Nice	43	Todd	39
Conley	41	Krist	81	Omley	43	Van Valey	50
Eagrin	68	Long	27	Pratt	54	Wiseman	64
Feinberg	37	Lonney	37	Pulley	62	Wood	76
Friendly	60	Mace	56	Quigley	67	Young, B.	63
Funk	41	Mathews	71	Rich	48	Young, H.	29
Geist	70	Matthews	39	Roster	32		
Good	47	Morse	46	Rush	42		

a. Draw a histogram of the population distribution of the ages of all heads of households.

b. Using a random number table (see Table 2.2), each student should be assigned nine random numbers between 01 and 50. Using these numbers, each student should sample nine of the heads of households and compute the corresponding sample mean age. Using the intervals 31.01–34.00, 34.01–37.00, 37.01–40.00, and so forth to 61.01–64.00, construct the empirical sampling distribution of the $\bar{Y}$-values. Compare it to the distribution in part **a**.

c. Find the mean of the $\bar{Y}$-values generated in part **b**. What value would you expect for this mean in a long run of repeated samples of size 9?

d. Find the standard deviation of the $\bar{Y}$-values generated in part **b**. What value would you expect for this standard deviation in a long run of repeated samples of size 9?

Bibliography   Mendenhall, W. (1983). *Introduction to Probability and Statistics*. 6th ed. Boston: Duxbury Press. Chaps. 4, 5, and 7.

CHAPTER 5

Statistical Inference: Estimation

Contents

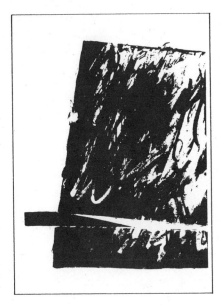

We now consider the subject of estimating parameters of a population distribution using sample data. For an interval variable, interest usually focuses on estimation of the mean μ of its distribution. For example, given access to a sample of building permits, we might want to estimate the mean sales price of homes built within the past year in some city. For a categorical variable, interest usually focuses on estimating the proportions of measurements in the various categories. For example, we might wish to estimate the proportion of adults in some community who rate the cultural programs of the community good or excellent, as opposed to fair or poor. The estimation procedures introduced in this chapter will be illustrated in detail for means and proportions.

There are two types of estimation procedures used in statistical inference. A *point estimate* consists of a single number that is used as the best estimate of a parameter. For example, using information contained in a sample of marriage records, we might decide that our best estimate of the mean age at first marriage for all women married within the previous year in a particular county is 22.5. An *interval estimate* consists of an interval of numbers around the point estimate, within which the parameter is believed to be contained. For example, we might predict that the mean age at first marriage for this population of women is somewhere between 21 and 24. We would then be concluding that the point estimate of 22.5 years is probably off by no more than 1.5 years. Thus, an interval estimate gives us a way of gauging the probable accuracy of a sample point estimate. Point estimation is introduced in the following section, and interval estimates for population means and proportions are given in Sections 5.2 and 5.3.

5.1 Point Estimation

Basic Concepts

Let us suppose that we have a random sample on which we have taken measurements on some variable. Often we are particularly interested in estimating a parameter of the population distribution of that variable. For example, based on election returns from key precincts, we might want to predict the proportion of a voting population that has cast a vote for the Democratic candidate in a congressional election. Since the process of forming a prediction about a parameter value involves reducing the data set of sample observations to one number, the statistic used as the prediction is referred to as a *point estimate* of the parameter.

Point Estimate

A *point estimate* of a parameter is a sample statistic that is used to predict the value of that parameter.

In this section, we formulate point estimates for some of the parameters introduced in Chapter 3. There are several estimates that could be proposed for any particular parameter. To estimate the population mean μ, for example, we could use the sample mean $\bar{Y}$, the sample median, Y_1 (the first observation), or a trimmed mean formed by deleting the largest and smallest measurements and averaging the other $(n - 2)$ measurements, among many possibilities. Some potential estimates are clearly nonsensical, such as Y_1, which uses the first observation as the estimate of μ and ignores all the information provided by the other observations. However, it is easy to propose several seemingly reasonable estimates for a parameter, and we need some way to choose among them.

Over the past several decades, statisticians have formulated various criteria for choosing among estimators. These criteria involve comparing certain statistical properties of the estimators. Basically, a good estimator is one with a sampling distribution that (a) is centered around the parameter and (b) has as small a standard error as possible. An estimator is *unbiased* if its sampling distribution is centered around the parameter in the sense that it has the parameter as its mean. If we repeatedly took samples of some fixed size n and used an unbiased estimator each time to obtain an estimate of the parameter, then, in the long run, the average of these estimates would equal the parameter value. A *biased* estimator, on the other hand, tends to either underestimate or overestimate the parameter, on the average. Generally, statisticians prefer to use estimators for which the bias (if any) tends to disappear as the sample size increases.

A second desirable property for an estimator to have is a small degree of sampling error compared with other estimators. An estimator with a small standard error relative to other estimators of the parameter is *efficient*. An efficient estimator, therefore, is one that tends to be relatively close to whatever population characteristic it estimates. Thus, a good estimator of a parameter has the properties of being unbiased (or nearly so) and efficient.

To illustrate, $\overline{Y}$ is an unbiased estimator of the population mean μ. However, $\overline{Y} - 10$ is a biased estimator, since the point estimates based on this formula would tend to underestimate μ. In fact, their values in repeated sampling would tend to fall around $\mu - 10$ (see Figure 5.1). The estimator Y_1 is unbiased for μ but it is not efficient, since its standard error is much larger than the standard error of other estimators. (Note that the sampling distribution of Y_1 is the same as the population distribution of Y.) If we always used just the first measurement, Y_1, in the estimation of means, we would not tend systematically to underestimate or overestimate those means; but we would tend to make a larger error than if we used a more efficient estimator, such as $\overline{Y}$.

Fig. 5.1 Sampling Distributions of Three Point Estimates of the Mean of a Variable Y

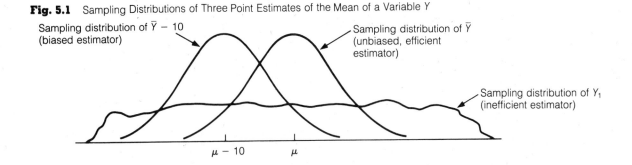

Sampling distribution of $\overline{Y} - 10$
(biased estimator)

Sampling distribution of $\overline{Y}$
(unbiased, efficient estimator)

Sampling distribution of Y_1
(inefficient estimator)

$\mu - 10$ μ

The concept of bias refers to what occurs in repeated sampling, not in one particular sample. In any one sample of n measurements, for example, $\bar{Y}$ may be less than or greater than μ; we certainly do not expect it to equal μ exactly. In this textbook, we discuss only the point estimates most commonly used. These perform well with respect to criteria such as unbiasedness and efficiency.

Point Estimates of the Mean and Standard Deviation

The sample mean $\bar{Y}$ is the most intuitively appealing point estimate of the mean μ of the population distribution of a variable, since the formulas for the two measures are similar. In fact, $\bar{Y}$ is unbiased and generally quite efficient, and it is the point estimate we shall use in this textbook.

We use the symbol "^" over a parameter symbol to represent an estimate of that parameter.* For instance, $\hat{\mu} = \bar{Y}$ is the estimate of the population mean μ, and $\hat{\sigma}$ denotes an estimate of the population standard deviation σ. The sample standard deviation s is the most commonly used point estimate of σ. That is,

$$\hat{\sigma} = s = \sqrt{\frac{\Sigma(Y_i - \bar{Y})^2}{n - 1}}$$

We shall use the $\hat{\sigma}$ notation for s in the next few chapters to emphasize that we are using this measure to estimate the population standard deviation.

Example 5.1

Suppose that the following household sizes were recorded for a small sample from a 1750 census listing for a New England Puritan community: 2, 6, 3, 5, 7, 7, 8, 10, 5, 7. Then the point estimate of the mean household size μ for that community is

$$\hat{\mu} = \bar{Y} = \frac{2 + 6 + 3 + 5 + 7 + 7 + 8 + 10 + 5 + 7}{10} = \frac{60}{10} = 6$$

Also,

$$\sum_{i=1}^{10} (Y_i - \bar{Y})^2 = (2 - 6)^2 + (6 - 6)^2 + (3 - 6)^2 + \cdots + (7 - 6)^2 = 50$$

so that the point estimate of the population variance σ^2 is

$$\hat{\sigma}^2 = s^2 = \frac{\sum_{i=1}^{n} (Y_i - \bar{Y})^2}{n - 1} = \frac{50}{9} = 5.56$$

The corresponding point estimate of the population standard deviation is

$$\hat{\sigma} = \sqrt{\hat{\sigma}^2} = \sqrt{5.56} = 2.36$$

In summary, we would estimate that the mean household size in that community was six persons and that the standard deviation was 2.36. ■

---

*The symbol "^" is called a caret, and is usually read as "hat." For example, $\hat{\sigma}$ is read as "sigma-hat."

5.2 Confidence Interval for a Mean—Large Samples

Most inferences reported by the mass media take the form of point estimates. For example, we may be informed that a recent survey reveals that 53% of the American public approves of the president's performance in office, or that the mean annual family income of Americans is $26,000. These are *estimates* of parameters, since they are based on sample data. To be truly meaningful, though, an inference concerning a parameter must consist not only of a simple point estimate, but also of a measure of the probable accuracy of the estimate. We need to provide a statement concerning how close that estimate is likely to be to the actual value of the parameter.

One way of accomplishing this is to use characteristics of the sampling distribution of the point estimate. For example, we can calculate the probability that the value of the estimator lies within a certain distance of the parameter. If the sampling distribution is approximately normal about the parameter, then with high probability (about .95), the estimate will be within a distance of two standard errors of that parameter, and almost certainly it will be within three standard errors. The smaller the standard error of the sampling distribution, the more accurate an unbiased estimate tends to be. If we know or can approximate the value of the standard error, then this type of reasoning gives us a mechanism for judging the accuracy of the estimate.

Confidence Intervals

Given access to a sample, we can use properties of the sampling distribution to form an *interval estimate* of the parameter, that is, an interval of numbers that we believe contains the unknown parameter. An interval estimate for a parameter is customarily referred to as a *confidence interval*.

Confidence Interval; Confidence Coefficient

A *confidence interval* for a parameter is an interval of numbers within which the value of the parameter is believed to lie. The likelihood that the interval contains the true value of the parameter is called the *confidence coefficient*.

A common approach for constructing a confidence interval consists of taking the point estimate of the parameter and adding and subtracting some multiple (such as a z-value) of the standard error of that estimate. We shall illustrate the notion of a confidence interval in this section for the case of estimating a population mean μ from the sample mean $\bar{Y}$. The formula for this confidence interval has the Central Limit Theorem as its foundation, so it is appropriate whenever the sample size is *large*, say, $n \geq 30$.* The reason for 30 as the cutoff point will become more apparent in Section 6.4 when we consider an analogous procedure for *small* samples.

*The terminology *large sample* does not refer to the sample being of such a size to produce a necessarily accurate estimate of μ, but merely of such a size that we can apply the Central Limit Theorem to describe the form of the sampling distribution of $\bar{Y}$. With a sample size of $n \geq 30$, we are able to use the formulas that follow, but we might not obtain a very exact estimate of μ.

**Confidence Interval
for a Mean**

From Section 4.4, the Central Limit Theorem states that the sampling distribution of $\bar{Y}$ is approximately normal about μ with standard error $\sigma_{\bar{Y}} = \sigma/\sqrt{n}$. Thus, with probability .95, for example, $\bar{Y}$ will occur within a distance of $1.96\sigma_{\bar{Y}}$ units of the parameter μ, that is, between $\mu - 1.96\sigma_{\bar{Y}}$ and $\mu + 1.96\sigma_{\bar{Y}}$ (see Figure 5.2). Now, if the sample is selected and $\bar{Y}$ *is* in fact between those values, then the interval from $\bar{Y} - 1.96\sigma_{\bar{Y}}$ to $\bar{Y} + 1.96\sigma_{\bar{Y}}$ contains μ (see Figure 5.2, Line 1). In other words, the probability is .95 that the value of $\bar{Y}$ based on a particular random sample will be such that the interval $\bar{Y} \pm 1.96\sigma_{\bar{Y}}$ contains the unknown population mean μ. Equivalently, if random samples of size n were repeatedly selected, then in the long run 95% of the intervals $\bar{Y} \pm 1.96\sigma_{\bar{Y}}$ would contain μ. On the other hand, the probability is .05 that the value of $\bar{Y}$ will not occur within $1.96\sigma_{\bar{Y}}$ of μ. If the sample is chosen and that happens, then the interval from $\bar{Y} - 1.96\sigma_{\bar{Y}}$ to $\bar{Y} + 1.96\sigma_{\bar{Y}}$ does *not* contain the parameter value μ (see Figure 5.2, Line 2). Thus, the probability is .05 that $\bar{Y}$ will be such that the interval $\bar{Y} \pm 1.96\sigma_{\bar{Y}}$ does *not* contain μ.

Fig. 5.2 Sampling Distribution of $\bar{Y}$, and Possible 95% Confidence Intervals for μ

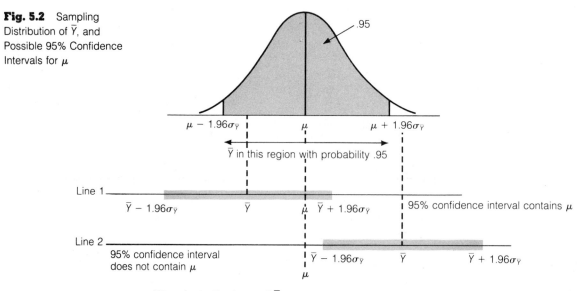

We refer to the interval $\bar{Y} \pm 1.96\sigma_{\bar{Y}}$ as a confidence interval for μ with confidence coefficient .95, or a **95% confidence interval** for μ. Similarly, a 99% confidence interval for μ would be $\bar{Y} \pm 2.58\sigma_{\bar{Y}}$. The reason for this is that 99% of the probability of a normal distribution occurs within 2.58 standard deviations of the mean, so the probability is .99 that the value of $\bar{Y}$ for a sample will be within $2.58\sigma_{\bar{Y}}$ of μ. The general form for the confidence interval is

$$\bar{Y} \pm z\sigma_{\bar{Y}}$$

where the z-value depends on the desired confidence coefficient. The higher the confidence coefficient selected, the more confident we can be that the value of the parameter is in fact enclosed by the corresponding interval. Researchers usually choose high confidence coefficients, such as .95, .98, or .99, so that there is a small chance of error—that is, a small probability that the interval will not contain the value of the parameter.

Let us consider in more detail the formula $\bar{Y} \pm z\sigma_{\bar{Y}}$ for obtaining the confidence interval. Notice that the standard error $\sigma_{\bar{Y}}$ is multiplied by a z-value, and then that product is added to and subtracted from $\bar{Y}$. The z-value is determined so that the probability concentrated within z standard errors of the center of the normal sampling distribution is the desired confidence coefficient. For example, a 98% confidence interval is $\bar{Y} \pm 2.33\sigma_{\bar{Y}}$, since $z = 2.33$ in Table A yields a probability of .01 in one tail of the normal distribution and .02 in the two tails; hence, .98 is the probability concentrated within 2.33 standard deviations of the center of a normal curve, and equals the probability that $\bar{Y}$ is within $2.33\sigma_{\bar{Y}}$ of μ.

Unfortunately, the exact value of the standard error $\sigma_{\bar{Y}} = \sigma/\sqrt{n}$ needed to use this formula is typically unknown, since the standard deviation σ of the population distribution is usually an unknown parameter whenever μ is unknown. However, for $n \geq 30$, a very good approximation for $\sigma_{\bar{Y}}$ can be obtained by using the point estimate $\hat{\sigma}$ of the population standard deviation σ in the standard error formula. This substitution yields

$$\hat{\sigma}_{\bar{Y}} = \frac{\hat{\sigma}}{\sqrt{n}}$$

as an estimate of the standard error in the formula for a confidence interval. The error in substituting the point estimate $\hat{\sigma}$ for σ is relatively negligible when $n \geq 30$. Thus, for practical purposes we have the result stated in the accompanying box.

Large-Sample Confidence Interval for μ

A large-sample* confidence interval for μ is

$$\bar{Y} \pm z\hat{\sigma}_{\bar{Y}} = \bar{Y} \pm z\left(\frac{\hat{\sigma}}{\sqrt{n}}\right)$$

The z-value is chosen so that the probability concentrated under a normal curve within z standard deviations of the mean equals the confidence coefficient. To illustrate, for 95%, 98%, and 99% confidence intervals, we would use the z-values 1.96, 2.33, and 2.58, respectively.

Example 5.2 Let us return to the problem presented in Example 5.1, that of estimating the mean household size of an early American community. In practice, we would use more than ten observations in order to estimate this. Suppose, then, that we take a random sample of 100 households from the 1750 census for that community and calculate

---

*The probability that the interval contains μ is *approximately* equal to the confidence coefficient selected. The approximation improves for larger samples, as the sampling distribution of $\bar{Y}$ is more closely normal in form and the estimated standard error $\hat{\sigma}_{\bar{Y}}$ converges to the true standard error $\sigma_{\bar{Y}}$.

the mean and standard deviation of household size for that sample to be $\bar{Y} = 5.5$ and $\hat{\sigma} = s = 2.2$. Then the estimated standard error of the sampling distribution of $\bar{Y}$ is

$$\hat{\sigma}_{\bar{Y}} = \frac{\hat{\sigma}}{\sqrt{n}} = \frac{2.2}{\sqrt{100}} = .22$$

and a 95% confidence interval for μ is

$$\bar{Y} \pm 1.96\hat{\sigma}_{\bar{Y}} = 5.5 \pm 1.96(.22) = 5.5 \pm .4 \quad \text{or} \quad (5.1, 5.9)$$

We can be 95% confident that this interval contains the value μ of the mean household size in the Puritan community being studied. The best point estimate of μ is 5.5, and we believe that μ is most likely no smaller than 5.1 and no greater than 5.9.

Alternatively, to be more sure that the inference is correct (i.e., that the interval actually contains μ), we could use a larger confidence coefficient. For example, a 99% confidence interval for μ is

$$\bar{Y} \pm 2.58\hat{\sigma}_{\bar{Y}} = 5.5 \pm 2.58(.22) = 5.5 \pm .6 \quad \text{or} \quad (4.9, 6.1)$$

We obtain a less precise estimate, in the sense that the interval is wider, as a sacrifice for gaining greater assurance of making a correct inference. ∎

Properties of the Confidence Interval for a Mean

We next consider some of the basic properties of confidence intervals for means. These properties are characteristic of confidence intervals for other parameters as well.

A relative frequency interpretation can be provided for confidence intervals. We should keep in mind that the unknown mean μ is a fixed number. A confidence interval corresponding to any particular sample either does or does not actually contain μ. However, if we repeatedly obtained random samples of some size n and each time calculated the corresponding 95% confidence interval, for example, then in the long run, approximately 95% of these intervals would actually contain μ. This is because about 95% of the sample means would fall within $1.96\sigma_{\bar{Y}}$ of μ, as does the $\bar{Y}$ in Line 1 of Figure 5.2. Thus, when we say that we are 95% confident that a particular interval contains the mean μ, this signifies that, *in the long run*, 95% of such intervals would actually contain μ.

Of course, in practice, we would choose just *one* sample of some size n, and form *one* confidence interval based on the n measurements in that sample. We would not know for sure whether that particular interval contained μ. We can control the likelihood of enclosing μ in the interval by an appropriate choice of the confidence coefficient. We have observed that the greater the desired confidence, the wider the confidence interval. To be more sure of enclosing μ, we must sacrifice precision of estimation by permitting a wider interval. Equivalently, narrowing the width of the interval for a given sample size leads to a decrease in the level of the confidence coefficient. In forming an interval estimate, we must achieve a balance between the desired precision of estimation and the desired confidence that the inference is correct.

It makes intuitive sense that we should be able to obtain a better estimate of μ with a larger sample size. The width of a confidence interval is the difference between the upper endpoint $\bar{Y} + z\sigma/\sqrt{n}$ and the lower endpoint $\bar{Y} - z\sigma/\sqrt{n}$. This width equals $2z\sigma/\sqrt{n}$, which is inversely proportional to the square root of the sample size. The larger n is, the narrower is the width of the interval. Thus, improved precision for a given confidence coefficient can in fact be obtained by increasing the sample size.

Example 5.3 Suppose that the values of $\bar{Y} = 5.5$ and $\hat{\sigma} = 2.2$ in Example 5.2 had been calculated from a sample of size $n = 400$. Then, the estimated standard error $\hat{\sigma}_{\bar{Y}}$ of the sampling distribution of $\bar{Y}$ is

$$\hat{\sigma}_{\bar{Y}} = \frac{\hat{\sigma}}{\sqrt{n}} = \frac{2.2}{\sqrt{400}} = .11$$

half as large as in that example. The resulting 95% confidence interval is

$$\bar{Y} \pm 1.96\hat{\sigma}_{\bar{Y}} = 5.5 \pm 1.96(.11) = 5.5 \pm .2 \quad \text{or} \quad (5.3, 5.7)$$

which is half as wide as the interval formed from the sample of size $n = 100$ in Example 5.2. In other words, an interval estimate based on $n = 400$ is half as wide as one based on $n = 100$, for a fixed confidence coefficient. ∎

Since the width of a confidence interval for μ is inversely proportional to the square root of n, and since $\sqrt{4n} = 2\sqrt{n}$, one must *quadruple* the sample size in order to *double* the precision. We shall show in Section 5.4 how to calculate the sample size needed to achieve a certain precision.

The width of a confidence interval:

1. Increases as the confidence coefficient increases
2. Decreases as the sample size increases

5.3 Confidence Interval for a Proportion— Large Samples

Suppose now that each observation in a sample is classified into one of two or more categories. This is the standard type of measurement that occurs when the variable is nominal (such as religion, with categories Protestant, Catholic, Jewish, other) or ordinal categorical (such as opinion concerning defense spending, with categories increase, keep the same, decrease). It can also be used when interval scales are collapsed into cruder levels, as, for example, when income is classified into $0–$5,000, $5,000–$10,000, and so forth.

A natural way to summarize the information in the total sample for a categorical variable is to count the number of observations in each category. Equivalently, we could use the *proportions* of observations in the various categories, which are simply these counts divided by the total sample size. For example, we might be interested in a point or interval estimate of the following:

1. The proportion of voters who are registered Democrats (versus Republicans or Independents)
2. The proportion of Americans who favor (versus oppose) decriminalization of marijuana
3. The proportion of Mexican-American adults who have attended college (versus those with no college experience)
4. The proportion of families in some city who have changed residence (versus kept the same residence) during the past year
5. The proportion of American families with income below the poverty level (versus above the poverty level)

Point and Interval Estimation for a Proportion

Let π denote the parameter representing the proportion of the defined population classified in some specific category. A sample statistic that makes intuitive sense for use as a point estimate of the population proportion π is the *sample proportion* of observations classified in that category. Suppose that we have observations on a random sample of size n. We let X denote the number of these observations that are classified in the category of interest. Then $\hat{\pi} = X/n$ is the proportion of the sample classified in that category. The sample proportion $\hat{\pi}$ is, in fact, an unbiased point estimate of π.

The sample proportion is shown in Note 5.5 to be a type of sample mean. Therefore, the sampling distribution of $\hat{\pi}$ is, for sufficiently large n, approximately normal (see Figure 5.3) about the parameter π it estimates. The formula for the standard error of the sample proportion $\hat{\pi}$ is

$$\sigma_{\hat{\pi}} = \sqrt{\frac{\pi(1 - \pi)}{n}}$$

The symbol $\sigma_{\hat{\pi}}$ signifies the standard error of the sampling distribution of $\hat{\pi}$, and it is an analog of the symbol $\sigma_{\bar{Y}}$ ($= \sigma/\sqrt{n}$) for the standard error of the sampling distribution of the sample mean $\bar{Y}$. As in that case, the standard error is inversely proportional to the square root of the sample size.

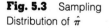

Fig. 5.3 Sampling Distribution of $\hat{\pi}$

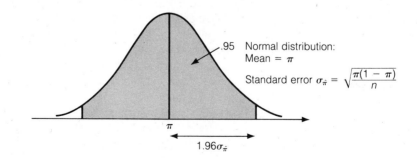

.95   Normal distribution:
Mean = π

Standard error $\sigma_{\hat{\pi}} = \sqrt{\frac{\pi(1 - \pi)}{n}}$

π

1.96$\sigma_{\hat{\pi}}$

As with the standard error of $\bar{Y}$, the formula for the standard error of $\hat{\pi}$ can be derived theoretically using mathematical arguments, and its exact value depends on an unknown parameter (in this case, π). Thus, in practice we obtain an estimate of this standard error, by using

$$\hat{\sigma}_{\hat{\pi}} = \sqrt{\frac{\hat{\pi}(1 - \hat{\pi})}{n}}$$

which can be used in constructing a confidence interval. Based on the same reasoning as in the previous section, a 95% confidence interval for π is

$$\hat{\pi} \pm 1.96\hat{\sigma}_{\hat{\pi}} = \hat{\pi} \pm 1.96 \sqrt{\frac{\hat{\pi}(1 - \hat{\pi})}{n}}$$

Example 5.4 A national television network takes a sample of 1,400 voters after each has cast a vote in a state gubernatorial election. Of these 1,400 voters, 742 claim to have voted for the Democratic candidate and 658 for the Republican candidate. There are only two candidates in the election. Assuming that each of the sampled voters actually voted as claimed, and assuming that the sample is a random sample from the population of all voters, is there enough evidence to predict the winner of the election?

Let us use π to represent the proportion of votes that the Democratic candidate will receive in the election. Now, of the $n = 1,400$ voters sampled, $X = 742$ of them voted for the Democratic candidate, so that $\hat{\pi} = 742/1,400 = .530$, and $1 - \hat{\pi} = .470$. That is, 53.0% of those sampled voted for the Democratic candidate and 47.0% of those sampled voted for the Republican candidate.

The estimated standard error of the estimate $\hat{\pi}$ of π equals

$$\hat{\sigma}_{\hat{\pi}} = \sqrt{\frac{\hat{\pi}(1 - \hat{\pi})}{n}} = \sqrt{\frac{(.53)(.47)}{1,400}} = \sqrt{.000178} = .013$$

A 95% confidence interval for π is

$$\hat{\pi} \pm 1.96\hat{\sigma}_{\hat{\pi}} = .530 \pm 1.96(.013) = .530 \pm .026 \quad \text{or} \quad (.504, .556)$$

We can be 95% confident that the overall percentage of votes that the Democratic candidate will receive is at least 50.4% but no more than 55.6%. Based on these sample returns, we might project that the Democratic candidate will be the winner of the election, assuming that the sample of voters was randomly selected. ■

Example 5.5 When $n = 1,400$ and $\hat{\pi} = .530$, we have just seen that the estimated standard error of $\hat{\pi}$ is $\hat{\sigma}_{\hat{\pi}} = \sqrt{\hat{\pi}(1 - \hat{\pi})/n} = .013$. Similarly, the estimated standard error for $1 - \hat{\pi}$, the proportion of voters favoring the Republican candidate, is $\hat{\sigma}_{1-\hat{\pi}} = \sqrt{(1 - \hat{\pi})\hat{\pi}/n} = .013$. Thus, a 95% confidence interval for the proportion of votes that the Republican candidate will receive out of the entire population of voters is

$$.470 \pm 1.96(.013) = .470 \pm .026 \quad \text{or} \quad (.444, .496)$$

Now $.444 = 1 - .556$ and $.496 = 1 - .504$, where $(.504, .556)$ is the 95% confidence interval for π. Thus, inferences for the proportion $1 - \pi$ follow directly from those for the proportion π. ∎

More generally, we can express the formula for the confidence interval as $\hat{\pi} \pm z\hat{\sigma}_{\hat{\pi}}$, where the z-value depends on the confidence coefficient in exactly the same way as in the case of a confidence interval for μ.

Example 5.6   A more cautious observer of the above results would not be prepared to forecast a winner in the election. For example, a 99% confidence interval for π is

$$\hat{\pi} \pm 2.58\hat{\sigma}_{\hat{\pi}} = .530 \pm 2.58(.013) = .530 \pm .034 \quad \text{or} \quad (.496, .564)$$

At this confidence level, we would infer that the Democratic candidate might receive less than half the total votes, since the lower limit of the confidence interval is 49.6%. ∎

Like the behavior of the confidence interval for a mean considered in the previous section, the width of a confidence interval for a proportion depends on the sample size n, as well as on the confidence coefficient.

Example 5.7   Suppose that 53.0% of a random sample of size $n = 2,000$ voted for the Democratic candidate. Then $\hat{\sigma}_{\hat{\pi}} = \sqrt{(.53)(.47)/2,000} = .011$, and a 99% confidence interval for π is

$$\hat{\pi} \pm 2.58\hat{\sigma}_{\hat{\pi}} = .530 \pm 2.58(.011) = .530 \pm .029 \quad \text{or} \quad (.501, .559)$$

In other words, if the proportions in Examples 5.4, 5.5, and 5.6 had been calculated from a sample of size 2,000 instead of 1,400, we could have been confident even at the 99% level that the Democratic candidate would receive more than half of the votes. ∎

Naturally, even for the larger sample size in Example 5.7, there are confidence intervals corresponding to yet larger confidence coefficients that would result in the interpretation that the election is too close to call. To illustrate, a 99.5% confidence interval for π in Example 5.7 is

$$\hat{\pi} \pm 2.81\hat{\sigma}_{\hat{\pi}} = .530 \pm .031 \quad \text{or} \quad (.499, .561)$$

Being 100% sure of enclosing π would necessitate using the trivial and consequently uninformative interval $(0, 1)$ (see Problem 40 at the end of the chapter).

In the case of the proportion, the sample size requirement for a large-sample inference to be valid is slightly different from the one given for the mean. There must be more than 5 observations both in the category of interest and not in it. In Example 5.4, there were 742 observations in the category for which the population proportion was estimated, and there were 658 observations not in it. Thus, the sample size requirement was easily satisfied.

A formula may be given for the confidence interval $\hat{\pi} \pm z\hat{\sigma}_{\hat{\pi}}$ that explicitly represents the dependence of the z-value on the confidence coefficient. We first introduce some new notation in the box.

Notation

Let α denote the probability that the confidence interval does not contain the population proportion π.

Since α denotes the error probability for the interval, $1 - \alpha$ represents the confidence coefficient. The z-value that is used for a $100(1 - \alpha)\%$ confidence interval is such that the probability is $1 - \alpha$ that $\hat{\pi}$ falls within z standard errors of π. Equivalently, the probability is α that $\hat{\pi}$ falls more than z standard errors from π. Thus, the z-value corresponds to a total area of α in the two tails of a normal distribution or an area of $\alpha/2$ in each of the tails. From Figure 4.7, the z-value corresponding to an area of $a = \alpha/2$ in each tail is denoted $z_{\alpha/2}$. Thus, we have the formula given in the next box.

Large-Sample Confidence Interval for π

A large-sample $100(1 - \alpha)\%$ confidence interval for the population proportion π is $\hat{\pi} \pm z_{\alpha/2}\hat{\sigma}_{\hat{\pi}}$, which equals

$$\hat{\pi} \pm z_{\alpha/2} \sqrt{\frac{\hat{\pi}(1 - \hat{\pi})}{n}}$$

where $\hat{\pi}$ is the sample proportion. There must be more than 5 observations both in the category and not in it.

As an illustration of the $z_{\alpha/2}$ notation, note that an error probability of $\alpha = .05$ corresponds to a confidence coefficient of $1 - \alpha = .95$, for which the appropriate z-value is $z_{\alpha/2} = z_{.05/2} = z_{.025} = 1.96$. Similarly, $\alpha = .02$ and $\alpha = .01$ lead to 98% and 99% confidence intervals, respectively. The $z_{\alpha/2}$ values for those levels are $z_{.02/2} = z_{.01} = 2.33$ and $z_{.01/2} = z_{.005} = 2.58$, respectively.

The same dependence of the z-value on the confidence coefficient $(1 - \alpha)$ occurs in the confidence interval for a mean. The formula for that interval can be written as

$$\bar{Y} \pm z_{\alpha/2}\hat{\sigma}_{\bar{Y}} \quad \text{or} \quad \bar{Y} \pm z_{\alpha/2} \frac{\hat{\sigma}}{\sqrt{n}}$$

**5.4
Choice of
Sample Size**

Samples taken by professional polling organizations such as the Gallup and Harris polls typically contain 1,000–2,000 sampling units. We have seen in the previous section that this is large enough to obtain an estimate of a proportion that is very probably within about .03 of the actual population value. The sampling procedures used by these organizations are usually more complex than simple random samples; however, the formulas for the standard errors of the estimates under their sampling plans are approximated reasonably well by the ones based on random sampling that we have been using.

To many people, it is astonishing that a sample on the order of 1,000 out of a population of perhaps many millions (which we are treating as actually *infinite* in size) can be used to predict outcomes of elections, analyze the relative sizes of television audiences, and so forth. The basis for such inferential power lies in the formulas for the standard errors of the sample point estimates that we have studied in this chapter. As long as the sampling is properly executed, excellent estimates can be obtained using relatively small samples, no matter how large the population size.

Before collecting the data, it is usually important to determine the size of the sample that must be chosen in order to achieve a certain degree of accuracy in estimation. For example, we might wish to know the size of the sample needed so that a confidence interval for a particular parameter is no wider than some specified width. In this section, we provide approximate solutions for estimating a mean or proportion when the sample is to be selected randomly. We use the facts that the width of the confidence interval depends directly on the standard error of the sampling distribution of the estimate and that the standard error itself is a function of the sample size. We then discuss some other considerations in choosing sample size.

Sample Size for Estimating Proportions

Before computing the sample size, we must first decide on the degree of **precision** desired. In other words, we must decide how close the estimate should be to the parameter. In some studies, the degree of precision is not as important as in others. For example, if we were estimating the proportion of voters who intend to vote for a certain candidate in a very close election, it is necessary to have a fairly accurate estimate in order to predict the winner. If, on the other hand, the goal is to estimate the proportion of the residents of a city who have rural origins, a larger margin of error might be acceptable. So, we must first decide whether the error should be no more than .03 (three percentage points), .04, or whatever.

Second, a decision must be made concerning the *probability* with which the specified amount of error will not be exceeded. The probability that the error will be no more than the specified amount (.04, say) must be stated, since it is possible with *any* sample size to have an error of no more than .04 with *some* probability—though perhaps a very small probability.

In Example 5.8, we will illustrate the reasoning used to select the sample size for obtaining a certain accuracy with some given probability in estimating a proportion.

Example 5.8

A group of social scientists was interested in estimating the proportion of school children in Boston who were living with only one parent. Since their report was to be published, they wanted to obtain a reasonably accurate estimate. However, since their resources were somewhat limited, they did not want to gather more information than necessary. They finally decided that they would use a sample size such that the probability would be .95 of making an error of no more than .04. In other words, they decided that they wanted to estimate the proportion to within .04 of the true value, with probability .95. Thus, they wanted to determine how large n should be so that their 95% confidence interval for π equals $\hat{\pi} \pm .04$. Let us now consider how to gauge the sample size necessary for this degree of accuracy.

Since the sampling distribution of $\hat{\pi}$ is approximately normal, we know that the sample proportion $\hat{\pi}$ will occur within $1.96\sigma_{\hat{\pi}}$ of π with probability .95. Thus, if the sample size is such that $1.96\sigma_{\hat{\pi}} = .04$, then with probability .95, $\hat{\pi}$ will fall within .04 units of π, so that the error of estimation will not exceed .04 (see Figure 5.4).

Fig. 5.4 Sampling Distribution of $\hat{\pi}$ with the Error of Estimation No Greater Than .04, with Probability .95

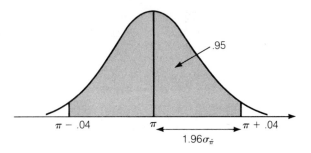

We need to solve algebraically for the value of n that produces a value of $\sigma_{\hat{\pi}}$ for which $.04 = 1.96\sigma_{\hat{\pi}}$; that is, we must solve for n in the expression

$$.04 = 1.96 \sqrt{\frac{\pi(1 - \pi)}{n}}$$

Multiplying both sides of the expression by $\sqrt{n}$ and dividing both sides by .04, we get

$$\sqrt{n} = \frac{1.96 \sqrt{\pi(1 - \pi)}}{.04}$$

Squaring both sides, we obtain the formula

$$n = \frac{(1.96)^2 \pi(1 - \pi)}{(.04)^2}$$

Since π is unknown, an educated guess must be substituted for it in this equation to yield a numerical solution for n. Alternatively, it can be shown that the largest possible value for $\pi(1 - \pi)$ is .25, which occurs when $\pi = .5$. We note that $\pi(1 - \pi)$ is, in fact, fairly close to .25 unless π is quite far from .5. For example, $\pi(1 - \pi) = .24$ when $\pi = .4$ or $\pi = .6$, and $\pi(1 - \pi) = .21$ when $\pi = .7$ or $\pi = .3$. Thus, by taking a sample of size

$$n = \frac{(1.96)^2(.25)}{(.04)^2} = 600.25 \approx 600$$

we are assured that the error will not exceed .04, with a probability of *at least* .95, no matter what the value of π. ∎

In general, the value of n obtained by setting $\pi(1 - \pi) = .25$ is a safe one. It is excessively large if π is not close to .5. Suppose, for example, that based on other studies, the social scientists discussed in Example 5.8 believed that the proportion π of school children in Boston who were living with only one parent was no more than .20. Then an adequate sample size would be

$$n = \frac{(1.96)^2 \pi (1 - \pi)}{(.04)^2} \approx \frac{(1.96)^2(.2)(.8)}{(.04)^2} = 384$$

If we substitute in the above safe formula a general value B (in place of .04) for the bound on the error, and a general z-value (in place of 1.96) determined by the probability with which the error is no greater than B, we obtain the result given in the accompanying box.

Sample Size Required for Estimating π

The sample size n needed to ensure that, with probability at least $1 - \alpha$, the error of estimation of π by $\hat{\pi}$ is no greater than B, is

$$n = .25 \left(\frac{z_{\alpha/2}}{B}\right)^2$$

Example 5.9   In estimating a proportion, suppose that we would like to ensure an error of no more than $B = .08$ with a probability of at least $1 - \alpha = .95$. In other words, we want the probability of making an estimation error of more than $B = .08$ to be at most $\alpha = .05$. Then, $\alpha/2 = .025$ and $z_{\alpha/2} = 1.96$, the z-value used in a 95% confidence interval. The required sample size is

$$n = .25 \left(\frac{z_{.025}}{.08}\right)^2 = .25 \left(\frac{1.96}{.08}\right)^2 = 150$$

The sample size here of 150 is one-fourth the sample size of 600 that is necessary to achieve a 95% confidence bound of .04. Again, we see that to reduce the bound on error by a factor of one-half, the sample size must be quadrupled.   ∎

Sample Size for Estimating Means   Using similar arguments with the sampling distribution of $\bar{Y}$, we obtain the following result for the sample size necessary for achieving a certain precision in the estimation of the population mean μ.

Sample Size Required for Estimating μ

The sample size n needed to ensure that, with probability $1 - \alpha$, the error of estimation of μ by $\bar{Y}$ is no greater than B, is

$$n = \sigma^2 \left(\frac{z_{\alpha/2}}{B}\right)^2$$

An educated guess for σ must be substituted in order to use this formula. Sometimes the results of a previously completed survey suggest a value.

Example 5.10   How large a sample size is needed so that the mean annual family income of Native Americans (i.e., American Indians) can be estimated correct to within $1,000 with probability .99?

Suppose that we have no prior information about the standard deviation of annual family income of Native Americans. As a crude approximation, we might guess that 95% of their family incomes are between $4,000 and $20,000. If this distribution of family incomes is approximately normal, then the difference $20,000 − $4,000 = $16,000 would equal about 4σ, since the range from $\mu − 2\sigma$ to $\mu + 2\sigma$ contains about 95% of a bell-shaped distribution. We could therefore use $16,000/4 = $4,000 as a crude guess for σ. For an error probability of $\alpha = .01$, $z_{\alpha/2} = z_{.01/2} = z_{.005} = 2.58$. Since $B = $1,000$, the required sample size is

$$n = \sigma^2 \left(\frac{z_{\alpha/2}}{B}\right)^2 = (4,000)^2 \left(\frac{2.58}{1,000}\right)^2 = 107 \text{ families}$$

A more conservative approach would involve selecting for σ a number that we are quite sure to be an upper bound for its value. For example, if we believe σ to be no greater than $6,000, we could sample $n = (6,000)^2(2.58/1,000)^2 = 240$ families. Then, if σ is actually less than $6,000, our estimate $\bar{Y}$ will be within $1,000 of μ with probability even greater than .99. ■

It should be reemphasized that these formulas apply to random sampling. The same formulas can be used with systematic sampling, if there is no trend or cyclical pattern in the values of the variable over the population listing. However, cluster samples must usually be larger than random or systematic samples in order to achieve the same precision, whereas smaller samples can usually be chosen with stratified random sampling.

Other Considerations in Determining Sample Size   From a practical point of view, determining sample size is not a simple matter of plugging numbers into a formula. There are several considerations that affect the number of observations needed in a study. We have just discussed two, **precision** and **confidence**. Precision corresponds to the width of a confidence interval, while confidence refers to the probability that the interval will contain the estimated parameter. In general, both of these improve as sample size increases, other things being equal.

A third characteristic affecting the sample size decision is the **degree of variability** in the population for the variables to be measured. We have already seen this with respect to estimating means, where the required sample size increases as σ increases. Generally, the more heterogeneous the population, the larger the sample needs to be. In the extreme case, if all population elements were alike (zero variability), we would need a sample of only *one* to accurately represent the population. On the other hand, if there are 15 ethnic groups, age variation from 18 to 85, and wide variation in income, we would need a relatively large sample to accurately reflect all the variation in these variables. In most social surveys of the general public, large samples (1,000 or more) are necessary, while more homogeneous population targets (e.g., residents of nursing homes) can often be represented well with smaller samples, due to reduced population variability.

A fourth consideration is the *amount and type of analysis* that is planned. Usually, the more complex the analysis (the more variables one analyzes simultaneously), the larger the sample needed to make the results meaningful. If one is to use simple univariate statistics (means, proportions, and so forth), a relatively small sample might be adequate. On the other hand, if we need to do a lot of comparisons among the groups using complex multivariate methods, we need a larger sample. One reason for the increase in average sample size in recent decades is the greater complexity of statistical analyses in social science research.

Finally, a fifth consideration has to do with time, money, and other *resources*. Larger samples are more expensive, more time-consuming, and may require more resources than the researcher commands. It is often the case that time, cost, and resource limitations are the major constraints on sample size. For example, we might apply the formulas and find that we need 1,000 cases for our desired purpose. However, perhaps we can afford to gather only 500. Should we go ahead with the smaller sample and sacrifice precision and/or confidence, or should we give up unless we can obtain more resources? We often are reduced to such questions as "Is it better to have some knowledge which is not very precise, or no knowledge at all?" or "Is it really important to study all population groups, or can I reduce the sample by focusing on some subsets?" The costs and benefits of large samples must be weighed against the importance of the study, the need for accuracy, and the complexity of the problem.

In summary, there is no simple formula that can always determine the "proper" sample size. While sample size is a very important matter, its choice depends on a careful assessment of needs and resources and requires good judgment on the part of the researcher.

Summary

A *point estimate* is a single number that is used as a best estimate of a parameter. The point estimates of μ, σ, and π are $\bar{Y}$, $\hat{\sigma}$, and $\hat{\pi}$.

A *confidence interval* is an interval of numbers around the point estimate, within which the parameter is believed to be contained. These intervals are theoretically derived using properties of the sampling distributions of the point estimates. The probability that the confidence interval will contain the parameter is called the *confidence coefficient*. The more sure we wish to be that the confidence interval includes the parameter, the higher we choose the confidence coefficient. Larger sample sizes lead to more precise estimates, in the sense of producing narrower confidence intervals.

Formulas were given for confidence intervals for μ and for π that apply whenever the sample size n is sufficiently large to use the Central Limit Theorem (see Table 5.1). An analogous small-sample ($n \leq 30$) confidence interval for μ is described in Section 6.4.

Table 5.1 Summary of Estimation Procedures for Means and Proportions

PARAMETER	POINT ESTIMATE	ESTIMATED STANDARD ERROR	$100(1 - \alpha)\%$ CONFIDENCE INTERVAL	SAMPLE SIZE NEEDED TO ESTIMATE PARAMETER TO WITHIN B
Mean μ	$\overline{Y}$	$\hat{\sigma}_{\overline{Y}} = \dfrac{\hat{\sigma}}{\sqrt{n}}$	$\overline{Y} \pm z_{\alpha/2}\, \hat{\sigma}_{\overline{Y}}$	$n = \sigma^2 \left(\dfrac{z_{\alpha/2}}{B}\right)^2$
Proportion π	$\hat{\pi} = \dfrac{X}{n}$	$\hat{\sigma}_{\hat{\pi}} = \sqrt{\dfrac{\hat{\pi}\,(1 - \hat{\pi})}{n}}$	$\hat{\pi} \pm z_{\alpha/2}\hat{\sigma}_{\hat{\pi}}$	$n = \pi(1 - \pi)\left(\dfrac{z_{\alpha/2}}{B}\right)^2$

Notes

Section 5.1

1. Compared to other mathematical sciences, statistical science is very young. Most of the methods described in this book were developed in the twentieth century. The inferential methods of hypothesis testing (presented in the next chapter) and confidence intervals were suggested in a series of articles beginning in 1928 by Jerzy Neyman (1894–1981) and E. S. Pearson (1895–1980).

The most important contributions to modern statistical science were made by the British statistician and geneticist R. A. Fisher (1890–1962). While working at an agricultural research laboratory in Rothamsted, England, he developed much of the theory of point estimation and the methodology for the design of experiments and analysis of data. He advocated the use of the *maximum likelihood estimate*. This is the estimate such that, if the parameter equaled that value, the observed data would have had greater likelihood of occurring than if the parameter equaled any other value. Fisher showed that, for large samples, maximum likelihood estimates tend to be efficient, with little (if any) bias, and have approximately normal sampling distributions. Most of the point estimates presented in this book are, under certain population assumptions, maximum likelihood estimates.

2. The existence of bias in an estimator is not necessarily a serious deficiency, as long as the degree of bias converges to 0 as the sample size increases (i.e., the estimator is *asymptotically unbiased*). In some situations there are slightly biased estimators that are as efficient (or even more efficient) than the best unbiased estimator. Hence, most statisticians do not consider it important to use estimators that are *exactly* unbiased. Biased estimators are especially useful for estimating large sets of means (e.g., mean income levels for all counties in a state). The biased estimators are obtained by "shrinking" the sample means toward the overall mean. See Efron and Morris (1977) for an interesting discussion of the benefits of this type of biased estimator.

Section 5.2

3. In the special case in which the population distribution of the variable is normal, a formula can be given for the standard error of the median that is similar to the one for the sample mean. Namely, for a large sample size n, the sample median M has approximately a normal sampling distribution with a standard error of $1.2533\sigma/\sqrt{n}$. It follows that a $100(1 - \alpha)\%$ confidence interval for the population median in that special case is

$$M \pm z_{\alpha/2} \frac{(1.2533\hat{\sigma})}{\sqrt{n}}$$

Now, the population median for a normal population distribution equals the population mean μ, so the sample median and sample mean are both point estimates of the same number. Since the confidence interval for μ based on the sample median is over 25% wider than the one based on the sample mean, the sample median is not as efficient an estimator. Thus, when the population distribution for a variable is symmetric and approximately bell-shaped, the sample mean tends to be a more precise estimate of the center of that distribution than the sample median. This is one of the reasons that the mean is more commonly used than the median in statistical inference.

4. Confidence intervals for medians can be constructed that make no assumption about the form of the population distribution. Suppose that the sample size exceeds 10 and let $Y_{(1)}, Y_{(2)}, \ldots, Y_{(n)}$ denote the ordered sample; that is, $Y_{(1)}$ is the smallest measurement, $Y_{(2)}$ is the second smallest, and so forth. Let r denote the integer part of the number $(n + 1)/2 - (z_{\alpha/2} \sqrt{n})/2$; that is, r is the greatest integer that is not larger than $(n + 1)/2 - (z_{\alpha/2} \sqrt{n})/2$. Then, a confidence interval for the median with confidence coefficient at least $(1 - \alpha)$ is given by $(Y_{(r)}, Y_{(n-r+1)})$. In other words, the lower endpoint of the confidence interval is just the rth smallest observation, while the upper endpoint of the confidence interval is the $(n - r + 1)$st smallest (rth largest) observation. See Problem 5.39.

Section 5.3

5. The sample proportion $\hat{\pi}$ can be treated as a special case of a sample mean, since it can be written as

$$\hat{\pi} = \frac{\displaystyle\sum_{i=1}^{n} Y_i}{n}$$

where $Y_i = 1$ if the ith observation is in the category of interest, and $Y_i = 0$ otherwise. That is, Y_i counts whether the ith observation is classified in the category, and thus $X = \Sigma_{i=1}^n Y_i$ is the count of the total number of units in the sample that are classified in that category.

Problems

1. The measurements on the number of children in six families selected at random from 1870 census records in a southern town are 1, 4, 0, 0, 6, 7. Calculate the point estimates of the population mean and standard deviation.

2. Explain what is meant for an estimator to be:
a. Unbiased　　　　　　　　　　　　**b.** Efficient

3. Explain the distinction between *point* estimation and *interval* estimation.

4. Fifty college students selected at random from the student directory were asked to respond to the question, "What is the ideal number of children for a family to have?" The responses were as shown in the accompanying table.

IDEAL NUMBER OF CHILDREN	FREQUENCY
0	4
1	9
2	25
3	8
4	3
5	1

a. Let μ denote the mean of this distribution for the population of all students at the college. Calculate a point estimate of μ.
b. Calculate the point estimate $\hat{\sigma}$ of the population standard deviation for this variable.

5. Refer to Problem 4.
a. Construct a 95% confidence interval for μ.
b. Construct a 99% confidence interval for μ.

6. A survey is taken to estimate the mean annual family income for families living in public housing in Chicago. For a random sample of thirty families, the family incomes (in hundreds of dollars) are as follows:

53	60	47	70	53	34	48	62	43	92
66	30	55	56	78	40	109	26	64	54
81	63	90	40	62	70	94	29	82	49

a. Compute the point estimates of μ and σ, the mean and standard deviation of the family incomes of all families living in public housing in Chicago.
b. Obtain a 95% confidence interval for μ.
c. Obtain a 99% confidence interval for μ. Interpret the interval and compare it to the one in part **b**.

7. A hospital administrator wants to estimate the mean length of stay for all in-patients who use that hospital. A systematic random sample of 400 records of patients for the previous year gives a sample mean of $\bar{Y} = 5.3$ and a sample standard deviation of $\hat{\sigma} = 5.0$. Construct a 95% confidence interval for the mean.

8. In an article in a sociological journal, the accompanying table is given for a random sample of employees in a particular profession.

SEX	MEAN ANNUAL INCOME	STANDARD ERROR
Men	$25,400	$400
Women	20,100	350

a. Find a 95% confidence interval for the mean annual income for all men in this profession.

b. Find a 95% confidence interval for the mean annual income for all women in this profession.

c. Interpret the results of the interval estimation procedure used in parts **a** and **b**.

9. A set of measurements representing the number of days an employee was absent in the previous year for a random sample of thirty-six employees who work on one of the assembly lines at an automobile plant is summarized by the sum $\Sigma\, Y_i = 720$ and the sum of squares $\Sigma\, (Y_i - \bar{Y})^2 = 5,040$.

a. Find $\bar{Y}$ and $\hat{\sigma}$.

b. Calculate a 95% confidence interval for μ, the mean number of days absent in the previous year for all assembly-line employees in this company.

c. Calculate a 99% confidence interval for μ. Interpret the interval and compare it to the 95% confidence interval.

10. In 1985, a random sample of thirty counties in the southern United States yielded a mean fertility ratio (number of children under 5 years of age per 1,000 women aged 15–45) of 340, and an estimated standard deviation of 40.

a. Find a 99% confidence interval for the mean fertility ratio for all southern counties.

b. Suppose that the estimated standard deviation had been 80. Find a 99% confidence interval for the mean, and compare it to the one obtained in part **a**.

c. Suppose that the sample size had been 120, with $\bar{Y} = 340$ and $\hat{\sigma} = 40$. Again, find a 99% confidence interval for μ, and compare it to the one obtained in part **a**.

11. A study of a random sample of 100 teenagers indicates that teenagers spend an average of 16 hours every week listening to the radio. Calculate a 98% confidence interval for the mean weekly time teenagers spend listening to the radio, if the estimated standard deviation of the listening time is 6.0 hours per week.

12. A study is conducted of the geographic distribution of the residences of the employees at a large factory, in order to determine the suitability of initiating mass transit operations to that factory. One variable considered is the distance the employee lives from the factory. For a random sample of 100 employees, it is determined that the mean distance is $\bar{Y} = 6.3$ miles and the estimated standard deviation is $\hat{\sigma} = 4.0$. Find a 90% confidence interval for the mean residential distance from the factory of all employees.

Select the best response(s) in Problems 13–15.

13. Increasing the confidence coefficient causes the width of a confidence interval to:
a. Increase.
b. Decrease.
c. Stay the same.

14. Other things being equal, quadrupling the sample size causes the width of a confidence interval to:
a. Double.
b. Halve.
c. Be one-quarter as wide.
d. Stay the same.

15. A random sample of eighty sixth-grade children results in a 95% confidence interval for the mean number of close friends of (2.4, 4.9). Which of the following interpretations is (are) correct?
a. We can be 95% confident that $\bar{Y}$ is between 2.4 and 4.9.
b. We can be 95% confident that μ is between 2.4 and 4.9.
c. Ninety-five percent of the values of Y = number of close friends (for this sample) are between 2.4 and 4.9.
d. If random samples of eighty sixth-grade children were repeatedly selected, then 95% of the time $\bar{Y}$ would be between 2.4 and 4.9.
e. If random samples of eighty sixth-grade children were repeatedly selected, then in the long run 95% of the confidence intervals formed would contain the true value of μ.

16. Find the z-score that is substituted into the formula for a:
a. 98% confidence interval
b. 50% confidence interval
c. 99.73% confidence interval

17. Explain why confidence intervals are wider when we use greater confidence coefficients.

18. A random sample of fifty records yields a 95% confidence interval for the age at first marriage of women in a certain county of 21.5 to 23.0 years. Explain what is wrong with each of the following interpretations of this interval.
a. If random samples of fifty records were repeatedly selected, then 95% of the time the sample mean age at first marriage for women would be between 21.5 and 23.0 years.
b. Ninety-five percent of the ages at first marriage for women in the sample are between 21.5 and 23.0 years.
c. We can be 95% confident that $\bar{Y}$ is between 21.5 and 23.0 years.

19. The National Opinion Research Corporation did a special survey of Black Americans in 1982, sampled to represent the adult Black noninstitutionalized population. In questions about attitude toward the Equal Rights Amendment, 271 of these respondents favored the amendment, 55 opposed it, and 29 had no opinion or no answer.

a. What is the point estimate of the proportion of Black Americans who favor the ERA?

b. Find a 95 percent confidence interval for the population proportion. Do you think a majority of Black Americans favored the ERA in 1982?

20. The General Social Survey of the National Opinion Research Corporation for 1983 shows the tabled responses to a question about the amount our country is spending on "the military, armaments, and defense."

RESPONSE	FREQUENCY
Spending too much	518
About right	603
Spending too little	385
Total	1,506

Give a 95% confidence interval for the proportion of Americans who believe we are "spending too much" for this purpose.

21. In the same national survey as described in Problem 20, respondents were asked if they smoke, to which 591 responded "yes" and 1,006 responded "no." Obtain a 90% confidence interval for the proportion of American adults who smoke.

22. An anthropologist wants to estimate the proportion of individuals in a tribe in the Philippines who die before reaching adulthood. For a sample of families who had children born between 1950 and 1960, it was found that 15 of 50 children died before reaching adulthood. Obtain a 95% confidence interval for the corresponding population proportion.

23. For every car passing a certain location during a particular 10-hour period, it was noted whether the driver was wearing a seat belt. For the 2,550 cars observed, 848 drivers were wearing seat belts.

a. Find a point estimate of the population proportion of drivers who wear seat belts in this community.

b. Construct a 99% confidence interval for the population proportion of drivers who wear seat belts.

c. Based on the answer in part **b**, can we conclude that a majority of drivers do not wear seat belts?

24. A random sample is taken of students at a large university to determine the proportion who own automobiles. If 34% of the students in the sample own automobiles, form a 99% confidence interval for the proportion of all students owning automobiles under the following conditions:

a. Sample size is 50
b. Sample size is 100
c. Sample size is 400

25. Out of a random sample of 400 individuals who are registered and planning to vote in a mayoral election, 160 plan on voting for Jones and 240 for Smith. Compute a 99% confidence interval for the proportion of votes that Jones will receive. Do you think that Jones will lose the election?

26. In Problem 25, suppose that 16 out of 40 sampled individuals plan to vote for Jones. Again, find the 99% confidence interval and, if possible, predict the winner. How does the result here compare to the result in Problem 25?

27. A city council votes to appropriate funds for a new civic auditorium. The mayor of the city threatens to veto this decision unless it can be shown that a majority of citizens would use it at least twice a year. The council commissions a poll to be taken of city residents. Out of a random sample of 400 residents, 230 plan to use the facility at least twice a year, if it is built. Find a 98% confidence interval for the proportion of all residents of the town who would use the proposed auditorium at least twice a year. Interpret the interval and advise the mayor.

28. An experiment was conducted to study the effect on pregnancies of exposure to a certain toxic substance. Of 100 pregnant rats that were exposed to a certain dose of the substance, 20 suffered spontaneous abortions (miscarriages).
a. Calculate a 90% confidence interval for the population proportion of pregnant rats that would suffer a spontaneous abortion in this situation.
b. Explain what is meant when we say that we have 90% confidence in this interval.
c. What must the sample size be to obtain a confidence interval about half as wide as the one obtained in part **a**?

29. Refer to Problem 22. Suppose that, before obtaining the sample, the anthropologist wanted to determine how large a sample would be necessary in order to estimate π to within .07 with 95% confidence. Assuming nothing about the value of π, calculate the sample size that will ensure at least this degree of accuracy.

30. It is desired to estimate the proportion of traffic deaths in Florida last year that were alcohol-related. Determine the necessary sample size, if we want our estimate of this proportion to be accurate to within .06 with probability .90.

31. A study is being planned for estimating the proportion of married women with living parents in the United States who live in the same state as their parents. Approximately how large a sample size is needed to estimate this proportion correct to within the following:
a. .10 with probability .95
b. .05 with probability .95
c. .05 with probability .99
d. .01 with probability .99
Compare sample sizes for parts **a** and **b**, **b** and **c**, and **c** and **d**.

32. Suppose that it is desired to estimate the proportion of the deaths in the previous year in New York City that were due to accidents. We want the estimate to be accurate to within .01 with probability .95, and we have access to death records for this past year.

a. Find the necessary sample size if we have reason to believe that this proportion does not exceed .10.

b. Suppose that, to determine the necessary sample size, we use the conservative approach that sets $\pi = .5$ in the appropriate formula. Then how many records would have to be sampled? Compare the result to the answer in part **a**, and note the reduction in sample size that could occur when an educated guess is made for π.

33. A tax assessor wants to estimate the mean property tax bill for all homeowners living in Madison, Wisconsin. A survey completed 3 years ago indicated that the mean and standard deviation were $1,100 and $400, respectively. Assuming that the standard deviation is still about $400, how large a sample of tax records should the tax assessor take in order to estimate the mean correct to within $50 with probability .95?

34. An estimate is needed of the mean acreage of farms in Brazil. The estimate is to be correct to within 5 acres with probability .95. Assuming that 50 acres is a reasonable guess for the standard deviation of farm size, how large a sample of farm sizes would be needed?

35. In Problem 34, suppose that we selected a sample of farms of the number believed to be required to produce an estimate correct to within 5 acres with probability .95. Suppose, however, that once the sample is selected, we see that the estimated standard deviation is 100 acres. Then, how close can we expect the sample mean to be to the true mean? In other words, what amount is added to and subtracted from the sample mean to get a 95% confidence interval for the mean acreage of farms in Brazil?

36. Give some examples of studies in which it would be very important to have:

a. A high degree of confidence

b. A high degree of precision

37. How does population heterogeneity affect the sample size required to estimate a population parameter? Illustrate with an example.

****38.** Based on data from a random sample of thirty-six records of patients in a particular hospital in a 3-year period, we are informed that a 95% confidence interval for the mean length of stay (in days) of a patient in that hospital is (3.5, 6.5). Find the point estimates of μ and σ, the mean and standard deviation, of length of stay for the population of all patients in those 3 years.

****39.** Suppose that a random sample of $n = 20$ private companies having at least 1,000 employees each is chosen to form the basis of a study of political contributions by industry. In particular, suppose we would like to form a 95% confidence interval for the median yearly total contribution to political campaigns by all companies with

at least 1,000 employees. Our interest in the median instead of the mean is due to our belief that this distribution may be very skewed to the right. The reported total contributions for the past year for the twenty companies sampled are (in thousands of dollars):

| 10 | 17 | 1 | 15 | 14 | 0 | 5 | 2 | 8 | 10 |
| 0 | 3 | 4 | 100 | 3 | 0 | 25 | 12 | 9 | 36 |

Using the formulas given in Note 5.4, show that a 95% confidence interval for the median contribution is ($3,000, $14,000). That is, the interval is determined by the ordered values $Y_{(6)} = 3$ and $Y_{(15)} = 14$.

*40. Show that the shortest 100% confidence interval for the proportion of population measurements in a certain category is

$$(X/N, 1 - (n - X)/N)$$

where X is the number of observations in the sample classified in that category, n is the sample size, and N is the population size. Notice that if the population size N is very large relative to the sample size n (and hence relative to X), this interval approximates the interval from 0 to 1 enclosing all possible proportions. Then, the only way of being 100% sure of enclosing π is to use the trivial and consequently uninformative interval (0, 1).

*41. Derive the formula for determining how large a sample size is necessary to estimate a population mean to within B units with probability .95.

Bibliography   Box, J. F. (1978). *R. A. Fisher, The Life of a Scientist*. New York: Wiley.
Efron, B. and C. Morris (1977). "Stein's Paradox in Statistics." *Scientific American 236*, 119–127.
Lehmann, E. L. (1983). *Theory of Point Estimation*. New York: Wiley.
Reid, C. (1982). *Neyman—From Life*. New York: Springer-Verlag.

CHAPTER 6

Statistical Inference: Testing Hypotheses

Contents

A large portion of social science research deals with testing *hypotheses* about variables.

Hypothesis

A *hypothesis* is a prediction about some aspect of a variable or a collection of variables.

Hypotheses are derived from theory and they serve as guides to research. When a hypothesis can be stated in terms of one or more parameters of the appropriate population distribution(s), statistical methods can be used to test its validity. A statistical test involves comparing what is expected according to the hypothesis with what is actually observed in the data. Examples of hypotheses that might be tested statistically are: "The mean age at marriage for men in colonial America was at least 25 years," "The rate of serious crimes has remained the same over the past 4 years," "Married women have more depression (as measured by some standard scale) than do married men," and "There is a difference between the probabilities that Democrats and Republicans vote with their party leadership."

To illustrate briefly what is meant by a statistical test, let us consider the following problem. The authorship of an old document is in doubt. A historian hypothesizes that the author was a journalist named Jane Anderson. Upon a thorough investigation of Anderson's known works, it is observed that one unusual feature of her writing was that she consistently began about 6% of her sentences with the word *whereas*. To test the historian's hypothesis, it is decided to count the number of sentences in the disputed document that begin with the word *whereas*.*

Out of the 300 sentences in the document, none begin with that word. We might be inclined to reject the historian's claim, based on this evidence. On the other hand, we might consider first whether it would be highly unlikely that out of 300 sentences selected at random from Anderson's known works, none of the sentences would begin with *whereas*. Due to sampling variation, we would not expect exactly 6% of the 300 sentences to have this characteristic. We need to develop some guidelines concerning how large or how small the percentage of sentences beginning with *whereas* would have to be before we could feel reasonably confident in rejecting the historian's hypothesis. Then, based on the information in the disputed essay, we would make the decision either to reject the historian's hypothesis (i.e., conclude that Anderson very likely was not the author) or not to reject the hypothesis (i.e., admit that Anderson may be, but is not necessarily, the author). The purpose of this chapter is to introduce the basic statistical procedures for making such decisions. The decision-making process is statistical in the sense that the probabilities of making incorrect decisions can be controlled.

---

*An investigation similar to the one described here, but in much greater depth, was carried out by Mosteller and Wallace (1964) to determine whether Alexander Hamilton or James Madison was the author of twelve of the "Federalist Papers."

In the next section, the elements of a statistical test of a hypothesis are described. The remainder of the chapter deals with testing a hypothesis about a population mean μ of an interval variable, or the population proportion π classified in some particular level of a categorical variable. Sections 6.2 and 6.3 deal with the case in which the sample size is large enough to apply the Central Limit Theorem. Sections 6.4 and 6.5 present analogous small-sample tests. In Section 6.6, we discuss how to control the probability of an incorrect decision in a statistical test. Section 6.7 gives some comments on the practical application of tests and estimation procedures.

The hypotheses tested in this chapter concern the value of a summary characteristic of a single variable. These hypotheses are somewhat simplistic, since social science researchers rarely study variables in isolation. However, their simplicity makes them suitable for introducing the basic elements of this type of statistical procedure. We encounter more complex hypotheses about relationships between variables in the remaining chapters of the text.

6.1 Elements of a Statistical Test

There are five basic elements of statistical tests of hypotheses about a parameter: assumptions, hypotheses, test statistic, *P*-value, and conclusion.

Assumptions

All statistical tests are based upon certain assumptions that must be met in order for the tests to be valid. These assumptions usually entail considerations such as the following:

1. The assumed *scale of measurement* of the variable: As with other statistical procedures, each test is specifically designed for a certain level of measurement.
2. The form of the *population distribution*: For many tests, the variable must be continuous, or even normally distributed in the population.
3. The *method of sampling*: The formulas for most tests require simple random sampling.
4. The *sample size*: Many tests rely on results similar to the Central Limit Theorem and require a certain minimum sample size in order to be valid.

Hypotheses

A statistical test focuses on two hypotheses about the value of a parameter.

Null Hypothesis; Alternative Hypothesis

The *null hypothesis* is the hypothesis that is actually tested.

The *alternative hypothesis* is accepted when the test results in rejection of the null hypothesis. It consists of an alternative set of parameter values to those given in the null hypothesis.

Notation

The symbol H_0 represents the null hypothesis, and the symbol H_a represents the alternative hypothesis.

The purpose of the test is to analyze, in probabilistic terms, how strong the sample evidence is against the null hypothesis. The researcher usually conducts the test to investigate whether the alternative hypothesis is true. The approach taken is the indirect one of *proof by contradiction*. The alternative hypothesis is judged to be acceptable if the null hypothesis can be shown to be inconsistent with the observed data. In other words, we reason that the alternative hypothesis is likely to be correct if the null hypothesis appears to be incorrect. Since the researcher usually conducts the test to gauge the amount of support for the alternative hypothesis, it is often referred to as the **research hypothesis**. The hypotheses should be formulated *before* observing or analyzing the data.

Test Statistic   After obtaining the sample, we form some sample statistic to help us test the null hypothesis. This **test statistic** typically involves a point estimate of the parameter about which the hypotheses are made. Knowledge of the sampling distribution of the test statistic allows us to calculate the probability that specific values of the statistic (e.g., values such as the one actually observed) would occur if the null hypothesis were actually true.

P-Value   Once the test statistic has been calculated for the sample, a measure is obtained of how unusual that observed value is relative to what would be expected for its value if H_0 were true. To calculate such a measure, we consider the collection of possible values for the test statistic that give at least as much evidence in favor of the alternative hypothesis as the observed test statistic. The **P-value** is defined to be the probability that the test statistic would occur in this collection of values, if H_0 were true.

P-Value

The **P-value** is the probability, when H_0 is true, of getting a test statistic value at least as favorable to H_a as the value actually observed.

Notation

The P-value is denoted by P and is sometimes referred to as the **attained significance level** of the test.

The P-value is used as a measure of the weight of evidence supporting the null hypothesis. A moderate to large P-value means that the data are consistent with H_0.

In other words, when P is a number such as .3 or .9, it would not be unusual to obtain data such as those we observed, if H_0 were true. On the other hand, a value for P such as .01 means that it would be very unlikely to obtain such data, if H_0 actually were true. The smaller the value of P, therefore, the more contradictory the sample results are to H_0.

Conclusion   The researcher should routinely report the P-value, so that an observer of the results can judge the extent of the evidence against H_0. In some situations, we may need to make a decision about the validity of H_0. If the P-value is sufficiently small, we might decide to reject H_0, and therefore accept H_a. In practice, researchers usually require very small P-values, such as $P < .05$, in order to conclude that the data contain sufficient evidence to reject H_0. The process of making a formal conclusion is an optional part of a statistical test, and we shall defer further discussion of it until Section 6.6. The elements of a statistical test are summarized in Table 6.1.

Table 6.1

Elements of a Statistical Test

1. Assumptions
   Measurement scale, population, sample

2. Hypotheses
   Null hypothesis, H_0
   Alternative hypothesis, H_a

3. Test statistic

4. P-value
   Weight of evidence supporting H_0

5. Conclusion
   Report P-value
   Formal decision (optional; see Section 6.6)

6.2
Test for a Mean—Large Samples

We next consider testing a hypothesis about the value of the population mean μ for an interval variable. When the sample size n is at least 30, we can utilize the fact that the sampling distribution of $\bar{Y}$ is approximately normal (no matter what the form of the distribution of the variable) in setting up this test. We now examine the five elements outlined in Section 6.1 as applied to this particular large-sample test.

Elements of the Test

1. *Assumptions*   A random sample of size $n \geq 30$ is selected. Measurements are obtained on a variable measured on at least an interval scale.

2. *Hypotheses*   It is perhaps easiest to set up the alternative hypothesis first. This hypothesis H_a can take on any one of three forms. The most general of these is

$$H_a: \quad \mu \neq \mu_0$$

where μ_0 is some particular number. For example, $H_a: \mu \neq 10$ illustrates this form of alternative hypothesis. It states that the population mean does not equal 10. The basic form H_a: $\mu \neq \mu_0$ is used whenever the purpose of the test is to detect whether μ equals some number *other than* μ_0. More specific alternative hypotheses are

$$H_a: \quad \mu > \mu_0 \qquad \text{and} \qquad H_a: \quad \mu < \mu_0$$

The alternative hypothesis H_a: $\mu > \mu_0$ is used whenever the purpose of the test is to detect whether μ is specifically *larger* than the particular number μ_0, whereas H_a: $\mu < \mu_0$ is used to detect whether μ is *smaller* than that value.

The null hypothesis in a test about a mean takes the form

$$H_0: \quad \mu = \mu_0$$

In other words, the hypothesized value of μ in H_0 is the single value with respect to which the alternative hypothesis is set up to detect a deviation. This hypothesis is explicitly tested to analyze the strength of the sample evidence against it.

The alternative hypothesis H_a: $\mu \neq \mu_0$ is called **two-sided**, since the values included in it fall both below and above the value μ_0 given in H_0. The alternative hypotheses H_a: $\mu > \mu_0$ and H_a: $\mu < \mu_0$ are **one-sided**. The choice of the form for H_a depends on whether the researcher wishes to detect *any* type of deviation of μ from μ_0 (in which case H_a: $\mu \neq \mu_0$ is used) or a deviation in a particular direction (in which case one of the one-sided alternatives is used). This choice must be made before analyzing the data.

3.   *Test Statistic*   When $n \geq 30$, we know by the Central Limit Theorem that the sampling distribution of $\overline{Y}$ is approximately normal about μ, with standard error $\sigma_{\overline{Y}} = \sigma/\sqrt{n}$. If H_0 is true, then the center of the sampling distribution is the number μ_0 (see Figure 6.1). The evidence regarding H_0 is based on the distance of the observed $\overline{Y}$ from the null hypothesis value μ_0, relative to the standard error. In other words, we would tend to doubt the validity of H_0 if the value of $\overline{Y}$ is well out in the tail of this sampling distribution. Our reasoning would be that the probability of observing a $\overline{Y}$ that far from μ_0 would be small if $\mu = \mu_0$.

Fig. 6.1   Sampling Distribution of $\overline{Y}$ if H_0: $\mu = \mu_0$ Is True

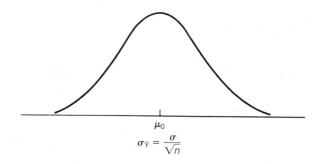

$$\mu_0$$

$$\sigma_{\overline{Y}} = \frac{\sigma}{\sqrt{n}}$$

As a test statistic, we use the z-score

$$z = \frac{\overline{Y} - \mu_0}{\sigma_{\overline{Y}}}$$

which gives the number of standard errors that the observed $\bar{Y}$ is from the hypothesized value μ_0. The sampling distribution of this test statistic is approximately the standard normal distribution (i.e., normal with mean equal to 0 and standard deviation equal to 1; see Section 4.2) when H_0 is true. The larger the observed absolute value of z, the farther $\bar{Y}$ is from μ_0 relative to what would be expected if μ_0 were the actual population mean, and the more suspect we would be of H_0.

In practice, we do not know the exact value of $\sigma_{\bar{Y}} = \sigma/\sqrt{n}$, because σ is also an unknown parameter. As in Chapter 5, we would substitute the sample point estimate $\hat{\sigma}$ for σ to get $\hat{\sigma}_{\bar{Y}} = \hat{\sigma}/\sqrt{n}$ as an estimated standard error. Then, we calculate

$$z = \frac{\bar{Y} - \mu_0}{\hat{\sigma}_{\bar{Y}}}$$

as the test statistic. For samples of size $n \geq 30$, $\hat{\sigma}$ is close enough to σ so that there is little sacrifice in making this substitution. This amended z statistic still has approximately the standard normal distribution when H_0 is true.

One reason for hypothesizing only one particular number in H_0 should now be apparent. The test statistic, and hence the result of the test, must be evaluated in terms of that one value.

4. *P-Value* So far, the sample evidence has been summarized in a test statistic. Different tests use different test statistics, though, and it is easier to interpret the results when they are transformed to a probability scale from 0 to 1. The *P*-value is used for this purpose.

For the two-sided alternative hypothesis H_a: $\mu \neq \mu_0$, we take the *P*-value to be the probability of obtaining a value of the z test statistic that is at least as large in absolute value as the observed test statistic. In other words, P is the probability of obtaining a value of $\bar{Y}$ at least as far from μ_0 *in either direction* as the observed value of $\bar{Y}$, when H_0 is true. A z-score of 0 would be most consistent with H_0, since it occurs when $\bar{Y} = \mu_0$. The *P*-value is the probability of observing a test statistic value at least as far from this consistent value as the one we observed. In summary, P is the probability of those $\bar{Y}$ values that are at least as favorable to H_a: $\mu \neq \mu_0$ as the observed $\bar{Y}$, in the sense that they are at least as many standard errors distant from μ_0.

Figure 6.2 shows the sampling distribution of the z test statistic when H_0 is true. To illustrate the calculation of P, suppose that we observed $z = -1.5$. This is the z-score

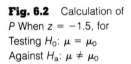

Fig. 6.2 Calculation of P When $z = -1.5$, for Testing H_0: $\mu = \mu_0$ Against H_a: $\mu \neq \mu_0$

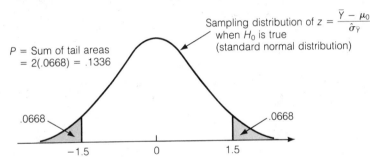

P = Sum of tail areas
= 2(.0668) = .1336

Sampling distribution of $z = \dfrac{\bar{Y} - \mu_0}{\hat{\sigma}_{\bar{Y}}}$
when H_0 is true
(standard normal distribution)

.0668   .0668

−1.5   0   1.5

corresponding to a sample mean $\bar{Y}$ that is 1.5 standard errors below the hypothesized value μ_0. The corresponding P-value for the two-sided alternative would be the probability that $z \geq 1.5$ or $z \leq -1.5$ (i.e., $|z| \geq 1.5$), which is $2(.0668) = .1336$. So, if μ_0 were the true value of μ, the probability of obtaining a sample mean at least 1.5 standard errors from that value (above *or* below) would be .1336.

For the one-sided alternative hypothesis H_a: $\mu > \mu_0$, P is the probability of obtaining a z-score above the observed z-score (i.e., to the right of it on the real number line) when H_0 is true. Equivalently, P is the probability that we would obtain a sample mean above the observed value of $\bar{Y}$. These $\bar{Y}$ values are the ones that provide at least as much evidence in favor of H_a: $\mu > \mu_0$ as the observed value. So, P equals the tail area to the right of the observed z-score under the standard normal curve (see Figure 6.3).

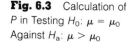
Fig. 6.3 Calculation of P in Testing H_0: $\mu = \mu_0$ Against H_a: $\mu > \mu_0$

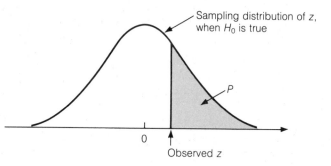

Sampling distribution of z, when H_0 is true

P

0

Observed z

The analogous result applies to the other one-sided alternative hypothesis. Namely, for H_a: $\mu < \mu_0$, P is the tail area to the left of the observed z-score under the standard normal curve. A z-score of -1.5 would result in $P = .0668$ for this alternative.

5. *Conclusion* Finally, the researcher should report the value of P, so that others may form an opinion about the results. The smaller P is, the more evidence there is against H_0 and in favor of H_a.

Next, we consider some examples of tests of hypotheses about a mean. In the first example, we will illustrate each of the five elements of this test.

Example 6.1 An extensive study of criminal recidivism was conducted in a Florida county in 1980. The mean number of prior convictions for all individuals convicted of a serious crime in that county in 1980 was 2.0. The county sheriff believes that the mean has increased since then, and a small investigation has been organized to check that hunch. A random sample of thirty-six records is examined out of the set of all conviction records involving serious crimes in that county in 1985.

1. Assumptions:　The sample is randomly selected, the sample size exceeds 30, and the number of previous convictions is an interval variable, so all of the assumptions are satisfied for a large-sample test about a mean.

2. Hypotheses: Let μ denote the mean number of prior convictions for those people convicted of serious crimes in the county in 1985. Since the mean number of prior convictions was 2.0 in 1980, and since the sheriff believes that the mean has *increased* since 1980, the appropriate alternative hypothesis is

H_a: $\mu > 2.0$

The null hypothesis must contain one specified value for μ. Since the sheriff wishes to compare the 1985 value of μ to the known 1980 value of 2.0, it is natural to set up the null hypothesis as

H_0: $\mu = 2.0$

The null hypothesis states that there has been no change since 1980 in the mean number of previous convictions. Notice that we have set up H_0 and H_a without knowing the results of the survey.

3. Test statistic: Suppose now that the distribution of the number of previous convictions for the thirty-six sampled records is summarized by the point estimates $\bar{Y} = 2.8$ and $\hat{\sigma} = 2.0$. The estimated standard error of the sampling distribution of $\bar{Y}$ is

$$\hat{\sigma}_{\bar{Y}} = \frac{\hat{\sigma}}{\sqrt{n}} = \frac{2.0}{\sqrt{36}} = .33$$

The value of the test statistic is therefore

$$z = \frac{\bar{Y} - \mu_0}{\hat{\sigma}_{\bar{Y}}} = \frac{2.8 - 2.0}{.33} = 2.4$$

That is, the observed sample mean is 2.4 estimated standard errors above the hypothesized value of the mean.

4. *P*-value: Since the alternative hypothesis is one-sided, the *P*-value is the probability that z would exceed 2.4 if H_0 were true (see Figure 6.4). From the normal curve area table (Table A), this right-hand tail area equals $P = .0082$. This *P*-value means that if the mean number of prior convictions *were* 2.0 in 1985, then the probability is only .0082 that a sample mean for $n = 36$ convictions would be at least as far above 2.0 as the observed $\bar{Y}$ of 2.8. In other words, if H_0 were true, the sample we have observed would be rather unusual.

Fig. 6.4 Calculation of *P*

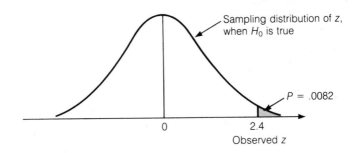

Sampling distribution of z, when H_0 is true

$P = .0082$

0

2.4
Observed z

5. Conclusion: As a measure of the strength of the evidence regarding the null hypothesis, the sheriff could report the *P*-value of *P* = .0082. This very small value for *P* provides strong evidence against the null hypothesis.   ∎

Example 6.2   In Example 6.1, suppose that we had been unsure before observing the data whether to expect an increase or decrease in the mean number of prior convictions. If we simply wanted to test for a change in the mean, we would use the two-sided alternative hypothesis

$$H_a: \quad \mu \neq 2.0$$

The test statistic would still be *z* = 2.4, but now *P* = 2(.0082) = .0164, since the *P*-value is the sum of probabilities in *both* tails of the standard normal sampling distribution (see Figure 6.5). Thus, if the researcher successfully predicts the direction of the deviation of the sample estimator from the value of the parameter hypothesized in H_0 (as was done in Example 6.1), the *P*-value is only half as large as when the general two-sided alternative hypothesis is used.   ∎

Fig. 6.5   Calculation of *P* for Two-Sided Test

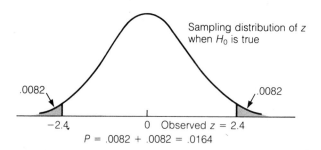

Sampling distribution of *z* when H_0 is true

.0082   .0082

−2.4   0   Observed *z* = 2.4
P = .0082 + .0082 = .0164

Comments   In deciding whether to use a one-sided or a two-sided alternative hypothesis in a particular problem, you should consider the object of the test. A statement such as "Test whether the mean has *changed*" suggests a two-sided alternative (to allow for increase *or* decrease), whereas "Test whether the mean has *increased*" suggests a one-sided alternative.

In Example 6.2, suppose that $\bar{Y}$ = 2.8 and $\hat{\sigma}$ = 2.0 had been calculated from a sample of size *n* = 50 instead of *n* = 36. Then

$$\hat{\sigma}_{\bar{Y}} = \frac{\hat{\sigma}}{\sqrt{n}} = \frac{2.0}{\sqrt{50}} = .283$$

so that

$$z = \frac{\bar{Y} - \mu_0}{\hat{\sigma}_{\bar{Y}}} = \frac{2.8 - 2.0}{.283} = 2.83$$

Then the *P*-value would be *P* = 2(.0023) = .0046 for $H_a: \mu \neq 2.0$. We see that the same difference between $\bar{Y}$ and μ_0 based on a larger sample size results in a smaller

P-value. Naturally, the larger the sample size is, the more certain we can be that sample deviations from H_0 are indicative of true population deviations. This corresponds to the observation in Chapter 5 that a confidence interval for the mean tends to decrease in width as *n* increases, leading to improved precision in estimating the value of μ.

Exercise Show that for testing H_0: $\mu = 2.0$ against H_a: $\mu \neq 2.0$, if $\hat{\sigma} = 2.0$ and $n = 50$ but $\bar{Y} = 2.3$ (instead of 2.8), then $P = .289$. Thus, when $n = 50$ and $\hat{\sigma} = 2.0$, a sample mean of $\bar{Y} = 2.3$ is not an unusual occurrence if μ equals 2.0. That is, $\bar{Y} = 2.3$ is not sufficiently greater than $\mu_0 = 2.0$ to give us reason to disbelieve H_0.

The *P*-value is sometimes misinterpreted as the probability that H_0 is true. In reality, the null hypothesis H_0 is either *true* or *not true*. In Example 6.2, either μ equals 2.0, or μ does not equal 2.0. Probability statements are made about statistics, never about parameters, in classical statistical procedures. We interpret $P = .0164$ in Example 6.2 as follows: "*If H_0 were true*, the probability would be .0164 of obtaining a sample mean at least as many standard errors from the null hypothesis value of 2.0 as the observed $\bar{Y}$." That is, *P* refers to the probability of getting a $\bar{Y}$ value at least as favorable to H_a as the observed $\bar{Y}$, *under the assumption that H_0 is true*.

The smaller the *P*-value is, the stronger the evidence against the null hypothesis. Generally, though, researchers do not regard the evidence against H_0 as being conclusive unless *P* is *very small*, say $P < .05$ or $P < .01$. The next example shows that conclusions reached using tests of hypotheses are consistent with conclusions reached using confidence intervals.

Example 6.3 An alternative inferential approach in Examples 6.1 and 6.2 is to use the data to construct a confidence interval for the population mean number of prior convictions in 1985. Since $\bar{Y} = 2.8$ and $\hat{\sigma}_{\bar{Y}} = .33$ for the data in those examples, a 95% confidence interval for μ is

$$\bar{Y} \pm 1.96\hat{\sigma}_{\bar{Y}} = 2.8 \pm 1.96(.33) = 2.8 \pm .7 \quad \text{or} \quad (2.1, 3.5)$$

At a 95% confidence level, these are the plausible values for μ. This confidence interval indicates that 2.0 is not a very plausible value for μ. Thus, it is not surprising that we obtained the small *P*-value of $P = .0164$ in testing H_0: $\mu = 2.0$ against H_a: $\mu \neq 2.0$ in Example 6.2. In fact, whenever we obtain $P < .05$ in a test of H_0: $\mu = \mu_0$ against H_a: $\mu \neq \mu_0$, it necessarily follows that a 95% confidence interval for μ does not contain the null hypothesis value μ_0 of μ. In this sense there is a consistency between results of confidence intervals and results of two-sided tests. If a confidence interval tells us that a particular number is an implausible value for μ, then we would obtain a small *P*-value in testing the null hypothesis that μ equals that number. The connection between hypothesis tests and confidence intervals will be further discussed in Section 6.6. ∎

Table 6.2 summarizes the elements of large-sample tests for population means.

Table 6.2

Elements of Large-Sample
Test for Population Mean

1. Assumptions

   $n \geq 30$

   Random sample

   Interval variable

2. Hypotheses

   H_0: $\mu = \mu_0$

   H_a: $\mu \neq \mu_0$ or H_a: $\mu > \mu_0$ or H_a: $\mu < \mu_0$

3. Test statistic

   $$z = \frac{\bar{Y} - \mu_0}{\hat{\sigma}_{\bar{Y}}} \quad \text{where } \hat{\sigma}_{\bar{Y}} = \frac{\hat{\sigma}}{\sqrt{n}}$$

4. *P*-value

   In standard normal curve, use:

   P = Two-tail probability for H_a: $\mu \neq \mu_0$

   P = Probability to right of observed *z*-value for H_a: $\mu > \mu_0$

   P = Probability to left of observed *z*-value for H_a: $\mu < \mu_0$

5. Conclusion

   Report *P*-value. Smaller *P* gives more evidence against H_0 and in favor of H_a.

6.3
Test for a
Proportion—
Large Samples

The large-sample test of a hypothesis about a proportion π is very similar to the one for a mean. It utilizes the fact that the sampling distribution of the sample proportion $\hat{\pi}$ is approximately normal, with mean π and standard error $\sigma_{\hat{\pi}} = \sqrt{\pi(1 - \pi)/n}$. We present this test, as before, by referring to its five elements.

Elements of the Test

1. *Assumptions*   We wish to test a hypothesis about the proportion of measurements occurring in a particular level of a categorical variable. The size of the random sample must be large enough so that the sampling distribution of $\hat{\pi}$ is approximately normal (see the discussion following the examples).

2. *Hypotheses*   The null hypothesis takes the form

   H_0: $\pi = \pi_0$

where π_0 denotes a particular number from which we wish to be able to detect a deviation in the population proportion π. The alternative hypothesis can take any of the three forms

   H_a: $\pi \neq \pi_0$ H_a: $\pi > \pi_0$ H_a: $\pi < \pi_0$

according to whether we are interested in detecting a deviation of π from π_0 in a certain direction.

3. *Test Statistic* When $\pi = \pi_0$, the sampling distribution of $\hat{\pi}$ is approximately normal, with mean π_0 and standard error $\sigma_{\hat{\pi}} = \sqrt{\pi_0(1 - \pi_0)/n}$. We use the test statistic

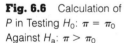

$$z = \frac{\hat{\pi} - \pi_0}{\sigma_{\hat{\pi}}}$$

which measures the distance of the sample proportion from the null hypothesis value of π, in standard error units. The parameter values of sampling distributions in tests are always based on the assumption that H_0 is true, so that π_0 is used as the value for π in the expression for the standard error, $\sigma_{\hat{\pi}} = \sqrt{\pi(1 - \pi)/n}$.* Therefore, the test statistic can be expressed as

$$z = \frac{\hat{\pi} - \pi_0}{\sqrt{\dfrac{\pi_0(1 - \pi_0)}{n}}}$$

The form of the z test statistic is identical to the one used in the test for a mean given in the previous section—namely,

$$z = \frac{\text{Estimate of parameter} - \text{Null hypothesis value of parameter}}{\text{Standard error of estimate}}$$

Here, the estimate $\hat{\pi}$ takes the place of $\bar{Y}$, the hypothesized value π_0 takes the place of μ_0, and the standard error $\sigma_{\hat{\pi}}$ takes the place of $\sigma_{\bar{Y}}$. The sampling distribution of the z test statistic is again the standard normal distribution when H_0 is true.

4. *P-Value* P is determined just as in the test for a mean. For example, for the alternative hypothesis H_a: $\pi > \pi_0$, P is the probability of obtaining a z-value above the observed z-value, when H_0 is true. This probability is just the tail area to the right of the observed value of z under the standard normal curve (see Figure 6.6). For the two-sided alternative H_a: $\pi \neq \pi_0$, the P-value is the two-tail probability.

Fig. 6.6 Calculation of P in Testing H_0: $\pi = \pi_0$ Against H_a: $\pi > \pi_0$

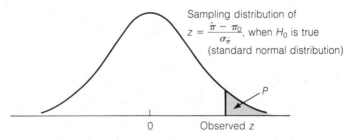

Sampling distribution of $z = \dfrac{\hat{\pi} - \pi_0}{\sigma_{\hat{\pi}}}$, when H_0 is true (standard normal distribution)

5. *Conclusion* The P-value should be reported in order to indicate the strength of evidence regarding H_0 and H_a. The smaller the P-value, the more the data contradict H_0.

*In setting up confidence intervals, there is no hypothesized value for π, so the point estimate $\hat{\pi}$ is substituted for π in this expression.

We end this section with a few examples of tests of hypotheses about proportions. As you read these examples, it may be instructive to notice the parallel between each element and the corresponding element of a test about a mean.

Example 6.4   An organization is set up for the purpose of banning smoking in public restaurants in Greenvale, Colorado. The members claim that a majority of adults in the community support such a ban for public health reasons. In an attempt to convince the city council of this support, they conduct a statistical test of H_0: $\pi = .5$ against H_a: $\pi > .5$, where π denotes the proportion of adults in the community who support the ban on smoking. The alternative hypothesis represents the claim of the organization that this proportion exceeds one-half. The null hypothesis contains the statement that this proportion is just one-half. The organization has set up the hypotheses in such a way that rejection of the null hypothesis will correspond to acceptance of its claim. However, the city council might decide not to reject the null hypothesis unless there is strong evidence against it and in favor of H_a, in the form of a small P-value.

Suppose that out of a random sample of 25 adults in this community, 15 support the smoking ban, so the point estimate of π is $\hat{\pi} = 15/25 = .60$. The standard error of $\hat{\pi}$ when H_0: $\pi = .5$ is true is

$$\sigma_{\hat{\pi}} = \sqrt{\frac{\pi_0(1 - \pi_0)}{n}} = \sqrt{\frac{(.5)(.5)}{25}} = .10$$

The value of the test statistic for this survey is therefore

$$z = \frac{\hat{\pi} - \pi_0}{\sigma_{\hat{\pi}}} = \frac{.60 - .50}{.10} = 1.0$$

The P-value for testing H_0: $\pi = .5$ against H_a: $\pi > .5$ is $P = .1587$, so there is not overwhelming evidence in favor of H_a as opposed to H_0. If only half the adults in the community favored the ban, there would still be a probability of .1587 that 60% or more of a random sample of size 25 would take that position. So, the city council might conclude that there is insufficient evidence to reject H_0. The organization formed to ban smoking has not demonstrated beyond a reasonable doubt that a majority of community residents support such a ban. ∎

We tend to disbelieve H_0 when we obtain a very small P-value, since the implication is that the observed sample result would be a rather rare event if H_0 actually were true. On the other hand, if we do not obtain an especially small P-value, this does not mean that we can *accept* H_0. The failure to obtain a small P-value could be due to the use of a small sample size. This is illustrated by the following two examples.

Example 6.5   We observed in Example 6.4 that $\hat{\pi} = .60$ for $n = 25$ measurements leads to a P-value of .1587 in testing H_0: $\pi = .5$ against H_a: $\pi > .5$. However, we would certainly agree that π might equal .55, .60, or .65 (for example), based on our sample information. In fact, a 95% confidence interval for π would be

$$\hat{\pi} \pm 1.96\sqrt{\frac{\hat{\pi}(1 - \hat{\pi})}{n}} = .60 \pm 1.96\sqrt{\frac{(.6)(.4)}{25}} = .60 \pm .19 \quad \text{or} \quad (.41, .79)$$

We see that there is a wide range of plausible values for π. Even though there is insufficient evidence to conclude that $\pi > .5$, then, it would be improper to conclude that necessarily $\pi = .5$ or $\pi < .5$. Thus, the data do not strongly contradict H_0, but we realize the need for a larger sample size to determine whether a majority of the community residents favor the ban on smoking in public restaurants. ∎

Example 6.6 If, in Example 6.4, we had observed $\hat{\pi} = .60$ for a random sample of $n = 200$ adults, then $\sigma_{\hat{\pi}} = \sqrt{(.5)(.5)/200} = .0354$, and

$$z = \frac{.60 - .50}{.0354} = 2.83$$

leading to a P-value of only $P = .0023$. In other words, for a random sample of size $n = 200$, the probability that $\hat{\pi} \geq .60$ when actually $\pi = .50$ is only .0023. Thus, if 60% of a sample of size 200 favored the smoking ban, we could be much more sure that a majority of the entire community favored the ban than if 60% of a sample of only 25 took this position. ∎

In Example 6.6, if $\pi < .5$ (i.e., if actually only a minority of the community favors the ban), then the probability of observing $\hat{\pi} \geq .60$ would be even smaller than .0023. For example, a sample value of $\hat{\pi} = .60$ is an even more unlikely occurrence when $\pi = .40$ than when $\pi = .50$, since .60 is farther out in the tail of the sampling distribution of $\hat{\pi}$ when $\pi = .40$ than when $\pi = .50$. Thus, in rejecting H_0: $\pi = .5$ in favor of H_a: $\pi > .5$, we are inherently rejecting the broader null hypothesis of H_0: $\pi \leq .5$. In other words, if we accept the alternative hypothesis that $\pi > .5$, we are concluding that $\pi = .5$ is false *and* that $\pi < .5$ is false.

We conclude this section by giving a guideline about how large the sample size must be in order to use this test for a proportion. The normal approximation for the sampling distribution of $\hat{\pi}$ is reasonably good when

$$n > 5/[\min(\pi, 1 - \pi)]$$

where the notation $\min(\pi, 1 - \pi)$ denotes the minimum of the numbers π and $1 - \pi$. For example, for testing H_0: $\pi = .5$, we need $n > 5/.5 = 10$, whereas for testing H_0: $\pi = .9$ (or H_0: $\pi = .1$), we need $n > 5/.1 = 50$. This sample size requirement reflects the fact that the sampling distribution of $\hat{\pi}$ tends to be more skewed when π is near 0 or near 1, and larger sample sizes are then needed before a symmetric bell shape is achieved. In Example 6.4, the sample size of $n = 25$ was adequately large to use this procedure to test H_0: $\pi = .5$. A test is introduced in Section 6.5 that can be used when this sample size requirement is not fulfilled.

**6.4
Small-Sample
Inference for a
Mean—The *t*
Distribution**

The confidence interval for a mean presented in Section 5.2 and the test of a hypothesis about a mean presented in Section 6.2 are both appropriate only for large sample sizes. This assumption is needed to ensure both that the sampling distribution of $\bar{Y}$ is approximately normal and that the point estimate $\hat{\sigma}_{\bar{Y}} = \hat{\sigma}/\sqrt{n}$ is close enough to $\sigma_{\bar{Y}} = \sigma/\sqrt{n}$ so that the z test statistic still has the standard normal distribution (when H_0 is true) when $\hat{\sigma}_{\bar{Y}}$ is substituted in the denominator for $\sigma_{\bar{Y}}$. As a rough guideline, we indicated that these approximations are usually sufficiently good if the sample size is at least 30.

However, we are sometimes limited in the size of the sample that can be practically obtained. For example, each observation may be the result of a long or expensive experimental procedure. A consumer group that decides to evaluate the mean repair cost resulting when a new-model automobile crashes into a brick wall at 10 miles per hour would probably not want to be restricted to large-sample statistical methods!

The *t* Distribution

For small sample sizes, the sampling distribution of $\bar{Y}$ might not be normal, and $\hat{\sigma}_{\bar{Y}}$ might not be very close to $\sigma_{\bar{Y}}$. Thus, the sampling distribution of the statistic $(\bar{Y} - \mu)/\hat{\sigma}_{\bar{Y}}$ is not in general the standard normal distribution. In this section, we restrict our attention to the special case in which the *population distribution* of the variable Y is normal. Then, the sampling distribution of the statistic $(\bar{Y} - \mu)/\sigma_{\bar{Y}}$ is normal even for small sample sizes (refer back to Figure 4.11). However, substitution of $\hat{\sigma}_{\bar{Y}}$ for $\sigma_{\bar{Y}}$ introduces more variability in the sampling distribution, which is no longer normal, but the *t distribution*.

---

t Statistic; t Distribution

Suppose that the population distribution of a variable is normal, with parameters μ and σ. Then, for a random sample of size n, the sampling distribution of the *t statistic*

$$t = \frac{\bar{Y} - \mu}{\hat{\sigma}_{\bar{Y}}}$$

is called the *t distribution with (n − 1) degrees of freedom*.

The form of the t statistic is exactly the same as that of the z statistic introduced in Section 6.2. However, we use a different symbol here for the test statistic in order to emphasize that the sampling distribution is different and that the test is appropriate in a different situation—when $n \leq 30$ and the population distribution is normal. The degrees of freedom for the t distribution, denoted by df, refers to the divisor in the point estimate $\hat{\sigma}^2$ of σ^2, namely, $n - 1$ (see Section 5.1).

The t distribution was discovered in 1908 by the statistician and chemist W. S. Gosset. At the time, Gosset was employed by Guinness Breweries in Dublin, and probably was supplied only with small samples. Due to company policy forbidding the publishing of trade secrets, Gosset used the pseudonym Student in publishing this result, and the *t* statistic is often referred to as *Student's t*.

Before returning to the subject of statistical inference for small samples, we shall consider a few of the major properties of the *t* probability distribution.

1. The *t* distribution is symmetric about 0. This property is analogous to the property that the sampling distribution of the *z* statistic (the standard normal distribution) is also symmetric about 0.
2. The dispersion of the *t* distribution depends on the degrees of freedom. The standard deviation of the *t* distribution always exceeds 1 (see Note 6.2), but decreases to 1 as df (and hence *n*) increases without limit.
3. The *t* distribution is mound-shaped about 0, but it has more probability concentrated in the tails than does the standard normal distribution. The larger the value of df, though, the more closely it resembles the standard normal distribution (see Figure 6.7). In the limit as df increases indefinitely, the two distributions are identical.

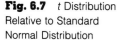

Fig. 6.7 *t* Distribution Relative to Standard Normal Distribution

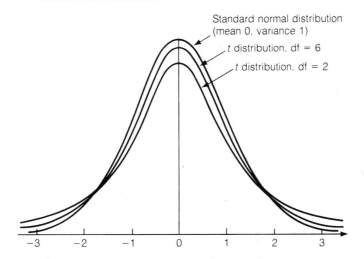

The change in the form of the *t* distribution as df increases is due to the increasing precision of $\hat{\sigma}$ as a point estimate of σ in the standard error formula $\hat{\sigma}_{\bar{Y}} = \hat{\sigma}/\sqrt{n}$. Because $\hat{\sigma}$ tends to be less accurate as an estimate of σ when df < 30, its presence in the denominator of the *t* statistic tends to produce additional sampling error. This greater degree of sampling error in the small-sample case results in the *t* sampling distribution being more disperse than the standard normal sampling distribution of the corresponding large-sample *z* statistic, in which $\hat{\sigma}$ tends to be nearly equal to σ. As the sample size increases, $\hat{\sigma}$ becomes a more accurate estimate of σ, and the *t* distribution becomes less disperse. When df $\geq$ 30, the *t* distribution is so similar to the standard normal distribution that inference procedures for the mean using the *t* distribution are practically equivalent to those described in Sections 5.2 and 6.2.

4. The *t*-values for various tail areas under the *t* distribution are listed in Table B at the end of the text. Since the *t* distribution has a slightly different shape for each distinct value of df, a different set of *t*-values is needed for each df value. Thus, there is room in this table to list only the *t*-values corresponding to the one-tail probabilities of .100, .050, .025, .010, and .005. These same values correspond to two-tail probabilities of .20, .10, .05, .02, and .01, respectively.

Notation

For a particular value of df, let t_a denote the *t*-value corresponding to a right-hand tail area of *a*.

Fig. 6.8 *t* Distribution with df = 6

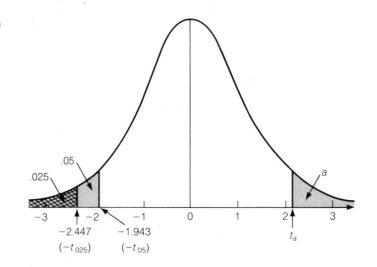

To illustrate, when df = 6, 2.5% of the *t* distribution with 6 degrees of freedom lies in the right-hand tail above $t_{.025} = 2.447$, and 2.5% lies in the left-hand tail below $-t_{.025} = -2.447$ (see Figure 6.8). We see in Table B that as df increases, t_a decreases to the z_a-value for a standard normal distribution. This reflects the fact that the *t* distribution becomes less disperse and more similar in appearance to the standard normal distribution as df increases. When df = 29 (*n* = 30), we see that $t_{.025} = 2.045$, whereas $z_{.025} = 1.96$. The *z*-values for these one-tail areas are given in the last row of the table, opposite df = ∞ (infinity). The t_a-values are not printed for df ≥ 30, since they are so close to the z_a-values. Hence, whenever df ≥ 30 for a procedure utilizing the *t* distribution, we can refer to the normal curve probability table (Table A) and proceed as if the procedure uses the standard normal distribution.

Elements of a *t* Test   We now give the elements of a test of hypothesis for a mean for the small-sample case.

1. *Assumptions* A random sample of size $n \leq 30$ is selected. The variable is measured on at least an interval scale and has a normal population distribution.

2. *Hypotheses* The hypotheses are the same as in the large-sample test for a mean. The null hypothesis has the form $H_0: \mu = \mu_0$, and the alternative hypothesis can take any of the forms, $H_a: \mu \neq \mu_0$, $H_a: \mu > \mu_0$, or $H_a: \mu < \mu_0$.

3. *Test Statistic* The t statistic with $\mu = \mu_0$, namely,

$$t = \frac{\bar{Y} - \mu_0}{\hat{\sigma}_{\bar{Y}}} = \frac{\bar{Y} - \mu_0}{\hat{\sigma}/\sqrt{n}}$$

is the test statistic. This statistic measures the distance from the sample mean to the null hypothesis value of the population mean, by the number of estimated standard errors between $\bar{Y}$ and μ_0. If H_0 is true, the sampling distribution of the t test statistic is the t distribution with df $= n - 1$.

4. *P-Value* The calculation of the *P*-value here is similar to the large-sample calculation. For example, for the two-sided alternative hypothesis $H_a: \mu \neq \mu_0$, *P* is the probability that we would obtain a *t*-value at least as large in absolute value as the observed one, if H_0 were true (see Figure 6.9).

Fig. 6.9 Calculation of *P* in Testing $H_0: \mu = \mu_0$ Against $H_a: \mu \neq \mu_0$, for a Small Sample

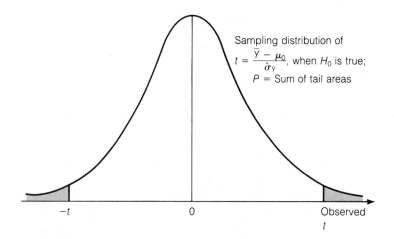

Sampling distribution of $t = \frac{\bar{Y} - \mu_0}{\hat{\sigma}_{\bar{Y}}}$, when H_0 is true; P = Sum of tail areas

$-t$ 0   Observed t

Table B is not detailed enough to calculate the exact value of *P*. If we observed a test statistic value of $t = 2.0$ when df $= 6$, we would know that $P < .10$ (since $|t| = 1.943$ corresponds to a two-tail area of .10) but $P > .05$ (since $t = 2.447$ corresponds to a two-tail area of .05). Thus, there is enough information in Table B to determine whether the two-tailed *P*-value is greater than or less than .20, .10, .05, .02, and .01.

For the one-sided alternative $H_a: \mu > \mu_0$, the *P*-value is the right-hand tail probability above the observed *t*-value. A small value of *P* then occurs when $\bar{Y}$ is much larger than μ_0, so we get a large positive *t*-value. If $t = 2.0$ and df $= 6$, then $P < .05$, but $P >$

.025, since $t = 1.943$ corresponds to a right-hand tail area of .05, and $t = 2.447$ corresponds to a right-hand tail area of .025. The analogous results apply to the left-hand tail of the t distribution for the one-sided alternative H_a: $\mu < \mu_0$.

5. *Conclusion* Since the exact P-value cannot be determined from Table B, we specify the smallest number that we know to exceed P. That is, it would be reported as $P < .10$, $P < .05$, $P < .01$, or whatever. As usual, small P-values give evidence against H_0 and in favor of H_a.

Example 6.7 An anthropological expedition discovers seven ancient animal skulls at several points along a river. The anthropologists immediately wonder whether these are the remains of a particular species of ape that they believe once inhabited the territory. It is known that the mean skull length for this species was 6.0 inches. The group decides to do a statistical test of the hypothesis that the remains are from that species. They do this by testing H_0: $\mu = 6.0$ against H_a: $\mu \neq 6.0$, where μ represents the mean skull length for the actual species of the remains.

The seven skull lengths (in inches) for the discovered skulls are 7.6, 8.2, 8.1, 7.6, 8.3, 8.0, and 8.2. Hence,

$$\bar{Y} = \frac{56}{7} = 8.0 \quad \text{and} \quad \hat{\sigma} = \sqrt{\frac{\Sigma \, (Y_i - \bar{Y})^2}{n - 1}} = \sqrt{\frac{.50}{6}} = .289$$

The estimated standard error of $\bar{Y}$ equals

$$\hat{\sigma}_{\bar{Y}} = \frac{\hat{\sigma}}{\sqrt{n}} = \frac{.289}{\sqrt{7}} = .109$$

so that the test statistic is calculated to be

$$t = \frac{\bar{Y} - \mu_0}{\hat{\sigma}_{\bar{Y}}} = \frac{8.0 - 6.0}{.109} = 18.35$$

Now, for df $= 6$, $t = 3.707$ corresponds to $P = .01$ for the two-sided alternative hypothesis. Since we observed $t = 18.35 > 3.707$, the P-value is $P < .01$. We have overwhelming evidence against the hypothesis that these skulls are a random sample from a population with mean skull length of 6 inches. The explorers might conclude that these skulls are not of the indicated species.* ■

Of course, for the statistical test in Example 6.7 to be valid, we must assume that the skulls are a random sampling of skulls of their species, and that the distribution of skull length for that species is normal. It would be impossible to verify these assumptions for this type of application. In most practical problems, in fact, we would not have a very clear notion of the form of the population distribution, especially when the sample size is small. Statistical researchers have shown, though, that the t test

*For another approach to this example, see Problem 47 at the end of the chapter.

for a mean is quite *robust* against violations of the assumption that the population distribution is normal. This means that even if the population is not normally distributed, the t distribution still provides a reasonably good approximation to the exact sampling distribution of the statistic $(\bar{Y} - \mu)/\hat{\sigma}_{\bar{Y}}$. The P-values seem to be fairly accurate except for the case when the population distribution is highly skewed and a one-sided alternative hypothesis is used. However, the result of the t test may be completely invalid if the sample is not random.

Small-Sample Confidence Interval

The t distribution can also be used to construct confidence intervals for a mean when the size of the random sample is too small to use the procedure in Section 5.2.

Small-Sample Confidence Interval for μ

If the population distribution is normal, a $100(1 - \alpha)\%$ confidence interval for μ is

$$\bar{Y} \pm t_{\alpha/2}\hat{\sigma}_{\bar{Y}} = \bar{Y} \pm t_{\alpha/2}\left(\frac{\hat{\sigma}}{\sqrt{n}}\right)$$

where df $= n - 1$ for the t-value.

The $t_{\alpha/2}$-value is used since the area under the t curve between $-t_{\alpha/2}$ and $t_{\alpha/2}$ is the desired confidence coefficient $(1 - \alpha)$. For example, a $t_{.025}$-value is used for a 95% confidence interval, since 95% of the probability for a t distribution falls between $-t_{.025}$ and $t_{.025}$. In that case, we identify .95 with the confidence coefficient $1 - \alpha$ and .05 with α, the probability that the confidence interval does not contain μ.

The approach here is analogous to the one used in Chapter 5 for large samples. To form the confidence interval, we take the point estimate of μ and add and subtract a table value multiplied by the estimated standard error. The only difference in the formula is the substitution of the t table value $t_{\alpha/2}$ for the z table value $z_{\alpha/2}$, to reflect the small sample size. We also have the additional assumption of a normal population distribution, although this procedure is also robust to violations of that assumption.

Example 6.8 Based on the data in Example 6.7, for which df $= 6$, a 99% confidence interval for μ is

$$\bar{Y} \pm t_{.005}\hat{\sigma}_{\bar{Y}} = 8.0 \pm 3.707(.109) = 8.0 \pm .40 \quad \text{or} \quad (7.6, 8.4)$$

That is, we infer with 99% confidence that this interval contains the mean skull length for the species of the sampled skulls. In the test in Example 6.7, we concluded that the mean skull length for that species was not equal to 6.0 inches. The confidence interval of (7.6, 8.4) is a way of inferring just how different from 6.0 the mean actually is. ■

6.5
Small-Sample
Inference for a
Proportion—
The Binomial
Distribution

The test for a proportion discussed in Section 6.3 is applicable when $n > 5/[\min(\pi_0, 1 - \pi_0)]$, in which case the sampling distribution of $\hat{\pi}$ is approximately normal when H_0 is true. The closer π_0 is to 0 or 1 for a given sample size, the more skewed the actual sampling distribution becomes, and the normal approximation may be poor. To illustrate, when π_0 equals .05 or .95, a sample size of about $n = 100$ would be needed before the normal distribution would provide a good approximation. Also, for small values of n, the sampling distribution of $\hat{\pi}$ is very discrete, in the sense that it is concentrated at very few points, and a continuous approximation such as the normal distribution is less appropriate. For example, if $n = 5$, the only possible values for $\hat{\pi}$ are 0, 1/5, 2/5, 3/5, 4/5, and 1. In this section, we introduce a small-sample test for a proportion that can be used when the normal approximation is inappropriate.

The Binomial Distribution

In Section 5.3, we saw that the sample proportion $\hat{\pi}$ of observations classified in a particular category can be expressed as $\hat{\pi} = X/n$, where X is the number of observations in that category. For example, when $n = 5$, the possible values for the variable X are 0, 1, 2, 3, 4, and 5. We will conduct a small-sample test about the value of π using the sampling distribution of X, which (under certain circumstances) is called the *binomial distribution*.

In general, the binomial distribution arises in the following context:

1. We take a sequence of n observations, and for each we observe the classification on some categorical variable.

2. The probability that an observation is classified in a particular category remains the same for each observation.

3. The outcome of each observation (i.e., the classification on this categorical variable) does not depend on the outcome of other observations.

Now, let X denote the number of these observations classified in a particular category. Each of the n observations either *is* or *is not* in that category, and the total number X classified in it is a variable (before the sample is selected). For a sequence of observations satisfying the above three conditions, the sampling distribution of X is the binomial distribution.

Example 6.9

It is known that 11% of all Americans are black. If a random sample of $n = 5$ Americans is selected and classified according to race, the probability that any particular person selected is black equals .11. Given that one particular person selected is black, the probability that some other particular person selected is black is also .11 due to the large size of the population. That selection does not depend on the first selection, due to the randomness of the selection process. Thus, the sampling distribution of the number of blacks selected in a sample of size 5 is a binomial distribution. ∎

The population size must be large for property 2 to hold (even approximately) in situations such as the one described in Example 6.9. To illustrate, suppose that a *population* of ten persons contains one black individual. If we randomly sample two (or more) separate individuals from this group, the second observation on race will depend on the first, probabilistically.* For example, if we know that the first person selected was black, then the probability that the second person selected is black equals 0, since there is only one black person in that population. Thus, the second selection is *not* independent of the first. One way in which the binomial distribution would still apply would be if the sampling were done with replacement—that is, if the same collection of people were used for each selection, so that the same person could be selected more than once.

The binomial variable X is discrete, since it counts the number of occurrences of a particular type. For a sample of size n, it must take on one of the integer values 0, 1, 2, . . . , n. The formula for the probabilities of a binomial distribution is given in the box.

Probabilities for a Binomial Distribution

If the probability of being classified in a given category equals π for each observation, then the probability that X out of n independent observations are classified in that category, denoted by $P(X)$, equals

$$P(X) = \frac{n!}{X!(n - X)!} \pi^X (1 - \pi)^{n-X} \qquad X = 0, 1, 2, \ldots, n$$

Notation

The symbol $n!$ is called **n factorial**, and represents $n! = 1 \cdot 2 \cdot 3 \cdot \cdots \cdot n$.

That is, $n!$ denotes the product of all of the integers from 1 to n. To illustrate, $1! = 1$, $2! = 1 \cdot 2 = 2$, $3! = 1 \cdot 2 \cdot 3 = 6$, $4! = 1 \cdot 2 \cdot 3 \cdot 4 = 24$, and so forth. Also, $0!$ is defined to be 1.

By substituting the $(n + 1)$ possible values for X into the formula for $P(X)$, we obtain the probabilities of the various outcomes. The sum of the probabilities, $P(0) + P(1) + P(2) + \cdots + P(n)$, equals 1.0. To calculate these probabilities, of course, we must have particular values for π and n.

Example 6.10   A jury list contains the names of 1,000 individuals who may be called for jury duty. The proportion of the available jurors on the list who are women is .53. If a jury of size 12 is to be selected at random from the list of available jurors, how many women would we expect to find in the jury?

---

*The sampling distribution of X for this situation is called the *hypergeometric distribution*, which is not discussed in this text.

The probability that any one person selected is a woman is $\pi = .53$, the proportion of available jurors who are women. Similarly, the probability that any one person selected is a man is $(1 - \pi) = .47$. The variable X, the number of women selected for the jury, has the binomial distribution with $n = 12$ and $\pi = .53$. For each X between 0 and 12, the probability that X of the 12 people selected are women equals

$$P(X) = \frac{12!}{X!(12 - X)!}(.53)^X(.47)^{12-X} \qquad X = 0, 1, 2, \ldots, 12$$

For example, the probability that no women would be chosen equals

$$P(0) = \frac{12!}{0!12!}(.53)^0(.47)^{12} = (.47)^{12} = .0001^*$$

Similarly, the probability that exactly one woman would be chosen is

$$P(1) = \frac{12!}{1!11!}(.53)^1(.47)^{11} = 12(.53)(.47)^{11} = .0016$$

This computation is simplified considerably by noticing that $12!/11! = 12$, since $12!$ is just $11!$ multiplied by 12. The entire binomial distribution for $n = 12$, $\pi = .53$ is listed in Table 6.3. If we had let X represent the number of *men* selected for the jury, we would have used the formula for $P(X)$ with $n = 12$ but $\pi = .47$, since .47 is the probability that a man is chosen on any particular selection.

Table 6.3

The Binomial Distribution for $n = 12$, $\pi = .53$

X	$P(X)$	X	$P(X)$
0	.0001	7	.2134
1	.0016	8	.1504
2	.0097	9	.0754
3	.0366	10	.0255
4	.0930	11	.0052
5	.1678	12	.0005
6	.2208		

We observe that more than 99% of the distribution in Table 6.3 is concentrated between $X = 2$ and $X = 10$, inclusive. The least likely values for X are 0, 12, 1, and 11, which have a combined probability of only .0074. Thus, if the sample were randomly selected, we would expect to find between about 2 and 10 women on the jury. It is especially unlikely that there would be 0 or 12 women on the jury. In this example, the binomial distribution is not symmetric about the modal value of 6. Since the proportion of women on the jury list exceeds .5, $X = 12$ is more likely to occur than $X = 0$. The binomial distribution is perfectly symmetric only when $\pi = .5$. ■

*Any number raised to the power of 0 equals 1. Also, $0! = 1$, and the $12!$ terms in the numerator and denominator cancel, leaving $P(0) = (.47)^{12}$.

The Binomial Test If a jury were selected that contained no women, even though 53% of the available jurors were women, we would be highly suspicious of the method of jury selection. We would reason that when a random sample of size $n = 12$ is selected from a population with proportion $\pi = .53$ in a certain category, then the probability is only .0001 that $X = 0$ out of the 12 measurements are in that category. This type of probabilistic argument has been used successfully in court appeals challenging the composition of juries or jury lists as being biased. For example, the conviction of Dr. Benjamin Spock for conspiracy to encourage draft evasion during the Vietnam War was overturned on these (and other) grounds. We now give an example of a formal statistical test of hypothesis, called the *binomial test*, which illustrates the above reasoning.

Example 6.11 A population of available jurors in a city contains 53% women. A local judge, who is responsible for randomly selecting individuals from this community for placement on a jury list, is suspected of choosing people for his jury list with bias against women. To check this suspicion, we test

$$H_0: \quad \pi = .53 \quad \text{versus} \quad H_a: \quad \pi < .53$$

where π represents the probability that any one person selected by the judge for the list is a woman. In H_0, the parameter π is hypothesized to equal the probability corresponding to random sampling. In H_a, the judge is claimed to be selecting potential jurors in such a way that the probability of selecting a woman on any one choice is less than it would be if he were using random sampling. Thus, we have set up H_a so that the test is designed to detect bias of the judge against women in his selections. Rejecting H_0 corresponds to confirming the suspicion of bias.

Suppose that we decide to observe the judge's next twelve choices for the list. Let X denote the number of women chosen for the list. This is a natural test statistic to use for this situation. Under the assumption of random sampling, the sampling distribution of X is the binomial distribution with $n = 12$ and $\pi = .53$, already tabulated in Table 6.3. For the one-sided alternative H_a: $\pi < .53$, the P-value is the probability of obtaining a value of the test statistic X that is as small as or smaller than the observed value—that is, the left-hand tail area for the binomial distribution.

Out of the twelve people chosen for the jury list, suppose that two are women. Thus, the P-value is the left-hand tail probability (see Figure 6.10 on the next page) of $X \leq 2$ for the binomial distribution with $n = 12$ and $\pi = .53$. From Table 6.3,

$$P = P(0) + P(1) + P(2) = .0001 + .0016 + .0097 = .0114$$

In other words, if the judge had selected the individuals randomly for the jury list, the probability that two or fewer women would have been chosen is only .0114. This result gives strong evidence against the null hypothesis of a random selection process. Similarly, $X = 1$ would yield a P-value of .0017, and $X = 0$ would yield $P = .0001$.

Fig. 6.10 Calculation of P in Testing $H_0: \pi = .53$ Against $H_a: \pi < .53$, When $n = 12$ and $X = 2$

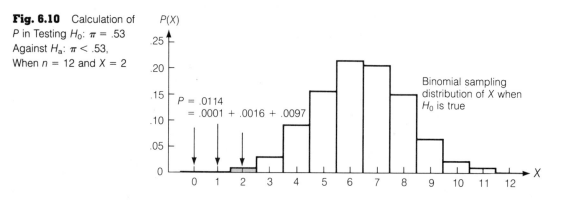

If we suspected bias against men in the selection procedure, right-hand tail probabilities would be summed to get the P-value. For example, $X = 9$ women corresponds to $P = .1066$, for the alternative $H_a: \pi > .53$. ∎

In summary, the assumptions for the binomial test are that the three elements needed to apply the binomial distribution are satisfied. The hypotheses take the same form as in the large-sample test for a proportion. The test statistic is the binomial variable X, and the P-value is calculated using its sampling distribution. For large n, the binomial sampling distribution of X is well approximated by the normal distribution, with mean $\mu = n\pi$ and standard deviation $\sqrt{n\pi(1 - \pi)}$. Equivalently, the sampling distribution of the sample proportion $\hat{\pi} = X/n$ is well approximated by the normal distribution with mean π and standard error $\sigma_{\hat{\pi}} = \sqrt{\pi(1 - \pi)/n}$. This approximation leads to the procedures described in Sections 5.3 and 6.3.

6.6 Making Decisions in Statistical Tests

In the tests presented in this chapter, we have used the P-value as a measure of the extent of the evidence about H_0 and H_a. The smaller the P-value, the more contradictory the data are to H_0. This is because a small P-value means that, if H_0 were true, it would be unusual to observe data such as those actually observed.

α-Level

In some applications it may be necessary to make a formal decision about whether the evidence against H_0 is so strong that it should be rejected. Usually the decision is based on whether the P-value falls below some previously specified cutoff point.

To illustrate, we might decide to reject H_0 if $P < .05$, and thus conclude that there is not enough evidence to reject H_0 if $P \geq .05$. The value .05 would then be referred to as the α-level of the test.

α-Level

The α-*level* is a number such that H_0 is rejected if the P-value is less than its value.*

The α-levels that are traditionally chosen by researchers are .10, .05, .01, and .001. As with confidence coefficients, the choice of the α-level reflects how careful the researcher wishes to be in making an inference. The smaller the α-level is chosen to be, the stronger the evidence must be before rejecting H_0. To avoid bias in the decision-making process, the researcher selects the α-level at which to conduct the test *before* analyzing the data. Table 6.4 summarizes the two possible conclusions for a test with α-level .05.

Table 6.4

Possible Conclusions in a Test of Hypothesis with α-Level .05

P-VALUE	CONCLUSION	
	H_0	H_a
$P < .05$	Reject	Accept
$P \geq .05$	Do not reject	Do not accept

The null hypothesis can be either *rejected* or *not rejected*. It is never "accepted," for reasons we will discuss. If the null hypothesis is not rejected, then the alternative hypothesis is not accepted; if the null hypothesis is rejected, then the alternative hypothesis is accepted.

Example 6.12

Suppose that in Example 6.1 we had set an α-level of $\alpha = .05$ to guide us in making a formal decision about H_0. Since we obtained a P-value of $P = .0082$ in that example, we have $P < .05$ and sufficient evidence to reject H_0: $\mu = 2.0$ in favor of H_a: $\mu > 2.0$. In other words, we can conclude that the mean number of prior convictions in 1985 exceeds the value for 1980. This type of conclusion is sometimes phrased as, "The increase in the mean is statistically significant."

In Example 6.4 we obtained $P = .1587$, so we would not be able to reject H_0: $\pi = .5$ using $\alpha = .05$, since $P > \alpha$. Failure to reject H_0, though, is very different from saying that we can "accept H_0," which is not the case. Although the observed sample proportion of $\hat{\pi} = .60$ is not sufficiently larger than .50 that we can conclude that a majority of residents favor the smoking ban, it certainly does not imply that $\pi = .50$. In fact, in Example 6.5 we observed that a confidence interval gave us a wide range of plausible values for π. ∎

We use the terminology "Do not reject H_0" instead of "Accept H_0" to emphasize that the null hypothesis value for the parameter is simply one of many plausible values. Because of sampling error, we can never accept a hypothesis consisting of a

---

*The α-level is sometimes referred to as the *significance level* (as distinguished from the *attained* significance level, or P-value).

single number. The reason we *can* use "accept H_a" terminology for the *alternative* hypothesis is that when the *P*-value is sufficiently small, the plausible values for the parameter are all contained within the broad range of numbers that are contained in H_a.

The collection of values of the test statistic that would lead a researcher to reject H_0 at a particular α-level is referred to as the **rejection region**. For example, the rejection region for a test of level $\alpha = .05$ is the set of values for the test statistic that produce $P < .05$. For the large-sample test of H_0: $\mu = \mu_0$ against H_a: $\mu \neq \mu_0$, this happens when $|z| > 1.96$. In other words, the rejection region for an $\alpha = .05$ level test consists of values of z for which $|z| > 1.96$—that is, values of z corresponding to an occurrence of $\bar{Y}$ more than 1.96 standard errors from the hypothesized value μ_0. Rejecting H_0 at the .05 level corresponds to concluding that if H_0 were true, the probability would be less than .05 of observing a test statistic value at least as favorable to the alternative hypothesis as the observed *z*-score.

Type I and Type II Errors

Since there is sampling error, we can never make a conclusion with certainty, and the procedure of testing a hypothesis could lead us to an erroneous conclusion. When a researcher makes a decision about whether to reject H_0 at the conclusion of a statistical test, there are two potential errors that may be made. These errors are conventionally referred to as *Type I* and *Type II* errors.

Type I Error; Type II Error

A *Type I error* occurs when H_0 is rejected even though it is true.

A *Type II error* occurs when H_0 is not rejected even though it is false.

The four possible outcomes when a conclusion is made in a test of a hypothesis are a result of the two possible decisions combined with the two possible conditions for H_0. These outcomes are illustrated in Table 6.5.

Table 6.5
The Four Possible Outcomes of a Test

		DECISION OF RESEARCHER	
		Reject H_0	Do not reject H_0
CONDITION OF H_0	H_0 true	Type I error	Correct decision
	H_0 false	Correct decision	Type II error

Suppose we decided to test H_0 at the $\alpha = .05$ level; that is, we reject H_0 if $P < .05$. For example, for the large-sample test of H_0: $\mu = \mu_0$ against H_a: $\mu \neq \mu_0$, we reject H_0 at the $\alpha = .05$ level when $|z| > 1.96$. For a continuous sampling distribution such as the normal distribution, the probability of rejecting H_0 when it is true is exactly .05, since the probability of the values in the rejection region is exactly the α-level. Hence, the probability of a Type I error is precisely the α-level at which the test is conducted.

The researcher can control the probability of a Type I error by the choice of the α-level at which the decision is made. Labovitz (1968) has written a good, non-technical article that provides guidelines for this choice of an α-level. The more serious the consequences of a Type I error, the smaller we would choose α to be. For preliminary, exploratory research conducted for data-snooping—scanning a large number of hypotheses to see which might warrant further investigation—we might not wish to be too stringent (say, $\alpha = .1$). On the other hand, suppose that rejection of H_0 has the consequence that a newly discovered drug is judged to be better than one currently used and will result in that new drug being prescribed to treat a serious ailment. Then, we might wish to impose tough standards, such as $\alpha = .001$. For that level, rejection of H_0 and acceptance of the new drug means that, if the new drug were no better (i.e., if H_0 were true), there would have been a .001 probability or less of obtaining a sample at least as favorable to the new drug as the observed sample.

Calculating P(Type II Error)* The probability of a Type II error (not rejecting H_0 when it is false) depends on just how false H_0 is. If the actual parameter value is nearly equal to the value hypothesized in H_0, the probability of a Type II error might be quite high, whereas it would tend to be smaller for more distant values of the parameter. The greater the deviation of the true value of the parameter from the value specified in H_0, the less likely the sample is to fail to detect the difference and lead to a Type II error. The calculation of the probability of a Type II error is illustrated in Example 6.13.

Example 6.13 The null hypothesis H_0: $\mu = 10$ is to be tested against H_a: $\mu > 10$, at the $\alpha = .05$ level. For a sample of size 50, assume the estimated standard error of $\bar{Y}$ is $\hat{\sigma}_{\bar{Y}} = 2.0$. Suppose that we consider it very important that we reject H_0 if μ is actually 14 or larger. Then we might calculate the probability of a Type II error for the alternative value of $\mu = 14$.

Now, H_0: $\mu = 10$ is rejected in favor of the one-sided alternative H_a: $\mu > 10$ if $z > 1.645$, since a test statistic value of $z = 1.645$ corresponds to a P-value of $P = .05$. In other words, H_0 is rejected if $\bar{Y}$ is more than 1.645 estimated standard errors above $\mu_0 = 10$, or when

$$\bar{Y} > 10 + 1.645\hat{\sigma}_{\bar{Y}} = 10 + 1.645(2.0) = 13.3$$

Similarly, H_0 is not rejected if $\bar{Y} \leq 13.3$ (see Figure 6.11 on the next page). If the actual value of μ is 14, then the probability of committing a Type II error is the probability that $\bar{Y} \leq 13.3$ (so H_0 is not rejected) when $\mu = 14$ (H_0 is false). For a normal sampling distribution with mean 14 and standard error 2.0, the $\bar{Y}$-value of 13.3 corresponds to a z-score of

$$z = \frac{13.3 - 14}{2.0} = -.35$$

---

*Sections marked with an asterisk are intended to be optional, and may be omitted at a first reading.

Fig. 6.11 Calculation of Probability of Type II Error for Testing H_0: $\mu = 10$ Against H_a: $\mu > 10$ at $\alpha = .05$ Level

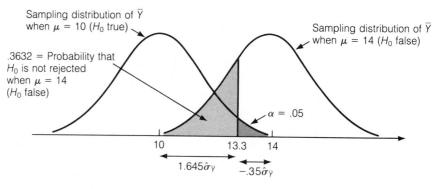

The left-hand tail probability below 13.3 for that normal distribution is therefore .3632. So, for the sample of size 50, there is a probability of .3632 of not rejecting H_0: $\mu = 10$, if in fact $\mu = 14$. The probability of making a Type II error for that alternative value is exactly that number, .3632.   ■

Exercise Show that for the alternative values of $\mu = 12$ and $\mu = 16$ in Example 6.13, the probabilities of a Type II error are .7422 and .0885, respectively. Observe that the probabilities decrease as alternative values further above 10 are considered.

The probability of a Type I error and the probability of a Type II error are inversely related. The smaller we fix the α-level in a test, the larger the probability of a Type II error will be for a particular alternative value, and vice versa. To illustrate, if we had set a probability of a Type I error of $\alpha = .01$ in Example 6.13, then a Type II error would have occurred if $\bar{Y} \leq 14.66$, which happens with a probability of .6293 when $\mu = 14$. Hence, the stronger the evidence we require before rejecting H_0 (i.e., the smaller the α-value), the more likely we are to fail to detect a real difference. For a fixed value of the probability of one of the types of error, we can decrease the probability of the other type of error by selecting a larger sample. In other words, the larger the sample size, the more likely we are to reject a false null hypothesis at a particular α-level (see Problem 42 at the end of the chapter).

When we make a decision after conducting a statistical test, we do not know whether we have made a Type I or Type II error, just as we do not know whether a confidence interval really contains the actual parameter value. However, the probability of an incorrect decision can be controlled in either case. Although we do not know whether the conclusion in a particular test is right or wrong, we justify the procedure in terms of the long-run proportions of Type I and Type II errors.

The probability of rejecting the null hypothesis when it is false is referred to as the *power* of the test. For a particular alternative value of the parameter, the power is simply one minus the probability of a Type II error. For example, the power of the test for the alternative $\mu = 14$ in Example 6.13 is $1 - .3632 = .6368$.

In later chapters, we shall usually omit examples of the calculation of the power or the probability of a Type II error, since these calculations are quite complicated for most statistical tests. It should be kept in mind, though, that the probability of a Type

II error may be fairly large for important alternatives, especially if the sample size is small. Partly because we do not calculate the size of this probability, we never, in fact, accept H_0. If there is insufficient evidence to reject H_0, we state the conclusion as *not rejecting* H_0. In other words, we recognize that the reason for not rejecting H_0 may be that the test simply does not have enough power to detect a deviation from H_0 for that size of sample.

6.7 Some Comments on Tests of Hypotheses

In this section, we first elaborate on the equivalence between conclusions made using hypothesis tests and conclusions made from confidence intervals, which was first alluded to in Example 6.3. Then we consider the distinction between a statistically significant result and practical significance. Also we discuss why estimation procedures such as confidence intervals often yield more substantive inferences than hypothesis tests.

An Equivalence Between Confidence Intervals and Tests of Hypotheses

Let us consider the large-sample test of

$$H_0: \quad \mu = \mu_0 \qquad \text{versus} \qquad H_a: \quad \mu \neq \mu_0$$

If $P < .05$, so that H_0 is rejected at the $\alpha = .05$ level, then this implies that the test statistic $z = (\bar{Y} - \mu_0)/\hat{\sigma}_{\bar{Y}}$ exceeds 1.96 in absolute value. That is, $\bar{Y}$ occurs more than $1.96\hat{\sigma}_{\bar{Y}}$ from the hypothesized value μ_0. But this also means that the 95% confidence interval for μ, namely, $\bar{Y} \pm 1.96\hat{\sigma}_{\bar{Y}}$, does not contain the null hypothesis value μ_0 (see Figure 6.12). In other words, the result of $H_0: \mu = \mu_0$ being rejected at the $\alpha = .05$ level is equivalent to the 95% confidence interval for μ not containing μ_0, in the sense that one result implies the other. These two inference procedures are therefore consistent. If a confidence interval with given confidence coefficient indicates that a specific number μ_0 is unrealistic for the value of μ, then $H_0: \mu = \mu_0$ is rejected in favor of $H_a: \mu \neq \mu_0$ in a corresponding statistical test. The null hypothesis H_0 would be rejected at the α-level equal to one minus the confidence coefficient. This relationship also holds for the small-sample t test and confidence interval for a mean.

Fig. 6.12   Relationship Between Confidence Interval and Hypothesis Test

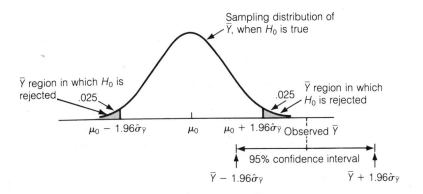

> Suppose that in testing H_0: $\mu = \mu_0$ against the two-sided alternative H_a: $\mu \neq \mu_0$, H_0 is rejected at the α-level. Then, the $100(1 - \alpha)\%$ confidence interval for μ does not contain μ_0. In fact, the $100(1 - \alpha)\%$ confidence interval for μ consists of exactly those values of μ_0 for which H_0: $\mu = \mu_0$ is not rejected at the α-level.

In Example 6.2, since $P = .0164$, H_0: $\mu = 2$ can be rejected in favor of H_a: $\mu \neq 2$ at the $\alpha = .05$ level, but not at the $\alpha = .01$ level. Thus, a 95% confidence interval for μ would not contain $\mu_0 = 2$, but a 99% confidence interval would.*

For other parameters as well, parallels can be drawn (at least approximately) between the results of confidence intervals and tests with two-sided alternatives. Parallels with tests with one-sided alternatives can be obtained by defining one-sided confidence intervals, which take the form of upper or lower bounds for a parameter.

Statistical and Practical Significance

Before leaving the topic of testing hypotheses, we should elaborate on the concept of statistical *significance*. If P is very small (say, $P = .001$), this does not imply that we have obtained an important finding. We simply know that, if H_0 were true, then the observed results would be very unusual. Even if H_0 is in fact false, though, the true value of the parameter may be very close to the hypothesized value. In such a case, the difference between the hypothesized and the true parameter values may not be considered significant in practical terms. If the sample size is very large, small P-values may occur even though the difference is very small.

Example 6.14

A statistical test is conducted of whether the mean score on a college entrance exam for students in 1985 is any different from the mean score of 500 for students who took the same exam in 1968. We test H_0: $\mu = 500$ against H_a: $\mu \neq 500$, where μ represents the mean score for all students who took the exam in 1985. For a nationwide random sample of 10,000 students who took the exam in 1985, we observe that $\bar{Y} = 497$ and $\hat{\sigma} = 100$. Then, $\hat{\sigma}_{\bar{Y}} = \hat{\sigma}/\sqrt{n} = 100/\sqrt{10,000} = 1.0$, and

$$z = \frac{\bar{Y} - \mu_0}{\hat{\sigma}_{\bar{Y}}} = \frac{497 - 500}{1.0} = -3.0$$

The P-value is $P = 2(.00135) = .0027$. Although the difference between the true mean in 1968 and the sample mean in 1985 is highly significant statistically, its magnitude would probably be considered trivial and unimportant in practice. ■

The result of Example 6.14 is simply a consequence of the fact that inferences are more powerful with larger sample sizes, and thus test statistics are able to detect deviations of smaller magnitude from H_0 than they would be able to for smaller samples. The point that should be stressed here is that the size of P is merely a measure of how certain we can be that H_0 is false, not how far from the truth H_0

*Since $P = .0164$ in that example, and since $1 - .0164 = .9836$, the 98.36% confidence interval ($\bar{Y} \pm 2.4\hat{\sigma}_{\bar{Y}}$) is the narrowest confidence interval centered about $\bar{Y}$ that contains $\mu_0 = 2$.

happens to be. The smaller the value of P, the more contradictory the observed result is to H_0. However, one should always inspect the difference between the sample estimate and the hypothesized value of the parameter (e.g., between $\bar{Y}$ and μ_0, between $\hat{\pi}$ and π_0) to gauge the practical implications of that result.

Testing Versus Estimation

A good case can be made for the argument that null hypotheses are rarely true in the social sciences, and hence that with large enough samples (so that Type II error is unlikely) they will be rejected. That is, rarely will the true value of the parameter be *exactly* equal to the value listed in H_0. What should be relevant to the researcher is whether the true value is sufficiently different from the null hypothesis value to be of importance.

Although there are situations in which tests of hypotheses yield useful decisions, many social scientists and statisticians agree that there has been an overemphasis on hypothesis testing in social science research, while estimation procedures such as confidence intervals have probably been underutilized. When the methodology is available for obtaining a confidence interval for a descriptively useful parameter, it may be preferable to form that interval instead of simply performing a statistical test. If the null hypothesis is rejected, then the confidence interval gives us numbers that *do* seem to be reasonable values for the parameter. This permits us to investigate the extent to which H_0 may be false, and thus whether its rejection is of practical importance. To illustrate, in Example 6.14, a 95% confidence interval for μ is $\bar{Y} \pm 1.96\hat{\sigma}_{\bar{Y}} = 497 \pm 2.0$, or (495, 499). This indicates that, although $P = .0027$, any change in the mean since 1968 is likely of tiny magnitude. On the other hand, if $\bar{Y}$ had been 450 (with $\hat{\sigma} = 100$), the 95% confidence interval would have been 450 ± 2.0, or (448, 452), which would have indicated a very substantial decrease since 1968.

If H_0 is not rejected, the computation of a confidence interval indicates whether that failure to reject may be due to a lack of power. A relatively wide confidence interval containing the null hypothesis value of the parameter indicates a strong possibility of a Type II error. In that case, the lack of precision of the interval estimate also indicates why it would not make sense to *accept* H_0, as we observed in Examples 6.5 and 6.12.

In the remaining chapters, we present a large number of statistical tests for various situations. It is important to become familiar with the terminology and elements of statistical tests, if for no other reason than that they are very frequently used in the social science literature. However, whenever possible, we shall introduce parameters that describe how far the true state of the situation is from the hypothesized state, as well as the confidence intervals for those parameters.

Summary

Statistical inference involves making conclusions about descriptive parameters of populations using sample data. In Chapters 5 and 6, we have studied the two primary mechanisms for making inferences—estimation and tests of hypotheses. Both of these procedures are based on the foundations of probability and probability distributions, as formulated in Chapter 4.

A statistical test of hypothesis is composed of five elements:

1. *Assumptions* about the scale of measurement of the variable, the form of the population distribution, the sampling method, and the sample size
2. *Null and alternative hypotheses* about the value of the parameter
3. A *test statistic* that can be used to describe how consistent the observed data are with what would be expected if the null hypothesis were true
4. The *P-value*, which describes in a particular sense how likely the observed result would be to occur if the null hypothesis were true
5. A *conclusion* based on the sample evidence about the null hypothesis

In this chapter, we have studied methods for testing hypotheses about a parameter, based on a single sample from a population. The large-sample tests for a mean and for a proportion are founded on the Central Limit Theorem and use the standard normal sampling distribution. The small-sample test for a mean uses the t sampling distribution, and the small-sample test for a proportion uses the binomial sampling distribution. In each test, small P-values occur when the test statistic is far from the mean of the sampling distribution under the null hypothesis. The elements of these tests are summarized in Table 6.6.

The sample size is a crucial factor in both the estimation and hypothesis-testing procedures. Small sample sizes tend to yield wide confidence intervals for a parameter, and thus imprecise estimations. With small sample sizes it is difficult to reject false null hypotheses, especially when the actual parameter value is not very different from the value stated in the null hypothesis.

Table 6.6 Summary of Tests for Means and Proportions

PARAMETER	MEAN		PROPORTION	
	$n > 30$	$n \le 30$	$n > 5/[\min(\pi_0, 1 - \pi_0)]$	$n \le 5/[\min(\pi_0, 1 - \pi_0)]$
1. Assumptions	Random sample, interval variable	Random sample, normal population distribution, interval variable	Random sample, categorical variable	Random sample, categorical variable
2. Hypotheses	$H_0: \mu = \mu_0$ $H_a: \mu \ne \mu_0$ $H_a: \mu > \mu_0$ $H_a: \mu < \mu_0$	Same	$H_0: \pi = \pi_0$ $H_a: \pi \ne \pi_0$ $H_a: \pi < \pi_0$ $H_a: \pi > \pi_0$	Same
3. Test statistic	$z = \dfrac{\bar{Y} - \mu_0}{\hat{\sigma}_{\bar{Y}}}$	$t = \dfrac{\bar{Y} - \mu_0}{\hat{\sigma}_{\bar{Y}}}$	$z = \dfrac{\hat{\pi} - \pi_0}{\sigma_{\hat{\pi}}}$	Binomial variable $X = n\hat{\pi}$
4. P-value	Two-tail area in sampling distribution for two-sided test ($H_a: \mu \ne \mu_0$ or $H_a: \pi \ne \pi_0$); one-tail area in sampling distribution for one-sided test			
5. Conclusion	Reject H_0 if P-value $P < \alpha$-level			

Notes

Section 6.4

1. The formula for the degrees of freedom for the t test for a mean is df $= n - 1$, which is the denominator of the point estimate $\hat{\sigma}^2$ of σ^2. Later in the text, we formulate other estimates of σ^2 in more general contexts, and the formula for the degrees of freedom changes somewhat. In general, though, it equals the sample size minus the number of parameters that must be estimated to compute the numerator of $\hat{\sigma}^2$ [in this case, $n - 1$, since $\bar{Y}$ estimates μ in the numerator $\Sigma (Y_i - \bar{Y})^2$]. The reasoning for the terminology *degrees of freedom* is discussed in Problem 46 at the end of this chapter.

2. The exact formula for the standard deviation of the t distribution is $\sqrt{\text{df}/(\text{df} - 2)}$. This value exceeds 1.0, but it converges downward to 1.0 as df increases.

Problems

1. A large-sample test of a hypothesis is conducted about the value of a mean. The observed z-value is 1.8. Find the P-value when the alternative hypothesis is each of the following:

a. H_a: $\mu > \mu_0$ **b.** H_a: $\mu \neq \mu_0$ **c.** H_a: $\mu < \mu_0$

2. The P-value for a large-sample test about a mean is reported to be $P = .100$. Find the value of the z test statistic when the alternative hypothesis is each of the following:

a. H_a: $\mu > \mu_0$ **b.** H_a: $\mu \neq \mu_0$ **c.** H_a: $\mu < \mu_0$

3. Each student at a university completed a questionnaire concerning the use of advising services. For the entire student body, the mean number of visits per year to an advisor was 3.1. It is hypothesized that this would decrease with the introduction of a student advising service. At the end of the next year, a random sample of thirty-six students was chosen, for which the mean number of visits was 2.9, with an estimated standard deviation of 1.0. Is this strong evidence that the mean number of visits has decreased? Show all steps of the appropriate test of the hypothesis, and calculate the P-value.

4. A social psychologist plans to conduct an experiment with a random sample of forty-nine children from some school. It is considered important that these children possess (on the average) IQ scores no different from 100, the nationwide average IQ. For these children, $\bar{Y} = 106$ and $\hat{\sigma} = 14$. Conduct a test of the hypothesis H_0: $\mu = 100$ against H_a: $\mu \neq 100$, where μ represents the mean IQ of all children in the population from which these students were sampled. Report the P-value, and give your interpretation.

5. The mean age at first marriage for married men in a particular community was 28.0 in 1900. For a random sample of thirty-six married men in that community in 1984, the estimated mean and standard deviation of age at first marriage were $\bar{Y} = 26.0$ and $\hat{\sigma} = 9.0$. Find the P-value for testing whether the mean has changed.

6. By law, an industrial plant is supposed to discharge no more than 600 gallons of hot water per hour, on the average, into a neighboring lake. A consumer group believes (based on other infractions they have noticed) that this limit is being exceeded. A random sample of 64 hours are selected over the period of a month for monitoring the plant. After the month is over, they calculate the summary statistics $\bar{Y} = 1{,}000$ and $\hat{\sigma} = 400$ for the 64 hourly measurements. Conduct a test of the null hypothesis that the mean discharge equals 600 gallons per hour. What is your conclusion?

7. Nationwide, the average cost of a new home is $80,000. A survey is conducted in Dayton, Ohio, to see if the mean is any different there.
a. Set up the appropriate null and alternative hypotheses for this investigation.
b. For a random sample of eighty-one homes sold in the previous year, the distribution of cost is characterized by $\bar{Y} = \$70{,}000$ and $\hat{\sigma} = \$18{,}000$. Find the P-value for this test and state your conclusion.

8. The P-value for testing H_0: $\mu = 100$ against H_a: $\mu \neq 100$ is reported to be $P = .057$ based on a random sample of size 40 with $\bar{Y} = 120$. Explain what is incorrect about each of the following interpretations of this level:
a. The probability that the null hypothesis is correct equals .057.
b. The probability that $\bar{Y} = 120$ if H_0 is true equals .057.
c. We would reject H_0 at the $\alpha = .05$ level.
d. The value of the z test statistic is $z = 1.58$.

9. Refer to Problem 8 and give the correct interpretation of $P = .057$.

10. A leader of a fundamentalist Christian denomination claims that a majority of Americans support a constitutional amendment outlawing abortion.
a. Set up hypotheses for a statistical test that can be used to analyze this claim.
b. Suppose that in a poll taken of a random sample of 900 Americans, 375 indicate support for such an amendment. Calculate the test statistic and P-value for the hypotheses presented in part **a**.
c. What is your conclusion about the claim?

11. A multiple-choice test question has four possible responses. The question is designed to be very difficult, with none of the four responses being obviously wrong, yet with only one correct answer. It is first placed on an exam taken by 400 students. The designers decide to test whether more people correctly answer the question than would be expected just due to chance (i.e., if everyone randomly guessed the correct answer).
a. Set up the hypotheses for the test.   *one tailed*
b. Out of the 400 students, 125 correctly answer the question. Find the P-value and interpret it.

12. A random sample of 100 residents in a large city is selected to test the claim that a majority of individuals want a larger portion of the transportation budget to be spent on developing a mass transit system.
a. Set up null and alternative statistical hypotheses that could be tested to determine whether a judgment can be made based on this sample.

b. Suppose that 60 out of the 100 prefer a larger budget for mass transit, and 40 out of the 100 prefer a smaller budget. Find the P-value for this test and interpret it.

13. There are two candidates in a mayoral election. Suppose that exactly half of the residents of the city prefer each candidate.

a. What is the probability that out of a random sample of 400 residents, at least 230 indicate a preference for one of the candidates, or the other? In other words, what is the P-value for $X = 230$ out of $n = 400$ in testing H_0: $\pi = .5$ against H_a: $\pi \neq .5$?

b. Suppose that out of a random sample of 400 voters, 230 indicate that they voted for a particular candidate. Would you be willing to predict the outcome of the election? Why?

c. Suppose that out of a random sample of 40 voters, 23 indicate that they voted for a particular candidate. Would you be willing to predict the outcome of the election? Why?

14. According to an extensive survey, only 20% of the residents in Rochester, New York, are aware of a new department store that has opened. A special advertising campaign is conducted for a week to increase awareness of the store. Before investing any additional money in advertising, the owner decides to take a survey to see if the proportion of residents of Rochester who have heard of the store has increased. Out of a random sample of 100 residents, 22 indicate that they have heard of the store. Conduct a test of H_0: $\pi = .2$ against H_a: $\pi > .2$ at the $\alpha = .05$ level, where π represents the proportion of residents who are aware of the store after the advertising campaign.

15. Consider the problem in the beginning of the chapter about the disputed authorship of the document. Let π denote the probability that any one sentence written by the unknown author of the document begins with the word *whereas*. Conduct a test of the hypothesis H_0: $\pi = .05$ against H_a: $\pi \neq .05$, using the fact that none of the 300 sentences in the document begins with that word. What conclusion can you make, and what assumption is needed for that conclusion to be valid?

16. A t test is to be conducted based on a sample of fifteen observations. What is the t-value corresponding to $P = .05$ when the alternative hypothesis is each of the following?

a. H_a: $\mu > \mu_0$ **b.** H_a: $\mu \neq \mu_0$ **c.** H_a: $\mu < \mu_0$

17. It is known that the mean income for all assembly-line workers with less than 5 years of experience in a large company is $300 per week. A representative of a women's group believes that the female employees are being underpaid. A random sample of sixteen female employees yields $\overline{Y} = \$270$ and $\hat{\sigma} = 36$. Conduct a statistical test that will give you evidence about whether the female employees have a mean income of less than $300 per week. Include all the assumptions on which the test is based.

18. A school board wants to get a rough idea of the absentee rate of students at a particular high school. A random sample is taken of twenty-five student records from the previous year. For each student, the number of days absent in the previous year is recorded. For these students, $\bar{Y} = 8.0$ and $\hat{\sigma} = 5$. State the necessary assumptions, and calculate a 95% confidence interval for the mean number of days absent for all students at that high school during the previous year.

19. A group of disabled veterans in New York City claims that their disability checks chronically arrive late. The local head administrator in the Veterans Administration claims that the checks, on the average, are no more than 3 days late. To test this claim against that of the veterans group, a test is conducted of H_0: $\mu = 3$ against H_a: $\mu > 3$, where μ represents the mean delay in time (in days) for all disability checks mailed to veterans in New York City during a particular month. For a random sample of seven veterans, the delay times for the checks are 8, 11, 2, 5, 8, 7, 8. What is the P-value for this test? Include all assumptions needed to justify the use of the test, and interpret the result.

20. A study conducted in 1965 indicated that adults spent an average of 16 hours every week watching television.
a. Suppose we wish to see if this has changed. Set up the hypotheses of an appropriate test.
b. In a new survey conducted in 1984 with a sample of twenty-five adults, the mean time spent watching television was $\bar{Y} = 14.5$ hours, with $\hat{\sigma} = 6.0$ hours. Conduct a test and indicate whether there is strong evidence of a change. What assumptions are made in conducting this test?
c. Give the 95% confidence interval for the mean time adults spent watching television per week in 1984.

21. A study was conducted of the effects of a special class designed to aid children with verbal skills. Each child was given a verbal skills test twice, both before and after a 3-week period in the class. Let Y be the second exam score minus the first exam score. Hence, if μ (the population mean for Y) is equal to 0, the class has no effect on the average. Test the null hypothesis of no effect against the alternative hypothesis that the effect is positive, if the scores on Y for a random sample of four children having learning problems were 3, 7, 3, 3.

22. The proportion of people in a particular society who attempt to commit suicide sometime during their life is .01. For a random sample of ten people from the society, what is the probability that
a. None of them attempts to commit suicide?
b. At most one attempts to commit suicide?

23. A binomial variable X is used to test H_0: $\pi = .5$ against H_a: $\pi > .5$ for a sample size of $n = 6$.
a. Calculate the probabilities in the binomial sampling distribution.
b. Find the P-value corresponding to $X = 5$.
c. Find the P-value corresponding to $X = 2$.

24. Refer to Problem 13. Find the P-value in testing H_0: $\pi = .5$ against H_a: $\pi \neq .5$ when five people are randomly selected and all of them prefer a particular one of the two candidates. Interpret the result.

25. A fraternal organization admits 80% of all applicants who satisfy certain requirements. Out of four members of a minority group who recently applied for admission, none was accepted.
a. Find the probability that none would be accepted if the same admissions standards were applied to the minority group (other things assumed to be equal).
b. Find the *P*-value for testing whether a minority group member is less likely to be accepted, and interpret the result.

26. The proportion of the residents of Washington, D.C. who are black is .70. A random sample of five residents of that city is to be selected for interview by a commission studying problems with race relations.
a. Find the probability that none of the five residents selected is black.
b. A citizen's group suspects bias against blacks in the selection process. Conduct the steps of a statistical test that is designed to detect bias, if in fact none of the five selected are black.

27. Refer to Problem 26.
a. What would be your decision about the null hypothesis, for each of the following α-levels?

   (i) .05   (ii) .001

b. Show that it is impossible to reject the null hypothesis for Problem 26 at the $\alpha = .001$ level, when there are only five observations.

28. Refer to Problem 1. For each of the three possible alternative hypotheses, indicate whether H_0 would be rejected at the $\alpha = .05$ level.

29. Refer to Problem 3. Suppose that a decision must be made about H_0. Indicate what decision would be made for each of the following α-levels:
a. $\alpha = .01$ **b.** $\alpha = .05$ **c.** $\alpha = .20$

30. Refer to Problem 4. Indicate what decision would be made for $\alpha = .01$. Interpret this decision in terms of the value of μ.

31. Refer to Problem 5.
a. If $\alpha = .05$, what decision would you make?
b. Would it made sense to "accept H_0" in part **a**? Why or why not?

32. Refer to Problem 17. For which of the α-levels listed in Table B (the *t* distribution) would you be able to reject H_0?

33. Refer to Problem 23. How large would *X* have to be in order to reject H_0 using $\alpha = .05$?

34. Suppose that we need to make a decision about whether to reject H_0 in a statistical test, but we are worried about the possibility of making a Type I error. Explain how the probability of a Type I error can be controlled when we make a decision in a statistical test.

Select the best response(s) in Problems 35–39.

35. A 95% confidence interval for μ is (96, 110). Which of the following statements about significance tests for the same data is (are) correct?

a. In testing H_0: $\mu = 100$ against H_a: $\mu \neq 100$, we would get $P > .05$.
b. In testing H_0: $\mu = 100$ against H_a: $\mu \neq 100$, we would get $P < .05$.
c. In testing H_0: $\mu = \mu_0$ against H_a: $\mu \neq \mu_0$, we would get $P > .05$ if μ_0 is any of the numbers inside the confidence interval.
d. In testing H_0: $\mu = \mu_0$ against H_a: $\mu \neq \mu_0$, we would get $P > .05$ if μ_0 is any of the numbers outside the confidence interval.

36. The P-value for testing H_0: $\mu = 100$ against H_a: $\mu > 100$ is $P = .001$. This indicates that:

a. There is strong evidence that $\mu = 100$.
b. There is strong evidence that $\mu > 100$.
c. There is strong evidence that $\mu < 100$.
d. If μ were equal to 100, it would be unusual to obtain data such as those observed.

37. A Type I error occurs when we:
a. Do not reject H_0 when it is false.
b. Do not reject H_0 when it is true.
c. Reject H_0 when it is false.
d. Reject H_0 when it is true.

38. A Type II error occurs when we:
a. Do not reject H_0 when it is false.
b. Do not reject H_0 when it is true.
c. Reject H_0 when it is false.
d. Reject H_0 when it is true.

39. Refer to Problem 6. If we make a conclusion using $\alpha = .05$, this means that:
a. If the plant is not exceeding the limit, but actually $\mu = 600$, there is only a 5% chance that we will conclude that they are exceeding the limit.
b. If the plant is exceeding the limit, there is only a 5% chance that we will conclude that they are not exceeding the limit.
c. The probability of getting a sample mean such as the one we obtained would be only .05 if H_0 were true.
d. If we reject H_0, the probability that it is actually true is .05.
e. All of the above

40. Define each of the following:
a. Type I error
b. Type II error
c. Power
d. P-value
e. α-level

41. A conclusion is to be made in a test of H_0: $\mu = \mu_0$ against H_a: $\mu > \mu_0$, using the $\alpha = .05$ level. For a value five units above the null hypothesis value of the mean, the probability of a Type II error is determined to be .10.

a. Explain the meaning of this last sentence.

b. If the test were conducted at the $\alpha = .01$ level, would the probability of a Type II error be less than, equal to, or greater than .10?

42. Refer to the hypotheses considered in Example 6.13. Suppose that a sample of size 200 were taken (instead of 50), and suppose that the estimated standard error of $\bar{Y}$ is $\hat{\sigma}_{\bar{Y}} = 1.0$. Compute the probabilities of a Type II error for the alternative μ values of 12, 14, and 16. Compare each of these to the probabilities of a Type II error when $\hat{\sigma}_{\bar{Y}} = 2.0$, and interpret the differences. (Again, use $\alpha = .05$.)

43.

a. Give an example of a situation in which a confidence interval would be a more informative procedure than a test of hypothesis.

b. Explain why the terminology "do not reject H_0" is preferred to "accept H_0."

44. The P-value for testing H_0: $\mu = 100$ against H_a: $\mu \neq 100$ is reported to be $P = .043$. Does this imply that a 95% confidence interval for μ contains 100?

*45. The P-value for testing H_0: $\mu = 100$ against H_a: $\mu > 100$ is reported to be $P = .043$. Does this imply that a 95% confidence interval for μ contains 100?

*46. Suppose that we know the mean $\bar{Y}$ of n sample measurements. Show that if $(n - 1)$ of those measurements are given to us, then we can determine the remaining observation. In other words, $(n - 1)$ of the measurements may take on any value, but once values are assigned to them and to $\bar{Y}$, the value of the remaining measurement is determined. Thus, in summarizing scores on a single variable, there are said to be $(n - 1)$ degrees of freedom.

*47. Refer to Example 6.7. Suppose that it is known that the median skull length for the species to which the remains are hypothesized to belong is 6.0 inches.

a. If the discovered skulls constitute a random sample from this species, then what is the probability that all seven skulls would exceed 6.0 inches in length? [*Hint:* Use the binomial distribution with π equal to the probability that a skull length exceeds 6.0 inches.]

b. Find the P-value for testing H_0: $\pi = .5$ against H_a: $\pi \neq .5$, where π represents the proportion of skulls of length over 6.0 inches for the species represented by the remains. Compare this result to the one in Example 6.7. (Notice that for this approach to the problem, we need not assume that the skull lengths for the hypothesized species are normally distributed. A test of this nature is sometimes referred to as a *sign test*, since the observations are summarized only in terms of the signs of their deviations from the median, not their distances.)

*48. Each year in a particular community, a public librarian takes a random sample of acquisition cards for ten new books in order to estimate the mean amount the library spends per book ordered. In each year, the librarian forms a 95% confidence interval for the mean cost of all books ordered within the previous year. This has been done for 20 years.

a. What is the probability that all the confidence intervals contain the true means?

b. What is the probability that at least one confidence interval does not contain the true mean?

*49. For an $\alpha = .05$ level test of H_0: $\mu = 100$ against H_a: $\mu > 100$ based on $n = 30$ observations, the probability of a Type II error is $\beta = .36$ at $\mu = 104$. Select the correct response(s).

a. At $\mu = 105$ we would get $\beta > .36$.

b. If $\alpha = .01$, at $\mu = 104$ we would get $\beta > .36$.

c. If $n = 50$, at $\mu = 104$ we would get $\beta > .36$.

d. The power of the test is .64 at $\mu = 104$.

e. This must be false, because it is necessary that $\alpha + \beta = 1$.

Bibliography   Labovitz, S. (1968). "Criteria for Selecting a Significance Level: A Note on the Sacredness of .05." *American Sociologist 3*, 220–222.

Morrison, D. E. and R. E. Henkel, eds. (1970). *The Significance Test Controversy: A Reader.* Chicago: Aldine.

Mosteller, F. and D. L. Wallace (1964). *Inference and Disputed Authorship: The Federalist.* Reading, Mass.: Addison-Wesley.

PART II

INTRODUCTION TO BIVARIATE STATISTICAL ANALYSIS

CHAPTER 7

Comparison of Two Groups

Contents

One of the most common types of analysis in the social sciences involves the comparison of two or more groups with respect to some characteristic. For example, we might be interested in comparing the mean income for men with that of women having similar jobs and experience. Or, we might wish to compare Democrats and Republicans with respect to the proportions responding yes when asked whether they favor comprehensive national health insurance. In such cases, the comparison is usually conducted by making inferences about the difference between two means or the difference between two proportions, depending on whether the characteristic is interval (e.g., income) or nominal (e.g., opinion, with levels yes and no) in measurement. As another possibility, the characteristic could be ordinal. For example, Democrats and Republicans could be compared on how they feel about the establishment of comprehensive national health insurance, when the possible responses consist of a set of ordered categories (e.g., definitely favorable, somewhat favorable, neutral, somewhat unfavorable, definitely unfavorable). In this case, we could compare the proportions of observations in the five categories for the two groups, or we could compare some aspect of the two sets of observations, such as the median response.

In this chapter, we present some basic statistical methods for comparing two groups. We primarily consider the situation in which *independent* random samples are taken from the two groups. By *independent samples*, we mean that the probability that a particular member of one population is chosen in the sample from that population is not dependent on which members are chosen in the other sample. That is, knowing which members were selected for one of the samples provides us with no information about which members were selected for the other sample. Many comparisons of two groups result from dividing a larger sample into subsamples according to classification on some variable (e.g., sex). If the overall sample was randomly selected, then the subsamples constitute independent random samples from the corresponding subpopulations.

Dependent samples occur when members of one sample are naturally matched with members of the other sample. An example of matched samples is a set of married couples, the husbands forming one group and the wives the other. As another example, we might consider the same sample of individuals at two different times, such as in testing whether a tutoring program substantially improves mathematical understanding for a sample of students. In this type of situation, the response on a variable for an individual is likely to be similar in some way to the response of the corresponding matched measurement, and different statistical methods must be used. Methods for dependent samples are described briefly at the end of Section 7.2 (for comparing means) and in Note 7.1 (for comparing proportions).

In practice, statistical tests of hypotheses are much more commonly applied to two-sample comparisons than to one-sample problems such as those considered in Chapter 6. For example, it is often artificial to test whether the population mean equals one particular value. However, we may be especially interested in testing whether there is a *difference* between the values of two population means. We may not have any idea what to hypothesize for the mean income of men in a particular type of employment, but we may wish to know whether that mean (whatever its value) is the same as, larger than, or smaller than the corresponding mean income for women. Comparison procedures focus on the nature and degree of differences between groups, not on the specification of exact values of characteristics of the separate distributions.

In essence, the two groups being compared constitute levels of a *dichotomous variable*—that is, a variable having only two categories. Hence, these procedures for comparing two groups are special cases of *bivariate* statistical methods, in the sense that a nominal, ordinal, or interval variable is analyzed within each of two levels of some other variable. The variable about which comparisons are made is sometimes referred to as the *dependent variable* or the *response variable*. The variable by which the groups are defined is referred to as the *independent variable*. In the first example mentioned above, for example, we are studying the relationship between the interval variable, income, and the dichotomous variable, sex. Income is the dependent variable and sex is the independent variable. Similarly, a comparison of Democrats and Republicans on the proportion who favor comprehensive national health insurance is a bivariate analysis of the dependent variable, opinion about national health insurance, and the independent variable, political party affiliation. The terminology *dependent variable* refers to the researcher's usual desire to investigate the degree to which the response on that variable *depends on* the group into which the member is classified. The methods described in the first three sections of this chapter are classified according to whether the dependent variable is nominal, interval, or ordinal in scale.

7.1 Nominal Scales: Difference of Proportions

In this section, we treat the case in which the dependent variable is measured on a nominal scale, and we consider how to compare two populations on the proportion of members classified in a particular category of that nominal scale. Let π_1 denote the proportion of the first population classified in that category, and let π_2 denote the proportion of the second population classified in that category. Suppose that independent random samples of sizes n_1 and n_2 are taken from the two respective populations, and let $\hat{\pi}_1$ and $\hat{\pi}_2$ denote the sample proportions that serve as point estimates of the population proportions. You may wish to refer to Section 5.3 to review the method for analyzing a proportion in the one-sample case.

Example 7.1

Out of a random sample of 1,600 Americans taken in January, 656 people indicate approval of the president's performance in office. A similar poll taken a month later of a separate random sample of 1,800 Americans yields a favorable rating by 810 people. These results are summarized in Table 7.1. Let π_1 represent the true proportion in January of Americans that approve of the president's performance in office, and let π_2 represent the corresponding proportion in February. From Table 7.1 (next page), we have

$$\hat{\pi}_1 = \frac{656}{1,600} = .410 \quad \text{and} \quad \hat{\pi}_2 = \frac{810}{1,800} = .450$$

Table 7.1

Performance of President

	APPROVE	DISAPPROVE	TOTAL
January	656	944	1,600
February	810	990	1,800

Similarly, the sample proportions of individuals expressing disapproval are $1 - \hat{\pi}_1 = .590$ in January and $1 - \hat{\pi}_2 = .550$ in February. We estimate, in other words, that 4% more Americans approve of the president's performance in February than in January. ∎

Confidence Interval for $\pi_2 - \pi_1$

A natural way to compare two population proportions is to describe the difference between them, $\pi_2 - \pi_1$. That is, we can treat $\pi_2 - \pi_1$ as a parameter, which may be estimated from the sample data by the point estimate $\hat{\pi}_2 - \hat{\pi}_1$. If n_1 and n_2 are sufficiently large, it follows from the Central Limit Theorem that the sampling distribution of $\hat{\pi}_1$ is approximately normal about π_1 and that the sampling distribution of $\hat{\pi}_2$ is approximately normal about π_2. Now, $\hat{\pi}_2 - \hat{\pi}_1$ also depends on the samples selected, and its sampling distribution is approximately normal about $\pi_2 - \pi_1$ (see Figure 7.1). Based on reasoning similar to that in Chapter 5, a large-sample confidence interval for $\pi_2 - \pi_1$ is given by

$$(\hat{\pi}_2 - \hat{\pi}_1) \pm z_{\alpha/2}\sigma_{\hat{\pi}_2 - \hat{\pi}_1}$$

where $\sigma_{\hat{\pi}_2 - \hat{\pi}_1}$ denotes the standard error of the sampling distribution of $\hat{\pi}_2 - \hat{\pi}_1$ and $z_{\alpha/2}$ is the z-score corresponding to a confidence coefficient of $(1 - \alpha)$.

Fig. 7.1 Sampling Distribution of $\hat{\pi}_2 - \hat{\pi}_1$

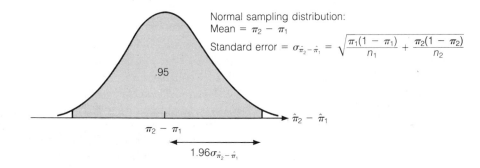

Normal sampling distribution:

Mean $= \pi_2 - \pi_1$

Standard error $= \sigma_{\hat{\pi}_2 - \hat{\pi}_1} = \sqrt{\dfrac{\pi_1(1 - \pi_1)}{n_1} + \dfrac{\pi_2(1 - \pi_2)}{n_2}}$

.95

$\pi_2 - \pi_1$

$\hat{\pi}_2 - \hat{\pi}_1$

$1.96\sigma_{\hat{\pi}_2 - \hat{\pi}_1}$

In order to calculate this confidence interval, we need to know the formula for the standard error $\sigma_{\hat{\pi}_2 - \hat{\pi}_1}$. The general rule given in the box enables us to obtain it.

> If two estimates are formed from two independent samples, the variance of the sampling distribution for their difference (or their sum) is the sum of the variances of the sampling distributions of the two separate estimates.

For example,

$$\sigma^2_{\hat{\pi}_2 - \hat{\pi}_1} = \sigma^2_{\hat{\pi}_1} + \sigma^2_{\hat{\pi}_2}$$

if $\hat{\pi}_1$ and $\hat{\pi}_2$ are computed from independent samples. There is sampling error associated with each of the estimates, and these errors must be added in describing the sampling error of a combination of the estimates.*

Since $\sigma_{\hat{\pi}}^2 = \pi(1 - \pi)/n$ (see Section 5.3), we have as a result

$$\sigma_{\hat{\pi}_2-\hat{\pi}_1} = \sqrt{\sigma_{\hat{\pi}_2-\hat{\pi}_1}^2} = \sqrt{\sigma_{\hat{\pi}_1}^2 + \sigma_{\hat{\pi}_2}^2} = \sqrt{\frac{\pi_1(1 - \pi_1)}{n_1} + \frac{\pi_2(1 - \pi_2)}{n_2}}$$

which may be estimated by

$$\hat{\sigma}_{\hat{\pi}_2-\hat{\pi}_1} = \sqrt{\frac{\hat{\pi}_1(1 - \hat{\pi}_1)}{n_1} + \frac{\hat{\pi}_2(1 - \hat{\pi}_2)}{n_2}}$$

Substituting this expression for the unknown parameter $\sigma_{\hat{\pi}_2-\hat{\pi}_1}$ in the formula for a confidence interval for $\pi_2 - \pi_1$, we obtain the result stated in the accompanying box. The form of this confidence interval is similar to the ones studied in Chapter 5— namely, point estimate ± z-score × estimated standard error.

Large-Sample Confidence Interval for $\pi_2 - \pi_1$

A large-sample $100(1 - \alpha)\%$ confidence interval for $\pi_2 - \pi_1$ is $(\hat{\pi}_2 - \hat{\pi}_1) \pm z_{\alpha/2}\hat{\sigma}_{\hat{\pi}_2-\hat{\pi}_1}$, or

$$(\hat{\pi}_2 - \hat{\pi}_1) \pm z_{\alpha/2} \sqrt{\frac{\hat{\pi}_1(1 - \hat{\pi}_1)}{n_1} + \frac{\hat{\pi}_2(1 - \hat{\pi}_2)}{n_2}}$$

The sample is generally large enough to use this formula if, for each group, more than 5 observations are in the category for which the proportion is estimated, and more than 5 observations are not in that category.

Example 7.1 (continued) In evaluating the change in the approval of the president's performance in office from January to February, we take the difference $\pi_2 - \pi_1$ as the parameter of interest. We have $\hat{\pi}_1 = .410$ and $\hat{\pi}_2 = .450$, so $\hat{\pi}_2 - \hat{\pi}_1 = .04$. We estimate that a 4% increase in the percentage of individuals approving the president's performance has occurred during 1 month. However, there is sampling error attached to each estimate, so it is wise to compute a confidence interval to gauge how small or large the actual change in support is likely to have been *in the entire population*. A 99% confidence interval for $\pi_2 - \pi_1$ is

$$(\hat{\pi}_2 - \hat{\pi}_1) \pm z_{.005} \sqrt{\frac{\hat{\pi}_1(1 - \hat{\pi}_1)}{n_1} + \frac{\hat{\pi}_2(1 - \hat{\pi}_2)}{n_2}}$$

---

*Notice that if $\hat{\pi}_1$ is above (below) π_1, and $\hat{\pi}_2$ is below (above) π_2, then $\hat{\pi}_2 - \hat{\pi}_1$ is even further below (above) $\pi_2 - \pi_1$. Thus, there is the potential for making a larger error in using $\hat{\pi}_2 - \hat{\pi}_1$ to estimate $\pi_2 - \pi_1$ than in using $\hat{\pi}_1$ to estimate π_1 or $\hat{\pi}_2$ to estimate π_2, so $\sigma_{\hat{\pi}_2-\hat{\pi}_1}^2$ is larger than either $\sigma_{\hat{\pi}_1}^2$ or $\sigma_{\hat{\pi}_2}^2$.

which equals

$$.040 \pm 2.58 \sqrt{\frac{(.41)(.59)}{1,600} + \frac{(.45)(.55)}{1,800}} = .040 \pm .044 \quad \text{or} \quad (-.004, .084)$$

Thus, we can be reasonably sure that the true increase in support was no larger than 8.4%. On the other hand, since 0 is contained in the interval $(-.004, .084)$, we infer that there may have been no change in support over 1 month; that is, 0 is considered to be a realistic value for the parameter $\pi_2 - \pi_1$ at this confidence level, and $\pi_2 - \pi_1 = 0$ translates to $\pi_1 = \pi_2$, or no change in support. Similarly, we infer from the lower bound of $-.004$ that there may have been an actual decrease in support [i.e., $\pi_1 > \pi_2$, or $(\pi_2 - \pi_1)$ is a negative number] in the overall population, although probably no more than .4%. ∎

Interpretation   If the confidence interval for $\pi_2 - \pi_1$ contains entirely positive (negative) numbers, we are essentially concluding that π_2 is larger (smaller) than π_1 at that confidence level. If 0 is contained in the interval, however, there is insufficient evidence to conclude which of π_1 or π_2 is the larger. As in the one-sample case, higher confidence coefficients yield wider confidence intervals, and larger sample sizes contribute to narrower confidence intervals.

Example 7.2   In a magazine article on sexual behavior, the author claims that 77% of male college seniors and 67% of female college seniors are sexually experienced. Upon further investigation, we discover that these results refer to a sample of 200 men and 200 women. Let π_1 represent the proportion of *all* male college seniors who are sexually experienced, and let π_2 be the analogous proportion of all female college seniors. Then, assuming that these samples were obtained randomly and independently, a 95% confidence interval for $\pi_2 - \pi_1$ is

$$(\hat{\pi}_2 - \hat{\pi}_1) \pm 1.96 \hat{\sigma}_{\hat{\pi}_2 - \hat{\pi}_1} = (.67 - .77) \pm 1.96 \sqrt{\frac{(.77)(.23)}{200} + \frac{(.67)(.33)}{200}}$$

$$= -.10 \pm 1.96(.045)$$

$$= -.10 \pm .09 \quad \text{or} \quad (-.19, -.01)$$

Both endpoints are negative, indicating that we can be confident at this level that $\pi_2 - \pi_1$ is a negative number; that is, we can conclude that the proportion of female college seniors who are sexually experienced is less than the proportion of male college seniors who are sexually experienced. However, since $-.01$ is quite close to 0, we infer that the true difference may be very small, and perhaps practically insignificant. ∎

Testing Hypotheses   The population proportions π_1 and π_2 can also be compared through a test of the
About $\pi_2 - \pi_1$ hypothesis H_0: $\pi_1 = \pi_2$, or equivalently, H_0: $\pi_2 - \pi_1 = 0$. This can be done by comparing the estimate $\hat{\pi}_2 - \hat{\pi}_1$ of $\pi_2 - \pi_1$ to the null hypothesis value of 0. For large samples, the test statistic is

$$z = \frac{\text{Estimate} - \text{Null hypothesis value}}{\text{Standard error}} = \frac{\hat{\pi}_2 - \hat{\pi}_1}{\hat{\sigma}_{\hat{\pi}_2 - \hat{\pi}_1}}$$

To illustrate, in Example 7.1, $\hat{\pi}_1 = .41$ and $\hat{\pi}_2 = .45$, and $\hat{\sigma}_{\hat{\pi}_2 - \hat{\pi}_1} = .017$. The test statistic for testing H_0: $\pi_1 = \pi_2$ is

$$z = \frac{\hat{\pi}_2 - \hat{\pi}_1}{\hat{\sigma}_{\hat{\pi}_2 - \hat{\pi}_1}} = \frac{.45 - .41}{.017} = 2.35$$

From the standard normal table, this result gives $P = 2(.0094) = .0188$ for the two-sided alternative hypothesis H_a: $\pi_1 \neq \pi_2$. Thus, there is fairly strong evidence of an increase in the support for the president's performance, though not enough evidence to reject H_0 at the $\alpha = .01$ level.

The null hypothesis H_0: $\pi_1 = \pi_2$ is a special case of one to be presented in Section 8.2 in the study of the **chi-square test.**[*] We shall defer further discussion of it to that section. For small sample sizes, π_1 and π_2 can be compared using **Fisher's exact test** (see Siegel, 1956, p. 96).

7.2 Interval Scales: Difference of Means

The most common procedure for comparing two groups on a characteristic measured on at least an interval scale is to make inferences about their means μ_1 and μ_2 and the difference between them, $\mu_2 - \mu_1$. We shall first consider the situation in which the samples are obtained independently and randomly, and the sample sizes are sufficiently large to obtain a normal sampling distribution.

Confidence Interval for $\mu_2 - \mu_1$

From the Central Limit Theorem, we know that if the sample size n_1 of the first group is sufficiently large, the sampling distribution of $\bar{Y}_1$ is approximately normal about μ_1 with variance $\sigma^2_{\bar{Y}_1} = \sigma_1^2/n_1$, where σ_1^2 is the population variance for that group. Similarly, the sampling distribution of $\bar{Y}_2$ is approximately normal about μ_2 with variance $\sigma^2_{\bar{Y}_2} = \sigma_2^2/n_2$, if n_2 is sufficiently large. Using the same reasoning as in Section 7.1, $\bar{Y}_2 - \bar{Y}_1$, an unbiased point estimator of $\mu_2 - \mu_1$, has a sampling distribution that is approximately normal about $\mu_2 - \mu_1$ (see Figure 7.2 at the top of the next page) with standard error

$$\sigma_{\bar{Y}_2 - \bar{Y}_1} = \sqrt{\sigma^2_{\bar{Y}_1} + \sigma^2_{\bar{Y}_2}} = \sqrt{\frac{\sigma_1^2}{n_1} + \frac{\sigma_2^2}{n_2}}$$

This leads us to the form for a confidence interval for $\mu_2 - \mu_1$

$$(\bar{Y}_2 - \bar{Y}_1) \pm z_{\alpha/2}\sigma_{\bar{Y}_2 - \bar{Y}_1}$$

As usual, we take the best point estimate of $\mu_2 - \mu_1$, and add and subtract a z-score (depending on the desired confidence coefficient) multiplied by the standard error of the estimate.

---

[*] An alternative standard error formula, based on the assumption that $\pi_1 = \pi_2$, is sometimes used in the z test statistic. The formula is

$$\hat{\sigma}_{\hat{\pi}_2 - \hat{\pi}_1} = \sqrt{\frac{\hat{\pi}(1 - \hat{\pi})}{n_1} + \frac{\hat{\pi}(1 - \hat{\pi})}{n_2}} = \sqrt{\hat{\pi}(1 - \hat{\pi})\left(\frac{1}{n_1} + \frac{1}{n_2}\right)}$$

where $\hat{\pi}$ is the proportion of the *total* sample in the category of interest. When this formula is used, the square of the z test statistic equals the chi-square statistic.

Fig. 7.2 Sampling Distribution of $\bar{Y}_2 - \bar{Y}_1$

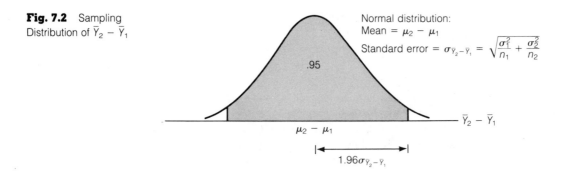

Normal distribution:

Mean $= \mu_2 - \mu_1$

Standard error $= \sigma_{\bar{Y}_2 - \bar{Y}_1} = \sqrt{\dfrac{\sigma_1^2}{n_1} + \dfrac{\sigma_2^2}{n_2}}$

As in previous cases, the theoretical formula for the standard error involves the population variances σ_1^2 and σ_2^2, which are nearly always unknown in applications. In the large-sample case considered here, we can substitute the sample variances $\hat{\sigma}_1^2$ and $\hat{\sigma}_2^2$ as point estimates for σ_1^2 and σ_2^2 in the formula for $\hat{\sigma}_{\bar{Y}_2 - \bar{Y}_1}$ without significantly affecting the results. Thus, for practical purposes, we would use the formula given in the box. As a guideline, this large-sample approach for a confidence interval for the difference $\mu_2 - \mu_1$ is usually acceptable if both n_1 and n_2 are at least 20.

Large-Sample Confidence Interval for $\mu_2 - \mu_1$

A large-sample $100(1 - \alpha)\%$ confidence interval for $\mu_2 - \mu_1$ is $(\bar{Y}_2 - \bar{Y}_1) \pm z_{\alpha/2}\hat{\sigma}_{\bar{Y}_2 - \bar{Y}_1}$, or

$$(\bar{Y}_2 - \bar{Y}_1) \pm z_{\alpha/2} \sqrt{\frac{\hat{\sigma}_1^2}{n_1} + \frac{\hat{\sigma}_2^2}{n_2}}$$

Example 7.3   A random sample of twenty-five retired workers in Minneapolis was selected in 1965 in order to study health care among the aged. A similar study was conducted in 1985 of fifty retired workers in that city. The individuals in each study were asked, among other things, to report their total medical expenses for the past year. In 1965, the results were $\bar{Y}_1 = \$270$ and $\hat{\sigma}_1 = \$300$, whereas in 1985, $\bar{Y}_2 = \$580$ and $\hat{\sigma}_2 = \$700$, expressed in 1965 dollars (adjusted for inflation).

As a point estimate of $\mu_2 - \mu_1$, the change in the mean yearly medical expenses over this 20-year period for retired workers in Minneapolis, we would use $\bar{Y}_2 - \bar{Y}_1 = \$580 - \$270 = \$310$. A 99% confidence interval for $\mu_2 - \mu_1$ is

$$(\bar{Y}_2 - \bar{Y}_1) \pm z_{.005} \sqrt{\frac{\hat{\sigma}_1^2}{n_1} + \frac{\hat{\sigma}_2^2}{n_2}} = \$310 \pm 2.58 \sqrt{\frac{(300)^2}{25} + \frac{(700)^2}{50}}$$

$$= \$310 \pm 2.58(116)$$

$$= \$310 \pm 299 \quad \text{or} \quad (\$11, \$609)$$

Since the interval contains only positive values, we conclude that the mean yearly medical bill has increased. However, we infer that the increase is as little as $11 or as much as $609. ■

The confidence interval obtained in Example 7.3 is very wide, due to the relatively small sample sizes and the variability in the sample scores. In both samples, $\hat{\sigma}$ is larger than $\bar{Y}$. This indicates that the distribution of medical expenses in both years was probably highly skewed to the right, since the lowest possible expense value is less than one $\hat{\sigma}$ below $\bar{Y}$. Perhaps there were many observations relatively close to 0, but some very large observations representing a long right-hand tail for each of the distributions. It would probably be of interest here to compare also the medians, if the unsummarized data were available.

Testing Hypotheses About $\mu_2 - \mu_1$

A large-sample ($n_1 \geq 20$, $n_2 \geq 20$) test of the hypothesis that $\mu_1 = \mu_2$ can also be based on $\bar{Y}_2 - \bar{Y}_1$ and $\hat{\sigma}_{\bar{Y}_2 - \bar{Y}_1}$. The standard form for the z test statistic is

$$z = \frac{\text{Estimate of parameter} - \text{Null hypothesis value of parameter}}{\text{Standard error of estimate}}$$

Treating the difference $\mu_2 - \mu_1$ as the parameter, we are in essence testing that $\mu_2 - \mu_1 = 0$; that is, the null hypothesis value of the parameter $\mu_2 - \mu_1$ is 0. The estimated value of $\mu_2 - \mu_1$ is $\bar{Y}_2 - \bar{Y}_1$, and the estimated standard error of $\bar{Y}_2 - \bar{Y}_1$ is

$$\hat{\sigma}_{\bar{Y}_2 - \bar{Y}_1} = \sqrt{(\hat{\sigma}_1^2/n_1) + (\hat{\sigma}_2^2/n_2)}$$

so the form of the z test statistic when $n_1 \geq 20$ and $n_2 \geq 20$ is

$$z = \frac{(\bar{Y}_2 - \bar{Y}_1) - 0}{\hat{\sigma}_{\bar{Y}_2 - \bar{Y}_1}} = \frac{\bar{Y}_2 - \bar{Y}_1}{\sqrt{\dfrac{\hat{\sigma}_1^2}{n_1} + \dfrac{\hat{\sigma}_2^2}{n_2}}}$$

The P-value for the test depends in the usual way on whether the alternative hypothesis is the two-sided one, H_a: $\mu_1 \neq \mu_2$ ($\mu_2 - \mu_1 \neq 0$), or one of the one-sided ones, H_a: $\mu_1 > \mu_2$ ($\mu_2 - \mu_1 < 0$) or H_a: $\mu_1 < \mu_2$ ($\mu_2 - \mu_1 > 0$).

Example 7.4

A study was carried out to determine whether nonworking wives from middle-class families have more voluntary association memberships than nonworking wives from working-class families. A random sample of housewives was obtained, and each was asked for information about her husband's occupation and her own memberships in voluntary associations. On the basis of their husbands' occupations, the women were divided into middle-class and working-class groups, and the mean number of voluntary association memberships was computed for each group.

For the fifty middle-class women, the mean number of memberships per woman was $\bar{Y}_1 = 3.4$, with $\hat{\sigma}_1 = 2.5$. For the forty-seven working-class wives, $\bar{Y}_2 = 2.2$, with $\hat{\sigma}_2 = 2.8$. How should the researcher proceed in deciding whether there is enough evidence to conclude that middle-class housewives average more voluntary association memberships than working-class housewives?

We wish to test $H_0: \mu_1 = \mu_2$ against $H_a: \mu_1 > \mu_2$ ($\mu_2 - \mu_1 < 0$), where μ_1 is the mean number of voluntary association memberships for middle-class wives and μ_2 is the corresponding mean for working-class wives. The alternative hypothesis reflects the researcher's belief that middle-class wives have the larger mean. Now,

$$\hat{\sigma}_{\bar{Y}_2 - \bar{Y}_1} = \sqrt{\frac{\hat{\sigma}_1^2}{n_1} + \frac{\hat{\sigma}_2^2}{n_2}} = \sqrt{\frac{(2.5)^2}{50} + \frac{(2.8)^2}{47}} = .54$$

so that

$$z = \frac{\bar{Y}_2 - \bar{Y}_1}{\hat{\sigma}_{\bar{Y}_2 - \bar{Y}_1}} = \frac{2.2 - 3.4}{.54} = -2.22$$

For this one-sided test, the P-value would be $P = .0132$. Thus, there is fairly substantial evidence that middle-class women have greater involvement with voluntary associations. If the researcher had set up the alternative hypothesis as $H_a: \mu_1 \neq \mu_2$ in order to detect *any* type of difference, the P-value would have been $P = 2(.0132) = .0264$. In either case, H_0 would be rejected if the α-level had been set at $\alpha = .05$, but not at $\alpha = .01$. ∎

The equivalence between the two-sided test of a hypothesis and the confidence interval for a mean mentioned in Section 6.7 also applies in the two-sample case. For example, $P < .05$ for the two-sided test of the hypothesis that $\mu_2 - \mu_1 = 0$ in Example 7.4, so that a 95% confidence interval for $\mu_2 - \mu_1$ would not contain 0 (the null hypothesis value). However, $P = .0264 > .01$, so a 99% confidence interval for the difference $\mu_2 - \mu_1$ *would* contain 0. Conversely, if a 95% confidence interval for the difference between two means does not contain 0, then 0 is not considered to be a likely value for $\mu_2 - \mu_1$, at the $\alpha = .05$ level; that is, the P-value for testing the hypothesis $H_0: \mu_2 - \mu_1 = 0$ against $H_a: \mu_2 - \mu_1 \neq 0$ would be less than .05. Thus, H_0 would be rejected at the .05 level and, in fact, at any α-level down to the P-value. A similar equivalence can be made for the case in which the difference $\mu_2 - \mu_1$ is hypothesized to be some nonzero value, but this case is rarely encountered in practical applications.

Small-Sample Inference for $\mu_2 - \mu_1$[*]   If either sample size n_1 or n_2 is less than 20, alternative formulas must be used for confidence intervals and tests. The procedure using the t distribution introduced in Section 6.4 can be extended to the two-sample case. As in that section, we must assume that the population distributions are normal. In the two-sample case, we must also assume that the population standard deviations are equal, that is, $\sigma_1 = \sigma_2$. The common value σ of σ_1 and σ_2 is estimated by

$$\hat{\sigma} = \sqrt{\frac{\Sigma (Y_{1i} - \bar{Y}_1)^2 + \Sigma (Y_{2i} - \bar{Y}_2)^2}{n_1 + n_2 - 2}}$$

Here, $\Sigma (Y_{1i} - \bar{Y}_1)^2$ represents the sum of squares of the measurements in the first sample about their mean and $\Sigma (Y_{2i} - \bar{Y}_2)^2$ represents the sum of squares of the measurements in the second sample about their mean. The degrees of freedom for this estimate is df $= n_1 + n_2 - 2$, representing the total number of measurements minus the number of parameters that are estimated in order to obtain $\hat{\sigma}$ (namely, the two means, μ_1 and μ_2, estimated by $\bar{Y}_1$ and $\bar{Y}_2$).

When the single value $\hat{\sigma}$ is used to estimate σ_1 and σ_2, the estimated standard error of $\bar{Y}_2 - \bar{Y}_1$ simplifies to

$$\hat{\sigma}_{\bar{Y}_2 - \bar{Y}_1} = \sqrt{\frac{\hat{\sigma}^2}{n_1} + \frac{\hat{\sigma}^2}{n_2}} = \hat{\sigma}\sqrt{\frac{1}{n_1} + \frac{1}{n_2}}$$

Then, a confidence interval for $\mu_2 - \mu_1$ has the form

$$(\bar{Y}_2 - \bar{Y}_1) \pm t_{\alpha/2}\hat{\sigma}_{\bar{Y}_2 - \bar{Y}_1}$$

and a test statistic for testing $H_0: \mu_1 = \mu_2$ is given by

$$t = \frac{(\bar{Y}_2 - \bar{Y}_1)}{\hat{\sigma}_{\bar{Y}_2 - \bar{Y}_1}}$$

Here, $t_{\alpha/2}$ is the value from the t table with single-tail probability $\alpha/2$ (two-tail probability α), and the t-scores are based on df $= n_1 + n_2 - 2$.

This method is a special case of the **analysis of variance** technique to be introduced in Section 13.1 as a method of comparing *several* groups. We shall defer further discussion of the assumptions and formulas for small-sample inference for means until then.

Example 7.5 A clinical psychologist wants to choose between two therapies for treating severe cases of mental depression. She selects six patients who are similar in their depressive symptoms and in their socioeconomic backgrounds and general health status. She randomly selects three of the patients to receive therapy 1, and the other three receive therapy 2. She selects small samples for ethical reasons; if her experiment indicates that one therapy is superior, that therapy shall be used on all her other patients having these symptoms. After 1 month of intense treatment, she subjectively gives a score on a 0–100 scale to describe the degree of improvement in the patient. The scores are 60, 70, 80 for the patients receiving therapy 1 and 80, 95, 95 for the patients receiving therapy 2.

For these data, $\bar{Y}_1 = 70$, $\bar{Y}_2 = 90$, and

$$\Sigma (Y_{1i} - \bar{Y}_1)^2 = (60 - 70)^2 + (70 - 70)^2 + (80 - 70)^2 = 200$$
$$\Sigma (Y_{2i} - \bar{Y}_2)^2 = (80 - 90)^2 + (95 - 90)^2 + (95 - 90)^2 = 150$$

Under the assumption that $\sigma_1 = \sigma_2 = \sigma$, the joint estimate is

$$\hat{\sigma} = \sqrt{\frac{\Sigma (Y_{1i} - \bar{Y}_1)^2 + \Sigma (Y_{2i} - \bar{Y}_2)^2}{n_1 + n_2 - 2}} = \sqrt{\frac{200 + 150}{4}} = 9.354$$

Now, $\bar{Y}_2 - \bar{Y}_1 = 90 - 70 = 20$ has an estimated standard error of

$$\hat{\sigma}_{\bar{Y}_2 - \bar{Y}_1} = \hat{\sigma}\sqrt{\frac{1}{n_1} + \frac{1}{n_2}} = 9.354\sqrt{\frac{1}{3} + \frac{1}{3}} = 7.64$$

Let μ_1 and μ_2 denote the mean improvement scores for these therapies for the hypothetical populations that the samples represent. For testing $H_0: \mu_1 = \mu_2$ against $H_a: \mu_1 \neq \mu_2$, the test statistic

$$t = \frac{\bar{Y}_2 - \bar{Y}_1}{\hat{\sigma}_{\bar{Y}_2 - \bar{Y}_1}} = \frac{90 - 70}{7.64} = 2.62$$

has df $= n_1 + n_2 - 2 = 6 - 2 = 4$ and gives $P < .10$ but $P > .05$. There is noticeable evidence (particularly given the small sample size) that this psychologist has better success using the second therapy, but not enough evidence to reject H_0 at the $\alpha = .05$ level. ∎

Paired Differences for Dependent Samples*

Dependent samples occur when each observation in sample 1 is naturally matched with an observation from sample 2, such as when the same subjects are in each sample. Let

$$D_i = \text{Observation in sample 2} - \text{Observation in sample 1}$$

for the ith subject in the sample. Then $\mu_2 - \mu_1 = \mu_D$ is the population mean of the difference scores. Thus, inferences about $\mu_2 - \mu_1$ can be based on inferences about μ_D using the single sample of difference scores. For instance, for small samples, a confidence interval for $\mu_D = \mu_2 - \mu_1$ has the form

$$\bar{D} \pm t_{\alpha/2} \frac{\hat{\sigma}}{\sqrt{n}},$$

assuming that the population distribution of difference scores is normal. Here, $\bar{D}$ is the sample mean of the difference scores, n is the number of observations in each sample (and hence, the number of differences), $\hat{\sigma} = \sqrt{\Sigma (D_i - \bar{D})^2/(n - 1)}$, and df $= n - 1$. The corresponding statistic for testing $H_0: \mu_1 = \mu_2$ (i.e., $\mu_D = 0$) against $H_a: \mu_1 \neq \mu_2$ ($\mu_D \neq 0$) is

$$t = \frac{\bar{D}}{\hat{\sigma}/\sqrt{n}}$$

This procedure is referred to as a *paired difference t test*.

Example 7.5 (continued)

In Example 7.5, the random choice of patients for each treatment would have been inadvisable if the patients differ in ways thought to affect the experimental results. For instance, if the patients selected for treatment 1 happened to have poor overall health quality and little potential for relief of depressive symptoms regardless of treatment (compared to those selected for treatment 2), results might have an inadvertent bias in favor of treatment 2. With this in mind, suppose the psychologist redesigned the experiment. She selects three pairs of subjects, such that the patients matched in any given pair are very similar in health and other factors. For each pair, one subject is randomly selected for each therapy. The sample results are as follows:

PAIR	THERAPY 1	THERAPY 2	DIFFERENCE (2) − (1)
1	60	80	+20
2	70	95	+25
3	80	95	+15

The three difference scores have a sample mean of $\bar{D} = 20$ and a sample standard deviation of

$$\hat{\sigma} = \sqrt{\frac{\Sigma (D_i - \bar{D})^2}{n - 1}} = \sqrt{\frac{(20 - 20)^2 + (25 - 20)^2 + (15 - 20)^2}{2}}$$

$$= \sqrt{25} = 5.0$$

The standard error of $\bar{D}$ is $\hat{\sigma}/\sqrt{n} = 5.0/\sqrt{3} = 2.887$. The statistic for testing H_0: $\mu_1 = \mu_2$ against H_a: $\mu_1 \neq \mu_2$ is

$$t = \frac{\bar{D}}{\hat{\sigma}/\sqrt{n}} = \frac{20}{2.887} = 6.93$$

based on df $= n - 1 = 2$. Table B reports $t_{01} = 6.965$ for df $= 2$, so the (two-tailed) P-value barely exceeds .02 for these data. There is fairly substantial evidence that therapy 2 is superior for use by this psychologist.

Notice that although the raw scores used here are the same as in the previous example, the analyses and results differ according to whether the samples are independent or dependent. The design of selecting dependent samples often has the benefits that (a) known sources of potential bias are controlled, and (b) the standard error of $\bar{Y}_2 - \bar{Y}_1$ may be reduced, because the variability in the difference scores is often much less than the variability in the original scores. ■

7.3
Ordinal Scales:
Wilcoxon Test

Let us now suppose that the characteristic on which the two groups are to be compared is measured using an ordinal scale. For example, a study may involve a comparison of northerners and southerners on attitudes toward school busing for the purpose of integration, when the possible responses are (support, support only in some cases, oppose).

Wilcoxon Test for Fully Ranked Data

Example 7.6 illustrates a commonly used procedure for comparing two groups when the observations can be ranked.

Example 7.6

In Example 7.5, a clinical psychologist compared two therapies for treating mental depression. She used the therapies on independent samples of three patients for 1 month, and then subjectively assigned a score to measure degree of improvement for each patient. It would probably be easier, however, for the psychologist to *rank* the six patients in terms of their improvement. In other words, it would be easier to treat change in mental depression as an ordinal variable than an interval variable.

We will assign ranks to the six patients so that the smallest rank (1) corresponds to the least improvement, and the largest rank (6) corresponds to the greatest improvement. Suppose that the psychologist gives ranks 1, 2, and 4 to the patients who had therapy 1 and ranks 3, 5, and 6 to the patients who had therapy 2. In other words, the patients who received therapy 1 were rated as having the two poorest and fourth poorest improvements.

We shall now test the null hypothesis that the therapies have identical effects, in the sense that all possible permutations of rankings of the six patients are equally likely. The **Wilcoxon test*** can be used to judge whether the observed ranking indicates a significant difference between the performances of the therapies. This test assumes independent random samples, but makes no assumption about the form of the population distribution. The Wilcoxon test statistic is the sum of the ranks assigned to subjects in the first group, denoted by R_1. In this example $R_1 = 1 + 2 + 4 = 7$. Table 7.2 contains the sampling distribution of R_1. The table lists the possible values for R_1 when the sample sizes are $n_1 = n_2 = 3$. It also lists their probability of occurrence under the null hypothesis that the therapies have identical effects. For instance, $R_1 = 6$ (the smallest possible sum for three ranks) with probability .05 and $R_1 = 7$ with probability .05.

Table 7.2

Sampling Distribution of R_1 for Wilcoxon Test, $n_1 = n_2 = 3$

R_1	PROBABILITY
6	.05
7	.05
8	.10
9	.15
10	.15
11	.15
12	.15
13	.10
14	.05
15	.05

For the one-sided alternative hypothesis that therapy 1 gives poorer results, the P-value is the probability of obtaining an R_1-value equal to or even smaller than the observed R_1-value, since these are the R_1-values corresponding to therapy 1 receiving small ranks (i.e., being rated relatively poor). In this case, since we obtained $R_1 = 7$, the P-value is

$$P = P(R_1 \leq 7) = P(6) + P(7) = .05 + .05 = .10$$

For the two-sided alternative, we also add the corresponding values in the right-hand tail of the sampling distribution, obtaining

$$P = P(R_1 \leq 7) + P(R_1 \geq 14) = .10 + .10 = .20$$

*The Wilcoxon test is also referred to as the *Mann–Whitney test*, since those two researchers proposed an equivalent test in an article published at about the same time (1947) as the one by Wilcoxon.

In either case, there is not strong evidence of a difference in the effects of the therapies. Note, however, that it is impossible to obtain $P < .10$ for the two-sided Wilcoxon test when n_1 and n_2 are only 3 ($P = .10$ occurs for $R_1 = 6$ or $R_1 = 15$, corresponding to group 1 receiving ranks 1, 2, 3 or else 4, 5, 6). ■

Tables such as Table 7.2 are available for the Wilcoxon test for n_1 and n_2 between 3 and 10 in most "nonparametric" statistics books, including Lehmann (1975). Even if the data are interval, this test is often applied (using the rankings of the interval scores) instead of the two-sample t test discussed in the previous section, because the Wilcoxon test does not require such strong assumptions as normal population distributions with equal standard deviations. This matter is discussed in Section 7.4.

Comparing Ordinal Categorical Distributions

In social science research, samples are usually quite large and it is usually impossible to fully rank subjects without any ties. It is much more common that ordinal variables are measured on a categorical scale. For instance, many social science surveys contain questions in which the respondent is asked to choose one from several ordered choices. A Likert-type scale item in which each individual expresses a degree of agreement or disagreement with some statement is an example of such a scale. Another ordinal categorical scale would be the set of categories often, occasionally, seldom, and never, as answers to questions such as "How often do you visit your parents-in-law?" Example 7.7 gives a data set that will be used to illustrate procedures for comparing two groups on an ordinal categorical variable.

Example 7.7

At Iowa State University, a random sample of forty freshmen and another random sample of thirty seniors are selected to compare the degree of political conservatism of the two groups. Each student in each sample is asked to respond to the question, "How would you rate your political philosophy?" The available responses are very liberal, slightly liberal, moderate, slightly conservative, and very conservative. The results of the study are shown in Table 7.3. Thus, as classified, the students can be ranked according to degree of political conservatism. Of the freshmen, three exhibit the highest level of conservatism, nine exhibit the next highest level, and so forth. ■

Table 7.3 Political Philosophy by Academic Class

	VERY LIBERAL	SLIGHTLY LIBERAL	MODERATE	SLIGHTLY CONSERVATIVE	VERY CONSERVATIVE	TOTAL
Freshmen	2	8	18	9	3	40
Seniors	6	11	7	4	2	30
Total	8	19	25	13	5	70

In situations such as the one described in Example 7.7, the primary statistical procedure is usually a test of whether there is a difference of some type between the two groups. In these tests, the null hypothesis is that the two underlying population distributions are identical. For a categorical scale, as in Table 7.3, this means that for each of the categories, the proportion of one population classified in that category equals the proportion of the other population classified in that category. For example, the proportion of freshmen who are very liberal equals the proportion of seniors who are very liberal, the proportion of freshmen who are slightly liberal equals the proportion of seniors who are slightly liberal, and so forth.

There are many ways in which the two populations could differ. The alternative hypothesis that is usually of greatest interest is that the distributions differ in *location*, in the sense that the observations from one of the population distributions tend to have a higher ranking, on the average, than those from the other population distribution. In many applications, it might make sense to imagine one of the distributions as being similar in form to the other, but *shifted* somewhat so that the rankings of the observations tend to be either larger or smaller on the average (see Figure 7.3).

Fig. 7.3 Two Population Distributions That Differ in Location; Group 2 Tends to Be Ranked Higher

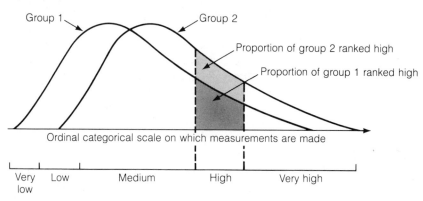

In the above example, we might wish to consider whether one class of students tends to be more conservative than the other class of students, for example. Since political philosophy is an ordinal variable, there are no given scores with which to compute a "mean conservatism" type of index for each group. We could proceed as in Example 7.6, assigning ranks to the seventy observations, taking account of the ties occurring for students falling in the same category of political philosophy. Instead, we shall give an approach that uses the data to generate a set of scores whose means are easier to interpret than mean ranks.

Ridit Scores   Let $\hat{\pi}_i$ denote the proportion of the sample observations that are in the ith category of the ordinal variable. For Table 7.3, for instance,

$\hat{\pi}_1 = 8/70$

$\hat{\pi}_2 = 19/70$

$\hat{\pi}_3 = 25/70$

$\hat{\pi}_4 = 13/70$

$\hat{\pi}_5 = 5/70$

Ridit scores are average cumulative proportions for these responses.

Ridit Score

The *ridit score* for a response category equals the proportion of observations below that category plus half the proportion in that category.

Notation

The sample ridit score for the *i*th category is denoted by $\hat{r}_i$.

For the very liberal category in Table 7.3, the ridit score is

$$\hat{r}_1 = \frac{\hat{\pi}_1}{2} = \frac{1}{2}\left(\frac{8}{70}\right) = .057$$

For the slightly liberal category, the ridit score is

$$\hat{r}_2 = \hat{\pi}_1 + \frac{\hat{\pi}_2}{2} = \frac{8}{70} + \frac{1}{2}\left(\frac{19}{70}\right) = .250$$

the proportion below the slightly liberal category (i.e., in the very liberal category) plus half the proportion in that category. The ridit scores for the remaining categories are

$$\hat{r}_3 = \hat{\pi}_1 + \hat{\pi}_2 + \frac{\hat{\pi}_3}{2} = \frac{8}{70} + \frac{19}{70} + \frac{1}{2}\left(\frac{25}{70}\right) = .564$$

$$\hat{r}_4 = \hat{\pi}_1 + \hat{\pi}_2 + \hat{\pi}_3 + \frac{\hat{\pi}_4}{2} = \frac{8}{70} + \frac{19}{70} + \frac{25}{70} + \frac{1}{2}\left(\frac{13}{70}\right) = .836$$

$$\hat{r}_5 = \hat{\pi}_1 + \hat{\pi}_2 + \hat{\pi}_3 + \hat{\pi}_4 + \frac{\hat{\pi}_5}{2} = \frac{8}{70} + \frac{19}{70} + \frac{25}{70} + \frac{13}{70} + \frac{1}{2}\left(\frac{5}{70}\right) = .964$$

Notice that the ridit scores fall between 0 and 1, and they increase as the degree of political conservatism increases. The *i*th score is calculated by

$$\hat{r}_i = \hat{\pi}_1 + \hat{\pi}_2 + \cdots + \hat{\pi}_{i-1} + \frac{1}{2}\hat{\pi}_i.$$

We can summarize degree of political conservatism for freshmen and for seniors by computing a mean of the ridit scores for each group. For freshmen, there are two students having ridit score $\hat{r}_1 = .057$ (i.e., two students in the very liberal category in Table 7.3), eight students having ridit score $\hat{r}_2 = .250$, and so forth, so the mean ridit score for the forty freshmen is

$$\bar{r}_1 = \frac{2(.057) + 8(.250) + 18(.564) + 9(.836) + 3(.964)}{40} = .567$$

Similarly, the mean ridit score for the thirty seniors is

$$\bar{r}_2 = \frac{6(.057) + 11(.250) + 7(.564) + 4(.836) + 2(.964)}{30} = .410$$

Since $\bar{r}_1 > \bar{r}_2$ for the sample in Table 7.3, freshmen tended to be more conservative than seniors.

Mean ridit scores fall between 0 and 1, and the mean ridit score for the combined sample must equal .5. For Table 7.3, for instance, the mean ridit score for the combined sample is

$$\frac{8(.057) + 19(.250) + 25(.564) + 13(.836) + 5(.964)}{70} = .500$$

A useful interpretation for the mean ridits is the following. Suppose that the categories of the ordinal variable represent intervals of an underlying continuous distribution, as in Figure 7.3. Then $\bar{r}_2 - \bar{r}_1 + .5$ approximates the probability that a randomly selected individual from group 2 ranks higher than a randomly selected individual from group 1, for the underlying continuous distributions. For Table 7.3, for instance,

$$\bar{r}_2 - \bar{r}_1 + .5 = .410 - .567 + .5 = .343$$

Hence, we estimate that the probability that a senior is more conservative than a freshman is .343 and that the probability that a freshman is more conservative than a senior is $1 - .343 = .657 = \bar{r}_1 - \bar{r}_2 + .5$.

In summary, sample mean ridits can be used to *describe* differences between groups measured on an ordinal variable. We next consider a test that can be used to compare mean ridits in the population.

Wilcoxon Test for Ordinal Categorical Distributions

Suppose we want to compare two groups with respect to an ordinal variable having c categories. We assume that independent random samples are selected. An ordinal categorical version of the Wilcoxon test can be used to compare the locations of the two groups, as described by their mean ridit scores. The null hypothesis that the two population distributions are identical implies that the mean ridits are equal in the population. The alternative hypothesis could be one-sided or two-sided, depending on whether one is willing to predict which group has the higher population mean ridit.

For large samples, roughly $n_1 \geq 20$ and $n_2 \geq 20$, the difference $\bar{r}_2 - \bar{r}_1$ in the sample mean ridits has approximately a normal sampling distribution. A test statistic* for comparing the mean ridits is

$$z = \frac{\bar{r}_2 - \bar{r}_1}{\sigma_{\bar{r}_2 - \bar{r}_1}}$$

---

*This statistic can be expressed equivalently in terms of the sum of ranks R_1 for the first group. The alternative form is used in many statistics texts, but we prefer this form because the mean ridits are more easily interpreted than sums of ranks.

where $\sigma_{\bar{r}_2-\bar{r}_1}$ denotes the standard error of the sampling distribution of $\bar{r}_2 - \bar{r}_1$. This statistic reflects whether the difference in sample mean ridits is large relative to what would be expected due to sampling error if H_0 were true. The value of the z test statistic can be referred to the normal curve area table to get a P-value, in the same way as with the z test for comparing two means in Section 7.2. The formula for the standard error of $\bar{r}_2 - \bar{r}_1$ is

$$\sigma_{\bar{r}_2-\bar{r}_1} = \sqrt{\frac{(n_1 + n_2 + 1)T}{12n_1n_2}}$$

where

$$T = \frac{(n_1 + n_2)^2\left(1 - \sum_{i=1}^{c} \hat{\pi}_i^3\right)}{(n_1 + n_2)^2 - 1}$$

The formula for $\sigma_{\bar{r}_2-\bar{r}_1}$ is based on theoretical properties of how ridit scores are related to rankings of observations. The factor T reflects the coarseness of the categorization for the ordinal variable. It converges upward toward 1.0 as the number of categories and the dispersion of the sample among them increases. These formulas will be illustrated by returning to the data in Example 7.7.

Example 7.7 (continued) We are now ready to test the null hypothesis that freshmen and seniors have the same distribution on political conservatism. We will use the two-sided alternative hypothesis of a difference in the mean ridits for the two groups. That is, we do not predict which class tends to be the more conservative.

We previously calculated for Table 7.3 the category proportions

$$\hat{\pi}_1 = \frac{8}{70} \quad \hat{\pi}_2 = \frac{19}{70} \quad \hat{\pi}_3 = \frac{25}{70} \quad \hat{\pi}_4 = \frac{13}{70} \quad \hat{\pi}_5 = \frac{5}{70}$$

based on $n_1 + n_2 = 40 + 30 = 70$ observations. The factor T needed for the standard error formula is therefore

$$T = \frac{(n_1 + n_2)^2\left(1 - \sum_{i=1}^{5} \hat{\pi}_i^3\right)}{(n_1 + n_2)^2 - 1}$$

$$= \frac{(70)^2\left\{1 - \left[\left(\frac{8}{70}\right)^3 + \left(\frac{19}{70}\right)^3 + \cdots + \left(\frac{5}{70}\right)^3\right]\right\}}{70^2 - 1}$$

$$= \frac{4,900(1 - .0738)}{4,899} = .9264$$

The standard error of $\bar{r}_2 - \bar{r}_1$ is

$$\sigma_{\bar{r}_2-\bar{r}_1} = \sqrt{\frac{(n_1 + n_2 + 1)T}{12n_1n_2}} = \sqrt{\frac{71(.9264)}{12(40)(30)}} = .0676$$

The sample mean ridits were previously calculated to be $\bar{r}_1 = .567$ and $\bar{r}_2 = .410$, so the test statistic for comparing the mean ridits is

$$z = \frac{\bar{r}_2 - \bar{r}_1}{\sigma_{\bar{r}_2 - \bar{r}_1}} = \frac{.410 - .567}{.0676} = -2.32$$

For the two-sided alternative hypothesis, the P-value is $P = 2(.0102) = .0204$, the probability of getting a z-score above 2.32 or below -2.32, if H_0 were true. Suppose that the alternative hypothesis had been the one-sided one that freshmen tend to be more conservative (i.e., that the mean ridit for freshmen is higher than for seniors). This alternative hypothesis would be corroborated by the sample if $\bar{r}_1$ were significantly larger than $\bar{r}_2$; in other words, if the sample z-score were a sufficiently large negative number. For this alternative, the P-value is the probability below the observed z-score in the left-hand tail of the standard normal sampling distribution. In this example, the P-value would have been $P = .0102$, the probability of getting a z-score below -2.32 if H_0 were true. For either alternative, there is strong evidence that freshmen tend to be more conservative than seniors at Iowa State. ∎

The five elements of the Wilcoxon test for ordered categories are summarized in Table 7.4 at the end of this chapter. The z test statistic and normal sampling distribution for $\bar{r}_2 - \bar{r}_1$ are generally appropriate when both n_1 and n_2 are at least 20. A generalization of the Wilcoxon test used to compare mean ridits for *several* groups is the **Kruskal–Wallis test**, discussed in Section 13.7.

Describing Differences Between Groups

As in Chapter 6, if the sample sizes are very large, one may observe a very small P-value even when the observed differences between the two groups are relatively small, in practical terms. One way of describing the size of that difference is to compare the two medians. In Example 7.7, the median response for freshmen is moderate, whereas for seniors the median response is slightly liberal. (Verify this.) Notice, though, that the two medians could be identical even though the two distributions are very different (as in Figure 7.4). This is particularly apt to happen if there is a crude categorization of the ordinal scale, such as a dichotomy or trichotomy. If one is restricted to an ordinal categorical scale in designing the measurement instrument for a variable, one should attempt to allow several (say, at least four) distinct responses. Conover (1980) and Lehmann (1975) present a method of obtaining a confidence interval for the difference between two medians in the more restrictive situation in which the variable has a symmetric distribution and is measured on an interval scale.

Another way of describing the difference between the two groups is to compare the two mean ridits $\bar{r}_1$ and $\bar{r}_2$. For instance, we could use $\bar{r}_2 - \bar{r}_1 + .5$ to estimate the probability that a randomly selected observation from group 2 is higher than a randomly selected observation from group 1. Unfortunately, the formula we gave for the standard error $\sigma_{\bar{r}_2 - \bar{r}_1}$ applies only when the two population distributions are identical, and it cannot be used to construct a confidence interval for differences between mean ridits. The formula needed for that purpose is quite complex and is discussed in Agresti (1984, pp. 188, 200).

Fig. 7.4 A Difference in Population Distributions That Would Not Be Detected by the Wilcoxon Test (Same Locations but Different Dispersions)

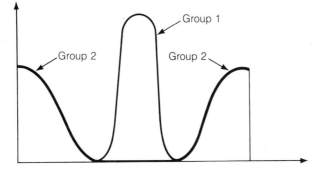

7.4 Comments Concerning Nonparametric Statistics

The Wilcoxon test is an inferential procedure that is one of a body of techniques referred to as *nonparametric* or *distribution-free* statistical procedures. These procedures, which have been developed primarily since 1940, rely on relatively few assumptions about the underlying form of the population distributions for the variables. Many of the traditional (so-called *parametric*) methods for interval dependent variables have very strict assumptions concerning these distributions. The term *nonparametric* statistical methods refers partly to the analogous ordinal methods that are based only on the rankings of the observations. These procedures can be used in situations where we believe that at least one of the assumptions required for use of a parametric technique is badly violated.

Comparing Parametric and Nonparametric Procedures

As an example, when n_1 or n_2 is less than 20, the t distribution procedure for comparing means, discussed in Section 7.2, requires that the population distributions be normal with identical standard deviations. Most comparisons of groups using ranks are based on the assumption of identical shapes for the population distributions, but the shapes are not required to be normal. Hence, the Wilcoxon test is used not only for comparing two groups on an ordinal variable, but also for comparing two groups on an interval variable when at least one of the sample sizes is small (say, $n < 20$) and there is doubt about whether the corresponding population distributions are normal in form.

One might wonder whether anything is sacrificed by using a nonparametric procedure when a parametric procedure is actually justified, in the sense that the assumptions are completely fulfilled for using that parametric procedure. Intuitively, we might believe that nonparametric procedures are not as good in that case, since they use only the ordinal characteristics of the data. However, statisticians have shown that some nonparametric procedures are very nearly as good even in the exact case for which the parametric tests are designed.

To illustrate, if two population distributions are normal in shape and have the same standard deviation but different means, the Wilcoxon rank test is very nearly as powerful in detecting this difference as the z test and t test procedures for interval variables. More precisely, the *relative efficiency* of the Wilcoxon test is approximately .95. This means that the parametric procedure requires about 95% as large a sample as does the Wilcoxon test in order to have the same power as the Wilcoxon test for rejecting H_0 when the two distributions are slightly different. In other words, the Wilcoxon test requires just a slightly larger sample size in order to have the same probability of rejecting the null hypothesis at a fixed α-level. This comparison is typical of many in which the nonparametric procedure is almost as efficient as the parametric procedure, even though it is based only on the ranks of the observations. Notice that the comparison we have given refers to the *best possible conditions* for the parametric procedure—that is, when the assumptions on which it is based are exactly fulfilled. In general, if both population distributions have the same shape but possibly different locations, the Wilcoxon test is never much less efficient than the parametric tests, yet it can be much more efficient than those tests if the population distributions are highly nonnormal.

Since many nonparametric procedures have been introduced only recently relative to well-established parametric procedures, they are often not as familiar to the social scientist. In addition, there are still some gaps in their development, although statisticians are working to remove these. For example, estimation techniques have not been as thoroughly developed as hypothesis tests in some areas of nonparametric statistics.

Treating Ordinal Variables as Interval Variables

Social scientists sometimes use statistical procedures designed for interval scale variables when the data themselves are only ordinal. Many researchers, for example, might compare the freshmen and seniors in Example 7.7 by assigning scores 1, 2, 3, 4, and 5 to the five categories of political philosophy and conducting the z test of Section 7.2. Such a scoring system assumes equal distances between the five categories. Alternative scoring systems (e.g., 1, 2, 5, 8, 9, if categories one and two are believed to be much more alike than two and three, and categories four and five much more alike than three and four) would lead to different conclusions in some applications (see Problem 33 at the end of the chapter). Thus, it can be dangerous to treat ordinal data as interval, and researchers who do so should at least try various score choices to check the dependence of the conclusions on that choice.

We shall study other nonparametric methods in Chapters 8 and 13. Whenever the assumptions for a procedure designed for interval variables appear to be grossly violated, the corresponding procedures for ordinal variables may be used as a nonparametric approach to the problem. These procedures based on ranks tend to be simple in concept and very widely applicable because of the generality of the assumptions.

Summary

In this chapter, we have considered methods for the comparison of two populations. The methods are summarized in Table 7.4 by measurement level of the response (dependent) variable, for the case of large, independent random samples.

For a nominal response variable, we compared the **proportions** of individuals in the two groups that were classified in a particular category of that nominal scale. A confidence interval was formulated for the difference between the proportions. The corresponding test of equality of the two proportions is a special case of the chi-square test introduced in the next chapter.

For an interval response variable, we compared the *means* for the two groups. A large-sample confidence interval and hypothesis test for the difference between the means were formulated as extensions of the one-sample z procedures introduced for the mean in Chapter 6. The corresponding t procedures when either n_1 or n_2 is less than 20 assume normal population distributions with equal standard deviations. If these assumptions are badly violated, one can still use the ordinal information in the data for the *Wilcoxon test*, which is an example of a *nonparametric* statistical procedure. We also used the Wilcoxon test to compare the *mean ridits* for two groups measured on an ordinal categorical variable.

Table 7.4 Summary of Comparison Methods for Two Groups, for Large, Independent Random Samples

| | SCALE OF MEASUREMENT OF DEPENDENT VARIABLE | | |
	Nominal	Ordinal	Interval
Estimation			
1. Parameter	$\pi_2 - \pi_1$	Difference of mean ridits	$\mu_2 - \mu_1$
2. Point estimate	$\hat{\pi}_2 - \hat{\pi}_1$	Sample difference of mean ridits	$\bar{Y}_2 - \bar{Y}_1$
3. Standard error of estimate	$\hat{\sigma}_{\hat{\pi}_2 - \hat{\pi}_1} = \sqrt{\dfrac{\hat{\pi}_1(1-\hat{\pi}_1)}{n_1} + \dfrac{\hat{\pi}_2(1-\hat{\pi}_2)}{n_2}}$		$\hat{\sigma}_{\bar{Y}_2 - \bar{Y}_1} = \sqrt{\dfrac{\hat{\sigma}_1^2}{n_1} + \dfrac{\hat{\sigma}_2^2}{n_2}}$
4. Confidence interval	$(\hat{\pi}_2 - \hat{\pi}_1) \pm z_{\alpha/2}\hat{\sigma}_{\hat{\pi}_2 - \hat{\pi}_1}$		$(\bar{Y}_2 - \bar{Y}_1) \pm z_{\alpha/2}\hat{\sigma}_{\bar{Y}_2 - \bar{Y}_1}$
Hypothesis testing			
1. Assumptions	More than 5 observations in each category, for each group	$n_1, n_2 \geq 20$	$n_1, n_2 \geq 20$
2. Hypotheses	$H_0: \pi_1 = \pi_2 \ (\pi_2 - \pi_1 = 0)$	H_0: Identical population distributions	$H_0: \mu_1 = \mu_2$ $(\mu_2 - \mu_1 = 0)$
	$H_a: \pi_1 \neq \pi_2$	H_a: Mean ridit$_1 \neq$ mean ridit$_2$	$H_a: \mu_1 \neq \mu_2$
	$H_a: \pi_1 < \pi_2$	H_a: Mean ridit$_1 <$ mean ridit$_2$	$H_a: \mu_1 < \mu_2$
	$H_a: \pi_1 > \pi_2$	H_a: Mean ridit$_1 >$ mean ridit$_2$	$H_a: \mu_1 > \mu_2$
3. Test statistic	$z = \dfrac{\hat{\pi}_2 - \hat{\pi}_1}{\hat{\sigma}_{\hat{\pi}_2 - \hat{\pi}_1}}$, or see Section 8.2	$z = \dfrac{\bar{r}_2 - \bar{r}_1}{\sigma_{\bar{r}_2 - \bar{r}_1}}$	$z = \dfrac{\bar{Y}_2 - \bar{Y}_1}{\hat{\sigma}_{\bar{Y}_2 - \bar{Y}_1}}$
4. *P*-value 5. Conclusion	Same as for z tests in Chapter 6 (see, e.g., Section 6.2)		

Notes

Section 7.1

1. The formula given for the standard error of $\hat{\pi}_2 - \hat{\pi}_1$ is based on *independent* samples. Suppose in Example 7.1 that we wanted to compare the president's popularity in January and February, but the same people were in each sample.

Then the samples are *dependent*, and a different formula must be used. The population proportions of different outcomes can be summarized as follows:

| | | FEBRUARY | | |
		Approve	Disapprove	
JANUARY	Approve	π_{++}	π_{+-}	π_1
	Disapprove	π_{-+}	π_{--}	$1 - \pi_1$
		π_2	$1 - \pi_2$	1.0

Here π_{++} is the proportion of people who approve of the president's performance both months, π_{+-} is the proportion who approve in the January survey but disapprove in the February survey, and so forth. Notice that

$$\pi_2 - \pi_1 = (\pi_{++} + \pi_{-+}) - (\pi_{++} + \pi_{+-}) = \pi_{-+} - \pi_{+-}$$

The estimated standard error of $\hat{\pi}_2 - \hat{\pi}_1$ for dependent samples is

$$\hat{\sigma}_{\hat{\pi}_2 - \hat{\pi}_1} = \sqrt{\frac{\hat{\pi}_1(1 - \hat{\pi}_1)}{n} + \frac{\hat{\pi}_2(1 - \hat{\pi}_2)}{n} - \frac{2(\hat{\pi}_{++}\hat{\pi}_{--} - \hat{\pi}_{+-}\hat{\pi}_{-+})}{n}}$$

where $n = n_1 = n_2$ is the number of subjects in each sample. Then, as usual, a large-sample confidence interval for $\pi_2 - \pi_1$ is

$$(\hat{\pi}_2 - \hat{\pi}_1) \pm z_{\alpha/2}\hat{\sigma}_{\hat{\pi}_2 - \hat{\pi}_1}$$

and the test statistic

$$z = \frac{\hat{\pi}_2 - \hat{\pi}_1}{\hat{\sigma}_{\hat{\pi}_2 - \hat{\pi}_1}}$$

can be used to test H_0: $\pi_1 = \pi_2$. Refer to Problem 7.34 for an example of this analysis. A small-sample test of H_0: $\pi_1 = \pi_2$ can be based on a binomial test that $\pi_{+-}/(\pi_{+-} + \pi_{-+}) = .5$, by identifying X with the number of negative changes n_{+-} and n with the total number of changes $n_{+-} + n_{-+}$. This test is referred to as *McNemar's test*.

Section 7.3

2. Occasionally, two populations do not differ in location but are very different in some other way. The two population distributions shown in Figure 7.4 differ in dispersion but not in central tendency, for example. Since samples from these populations would probably be similar in mean rank, we would not be likely to conclude that the populations are different using the Wilcoxon test. Other rank tests are more sensitive to such differences. These include the *runs test* and the *Kolmogorov–Smirnov* test. The reader is referred to the books by Conover (1980), Lehmann (1975), and Siegel (1956) for in-depth studies of these and other procedures based on ranks.

Problems

1. Find a 95% confidence interval for $\pi_2 - \pi_1$ for the data in Example 7.1. Compare the conclusion for the .95 confidence coefficient to the one made in the text using a .99 confidence coefficient.

2. Refer to Example 7.1. Find point estimates of the proportions of Americans who *disapprove* of the president's performance in January and February, respectively. Find a 99% confidence interval for the change in the disapproval rating, and compare it to the interval given in Example 7.1 for the change in approval rating.

3. One of the questions posed in a nationwide poll is whether the death penalty should be completely abolished. Out of 845 women interviewed, 400 favor abolition of the death penalty. Out of 825 men, 350 favor abolition. Assuming that these individuals were randomly selected, find a 95% confidence interval for the difference between the proportions of men and women favoring abolition. Interpret the interval.

4. In a random sample of voters in a presidential election, 300 give Democrat as their political party affiliation, whereas 200 give Republican as their affiliation. Of the 300 Democrats, 90 voted for the Republican candidate. Of the 200 Republicans, 20 voted for the Democratic candidate. Find a 90% confidence interval for the difference between the proportion of Democrats who voted Republican and the proportion of Republicans who voted Democratic. Interpret the interval.

5. In a study of the relationship between religious affiliation and political philosophy, it is noticed that 10 out of 20 Unitarians classify themselves as liberal, whereas 6 out of 30 Baptists in the sample classify themselves as liberal. The alternative choices were moderate and conservative.
   a. Are the sample sizes large enough that you can calculate large-sample confidence intervals?
   b. Find a 99% confidence interval for the difference between the proportions of Unitarians and Baptists who label themselves liberal. Interpret the interval.
   c. Can you conclude that there is a difference between Unitarians and Baptists in political philosophy? Why or why not?
   d. Suppose that the sample sizes for the two groups were 200 and 300 instead of 20 and 30, but that the sample proportions were the same. Recompute a 99% confidence interval for the difference in proportions. Interpret the interval, and compare your conclusions to the results in parts **b** and **c**.

6. In the 1974 and 1975 General Social Surveys, one question asked was "Do you believe that women should take care of running their homes and leave running the country up to men?" For 1,305 male respondents, 465 replied "yes" and 840 replied "no." For 1,566 female respondents, 555 replied "yes" and 1,011 replied "no." Find a 95% confidence interval for the difference between the proportion of males and the proportion of females who would respond "yes." Interpret the interval.

7. Refer to Problem 6. Of 487 respondents having 8 years or less education, 330 replied "yes." Of 902 respondents having at least 13 years of education, 153 replied "yes." Find a 95% confidence interval for the difference between the proportion at the low education level and the proportion at the high education level who would respond "yes." Interpret the interval.

8. Refer to Problems 6 and 7. Which variable, sex or educational level, seems to have the greater influence on opinion concerning whether women should take care of running their homes and leave running the country up to men?

9. *Newsweek* magazine (Sept. 19, 1983) reported the results of a poll taken to investigate whether there was a difference between the percentage of women and the percentage of men who approved of the way Ronald Reagan was handling his job as president. Of 511 women interviewed, 40% indicated approval. Of 507 men, 49% indicated approval.

a. Assuming that these can be treated as independent random samples, find a 90% confidence interval for the difference between the proportion of men and the proportion of women who approved of Reagan's performance.

b. Interpret the interval obtained in part **a**. Can you conclude that there is a gender gap?

10. For thirty female assistant professors selected at random from arts and science departments in a large state university system, the mean salary for the academic year is $27,000. The corresponding mean salary for a random sample of fifty male assistant professors is $27,800. The estimated standard deviations for the two samples are $1,000 and $1,400, respectively. Compute a 95% confidence interval for the difference in mean salary between male and female assistant professors in this system. What is your interpretation?

11. The accompanying table summarizes results of responses to a questionnaire designed to study the effect of educational attainment on attitudes toward women having executive positions in business. The results are summarized on a scale of 0 to 100, with larger values representing more positive attitudes toward women's roles.

EDUCATION LEVEL	n	$\bar{Y}$	$\hat{\sigma}$
1. No college	25	64	16
2. At least some college	25	76	12

a. Assuming these may be treated as independent random samples, find a 95% confidence interval for $\mu_2 - \mu_1$.

b. Find the P-value for testing $H_0: \mu_1 = \mu_2$ against $H_a: \mu_1 < \mu_2$. Is there strong evidence that the population mean is higher for those having some college education?

12. A study involves a comparison of the mean educational attainment for adults who grew up in a household with married parents to those who grew up in a household with divorced parents. Out of a random sample of 300 adults in a particular community, 255 had married parents and 45 had divorced parents. For the first group, the mean number of years of school attendance was 13.2, with an estimated standard deviation of 3.0 years. For the second group, the mean was 12.5, with an estimated standard deviation of 4.0 years. Conduct a test of the hypothesis that the two corresponding population means are equal. If we base our conclusion for a two-sided alternative on the α-level of .05, would the null hypothesis be rejected?

13. Find a 95% confidence interval for the difference in the means in Problem 12. Interpret the interval, and show how your interpretation relates to the conclusion made in that exercise.

14. A mathematics professor believes that the performance of students taking an elementary calculus course has declined in recent years. The professor decides to reuse a final exam that was first administered 10 years ago. At that time, the mean score was $\bar{Y}_1 = 81$, with $\hat{\sigma}_1 = 10$, for the fifty students in the section taught by that professor. When given to the current class of fifty-three students, who observed essentially the same set of lectures, the mean is $\bar{Y}_2 = 75$, with $\hat{\sigma}_2 = 15$. If we treat these students as random samples of the populations of all such students taking calculus at this college during these two years, do the results indicate a decline in performance on the average? Conduct the appropriate test at the $\alpha = .01$ level.

15. A study involves a comparison of the mean time needed to complete a task under two conditions, labeled experimental and control. For the twenty-five subjects in the control group, the sample mean was 4.2 minutes, with an estimated standard deviation of 3.0 minutes. For the twenty-five subjects in the experimental group, the sample mean was 6.2 minutes, with an estimated standard deviation of 4.0 minutes.
  a. Set up hypotheses that are designed to test whether there is any difference in the population means.
  b. Calculate the value of the appropriate test statistic.
  c. Give the P-value and interpret it.

16. Refer to Problem 15. Indicate whether H_0 would be rejected at the $\alpha = .01$ level.

17. Refer to Problem 11b. Is there sufficient evidence to reject H_0, using $\alpha = .01$?

18. Two new drugs have been proposed for treating subjects who suffer from high blood pressure. Two random samples of such subjects are obtained for an experiment designed to compare the drugs. Five subjects take drug A and five subjects take drug B for a period of 3 months, at which time the drop in blood pressure is measured. The sample values were as follows:

  Drug A: 0, 2, 2, 3, 3
  Drug B: 3, 6, 6, 7, 8

  a. Calculate the sample means, $\bar{Y}_1$ for drug A and $\bar{Y}_2$ for drug B.
  b. Calculate the estimated standard error of $\bar{Y}_2 - \bar{Y}_1$.
  c. Obtain a 99% confidence interval for $\mu_2 - \mu_1$, and interpret the result.
  d. Find the P-value for testing $H_0: \mu_1 = \mu_2$ against $H_a: \mu_1 \neq \mu_2$, and interpret its value.

19. Refer to Problem 18. Using an α-level of $\alpha = .01$, can you make a conclusion about which drug is better?

20. The property values for three homes selected at random in the Forest Ridge subdivision are (in thousands of dollars) 90, 100, 110. The property values for two homes selected at random in the Hermitage subdivision are 160, 180.

   a. Use small-sample procedures to construct a 90% confidence interval for the difference in mean property values between the Hermitage and Forest Ridge subdivisions.

   b. Find the P-value for testing H_0: $\mu_1 = \mu_2$ against H_a: $\mu_1 \neq \mu_2$.

21. Refer to Example 7.5. Construct and interpret a 95% confidence interval for $\mu_2 - \mu_1$:

   a. In the independent samples case.

   b. In the dependent samples case considered in the continuation example.

22. Suppose a mathematics aptitude test is taken by each of a random sample of ten college freshmen both before and after undergoing an intensive training course designed to improve such test scores. Then, the *before* score for each student is paired with the *after* score, as shown in the table.

STUDENT	BEFORE	AFTER
1	60	70
2	73	80
3	42	40
4	88	94
5	66	79
6	77	86
7	90	93
8	63	71
9	55	70
10	96	97

   a. Compare the mean scores before and after the training course by finding and interpreting the P-value for testing whether the mean change equals 0.

   b. Compare the mean scores before and after the training course by constructing and interpreting a 90% confidence interval for the population mean difference.

23. Give an example of a situation in which it would be more sensible to compare means using dependent samples than independent samples.

24. Three editors of large-city newspapers with circulations of over 100,000 are selected at random and asked to rate on a score of 0–100 the fairness of the news media in political investigative reporting (0 corresponds to very poor). The same question is posed to three editors of small-town papers with circulations of under 10,000. The large-city editors gave scores of 55, 90, 95, and the small-town editors gave scores of 40, 60, 80.

a. Test H_0: $\mu_1 = \mu_2$ against H_a: $\mu_1 > \mu_2$, where group 1 is the large-city editors. Interpret the P-value.

b. Construct a 95% confidence interval for $\mu_2 - \mu_1$, and note that precision of inference is poor for such small sample sizes.

c. Treat the data as ordinal by assigning ranks to the scores.

d. Calculate the Wilcoxon statistic R_1. Using Table 7.2, find the P-value when the alternative hypothesis predicts that large-city editors tend to give more favorable ratings to the news media. Interpret the result.

25. The data in the table were obtained from a sample of voters taken in the 1976 presidential primary in Wisconsin (see Agresti, 1984, p. 87). Democrats and Republicans were classified on the ordinal variable, political ideology.

		POLITICAL IDEOLOGY		
		Liberal	Moderate	Conservative
PARTY	Democrat	143	156	100
AFFILIATION	Republican	15	72	127

a. Calculate the ridit scores for the three levels of political ideology.

b. Calculate the mean ridit scores for Democrats and Republicans. In this sample, which party tended to be more conservative?

c. Find an estimate of the probability that a randomly selected Republican is more conservative than a randomly selected Democrat.

d. Use the Wilcoxon test to obtain a P-value for testing the hypothesis that Democrats and Republicans have identical distributions on political ideology. Use the alternative hypothesis that corresponds to the prior belief that Republicans tend to be more conservative.

e. Refer to the P-value in part **d**. Is there strong evidence that, in the population, Republicans are more conservative?

26. Each person in a random sample of 100 individuals from a community is classified according to political party affiliation and opinion as to whether criminal penalties for the use of marijuana should be eliminated, made more severe, made less severe, or remain as they presently are. The results are indicated in the table.

	MORE SEVERE	REMAIN SAME	LESS SEVERE	ELIMINATE
Republicans	8	18	7	4
Democrats	4	19	24	16

a. Find the P-value for testing whether there is a difference between the two groups concerning opinion on this subject.

b. What is the median response for each group?

27. A new drug is designed to treat a certain type of respiratory infection, and is believed to lead to a faster recovery than the standard drug used. Out of eighty people reporting to a particular health clinic with this type of infection over a 1-month period, forty are randomly selected to receive the standard treatment, whereas the remaining forty receive the new treatment. A team of doctors analyzes the recovery of each patient after 3 days. The results obtained are given in the table.

	EXCELLENT	VERY GOOD	GOOD	FAIR	POOR
New treatment	14	15	7	2	2
Standard treatment	6	9	10	10	5

a. Calculate the sample mean ridits for the two treatments. Interpret the values.
b. Report the *P*-value for testing whether the new drug produces better recovery than the standard one. Interpret the result, and state what conclusions, if any, you would make.

28. Each of fifty individuals in a random sample selected in Fernwood, Ohio, is asked to respond on a scale of 0–10 to the statement "Sex education should be provided to students in public high schools." A score of 10 designates complete agreement with the statement, whereas a score of 0 designates complete disagreement. It is decided to compare the responses of men and women. The frequencies of the various responses are given in the table.

	0	1	2	3	4	5	6	7	8	9	10	TOTAL
Men	5	3	1	1	0	0	1	1	2	3	8	25
Women	12	4	1	0	1	0	0	0	2	2	3	25

a. Calculate the mean ridits for men and women.
b. Using the Wilcoxon test, find the *P*-value for the two-sided test of the null hypothesis of identical distributions for men and women.

In Problems 29–32, select the correct response(s).

29. We calculate a 99% confidence interval for the difference $\pi_2 - \pi_1$ between the proportion of women in Florida who favor the Equal Rights Amendment (ERA) and the proportion of men in Florida who favor the ERA, obtaining (.02, .09).
a. We are 99% confident that the proportion who favor the ERA is between .02 and .09.
b. We are 99% confident that the proportion of women in Florida who favor the ERA is between .02 and .09 larger than the proportion of men in Florida who favor the ERA.
c. At this confidence level, there is insufficient evidence to infer that the population proportions are different.
d. We are 99% confident that a minority of Florida residents favor the ERA.
e. Since the confidence interval does not contain 0, it is impossible that $\pi_1 = \pi_2$.

30. The *Statistical Abstract of the United States 1984* reports that the mean income of adult males in the United States in 1981 was $\bar{Y}_1 = \$10,531$ for blacks and $\bar{Y}_2 = \$17,195$ for whites.

a. If these means are based on a census random sample, then the samples can be treated as independent random samples.

b. The center of the confidence interval for $\mu_2 - \mu_1$ would be 0.

c. If $\hat{\sigma}_1 = 5,000$ and $\hat{\sigma}_2 = 8,000$ and if $n_1 = 150$ and $n_2 = 1,300$, then the data would provide strong evidence that μ_2 is much larger than μ_1.

31. In order to compare the population mean annual incomes for Mexican-Americans (μ_1) and for whites (μ_2) having jobs in construction, we plan on constructing a 95% confidence interval for $\mu_2 - \mu_1$.

a. If the confidence interval is (3,000, 6,000), then at this confidence level we could conclude that the mean income for whites is higher than for Mexican-Americans.

b. If the confidence interval is ($-1,000$, 3,000), then in the corresponding $\alpha = .05$ level test of H_0: $\mu_1 = \mu_2$ against H_a: $\mu_1 \neq \mu_2$, we would reject H_0.

c. If the confidence interval is ($-1,000$, 3,000), then it is plausible that $\mu_1 = \mu_2$.

d. If the confidence interval is ($-1,000$, 3,000), then we are 95% confident that the mean annual income for whites is between $1,000 less and $3,000 more than the mean annual income for Mexican-Americans.

32. For small samples, the Wilcoxon test for comparing two distributions differs from parametric procedures (for means) in the sense that:

a. The alternative hypothesis cannot be one-sided.

b. It is unnecessary to assume that the population distribution is normal.

c. Random sampling is not assumed.

d. It can be used for ordinal as well as interval response variables.

*33. The accompanying table compares two hospitals on the outcomes of patient admissions for severe pneumonia. Although patient status is an ordinal variable, two researchers who analyze the data treat it as an interval variable. The first researcher assigns the equal-interval scores of (0, 5, 10) to the three categories. The second researcher, believing that the middle category should be treated as much closer to the third category than to the first, uses the scores of (0, 9, 10). Each researcher calculates the means for the two institutions and identifies the institution with the higher mean as the one having more success in treating its patients.

	PATIENT STATUS		
	Died in Hospital	Released After Lengthy Stay	Released After Brief Stay
Hospital A	1	29	0
Hospital B	8	8	14

a. Find the two means for the scoring system used by the first researcher.

b. Find the two means for the scoring system used by the second researcher.

c. Observe that the conclusion depends on the scoring system used; hence, if interval scale methods are to be applied to ordinal data, a great deal of care should be used in assigning scores to categories. In addition, different feasible scoring systems should be tested and their results compared in order to see their influence on the outcome of the analysis.

*34. Refer to Note 7.1 and Example 7.1. Suppose the same 1,600 people are interviewed in January and February, with the results shown in the accompanying table.

		FEBRUARY		
		Approve	Disapprove	
JANUARY	Approve	570	86	656
	Disapprove	150	794	944
		720	880	1,600

a. Find a 95% confidence interval for the difference between the proportion who approve in February and the proportion who approve in January.

b. At the 95% confidence level, can you conclude that the president's approval rating improved from January to February?

Bibliography

Agresti, A. (1984). *Analysis of Ordinal Categorical Data*. New York: Wiley.

Conover, W. J. (1980). *Practical Nonparametric Statistics*, 2nd ed. New York: Wiley.

Lehmann, E. L. (1975). *Nonparametrics: Statistical Methods Based on Ranks*. San Francisco: Holden-Day.

Siegel, S. (1956). *Nonparametric Statistics for the Behavioral Sciences*. New York: McGraw-Hill.

CHAPTER 8

Measuring Association for Categorical Variables

Contents

We now turn our attention to methods of detecting and describing relationships between variables. By *relationship* we mean the tendency for two variables to covary—vary together. For categorical variables, this means that the presence or absence of a certain attribute on one variable depends in part on the category into which the member is classified on the other variable. Certain values of one variable tend to go with certain values of another. For example, Anglo-Americans are more likely to be Protestant than are Mexican-Americans, who are overwhelmingly Catholic. Therefore, there is a relationship, or an association, between religious affiliation and ethnic group.

As another example, the likelihood of becoming pregnant is related to whether one uses contraceptives. The proportion of women who become pregnant is much higher among those who do not use contraceptives than among those who do. Of course, many other factors are also related to pregnancy—the experience of sexual intercourse, the type of contraceptive method, the health of the woman, the health of the man, and the desire to have children, among others. The probability of a pregnancy varies with different values of each of these variables, but some are much stronger in their effects than others. For example, whether a woman experiences sexual intercourse is much more strongly related to whether she becomes pregnant than is her health. Yet both variables have an effect on the probability of pregnancy.

In this chapter we will study methods for describing relationships between categorical variables. Most of the time when variables are categorical, *cross-classification tables* are used for at least part of the analysis. This chapter introduces some of the most common techniques for the analysis of cross-classifications for both nominal and ordinal variables. We begin our discussion in Section 8.1 by introducing some of the basic terminology for categorical data analysis. In particular, we define the concept of *statistical independence* in cross-classification tables. In Section 8.2, we introduce the *chi-square test of independence* for determining whether two nominal variables are associated. We then discuss in Sections 8.3 and 8.4 how to describe the strength of the relationship between two nominal variables, using the *difference of proportions* for two dichotomous variables and *Goodman and Kruskal's tau* for the general case. In Section 8.5, we present two important measures of association for ordinal variables, *gamma* and *Kendall's tau-b*, and a test of their significance follows in Section 8.6.

8.1 Cross-Classification Tables

One of the most useful tools for the bivariate or multivariate analysis of nominal and ordinal data is the **cross-classification table**. Such a table can be constructed when the observations in a sample have been classified according to their values on two or more categorical variables. Cross-classifications are usually presented in two-dimensional tables, each row representing a category of one variable and each column representing a category of the other variable. Each unique combination of categories of the variables is represented by a cell in the table.

Example 8.1 A number of sociologists have reported that racial prejudice varies according to religious group. Greeley (1974) found white Catholics to be less racially prejudiced than Protestants, and members of theologically liberal Protestant groups seem to be less prejudiced than those from the more conservative denominations. Other studies have found that Jews and the nonreligious may be the least prejudiced of all. We can examine this relationship by using the 1980 General Social Survey (GSS), which includes data on respondents' religious preferences as well as a number of questions about racial attitudes.

We can classify religious preference into four major categories: (a) Liberal Protestant, encompassing the theologically more liberal groups such as Presbyterians, Episcopalians, Methodists, and Congregationalists; (b) Conservative Protestant, consisting of conservative and fundamentalist denominations and sects such as Baptists and Pentacostals; (c) Catholic; and (d) None,* including those with no religious preference. As an indicator of racial prejudice, we use the survey question, "Do you think there should be laws against marriages between Blacks and Whites?" which had the response categories "yes" and "no." Table 8.1 shows the results of the cross-classification of these two variables for the 1980 GSS white respondents.

Table 8.1 Attitude Toward Laws Against Racial Intermarriage, by Religious Preference Type (1980 GSS White Respondents)

| | | RELIGIOUS PREFERENCE | | | | ROW TOTAL |
		Liberal Protestant	Conservative Protestant	Catholic	None	
ATTITUDE	Favor	103	182	80	16	381
	Oppose	187	238	286	74	785
COLUMN TOTAL		290	420	366	90	1,166

In examining the data in Table 8.1, we can see that there are 1,166 observations (respondents), all classified according to their values on both religious preference and attitude toward racial intermarriage. There are 103 individuals in the sample who are Liberal Protestants who favor laws prohibiting racial intermarriage, and 187 Liberal Protestants who oppose such laws, for example. In all, there are 381 respondents who favor legal bans on intermarriage and 785 who oppose them. This same set of individuals consists of 290 Liberal Protestants, 420 Conservative Protestants, 366 Catholics, and 90 respondents classified in the "None" category on religious preference. ■

There are a few conventions in presenting or describing cross-classification tables. First, tables are often identified by their size, in terms of their numbers of rows and columns. The number of rows (denoted by r) is given first, followed by the

*Jews were eliminated from this analysis because of the small number of cases in the sample. In addition, all other religious-preference responses were excluded.

number of columns (denoted by c). Table 8.1 is said to be a 2×4 (read "2 by 4") table, meaning two rows and four columns. The product of the numbers of rows and columns gives the number of cells in the table. The row totals and the column totals are called *marginal frequencies* or simply *marginals*. The two sets of marginals represent the univariate frequency distributions on the row variable and the column variable, respectively. The collection of marginal frequencies for a variable is called its *marginal distribution*. Just as there are both sample and population distributions in the univariate case, so there are both sample and population distributions for bivariate cross-classifications and their associated marginal distributions. For example, the sample marginal distribution for religious preference in Table 8.1 is the set of marginal frequencies (290, 420, 366, 90). The total sample size is the sum of all cell frequencies or, alternatively, the sum of the marginals for either the rows or the columns.

Cross-classifications are often used as a first step in detecting relationships between variables. They help answer such questions as "Does political conservatism vary by political party affiliation?" "How is marital status related to mental health?" "Are adolescents in different social class levels equally likely to have experienced premarital sex?" "Is there regional variation in the attitudes of people about federal aid toward education?" In the remainder of this section, we consider some descriptive procedures for summarizing the frequencies in a cross-classification table as the next step in investigating the association between two categorical variables.

Percentage Comparisons

In order to interpret the data found in Example 8.1, we need a way of describing how (if at all) the attitudes of members of the religious groups differ. To make comparisons among the groups, we can convert the frequencies to percentages within each column, as shown in Table 8.2. For example, of 366 Catholics in the sample, 80 or 21.9% favor the legal prohibition of interracial marriage, compared to 43.3% (182 out of 420) of Conservative Protestants, 35.5% (103 out of 290) of Liberal Protestants, and 17.8% (16 out of 90) of the "no preference" group. The column totals in Table 8.1 are used as the basis of these percentage calculations. Thus, the percentage comparisons favor the interpretation that the nonreligiously affiliated and Catholics are less likely to be prejudiced than Protestants, with Liberal Protestants less prejudiced than Conservative Protestants.

Table 8.2

Attitude Toward Laws Against Racial Intermarriage by Religious Preference Type: Percentages

| | | RELIGIOUS PREFERENCE | | | |
		Liberal Protestant	Conservative Protestant	Catholic	None
ATTITUDE	Favor	35.5	43.3	21.9	17.8
	Oppose	64.5	56.7	78.1	82.2
TOTAL PERCENTAGE		100.0	100.0	100.0	100.0
SAMPLE SIZE		290	420	366	90

We refer to the four sets of percentages for the different religious categories as the *conditional distributions* on the variable, attitude toward interracial marriage. For example, the conditional distribution on this variable for Conservative Protestants is the set of percentages (43.3, 56.7) for the responses favor and oppose, respectively.

In a similar way, it is possible to compute conditional distributions on religious affiliation for each attitude category. Then each row would contain a percentage distribution. The first row would indicate, for example, what percentages of those who favor antimiscegenation laws are Catholic, Liberal Protestant, and so on. In this example, though, we would probably be more interested in comparing attitudes among religious groups than in comparing the religious distributions of the separate attitude categories. Therefore, we have computed conditional distributions within columns only.

One other way in which it is sometimes informative to report percentages is over all cells in the table, using the total sample size as the base. To illustrate, out of the 1,166 individuals sampled, 80 people or 6.9% are classified in the cell (Catholic, favor), 286 people or 24.5% are classified in the cell (Catholic, oppose), and so forth. This type of percentage distribution (often referred to as the sample *joint distribution* of the variables) is useful for comparing the relative frequencies of occurrences for combinations of variable levels.

There are certain considerations to keep in mind when constructing percentage cross-classification tables. First, one should compute percentages within the categories of the independent variable. If one makes the independent variable the column variable (listing its categories across the top of the table) and the dependent variable the row variable (listing its categories down the left side of the table), this means that one computes percentages within each column. Each cell frequency is divided by the column total and the result is multiplied by 100. The sum of the cell percentages within columns is then 100, apart from slight variations due to rounding.

Second, one should give the table a title that specifies the variables that are cross-classified, and any other relevant information for understanding the table. In addition, the two variables and each of their categories should be clearly labeled, so that a person can read the table without having to refer to variable definitions elsewhere.

Third, the base frequencies for the percentages in the table should always be included in the table, so that a person can recompute the frequencies in the cells if needed, and so that one can judge how stable the percentages are likely to be (10% of 1,000 has less sampling error than 10% of 10).

Independence and Dependence

Whether members of different religious groups vary in their attitudes about racial intermarriage is a matter of whether there is an association between the two variables. A question such as "Is one's religious affiliation related to one's racial attitudes?" is best answered with reference to the concepts of statistical independence and dependence.

Statistical Independence and Dependence

Two categorical variables are *statistically independent* if the population conditional distributions on one of them are identical for each of the levels of the other.

Variables are *statistically dependent* if the conditional distributions are not identical.

In other words, two variables are statistically independent if the percentage of population observations classified in any given level of one variable is the same for each level of the other variable. In Table 8.2, the four conditional distributions are not identical. For example, there is a difference of 21.4% in the percentages of Conservative Protestants and Catholics who favor laws against racial intermarriage. If the observations summarized there represented the entire population of interest, then the variables would be statistically dependent in that population. An example of a (population) cross-classification table corresponding to independence is given in Table 8.3. In that table, the percentage of people in the Favor category does not depend on which religious group they are in—it is 30% in each case (verify). The conditional distribution on attitude consists of the percentages (30, 70) for all religious affiliations. In other words, the probability that a person favors laws against intermarriage would be the same for all religious affiliations, and hence attitude is independent of religious affiliation.

Table 8.3   Cross-Classification of Population Measurements Exhibiting Statistical Independence

		RELIGIOUS PREFERENCE				TOTAL
		Liberal Protestant	Conservative Protestant	Catholic	None	
ATTITUDE	Favor	750	1,200	900	150	3,000
	Oppose	1,750	2,800	2,100	350	7,000
TOTAL		2,500	4,000	3,000	500	10,000

Statistical independence is a symmetric property between two variables. That is, if the conditional distributions within columns are identical, then so are the conditional distributions within rows. In Table 8.3, for example, the conditional distribution within each of the two rows equals (25%, 40%, 30%, 5%).

8.2 Chi-Square Test of Independence

We will now specifically treat the data in Example 8.1 (Tables 8.1 and 8.2) as *sample* data from some population of interest. We might then wonder, "Could the observed percentage differences among religious groups be due to sampling variation?" In other words, is it a realistic hypothesis that attitude is independent of religious affiliation in the entire population from which the sample was drawn? We observed large differences in the sample conditional distributions summarized in Table 8.2, but we might wonder whether those sample differences are the result of sampling variation. Even if the variables were independent in the population, we would not expect to observe exact independence in the sample due to sampling variability, so we need a statistical test to answer these questions.

The *chi-square test* is designed to test for independence between two nominal variables. As described here, it is appropriate for random samples or stratified random samples in which the categories of one variable are the strata. The sample size must also be large, in a certain sense to be described below. The hypotheses for the chi-square test are H_0: The variables are statistically independent, and H_a: The variables are statistically dependent.

Expected Frequencies The chi-square test is based on a comparison between the frequencies that are observed in the cells of the cross-classification table and those that we would expect to observe if the null hypothesis of independence were true.

Notation

Let f_o denote the observed frequency in a cell of the table.

Let f_e denote the frequency expected in that cell if the variables were independent.

To illustrate, the value of f_o for the cell in the upper left-hand corner of Table 8.1 is 103. The expected frequencies are the cell entries that would have exactly the same row and column marginals as the observed frequencies, but that would represent independence. A rule for calculating the f_e terms is given in the next box.

Calculation of Expected Frequency

The expected frequency f_e for a cell equals the product of the row and column totals for that cell, divided by the total sample size.

For illustration of this rule, consider the cell in Table 8.1 corresponding to the Catholic religion and the Favor attitude category. Its expected frequency is $(381)(366)/1,166$, the product of the row and column totals divided by the overall sample size. To see why this rule makes sense, note that in the entire sample, 381 out of 1,166 people (32.7%) favor laws against interracial marriage. So, if the variables were independent, we would expect 32.7% of those in each religious category to favor such laws. In particular, we would expect 32.7% of the 366 people who are Catholic to be classified in the Favor category. In other words, the expected frequency for the cell is

$$f_e = \left(\frac{381}{1,166}\right)366 = .327(366) = 119.6$$

The expected frequencies for the remainder of the table are worked out in the same way. For example, for the cell corresponding to the Catholic conditional distribution and the attitude Oppose, the expected frequency is

$$f_e = (785)(366)/1,166 = 246.4$$

In Table 8.4, the expected frequencies are shown in parentheses next to the corresponding observed frequencies.

Table 8.4 Attitude by Religious Preference, with Expected Frequencies in Parentheses

| | | \multicolumn{4}{c}{RELIGIOUS PREFERENCE} | TOTAL |
		Liberal Protestant	Conservative Protestant	Catholic	None	
ATTITUDE	Favor	103 (94.8)	182 (137.2)	80 (119.6)	16 (29.4)	381
	Oppose	187 (195.2)	238 (282.8)	286 (246.4)	74 (60.6)	785
SAMPLE SIZE		290	420	366	90	1,166

The test statistic for the test of independence helps to summarize how close the expected frequencies are to the observed frequencies. The form of the test statistic, symbolized by χ^2 and referred to as the (Pearson) *chi-square statistic*, is

$$\chi^2 = \sum \frac{(f_o - f_e)^2}{f_e}$$

where the summation is taken over all the cells in the cross-classification. That is, for each cell we square the difference between the observed and expected frequencies, and we divide that square by the expected frequency. After calculating this term for every cell, we sum them to get the χ^2 statistic. If H_0 is true, the f_o and f_e values should be relatively close for each cell, and the χ^2 value should be relatively small. If H_0 is false, at least some of the f_o and f_e values should not be very close, leading to large $(f_o - f_e)^2$ values and a large test statistic. Thus, the larger the χ^2 value, the more evidence there is against the null hypothesis of independence.

Substituting the f_o and f_e values from Table 8.4 into the formula for the χ^2 test statistic, we get

$$\chi^2 = \sum \frac{(f_o - f_e)^2}{f_e}$$

$$= \frac{(103 - 94.8)^2}{94.8} + \frac{(182 - 137.2)^2}{137.2} + \frac{(80 - 119.6)^2}{119.6} + \frac{(16 - 29.4)^2}{29.4}$$

$$+ \frac{(187 - 195.2)^2}{195.2} + \frac{(238 - 282.8)^2}{282.8} + \frac{(286 - 246.4)^2}{246.4} + \frac{(74 - 60.6)^2}{60.6}$$

$$= 0.71 + 14.63 + 13.11 + 6.11 + 0.34 + 7.10 + 6.36 + 2.96$$

$$= 51.3$$

We shall next consider how to interpret the magnitude of this χ^2 value.

The Chi-Square Distribution   Naturally, we need a gauge of how large χ^2 must be before we can feel confident that H_0 is false. This can be determined from the sampling distribution of the χ^2 statistic. If H_0 is true and if the sample size is sufficiently large, the sampling distribution of χ^2 is approximately the *chi-square probability distribution*. The name of the test and the symbol for the test statistic are derived from the name of the sampling distribution. The chi-square distribution is used in many important statistical procedures in the social sciences. Figure 8.1 is a sketch of a chi-square distribution. Some of its main properties are described beneath the figure.

Fig. 8.1 The Chi-Square Distribution

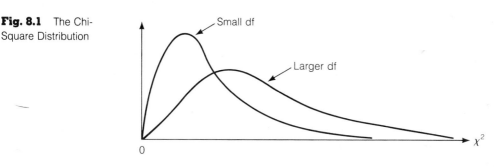

1. It is skewed to the right.
2. It is concentrated on the positive part of the real line. It is impossible to get a negative χ^2 test statistic value, since it involves a sum of squared differences divided by positive expected frequencies. The minimum possible value, $\chi^2 = 0$, occurs when the observed frequency in each cell equals the expected frequency for that cell, that is, when the variables are completely independent in the sample.
3. The exact shape of the distribution depends on the *degrees of freedom*. For the test of independence, the formula for the degrees of freedom is df = $(r - 1)(c - 1)$. For a 2 × 4 table, for example, df = $(2 - 1)(4 - 1) = 1(3) = 3$.
   The mean and standard deviation of the chi-square distribution depend on the value of df. Larger table dimensions produce larger values for df = $(r - 1)(c - 1)$. Since larger tables yield more terms in the summation for the χ^2 statistic, the values of the test statistic also tend to be larger and more variable. Thus, the distribution tends to shift to the right and become more disperse for larger values of df. In fact, the mean of the chi-square distribution is exactly the value of df, and the standard deviation equals $\sqrt{2(df)}$. As df increases, the shape of the chi-square curve more closely resembles a normal curve.
4. The χ^2 values corresponding to various P-values are listed in Table C in the back of the text. For example, Table 8.4 is of size 2 × 4, so df = 3. The χ^2 value of 7.815 corresponds to $P = .05$ when df = 3, whereas the χ^2 value of 11.341 corresponds to $P = .01$. In general, since large values of χ^2 are incompatible with H_0, we define P to be the probability, when H_0 is true, of getting a value at least as large as the observed χ^2 (see Figure 8.2). That is, P is the right-hand tail area

under the chi-square curve above the observed x^2 value. The larger the table size (and thus, the larger the value of df), the larger the x^2 value needs to be to achieve a certain P-value.

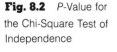

Fig. 8.2 P-Value for the Chi-Square Test of Independence

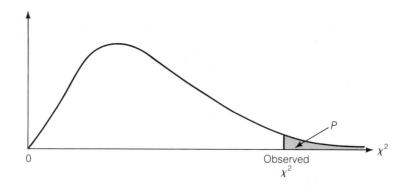

Example 8.2   If we assume that the sample cross-classified in Tables 8.1 and 8.4 was randomly selected, then we can test H_0: Statistical independence of religious preference and attitude about intermarriage, against H_a: Statistical dependence of religious preference and intermarriage attitude.

We obtained a test statistic value of $x^2 = 51.3$ for these data. In Table C, for df = 3 the largest value listed is $x^2 = 16.268$, which yields a P-value of $P = .001$. Since $x^2 = 51.3$ is greater than 16.268, we know that $P < .001$. Thus, we would reject the null hypothesis of independence at the $\alpha = .001$ level, and at even much smaller levels if we had more complete tables. In fact, the SPSS^X computer package calculates this probability to be less than .0001. In other words, there is very strong evidence that a person's racial attitude is associated with which religious group he or she belongs to. We should keep in mind, though, that this is a *statistical* dependence and not necessarily a *causal* dependence. We are not implying that a person's religious preference determines that person's racial attitudes. Association does not imply causation (see, for instance, the data in Problem 1).   ∎

The df term in a chi-square test may be interpreted in the following manner: If one knows the two sets of marginal frequencies and the observed frequencies in a rectangular block of size $(r - 1) \times (c - 1)$ in the table, then the other cell frequencies are automatically determined. For given marginal frequencies, the frequencies in a block of just df $= (r - 1)(c - 1)$ cells of the table determine the whole table. To illustrate, in Table 8.4, suppose we were given the two sets of marginal frequencies and the three frequencies 103, 182, and 80 in the upper left-hand part (of size 1 × 3) of the table (see Table 8.5). Then, since 103 of the 290 Liberal Protestants are classified Favor, the other 187 must be classified Oppose. Similarly, since the total of the Favor row is 381, and since we know that the first three cells contain a total of 365 (103 + 182 + 80) subjects, then we know that the remaining cell must have 16 (381 − 365) observations. Using this and the fact that the last column has a total of

90 observations, we conclude that there must be 74 observations in the second cell in that column. Similarly, the other unknown cell entries can be determined from the original three cells and the marginal distributions. It follows that once the marginal frequencies are fixed, a block of only $(r - 1) \times (c - 1)$ cell entries is free to vary, since these cell entries determine the remaining ones. The degrees of freedom value equals the number of cells in this block, or $df = (r - 1)(c - 1)$.

Table 8.5

Illustration of Degrees of Freedom

	LIBERAL PROTESTANT	CONSERVATIVE PROTESTANT	CATHOLIC	NONE	TOTAL
Favor	103	182	80		381
Opposes					785
Total	290	420	366	90	1,166

Sample Size Requirements

We complete this section with a few remarks about the use and misuse of the chi-square test of independence. First, we mentioned earlier that the chi-square probability distribution is appropriate as the sampling distribution of the χ^2 statistic only if the sample size is sufficiently large. A rough guideline for this requirement is as follows: For 2×2 tables, the expected frequency f_e should be at least 5 in each cell. If this is not fulfilled, **Fisher's exact test** should be used (see Blalock, 1979, pp. 292–297; Siegel, 1956, pp. 96–104). This procedure gives the exact P-value for the table. The calculation of Fisher's exact test is somewhat more complicated than that of the chi-square test, and we omit it in this book. The results of this test are available as an option in the CROSSTABS routine in the SPSS^X (SPSS Inc., 1983) computer package.

For larger tables, f_e should be at least 5 in most (say, 75%) of the cells, and f_e should exceed 1 in all other cells. If this condition is not fulfilled, it may be necessary to omit one or more categories of one or both variables. Alternatively, we might combine categories, if it makes sense, so that we have the necessary expected frequencies in each cell. Neither of these alternatives is really desirable, since both involve a reduction in the amount of information available. If practically possible, we might obtain a larger sample so that the conditions are fulfilled for the original classification. Another alternative is to perform an analog of Fisher's exact test for the $r \times c$ table (see Agresti and Wackerly, 1977). This test usually requires the use of a computer. Both this exact test for $r \times c$ tables and Fisher's exact test for 2×2 tables utilize a sampling distribution of all possible χ^2 values corresponding to tables that have the same marginal distributions as the observed table. When n is small, this sampling distribution is highly discrete, and is not well approximated by the continuous chi-square curve.

2×2 Tables and Difference of Proportions

For the special case of a 2×2 table, the chi-square test of independence is equivalent to testing the equality of two proportions, π_1 and π_2. Specifically, suppose that the 2×2 table represents the responses of two populations on a dichotomous variable with possible responses A and B (see Table 8.6). The responses could be, for example, (college education, no college), (support president, do not support

8 MEASURING ASSOCIATION FOR CATEGORICAL VARIABLES

Table 8.6
2 × 2 Table for Comparing Two Populations on a Dichotomous Response

| RESPONSE | PROPORTION MAKING EACH RESPONSE | |
	Population 1	Population 2
A	π_1	π_2
B	$1 - \pi_1$	$1 - \pi_2$
Total	1.0	1.0

president), or (yes, no) on some opinion question. Let π_1 represent the proportion of population 1 making response A, and let π_2 represent the proportion of population 2 making response A. Then $(1 - \pi_1)$ and $(1 - \pi_2)$ are the proportions making response B for the two populations. If the response is statistically independent of the populations considered, then $\pi_1 = \pi_2$; that is, the probability of making response A does not depend on whether a person is from population 1 or population 2. The null hypothesis of independence in the chi-square test corresponds to H_0: $\pi_1 = \pi_2$ in this case.

The inferential operation of obtaining a confidence interval for the difference $(\pi_2 - \pi_1)$ between two proportions was considered in Section 7.1. In that section, we used the confidence interval for $(\pi_2 - \pi_1)$ as a method of comparing two groups on a dichotomous variable, but we did not consider in detail the z test of the null hypothesis H_0: $\pi_1 = \pi_2$. Also, in Section 7.1 we did not discuss the problem of comparing two groups on a nominal scale with *more than* two categories. We have seen in this section that the null hypothesis that two groups have identical distributions on a nominal response variable can be tested using the chi-square test of independence. Thus, the procedure for comparing two groups on a nominal variable is a special case of the chi-square test in which one of the classifications (the one defining the groups to be compared) has only two levels. For example, we could compare Democrats and Republicans with respect to their distributions over four categories of religious affiliation by conducting a chi-square test on a 2 × 4 cross-classification of frequencies.

Misuses It should be apparent by now that the value of the χ^2 statistic depends on the way the categories are defined for the two variables. If religion were classified as Protestant and non-Protestant, the basic conclusion of the chi-square test might be different than if the categories were Protestant, Jewish, Catholic, None and Other, or Methodist, Presbyterian, Episcopalian, Baptist, Catholic, Lutheran, and so forth. In reporting the result of a chi-square test, therefore, it is important to mention the ways in which the variables were classified.

Finally, we should mention that the chi-square test is one of the most frequently misused statistical tests. One of the most common misuses is to apply the test when the expected frequencies are too small. Another misuse is to compute the χ^2 statistic for percentages or numbers other than the actual observed frequencies and their corresponding expected frequencies. The chi-square test is sometimes mistakenly applied to classifications in which some members are classified in more than one category, as when each person is asked to indicate which factors (one or more) are most responsible for economic inflation. In addition, χ^2 is often applied as a test for detecting association when the variables are ordinal or interval. In these cases it would usually be better to use stronger statistical procedures that use the additional information given by the higher level of measurement. The chi-square test can be computed very easily using computer packages such as SPSS^X, regardless of whether the test is justified. It is the responsibility of the researcher to check that the assumptions required for use of that test are satisfied.

The five elements of the chi-square test of independence are summarized in Table 8.7.

Table 8.7

The Five Elements of the Chi-Square Test of Independence

1. Assumptions:	Two nominal variables
	Random sample or stratified random sample
	2 × 2 table: $f_e \geq 5$ in all cells
	Larger tables: $f_e \geq 5$ in at least 75% of cells
	$f_e \geq 1$ in remaining cells
2. Hypotheses:	H_0: Statistical independence of variables
	H_a: Statistical dependence of variables
3. Test statistic:	$\chi^2 = \sum \frac{(f_o - f_e)^2}{f_e}$, where $f_e = \dfrac{(\text{Row total})(\text{Column total})}{\text{Total sample size}}$
4. P-Value:	P = right-hand tail area beyond observed χ^2 value, for chi-square distribution with df $= (r - 1)(c - 1)$
5. Conclusion:	Reject H_0 at α-level if $P < \alpha$

8.3 Measuring Association: 2 × 2 Tables

We observed in Section 6.7 that if a null hypothesis appears to be false, it is important to assess how false. In the context of bivariate analyses, if two variables appear to be statistically dependent, it is informative to provide a descriptive measure of the *degree* of the dependence. Such a measure helps us to determine if the association is a strong, important one, or if it is statistically significant but relatively weak and unimportant.

Measure of Association

A *measure of association* is a statistic that summarizes some aspect of the degree of the statistical dependence between two or more variables.

In this section and the next, we study measures of association for cross-classifications of nominal variables.

Difference of Proportions

Let us first consider what is meant by *strong* association relative to *weak* association. Tables 8.8 and 8.9 show two hypothetical sets of frequencies for cross-classifications relating political party preference to occupational level. The weakest possible association is represented by Table 8.8, which displays statistical independence. Both white-collar and blue-collar workers are 60% Democrats and 40% Republicans; both Democrats and Republicans are 50% white-collar workers and

Table 8.8

Cross-Classification of
Political Party by
Occupational Level,
Showing No Association

		OCCUPATIONAL LEVEL		TOTAL
		White-collar	Blue-collar	
POLITICAL PARTY	Democrat	300	300	600
	Republican	200	200	400
TOTAL		500	500	1,000

50% blue-collar workers. The strongest possible association is represented by Table 8.9, in which a person's classification on one of the variables is completely dependent on the classification on the other variable. All white-collar workers are Republicans; all blue-collar workers are Democrats. For these individuals, in other words, knowledge of a person's occupational level is equivalent to knowledge of his or her political party preference. A measure of association describes how similar a particular table is to the tables representing the strongest and weakest associations.

Table 8.9

Cross-Classification of
Political Party by
Occupational Level,
Showing Maximum
Association

		OCCUPATIONAL LEVEL		TOTAL
		White-collar	Blue-collar	
POLITICAL PARTY	Democrat	0	500	500
	Republican	500	0	500
TOTAL		500	500	1,000

By convention, it is usually required that a measure of association (**a**) take a minimum absolute value (usually 0) for a table such as Table 8.8, in which there is the weakest possible association; and (**b**) take a maximum absolute value (usually 1) for a table such as Table 8.9, in which there is the strongest possible association.

Many 2×2 tables summarize the responses of two groups on a dichotomous variable. In such cases, an easily interpretable measure of association is the difference between the proportions for the two groups at a given response level. For example, we could consider the difference between the proportions of blue-collar workers and white-collar workers who classify themselves as Democrats. For Table 8.8, this difference is

$$\frac{300}{500} - \frac{300}{500} = 0$$

The population difference of proportions is 0 whenever the conditional distributions are identical—that is, when the variables are independent. For Table 8.9, the difference is

$$\frac{500}{500} - \frac{0}{500} = 1.0$$

This is the maximum possible absolute value for the difference.

As we observed in Section 7.1, the difference of proportions must fall between -1 and $+1$. The stronger the association, the larger the difference is in absolute value.

The increase in this measure as the degree of association increases is illustrated by the following cross-classifications:

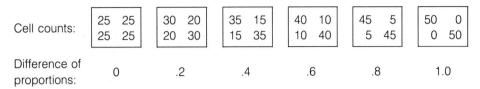

Cell counts:	25 25	30 20	35 15	40 10	45 5	50 0
	25 25	20 30	15 35	10 40	5 45	0 50

Difference of proportions: 0   .2   .4   .6   .8   1.0

The formula for a confidence interval for the difference between two proportions was given in Section 7.1.

Chi-Square and Association

Some people mistakenly assume that a large value for the χ^2 statistic in the test of independence implies that the variables have a strong association. The χ^2 statistic provides a measure of how close the observed frequencies are to the frequencies that would be expected if the variables were independent. Note, however, that this statistic merely indicates *how certain* we can be that the variables are dependent, not *how strong* that dependence is. Large χ^2 values can be obtained for weak associations, if the sample size is large. For example, consider cross-classifications A, B, and C in Table 8.10. The association in each table is very weak, in the sense that the conditional distribution for white-collar workers on party preference (49% Democrat, 51% Republican) is nearly identical to the conditional distribution for the blue-collar workers (51% Democrat, 49% Republican). All three tables show exactly the same degree of association, with the difference between the proportions of blue-collar workers and white-collar workers who classify themselves as Democrats being 0.51 − 0.49 = 0.02 in each table.

Table 8.10 Cross-Classifications of Political Party with Occupational Level

	A			B			C		
	White-collar	Blue-collar	Total	White-collar	Blue-collar	Total	White-collar	Blue-collar	Total
Democrat	49	51	100	98	102	200	4,900	5,100	10,000
Republican	51	49	100	102	98	200	5,100	4,900	10,000
Total	100	100	200	200	200	400	10,000	10,000	20,000
	$\chi^2 = .08$			$\chi^2 = .16$			$\chi^2 = 8.0$		
	$P < .80$			$P < .70$			$P < .01$		

For the sample of size 200 in cross-classification A, χ^2 equals only .08, leading to a P-value of $P < .80$. For the sample of size 400 in cross-classification B, $\chi^2 = .16$, for which $P < .70$. So, doubling the frequencies in the cells leads to a doubling of the chi-square statistic. Similarly, for the sample size of 20,000 (100 times as large as $n = 200$) in cross-classification C, $\chi^2 = 8.0$ (100 times as large as $\chi^2 = .08$) and $P <$

.01. Thus, for a particular assignment of percentages to the cells of a cross-classification table, the value of the χ^2 statistic is directly proportional to the sample size. As with other test statistics we have used, the larger the χ^2 statistic, the smaller the P-value and the more sure we can be that the null hypothesis is false. However, one can obtain a very small P-value for a relatively weak association when the sample size is large, as illustrated by cross-classification C.*

Thus, there are at least two questions that should always be addressed in analyzing a table from sample data. First, we ask how strong the association is between the two variables in the observed data. For this we use a measure of association such as a difference of proportions. Second, we ask how likely it is that we could obtain at least the observed degree of association in a sample, if in fact the variables are independent in the population. For this question of whether we have strong evidence that an association exists in the population, we use a significance test, chi-square in this case.

Other Measures for 2 × 2 Tables

The difference of proportions is the most easily interpretable measure of association for most 2 × 2 tables. However, there are several other measures that are occasionally used. The **phi-squared** measure has sample value

$$\hat{\phi}^2 = \frac{\chi^2}{n}$$

This measure falls in the range from 0 to 1 (see Problem 32), with a population value of 0 corresponding to independence. It is a special case (for 2 × 2 tables) of the *Goodman and Kruskal tau* measure to be defined in the next section. The measure *Yule's Q* is a special case of the *gamma* measure to be defined in Section 8.5. The *odds ratio*, a measure that is particularly useful for describing properties of multidimensional cross-classifications of several variables, is thoroughly discussed in Section 15.4.

**8.4
Measuring
Association:
r × c Tables**

**Proportional
Reduction in
Error Measures**

Before introducing a measure of association for cross-classification tables larger than 2 × 2, we need to discuss a concept that unifies the treatment of measuring association for nominal, ordinal, and interval variables. For the measures that are formulated according to this concept, the degree of the association is described by how well one can make predictions about the values for members on one variable based on their values on the other variable. For example, we might say that race and attitude toward capital punishment are highly associated if race is a good predictor of attitude; that is, if based on classification on race, we can make much better predictions about people's attitudes toward capital punishment than if we did not know their race. Different measures of association based on this concept vary in the way the predictions are made and in the way the goodness of the predictions is described.

*This corresponds to the observation in Example 6.14 that a small P-value may occur in testing H_0: $\mu = \mu_0$ when $\bar{Y}$ is not very different from μ_0 in practical terms, especially when n is large.

We refer to the variable about which the predictions are made as the *dependent variable*.* The variable used to make the predictions is called the *independent variable*. The measures of association we discuss can be defined in terms of a comparison of two summaries of prediction error. One summary refers to errors that are made in using the independent variable to predict the dependent variable. This is compared to an analogous summary of the prediction errors made in predicting measurements on the dependent variable *without* using the corresponding measurements on the independent variable. The measure is defined as the proportion fewer errors made when information on the independent variable is used instead of ignored in making the predictions. In other words, the magnitude of the measure of association may be interpreted as the *proportional reduction in error*.

For example, suppose that we make 100 errors in predicting attitude toward capital punishment when our prediction rule is not based on the values of the sample on other variables. Suppose also that 70 errors are made for that sample when information on the independent variable, race, is used in predicting attitude. Then there are 30% fewer prediction errors made when the independent variable is utilized in making the predictions, so the degree of association can be summarized by the number .30.

The four elements of a measure of association for nominal variables having a proportional reduction in error interpretation are as follows:

1. *A rule for predicting the classification of each member on the dependent variable, ignoring information about the classification of that member on the independent variable.* These predictions are based on the marginal distribution of the dependent variable. For example, predictions about individuals' attitudes toward capital punishment must be based just on the relative numbers of individuals favoring and opposing it. We refer to the rule for making these predictions as Rule 1.

2. *A rule for predicting the classification of each member on the dependent variable, using the information about the classification of that member on the independent variable.* These predictions using Rule 2 are based on the frequencies of observations in the various categories of the dependent variable *within* each level of the independent variable. For example, we might base predictions about an individual's attitude toward capital punishment on the frequency of individuals *of that person's race* favoring and opposing it.

3. *A definition of what is meant by a prediction error.* For nominal variables, an error consists of a misclassification of a member on the dependent variable—for instance, predicting that a person favors capital punishment when actually that person opposes it. The total number of times that the wrong category of the dependent variable is predicted using Rule 1 is denoted by E_1. The total number of classification errors using Rule 2 is denoted by E_2.

4. *The definition of the measure.* The difference between the total numbers of classification errors committed using the two rules is $E_1 - E_2$. There are $(E_1 - E_2)$

*The terminology of independent and dependent variables here is used as in Chapter 7, not in the sense of statistical dependence or independence.

fewer errors made when the independent variable is used in making the predictions, so $E_1 - E_2$ is the reduction in error obtained by using Rule 2 instead of Rule 1. The reduction in error is standardized by dividing by E_1. This yields the measure of association given by the proportional reduction in error (PRE),

$$PRE = \frac{E_1 - E_2}{E_1}$$

The PRE value describes how much better the predictions are using Rule 2 than using Rule 1. For example, PRE = .30 between race and attitude means that 30% fewer prediction errors on attitude are made using Rule 2 (with race as a predictor) than using Rule 1 (ignoring race in forming the predictions). The larger the relative reduction in error, the better the dependent variable can be predicted using the independent variable, and the stronger the association between the variables. The weakest possible association, PRE = 0, occurs when there is no reduction in error ($E_1 = E_2$) obtained by having the additional information about the members' classifications on the independent variable. In that case, the classification on the dependent variable is not associated with the classification on the independent variable. The strongest possible association, PRE = 1, occurs when $E_2 = 0$. In that case, the classification on one of the variables is completely associated with the classification on the other, in the sense that the classification of a member on the dependent variable can be predicted perfectly from the classification on the independent variable.

We next consider an example of a nominal measure of association having this type of PRE structure. It is usually referred to as *Goodman and Kruskal's tau,** or as the *concentration measure*.

Goodman and Kruskal's Tau   We shall define tau by describing each of the four elements of a PRE measure for this particular measure of association. To illustrate these elements, we refer to Example 8.1 concerning religious preference and attitude toward racial intermarriage (see Table 8.11). We treat attitude as the dependent variable and use tau to describe the degree to which it depends on religious preference for this 2 × 4 cross-classification.

Table 8.11   Cross-Classification Used to Illustrate Tau

| | | RELIGIOUS PREFERENCE | | | | TOTAL |
		Liberal Protestant	Conservative Protestant	Catholic	None	
ATTITUDE	Favor	103	182	80	16	381
	Oppose	187	238	286	74	785
TOTAL		290	420	366	90	1,166

*This measure was suggested by W. Allen Wallis to L. A. Goodman and W. Kruskal, and first appeared in an article by Goodman and Kruskal (1954).

Rule 1   The rule for predicting attitude without using religious preference is defined on the marginal distribution for that dependent variable. The frequencies for the levels (Favor, Oppose) are (381, 785). Tau is based on *proportional prediction* rules. To illustrate, since the proportion $381/1,166 = .3268$ of the sample is classified Favor, we guess a classification of Favor for that same proportion of the sample when we make our predictions. Since we have no other information on which to base our predictions about which of the 1,166 people are classified Favor, we would randomly select 381 of the 1,166 people and predict Favor for them. We would predict Oppose for the remaining 781 people.

Rule 2   Suppose now that we know the religious classification of each person. We again use the proportional prediction rule for predicting attitudes, but we do it for the conditional distribution of the dependent variable *within* each level of the independent variable. For example, we would predict Favor for a random sample of 103 of 290 Liberal Protestants, and predict Oppose for the other 187 Liberal Protestants. Thus, the proportions of predictions of the two different types on the dependent variable would now change according to the level of the independent variable.

Prediction Errors E_1 is the number of errors one would expect to make in predicting attitude for the 1,166 people without knowing their religious preferences. Now, 67.32% of the sample is classified Oppose. This is the probability of making an error when we predict that a person is classified Favor. Thus, when the prediction Favor is made for 381 randomly chosen individuals, the expected number of errors is $381(.6732) = 256.5$. In other words, we would expect to be wrong 67.32% of the time when we predict Favor. Similarly, $785(.3268) = 785(381/1,166) = 256.5$ is the expected number of errors in predicting Oppose for 785 people in the sample, since we would expect to be wrong with those predictions the same proportion of the time as there are Favor classifications. So,

$$E_1 = 256.5 + 256.5 = 513.0$$

is the total expected number of errors using Rule 1. E_2 is obtained in a similar manner by doing this calculation within each level of the independent variable, and then summing over the levels.* For example, the expected number of errors in making proportional predictions among Liberal Protestants is

$$187(103/290) + 103(187/290) = 132.8$$

For predictions within the other categories, the expected numbers of errors are

$$238(182/420) + 182(238/420) = 206.3 \quad \text{(Conservative Protestants)}$$
$$286(80/366) + 80(286/366) = 125.0 \quad \text{(Catholics)}$$
$$74(16/90) + 16(74/90) = 26.3 \quad \text{(None)}$$

---

*Notice that we do not actually go through the process of making individual predictions for either rule. Instead, we reason what the *expected* numbers of errors would be *if* we were to make the predictions.

Summing over the categories of religious affiliation yields the total expected number of errors using Rule 2:

$$E_2 = 132.8 + 206.3 + 125.0 + 26.3 = 490.4$$

Definition of Measure   Tau, denoted by τ, is defined to be the proportional reduction in error,

$$\tau = \frac{E_1 - E_2}{E_1}$$

for the proportional prediction rule. A sample value of the parameter τ is denoted by $\hat{\tau}$. For this example, there are $E_1 - E_2 = 513.0 - 490.4 = 22.6$ fewer expected prediction errors when one has the additional information on religious affiliation to help in making the predictions. Thus,

$$\hat{\tau} = \frac{513.0 - 490.4}{513.0} = \frac{22.6}{513.0} = .044$$

In other words, we would expect to make about 4.4% fewer errors in predicting attitude when we can utilize the information on religious preference. Equivalently, $(100 - 4.4)\% = 95.6\%$ as many errors are made when religious preference is used to predict attitude toward interracial marriage than when religious preference is unknown.

The general properties of tau (the population or sample version) are as follows:

1. $0 \leq \tau \leq 1$. E_2 is at least 0 but can be no larger than E_1, since predictions are at least as good overall when additional information on another classification is available. When $E_2 = 0$, $\tau = (E_1 - E_2)/E_1 = E_1/E_1 = 1$; when $E_2 = E_1$, $\tau = 0$.
2. $\tau = 0$ corresponds to independence. If the proportional allocation of the observations among the categories of the dependent variable is the same within each level of the independent variable, then the predictions about the dependent variable do not vary as the level of the independent variable changes. Hence, $E_1 = E_2$ and $\tau = 0$. The value $\tau = 0$ occurs for exactly the same set of tables for which $\chi^2 = 0$.
3. $\tau = 1$ when for each category of the independent variable, *all* the observations occur in one category of the dependent variable. For example, if the data in Example 8.1 had been classified as in Table 8.12, then we would have been able

Table 8.12   A Cross-Classification with $\tau = 1$ (Attitude Is Dependent Variable)

| | | RELIGIOUS PREFERENCE | | | | TOTAL |
		Liberal Protestant	Conservative Protestant	Catholic	None	
ATTITUDE	Favor	290	420	0	0	710
	Oppose	0	0	366	90	456
TOTAL		290	420	366	90	1,166

to predict attitude perfectly if we knew religious preference. To illustrate, all Liberal Protestants are classified Favor, so Rule 2 would have predicted Favor for all Liberal Protestants, leading to no prediction errors. It follows that $E_2 = 0$ and $\hat{\tau} = 1$. Attitude is then completely dependent on religion, in the sense that classification on attitude can be predicted without error based on the classification on religion.

4. The stronger the association, the larger the value of τ. Differences in values may be easily interpreted for PRE measures. For example, suppose that Y is a dependent variable and X_1 and X_2 are independent variables. Suppose also that $\tau = .30$ for Y and X_1 and $\tau = .15$ for Y and X_2. Then, Y and X_1 are twice as strongly related as Y and X_2, in the sense that there is twice the reduction in error when X_1 is used to predict Y as when X_2 is used to predict Y.

5. Tau may be applied to a cross-classification table of any dimensions $r \times c$, with any cell frequencies. It is most appropriate for nominal variables, since it does not assume an ordering of the categories of either classification.

6. For the 2×2 table, $\hat{\tau} = \hat{\phi}^2$. Thus, $\hat{\tau}$ can be considered a generalization to larger dimensions of the measure $\hat{\phi}^2 = \chi^2/n$ for 2×2 tables.* This property also implies that a PRE interpretation can be given to the magnitude of $\hat{\phi}^2$.

7. For a sufficiently large random sample, $\hat{\tau}$ has an approximately normal sampling distribution. It follows that a confidence interval for τ has the form $\hat{\tau} \pm z\hat{\sigma}_{\hat{\tau}}$, where $\hat{\sigma}_{\hat{\tau}}$ is the estimated standard error of $\hat{\tau}$. The formula for the standard error, which unfortunately is rather complicated, is given by Goodman and Kruskal (1972). The $\hat{\tau}$ measure and its standard error are printed out by the 4F program in the BMDP statistical computer package (Dixon, 1981). Since $\tau = 0$ is equivalent to independence of the variables, the null hypothesis H_0: $\tau = 0$ can be tested using the chi-square test of independence.

8. Tau is *asymmetric* for tables larger than 2×2. This means that the value of τ changes according to which variable is treated as the dependent variable. Variable X may be a better predictor of variable Y than Y is of X, as illustrated in Example 8.3.

Example 8.3 If we use attitude to predict religious preference in Table 8.11, we obtain

$$E_1 = 290\left(\frac{876}{1,166}\right) + 420\left(\frac{746}{1,166}\right) + 366\left(\frac{800}{1,166}\right) + 90\left(\frac{1,076}{1,166}\right) = 820.75$$

and

$$E_2 = \left[103\left(\frac{278}{381}\right) + 182\left(\frac{199}{381}\right) + 80\left(\frac{301}{381}\right) + 16\left(\frac{365}{381}\right)\right]$$
$$+ \left[187\left(\frac{598}{785}\right) + 238\left(\frac{547}{785}\right) + 286\left(\frac{499}{785}\right) + 74\left(\frac{711}{785}\right)\right] = 805.87$$

*However, for tables larger than 2×2, τ cannot be expressed in terms of the χ^2 statistic.

The term $290(876/1{,}166)$ in E_1 represents the expected number of errors when Liberal Protestant is predicted for a random sample of 290 of the 1,166 in the sample. The other terms have similar interpretations. Thus,

$$\hat{\tau} = (820.75 - 805.87)/820.75 = .018$$

meaning that belief provides only a 1.8% reduction in error as a predictor of religious preference, whereas we observed that religious preference provides a 4.4% reduction in error as a predictor of attitude. ■

Often, students wonder how large a measure such as τ needs to be before one can conclude that there is an important degree of association between two variables. There is no general response that can be given. In part, the answer depends on the discipline and the types of variables being considered. A value of $\tau = .2$ might be considered small for the purposes of an advertising agency investigating which variable (e.g., sex or race) has the greatest influence on whether a person buys a certain product. However, it would probably be quite large for most sociological studies. For example, suppose we are investigating the influence of several variables on the presence or absence of some mental illness. There may be few, if any, variables that are good enough indicators of the presence of mental illness to produce a τ-value as large as .2.

It is often an oversimplification to describe a table using a single value of a measure of association. One can often get a better "feel" for the degree of association in a table by making percentage comparisons across categories of the independent variable, in addition to computing $\hat{\tau}$. In our example, the percentage of Conservative Protestants who favor laws against interracial marriage is greater than the percentage of "None's" who favor such laws by 25.5% and greater than the percentage of Catholics by a difference of 21.5%. For a variable such as this, in which we would not expect wide variations, these percentage differences are large and important.

Other Nominal Measures

Another PRE measure for nominal variables, *lambda*, is defined in Problem 31 at the end of the chapter. It is based on a somewhat different prediction rule. The main difference between its properties and those of tau is that lambda may equal 0 even when the variables are not statistically independent.

Other nominal measures of association that have been proposed over the years are available in computer packages such as $SPSS^X$, BMDP, and the SAS System. Some of these measures are based directly on the value of the χ^2 test statistic. The most popular of these are *Cramér's V^2*, defined by

$$V^2 = \frac{\chi^2}{n[\min(r,\,c) - 1]}$$

where $\min(r,\,c)$ denotes the minimum of r and c, and *Pearson's contingency coefficient*, defined by

$$C = \sqrt{\frac{\chi^2}{\chi^2 + n}}$$

Cramér's V^2 simplifies to the ϕ^2 measure for 2×2 tables. These measures do not have PRE interpretations. Neither measure is reliable for comparisons between tables of different dimensions, and neither is intuitively meaningful, so it is preferable to use τ and percentage comparisons.

One other measure that has become somewhat popular in recent years is the *entropy measure*, sometimes referred to as the *uncertainty coefficient* (see Problem 41). This measure is also not simple to interpret, but it has some useful properties for multidimensional tables. See Theil (1970) for details.

8.5 Measuring Association for Ordinal Variables

We now turn our attention to the bivariate analysis of ordinal variables. Ordinal scales have high values and low values. When ordinal variables are associated, it is natural to consider whether subjects who are classified at the high end of one ordinal scale tend also to be classified at the high end of the other scale. Ordinal measures of association describe the extent to which the ranking of a subject on one variable is statistically related to the ranking of the subject on the other variable.

Common Properties of Ordinal Measures

Among the several ordinal measures of association that have been proposed are *gamma*, *Kendall's tau-b* and *tau-c*, *Spearman's rho-b* and *rho-c*, and *Somers' d*. All of these measures are quite similar in their basic purposes and characteristics. We now discuss some of their common properties.

1. Ordinal measures of association take on values between -1 and $+1$. When the variables are at least ordinal in level, it is possible to distinguish between two types of association—positive and negative. *Positive association* between variables X and Y results when a member ranked high on X tends also to be ranked high on Y, and those ranked low on X tend to be ranked low on Y. For example, we might expect an ordinal measure of association to be positive for variables such as degree of political conservatism and degree of social conservatism. *Negative association* occurs when a member ranked high on X tends to be ranked low on Y, and vice versa. This might result for variables such as degree of political conservatism and willingness to cut the defense budget. We would expect that persons ranked high in political conservatism might tend to be ranked low in willingness to reduce the national defense budget.

2. The population values of ordinal measures equal 0 if the variables are statistically independent. If an ordinal measure equals 0, however, the variables need not be statistically independent. For example, a dependence relationship for which all ordinal measures equal 0 will be illustrated in Table 8.16.

3. The stronger the relationship, the larger the absolute value of the measure. A value of .6 or $-.6$ represents a stronger association than a value of .3 or $-.3$, for example. When the value of 1.0 occurs, a subject who is ranked higher than another subject on X cannot be ranked lower on Y than that other subject.

4. With the exception of Somers' d (see Problem 36 at the end of the chapter), the ordinal measures of association named above are *symmetric*. By this, we mean

that their values are not based on the identification of a dependent and independent variable. The measures assume the same value when variable Y is called the dependent variable as when variable Y is called the independent variable.

5. Proportional reduction in error interpretations can be given to the measures or to their squares.

Concordance and Discordance

Most ordinal measures of association are based on the information contained in the relative rankings for all pairs of observations.

Concordant Pair; Discordant Pair

A pair of observations is *concordant* if the member that ranks higher on one variable also ranks higher on the other variable.

A pair of observations is *discordant* if the member that ranks higher on one variable ranks lower on the other.

Two observations are concordant whenever the order of the rankings of the observations for one of the variables is the same as the order for the other variable. Concordant pairs of observations provide evidence of positive association since, for such a pair, the observation ranked higher on one variable is also ranked higher on the other. On the other hand, the more prevalent the occurrence of discordant pairs, the more evidence there is of a negative association.

Notation

Let C denote the total number of concordant pairs of observations, and let D denote the total number of discordant pairs of observations.

When the variables are ordinal categorical, the frequencies of the various combinations of categories can be summarized in the cells of a cross-classification table. In that case, relatively simple rules can be given for calculating C and D, as illustrated by Example 8.4.

Example 8.4

The data in Table 8.13 are from a study of economic conditions and political attitudes of Cuban workers toward the Cuban revolution. The categories in both classifications are naturally ordered, so an ordinal measure of association is appropriate for describing the extent to which attitude toward the revolution depends on extent of employment in the year before the revolution. We shall refer to favorable as the high end of the scale on Y = attitude toward the revolution, and 10 or more as the high end of the scale on X = months worked in the year before the revolution. By convention, we set up cross-classification tables for ordinal variables so that the high end of the row variable is represented by the top row and the high end of the column variable is represented by the rightmost column.

Table 8.13 Attitudes of Cuban Workers Toward Revolution by Prerevolutionary Employment

| | | MONTHS WORKED IN YEAR BEFORE REVOLUTION | | | TOTAL |
		6 or Less	7–9	10 or More	
	Favorable	54 (85.7)	14 (73.7)	65 (61.9)	133
ATTITUDE	Indecisive	6 (9.5)	2 (10.5)	14 (13.3)	22
	Hostile	3 (4.8)	3 (15.8)	26 (24.8)	32
TOTAL PERCENT		100.0	100.0	100.0	
SAMPLE SIZE		63	19	105	187

Source: Zeitlin, M. *Revolutionary Politics and the Cuban Working Class* (Princeton: Princeton University Press, 1967), p. 55. Reprinted by permission of Princeton University Press.

In parentheses in Table 8.13, we have indicated the conditional distributions on attitude for the three levels of months worked. For example, the conditional distribution (85.7, 9.5, 4.8) refers to the percentages in the attitude categories for those who worked 6 months or less. Notice that only 4.8% of the individuals who worked 6 or fewer months are hostile toward the revolution, but 24.8% of those who worked at least 10 months are hostile. Conversely, a higher percentage (85.7%) of those who worked 6 or fewer months are favorable toward the revolution than of those who worked at least 10 months (61.9%). Hence, there is evidence that the association is negative, in the sense that people who worked more tend to have less favorable attitudes.

Consider a pair of individuals, one of whom is classified (favorable, 10 or more) on the variables, and the other of whom is classified (indecisive, 7–9). The first individual is one of the 65 classified in the upper right-hand corner of Table 8.13 and the second individual is one of the 2 classified in the middle cell in the table. This pair of individuals is concordant, since the first individual is ranked higher than the second individual both in attitude (favorable versus indecisive) and in months worked (10 or more versus 7–9). Now, each of the 65 such individuals classified (favorable, 10 or more) can be paired with both of the individuals classified (indecisive, 7–9), so there are 65 × 2 = 130 pairs of individuals who may be matched from these two cells. All of these pairs are concordant. Similarly, the 65 individuals in the cell (favorable, 10 or more) are part of a concordant pair when matched with each of the 3 individuals classified (hostile, 7–9), each of the 6 individuals classified (indecisive, 6 or less), and each of the 3 individuals classified (hostile, 6 or less). In summary, these 65 (2 + 3 + 6 + 3) pairs described above are concordant because each of the 65 individuals ranks higher on both variables than the other 2 + 3 + 6 + 3 individuals in cells below and to the left of the cell (favorable, 10 or more). See Table 8.14 (next page) for a representation of this fact.

Using the same reasoning, the 14 individuals in the cell (indecisive, 10 or more) are part of concordant pairs when matched with the 3 individuals classified (hostile, 7–9) and the 3 individuals classified (hostile, 6 or less); similarly for the 14 individuals in cell (favorable, 7–9) when paired with the 6 individuals classified (indecisive, 6 or less) and the 3 individuals classified (hostile, 6 or less); similarly for the 2 individuals in cell (indecisive, 7–9) when paired with the 3 individuals classified (hostile, 6 or

Table 8.14

Illustration of Concordant
Pairs

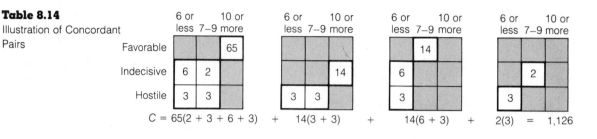

$$C = 65(2 + 3 + 6 + 3) \quad + \quad 14(3 + 3) \quad + \quad 14(6 + 3) \quad + \quad 2(3) \quad = \quad 1{,}126$$

less). There are no observations that rank lower on *both* variables than the observations classified in the cells (hostile, 10 or more), (hostile, 7–9), (hostile, 6 or less), (indecisive, 6 or less), and (favorable, 6 or less). Thus, there are no other concordant pairs in this table, and the total number of concordant pairs is (see Table 8.14)

$$C = 65(2 + 3 + 6 + 3) + 14(3 + 3) + 14(6 + 3) + 2(3) = 1{,}126$$

As a general rule for finding the total number of concordant pairs, the following strategy can be used. Start at the corner of the table corresponding to the high level for each variable (the upper right-hand corner for the convention we use in setting up the tables). Multiply the frequency in that cell by the sum of the frequencies in the cells that are ranked lower on both variables (those cells below and to the left in Table 8.13). Similarly, for every other cell, multiply the frequency in the cell by the sum of the frequencies in the cells that are ranked lower on both variables.* The number of concordant pairs is the sum of these totals.

To find the total number of discordant pairs, we start at the corner of the table corresponding to the high level of one of the variables and the low level of the other variable. For example, the 54 individuals in the cell (favorable, 6 or less) are part of a discordant pair when combined with the $(2 + 14 + 3 + 26)$ individuals classified higher on months worked but lower on attitude (see Table 8.15). Multiplying the frequency in each cell by the sum of the frequencies in the cells that are ranked higher on months worked but lower in attitude, we see that the total number of discordant pairs is

Table 8.15

Illustration of Discordant
Pairs

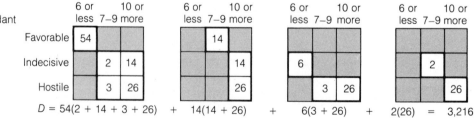

$$D = 54(2 + 14 + 3 + 26) \quad + \quad 14(14 + 26) \quad + \quad 6(3 + 26) \quad + \quad 2(26) \quad = \quad 3{,}216$$

*For the cells in the row or in the column corresponding to the lowest level of a variable (e.g., row hostile or column 6 or less in Table 8.13), there are no observations ranked lower on *both* variables.

$$D = 54(2 + 14 + 3 + 26) + 14(14 + 26) + 6(3 + 26) + 2(26) = 3{,}216$$

In other words, we calculate D for Table 8.13 by multiplying each frequency by the sum of the frequencies occurring below and to the right in the table, and then summing.

In summary, for these data there are many more pairs that give evidence of a negative association (i.e., discordant pairs) than there are that give evidence of a positive association (concordant pairs). ∎

Gamma   All of the ordinal measures of association that we define in this text refer in some way to $C - D$. A positive difference for $C - D$ indicates a positive association, in the sense that there are more concordant than discordant pairs. A negative difference reflects a negative association. Larger sample sizes would lead to larger numbers of pairs with, typically, larger absolute differences in $C - D$. Therefore, it is necessary to standardize this difference so that it is easier to interpret how strong the association is. To do this, we can divide $C - D$ by its maximum possible value, $C + D$, which is the total number of pairs that are either concordant or discordant. This gives the measure of association referred to as *gamma*, introduced by Goodman and Kruskal (1954). Its sample formula is

$$\hat{\gamma} = \frac{C - D}{C + D}$$

The value of gamma falls between -1 and $+1$. Strongest positive association (a value of $+1$) for gamma corresponds to there being no discordant pairs ($D = 0$). Gamma equals -1 when $C = 0$, and it equals 0 when $C = D$.

The sign of gamma indicates whether there is a positive or negative association between the variables. The magnitude of gamma indicates the strength of the association. Its magnitude can also be interpreted by noting that it can be expressed as

$$\hat{\gamma} = \frac{C - D}{C + D} = \frac{C}{C + D} - \frac{D}{C + D}$$

Now, $C/(C + D)$ is the proportion of the $C + D$ pairs that are concordant, $D/(C + D)$ is the proportion of the $C + D$ pairs that are discordant, and $\hat{\gamma}$ is the difference between these two proportions. For example, $\hat{\gamma} = .6$ means that 80% of the pairs are concordant and 20% are discordant (.8 and .2 are the two proportions that sum to 1.0 and have a difference of .6). Thus, $\hat{\gamma} = .6$ indicates that there are four times more pairs representing positive association than there are pairs representing negative association. Similarly, $\hat{\gamma} = -.333$ indicates that one-third of the pairs are concordant and two-thirds of the pairs are discordant (since $1/3 + 2/3 = 1$ and $1/3 - 2/3 = -.333$).

To illustrate the use of gamma, for Table 8.13, $C = 1{,}126$ and $D = 3{,}216$, so that

$$\hat{\gamma} = \frac{1{,}126 - 3{,}216}{1{,}126 + 3{,}216} = -.481$$

For this sample of 187 individuals, we observe a negative association between attitude and number of months worked. The more a person worked in the year before the revolution, the less favorably that person tends to react to the revolution. Out of the 1,126 + 3,216 = 4,342 pairs that are concordant or discordant, the proportion 1,126/4,342 = .259 of the pairs are concordant, and the proportion 3,216/4,342 = .740 are discordant; $\hat{\gamma} = -.481$ is the difference between the proportions.

For a 2 × 2 table, the measure of this form was first proposed by the statistician G. Udny Yule (see Yule and Kendall, 1950). In that special case, gamma is referred to as *Yule's Q*.

Kendall's Tau-*b*   In cross-classifications of ordinal variables, not all pairs of variables are concordant or discordant. Individuals placed in the same category of a variable are said to be *tied* on that variable. Two observations that fall in the same row of a table are tied with respect to the row variable, and two observations that fall in the same column of a table are tied with respect to the column variable.

For a sample of size *n*, there are $n(n - 1)/2$ pairs of observations.* Of these, the $C + D$ concordant or discordant pairs are untied on both variables, and the remaining pairs are tied on at least one of the variables.

Notation

For two variables *X* and *Y*, let T_x denote the number of pairs tied on *X*, let T_y denote the number of pairs tied on *Y*, and let T_{xy} denote the number of pairs tied on *X* and *Y*.

Now, $T_x + T_y - T_{xy}$ is the total number of tied pairs of observations. The reason for subtracting T_{xy} in this expression is that it represents the number of pairs that are tied on both variables and hence are counted twice in the sum $T_x + T_y$. The total number of pairs may therefore be expressed as

$$\frac{n(n - 1)}{2} = \text{(Number of untied pairs)} + \text{(Number of tied pairs)}$$

$$= C + D + T_x + T_y - T_{xy}$$

Also, observe that $n(n - 1)/2 - T_x$ is the total number of pairs minus the number of pairs tied on *X*, which is the number of pairs that are untied on *X*. Similarly, the number of pairs that are untied on *Y* is $n(n - 1)/2 - T_y$.

Kendall's tau-b is a measure of the association between two ordinal variables that takes into account the number of tied pairs on each of the variables. Its sample value is given by the formula

$$\hat{\tau}_b = \frac{C - D}{\sqrt{[n(n - 1)/2 - T_x][n(n - 1)/2 - T_y]}}$$

*The formula for the number of distinct sets of size *k* out of *n* members is $n!/[k!(n - k)!]$. This number is called the number of *combinations* of *n* things taken *k* at a time. Letting $k = 2$, we get the number of pairs, $n!/[2!(n - 2)!] = n(n - 1)/2$.

The magnitude of $\hat{\tau}_b$ can be interpreted in much the same way as gamma. It falls between -1 and $+1$, and the stronger the sample association, the larger the absolute value of $\hat{\tau}_b$. Before discussing why tau-b is sometimes preferred over gamma, we will illustrate its calculation using the data in Table 8.13, for which we have observed $C = 1,126$ and $D = 3,216$.

In order to complete the computation of $\hat{\tau}_b$, we need to calculate T_x, the number of pairs tied on X, and T_y, the number of pairs tied on Y. Since there are 105 people classified 10 or more on months worked, there is a total of $105(104)/2 = 5,460$ pairs tied at that level on that variable. In general, if t_i denotes the number of observations in the ith of c columns of a cross-classification, then there are $t_i(t_i - 1)/2$ tied pairs at the ith level of that column variable. When this is calculated for every column and then summed, we get the total number of pairs of ties on the column variable (call it X), namely,

$$T_x = \sum_{i=1}^{c} \frac{t_i(t_i - 1)}{2}$$

Also, if there are u_i observations in the ith of r rows of a cross-classification, the total number of pairs of ties on the row variable (call it Y) is

$$T_y = \sum_{i=1}^{r} \frac{u_i(u_i - 1)}{2}$$

For the marginal frequencies in Table 8.13,

$$T_x = \frac{(105)(104)}{2} + \frac{19(18)}{2} + \frac{63(62)}{2} = 7,584$$

$$T_y = \frac{133(132)}{2} + \frac{22(21)}{2} + \frac{32(31)}{2} = 9,505$$

In other words, for this sample of 187 people, there are 7,584 pairs of individuals who are tied on number of months worked and 9,505 pairs tied on attitude toward the revolution, as measured in this study. Due to the crudeness of the measurement, there are many more tied pairs than concordant or discordant pairs.

The total number of pairs of observations is $n(n - 1)/2 = 187(186)/2 = 17,391$. The total number of pairs untied on X is $n(n - 1)/2 - T_x = 17,391 - 7,584 = 9,807$, and the total number of pairs untied on Y is $n(n - 1)/2 - T_y = 17,391 - 9,505 = 7,886$. We finally compute the value of $\hat{\tau}_b$ to be

$$\hat{\tau}_b = \frac{C - D}{\sqrt{[n(n - 1)/2 - T_x][n(n - 1)/2 - T_y]}} = \frac{1,126 - 3,216}{\sqrt{(9,807)(7,886)}} = -.238$$

As does gamma, tau-b indicates that there was a negative association in the sample between attitude and number of months worked.

Relationship of Gamma and Tau-b to Kendall's Tau

Commonly in the social sciences, the measuring instrument for ordinal variables is fairly crude, with a wide range of possible responses forced into a few categories, such as often, seldom, and never. Hence, ordinal variables are usually *categorical*, and ties occur whenever two subjects are placed in the same category. It is occasionally the case, however, that each member in the sample can be distinctly ranked with respect to each variable. For each variable, we can assign the rank 1 to the observation that ranks lowest, the rank 2 to the observation that ranks second lowest, and so forth, continuing to the rank n for the observation that ranks highest in the sample. In such a situation we say that the data are **fully ranked**.

There are no tied pairs when the data can be fully ranked, so that $T_x = T_y = 0$ and $C + D = n(n - 1)/2$. In this case, gamma and tau-b simplify to the same measure,

$$\hat{\gamma} = \hat{\tau}_b = \frac{C - D}{n(n - 1)/2} = \hat{\tau}$$

referred to as **Kendall's tau**. This measure and one known as **Spearman's rho** are the two most popular ways of describing association for fully ranked data. Gamma and Kendall's tau-b can be regarded as generalizations of Kendall's tau that are used when ties occur.

If two variables are inherently continuous but are measured using ordered categories, we might conceive of Kendall's tau (the analogous measure when there are no tied pairs) as describing the underlying association. In other words, if we could break all the ties through finer measurement and identify each pair of observations as concordant or discordant, we could compute Kendall's tau to represent the difference between the proportion of concordant pairs and the proportion of discordant pairs. Kendall's $\hat{\tau}_b$ computed when there are ties can be interpreted as an approximation for the difference between these two proportions that would be obtained if these finer measurements were made. For example, if $\hat{\tau}_b = .40$, then (since .70 + .30 = 1 and .70 - .30 = .40) we would estimate that approximately 70% of the pairs would be characterized as concordant and 30% of the pairs would be discordant, if we could refine the measurement of the variables so that there would be no ties. We are estimating that we would obtain $\hat{\tau} = .40$ for the fully ranked case.

Gamma has the advantage, relative to $\hat{\tau}_b$, of being easier to calculate, since the ties pairs are omitted from the calculation. This is only a minor advantage today, however, given the accessibility of pocket calculators and computer program packages. An important deficiency of gamma is that its value depends crucially on how the variables are categorized. Its value tends to be larger for tables with relatively more ties, such as tables with few rows and columns. For *any* table, its value is always at least as large as the value of $\hat{\tau}_b$. We pointed out that $\hat{\gamma}$, $\hat{\tau}_b$, and Kendall's tau are all identical if there are no tied pairs. However, if two variables that are inherently continuous are grouped into ordered categories, the value of gamma tends to be inflated above the common value that occurs when there are no ties. In that sense, gamma can provide a misleading indication of the degree of association. A large value of gamma could occur for a table when finer measurement of these variables would produce a considerably smaller value. Thus, different researchers could reach different conclusions if they studied the same variables but used different categorizations. Tau-b tends to be more stable than gamma under different categorizations (see Agresti, 1976). Tau-b usually gives a closer approximation than other ordinal measures do for the value of Kendall's tau for the underlying fully ranked case. Problems 27, 28, and 40 at the end of the chapter illustrate the tendency of gamma to be inflated for small table sizes.

For the special case of the 2×2 table, the absolute value of $\hat{\tau}_b$ equals exactly the square root of the nominal measure $\hat{\phi}^2$ (i.e., $|\hat{\tau}_b| = \sqrt{\chi^2/n} = \sqrt{\hat{\phi}^2}$). Thus, for the 2×2 table, the square of $\hat{\tau}_b$ equals $\hat{\phi}^2$ and Goodman and Kruskal's tau, and has the same PRE interpretation as the one discussed in Section 8.4.

8.6 Testing for Association for Ordinal Variables

In Section 8.2 we studied the chi-square test for investigating whether two nominal variables are associated. In this section we give a test that is usually more appropriate than the chi-square test when the variables are ordinal. The null hypothesis states that the variables are not associated, in the sense that the population proportion of concordant pairs equals the population proportion of discordant pairs.

Common Test for Ordinal Measures

Let γ and τ_b denote the population values of gamma and tau-b. The null hypothesis can be expressed as H_0: $\gamma = 0$, or equivalently as H_0: $\tau_b = 0$. In fact, the procedure that we will describe can be used for *any* ordinal measure that is based on the difference between the numbers of concordant pairs and discordant pairs. In all of these cases, we can use this procedure to test the null hypothesis that the measure equals 0, since all of these measures equal 0 in the same situations. The alternative hypothesis in the test may take the form H_a: $\tau_b \neq 0$ ($\gamma \neq 0$), H_a: $\tau_b > 0$ ($\gamma > 0$), or H_a: $\tau_b < 0$ ($\gamma < 0$), according to whether the sign of the association is predicted.* The test is best applied to a relatively large random sample. As a rough guideline, $C + D$, the total number of untied pairs, should exceed 100.

The test statistic for testing H_0: $\tau_b = 0$ is most easily expressed in terms of $C - D$ and its approximate standard error, σ_{C-D}, which applies when H_0 is true. Specifically, it is

$$z = \frac{C - D}{\sigma_{C-D}}$$

where

$$\sigma_{C-D}^2 = \frac{n^3}{9} \left(1 - \frac{\sum_{i=1}^{c} t_i^3}{n^3} \right) \left(1 - \frac{\sum_{i=1}^{r} u_i^3}{n^3} \right)$$

and t_i and u_i are the ith column and row totals, as defined previously. In forming z, we take the difference $C - D$, which summarizes the tendency in the sample toward positive or negative association, subtract the value of 0 that we would expect for $C - D$ if the null hypothesis of no association were true, and divide by the standard error of $C - D$. The test statistic has approximately the standard normal distribution, when H_0 is true.

*For nominal variables, it did not make sense to differentiate between positive and negative association, so there was only one possible alternative hypothesis.

Example 8.5   To illustrate the formula for testing H_0: $\tau_b = 0$, we again consider the data from Table 8.13 relating attitude toward the Cuban revolution to number of months worked in the previous year, for $n = 187$ individuals. In Example 8.4, we obtained $C = 1{,}126$ concordant pairs and $D = 3{,}216$ discordant pairs. The $c = 3$ column totals in Table 8.13 are $t_1 = 63$, $t_2 = 19$, and $t_3 = 105$, so that

$$\sum_{i=1}^{c} t_i^3 = (63)^3 + (19)^3 + (105)^3 = 1{,}414{,}531$$

The $r = 3$ row totals in Table 8.13 are $u_1 = 133$, $u_2 = 22$, and $u_3 = 32$, so that

$$\sum_{i=1}^{r} u_i^3 = (133)^3 + (22)^3 + (32)^3 = 2{,}396{,}053$$

Thus, when H_0 is true, the variance of the sampling distribution of $C - D$ is approximately

$$\sigma_{C-D}^2 = \frac{n^3}{9}\left(1 - \frac{\sum t_i^3}{n^3}\right)\left(1 - \frac{\sum u_i^3}{n^3}\right)$$

$$= \frac{(187)^3}{9}\left[1 - \frac{1{,}414{,}531}{(187)^3}\right]\left[1 - \frac{2{,}396{,}053}{(187)^3}\right]$$

$$= 360{,}769.16$$

Finally, the approximate standard error is

$$\sigma_{C-D} = \sqrt{360{,}769.16} = 600.64$$

and the value of the test statistic is

$$z = \frac{C - D}{\sigma_{C-D}} = \frac{1{,}126 - 3{,}216}{600.64} = -3.48$$

There is enough evidence to reject the null hypothesis that $\tau_b = 0$, at the usual α-levels, in favor of the alternative hypothesis H_a: $\tau_b \neq 0$ or H_a: $\tau_b < 0$. We would conclude that there is a negative association between how favorable one's attitude was toward the revolution and the number of months worked in the previous year, assuming that the sample was randomly drawn from the population of interest. ■

The test of no association illustrated in Example 8.5 would usually be preferred to the chi-square test of independence when the variables are ordinal categorical, since the chi-square test does not utilize the ordering of the categories. If there is a positive or negative trend for the relationship, concordance–discordance measures are usually more powerful for detecting the association than the χ^2 statistic, which is the same no matter how the levels are ordered. Problem 30 at the end of the chapter illustrates this point.

It should be emphasized that τ_b (or γ) may equal 0 even though the variables are not statistically independent. For example, Table 8.16 presents a situation in which the relationship between two variables is U-shaped instead of having a single trend. Over the first two columns there is a negative relationship, since Y decreases in rank when X increases in rank. In fact, $\tau_b = \gamma = -1$ over this restricted range. Similarly, over the last two columns there is a positive relationship ($\tau_b = \gamma = 1$), as Y increases in rank when X increases in rank. For the entire table, $C = 25(25 + 25) = 1{,}250 = D$, so $\tau_b = \gamma = 0$. The proportion of concordant pairs equals the proportion of discordant pairs, although the two conditional distributions on Y for the low and high levels of X are completely different from the two conditional distributions on Y for the very low and very high levels of X. Thus, an ordinal measure of association may equal 0 when the variables are statistically dependent, but the dependence does not have an overall positive or overall negative trend. Hence, the chi-square test is typically better than the test based on $C - D$ when the relationship does not have a single trend, and neither test is best in all situations.

Table 8.16
A U-Shaped Relationship for Which Ordinal Measures of Association Equal 0

		LEVEL OF X			
		Very low	Low	High	Very high
LEVEL OF Y	High	25	0	0	25
	Low	0	25	25	0

Confidence Intervals for Measures of Association

Tests of hypothesis help us to determine whether there is an association between two variables, but confidence intervals are needed to gauge the strength of that association in the population. Confidence intervals for measures of association have the usual form—for instance, $\hat{\gamma} \pm z_{\alpha/2}\hat{\sigma}_{\hat{\gamma}}$ for γ, where $\hat{\sigma}_{\hat{\gamma}}$ is the estimated standard error of $\hat{\gamma}$. The formulas for the standard errors of various ordinal categorical measures are given in Agresti (1984, Section 10.3), in the BMDP manual (Dixon, 1981), and in Noether (1967) for Kendall's tau for fully ranked data. Unfortunately, the formulas are very complicated. However, standard error values are printed out by many computer packages that have programs for analyzing cross-classification tables.

Figure 8.3 (page 230) is an example of part of a BMDP-4F printout for the analysis of the data in Table 8.13. From the printout, we see that the sample value of gamma is $\hat{\gamma} = -.481$. Its standard error of .117 is given under the heading ASE1, where ASE denotes "asymptotic (large-sample) standard error." Hence, we can calculate a 95% confidence interval for γ of $\hat{\gamma} \pm 1.96\hat{\sigma}_{\hat{\gamma}}$, or $-.481 \pm 1.96(.117)$, or $-.481 \pm .229$, or $(-.710, -.252)$. Similarly, using Figure 8.3, we obtain a 95% confidence interval for τ_b of $-.238 \pm 1.96(.059)$, or $-.238 \pm .116$, or $(-.354, -.122)$. Our conclusion with these intervals is consistent with the one made in the test given in this section. Namely, we conclude that the association between the two variables is negative, since the confidence interval contains only negative values. The BMDP-4F printout also contains the χ^2 statistic (12.9) and its df value (4) and P-value (.0118), and a test statistic value (denoted T-VALUE) for testing H_0: $\gamma = 0$ (or $\tau_b = 0$). The statistic is a slightly different one from the z statistic we gave, but it is equally valid.

Fig. 8.3 Part of a
BMDP-4F Printout for
Analyzing Table 8.13

```
ATTITUDE                    MONTHS
------                      ------
           6 OR LES      7-9   10 OR MO    TOTAL
-------------------------------------------------
FAVORABL       54         14       65       133
INDECISI        6          2       14        22
HOSTILE         3          3       26        32
-------------------------------------------------
TOTAL          63         19      105       187

MINIMUM ESTIMATED EXPECTED VALUE IS      2.24

STATISTIC                      VALUE    D.F.    PROB.
PEARSON CHISQUARE             12.897      4   0.0118

STATISTIC                      VALUE   ASE1  T-VALUE
-------------------------------------------------
GAMMA                         -0.481   0.117  -3.884
KENDALL TAU-B                 -0.238   0.059  -3.884
```

We conclude with an important comment about the analysis of ordinal variables using cross-classifications. Whenever possible, it is best to choose the categories for ordinal categorical variables as finely as possible. The fewer tied observations in the table, the more information there is available about the relative numbers of concordant and discordant pairs. Variables with many categories tend to have fewer tied observations than those with few categories. Also, the sampling distributions of ordinal measures of association tend to have smaller standard errors when there are fewer ties for a given sample size. Thus, the finer the categorizations of the variables, the shorter the confidence interval for a population measure of association tends to be.

Summary

Most analyses of relationships between categorical variables involve the construction of *cross-classification tables* and percentage distributions (called *conditional distributions*) within rows or columns. Two variables are said to be *independent* if the conditional distributions on one variable are equal for each level of the other variable. The *chi-square test* is used to test for independence between two nominal variables, based on sample data. The strength of association between two nominal variables can be measured by the difference of proportions for 2 × 2 tables and by *Goodman and Kruskal's tau* for larger tables.

In this chapter we have also considered methods for analyzing the association between two ordinal variables. *Ordinal measures of association* measure the extent to which subjects' rankings on one variable are associated with their rankings on the other variable. Most of these measures are based on the relative occurrences of *concordant* and *discordant pairs*. We studied *gamma* and *Kendall's tau-b* for the case in which the variables are ordinal categorical.

In Chapter 9 we will consider similar procedures for describing the association between interval variables.

Notes

Section 8.1

1. One should never use as a dependent variable in a percentage table a variable that has been sampled in an unrepresentative manner (for example, a stratification variable for a disproportionate stratified sample) without proper weighting procedures to re-create representative proportionality. It is perfectly legitimate to use the disproportionately sampled groups as categories of the independent variable, computing percentage distributions *within* the categories and comparing them. But if one computes percentages in the other direction, the results will be misleading due to the unrepresentative sampling proportions. The same is true for computing percentages of the *total* sample within each cell, if one wants to estimate the population percentages for those variable combinations.

Section 8.4

2. We did not give a test of H_0: $\tau = 0$ for Goodman and Kruskal's tau, since this hypothesis is equivalent to the hypothesis of independence. Thus, the P-value for that test is the same as the P-value of the chi-square test. For example, for cross-classification C in Table 8.10, $\hat{\tau} = \hat{\phi}^2 = .0004$ is significant at the $P < .01$ level, since $\chi^2 = 8$ is based on df = 1 for that table.

Section 8.5

3. Gamma can be easily interpreted as a difference of two proportions, but it also has a proportional reduction in error interpretation, in terms of predictions about pairs. As in Section 8.4, there are two prediction rules that we compare. According to Rule 1, we must predict which of a pair of observations is higher on variable Y without knowing which is higher on variable X. In essence, with Rule 1 we randomly predict for each pair whether it is concordant or discordant—with probability .5 concordance is predicted, and with probability .5 discordance is predicted. Using this rule, we would expect to make an incorrect prediction half of the time. Since there are $C + D$ predictions made (one for each untied pair), the expected number of errors we would make using this rule is $E_1 = (C + D)/2$.

   With Rule 2, we predict which member in a pair ranks higher on variable Y based on knowing which member ranks higher on variable X. For example, suppose that there are more concordant than discordant pairs. Then, if the first member in a pair ranks higher on X than the second member, we would predict that member also to rank higher on Y than the second member. In other words, we would predict the pair to be concordant. Rule 2 specifies that we always predict concordance if $C > D$ and that we always predict discordance if $C < D$. Now, if every pair is predicted to be concordant, a prediction error is made whenever a pair is discordant. Hence, the number of errors using Rule 2 is $E_2 = D$, the total number of discordant pairs. The proportional reduction in error obtained from using the ordering of rankings on X to predict the ordering of rankings on Y is

$$\frac{E_1 - E_2}{E_1} = \frac{(C + D)/2 - D}{(C + D)/2} = \frac{C - D}{C + D} = \hat{\gamma}$$

Thus, we can interpret $\hat{\gamma} = .4$ as meaning that there are 40% fewer prediction errors made in predicting whether each pair is concordant or discordant, when we know which type of pair occurs more frequently.

When $\hat{\gamma} < 0$, the absolute value of gamma has a PRE interpretation. In that case $C < D$, so we predict that every pair is discordant. Hence, $E_2 = C$ and

$$\frac{E_1 - E_2}{E_1} = \frac{D - C}{C + D} = -\hat{\gamma} = |\hat{\gamma}|$$

For example, if $\hat{\gamma} = -.2$, then $|\hat{\gamma}| = .2$, and there is a 20% reduction in error in predicting pair orderings.

A similar PRE interpretation applies to Kendall's tau, using all $n(n - 1)/2$ pairs for fully ranked data. Since Kendall's tau-b can be interpreted as an approximation for the value one would obtain for tau if the data could be fully ranked, this PRE interpretation also extends to it.

4. Ordinal measures of association can also be used for cross-classifications of ordinal with nominal variables, when the nominal variable has only two categories. In that case, the sign of the measure indicates which level of the nominal variable is associated with higher responses on the ordinal variable. For tables in which the nominal variable has an arbitrary number of categories, the mean *ridit* measure introduced in Section 7.3 is useful for describing ordinal–nominal association.

5. For 2× 2 tables, Kendall's tau-b, the phi coefficient, and the Pearson correlation r (to be introduced in Section 9.3 for interval variables) are identical. Also, $\hat{\tau}_b^2 = r^2 = \hat{\phi}^2 = \chi^2/n$ are all identical to Goodman and Kruskal's tau for 2×2 tables.

Problems

1. A young child wonders what causes women to have babies. For the women who live on her block, she observes whether their hair is gray and whether they have young children, with the results shown in the accompanying table.

a. Obtain the cell frequencies for the 2 × 2 cross-classification of "gray hair" (yes, no) with "young children" (yes, no), for these nine women.

b. Treating "young children" as the dependent variable, obtain the conditional distributions for those women who have gray hair and for those who do not. Does there seem to be an association?

c. Realizing this association, the child concludes that not having gray hair is what causes women to have children. Use this example to explain why association does not imply causation.

WOMAN	GRAY HAIR	YOUNG CHILDREN
Andrea	No	Yes
Mary	Yes	No
Linda	No	Yes
Jane	No	Yes
Maureen	Yes	No
Judy	Yes	No
Margo	No	Yes
Carol	Yes	No
Donna	No	Yes

2. Shortly before a gubernatorial election, a random sample of fifty potential voters are contacted and asked the following questions:

Do you consider yourself to be a Democrat (D), a Republican (R), or Independent (I)?

If you were to vote today, would you vote for the Democratic candidate (D), the Republican (R), or would you be undecided (U) about how to vote?

Do you plan on voting in the election? Yes (Y) or No (N)?

For each person interviewed, the answers to the three questions are recorded on a postcard. For example, the record (D, U, N) represents a registered Democrat who is undecided and who does not expect to vote. The results of the fifty interviews are summarized below:

(D, U, N)	(R, R, Y)	(I, D, Y)	(I, U, N)	(R, U, N)
(I, D, N)	(R, R, Y)	(I, U, N)	(D, U, Y)	(D, R, N)
(I, D, N)	(D, D, Y)	(D, D, Y)	(I, D, Y)	(R, U, N)
(D, R, N)	(R, D, N)	(D, U, N)	(D, D, Y)	(R, R, Y)
(R, R, Y)	(D, D, N)	(D, D, Y)	(I, D, Y)	(R, R, N)
(D, D, Y)	(D, R, Y)	(I, U, N)	(D, D, N)	(D, D, Y)
(R, R, Y)	(R, R, Y)	(D, U, N)	(I, R, N)	(I, R, Y)
(R, R, Y)	(I, U, Y)	(D, D, Y)	(D, R, Y)	(D, D, N)
(D, D, Y)	(I, R, Y)	(R, R, Y)	(I, D, Y)	(R, R, N)
(R, R, Y)	(D, D, Y)	(I, D, Y)	(I, R, N)	(R, R, Y)

a. Find the frequencies for the 3 × 3 cross-classification table relating political party affiliation to intended vote (the first two variables listed).

b. Find the conditional distributions on intended vote for each of the three political party affiliations. Are they very different?

c. Test the null hypothesis that intended vote is independent of political party affiliation, using the $\alpha = .01$ level. Interpret the result.

3. Refer to Problem 2.

a. Find the frequencies for the 2 × 3 cross-classification table relating expectation of voting to political party affiliation (the first and third variables listed).

b. Find the conditional distributions on expectation of voting for each of the political party affiliations.

c. Test the null hypothesis that these two variables are independent, using the α = .01 level.

4. Refer to Problem 2.

a. Find the frequencies for the 2 × 3 cross-classification table relating expectation of voting to voting intention.

b. Find the conditional distributions on expectation of voting for each of the three present voting intention categories.

c. Test the null hypothesis that these two variables are independent, using the α = .01 level.

5. Summarize the implications of the test results in Problems 2–4.

6. Give an example of a cross-classification for which the chi-square test of independence should *not* be used, because of:

a. Sample size

b. Measurement scale

c. Another reason

7. How large a χ^2-value is needed to reject the null hypothesis of independence at the α = .05 level for the following table dimensions?

    a. 2 × 2   **b.** 3 × 3   **c.** 5 × 5   **d.** 3 × 9

8. Fill in the missing cell frequencies in the following cross-classification table with four degrees of freedom.

10	20	30	60
30	40	30	100
10	20	10	40
50	80	70	

9. A company test markets three new brands of a chocolate drink. One hundred individuals are randomly chosen in a typical urban market, a typical suburban market, and a typical rural market. Each person specifies which brand is preferred over the others. Using the results in the table, find the P-value for testing whether consumer preference is independent of market location. What do you conclude?

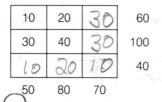

		MARKET LOCATION		
		Urban	Suburban	Rural
	A	53	57	55
PREFERRED BRAND OF DRINK	B	16	21	23
	C	31	22	22

10. A random sample of 300 adults living in a state not having a state income tax are classified according to their political party and according to their opinion about initiating that type of tax. Using the results in the table, find the *P*-value for testing whether opinion is independent of political party affiliation. Which party seems to be most opposed to the tax?

| | | POLITICAL PARTY | | |
		Democrat	Republican	Independent
OPINION ON TAX	Favor	35	10	30
	Oppose	65	70	90

11. Out of 10,000 people who have taken a flu shot, 15 develop a particular illness within the next month. Out of a comparable group of 10,000 people who have not had the flu shot, five acquire that illness within the next month. Assuming that it is reasonable that these groups represent random samples of the corresponding populations of people who have and who have not had the flu shot, test at the $\alpha = .05$ level whether there is a difference in the probability of getting the illness for the two groups. How do you interpret this result?

12. A study is conducted to compare salaries of men and women having sanitation jobs in a large corporation. In a random sample of 100 men, 65 have incomes exceeding $10,000, and in a random sample of 50 women, 25 have incomes over $10,000.
a. Conduct a chi-square test of the hypothesis that income is independent of sex. Report the *P*-value and indicate what your conclusion would be for an $\alpha = .05$ level test.
b. Estimate the difference between the proportions of men and women earning over $10,000, and set up a 95% confidence interval for this difference in the population of all people in this corporation having sanitation jobs (see Section 7.1). Compare the result to the conclusion in part **a**.

13. Interchanging two rows in a cross-classification table will cause the chi-square statistic to do which of the following?
a. Definitely change in value
b. Possibly change in value
c. Stay the same

14. When the sample size is very large, we have not necessarily established an important result when we show there is a statistically significant relationship between two variables. Why? Illustrate your reasoning using the accompanying table.

| | | OPINION ABOUT LEGALIZING POSSESSION OF MARIJUANA | |
		Favor	Oppose
SEX	Female	2,900	7,100
	Male	3,100	6,900

15. Calculate Goodman and Kruskal's tau for the accompanying table under each of the following conditions:
a. Treating belief as the dependent variable
b. Treating religious affiliation as the dependent variable
Account for the difference in the two values.

| | | RELIGIOUS AFFILIATION | | | | ROW TOTAL |
		Protestant	Catholic	Jewish	Other	
BELIEF IN LIFE	Yes	150	130	5	15	300
AFTER DEATH	No or uncertain	50	20	45	85	200
COLUMN TOTAL		200	150	50	100	500

16. Refer to Problem 2. Calculate Goodman and Kruskal's tau for the cross-classification table constructed there, treating present voting intention as the dependent variable.

17. Calculate an appropriate measure of association for the table in Problem 9, treating preferred brand of drink as the dependent variable. Interpret its value.

18. Give an example of a 3 × 3 table for which Goodman and Kruskal's tau satisfies the following conditions:
a. $\tau = 1$, no matter which variable is treated as the dependent variable
b. $\tau = 1$ only when the row variable is treated as the dependent variable
c. $\tau = 0$

19. If $\hat{\gamma} = .30$ for the relationship between two ordinal variables, what proportion of the untied pairs of observations are concordant? Discordant?

20. A study of political opinions of individuals in Los Angeles produces the following cross-classification:

| | | POLITICAL PHILOSOPHY | | |
		Liberal	Moderate	Conservative
OPINION ABOUT	Increase	5	14	12
DEFENSE BUDGET	Keep same	10	20	8
	Decrease	15	16	0

Compute:
a. The number of concordant pairs
b. The number of discordant pairs
c. The value of gamma   (Interpret the sign and magnitude of the measure.)
d. The number of pairs tied on opinion, and the number of pairs tied on political philosophy
e. The value of Kendall's tau-b   (Interpret the sign and magnitude of the measure.)

21. In the draft lottery conducted in 1970, the lottery numbers 1 through 366 were supposedly randomly assigned to the days of the year. Individuals having the birthday receiving lottery number 1 were first in priority to be drafted, and so forth down to those having the birthday with lottery number 366, who were last in priority to be drafted. The results of the lottery are summarized in the table.

		BIRTH DATE NUMBER (JAN. 1 = 1, . . . , DEC. 31 = 366)	
		1–183	*184–366*
DRAFT LOTTERY NUMBER	*184–366*	109	74
	1–183	74	109

a. If the numbers were truly randomly assigned (i.e., if lottery number were independent of birth date number), what frequencies would you expect to find in the four cells?

b. Use chi-square to test the hypothesis that the lottery numbers were in fact randomly assigned. Report the P-value and interpret it.

c. Compute Kendall's tau-*b* and observe whether there is a positive or negative association between birth date number and lottery number. How could you measure this more precisely if all 366 birth date numbers with corresponding lottery numbers were available?

22. If Kendall's $\tau_b = 0$ for the relationship between two variables, then which of the following is true?

a. The variables must be statistically independent.

b. The variables need not necessarily be independent, but the relationship does not have an overall increasing or overall decreasing trend.

c. One cannot tell whether there are more concordant pairs or discordant pairs.

23. Interchanging two rows in a cross-classification table will cause gamma and Kendall's tau-*b* to do which of the following?

a. Definitely change in value

b. Possibly change in value

c. Stay the same

The correct answer here and in Problem 13 implies that if the chi-square statistic is used for a cross-classification table having ordered categories in both directions, then [select the correct response(s)]:

a. The statistic actually treats the variables as nominal.

b. Information about the ordering is ignored.

c. The test will usually not be as powerful for detecting association as a test statistic based on numbers of concordant and discordant pairs.

d. The statistic cannot differentiate between positive and negative associations.

24. Compute the value of Kendall's tau-*b* to describe the degree of association between age and opinion concerning legalized gambling, based on the table at the top of the next page. Interpret the sign of the value you obtain.

		AGE		
		18–30	31–50	Over 50
OPINION ABOUT GAMBLING	Highly favorable	15	10	5
	Favorable	10	10	10
	Unfavorable	10	10	10
	Highly unfavorable	5	10	15

25. Compute and interpret the value of gamma for the table in Problem 24.

26. Using the accompanying data, calculate and interpret the value of tau-*b*.

		NUMBER OF CHILDREN	
		0–2	More than 2
ATTITUDE TOWARD LEGALIZED ABORTION	Favorable	120	80
	Unfavorable	80	120

27. Compute gamma for the table in Problem 26. Compare its value to tau-*b* computed in that problem.

28. Consider the accompanying table relating educational level to opinion about a Socialist Workers' Party candidate in a U.S. election.

		EDUCATIONAL LEVEL		
		Grammar school	High school graduate	College graduate
OPINION ABOUT S.W.P. CANDIDATE	Approve	0	0	1
	Disapprove	6	10	24

a. Compute the conditional distribution on opinion for each educational level. Does the degree of association appear to be strong or weak?
b. Compute tau-*b*.
c. Compute gamma.
d. Explain the large difference between gamma and tau-*b*. Which measure do you think more realistically describes the association?

29. Refer to Problem 20. Test H_0: $\gamma = 0$ against H_a: $\gamma > 0$, using the $\alpha = .01$ level. What can we conclude?

30. Refer to Problem 24.
a. Find the *P*-value for testing H_0: $\tau_b = 0$ against H_a: $\tau_b \neq 0$ for the data in that problem.
b. Find the *P*-value for testing H_0: Independence of age and opinion about gambling, against H_a: Dependence, using the chi-square test of independence.
c. Give the conclusions for the above tests, using the $\alpha = .05$ level.
d. Which test is more powerful for detecting an association between the variables? Why?

*31. Another PRE measure of association for nominal variables is called *lambda*. For this measure, Rule 1 predicts for each observation the *modal category* for the marginal distribution of the dependent variable. For the table in Problem 15, for example, Rule 1 predicts yes always for belief. The resulting number of errors is $E_1 = 200$. Rule 2 predicts the modal category for the conditional distribution of the dependent variable, within each level of the independent variable. For the Protestant and Catholic categories in Problem 15, yes is always predicted, whereas no or uncertain is always predicted for the Jewish and Other categories, using Rule 2. Hence, $E_2 = 50 + 20 + 5 + 15 = 90$, so that

$$\hat{\lambda} = (E_1 - E_2)/E_1 = (200 - 90)/200 = .55$$

for this prediction rule.

a. Calculate lambda for the data in Table 8.11, treating attitude as the dependent variable.

b. Compare lambda with the value of tau for Table 8.11.

c. What can be said about the value of lambda when the modal category of the dependent variable is the same for each level of the independent variable?

*32. The accompanying table exhibits the maximum possible association between two dichotomous variables for a sample of size n. Show that $\chi^2 = n$ for this table, and hence that the maximum value of χ^2 is n for a 2 × 2 table. Thus, $\phi^2 = \chi^2/n = 1$ for such a table.

$n/2$	0
0	$n/2$

*33.

a. Calculate the difference of proportions $\hat{\pi}_2 - \hat{\pi}_1$ for the data in Problem 11, and interpret its magnitude.

b. An alternative measure for 2 × 2 tables, called the *relative risk*, equals $\hat{\pi}_1/\hat{\pi}_2$. Calculate this measure for Problem 11, interpret its value, and indicate why it may be a more meaningful measure than $\hat{\pi}_2 - \hat{\pi}_1$ when both proportions are close to 0.

*34. Construct a 3 × 3 table for each of the following conditions:

a. Tau-*b* equals 1.

b. Tau-*b* equals −1.

c. Tau-*b* equals 0.

*35. Show that the absolute value of gamma equals 1 for *any* 2 × 2 table in which one of the cell frequencies is 0.

*36. An asymmetric measure of ordinal association is *Somers' d*. Treating Y as the dependent variable and X as the independent variable, d is defined as

$$d_{Y \cdot X} = \frac{C - D}{n(n - 1)/2 - T_x}$$

Obtain $d_{Y \cdot X}$ for the table in Problem 24.

*37. Refer to Problem 36. Show that $\hat{\tau}_b^2 = d_{Y \cdot X} d_{X \cdot Y}$, where $d_{X \cdot Y}$ denotes Somers' d when X is treated as the dependent variable. Tau-b is said to be a *geometric average* of the two asymmetric Somers' d values.

*38. Refer to Problem 20. Using the BMDP computer package to obtain the standard error, obtain and interpret a 95% confidence interval for:
a. Gamma
b. Kendall's tau-b

*39. The accompanying table presents ten cities with their ranking in population and the percentage vote cast for Johnson in the 1964 presidential election.

CITY	POPULATION RANK	PERCENTAGE FOR JOHNSON
Buffalo, N.Y.	10	72.6
Lansing, Mich.	7	61.0
Odessa, Tex.	3	48.6
San Jose, Ca.	8	63.1
Albany, Ga.	2	29.1
York, Pa.	6	62.0
Tucson, Ariz.	5	53.4
Cincinnati, Ohio	9	55.7
Pine Bluff, Ark.	1	56.0
Albuquerque, N.Mex.	4	56.1

a. List the concordant and discordant pairs of cities.
b. Use Kendall's tau to determine the strength of the association between population size and percentage vote for Johnson in these cities. Interpret the sign and magnitude of the measure.

*40. Refer to Problem 39. Suppose that instead of knowing the individual ranks, we know only whether a city is in the top five or lower five ranks with respect to population, and whether more than 56.0%, or 56.0% or fewer, voted for Johnson in that city.
a. Fill in the cell frequencies for the 2×2 table that could then be used to display the results.

| | | POPULATION RANK | |
		1–5	6–10
PERCENTAGE VOTE FOR JOHNSON	56.1–100		
	0–56.0		

b. Compute Kendall's tau-b and compare its value to the Kendall's tau value you computed in Problem 39.
c. Compute gamma and compare its value to the Kendall's tau value computed in Problem 39. Which measure, gamma or tau-b, is a better approximation for tau for the fully-ranked case?

*41. Let π_{ij} denote the proportion of the population classified in the cell falling in row i and column j. Let π_{i+} denote the proportion in the ith row and π_{+j} denote the proportion in the jth column. When the row variable is the dependent variable, the *uncertainty coefficient* for describing association is

$$ H = -\frac{\sum_i \sum_j \pi_{ij}\log(\pi_{ij}/\pi_{i+}\pi_{+j})}{\sum_i \pi_{i+}\log \pi_{i+}} $$

a. The condition of statistical independence can also be defined as $\pi_{ij} = \pi_{i+}\pi_{+j}$ for all cells. Show that $H = 0$ if the variables are independent.

b. Compute H for Table 8.11.

c. Compute H for Table 8.12. (Take 0 log 0 to equal 0.) What can you conclude about the conditions needed to obtain $H = 1$?

Bibliography

Agresti, A. (1976). "The Effect of Category Choice on Some Ordinal Measures of Association." *Journal of the American Statistical Association, 71* (March): 49–55.

Agresti, A. (1984). *Analysis of Ordinal Categorical Data.* New York: Wiley.

Agresti, A. and D. Wackerly (1977). "Some Exact Conditional Tests of Independence for $r \times c$ Cross-Classification Tables." *Psychometrika, 42* (March): 111–125.

Blalock, H. M. (1979). *Social Statistics*, revised 2nd ed. New York: McGraw-Hill. Chap. 15.

Dixon, W. J., ed. (1981). *BMDP Statistical Software 1981.* Berkeley: University of California Press.

Goodman, L. A. and W. H. Kruskal (1954). "Measures of Association for Cross-Classifications." *Journal of the American Statistical Association, 49* (December): 732–764.

Goodman, L. A. and W. H. Kruskal (1972). "Measures of Association for Cross-Classifications, IV: Simplification of Asymptotic Variances." *Journal of the American Statistical Association, 67* (June): 415–421.

Greeley, A. (1974). *Ethnicity in the United States: A Preliminary Reconnaissance.* New York: Wiley.

Kendall, M. G. (1970). *Rank Correlation Methods*, 4th ed. London: Charles W. Griffin.

Noether, G. E. (1967). *Elements of Nonparametric Statistics.* New York: Wiley.

Siegel, S. (1956). *Nonparametric Statistics for the Behavioral Sciences.* New York: McGraw-Hill. Chaps. 6, 9.

SPSS Inc. (1983). *SPSS^X Users Guide.* New York: McGraw-Hill.

Theil, H. (1970). "On the Estimation of Relationships Involving Qualitative Variables." *American Journal of Sociology, 76*: 103–154.

Yule, G. U. and M. G. Kendall (1950). *An Introduction to the Theory of Statistics.* New York: Hafner.

CHAPTER 9

Linear Regression and Correlation

Contents

In this chapter, we study methods of describing relationships between variables measured at the interval level. There are three different, but related, aspects of such relationships that we will consider. For one, we investigate *whether an association exists* between the two variables by using a test of the hypothesis of statistical independence. If two variables are related, then we will be interested in a second aspect, the *strength* of their association. These first two aspects of describing relationships between interval variables have the same purpose as the procedures studied in the last chapter for lower levels of measurement: Goodman and Kruskal's tau and the chi-square test for nominal variables, and Kendall's tau-*b*, gamma, and the related *z* tests for ordinal variables.

The third aspect of the relationships that we study in this chapter is unique to the interval level of measurement. This involves the specification of the *form* of the relationship between two variables. For interval variables, it is often possible to find a mathematical expression that enables us to predict a subject's score on one variable from knowing the score on the other variable. For instance, we might predict the college grade point average (GPA) that will be achieved by an entering freshman from his or her high school GPA or college entrance exam scores. Or we might try to develop a formula for predicting burglary rates for cities on the basis of such factors as city population size, the relative size of the police force, the unemployment rate, average income levels, population heterogeneity, the conviction rate in grand larceny trials, the average length of sentences for convicted burglars, and so forth. When we have numerical scores on two or more variables for a sample, we can describe the form of the relationship through the use of **regression analysis**. The search for a good mathematical formula to describe how a score on one variable depends on a score on a second variable makes sense only for numerical-valued variables, so we did not consider it in the previous chapter.

In this chapter, we shall consider how to use a *linear regression function* to model the form of the relationship between two variables. In Section 9.1, we introduce the basic idea of using a straight line to describe how the value on one variable depends on the value of another variable. In Section 9.2, the *method of least squares* is presented for finding the best straight-line equation to describe the relationship. In Section 9.3, we define a measure of association that is related to the linear regression function and can be given a proportional reduction in error interpretation. The square root of that measure is referred to as the *Pearson correlation* and is also discussed as a useful bivariate measure. In Section 9.4, we see how these measures of association can be used to test the hypothesis of statistical independence in the population from which the sample is drawn. In the final section, we discuss some basic assumptions for using linear regression functions, and we present a typical printout from a computer program for regression analyses.

9.1
The Linear
Regression
Model

In discussing inferential procedures in Chapters 5–7, we summarized univariate distributions of interval variables by their means. In many studies, we are interested in much more than descriptive measures for univariate distributions. For interval variables, it is often useful to see how the mean of a certain variable changes from one subset of the population to another, as defined by values of a second variable. For example, we might want to compare the mean yearly income values for fully employed people who have had (say) 8, 10, 12, 14, 16, and 18 years of formal education. We would not expect the individuals with 8 years of formal education to have exactly the same mean yearly income as those with 12 or 18 years of education. Instead, we would expect the mean of yearly income to vary in some way as we consider each of the subpopulations defined by the different values of years of formal education. Using bivariate methods, we can describe how the distribution of one variable changes as we look at various values of another variable. For nominal and ordinal categorical variables, we saw how to do this by comparing the conditional distributions on one variable for the various levels of the other variable, in a cross-classification table. For interval variables, we will obtain a mathematical formula that describes how the mean of the conditional distribution of a dependent variable varies across different values of an independent variable. We could do this, for instance, to describe how the dependent variable of yearly income varies for different levels of education, how birth rate varies by proportion of the nation's population using contraceptives, or how college GPA varies according to the score on a college entrance exam.

Notation

Let Y represent the dependent variable and let X denote the independent variable.

Linear Functions

There are many different mathematical formulas that could be used to describe how the dependent variable Y is related to the independent variable X. Some might provide a good representation of the relationship, others a poor one. We restrict our attention in this chapter to the simplest class of such mathematical formulas, those corresponding to *linear functions*.

Linear Function

The formula $Y = \alpha + \beta X$ expresses the dependent variable Y as a *linear function* of the independent variable X, with slope β (beta) and Y-intercept α (alpha).

The term *linear function* refers to the fact that the formula $Y = \alpha + \beta X$ maps out a straight-line graph when various X-values are substituted into the formula, for particular values of α and β.

Example 9.1

The formula $Y = 3 + 2X$ represents the linear function specified by the Y-intercept $\alpha = 3$ and the slope $\beta = 2$. The value $X = 1$ corresponds to $Y = 3 + 2(1) = 5$; the value $X = 4$ corresponds to $Y = 3 + 2(4) = 11$. Similarly, each real number X, when substituted into the formula, yields a distinct corresponding value for Y. We have graphed this function on the two-dimensional plane represented in Figure 9.1, where possible X-values are given on the horizontal axis (the X axis) and possible values of Y are indicated on the vertical axis (the Y axis). The straight line can be obtained by finding any two separate sets of (X, Y) values and then drawing the line through the points represented by those values. To illustrate, let $(1, 5)$ denote the point represented by the values $X = 1$, $Y = 5$. This point is located on the graph by starting at the point $(0, 0)$ (i.e., $X = 0$, $Y = 0$), and moving one unit to the right on the X axis and five units upward parallel to the Y axis (see Figure 9.1). After plotting the points $(1, 5)$ and $(4, 11)$, we draw the straight line that passes through these two points to yield the graph of the function $Y = 3 + 2X$. ■

Fig. 9.1 A Plot of the Equation $Y = 3 + 2X$

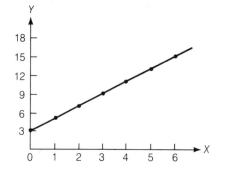

The **Y-intercept** α represents the value of the linear function when it crosses the Y axis. Points on the Y axis correspond to $X = 0$, so the linear function equals $Y = \alpha + \beta X = \alpha + \beta(0) = \alpha$ at the point of intersection. In Example 9.1, the straight line $Y = 3 + 2X$ intersects the Y axis at $\alpha = 3$. The **slope** β represents the change in Y for a 1-unit increase in X. That is, if we consider two X-values that differ by 1.0 (for example, $X = 3.4$ and $X = 4.4$), the corresponding Y-values will differ by β. Similarly, two X-values that are 10 units apart differ by 10β in their Y-values. For example, when $X = 1$, $Y = \alpha + \beta$, and when $X = 11$, $Y = \alpha + 11\beta$ (see Figure 9.2). As an illustration of the α and β terms, suppose that the line $Y = 40,000 + 2X$ serves as an approximation for the relationship between $Y = $ number of votes received and $X = $ campaign expenditures (in dollars) in congressional elections. Then, $X = 0$ expenditures corresponds to $\alpha = 40,000$ votes. Each additional dollar spent corresponds to $\beta = 2$ additional votes.

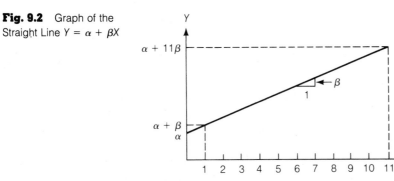

Fig. 9.2 Graph of the Straight Line $Y = \alpha + \beta X$

The slope gives the rate of change of the Y-values as X increases. Linear functions are distinguished by the fact that the rate of change of Y is the same over all X-values. That is, a 1-unit increase in X corresponds to a change of β units in Y, *no matter what the value of X.* The larger the absolute value of β, the steeper the line. If β is a positive number, then Y increases as X increases; that is, relatively large values of Y tend to occur with relatively large values of X, and relatively small values of Y tend to occur with relatively small values of X. In this case, the straight line goes upward, as with the line just given relating campaign expenditures to votes. To the extent that a relationship between two variables can be represented by a straight line with $\beta > 0$, we say that the relationship is *positive.* Similarly, if β is a *negative* number, then Y decreases as X increases and the straight line goes downward. The equation $Y = 10 - .1X$, which might approximate the relationship for several countries between Y = average family size and X = percentage of women in the labor force, represents a negative relationship between X and Y with slope $-.1$. This line is shown in Figure 9.3, together with other relationships representing various combinations of values of α and β. In the particular case in which $\beta = 0$, the linear function has the form $Y = \alpha$; the graph of the function is then a horizontal line. The value of Y is constant and does not vary as X varies. If two variables are independent, in the sense that the value of Y does not depend on the value of X, then a straight line with $\beta = 0$ would represent their relationship.

Fig. 9.3 Graphs of Lines Corresponding to Positive Relationships ($\beta > 0$), a Negative Relationship ($\beta < 0$), and Independence ($\beta = 0$)

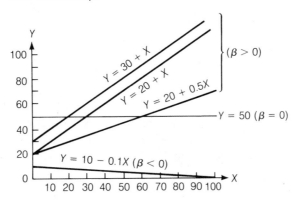

The linear function or straight line is the simplest type of mathematical function and thus provides the simplest basic *model* for the form of the relationship between two interval variables. In calling a function such as $Y = \alpha + \beta X$ a *model* for the relationship, we mean that the formula can be used to represent to a certain extent the relationship between the values of X and the values of Y for members of the population of interest. If we know the measurement for a person on the independent variable X, then we can use the model to predict the measurement on the dependent variable Y for that person. The better these predictions tend to be, the better we would judge the model to be.

A model of the form $Y = \alpha + \beta X$ is said to be *deterministic*, meaning that for each particular value of X, there is only one fixed corresponding value of Y. Without some modifications, such a model would be unrealistic in social science research, since we would expect variability in the Y-values among subjects with the same X-values. For example, we would not expect all individuals with 12 years of education to have exactly the same yearly income, since income is not completely dependent upon education. However, we could imagine a conditional distribution for yearly income for those with $X = 12$ years of education, another for those with $X = 13$ years of education, and others for those with each possible value of years of education. The conditional distributions of income would probably be different for the different levels of education, since the mean income would tend to be higher for higher values of education. A *probabilistic model* for the relationship between two interval variables X and Y is one that allows for variability in the values of Y for each value of X. We now consider how we can use a linear function as the basis for such a probabilistic model.

The Linear Regression Model

Instead of using $\alpha + \beta X$ to represent the exact value of a dependent variable Y as a function of an independent variable X, in a probabilistic model it represents the *mean* of those values. Thus, for a given value of X, $\alpha + \beta X$ is the mean of the conditional distribution of Y for the portion of the population having that value on the independent variable X.

Notation

Let $E(Y|X)$ denote the mean of the conditional distribution of Y for a given value of X. The symbol E represents *expected value*, which is another term for the mean. The vertical slash between Y and X represents the word *given*. $E(Y | X)$ is read "the expected value (mean) of Y, for a given value of X."

To illustrate, $E(Y|X = 10)$ represents the mean of the conditional distribution of Y-values at the particular X-value of 10. Unless we wish to refer to a certain X-value, we will usually abbreviate the $E(Y | X)$ notation as $E(Y)$.

In this chapter, we use the equation $E(Y) = \alpha + \beta X$ to model the relationship between X and the mean of Y. This equation is an example of what is referred to as a *regression function*.

Regression Function

A *regression function* is a mathematical function that describes how the mean of the values of a dependent variable changes according to the value of an independent variable.

The function $E(Y) = \alpha + \beta X$ is called a *linear regression function*, since it expresses a linear relationship between the mean of Y and the values of X. For a linear relationship, the difference between the mean values of Y at $X = 1$ and $X = 2$ is the same as the difference between the mean values of Y at $X = 101$ and $X = 102$, or for any X-values that are 1 unit apart. The Y-intercept α and the slope β are called the *regression coefficients* for the linear regression function.

For each fixed value of X, there is a conditional distribution of Y-values around the mean of $\alpha + \beta X$, with some standard deviation σ. The measure of dispersion σ in this context is a measure of the variability of all Y observations that have the same X-value.

Example 9.2   One possible model for the relationship between Y = yearly income in thousands of dollars and X = years of education is given by the linear regression function $E(Y) = 2.0 + 1.5X$, with $\sigma = 7$. According to this model, people with a high school education $(X = 12)$ would have a mean income of $20,000, since $E(Y \mid X = 12) = 2.0 + 1.5(12)$ = $20.0 thousand, with a standard deviation of $7,000. If the conditional distributions on income are approximately bell-shaped, then (by the Empirical Rule) about 95% of the people with 12 years of education earn between $6,000 [i.e., $20,000 - 2(7,000)$] and $34,000 [$20,000 + 2(7,000)$], or within two standard deviations of the mean. Similarly, people with a college education $(X = 16)$ would have a mean yearly income of $26,000, with about 95% of the incomes falling between $12,000 and $40,000. The slope of $\beta = 1.5$ implies that mean income tends to increase $1.5 thousand for each year increase in education. This linear regression model with $\alpha = 2.0$, $\beta = 1.5$, and $\sigma = 7$ is pictured in Figure 9.4 (page 250). In that figure, we have plotted the regression function $E(Y) = 2.0 + 1.5X$ and the conditional income distributions at $X = 8$, 12, and 16 years; each of these conditional distributions is approximately normal with $\sigma = 7$.   ∎

Error Terms*   Any specific observation on the variable Y is likely to deviate from $\alpha + \beta X$, the mean of all such Y-values for the corresponding value of X. The standard deviation component σ of the model is included to summarize the typical sizes of these deviations. We can provide a regression equation for a specific observation on Y by including a term for the deviation of the observation from the mean. For example, we can model the observation on Y as

$$Y = \alpha + \beta X + \varepsilon$$

where ε (epsilon) represents the deviation of that particular observation from the mean, $\alpha + \beta X$. If ε is positive, then $\alpha + \beta X + \varepsilon$ is larger than $\alpha + \beta X$, and the

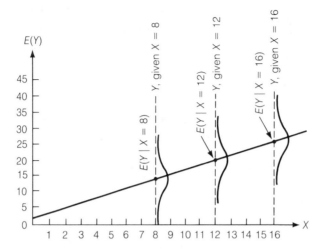

observation falls above the mean (see Figure 9.5). A negative value for ε corresponds to an observation that falls below the mean. When $\varepsilon = 0$, the observation falls exactly at the mean. There is a particular value of ε for each member in the population. In Example 9.2, a person with 12 years of education and $16,000 income would have $\varepsilon = -4.0$, since then $Y = 2.0 + 1.5X + \varepsilon$, or $16 = 2.0 + 18.0 + \varepsilon$. Since the values of $Y = \alpha + \beta X + \varepsilon$ have an average of $\alpha + \beta X$ at each fixed value of X, the average of the ε-values is 0.

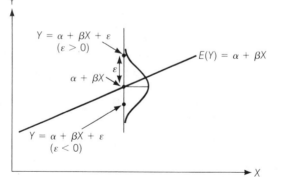

The ε term in the equation $Y = \alpha + \beta X + \varepsilon$ accounts for the fact that the variables are not perfectly related, or in other words, that observations with the same X-values do not all have the same Y-values. We could conceptualize ε as representing the cumulative effect on the dependent variable Y of all the other influences not represented in the regression model. The model $Y = \alpha + \beta X + \varepsilon$ is a probabilistic one. For each X, variability in the Y-values corresponds to variability in ε. The ε term is sometimes referred to as the *error term*, since it represents the error that would occur if we used the mean value $(\alpha + \beta X)$ of Y at a certain value of X for the prediction of an observation on Y.

Models and Reality In concluding this section, we should emphasize that a model such as $E(Y) = \alpha + \beta X$ (or equivalently, $Y = \alpha + \beta X + \varepsilon$), where the conditional distribution of Y is normal with standard deviation σ, is used to *approximate* the actual relationship between the two variables. No sensible researcher would expect most relationships to be *exactly* linear, with *exactly* normal conditional distributions at each X, and with *exactly* the same standard deviation of Y-values at each X-value. However, the model-building process always begins by proposing a simple model and testing it by applying it to real data. If the model is too crude, the data may suggest ways of improving its adequacy by making it more complex. It can then be retested and perhaps modified further. Model-building, then, is an iterative process. Its general goals are to find a realistic model that is useful for representing the bivariate relationship but is still simple enough to be easily interpreted.

The model that has been discussed in this section is actually a set of models indexed by the values of the parameters α, β, and σ. For a sample of observations on two variables, we could estimate the values of these parameters that yield the equation best representing the data, in some sense. We shall see how to do this for the linear regression function in the next section. In Chapters 11 and 12, we discuss some ways in which this simple model can be extended so that it can be applied to situations in which the assumptions we have made are violated.

9.2 Method of Least Squares and Prediction Equation

In this section, we present a method for estimating the linear function that provides the best approximation of the relationship between two interval variables, based on observations from a random sample. We treat α, β, and σ in the model described in Section 9.1 as the unknown parameters. These must be estimated in order to estimate the regression equation $E(Y) = \alpha + \beta X$ for the population. The estimated regression equation can then be used to make predictions about the dependent variable Y and its mean at specific values for the independent variable X.

Notation
Let X_i and Y_i denote the values of the independent variable and the dependent variable, respectively, for the ith member in the sample. The index i can take on values from 1 to n, the sample size.

For example, (X_1, Y_1) represents the pair of measurements on the two variables for the first member sampled. The values (X_i, Y_i) of the two variables for any particular member can be viewed as a point in the plane relative to the pair of X and Y axes. The n observations on the two variables can be represented as n points $(X_1, Y_1), \ldots, (X_n, Y_n)$, which can be plotted relative to the coordinate axes to portray graphically the relationship as observed in the sample. This type of graphical plot is usually referred to as a *scatter diagram* or *scattergram* of the points. A scatter diagram is illustrated using the data in Example 9.3. These data will be referred to throughout the chapter to illustrate various aspects of regression analysis.

Example 9.3   The data given in Table 9.1 are the values for twelve nations in 1970 on the percentage of women aged 14 and older who are economically active and on the crude birth rate. Suppose that we would like to describe the relationship of the birth rate of a nation in 1970 to the percentage of its women who were economically active. We treat birth rate as the dependent variable Y and the percentage of economically active women as the independent variable X. To check whether Y is approximately linearly dependent on X, we would first draw a scatter diagram for the twelve observations, as shown in Figure 9.6. In terms of the notation just given, the data are represented by the plotted points $(X_1, Y_1) = (2, 48)$, $(X_2, Y_2) = (19, 21)$, and so forth. For instance, we plot the point $(X_1, Y_1) = (2, 48)$ by moving from the origin $(0, 0)$ two units in the X (horizontal) direction and 48 units in the Y (vertical) direction. This brings us to the spot labeled Algeria in Figure 9.6. This figure provides some evidence that there is a negative relationship between the two variables, since the crude birth rates tend to be lower when the percentages of women who are econom-

Table 9.1

Data for Linear
Regression Analysis

NATION	PERCENTAGE OF ECONOMICALLY ACTIVE WOMEN	CRUDE BIRTH RATE[a]
Algeria	2	48
Argentina	19	21
Denmark	34	14
East Germany	40	11
Guatemala	8	41
India	12	37
Ireland	20	22
Jamaica	20	31
Japan	37	19
Philippines	19	42
United States	30	15
U.S.S.R.	46	18

[a]The crude birth rate is defined to be the number of births in the year per 1,000 population size. Sources: United Nations, *Statistical Yearbook 1975*; and U.S. Bureau of the Census, *World Population Statistics in Brief: 1975*, June 1976.

Fig. 9.6 Scatter
Diagram for Y = Crude
Birth Rate and X =
Percentage of Women
Who Are Economically
Active, for 12 Nations

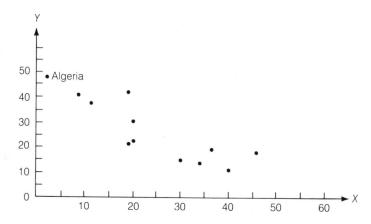

ically active are relatively higher. This pattern of points would seem to be approximated reasonably well by a linear function with negative slope. ∎

The scatter diagram provides a visual means of checking whether the relationship between the two variables is approximately linear. If the relationship appears to be strongly nonlinear, as in Figure 9.7, it would not make sense to try to find a straight line that best represents the observed points.

Fig. 9.7 A Strong Nonlinear Relationship

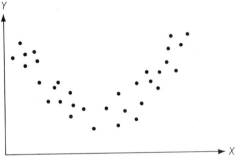

Prediction Equation

If it seems reasonable to assume that there is a linear regression equation $E(Y) = \alpha + \beta X$ relating the mean of Y to X for the population that has been sampled, then we can proceed with the problem of finding a sample equation that provides a good estimate of this unknown regression line. We use the notation $\hat{Y} = a + bX$ to represent a sample regression equation, based on the observations, that estimates the population regression equation $E(Y) = \alpha + \beta X$. In the sample equation, the Y-intercept (a) represents an estimate of the unknown Y-intercept α of the population regression equation, and the slope (b) represents an estimate of the corresponding population slope β. If a particular value of X is substituted into the formula $a + bX$, we get a number (denoted by $\hat{Y}$) that is an estimate of the mean of Y at that value of X. The sample regression equation $\hat{Y} = a + bX$ is often referred to as the *prediction equation*, since it can be used to generate predictions about the dependent variable Y at various values of X.

We have yet to see how to calculate the point estimates (a and b) of α and β, which are needed to obtain the prediction equation. Our objective is to find the values of a and b corresponding to the line that falls closest, in some sense, to the points in the scatter diagram. For the moment, we will provide the formula for the prediction equation that is best, according to a criterion discussed later in this section. The point estimates that we use in the prediction equation are as follows:

$$b = \frac{\sum (X_i - \bar{X})(Y_i - \bar{Y})}{\sum (X_i - \bar{X})^2} \qquad a = \bar{Y} - b\bar{X}$$

If an observation has both X- and Y-values above their means, or both X- and Y-values below their means, then $(X_i - \bar{X})(Y_i - \bar{Y})$ is positive. The numerator of b (and thus b) tends to be positive when points with large X-values also tend to have large Y-values, and points with small X-values tend to have small Y-values. An alternative formula for b that is usually simpler to use computationally is

$$b = \frac{\sum X_i Y_i - \left(\sum X_i\right)\left(\sum Y_i\right)/n}{\sum X_i^2 - \left(\sum X_i\right)^2/n}$$

This formula is now illustrated by using the data given in Example 9.3.

Example 9.4　To compute the slope of the best prediction line relating Y = birth rate to X = percentage of women who are economically active, we use the summary statistics in Table 9.2. In the columns labeled X and Y, we have repeated the values of X and Y for the twelve nations. The last three columns give the squares of the X-values (X^2), the squares of the Y-values (Y^2), and the products of the X- and Y-values (XY) for all twelve nations.

Table 9.2

Calculations for Linear Prediction Equation

NATION	X	Y	X^2	Y^2	XY
Algeria	2	48	4	2,304	96
Argentina	19	21	361	441	399
Denmark	34	14	1,156	196	476
East Germany	40	11	1,600	121	440
Guatemala	8	41	64	1,681	328
India	12	37	144	1,369	444
Ireland	20	22	400	484	440
Jamaica	20	31	400	961	620
Japan	37	19	1,369	361	703
Philippines	19	42	361	1,764	798
United States	30	15	900	225	450
U.S.S.R.	46	18	2,116	324	828
Total	287	319	8,875	10,231	6,022

The term $\sum X_i$ represents the sum of the values on the independent variable. In this example, the sum of the values of the percentage of women who are economically active is

$$\sum X_i = 2 + 19 + 34 + \cdots + 46 = 287$$

Similarly, $\sum Y_i$ represents the sum of the crude birth rate observations, which is

$$\sum Y_i = 48 + 21 + 14 + \cdots + 18 = 319$$

The term $\sum X_i^2$ represents the sum of the squared X-values, or

$$\sum X_i^2 = 2^2 + 19^2 + 34^2 + \cdots + 46^2 = 8,875$$

The term $\sum Y_i^2$ is not needed to obtain the prediction equation, but we have included its calculation since we will need it for the next section. The last column in the table is used to obtain the term $\sum X_i Y_i$. To calculate this term, we multiply the X-value by the Y-value for each observation, and then sum over all n observations. For these twelve nations,

$$\sum X_i Y_i = 2(48) + 19(21) + 34(14) + \cdots + 46(18) = 6{,}022$$

Substituting $\sum X_i = 287$, $\sum Y_i = 319$, $\sum X_i^2 = 8{,}875$, and $\sum X_i Y_i = 6{,}022$ into the formula for the slope b, we get

$$b = \frac{\sum X_i Y_i - \left(\sum X_i\right)\left(\sum Y_i\right)/n}{\sum X_i^2 - \left(\sum X_i\right)^2/n}$$

$$= \frac{6{,}022 - 287(319)/12}{8{,}875 - (287)^2/12} = \frac{6{,}022 - 7{,}629.42}{8{,}875 - 6{,}864.08} = \frac{-1{,}607.42}{2{,}010.92} = -.80$$

Also, $\bar{Y} = \sum Y_i/n = 319/12 = 26.58$, and $\bar{X} = \sum X_i/n = 287/12 = 23.92$, so that the Y-intercept is

$$a = \bar{Y} - b\bar{X} = 26.58 - (-.80)(23.92) = 45.70$$

Therefore, the prediction equation relating Y = crude birth rate to X = percentage of women who are economically active is $\hat{Y} = a + bX = 45.7 - .8X$. ∎

The prediction line from Example 9.4 is plotted over the corresponding scatter diagram in Figure 9.8. Since the slope is a negative number, the relationship between the variables is negative, at least as observed for these twelve nations. In other words, the larger the percentage of women who are economically active, the smaller the crude birth rate tends to be for the nations in the sample. The value $b = -.8$ indicates that (on the average) an increase of 1% of economically active women corresponds to a decrease of .8 in the crude birth rate. Similarly, an increase of 10% of economically active women would correspond to an 8-unit decline in the birth rate. This implies that if one nation has 20% of its women classified economically active and another has 30%, for example, the second nation would be predicted to have 8 fewer births per 1,000 population than the first nation.

Fig. 9.8 Prediction Equation and Residuals

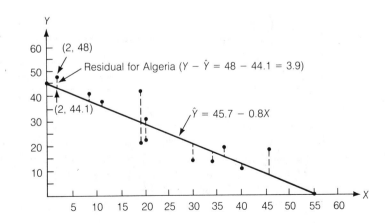

Residuals   The prediction equation $\hat{Y} = 45.7 - .8X$ can be used to generate predictions for crude birth rates for nations with various levels of X = percentage of women who are economically active. For the sample data, we can compare the predicted values to the actual values of the crude birth rates to get some notion of the goodness of the prediction equation. For example, let us consider Algeria, for which $X = 2$ and $Y = 48$. The predicted crude birth rate ($\hat{Y}$) according to the prediction equation is $\hat{Y} = 45.7 - .8X = 45.7 - .8(2) = 45.7 - 1.6 = 44.1$. The prediction error is the difference between the actual and predicted values. For Algeria, the prediction error is $Y - \hat{Y} = 48 - 44.1 = 3.9$. Thus, the prediction equation underestimates the crude birth rate by 3.9 for Algeria. Similarly, for Argentina, $\hat{Y} = 45.7 - .8(19) = 30.5$. The actual birth rate for Argentina is $Y = 21$, so the prediction error is $Y - \hat{Y} = 21 - 30.5 = -9.5$. The predictions, the observed values, and the prediction errors for all twelve nations are given in Table 9.3. The prediction errors are commonly referred to as *residuals*.

Table 9.3   Predictions on Crude Birth Rate and Corresponding Residuals

NATION	PERCENTAGE OF ECONOMICALLY ACTIVE WOMEN X	CRUDE BIRTH RATE Y	PREDICTED CRUDE BIRTH RATE $\hat{Y} = 45.7 - .8X$	RESIDUAL $Y - \hat{Y}$
Algeria	2	48	44.1	3.9
Argentina	19	21	30.5	−9.5
Denmark	34	14	18.5	−4.5
East Germany	40	11	13.7	−2.7
Guatemala	8	41	39.3	1.7
India	12	37	36.1	.9
Ireland	20	22	29.7	−7.7
Jamaica	20	31	29.7	1.3
Japan	37	19	16.1	2.9
Philippines	19	42	30.5	11.5
United States	30	15	21.7	−6.7
U.S.S.R.	46	18	8.9	9.1

Residual

The difference between the actual and predicted values of the dependent variable for the *i*th member in a sample is called the *ith residual*.

For the *i*th member of the sample, the value of the independent variable has been denoted by X_i, and we could denote the corresponding predicted value of the dependent variable as $\hat{Y}_i$. That is, $\hat{Y}_i = a + bX_i$ is the predicted value of Y for the *i*th member. We have denoted the actual value of the dependent variable Y for the *i*th member by Y_i, so the difference $Y_i - \hat{Y}_i$ is just the prediction error for the *i*th member, or the *i*th residual.

A positive residual results when the prediction is too small, so that the observed value Y_i is larger than the predicted value $\hat{Y}_i$, and $Y_i - \hat{Y}_i > 0$. Similarly, a negative residual means that the predicted value is larger than the observed value. The smaller the absolute value of the residual, the better is the prediction, since the predicted value is closer to the observed value. Graphically, the residual for an observation can be represented in the scatter diagram by the vertical distance between the point representing the observation and the prediction line (see Figure 9.8). For example, the observation for Algeria is represented by the point with coordinates $(2, 48)$. The prediction for Algeria can be represented by the point $(2, 44.1)$ on the prediction line corresponding to substituting $X = 2$ into the prediction equation $\hat{Y} = 45.7 - .8X$. The residual is the difference between the observed and predicted points, which is the vertical distance $Y - \hat{Y} = 48 - 44.1 = 3.9$.

Letting e denote a particular sample residual, we have $Y - \hat{Y} = e$. Since $\hat{Y} = a + bX$, this is equivalent to $Y - (a + bX) = e$, or $Y = a + bX + e$. The basic regression model for an observation is $Y = \alpha + \beta X + \varepsilon$, so we can interpret the sample residual e as being an estimate of a population residual ε. The residual ε is the difference between the observation Y and the mean $\alpha + \beta X$ of all observations on Y at that value of X—that is, the vertical distance between the observed point and the *true* regression line.

Method of Least Squares

There is a residual for each observation in a sample. Collectively, these are $Y_1 - \hat{Y}_1$, $Y_2 - \hat{Y}_2, \ldots, Y_n - \hat{Y}_n$. For the prediction equation with the formula we have just given, some of the residuals will be positive, some will be negative, and their average will be 0.* If the prediction line lies close to the points in the scatter diagram, the residuals will tend to be small. The usual way to summarize the size of the residuals is to calculate the sum of their squared values. This quantity, denoted by SSE, is given by the formula

$$SSE = \sum_{i=1}^{n} (Y_i - \hat{Y}_i)^2$$

In other words, the residual is computed for every observation in the sample; each residual is squared, and then SSE is computed by summing these squares. The symbol SSE is an abbreviation for the **sum of squared errors**. This terminology is based on the fact that each residual can be viewed as the prediction error that results from using $\hat{Y}$ to predict Y. The measure SSE is also referred to as the **residual sum of squares**. It describes the variation of the observed points around the prediction line. The better the prediction equation, the smaller the residuals tend to be and, hence, the smaller the summary measure SSE tends to be. For any particular prediction equation, there is a corresponding set of residuals and a value of SSE. The prediction equation that we have specified in this section is the one with the *smallest* value of SSE out of all possible linear prediction equations.

*They could not *all* be positive, for example, or we would be consistently underestimating the dependent variable and we could get a better fit by shifting the line upward. Just as $\bar{Y}$ is defined so that $\Sigma (Y_i - \bar{Y}) = 0$, so the prediction equation is defined so that $\Sigma (Y_i - \hat{Y}_i) = 0$.

> ### Method of Least Squares; Least Squares Estimates
>
> The *method of least squares* is a procedure for obtaining the linear prediction equation $\hat{Y} = a + bX$ having the minimal value of $SSE = \sum (Y_i - \hat{Y}_i)^2$.
>
> The *least squares estimates* a and b are the values determining the prediction equation for which the sum of squared errors in using the $\hat{Y}_i$ as predictors of the Y_i is a minimum.

Thus, the best prediction equation, according to the least squares criterion, is the one with the smallest sum of squared residuals. Because of this criterion, the prediction line $\hat{Y} = a + bX$ is often referred to as the *least squares line*. If the residuals in Table 9.3 are each squared and then summed, we get

$$SSE = \sum (Y_i - \hat{Y}_i)^2 = (3.9)^2 + (-9.5)^2 + \cdots + (9.1)^2 = 466.04$$

This value of SSE is smaller than the value of SSE for *any* other linear prediction equation we might use. In this sense, the observed points tend to be less spread out around this line than around *any* other line.

Estimating Conditional Variation

The actual numerical value for SSE is useful for other purposes as well. For one, this measure of variability of the points about the least squares line is used in estimating the standard deviation σ of the conditional Y distributions for fixed X-values. In this section, we have been assuming that the mean of Y is related to X by the linear regression equation $E(Y) = \alpha + \beta X$, and that it therefore makes sense to calculate a least squares line $\hat{Y} = a + bX$ to estimate that equation. The optimality of the estimates a and b of α and β and of the inference procedures to be introduced in Section 9.4 is based partly on the further assumption that the standard deviations σ of the conditional distributions of Y at the various values of X are identical.* If this assumption appears to be reasonable, it is useful to estimate this parameter σ to get a descriptive measure of the variability of the observations about the regression line at each fixed value of X.

In Section 5.1, we saw that a sample point estimate of the standard deviation of the distribution of a variable Y is given by

$$\sqrt{\frac{\sum (Y_i - \bar{Y})^2}{n - 1}}$$

The standard deviation estimated there was the standard deviation of the *marginal* distribution of Y, since no reference was made to any other variable X. Here, we wish to estimate the standard deviation of the *conditional* distribution of Y, for a fixed value of X. To distinguish this standard deviation from the one considered earlier for the marginal distribution, we shall refer to it as the *conditional standard deviation*.

---

*We will see how to check this assumption in Chapter 12, through analysis of the residuals. A quick check of the scatter diagram to see if the variability around the predicted line is fairly constant for various values of X would also be a way to evaluate whether the assumption is reasonable.

Whereas the univariate (unconditional) population variance represented the average squared deviation of Y about its overall population mean μ, the conditional variance represents the average squared deviation of Y about the population mean $\alpha + \beta X$ for all members with the same value of X. If the variables X and Y are strongly related, the variation in the conditional distributions will be considerably smaller than the variation in the marginal distribution. For example, college GPAs (Y) at a particular university may be primarily clustered between about 1.0 and 4.0. However, for those individuals with a high school GPA (X) of 3.8, the college GPAs might be clustered between (say) 2.8 and 3.9 (see Figure 9.9).

Fig. 9.9 Marginal and Conditional Distributions of College GPA

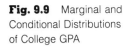

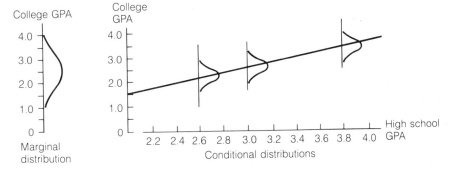

A sample unbiased estimate of the conditional variance of Y that uses the information on the relationship between X and Y is given by

$$\hat{\sigma}^2 = \frac{SSE}{n-2} = \frac{\sum (Y_i - \hat{Y}_i)^2}{n-2}$$

The denominator of this expression is called the **degrees of freedom** for the estimate. When the least squares line is used to estimate the regression equation $E(Y) = \alpha + \beta X$, the degrees of freedom is df $= n - 2$. In general, if the regression equation involves p unknown parameters, then df $= n - p$. For the model we are considering in this chapter, two parameters (α and β) must be estimated before we can calculate SSE, so df $= n - 2$. [In estimating the variance of the marginal distribution in Section 5.1, only one parameter (μ) had to be estimated before calculating the sum of the squared deviations, so we had df $= n - 1$.] The corresponding estimate of the standard deviation for the conditional distributions is

$$\hat{\sigma} = \sqrt{\frac{SSE}{n-2}}$$

Example 9.5   The sum of squared errors in using X = percentage of women who are economically active to predict Y = crude birth rate for twelve nations was SSE $= 466.0$. The estimate of the conditional variance is

$$\hat{\sigma}^2 = \frac{SSE}{n-2} = \frac{466.0}{12-2} = 46.60$$

The corresponding estimate of the conditional standard deviation, which is easier to interpret since it has the same units of measurement as Y, is given by $\hat{\sigma} = \sqrt{46.60} = 6.83$. Now for an approximately bell-shaped distribution, we know that most (about 95%) of the observations are within two standard deviations of the mean. Therefore, we could estimate that for a particular value of X, most birth rates would be within about $2\hat{\sigma} = 2(6.8) = 13.6$ of the conditional mean given by the true regression equation at that value of X. ∎

Extrapolation　　It is dangerous to apply the prediction equation to values of X outside the range of observed values of X. The main reason for this is that the relationship might not be linear outside that range. To illustrate, as the percentage of women who are economically active gets above a certain point, the crude birth rate probably does not continue to drop as fast, if at all. We might get very bad or even absurd predictions if we made them by extrapolating beyond our limited range of values of X. For example, according to the prediction equation $\hat{Y} = 45.7 - .8X$, the predicted crude birth rate for a nation with $X = 60\%$ of its women economically active is $\hat{Y} = 45.7 - .8(60) = -2.3$, an impossible value for crude birth rate.

**9.3
Measuring
Linear
Association—
The Correlation
Coefficient and
Its Square**

In the previous section, we represented the form of the sample relationship between two interval variables with a linear prediction equation. We now will introduce a measure for describing the strength of the association between the two variables. The slope b of the prediction equation tells us the *direction* of the association, since its sign describes whether the prediction line slopes upward (positive association) or downward (negative association) as X increases. However, unless the slope is standardized in some way, it cannot be used as a measure of the strength of the association between the variables. The reason for this is that the value of the slope can be any real number (not restricted to values between -1 and $+1$) and is intrinsically linked to the units of measurement of the variables. For example, if the crude birth rate in Example 9.4 had been measured in terms of the number of births per 10,000 population (instead of 1,000 population), the slope of the least squares line would have been $b = -8.0$ instead of $-.80$.* The degree of the association is the same in each case, since the same variables are used; only the way in which the dependent variable is measured is different. Hence, the slope depends on the units of measurement. To summarize, the slope is very useful for describing the *form* of the relationship and for predictive purposes (through its contribution to the prediction equation), but it is not appropriate as a measure of association. The measures we are about to consider do not vary according to the units of measurement and (as with the nominal and ordinal measures of association already presented) they are bounded between a minimum and maximum value so that their magnitudes can be used to interpret the degree of association between the variables.

---

*A 1-unit increase in the percentage of women who are economically active results in a predicted change of $-.8$ in the mean number of births per 1,000 people, which is equivalent to a predicted change of -8.0 in the mean number of births per 10,000 people.

The Pearson Correlation

The measure of association for interval variables known as the **Pearson correlation** is very commonly used in social science research.[*] The Pearson correlation can be interpreted as being a *standardized slope*; that is, the correlation is a type of slope whose value, unlike that of b, does not depend on the units of measurement. The standardization is accomplished by adjusting the slope b for the fact that the marginal distributions of the observations on X and Y have dispersions that depend on the respective units in which X and Y are measured. In general, the correlation can be interpreted as the value we would get for the slope of the regression equation for Y and X if we used measurement units for the two variables such that their standard deviations were equal.

Now, let $\hat{\sigma}_X$ and $\hat{\sigma}_Y$ denote the sample point estimates of the marginal standard deviations of X and Y, respectively. In other words,

$$\hat{\sigma}_X = \sqrt{\frac{\Sigma\,(X_i - \bar{X})^2}{n-1}} \quad \text{and} \quad \hat{\sigma}_Y = \sqrt{\frac{\Sigma\,(Y_i - \bar{Y})^2}{n-1}}$$

These are just the values of the point estimate of a standard deviation defined in Section 5.1, as calculated for the n observations on X and again for the n observations on Y. The Pearson correlation, which we denote by the symbol r (or by r_{YX} if we want to emphasize the variables to which the measure refers), is related to the slope by the formula

$$r = \left(\frac{\hat{\sigma}_X}{\hat{\sigma}_Y}\right) b$$

By multiplying the slope by the ratio of the two estimated marginal standard deviations, then, we get a standardized measure. In the special case in which the sample dispersions are equal ($\hat{\sigma}_X = \hat{\sigma}_Y$), the correlation is exactly the same as the slope of the least squares line. Because of this relationship between r and b, the Pearson correlation is often referred to as the *standardized regression coefficient* for the bivariate regression model.

Example 9.6

Before considering in detail the properties of the correlation, we will illustrate the calculation of its value using the data already given on crude birth rate and the percentage of women who are economically active. The prediction equation based on the data for the twelve nations listed in Table 9.1 was seen to be $\hat{Y} = 45.7 - .8X$. Now, $\Sigma\,(X_i - \bar{X})^2$ and $\Sigma\,(Y_i - \bar{Y})^2$ can be calculated from the summary statistics in Table 9.2 by the computational formulas[†]

$$\Sigma\,(X_i - \bar{X})^2 = \Sigma\,X_i^2 - \frac{\left(\Sigma\,X_i\right)^2}{n} = 8{,}875 - \frac{(287)^2}{12} = 2{,}010.92$$

$$\text{and } \Sigma\,(Y_i - \bar{Y})^2 = \Sigma\,Y_i^2 - \frac{\left(\Sigma\,Y_i\right)^2}{n} = 10{,}231 - \frac{(319)^2}{12} = 1{,}750.92$$

[*]We shall often refer to the Pearson correlation as simply the *correlation* in contexts where it would not be confused with another measure. The development of the concepts of correlation and regression is due primarily to the Englishmen Karl Pearson (1857–1936) and Sir Francis Galton (1822–1911).

[†]See Note 9.2 for a computational formula for r.

Therefore, the estimated standard deviations of the marginal distributions are

$$\hat{\sigma}_X = \sqrt{\frac{\Sigma\,(X_i - \bar{X})^2}{n - 1}} = \sqrt{\frac{2{,}010.92}{11}} = 13.52$$

and

$$\hat{\sigma}_Y = \sqrt{\frac{\Sigma\,(Y_i - \bar{Y})^2}{n - 1}} = \sqrt{\frac{1{,}750.92}{11}} = 12.62$$

The value of the Pearson correlation for these data is

$$r = \left(\frac{\hat{\sigma}_X}{\hat{\sigma}_Y}\right) b = \left(\frac{13.52}{12.62}\right)(-.80) = -.857$$

We will interpret this value for the Pearson correlation between birth rate and the percentage of economically active women in Example 9.7, after we have studied the general properties of this measure. ∎

Properties of _r_   The properties of the Pearson correlation are quite similar in many respects to those of the ordinal measures of association studied in Chapter 8.

1. $-1 \leq r \leq 1$. The standardized version of the slope, unlike b, is constrained to fall between -1 and $+1$. The reason for this will be seen later in the section.

2. r has the same sign as b. Since r is just the slope b multiplied by the ratio of two (positive) estimated standard deviations, the sign is preserved. Thus, $r > 0$ when the variables are positively related and $r < 0$ when the variables are negatively related. Clearly, $r = 0$ for exactly those lines having $b = 0$. So, when $r = 0$, there is not a linear increasing or linear decreasing trend in the relationship between X and Y.

3. $r = \pm 1$ when all the sample points fall exactly on the prediction line. These correspond to perfect positive and perfect negative linear associations. There is then no prediction error when the prediction equation $\hat{Y} = a + bX$ is used to predict the dependent variable.

4. The larger the absolute value of r, the stronger the degree of linear association. Two variables with a correlation of $-.80$ are more strongly related than two variables with a correlation of $.40$, for example. Figure 9.10 shows scatter diagrams corresponding to some possible values of r.

5. The value of r is not dependent on the units in which the variables are measured. For example, if Y had been measured in terms of the number of births per 10,000 population instead of per 1,000 population, we would have obtained the same value of $r = -.857$. Similarly, if one of the variables in a bivariate analysis is income, the correlation is identical regardless of whether the observations are in dollars, thousands of dollars, francs, pounds, or whatever unit we might use.

6. The correlation is a symmetric measure. If we formed a prediction equation that used Y to predict X, the correlation would be the same as in using X to predict Y.

Fig. 9.10 Scatter Diagrams for Different Correlation Coefficients

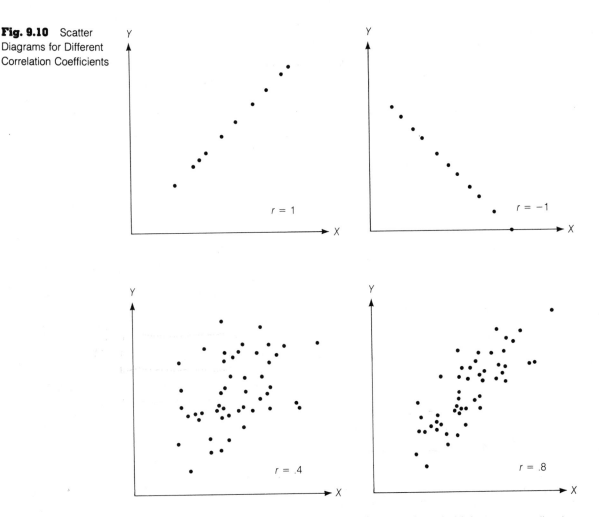

For the main example in this chapter, if we used crude birth rate to predict the percentage of women who are economically active, the correlation would be the same as in predicting the crude birth rate from the percentage of economically active women; i.e., $r = -.857$ in both cases.

7. The correlation is appropriate for use only when a straight line is a reasonable model for the relationship. Since r is proportional to the slope of a linear prediction equation, it measures the strength of the *linear association* between X and Y. If there is a curvilinear relationship between X and Y (as, for example, that shown in Figure 9.11 on page 264), then r may fail to indicate it since the least squares line may be completely or nearly horizontal, and $r = 0$ when $b = 0$. In such a case, a low absolute value for r does not imply that the variables are unassociated, but that the association is not a linear one.

Fig. 9.11 Scatter Diagram for Which $r = 0$, Even Though There Is Strong Curvilinear Relationship

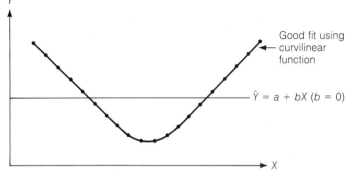

8. The interpretation of the correlation as a type of slope may be further illustrated as follows. We can rewrite the equality $r = (\hat{\sigma}_X/\hat{\sigma}_Y)b$ as $\hat{\sigma}_X b = r\hat{\sigma}_Y$. Now, the slope b is interpreted as the estimated change in the mean of Y for a 1-unit increase in X. Therefore, an increase in X of $\hat{\sigma}_X$ units corresponds to an estimated change in the mean of Y of $\hat{\sigma}_X b$ units (see Figure 9.12). Since $\hat{\sigma}_X b = r\hat{\sigma}_Y$, this implies that an increase of one estimated standard deviation (of X) in X corresponds to a change of r estimated standard deviations (of Y) in the Y variable. Thus, we can interpret the Pearson correlation as the estimated change in the mean of the dependent variable, in terms of the number of standard deviations, for an increase of one standard deviation in the independent variable. Hence, the larger the absolute value of r, the stronger the association, in the sense that for a particular change in the distribution of X, the greater the predicted (standardized) change in the mean of the distribution of Y.

Fig. 9.12 An Increase of $\hat{\sigma}_X$ Units in X Corresponds to a Change of $r\hat{\sigma}_Y$ Units in Y

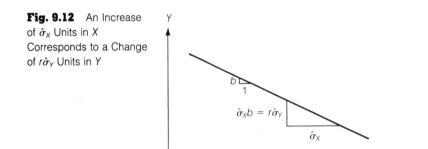

Example 9.7   Again, consider the data on X = percentage of women who are economically active and Y = crude birth rate. The correlation of $r = -.857$ implies that the variables are negatively related in the sample. Also, the least squares line is such that a one standard deviation increase in the percentage of women who are economically active ($\hat{\sigma}_X = 13.52\%$) corresponds to a $-.857$ standard deviation change in crude birth rate (i.e., $r\hat{\sigma}_Y = -.857(12.62) = -10.8$ births per 1,000 population). The change

of $-.857$ standard deviations is independent of whether the birth rate is measured as births per 1,000 population, births per 10,000 population, or whatever. It is the same *real* amount regardless of the units of measurement. If r had been only $-.20$, say, the association would have been much weaker in the sense that a one standard deviation increase in the percentage of women who are economically active would have corresponded to less than one-fourth as large a change in the crude birth rate.

∎

As with other measures of association, the correlation is especially useful for comparisons, since we can compare relationships between variables measured with different units. Suppose that we have two independent variables, X_1 and X_2, that are separately analyzed in bivariate linear models with Y. The two correlation values (denoted by r_{YX_1} and r_{YX_2}) are directly comparable, whereas the b-values may not be. Apart from sampling error, X_1 is more strongly related to Y than is X_2 if $|r_{YX_1}| > |r_{YX_2}|$.

A Proportional Reduction in Error Measure

To obtain another measure of association between two interval variables, we will return to the proportional reduction in error (PRE) formulation introduced in Section 8.4. The basis of such a measure is that the degree of association between two variables X and Y is judged by the goodness of the independent variable X as a predictor of the dependent variable Y. To the extent that the dependent variable Y tends to be predicted much better by substituting the corresponding values of X for the sample members into the equation $\hat{Y} = a + bX$ than it could be predicted without knowing the X-values, the variables are considered to be strongly related. In the following paragraphs, we describe each of the four elements of a PRE measure of association for two interval variables: Rule 1 for predicting Y using only its marginal distribution; Rule 2 for predicting Y using information on X; a summary measure of prediction error for each rule, E_1 for errors by Rule 1 and E_2 for errors by Rule 2; and the definition of the measure of association as the proportional reduction in error, $(E_1 - E_2)/E_1$.

Rule 1 Suppose that we know the distribution of the Y-values in the sample (without knowing which Y-values correspond to particular members), but that we cannot make reference to the values of the independent variable to make predictions about the values of Y for the members in the sample. Then, the best predictor is simply $\bar{Y} = \Sigma Y_i/n$, the sample mean of the observations on the dependent variable. In other words, the one number that tends to be closest to all of the observations, in an aggregate sense, is $\bar{Y}$.

Rule 2 If we know the value of X for each member and if we assume that the relationship between X and Y is linear, then the best predictor of the Y-values for the various members is the least squares prediction equation, $\hat{Y} = a + bX$. For each member, we substitute the appropriate X-value into the prediction equation to get the predicted value of Y. If X is related to Y, this should generally provide better predictions than the crude predictor $\bar{Y}$ used in Rule 1, which completely ignores the fact that the Y-values may tend to change as X changes.

Prediction Errors We define the prediction error for a particular member to be the difference between the observed value on Y and the predicted value on Y. For the ith observation, the prediction error using Rule 1 is $Y_i - \bar{Y}$, and the prediction error using Rule 2 is $Y_i - \hat{Y}_i$, the ith residual. For each predictor, some of the prediction errors will be positive, some will be negative, and the overall sum of the errors will be 0. Thus, it is usual to summarize the prediction errors in each case by the sum of their *squared* values. In other words, the summary measure of prediction error that we use is

$$E = \sum_{i=1}^{n} (i\text{th observed value} - i\text{th predicted value})^2$$

For Rule 1, the predicted values are all $\bar{Y}$, while for Rule 2, they are the $\hat{Y}_i$ values obtained from the least squares equation. The total error by Rule 1 is

$$E_1 = \sum_{i=1}^{n} (Y_i - \bar{Y})^2$$

which is commonly referred to as the **total sum of squares** of the Y-values about their mean and is denoted by TSS. For Rule 2, the measure of the total prediction error is

$$E_2 = \sum_{i=1}^{n} (Y_i - \hat{Y}_i)^2$$

which we have previously denoted by SSE, the *sum of squared errors*. Now a strong relationship between X and Y corresponds to the linear prediction equation yielding predictions ($\hat{Y}_i$) that are much better than $\bar{Y}$, in the sense that the sum of squared prediction errors is substantially less. Graphical interpretations of the two predictors and the corresponding prediction errors are shown in Figure 9.13 for the data on $Y =$ birth rate and $X =$ percentage of women who are economically active. Note that for Rule 1, the same prediction ($\bar{Y}$) is always made for the value of Y, regardless of the value of X.

Fig. 9.13 Graphical Representation of Rule 1 and E_1, Rule 2 and E_2

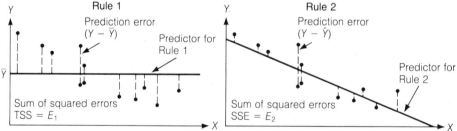

Definition of Measure The proportional reduction in error achieved by using the linear prediction equation instead of $\bar{Y}$ to make the predictions is referred to as the **coefficient of determination** and is customarily denoted by r^2. The PRE formula for r^2 is

$$r^2 = \frac{E_1 - E_2}{E_1} = \frac{\text{TSS} - \text{SSE}}{\text{TSS}}$$

The coefficient of determination, like the Pearson correlation, is also a measure of the degree of *linear* association between X and Y. We emphasize the adjective *linear* here because r^2 is based on how much better a predictor the linear prediction equation is than $\bar{Y}$. Other types of mathematical functions (i.e., nonlinear functions) would yield different predictions, sums of squared errors, and PRE values, as we shall see in Chapter 12. The reason that we use the notation r^2 for this measure is that it is in fact the square of the Pearson correlation r. Once the correlation has been obtained, it is therefore simple to calculate the coefficient of determination. The PRE formula above is useful for interpreting r^2 but is not needed for its calculation.

Example 9.8

In Example 9.6, we observed that the correlation between the percentage of women who are economically active and crude birth rate is $r = -.857$ for the twelve nations in our sample. The coefficient of determination is therefore $r^2 = (-.857)^2 = .734$. Alternatively, we observed that the sum of squared errors using the prediction equation $\hat{Y} = 45.7 - .8X$ is $SSE = \Sigma (Y_i - \hat{Y}_i)^2 = 466.04$. In Example 9.6, we calculated the total sum of squares of the Y-values about their mean to be $\Sigma (Y_i - \bar{Y})^2 = 1{,}750.92$. The sum of squared errors (SSE) using the linear prediction equation is in fact substantially smaller than the sum of squared errors (TSS) using $\bar{Y}$ as the predictor. So, by the definition of the coefficient of determination,

$$r^2 = \frac{TSS - SSE}{TSS} = \frac{1{,}750.92 - 466.04}{1{,}750.92} = \frac{1{,}284.88}{1{,}750.92} = .734$$

We interpret $r^2 = .734$ as follows: Using the function of X given by the linear prediction equation $\hat{Y} = 45.7 - .8X$ to predict the crude birth rates, the amount of error (as measured by the sum of squared errors) is 73.4% smaller than when $\bar{Y}$ is used as the predictor. Equivalently, the amount of error using $\hat{Y}$ as the predictor ($SSE = 466.04$) is only 26.6% [i.e., $(100 - 73.4)\%$] as large as the amount of error using $\bar{Y}$ as the predictor ($TSS = 1{,}750.92$). Since $\Sigma (Y_i - \bar{Y})^2$ summarizes the *variability* of the observations on the dependent variable (this quantity divided by $n - 1$ is the estimated variance $\hat{\sigma}_Y^2$ of the Y-values), the r^2 result is often expressed as X explains 73% of the variability in the dependent variable Y, or 73% of the variance in Y is explained by its linear relationship with X. Roughly speaking, the conditional distribution of Y for a given X has a 73% smaller variance than the marginal distribution of Y. ∎

The properties of the coefficient of determination r^2 follow directly from those of the Pearson correlation r. Since $-1 \leq r \leq 1$, this coefficient is constrained to fall between 0 and 1. SSE can be no larger than TSS, since predictions are at least as good overall when additional information on another variable is available. When $SSE = TSS$, we obtain $r^2 = 0$, in which case $b = 0$ also. When the least squares line has slope 0, the Y-intercept equals $\bar{Y}$ (since $a = \bar{Y} - b\bar{X} = \bar{Y}$ when $b = 0$), so that $\hat{Y} = \bar{Y}$ for all X. The two prediction rules are then identical, so that $SSE = TSS$ and $r^2 = 0$. The minimum possible value for SSE is 0, in which case $r^2 = TSS/TSS = 1$. In order to achieve $SSE = 0$, all sample points must fall exactly on the prediction line so that there is no prediction error using X to predict Y. This condition corresponds to $r =$

± 1. The closer r^2 is to 1, the stronger the linear association, in the sense that the more effective the least squares line $\hat{Y} = a + bX$ is relative to $\bar{Y}$ in predicting the dependent variable. Finally, as with the correlation, r^2 does not depend on the units of measurement, and it is a symmetric measure in terms of the identification of a dependent variable.

To summarize, the Pearson correlation r indicates the direction of the association (positive or negative) through the sign of its value. It falls between -1 and $+1$, and it can be interpreted as a standardized slope, that is, what the slope would be if the units of measurement were such that X and Y were equally disperse. A one standard deviation $(\hat{\sigma}_X)$ increase in X is associated with an r standard deviation $(\hat{\sigma}_Y)$ change in Y. The square of the correlation has a PRE interpretation and is therefore similar in structure to some of the measures of association we studied in Chapter 8. For example, $r = -.3$ indicates that two variables are negatively linearly related, but not very strongly since there is only a 9% $(r^2 = .09)$ reduction in error in using the least squares equation, rather than $\bar{Y}$, to predict Y. For most pairs of variables studied in the social sciences, it is unusual to observe r^2-values greater than .25 or r-values greater than .5 in absolute value.

9.4 Inferences for the Slope and Correlation

Our treatment of the bivariate analysis of interval variables has been primarily descriptive. We have studied how a linear function may be used to represent the *form* of many relationships. We have introduced the Pearson correlation and its square, the coefficient of determination, to describe two aspects of the *strength* of the association between the variables. We now consider inferential procedures for the parameters that characterize the relationship in the population represented by the sample. An inference that is usually of primary interest is the test of whether the variables are in fact associated. This type of test has the same purpose as the chi-square test for nominal variables and the test of the null hypothesis that Kendall's tau-*b* or gamma equals 0 for ordinal variables. In addition, we might be interested in forming a confidence interval for the slope β of the regression equation or for the population value of the Pearson correlation. These inferences enable us to test for the statistical independence of the variables and to estimate the direction and strength of the relationship.

Test of Independence

In this section, we consider situations in which the following assumptions are appropriate for the variables of interest:

1. The mean of Y is related to X by the linear equation $E(Y) = \alpha + \beta X$.
2. The conditional distribution of Y at each value of X is normal.
3. The conditional standard deviation is identical at each X-value.

Under these assumptions, if the conditional mean of Y is identical at each X-value, then the normal conditional distribution of Y is the same at each X-value, and the variables would be described as being statistically independent. For the linear regression model $E(Y) = \alpha + \beta X$, all of the conditional means are equal only when the slope β of the regression line equals 0 (see Figure 9.14). So the null hypothesis that the distribution of the dependent variable does not depend on the value of the independent variable is precisely equivalent to the null hypothesis that the slope of the regression line equals 0.

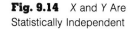

Fig. 9.14 *X* and *Y* Are Statistically Independent

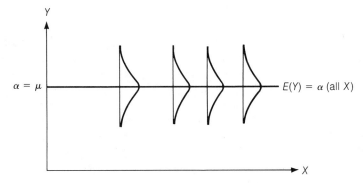

We can test the null hypothesis of independence, H_0: $\beta = 0$, against the two-sided alternative hypothesis H_a: $\beta \neq 0$ or one of the one-sided alternatives H_a: $\beta > 0$ or H_a: $\beta < 0$, depending on whether we are willing (before seeing the data) to predict the direction of the association. If the sample is randomly selected and of size $n \geq 3$, the test statistic takes the form

$$t = \frac{b}{\hat{\sigma}_b}$$

and has the *t* sampling distribution with df $= n - 2$, if H_0 is true. The form of the test statistic is the usual one for a *t* (or *z*) test. We take the point estimate *b* of the parameter β, subtract the null hypothesis value of the parameter (0, corresponding to independence), and divide by the estimated standard error of the point estimate *b*, which we denote by $\hat{\sigma}_b$.

The formula for the estimated standard error of *b* is

$$\hat{\sigma}_b = \frac{\hat{\sigma}}{\sqrt{\Sigma (X_i - \bar{X})^2}}$$

This standard error depends on the point estimate $\hat{\sigma}$ of the standard deviation of the conditional distributions of *Y*. From Section 9.2, this estimate is $\hat{\sigma} = \sqrt{\text{SSE}/(n - 2)}$. Thus, the less disperse these conditional distributions are (i.e., the less the variability of the points about the regression line), the more precise *b* tends to be as an estimate of β. The standard error of *b* is inversely related to $\Sigma (X_i - \bar{X})^2$, the sum of squares of the observed *X*-values about their mean. The larger the sample size *n* (and the more disperse the *X*-values about $\bar{X}$), the larger this sum becomes and the more precise *b* tends to be as an estimate of β. The *P*-value for the test is determined exactly as in the test for a mean, according to whether the alternative hypothesis is one-sided or two-sided. The degrees of freedom for the t sampling distribution are the same as the degrees of freedom of the estimate $\hat{\sigma}^2$, namely, the denominator $n - 2$. When df > 30, recall from Section 6.5 that the t distribution is so similar to the standard normal distribution that we can treat the t test statistic as a z statistic and use the normal probability table to determine the P-value.

Example 9.9   If a society has a "flat" income tax system, then the percentage of income that is paid in taxes is about the same at all income levels. By contrast, a progressive income tax implies that the percentage paid in taxes increases as income increases. Regardless of how the system is designed, in practice it may operate differently because of deductions, tax loopholes, failure to report income, and other factors.

Let X = gross annual income (in thousands of dollars) and let Y = percentage of gross income paid in federal taxes, measured for a random sample of individuals. The model $E(Y) = \alpha + \beta X$ corresponds to the flat tax system if $\beta = 0$ and a progressive tax system if $\beta > 0$. We will use the data in Table 9.4 to test the null hypothesis of a flat tax system ($H_0: \beta = 0$) against the alternative of a progressive tax system ($H_a: \beta > 0$). For an exercise, you can verify that the scatter diagram for these data indicates linearity, that the prediction equation is $\hat{Y} = 1.801 + .410X$, and that some basic statistics are $\Sigma\,(X_i - \bar{X})^2 = 1{,}344$, $\Sigma\,(Y_i - \bar{Y})^2 = 292$, $\text{SSE} = \Sigma\,(Y_i - \hat{Y}_i)^2 = 66.106$, and $r = .880$. The sample data predict that, on the average, the percentage of income taxed increases by $b = .41$ for every thousand dollar increase in gross income.

Table 9.4
Data for Linear Regression of X = Gross Income and Y = Percentage Taxed

OBSERVATION	GROSS INCOME	PERCENTAGE OF INCOME TAXED
1	7	2
2	9	4
3	10	4
4	13	7
5	18	10
6	18	13
7	20	15
8	24	12
9	36	13
10	45	20

The estimated conditional standard deviation of Y for fixed X is

$$\hat{\sigma} = \sqrt{\frac{\text{SSE}}{n - 2}} = \sqrt{\frac{66.106}{8}} = 2.875$$

Therefore, the estimated standard error of the estimate b of β is

$$\hat{\sigma}_b = \frac{\hat{\sigma}}{\sqrt{\Sigma\,(X_i - \bar{X})^2}} = \frac{2.875}{\sqrt{1{,}344}} = .0784$$

This gives us an estimate of the variability in sample slope values that would occur if we repeatedly selected random samples of ten people and calculated prediction equations. The value of the test statistic for testing H_0: $\beta = 0$ is

$$t = \frac{b}{\hat{\sigma}_b} = \frac{.410}{.0784} = 5.23$$

The degrees of freedom when $n = 10$ are df $= n - 2 = 8$, so (from Table B at the end of the text) the P-value is $P < .005$ for the one-sided alternative H_a: $\beta > 0$. Even though the sample is quite small, we can feel confident in rejecting the hypothesis that the tax system operates like a flat tax. There is strong evidence that, on the average, percentage of income taxed increases as gross income increases. ■

One should keep in mind that this test of independence is based on the linear model and is therefore appropriate for detecting positive or negative *linear* associations. If the true relationship were U-shaped, for example, the variables would be statistically dependent, since the mean of Y would change according to the value of X. This t test is not designed to detect it, however, since the slope b of the least squares line would be 0 or relatively close to 0. In other words, we would probably not reject the null hypothesis H_0: $\beta = 0$ even though there is a certain type of association between the variables. In summary, $\beta = 0$ need not correspond to independence if the assumptions we made at the beginning of the section are violated. The null hypothesis H_0: $\beta = 0$ is often described as no *linear* association between X and Y, since β could equal 0 even when the variables are associated in a *nonlinear* manner.

Confidence Interval for the Slope When we reject H_0: $\beta = 0$ in the test of independence, we conclude that the regression line has a nonzero slope. However, we may be more interested in the size of the slope than in knowing merely that it is not 0. If the absolute value of the slope is relatively small, the association could be a statistically significant but practically unimportant one. We might find it more informative, therefore, to obtain a confidence interval for the regression coefficient β. This can be obtained readily from statistics already calculated, according to the formula

$$b \pm t_{\alpha/2}\hat{\sigma}_b$$

where $t_{\alpha/2}$ represents the value from Table B corresponding to the confidence coefficient $(1 - \alpha)$, with df $= n - 2$. This interval is similar in form to the confidence interval for a mean (see Section 6.4). We take the point estimate b and add and subtract some t multiple of the estimated standard error of the point estimate.

Example 9.10 For the data in Example 9.9 on X = gross income and Y = percentage of income taxed, we obtained $b = .410$ and $\hat{\sigma}_b = .0784$. To obtain a 95% confidence interval for

β, the change in the mean percentage of income taxed for a $1,000 increase in gross income (i.e., a 1-unit increase in X), we use the $t_{.025}$ value for df $= n - 2 = 8$, which is $t_{.025} = 2.306$. The interval is

$$b \pm t_{.025}\hat{\sigma}_b = .41 \pm 2.306(.0784)$$
$$= .41 \pm .18 \quad \text{or} \quad (.23, .59)$$

We can be 95% confident that β lies between .23 and .59. The mean of the percentage of income taxed is predicted to increase by between .23 and .59 for every $1,000 increase in gross income. The interval contains only positive numbers, so we can be confident that the relationship is positive in direction. ■

A confidence interval for β may not be very meaningful if a 1-unit increase in X is small, in practical terms. Then it may be more useful to make inferences about the change in $E(Y)$ for an increase in X that is a larger portion of the actual range of X values. To get a confidence interval for a constant multiple of the slope (e.g., 10β, the change in the mean of Y for an increase of 10 units in X), we would multiply the endpoints of the interval for β by the same constant.

Example 9.11   Suppose we want to compare the mean percentage of income taxed for people at $X = 20$ and at $X = 30$. The change or difference in the mean of Y for a difference in X-values of 10 is simply the slope multiplied by 10. That is, the difference between $E(Y \mid X = 20)$ and $E(Y \mid X = 30)$ is 10β, assuming that the linear regression equation is appropriate. A confidence interval for 10β is given by $10b \pm 10t_{\alpha/2}\hat{\sigma}_b$, or from $10(b - t_{\alpha/2}\hat{\sigma}_b)$ to $10(b + t_{\alpha/2}\hat{\sigma}_b)$. For the data in Example 9.9, a 95% confidence interval for 10β goes from $10(.23) = 2.3$ to $10(.59) = 5.9$, since $(.23, .59)$ is the 95% confidence interval for β. We feel 95% confident, in other words, that the mean percentage of income taxed for people having $30,000 gross income is between 2.3% and 5.9% higher than for people having $20,000 gross income. ■

Inference for the Pearson Correlation*   We observed in Section 9.3 that the Pearson correlation r (or its square, the coefficient of determination) is 0 in exactly the same situations in which the slope b of the least squares line is 0. Similarly, letting ρ (rho) denote the value of the Pearson correlation corresponding to the regression equation $E(Y) = \alpha + \beta X$ (i.e., ρ is the population value of r), $\rho = 0$ precisely when $\beta = 0$. Thus, a test of H_0: $\rho = 0$ using the sample value r is equivalent to the test we have seen of H_0: $\beta = 0$ using the sample value b. The test statistic for testing H_0: $\rho = 0$ is

$$t = \frac{r}{\sqrt{\dfrac{1 - r^2}{n - 2}}}$$

which gives exactly the same value as the test statistic $t = b/\hat{\sigma}_b$. Either test statistic may be used to test the null hypothesis of independence, since each has the t sampling distribution with df $= n - 2$ when H_0 is true and yields the same P-value.

For example, the Pearson correlation of .880 for the tax data in Example 9.9 leads

$$t = \frac{r}{\sqrt{\dfrac{1 - r^2}{n - 2}}} = \frac{.880}{\sqrt{\dfrac{1 - .774}{8}}} = 5.23$$

and $P < .005$ for the one-sided alternative H_a: $\rho > 0$. These are the same t- and P-values observed in Example 9.9 for testing H_0: $\beta = 0$ against H_a: $\beta > 0$.

The method of obtaining a confidence interval for ρ is slightly more complicated than that for obtaining a confidence interval for the slope β, however. The reason for this is that the sampling distribution of r is not symmetric except in the special case when $\rho = 0$. The lack of symmetry is caused by the restricted range of $[-1, 1]$ for r values. If the true ρ is close to 1.0, for instance, then the sample r cannot fall much above ρ, but it can fall well below ρ, and the sampling distribution of r is skewed to the left.

The approach that is used for confidence intervals is to obtain a mathematical transformation of r for which the sampling distribution is simple (a normal distribution), and then to calculate a confidence interval for the corresponding mathematical transformation of ρ. The transformation of r has the form $T(r) = 1.151 \log[(1 + r)/(1 - r)]$ where log denotes the (base-10) logarithm. The corresponding transformation of the population value ρ is denoted by $T(\rho)$. The values of $T(r)$ corresponding to various r-values* are given in Table E at the end of the text. The variable $T(r)$ is approximately normally distributed about $T(\rho)$ with standard error $\sigma_T = 1/\sqrt{n - 3}$. The normal approximation is quite good when the sample size is at least 25, and is used in practice for sample sizes as small as 10. Thus, a $100(1 - \alpha)\%$ confidence interval for $T(\rho)$ is $T(r) \pm z_{\alpha/2}\sigma_T$. The larger the sample size, the narrower the width of this interval. Once we get the endpoints of the interval for $T(\rho)$, we see which two ρ values are transformed into those endpoints in Table E. These two values are then the endpoints of the corresponding confidence interval for ρ.

In estimating the correlation, the sample (X, Y) values must be a random sample from the *joint* (X, Y) distribution; that is, it is important to sample properly the X variation as well as the Y variation. If a sample were selected that had a much narrower range of variation in X than did the population, for example, then the sample correlation could underestimate drastically (in absolute value) the population correlation.

Example 9.12   The sample we have used to illustrate the analyses in this chapter has only ten observations. For such a small sample size, the confidence interval approach we just mentioned is very approximate. With this fact in mind, we will again use those data to illustrate the basic method and the use of Table E.

We observed a sample correlation of $r = .880$ between percentage of income taxed and gross income for the ten people sampled. From Table E, this corresponds

---

*Table E lists only positive values of r and $T(r)$, but a similar relationship applies to negative r and $T(r)$ values.

to a value of $T(r) = 1.3758$. The standard error of $T(r)$ is $\sigma_T = 1/\sqrt{n-3} = 1/\sqrt{7} = .378$. A 95% confidence interval for $T(\rho)$ is

$$T(r) \pm 1.96\sigma_T = 1.3758 \pm 1.96(.378) \quad \text{or} \quad (.635, 2.117)$$

From Table E, $T(\rho) = .635$ corresponds to a correlation of about .561 and $T(\rho) = 2.117$ corresponds to a correlation of about .971. The 95% confidence interval for ρ is therefore $(.561, .971)$. Again, the fact that the interval contains only positive values reaffirms our belief that the association between the variables is positive. Since the values in the interval are relatively far from 0, we can be quite confident that there is a substantial positive association. ∎

Unless $r = 0$, the confidence interval for ρ is not symmetric about the point estimate r, due to the nonsymmetry of the sampling distribution of r. For the interval in the previous example, the upper endpoint of .971 is much closer to the sample value $r = .880$ than is the lower endpoint of .561.

We can get a confidence interval for the population value ρ^2 of the coefficient of determination directly from the confidence interval for ρ. If we are 95% sure that ρ is between .561 and .971, then this corresponds to being 95% sure that ρ^2 is between $(.561)^2 = .31$ and $(.971)^2 = .94$. We can be confident that there is at least a 31% reduction in prediction error in using gross income to predict percentage of income taxed.

If the confidence interval for ρ includes 0, then the lower endpoint of the confidence interval for ρ^2 is also 0, and the upper endpoint is the larger of the squared endpoints of the confidence interval for ρ. For example, the confidence interval of $(-.4, .1)$ for ρ translates to the confidence interval $(0, .16)$ for ρ^2.

9.5
Some Practical
Considerations

Before ending this chapter, we shall reconsider some of the basic assumptions underlying linear regression analysis. In addition, we illustrate the interpretation of a typical computer output from a canned regression program.

Comments About Assumptions

Our use of the linear regression model rests upon the assumption that a straight line can provide a reasonable approximation for the true (unknown) form of the relationship between X and Y. Even though we would not expect the relationship to be exactly linear, especially if the range of X-values is large, a linear function often provides a reasonable *approximation* for the actual form (as in Figure 9.15). If the assumption is badly violated (as with a U-shaped relationship), our results and conclusions using the linear model will be very misleading. For this reason, it is always important to look at a scatter diagram as a check on this fundamental assumption.

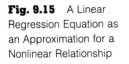

Fig. 9.15 A Linear
Regression Equation as
an Approximation for a
Nonlinear Relationship

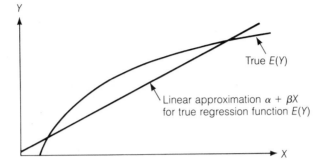

The least squares line and the measures of association r and r^2 are informative descriptive statistics no matter what the form of the conditional distribution of Y-values for each X-value. However, the inferences we made in Section 9.4 about the slope β require the additional assumption that the conditional distributions of Y must be normal with identical standard deviation σ for each X-value. This assumption is again one that would never be *exactly* satisfied in practice. However, the closer the real situation is to this ideal model, the more appropriate are the confidence interval and test procedures we introduced in the previous section. Also, as usual, we need to assume that the sample was randomly selected.

For any use of regression, it is important to think carefully about whether the linearity specification or the inferential assumptions are likely to be badly violated. For example, consider the variables X = gross income and Y = percentage of income taxed, for which data were analyzed in Examples 9.9–9.12. First, nearly all people at low incomes have a low percentage taxed, whereas at high incomes some people pay a high percentage but some (because of itemized deductions and loopholes) pay little or even no taxes. Thus, the variation in Y-values is very likely to increase dramatically as X increases. Second, the *nominal* tax rate (in 1985) is approximately linearly related to income (more accurately, to the *logarithm* of income) over most of its range. Because of deductions and loopholes that the wealthy are more able to exploit, however, the *effective* tax rate is curvilinear, with a leveling off or even a decline beyond a certain point. Thus, we must realize that our simple linear model is completely inappropriate for very large X-values, and that for other X-values it is only a very crude approximation for reality. In the last section of Chapter 12, we shall see how the residuals can be examined to check some of the assumptions made in regression modeling.

A Computer Printout

The calculations for the techniques discussed in this chapter are more numerous and complicated than those encountered in previous chapters. For even a moderate sample size, a calculator is almost a necessity for computing the least squares line, the correlation, and the related inference procedures. For the models that we consider in Chapter 11, it can be very tedious to calculate the corresponding statistics even with a hand calculator. The calculations can be handled very quickly and easily by a computer, however. There are many computer packages that will perform regression analyses, and most college campuses have access to at least one of them. Also, many small home (personal) computers have software available for performing statistical methods such as regression. In order to use such programs, the user simply supplies certain statements defining the variables to be used and others specifying the procedure to be performed (e.g., regression) and the options desired (e.g., scatter diagrams, correlation coefficients). The specific program statements needed depend, of course, on the computer installation and the program package used.

Most regression programs have fairly similar output, and we conclude this chapter with an illustration of what the printout is likely to resemble if we run such a program to analyze the data presented in this section on X = gross income and Y = percentage of income taxed. For most packaged programs, there is a page or two of output listing the sums of squares, the descriptive measures, and the corresponding inference procedures considered in regression analysis. These usually include the Y-intercept (a) and slope (b) of the least squares line, the total sum of squares (TSS) for the dependent variable, the sum of squared errors (SSE) for the prediction equation, the coefficient of determination (r^2), the Pearson correlation (r), the point estimate $\hat{\sigma}$ of the conditional standard deviation σ, the degrees of freedom for that estimate, the t test statistic value and its P-value for the test of independence, and a variety of other items. Figure 9.16 is a typical output for the example considered in this chapter.[*]

In the upper part of the printout, the total sum of squares, TSS $= \Sigma (Y_i - \bar{Y})^2 = 292.0$ is partitioned into two parts, the sum of squared errors (SSE = 66.106) and the difference between TSS and SSE, TSS $-$ SSE $= 225.894$. This difference is the numerator of the r^2 measure and is commonly referred to as the *regression sum of squares*. It represents the amount of the total variation TSS in Y that is explained by X in using the least squares line. The ratio of the regression sum of squares to the total sum of squares is just r^2, which is listed in the upper part of the printout under R-SQUARE. If SSE = 66.106 is divided by its degrees of freedom, df $= n - 2 = 8$, we get $\hat{\sigma}^2 = 8.263$. On the printout this is referred to as the MEAN SQUARE ERROR (sometimes abbreviated by MSE). Its square root is the estimate of the standard deviation of the conditional distributions of Y, $\hat{\sigma} = \sqrt{8.263} = 2.875$, which is listed under the heading ROOT MSE. The degrees of freedom for the total sum of squares TSS $= \Sigma (Y_i - \bar{Y})^2$ is $n - 1 = 9$, since one parameter (μ, the mean of the marginal distribution of Y) is estimated before its computation. The regression sum of squares is said to have one degree of freedom, corresponding to the fact that there is one independent variable in the model. In general, the sum of df for the regression sum of squares and df for the sum of squared errors equals df $= n - 1$ for the total sum of squares.

---

[*] This sample output is patterned somewhat after the standard output for the SAS System program using the General Linear Model (GLM) or Regression (REG) procedures. Other programs use somewhat different formats. For instance, in SPSS[X], ROOT MSE is labeled STANDARD ERROR.

Fig. 9.16 Regression Analysis for Y = Percentage of Income Taxed and X = Gross Income

```
                          SUM OF                      ROOT      R-SQUARE
SOURCE            DF      SQUARES    MEAN SQUARE       MSE
   REGRESSION     1       225.894      225.894       2.875        .774
   ERROR          8        66.106        8.263
   TOTAL          9       292.000

                                   T FOR H0:                   STD ERROR
PARAMETER         ESTIMATE      PARAMETER=0     PROB>|T|     OF ESTIMATE
   INTERCEPT       1.801
   INCOME           .410            5.23          .0008         .0784

                          OBSERVED        PREDICTED
OBSERVATION                VALUE            VALUE          RESIDUAL
     1                     2.000            4.670           -2.670
     2                     4.000            5.490           -1.490
     3                     4.000            5.900           -1.900
     4                     7.000            7.130           -0.130
     5                    10.000            9.180            0.820
     6                    13.000            9.180            3.820
     7                    15.000           10.000            5.000
     8                    12.000           11.640            0.360
     9                    13.000           16.560           -3.560
    10                    20.000           20.249           -0.249

   SUM OF RESIDUALS            = 0.000
   SUM OF SQUARED RESIDUALS  = 66.106

   CORRELATION COEFF./PROB>|R| UNDER H0: RHO=0
                  .880
                  .0008
```

The least squares estimates of α and β are listed under the heading ESTIMATE. The estimate of the Y-intercept is $a = 1.801$ (listed opposite INTERCEPT) and the estimate of the slope is $b = .410$ (listed opposite the variable name of which it is the coefficient in the prediction equation, INCOME). The estimated standard error of b, $\hat{\sigma}_b = .0784$, is given under STD ERROR OF ESTIMATE. The corresponding t test statistic value, $t = b/\hat{\sigma}_b = .410/.0784 = 5.23$, for the test of independence $H_0: \beta = 0$, is listed under T FOR H0: PARAMETER = 0. The number under PROB > |T| is the P-value, $P = .0008$,* for the two-sided alternative $H_a: \beta \neq 0$; that is, it is the (two-tailed) probability of observing a t statistic at least as large in absolute value as the absolute value of the observed t, $|t| = 5.23$, if H_0 were true. For the one-sided alternative $H_a: \beta > 0$, this level would be halved (to .0004), since P is then just the right-hand tail probability corresponding to getting $t > 5.23$, if H_0 were true.

*The P-values are completely tabulated for most standard distributions and are stored within the memory of the computer, so that exact values may be given. Hence, we have $P = .0008$ instead of just $P < .01$, for example.

At the bottom of Figure 9.16 are listed the observed values for the dependent variable Y = percentage of income taxed for the ten people sampled. Opposite these are listed the ten predicted values as obtained from the prediction equation $\hat{Y} = 1.80 + .41X$. The residuals, $Y_i - \hat{Y}_i$, are also given for the ten values. Finally, the sum of the residuals is given (this should be 0) as well as the sum of squared residuals, which is identical to the SSE term given near the top of the printout. As an option, the Pearson correlation can also be listed, together with its P-value for testing $H_0: \rho = 0$ against $H_a: \rho \neq 0$. This is the same as the P-value for testing $H_0: \beta = 0$ against $H_a: \beta \neq 0$.

Summary

Chapters 8 and 9 have dealt with the detection and description of association between two variables. In Chapter 8, we used the chi-square statistic to test for independence and the difference of proportions and Goodman and Kruskal's tau to measure the strength of the association between two nominal variables. We used gamma and Kendall's tau-b to describe the degree of association between two ordinal variables, and we used z tests based on their values to test for the existence of an association in the population. In this chapter, we used the Pearson correlation r and its square, the coefficient of determination, to describe the degree of the linear association between two interval variables. A t test was formulated based on the sample values of r and r^2 to test the null hypothesis of no association, namely, that the corresponding population values of ρ and ρ^2 are 0. These procedures are summarized by the measurement level of the variables in Table 9.5.

Table 9.5   Summary of Tests of No Association and Measures of Association

| | MEASUREMENT LEVELS OF VARIABLES | | |
	Nominal	Ordinal	Interval
Null hypothesis for test of no association	H_0: Independence	$H_0: \tau_b = 0$ or $H_0: \gamma = 0$	$H_0: \beta = 0$ or $H_0: \rho = 0$
Test statistic	$\chi^2 = \sum \dfrac{(f_o - f_e)^2}{f_e},$ $\text{df} = (r - 1)(c - 1)$	$z = \dfrac{C - D}{\sigma_{C-D}}$	$t = \dfrac{b}{\hat{\sigma}_b},$ or $t = \dfrac{r}{\sqrt{\dfrac{1 - r^2}{n - 2}}}$ $\text{df} = n - 2$
Measure of association	$\hat{\pi}_2 - \hat{\pi}_1$ (2 × 2 tables) $\hat{\tau} = \dfrac{E_1 - E_2}{E_1}$ (Goodman and Kruskal's tau)	$\hat{\gamma} = \dfrac{C - D}{C + D}$ (gamma) $\hat{\tau}_b = \dfrac{C - D}{\sqrt{[n(n-1)/2 - T_x][n(n-1)/2 - T_y]}}$ (Kendall's tau-b)	$r = b\left(\dfrac{\hat{\sigma}_X}{\hat{\sigma}_Y}\right),$ $r^2 = \dfrac{E_1 - E_2}{E_1}$

A new element considered in this chapter was that of describing the mathematical form of the relationship between the independent variable and the mean of the dependent variable. We used the *linear regression equation* $E(Y) = \alpha + \beta X$ for this purpose. This model is appropriate whenever the rate of change in the mean of the dependent variable is the same over the entire range of values of the independent variable. The *method of least squares* was used to estimate the Y-intercept α and the slope β and to generate a linear prediction equation $\hat{Y} = a + bX$. The *Pearson correlation r* is a standardized slope, constrained to fall between -1 and $+1$, with its square having a proportional reduction in error interpretation. A *scatter diagram* should be used to check whether the relationship is approximately linear in form. If it is clearly nonlinear, then a different regression model must be used.

In Chapter 11, we will introduce the *multiple* regression model for generalizing this approach so that *several* independent variables may be included in the model. Then, in Chapter 12, we will consider methods for modeling nonlinear relationships and more complex relationships between a dependent variable and a collection of independent variables. Before discussing multivariate models, though, in Chapter 10 we introduce some new concepts that help us to interpret multivariate relationships.

Notes

Section 9.2

1. The formula for the Y-intercept, $a = \bar{Y} - b\bar{X}$, can be expressed as $\bar{Y} = a + b\bar{X}$. This shows that if the X-value of $\bar{X}$ is substituted into the prediction equation, the predicted Y-value is $\hat{Y} = \bar{Y}$. In other words, the least squares prediction equation passes through the point with coordinates $(\bar{X}, \bar{Y})$, the center of gravity of the data.

Section 9.3

2. The Pearson correlation can also be defined in terms of the original data, using formulas similar to the ones given for b:

$$r = \frac{\Sigma\,(X_i - \bar{X})(Y_i - \bar{Y})}{\sqrt{[\Sigma\,(X_i - \bar{X})^2][\Sigma\,(Y_i - \bar{Y})^2]}}$$

$$= \frac{\Sigma\,X_i Y_i - (\Sigma\,X_i)(\Sigma\,Y_i)/n}{\sqrt{[\Sigma\,X_i^2 - (\Sigma\,X_i)^2/n][\Sigma\,Y_i^2 - (\Sigma\,Y_i)^2/n]}}$$

In the population, the correlation is often defined as

$$\frac{\text{Covariance of } X \text{ and } Y}{(\text{Standard deviation of } X)(\text{Standard deviation of } Y)}$$

where the *covariance* between X and Y is the average of the cross-products $(X - \mu_X)(Y - \mu_Y)$ about the population means.

3. To see why r does not depend on the units of measurement, suppose that the values of Y are multiplied by a constant c. Then the slope is multiplied by c and $\hat{\sigma}_Y$ is multiplied by c, so that

$$r = (cb)\hat{\sigma}_X / (c\hat{\sigma}_Y) = b\hat{\sigma}_X / \hat{\sigma}_Y$$

remains the same.

Section 9.4

4. Suppose that the linear regression equation $E(Y) = \alpha + \beta X$ with constant standard deviation σ is truly appropriate for the relationship between Y and X. Then, as the sample size increases, the least squares equation $\hat{Y} = a + bX$ becomes a better estimate of that line, since a and b become more precise estimates of α and β. Our best prediction for a value of Y (or for the mean of the conditional distribution of Y) at a particular value of X is $\hat{Y} = a + bX$. The interval of numbers

$$\hat{Y} \pm t_{\alpha/2}\hat{\sigma}\sqrt{1 + \frac{1}{n} + \frac{(X - \bar{X})^2}{\Sigma (X_i - \bar{X})^2}}$$

can be used to predict where a new observation on Y will fall at that value of X. This interval is called a $100(1 - \alpha)\%$ *prediction interval* for Y. To make an inference about the mean of Y (rather than a single value of Y) at that value of X, one can use the *confidence interval*

$$\hat{Y} \pm t_{\alpha/2}\hat{\sigma}\sqrt{\frac{1}{n} + \frac{(X - \bar{X})^2}{\Sigma (X_i - \bar{X})^2}}$$

The $t_{\alpha/2}$ value in these intervals is based on df $= n - 2$. For the data in Table 9.1, for instance, $\hat{Y} = 29.7$ at $X = 20$, and a 95% confidence interval for the mean birth rate at $X = 20$ is

$$29.7 \pm 2.228(6.83)\sqrt{\frac{1}{12} + \frac{(20 - 23.92)^2}{2{,}010.92}}$$

$$= 29.7 \pm 4.6 \quad \text{or} \quad (25.1, \, 34.3)$$

5. If natural logs (log to base e) are used instead of base-10 logs, the formula for the transformation used in obtaining a confidence interval for the Pearson correlation is

$$T(r) = \frac{1}{2}\log_e\left(\frac{1 + r}{1 - r}\right)$$

Problems

1. Plot the following lines on a pair of coordinate axes:
a. $Y = 2 + .5X$
b. $Y = 3 + .5X$
c. $Y = 3 + X$

d. $Y = X$

e. $Y = 3 - X$

f. $Y = 3 - .5X$

2. For data in certain congressional elections in 1984, the least squares line relating Y = percentage of vote for Democratic candidate to X = percentage of residents in district voting is claimed to be $\hat{Y} = 48.9 + .1X$.

a. Interpret the slope of this equation.

b. Is the Y-intercept meaningful in this example? Why?

3. For a sample of fifty families, data are obtained on X = number of children in family and Y = weekly expenditure for food (in dollars). The data are well described by the prediction equation $\hat{Y} = 50 + 15X$.

a. Interpret the Y-intercept of the prediction equation.

b. Interpret the slope of the prediction equation.

c. Find the predicted weekly expenditure for food for a family having two children.

d. Find the difference in estimated mean weekly food expenditures for families having five children and families having two children.

4. A college admissions officer claims that the relationship between Y = college GPA and X = high school GPA (both measured on a 4-point scale) for students at that college can be approximated by the prediction equation $\hat{Y} = -2 + 8X$. Is this equation realistic? Why or why not?

5. Suppose that the prediction equation relating Y = college GPA to X = high school GPA is $\hat{Y} = .5 + .7X$.

a. Interpret the values of the Y-intercept and the slope of the prediction line.

b. Suppose the prediction equation were $\hat{Y} = X$. Identify the Y-intercept and slope, and interpret their values.

6. Data are obtained on the variables X = proportion of labor force with agricultural occupations and Y = proportion of households with nuclear family members only, for a sample of nations. The least squares line that is fitted to the data is $\hat{Y} = .97 - .20X$.

a. Plot the least squares line.

b. Find the predicted value of Y for a nation with $X = .50$, and interpret that value.

c. What can be said about the Pearson correlation between X and Y?

d. As X ranges from 0 to 1, what is the range of predicted proportion values for Y?

7. Refer to Problem 3. The data can also be described by $\bar{X} = 2.4$, $\hat{\sigma}_X = 1.3$, $\bar{Y} = 86.0$, and $\hat{\sigma}_Y = 39.0$. Using this information and the formula $\hat{Y} = 50 + 15X$ for the prediction equation:

a. Find the correlation between X and Y.

b. Interpret the sign of the correlation.

c. Interpret the correlation as a standardized slope.

d. Interpret the square of the correlation.

8. Describe a situation in which it would be inappropriate to use the Pearson correlation to measure the association between two interval variables.

9. A high school student decides to see if there is any relationship between X = number of books read for pleasure in the previous year, and Y = number of hours spent watching television (daily average). For her three best friends, the observations are as follows:

X	Y
0	5
5	3
10	1

a. Draw a scatter diagram for the data.
b. Find the least squares prediction equation.
c. Find the sample correlation between X and Y.

10. Refer to Problem 2. Suppose that the sample correlation between Y and X is $r = .05$.
a. Interpret the sign of the correlation.
b. Interpret the square of the correlation. Would you conclude that the sample association is strong, or weak?
c. Suppose that when Y is predicted using X = average annual income of residents in district, the sample correlation is $r = -.40$. Which of these two independent variables seems to be a better predictor of Y = percentage of vote for the Democratic candidate?

11. The least squares line fitted to a collection of data involving X = years of education and Y = annual income (in dollars) is $\hat{Y} = 1,000 + 1,500X$.
a. If the sum of squares of deviations about the least squares line is three-fourths as large as the sum of squares of deviations about $\bar{Y}$, then what does r equal?
b. Suppose now that Y refers to annual income, in thousands of dollars. Give the prediction equation and the correlation.
c. Suppose that Y is treated as the independent variable and X is treated as the dependent variable. Then could the correlation coefficient change in value? Could the slope be different than when Y is treated as the dependent variable?

12. The variables Y = annual income (thousands of dollars), X_1 = number of years of education, and X_2 = number of years in job are measured for all the employees having city-funded jobs, in Knoxville, Tennessee. The following prediction equations and correlations are obtained:

$$\hat{Y} = 5 + 1.0X_1 \qquad r_{YX_1} = .30$$
$$\hat{Y} = 9 + .4X_2 \qquad r_{YX_2} = .60$$
$$r_{X_1X_2} = -.40$$

Which of the following statements are true?
a. The strongest association is between Y and X_2.
b. The weakest association is between X_1 and X_2.
c. The least squares prediction equation for using X_2 to predict X_1 would have negative slope.

d. A standard deviation increase in education corresponds to a predicted increase of .3 standard deviation in income.

e. There is a 30% reduction in error in using education (instead of $\bar{Y}$) to predict income.

f. Each additional year on the job is predicted to correspond to a $400 increase in income, on the average.

g. When X_1 is used to predict Y, the sum of squared residuals (SSE) is larger than when X_2 is used to predict Y.

h. The mean income for employees having 20 years experience is predicted to be $4,000 higher than the mean income for employees having 10 years experience.

i. If $\hat{\sigma} = 5$ for the model where X_1 is used to predict Y, then it is not unusual to observe an income of $45,000 for an employee who has 10 years of education.

*j. It is possible that $\bar{Y} = 20$ and $\bar{X}_1 = 13$.

*k. It is possible that $\hat{\sigma}_Y = 8.0$ and $\hat{\sigma}_{X_1} = 2.4$.

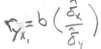

Select the best response(s) in Problems 13–15.

13. We can interpret $r = .3$ as follows:

a. There is a 30% reduction in error when we use X to predict Y.

b. There is a 9% reduction in error when we use X to predict Y.

c. 9% of the time $\hat{Y} = Y$.

d. Y changes .3 unit for every 1-unit increase in X.

e. When we use X to predict Y, the average residual is .3.

14. The correlation is inappropriate as a measure of association between two interval variables:

a. When different people measure the variables using different units.

b. When the relationship between the variables is highly nonlinear.

c. When the data points fall exactly on a straight line.

d. When the slope of the least squares line is 0.

e. When Y tends to decrease as X increases.

15. The slope of the least squares prediction equation and the Pearson correlation coefficient are similar in the sense that:

a. They do not depend on the units of measurement of the variables.

b. They both must fall between -1 and $+1$.

c. They both have the same sign.

d. They both equal 1 when there is the strongest association.

e. Their squares both have PRE interpretations.

f. They give the same t statistic value for testing H_0: Independence.

16. In an article in *USA Today* (Dec. 28, 1984), sociologists Norval Glenn and Beth Ann Shelton are quoted as showing a strong link between residential mobility and divorce rates. The accompanying data (next page) are based on surveys by the National Opinion Research Center. Divorce rate is the annual number of divorces and annulments per 1,000 population. Mobility rate is the percentage of people living in a different house from 5 years ago.

REGION	MOBILITY RATE	DIVORCE RATE
New England	41	4.0
Middle Atlantic	37	3.4
East North Central	44	5.1
West North Central	46	4.6
South Atlantic	47	5.6
East South Central	44	6.0
West South Central	50	6.5
Mountain	57	7.6
Pacific	56	5.9

a. Treating divorce rate as the dependent variable, construct a scatter diagram. Do these variables seem to be linearly associated?

b. Find the prediction equation, and interpret the slope.

c. Find the Pearson correlation, and interpret its value.

d. Calculate the coefficient of determination, and interpret its value.

17. A study is conducted using forty-nine Catholic female undergraduates at a large southwestern university. The variables measured refer to the parents of these students. The dependent variable is the number of children that the parents have. One of the independent variables is the mother's educational level, measured in terms of the number of years of formal education. For the forty-nine observations on these variables, we get $\Sigma X = 484$, $\Sigma Y = 164$, $\Sigma X^2 = 5,462$, $\Sigma Y^2 = 780$, $\Sigma XY = 1,479$, and $\Sigma (Y - \hat{Y})^2 = 201.95$.

a. Find the estimated mean and standard deviation for mother's education, and the estimated mean and standard deviation for number of children.

b. Find the prediction equation and interpret the Y-intercept and slope.

c. Give the predicted numbers of children for women with 8, 12, and 16 years of education.

d. Find the Pearson correlation and interpret its value.

e. Find the coefficient of determination and interpret its value.

f. Conduct a test of the null hypothesis that mean number of children is independent of mother's educational level, and report the P-value.

g. Find a 95% confidence interval for the slope of the regression equation.

h. Find a 95% confidence interval for the difference between the mean number of children for two sets of mothers who are eight years apart in educational level.

18. To determine which students should receive scholarships, a university admissions officer decided to study the relationship between a student's score on the SAT verbal test (taken in the final year of high school) and the student's college GPA at the end of the sophomore year. Ten student records were examined with the results shown in the accompanying table. The reported exam scores are the actual scores divided by 100.

STUDENT	SAT	GPA
1	4.8	2.4
2	6.6	3.5
3	5.9	3.0
4	7.4	3.8
5	3.8	2.7
6	5.2	2.4
7	6.6	3.0
8	5.0	2.8
9	7.2	3.4
10	6.0	3.2

Let X = SAT score and Y = GPA. Then $\Sigma X^2 = 354.05$, $\Sigma Y^2 = 93.14$, $\Sigma XY = 180.66$, $\Sigma X = 58.5$, $\Sigma Y = 30.2$, and $\Sigma (Y - \hat{Y})^2 = .5927$.

a. Draw a scatter diagram displaying the observed relationship between X and Y.

b. Find the least squares prediction equation, and graph it on the scatter diagram.

c. Interpret the slope of the prediction equation.

d. Find the predicted GPA and residual for the first student in the sample.

e. Find the Pearson correlation, and interpret the sign and magnitude of its value.

f. Find the coefficient of determination and interpret its magnitude.

g. The admissions officer believed that there would be a positive association between SAT and GPA. Can we accept his hypothesis at the $\alpha = .01$ level, based on the data?

h. Find a 95% confidence interval for the slope of the regression equation. Interpret this interval.

i. Could you make a statistical conclusion about the mean GPA of students who score 800 ($X = 8$) on the SAT, based on the data? Why?

19. For the nations listed in Table 9.1, their per capita gross national product (GNP) values (in dollars) at a comparable date were, respectively, 990, 1550, 7450, 4220, 630, 150, 2560, 1070, 4910, 410, 7890, and 2760. Use a computer package to do the following analyses, for Y = crude birth rate and X = GNP.

a. Obtain a scatter diagram, and indicate whether a linear model seems appropriate.

b. Find the prediction equation, and interpret the Y-intercept and slope.

c. Find r and r^2, and interpret their values.

20. Refer to Example 9.9. The values of the independent variable X = number of deductions claimed are (in order) for the same sample: 5, 3, 4, 6, 4, 5, 1, 2, 4, 3. Use a computer package to do the following analyses, for X and Y = percentage of income taxed.

a. Find the prediction equation, and interpret the Y-intercept and slope.

b. List the predicted values and residuals, and find SSE.

c. Find the Pearson correlation, and interpret its value.

d. Find the coefficient of determination, and interpret its value.

e. Find the P-value for testing H_0: $\beta = 0$ against H_a: $\beta < 0$, and interpret.

f. Construct a 95% confidence interval for β, and interpret it.

g. Use the result of part f to obtain a 95% confidence interval for the difference in the mean percentage of income taxed at $X = 6$ deductions and at $X = 1$ deduction. Interpret.

*h. Construct a 95% confidence interval for the population Pearson correlation.

21. For a random sample of U.S. counties, data are obtained on $X =$ percentage of the population aged over 50 and $Y =$ per student expenditure on education. The following results are taken from the computer printout for the packaged program used to analyze the data.

SOURCE	DF	SUM OF SQUARES	R-SQUARE		
REGRESSION	1	-------	--------		
ERROR	--	400,000	ROOT MSE		
TOTAL	49	500,000	--------		
PARAMETER	ESTIMATE	T FOR H0: PARAMETER=0	PROB>¦T¦	STD ERR OF ESTIMATE	CORRELATION
INTERCEPT	1300				
% OVER 50	-5	---------	---------	1.443	------

SUM OF SQUARED RESIDUALS = ---------

a. What was the sample size for this study?

b. Fill in the blanks in the above results.

22. Describe the assumptions that are made in using the regression equation $E(Y) = \alpha + \beta X$ to represent the relationship between two variables, and in making inferences about that equation using the least squares line.

23. Refer to Problem 22. In view of these assumptions, indicate why such a model would or would not be good in the following situations.

a. $X =$ time; $Y =$ percent unemployed workers in the United States

b. $X =$ income; $Y =$ charitable and political contributions within the previous year

c. $X =$ age; $Y =$ annual medical expenses

24. Explain carefully the interpretations of the following standard deviations:

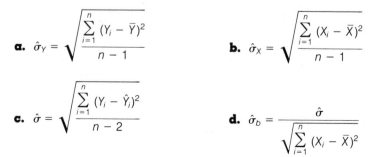

a. $\hat{\sigma}_Y = \sqrt{\dfrac{\sum\limits_{i=1}^{n} (Y_i - \bar{Y})^2}{n - 1}}$

b. $\hat{\sigma}_X = \sqrt{\dfrac{\sum\limits_{i=1}^{n} (X_i - \bar{X})^2}{n - 1}}$

c. $\hat{\sigma} = \sqrt{\dfrac{\sum\limits_{i=1}^{n} (Y_i - \hat{Y}_i)^2}{n - 2}}$

d. $\hat{\sigma}_b = \dfrac{\hat{\sigma}}{\sqrt{\sum\limits_{i=1}^{n} (X_i - \bar{X})^2}}$

*25. In a report summarizing the results of a study on the relationship between scores for students on a verbal aptitude test X and a mathematics aptitude test Y, it is stated that $\bar{X} = 480$, $\bar{Y} = 500$, $\hat{\sigma}_X = 80$, $\hat{\sigma}_Y = 120$, and that the Pearson correlation between the two sets of scores is $r = .60$.
   a. What is the least squares line for these two sets of scores?
   b. What is the predicted score on the mathematics test for someone who scores 400 on the verbal test? 600 on the verbal test?

*26. Refer to Problem 9. Suppose that for a fourth friend, $X = 9$ books and $Y = 7$ hours. Recompute the prediction equation and correlation using all four observations. Compare the results to those obtained in Problem 9. Notice the effect of a single outlying observation on the result.

*27. When both the independent variable X and the dependent variable Y have estimated means of 0 and standard deviations of 1 (as is the case when the variables are standardized—see Section 4.2), show that the prediction equation has the form $\hat{Y} = rX$, where r is the sample correlation between X and Y.

*28. Refer to Problem 17, part **d**. Find a 95% confidence interval for the population Pearson correlation.

*29. Refer to Problem 18, part **e**. Find a 99% confidence interval for each of the following:
   a. The population Pearson correlation
   b. The population coefficient of determination

*30. Suppose we want to test the hypothesis $H_0: \rho_1 = \rho_2$ that the correlation between two variables is the same for two populations, and suppose that we have sample correlation values r_1 and r_2 based on independent random samples from each of the populations. For relatively large samples (say, $n_1 > 10$ and $n_2 > 10$), we can use the test statistic

$$z = \frac{T_2 - T_1}{\sigma_{T_2 - T_1}}$$

where T_1 and T_2 are the transformed values of r_1 and r_2 using Table E, and

$$\sigma_{T_2 - T_1} = \sqrt{\frac{1}{n_1 - 3} + \frac{1}{n_2 - 3}}$$

is the standard error of $T_2 - T_1$. If H_0 is true, this test statistic has the standard normal distribution. Now, suppose that the correlation between murder rate and unemployment rate is $r_1 = .21$ for 15 northern cities and $r_2 = .12$ for 13 southern cities. Find the P-value for testing $H_0: \rho_1 = \rho_2$ against $H_a: \rho_1 \neq \rho_2$, assuming that these are random samples of all such cities in the two regions.

*31. Refer to Example 9.9 and to Note 9.4.
   a. At $X = 25$, give a prediction interval within which you would expect approximately 95% of the Y-values to fall.
   b. Give a 95% confidence interval for the mean percentage of income taxed at $X = 25$.

Bibliography   Afifi, A. A. and V. Clark (1984). *Computer-Aided Multivariate Analysis*. Belmont, Calif.: Lifetime Learning. Chap. 6.

Draper, N. R. and H. Smith (1981). *Applied Regression Analysis*, 2nd ed. New York: Wiley. Chap. 1.

Neter, J. and W. Wasserman (1974). *Applied Linear Statistical Models*. Homewood, Ill.: Richard D. Irwin. Chaps. 2 and 3.

Nie, N. H., et al. (1983). *SPSS^X User's Guide*. New York: McGraw-Hill.

SAS Institute Inc. (1982). *SAS User's Guide: Statistics*. Cary, N.C.: SAS Institute Inc.

Younger, M. S. (1979). *Handbook for Linear Regression*. North Scituate, Mass.: Duxbury Press.

PART III

INTRODUCTION TO MULTIVARIATE STATISTICAL ANALYSES

CHAPTER 10

Introduction to Multivariate Relationships

Contents

In the previous three chapters, we studied methods for analyzing relationships between two variables. In most social science research, these types of analyses are too simple taken by themselves, and they need to be incorporated into analyses involving other variables that might be related to the original two. In order to understand the effect of religious affiliation on attitudes about racial intermarriage, for example, we might want to consider whether educational differences among the religious groups are responsible for the observed difference in attitude. Or, we might want to know if the relationship between attitude and religious affiliation differs for different regions of the country—might data for Southerners show a stronger association than data for non-Southerners?

A number of types of questions can be asked that require the incorporation of additional variables in the analysis. These questions often involve theoretical notions of *causal* sequences among the variables. In Section 10.1 we consider the relationship of data analysis to the notions of causation, and we outline simple methods by which causal assumptions can be tested. Section 10.2 considers the important concept of *statistical control*, which allows us to view the association between two variables while removing the influence of other variables. That section and Section 10.3 also introduce some important types of multivariate relationships that can be revealed when variables are controlled. The final section discusses some matters dealing with the use of statistical inferential methods for multivariate relationships.

10.1 Criteria for Causality

The notion of causality is central to the scientific endeavor, guiding theoretical thinking and data analysis. Although most people are familiar with this concept, they often have only a vague understanding of how we can test a possible causal relationship. While this is not the place for a lengthy discussion on the concept of causation, we will present a few guidelines that scientific researchers have developed. These guidelines help one to assess a hypothesis of the form, "X causes Y."

In discussions of causation, letters such as X, Y, and Z stand for variables. To denote a causal association between two variables, X and Y, one draws an arrow between the symbols X and Y, pointing to the dependent variable. Thus,

$$X \rightarrow Y$$

specifies that X is an independent variable having a causal effect on Y. For example, suppose we suspect that whether one is a Boy Scout has a causal effect on whether one is a juvenile delinquent. We are hypothesizing* that $S \rightarrow D$, where S and D denote the dichotomous variables "whether a boy scout (yes, no)" and "whether a delinquent (yes, no)." Causal relationships usually imply an imbalance, in that one variable affects another, but not vice versa.

*More detailed notation is sometimes used, such as $S \Rightarrow D$, which predicts a negative association in the sense that scouting leads to lower delinquency rates.

If we suspect that one variable is causally related to another, how do we analyze if it is or not? There are three criteria that a relationship must satisfy for it to be considered a causal one. These criteria, which will be discussed next, are (a) association between the variables, (b) an appropriate time order, and (c) the elimination of alternative explanations. If all three criteria are met, then there is evidence to support the hypothesized relationship. If one or more criteria are not met, then we can often dismiss the hypothesized causal association as incorrect. We can never *prove* that one phenomenon is a cause of another, since causation is imputed by the observer but never actually observed. We can disprove causal hypotheses, however, by showing that empirical evidence contradicts them.

Association

The first of the three criteria is that of **association**. We must show that X and Y are statistically dependent if we are to support the hypothesis that X causes Y. If $X \rightarrow Y$, then as X changes, the distribution of Y should change in some way. If scouting causes lower delinquency rates, for example, then the population proportion of delinquents should be higher for nonscouts than for scouts. For sample data, we would use a statistical test (such as chi-square) or a confidence interval to see whether the association criterion is satisfied.

Time Order

The second necessary condition for causation is that the two variables have the appropriate *time order*, with the cause preceding the effect. Sometimes this is just a matter of logic. For instance, race, age, and sex exist prior to current attitudes or achieved statuses, so any causal association must treat them as independent variables. In other cases, the causal direction is not as obvious. The example of scouting and delinquency is one such case. It is possible and logically reasonable that scouting could reduce delinquency tendencies. On the other hand, it is just as reasonable to assume that delinquent boys avoid scouting whereas nondelinquent boys do not. Thus, the time order is not clear, and both possibilities, $S \rightarrow D$ and $D \rightarrow S$, are reasonable. Just showing that an association exists does not solve this dilemma, since a lower proportion of delinquents among scout members is consistent with both explanations. Methods of determining time order are beyond the scope of this book, but usually involve a research design that has some type of longitudinal data collection.

Elimination of Alternative Explanation

This last criterion is usually the most important in rejecting hypotheses of causal relationships, but it is also the most difficult to achieve. Suppose we find an association between two variables that are possibly causally related, and suppose we are satisfied that they have the proper time order. It is a common fallacy to deduce causality from association and time order alone. There may yet be an alternative explanation. Airplane pilots turn on the "fasten seat belt" sign just before their planes encounter turbulence, but this does not imply that turning on the sign causes turbulence.

The general types of *alternative explanations* that should be considered are the following:

1. The relationship may be *spurious*, both variables being dependent on a third variable, Z.
2. The relationship may be *conditional* on the values of another variable, perhaps disappearing at certain levels of that variable.
3. The relationship may be causal, but it might work through some other variable that intervenes between the two.
4. The observed relationship may be a result of sampling error.

The first three types of alternatives will be explained in the next two sections, and they form the focus of inquiry in most research. The fourth, the possibility that the observed relationship is a result of sampling variation and does not represent a true relationship in the population, is dealt with by means of inferential statistics as well as replication of research studies. One should also keep in mind that dependent variables in the social world usually have multiple causes, not just single ones, and that a data set can be consistent with different, conflicting causal theories. Before discussing these possible alternatives, we need to introduce the concept of *statistical control.* ·

10.2 Controlling for Other Variables

In evaluating whether X could be a cause of Y, it is important to study whether the association between them remains when the effects of other variables on this association are removed. A variable is said to be *controlled* in a multivariate analysis when its influence on the other variables is removed. For instance, for a random sample of students taken from schools in a certain school district, we might observe an association between X = height and Y = score on a math achievement test, with taller students tending to have higher scores. This association may well be explained by the sample having students of various ages (perhaps 5–18), since as Z = age increases, both height and test score would tend to increase. We would remove the effects of age (i.e., *control for age*) by studying the association between X and Y for students who have the same age. There is then unlikely to be an association between height and test score.

Thus, we can control a variable Z by holding its value constant or by considering only cases with equal (or similar) values of Z at a time. For instance, we can control for Z = age by analyzing the association between X and Y separately at each age level. In holding the control variable constant, we remove the part of the association between X and Y that is caused by variation in Z.

Statistical Control in Social Research

In a laboratory experiment, we can control a variable (e.g., the temperature at which the experiment is conducted) by setting a fixed value for it and observing the relationships among the other variables for that fixed value. We can then repeat the experiment at other fixed values of the control variable and see whether the same results occur. Social science research is usually observational rather than experimental, however, in the sense that we cannot usually fix values of variables such as intelligence, education, age, and income before obtaining the sample data. Therefore, in an attempt to approximate an experimental type of control, we group together observations with similar or equal values on the control variable.

In order to investigate the relationship between two categorical variables when a third variable is controlled, we could consider the cross-classification tables relating the original two variables for the subsets of the sample in each level of that controlled variable. The separate tables that display the relationship between the variables within the levels of the control variable are called *partial tables*.

Example 10.1   Suppose we observe that Boy Scouts have a significantly lower delinquency rate than nonscouts. In considering possible alternative explanations for the association, we might decide to control for variables such as church attendance or social class. For example, suppose that boys who attend church are more likely to be scouts than nonattenders, and suppose also that boys who attend church are less likely to be delinquent. Then the observed difference in delinquency rates between scouts and nonscouts might be due to variation in church attendance, not scouting per se.

Table 10.1 shows a hypothetical table relating scouting to delinquency. For this table, the percentage of delinquents among scout members is lower than among nonscouts. To control for church attendance, we could examine the association between scouting and delinquency within partial tables corresponding to various levels of church attendance. Table 10.2 gives possible partial tables for three levels of church attendance—low, medium, and high. You can verify that when these three partial tables are added together, we recover the *bivariate* table (Table 10.1) in which church attendance is ignored rather than controlled. For instance, the number of boy scouts who are delinquents is 36 = 10 + 18 + 8. When we control for church attendance, we no longer observe an association between scouting and delinquency. In each partial table, the percentage of delinquents is the same for scouts as for nonscouts. ∎

Table 10.1
Cross-Classification of
Scouting and Delinquency

		BOY SCOUT	
		Yes	No
DELINQUENT	Yes	36 (9%)	60 (15%)
	No	364 (91%)	340 (85%)
TOTAL		400 (100%)	400 (100%)

Table 10.2   Cross-Classification of Scouting and Delinquency, Controlling for Church Attendance

		CHURCH ATTENDANCE					
		Low		Medium		High	
SCOUT		Yes	No	Yes	No	Yes	No
DELINQUENCY	Yes	10 (20%)	40 (20%)	18 (12%)	18 (12%)	8 (4%)	2 (4%)
	No	40 (80%)	160 (80%)	132 (88%)	132 (88%)	192 (96%)	48 (96%)
TOTAL		50 (100%)	200 (100%)	150 (100%)	150 (100%)	200 (100%)	50 (100%)

**Spurious
Associations**

An association between two variables is said to be *spurious* if both variables are dependent on a third variable *Z*, so that the association disappears when *Z* is controlled. When two variables have a spurious association, it is an effect of the relationship of those variables to another variable, rather than indicative of a causal connection. There is then no association between them in the partial tables calculated within the levels of *Z*.

Figure 10.1 is a graphical depiction of a spurious association between *X* and *Y*. They vary together only because they both depend on a common cause, *Z*. If *Z* changes, it produces changes simultaneously in *X* and *Y*, so that *X* and *Y* appear to be statistically dependent. In reality they *are* related, but only because of their common dependence on the third variable. They are not *causally* related, because the variable *Z* provides an *alternative explanation* for their association. Thus, showing that the association between two variables is spurious disproves the hypothesis of a causal connection between them.

Fig. 10.1 Graphical
Depiction of a Spurious
Association Between *X*
and *Y*

Example 10.2

Table 10.1 displayed an association between scouting and delinquency. The partial tables shown in Table 10.2 indicated that this association disappears when we control for church attendance. This is consistent with the interpretation of spuriousness. One can show using Table 10.2 that as church attendance increases, the percentage of delinquents decreases (compare percentages across the partial tables) and also that the percentage of scout members increases. By the nature of these two associations, it is not surprising that scouts exhibit lower delinquency rates than nonscouts in Table 10.1. Since this association is explained by their dependence on church attendance, there is no causal link between scouting and delinquency. ∎

In practice, of course, even if there is a spurious association between two variables in some population, we would not expect to see *sample* partial tables like those in Table 10.2 (showing *exactly* no association) because of sampling error. Also, it is not always obvious which variables we should control in attempting to observe whether an association is spurious. One reason for having a thorough knowledge of the theory and previous work relating to a field of research is so that one will be more likely to recognize possible spurious relationships and control relevant variables, thus not giving too much importance to an observed bivariate association.

Concepts such as statistical control and spuriousness apply to all measurement scales, not just to categorical variables. For instance, they apply to regression analyses of interval variables. They also apply to comparisons of groups on mean responses, the nominal–interval type of bivariate association discussed in Section 7.2. The next example illustrates spurious association for that type of analysis.

Example 10.3   Table 10.3 shows a bivariate association between the interval variable "math achievement test score" and the nominal variable "home computer ownership (yes, no)." Students with home computers have higher mean test scores. Should we conclude that the use of a home computer improves the math test score? First, we should try to eliminate the alternative explanation that some other variable might be causally related to both of these. Social class or one of its relatives is almost always a candidate for control in social science research. We could reason that students with home computers almost all come from middle class or higher backgrounds, rather than lower class. Therefore, in comparing test scores for students on the basis of home computer ownership, we are likely to be comparing groups with very different social class composition. Since social class is also known to be a factor in school performance, we need to remove its effect in order to focus better on the home-computer effect.

Table 10.3

Relationship Between Math Test Score and Home Computer Ownership

		MEAN TEST SCORE	n
HOME COMPUTER	Yes	84.3	270
	No	75.5	1,150
TOTAL		77.2	1,420

The hypothetical data in Table 10.4 show the results of controlling social class of family. That table suggests that home computers do not help math test scores. Controlling for social class, there is essentially no association between home computer ownership and the math test score, in the sense that the mean score is about the same for those who have home computers as for those who do not, at each level of social class. Table 10.4 also indicates that social class has an effect on test score and on computer ownership, in that higher social class tends to correspond to higher mean test score and to higher probability of owning a computer. Thus, the evidence is that the original relationship is spurious, as depicted in Figure 10.2 (next page). ■

Table 10.4

Relationship Between Math Test Score and Home Computer Ownership, Controlling for Social Class

SOCIAL CLASS	HOME COMPUTER	MEAN TEST SCORE	n
Lower	Yes	69.5	10
	No	68.7	420
Middle	Yes	73.7	50
	No	72.3	370
Upper	Yes	87.5	210
	No	86.8	360

Fig. 10.2 Graphical
Depiction of Spurious
Association Between
Home Computer
Ownership and Math Test
Score

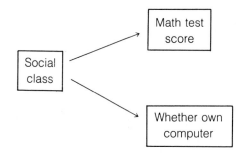

Note that the partial tables in Table 10.4 do not show exactly zero association (i.e., no difference in means), but all are close enough to 0 to be substantively non-significant. Even if the *true* relationship is spurious, one does not expect to see an exact zero *sample* association, because of random sampling variations. Remember also that several causal explanations can all be consistent with a particular data set. For instance, the association in Table 10.3 might also be explained by the joint dependence of math test score and home computer ownership on the degree of parental emphasis on education. Or, the students having home computers may have been ones encouraged to pursue computer-related studies because of high math test scores in previous years.

Statistical Interaction

Sometimes three or more variables are related in such a way that the association between two depends on the value of the third. In other words, the association appears when certain conditions hold, and it disappears or changes in intensity or direction when other conditions hold. Those conditions can usually be viewed as levels of a third variable. For example, having a mother who is employed outside the home seems to have significant positive effects on daughter's school achievement in high school, but no significant effect on son's achievement. We could say that the association between mother's employment and child's achievement *depends on* the sex of the child. When the population association between X and Y changes at different levels of the variable Z, the three-variable relationship is said to exhibit *statistical interaction*.

Statistical Interaction

Statistical interaction exists when the association between two variables changes as the level of a third variable changes.

This type of three-variable relationship can be depicted as in Figure 10.3, where the effect of variable Z is on the *relationship* between X and Y. There is *no* statistical interaction when the association between X and Y is the same at every level of Z. It is possible for there to be no statistical interaction even when all the variables are associated.

Fig. 10.3 Graphical Depiction of Statistical Interaction

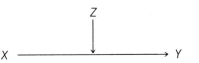

In assessing whether there is sample evidence of interaction, we need to select a measure of association to compare among the partial tables. For instance, we might use a difference of proportions (if each partial table is 2 × 2), a difference of means (for nominal–interval data), a slope or correlation (if both variables are interval), or gamma or Kendall's tau-*b* (if the partial tables are cross-classifications of ordinal variables).

Example 10.4   If interaction is suspected, we need to control the variable whose levels provide the conditions under which the relationship between X and Y varies. Suppose, for example, that we want to test whether child's achievement (as measured by GPA) is related to mother's employment (yes, no), and we suspect an interaction with sex of student. We then need to control sex of student by looking at the association between mother's employment and GPA separately for males and for females. Our results might look like those in Table 10.5.

Table 10.5   Cross-Classification of Mother's Employment and Child's GPA, Controlling for Sex of Student

		MALES		FEMALES	
		MOTHER NOT EMPLOYED	MOTHER EMPLOYED	MOTHER NOT EMPLOYED	MOTHER EMPLOYED
	3.31–4.00	16 (17.4%)	20 (17.2%)	12 (11.5%)	30 (25.4%)
GPA	2.61–3.30	40 (43.5%)	50 (43.1%)	50 (48.1%)	60 (50.8%)
	1.91–2.60	28 (30.4%)	34 (29.3%)	36 (34.6%)	24 (20.3%)
	Below 1.91	8 (8.7%)	12 (10.3%)	6 (5.8%)	4 (3.4%)
		92 (100.0%)	116 (99.9%)	104 (100.0%)	118 (99.9%)

Gamma = −.016   Gamma = .352
Standard error = .111   Standard error = .101

Kendall's tau-*b* = −.010   Kendall's tau-*b* = .202
Standard error = .064   Standard error = .060

Here we see that for males there is no substantive relationship between mother's employment and GPA. Specifically, the conditional distribution of GPA for males with employed mothers is similar to that for males not having employed mothers, and the sample value of gamma (see Section 8.5) is close to 0. For females, on the other hand, the relationship is clear and moderate in size. The positive value for gamma (.352) represents the fact that females with employed mothers tend to have higher GPA. Since the values of gamma are quite different for males and females, this sample gives evidence of statistical interaction.

When the tables for males and females are combined, we obtain Table 10.6, in which sex of student is ignored rather than controlled. This table is somewhat misleading, since we might conclude from it that the relationship between mother's employment and GPA is weak. This would be incorrect for both males and females, since there is essentially no association for males but a moderate one for females. When interaction such as this exists, it is important to describe the partial tables separately, since the association changes according to the level of the third variable. We must include the third variable (Z) in our description of how X is related to Y.

■

Table 10.6

Cross-Classification of Mother's Employment and Child's GPA

		MOTHER NOT EMPLOYED		MOTHER EMPLOYED	
GPA	3.31–4.00	28	(14.3%)	50	(21.4%)
	2.61–3.30	90	(45.9%)	110	(47.0%)
	1.91–2.60	64	(32.7%)	58	(24.8%)
	Below 1.91	14	(7.1%)	16	(6.8%)
		196	(100.0%)	234	(100.0%)

Gamma = .162
Standard error = .077

Kendall's tau-b = .093
Standard error = .045

In some cases, the interaction is such that opposite-directional associations exist within the levels of a third variable. In that case, there may be no bivariate association, even though control of the third variable reveals associations.

Example 10.5   Table 10.7 shows an example of opposite-directional associations. In that table, nuclear freeze attitude is associated with church attendance, but differently for different educational levels of the respondents. Since each partial table is of size 2×2, we can easily assess association by the difference of proportions $\hat{\pi}_2 - \hat{\pi}_1$ (see Section 7.1). With lower education, higher church attendance means a less favorable attitude toward a freeze, since the proportion favoring a freeze is .103 lower for those who often attend church than for those who seldom or never attend. The opposite is true for those at the higher level of education, with the proportion favoring a freeze being .113 higher for those who often attend church than for those who seldom or never attend. Without the control for education, it appears that freeze attitude and church attendance are unrelated, which is not really correct. They *are* related, but the nature of the relationship varies with educational level. In order to adequately describe their relationship, we must specify which educational level we are referring to.

■

Table 10.7 Cross-Classification of Attitude Toward Nuclear Freeze by Church Attendance

a. Controlling for Education

		EDUCATION			
		12 years or less		More than 12 years	
		Seldom or never attend	Often attend church	Seldom or never attend	Often attend church
ATTITUDE	Favor	82 (55.4%)	96 (45.1%)	140 (63.6%)	164 (74.9%)
	Oppose	66 (44.6%)	117 (54.9%)	80 (36.4%)	55 (25.1%)
TOTALS		148 (100.0%)	213 (100.0%)	220 (100.0%)	219 (100.0%)

$$\hat{\pi}_2 - \hat{\pi}_1 = -.103 \qquad\qquad \hat{\pi}_2 - \hat{\pi}_1 = .113$$

Standard error = .053   Standard error = .044

b. Ignoring Education

		CHURCH ATTENDANCE	
		Seldom or never	Often
ATTITUDE	Favor	222 (60.3%)	260 (60.2%)
	Oppose	146 (39.7%)	172 (39.8%)
TOTALS		368 (100.0%)	432 (100.0%)

$$\hat{\pi}_2 - \hat{\pi}_1 = -.001$$

10.3 Other Types of Multivariate Relationships

In Section 10.2 we discussed two types of partial association between X and Y that may be revealed when we control for a variable Z. A *spurious relationship* occurs when Z affects both X and Y and explains their association. *Statistical interaction* occurs when the association between X and Y is not the same at all levels of Z. This section describes some other types of multivariate relationships that are often encountered in social science research.

Chain Relationships

A third way in which three variables can be associated is in a chain of causation, in which X affects Z, which in turn affects Y. This is depicted in Figure 10.4. In such a situation, X is an *indirect* (rather than direct) cause of Y. The variable Z in Figure 10.4 is referred to as an *intervening variable*. In order to elaborate clearly how X is related to Y, we need to identify the intervening variable.

Fig. 10.4 A Chain Relationship, in Which X Indirectly Affects Y Through the Intervening Variable Z

$$X \longrightarrow Z \longrightarrow Y$$

If the hypothesized causal chain is correct, there will be a bivariate association between X and Y, but that association will disappear when we control for Z. For instance, suppose that race is related to one's number of juvenile arrests, but suppose we believe this to be primarily an effect of different family income levels of blacks and whites. We could hypothesize that race affects one's probability of being poor, and that being poor increases one's chance of being arrested as a juvenile. We then have the causal chain model depicted in Figure 10.5. To support this, we would need to show that the differential arrest rate between whites and blacks disappears when we control for family income. That is, within fixed levels of family income, the intervening variable, we should find no significant difference in the arrest rates of blacks and whites. If this happens, we would know that race does not directly affect arrest rate, but that it could be an indirect cause through the intervening variable, family income.

Fig. 10.5 Example of a Chain Relationship

You may have noticed that for both spurious relationships and chain relationships, the association between X and Y disappears when we control for Z. The difference is in the causal order among the variables and in the interpretation of the relationships. For a spurious association, Z is causally prior to both X and Y, whereas in a chain association Z intervenes between the two (refer to Figures 10.1 and 10.4). To illustrate, suppose that X = father's education is associated with Y = son's income at age 40, but suppose that this association disappears when we control for Z = son's education. We would expect that father's education affects son's income mainly through its effects on other factors, such as son's education. Thus, it is natural to treat this as a chain relationship. In order for us to conclude that the relationship was spurious, we would have to assume that Z = son's education was causally prior to both father's education and son's income, an improbable situation. It usually helps to draw arrow diagrams of how variables are believed to be related in order to help guide data analysis and interpretations.

Multiple Causes　　The actual relationships among three variables might also be as depicted in Figure 10.6. This figure indicates that X and Z are separate, independent causes of Y. If X and Z are statistically independent, then when we control for Z, the partial association between X and Y will be similar to the bivariate association observed when Z is ignored rather than controlled.* So, if we control for Z and the original association remains, we might have a case of two independent direct causes of Y, assuming that both X and Z are associated with Y to begin with.

*Correspondences between associations in the partial tables and the original bivariate table will be discussed in detail in Section 15.4.

Fig. 10.6 Graphical Depiction of Multiple Causes of Y

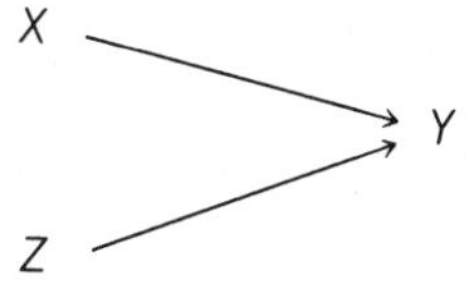

In practice, it often happens that when Z is controlled, the $X-Y$ association is reduced but does not disappear. Then the original $X-Y$ association might be only partially a chain, and also partially a valid causal association (see Figure 10.7). It is possible, however, that the associations in the partial tables could all have the opposite direction as the original $X-Y$ association. This is referred to as *Simpson's paradox* (see Problems 15 and 18 for examples). In reality, most dependent variables in social research have many causes, both direct and indirect, so that three-variable models are hardly ever adequate. However, once you understand the basic concepts presented in this chapter, you can better handle their extensions to more than three variables.

Fig. 10.7 Graphical Depiction of a Direct and Indirect Effect of X on Y

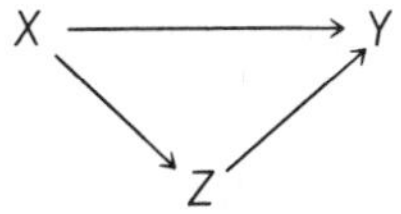

Suppressor Variables

Sometimes two variables are related in such a way that no association is apparent between them until a third variable is controlled. That control variable is referred to as a *suppressor variable*. We already saw one example of this in the discussion of interaction in Example 10.5, when the signs of the association were opposite for two levels of a suppressor variable. However, interaction is not necessary in order for this phenomenon to exist, as is shown in the following example.

Example 10.6

In a study of attitudes toward capital punishment in a large, industrial Northern city, we survey a random sample of registered voters and ask how they plan to vote on a proposed referendum on the death penalty. We believe that Catholics are more opposed to capital punishment than are Protestants. In the bivariate table shown in Table 10.8, however, the difference between the sample proportion of Protestants who favor the death penalty and the sample proportion of Catholics who favor the death penalty is only $\hat{\pi}_2 - \hat{\pi}_1 = .02$.

Table 10.8
Cross-Classification of Death Penalty Attitude and Religion

| | | RELIGION | |
		Catholic	Protestant
DEATH PENALTY	Favor	270 (54%)	280 (56%)
	Oppose	230 (46%)	220 (44%)
TOTAL		500 (100%)	500 (100%)
		$\hat{\pi}_2 - \hat{\pi}_1 = .56 - .54 = .02$	

Table 10.9 gives the results when the association is considered separately for working-class voters and for middle-class voters. Table 10.8, the bivariate table, is obtained by combining the two partial tables in Table 10.9. These partial tables show that Catholics are indeed more opposed to the death penalty than Protestants, within class levels. The difference in the proportions favoring the death penalty is .20 in each partial table, so there is no evidence of statistical interaction. Because the association is suppressed until social class is controlled, social class is a suppressor variable.

Table 10.9   Cross-Classification of Death Penalty Attitude and Religion, Controlling for Social Class

| | | SOCIAL CLASS | | | | |
| | | Working class | | | Middle class | |
		Catholic	Protestant		Catholic	Protestant
DEATH PENALTY	Favor	240 (60%)	80 (80%)		30 (30%)	200 (50%)
	Oppose	160 (40%)	20 (20%)		70 (70%)	200 (50%)
TOTAL		400 (100%)	100 (100%)		100 (100%)	400 (100%)
		$\hat{\pi}_2 - \hat{\pi}_1 = .80 - .60 = .20$			$\hat{\pi}_2 - \hat{\pi}_1 = .50 - .30 = .20$	

The reason that the association changes when we control for social class can be understood by noting how social class is associated with religion and with death penalty attitude. Using Table 10.9, one can see that working-class voters are moderately more in favor of capital punishment than are middle-class voters. At the same time, one can see that working-class voters are much more likely to be Catholics than are middle-class voters. Given this information, we expect Catholics to be relatively more favorable to the death penalty (compared to Protestants) when class is ignored than when it is controlled. Alternatively, since Protestants are more likely to be middle class than are Catholics, and since members of the middle class are less likely to favor the death penalty than are the working class, Protestants tend to be relatively less in favor of the death penalty (compared to Catholics) when class is ignored than when it is controlled.   ∎

Example 10.6 shows that it can be important to analyze partial associations even when corresponding bivariate associations are consistent with statistical independence. Again we see the importance of theory and careful thought about the relationships among the variables. We should control for a third variable if we think it is related to both the independent and dependent variables, even though there is no bivariate association. What we have seen in Example 10.6 is a *spurious non-association*, since religion and attitude both depend on the third variable, social class.

One must know when to use controls, what variables to control, and how to interpret the results in order to master data analysis. This is probably the most difficult, as well as the most crucial, task of learning research technique. Further discussions of these considerations can be found in Hyman (1955), McGaw and Watson (1976), and Rosenberg (1968).

10.4 Inferential Issues in Statistical Control

In the first three sections of this chapter, we have purposely ignored sampling variation and inferential matters in our analyses, so as not to confuse them with the new concepts presented. We shall now discuss some of these issues that arise in controlling variables.

Effects of Sample Size and Categorization

Since partial tables contain subsets of the total data set, sample sizes in the partial tables can be much smaller than in the original bivariate table. Even if there is no reduction in association in the partial tables relative to the original table, the test statistic values may be much smaller. For example, we could compute the χ^2 statistic within a particular partial table to test whether the variables are independent at that control level. This χ^2 value may be quite small relative to the χ^2 value for the original table. This could be due partly to a decrease in the degree of association, but it could also be due to the reduction in sample size. We saw in Section 8.3 that larger sample sizes tend to produce larger χ^2-values for a particular degree of association. Hence, a statistic may become nonsignificant under a control simply because of the reduction in sample size. It is therefore very important to compare the value of a measure of association from the original table to those from the partial tables even if the values from the partial tables are not statistically significant. The measure of association values in the control tables need not necessarily be smaller than in the overall table, even if the χ^2 values are smaller.

For simplicity of exposition, the control variables used in our examples were chosen to have only a few categories. However, in practice, it is important to avoid the use of overly crude categorizations of the control variable. The greater the number of control levels, the more nearly constant Z is forced to be within each partial table. The association between X and Y over a broad range of values of the control variable may be very different from the association over a more restricted range. A spurious association between X and Y may not be detected, for example, if only two control levels are used. Unless the control variable *naturally* has only two levels (e.g., sex), it is usually best to use several partial tables.

It is often of interest to control simultaneously for two or more variables. We might wish to look at the relationship between X and Y separately for white men, white women, black men, and black women. In that case, we would be controlling for both sex and race. One problem that we find in controlling for many variables (and in choosing several categories for the control variables) is that the sample sizes in some of the partial tables may be very small. For example, if there were three control variables, the first with three levels, the second with four levels, and the third with two levels, there would be $3 \times 4 \times 2 = 24$ separate partial tables, one for each combination of levels of the control variables. If some combinations of levels are sparsely represented by the sample (perhaps black Jewish men), it will be difficult to make precise inferences within the corresponding partial tables; that is, measures computed for the partial tables with small sample sizes will have large standard errors. Also, when there is a large number of partial tables, it becomes very difficult to assimilate the results, because there are many comparisons to be made. Fortunately, most of the advanced methods to be discussed in the remainder of the text allow us to assess patterns of partial association without doing separate analyses at the various combinations of levels of the control variables.

Comparing and Pooling Measures

When we control for a variable, it is often useful to compare certain parameters for different partial tables. For instance, we might wish to compare men and women on the value of the ordinal measure of association gamma between marital satisfaction and level of education. Confidence intervals can be given for a difference between two parameter values in much the same way as they were in Chapter 7 for a difference in proportions or a difference in means. Suppose that the two sample estimates are based on independent random samples, with standard errors denoted by $\hat{\sigma}_1$ and $\hat{\sigma}_2$. If the estimates have approximately normal sampling distributions, then a $100(1 - \alpha)\%$ confidence interval for the difference between the parameters is

$$(\text{Estimate}_2 - \text{Estimate}_1) \pm z_{\alpha/2} \sqrt{\hat{\sigma}_1^2 + \hat{\sigma}_2^2}$$

If the interval does not include 0, then we can conclude that the parameter values differ.

Example 10.7

In Table 10.5 we controlled for sex in studying the association between mother's employment and child's GPA. For males, we obtained $\hat{\gamma}_1 = -.016$ with $\hat{\sigma}_1 = .111$, whereas for females we obtained $\hat{\gamma}_2 = .352$ with $\hat{\sigma}_2 = .101$. For such large sample sizes, the gamma estimates have approximately normal sampling distributions, as does $\hat{\gamma}_2 - \hat{\gamma}_1$. A 95% confidence interval for the population difference $\gamma_2 - \gamma_1$ is

$$(\hat{\gamma}_2 - \hat{\gamma}_1) \pm z_{.025} \sqrt{\hat{\sigma}_1^2 + \hat{\sigma}_2^2}$$
$$= (.352 - (-.016)) \pm 1.96 \sqrt{(.111)^2 + (.101)^2}$$
$$= .368 \pm .294 \quad \text{or} \quad (.07, .66)$$

At this confidence level, we can conclude that the population gamma value is higher for females than for males. In this sense, there is significant evidence of statistical interaction for this three-variable relationship. ∎

When the association appears to be similar in various partial tables, it may be useful to pool measure values into a single summary measure of the strength of association in those tables. The term *measure of partial association* is used to refer to a statistic that describes the strength of the association between two variables after the influence of another variable has been controlled. To construct such a measure, one usually calculates some weighted average of the values from the separate partial tables, often weighting by sample size. See Problem 10.19 and Agresti (1984, Sections 9.4, 10.4–10.5) for examples of partial association measures for categorical variables.

Summary

The use of more than two variables in statistical analysis of relationships is almost always necessary. Causal logic requires not only that we demonstrate *associations* between variables, but also that we demonstrate proper *time order* and *eliminate alternative explanations* of the associations. In order to rule out alternative explanations, we must usually introduce *control variables* into the analysis. Control of variables can be used to detect *spuriousness*, *statistical interaction*, *causal chain models*, and to help to identify *suppressor variables*. Table 10.10 summarizes some of the possible three-variable relationships. The remainder of this text is concerned with statistical methods for analyzing multivariate relationships.

Table 10.10
Some Three-Variable Relationships

GRAPH	NAME OF RELATIONSHIP	WHAT HAPPENS WHEN WE CONTROL FOR Z
$Z \nearrow X \searrow Y$	Spurious X–Y association	Association between X and Y disappears.
$X \longrightarrow Z \longrightarrow Y$	Z intervenes; X is indirect cause of Y.	Association between X and Y disappears.
$Z \downarrow$ $X \longrightarrow Y$	Interaction	Association between X and Y varies according to level of Z.
$Z \searrow Y$ $X \nearrow$	Multiple causes	Association between X and Y does not change.
$X \longrightarrow Y$ $\searrow Z \nearrow$	Both direct and indirect effect of X on Y	Association between X and Y is reduced, but does not disappear.

Problems

1. What are the criteria for inferring *causation* between two variables?

2. Give an example of a situation in which the time order between variables is ambiguous.

3. Explain clearly what it means to *control* for a variable. Give an example of a situation in which it would be important to use a control variable.

4. Explain what is meant by a *spurious* association. Illustrate using the variables $X =$ height, $Y =$ test score, and $Z =$ age, for the situation discussed at the beginning of Section 10.2.

5. The news media report that a study has found that children who eat breakfast get better math grades than those who do not eat breakfast. Suppose that this result was based on a simple bivariate association. How might this result be spurious, and how could you check for that possibility?

6. Give an example of three variables, X, Y, and Z, for which you would expect the association between X and Y to be:
a. Spurious, disappearing when Z is controlled.
b. Part of a chain relationship, disappearing when Z is controlled.

7. Give a clear definition and an example of each of the following:
a. A spurious association
b. Statistical interaction
c. An intervening variable
d. A suppressor variable

8. Statistical interaction refers to which of the following?
a. Association exists between two variables.
b. The degree of association between two variables varies greatly over the partial levels of a control variable.
c. The partial association is the same at each level of the control variable, but it is different from the overall bivariate association (ignoring the control variable).
d. For a collection of three variables, each pair of variables is associated.

9. Refer to Problem 2 in Chapter 8.
a. Treat expectation of voting as the control variable, and construct the partial tables relating political party affiliation to present voting intention.
b. Show how to combine the partial tables to obtain the bivariate table constructed in Problem 8.2.
c. From viewing the partial tables in part **a**, indicate whether there seems to be sample evidence of statistical interaction.

10. Opposition to the legal availability of abortion is stronger among the very religious than the nonreligious, and it is also stronger among those with conservative sexual attitudes than those with more permissive attitudes.
a. Draw a three-variable diagram of how these variables might be related, treating abortion attitude as the dependent variable. [*Note:* There is more than one diagram that is realistic for these variables.]

b. Explain how you would test your diagram, showing example tables that are consistent with it.

11. The accompanying table relates occupational level (white-collar, blue-collar) and political party choice, controlling for income.

		HIGH INCOME		MEDIUM HIGH INCOME		MEDIUM LOW INCOME		LOW INCOME	
		White-collar	Blue-collar	White-collar	Blue-collar	White-collar	Blue-collar	White-collar	Blue-collar
PARTY	Democrat	45	5	100	25	75	300	45	405
	Republican	405	45	300	75	25	100	5	45

a. Construct the bivariate table between occupational level and political party (ignoring income). Does there appear to be an association? If so, describe it.

b. Do the partial tables display an association? Interpret them.

c. Using the nature of the association between income and each of the other variables, explain why the bivariate table constructed in part **a** has such different association than the partial tables.

d. Do the partial tables exhibit statistical interaction? Why or why not?

e. Construct a chain diagram for these data, and identify the intervening variable.

f. Show that the data are also consistent with a spurious association between occupational level and political party, and draw the corresponding diagram.

g. Refer to parts **e** and **f**. Which diagram seems more appropriate for these variables? Why?

12. The accompanying table describes the association between smoking status and a breathing test result, by age, for Caucasians in certain industrial plants in Houston, Texas, from 1974 to 1975. Describe the associations, and indicate which three-variable relationship these data seem to satisfy.

		BREATHING TEST RESULTS	SMOKING STATUS	
			Never smoked	Current smoker
AGE	< 40	Normal	577 (94.4%)	682 (92.3%)
		Not normal	34 (5.6%)	57 (7.7%)
	40–59	Normal	164 (97.6%)	245 (76.8%)
		Not normal	4 (2.4%)	74 (23.2%)

Source: Based on table on page 21 in *Public Program Analysis*, by R. N. Forthofer and R. G. Lehnen (Belmont, Calif.: Lifetime Learning Publications, 1981).

13. A study of students at Oregon State University found an association between frequency of church attendance and favorability toward the legalization of marijuana. Both variables were measured in ordered categories. When sex of student was controlled, the resulting Kendall's tau-*b* measures for the two partial tables were as follows:

Males: tau-*b* = −.191, standard error = .054

Females: tau-*b* = −.387, standard error = .061

a. Interpret these results.

b. These results show a slight degree of _____.

14. The accompanying table shows the median annual salaries of full-time employed doctorates by sex and years of experience, for the United States in 1979.

FIELD OF DOCTORATE	ALL FEMALES	ALL MALES	2–5 YEARS OF EXPERIENCE, FEMALE	2–5 YEARS OF EXPERIENCE, MALE	6–10 YEARS OF EXPERIENCE, FEMALE	6–10 YEARS OF EXPERIENCE, MALE
All fields	$23,100	$30,000	$19,700	$22,300	$22,000	$26,000
Math	22,100	26,600	19,800	19,900	20,600	23,600
Computer sciences	25,200	28,500	—	22,300	24,600	28,300
Chemistry	24,300	31,300	22,200	24,600	22,700	27,800
Engineering	26,200	32,700	24,600	26,400	25,600	30,000
Medicine	25,600	32,800	23,100	24,500	23,300	29,200
Biology	22,400	28,200	18,300	20,500	21,100	24,700
Psychology	22,900	28,000	19,700	20,300	22,500	24,000
Social sciences	22,900	27,400	19,500	19,900	21,300	24,000

Source: *National Research Council, Science, Engineering, and Humanities Doctorates in the United States, 1979 Profile,* p. 21.

a. Suppose that sex is the independent variable. Identify the dependent variable and the control variable(s).

b. Describe the bivariate relationship between sex and salary.

c. Describe the relationship between sex and salary, controlling only for field of doctorate.

d. Describe the relationship between sex and salary, controlling only for experience.

e. Describe the relationship between sex and salary, controlling for both field of doctorate and experience.

f. A hypothesis of interest for these variables is "Controlling for field of doctorate and years of experience, there is no association between annual salary and sex." Draw a diagram that would be consistent with this hypothesis and that would make sense for these variables.

g. Refer to your interpretations in parts **b–e**, and comment on whether the hypothesis described in part **f** seems reasonable.

15. The accompanying table describes the association between death penalty verdict and defendant's race, by victim's race, for 326 subjects who were defendants in homicide indictments in twenty Florida counties during 1976–1977. (These data are analyzed in detail in Chapter 15.)

VICTIM'S RACE	DEATH PENALTY	DEFENDANT'S RACE White	Black
White	Yes	19 (12.6%)	11 (17.5%)
	No	132 (87.4%)	52 (82.5%)
Black	Yes	0 (0.0%)	6 (5.8%)
	No	9 (100.0%)	97 (94.2%)

Source: Taken from M. Radelet, "Racial Characteristics and the Imposition of the Death Penalty." *American Sociological Review, 46*:918–927, 1981.

a. Construct the bivariate table relating defendant's race to death penalty verdict (ignoring victim's race). Calculate the conditional distribution on the death penalty verdict, for each race of defendant.

b. Notice that the association changes direction when we control for victim's race, in the sense that relatively more whites receive the death penalty in the bivariate table, but relatively more blacks receive the death penalty in each partial table. By describing how victim's race is associated with each of these variables, explain why the partial association differs as it does from the bivariate association.

c. For these variables, indicate whether each of the following diagrams would seem to provide a reasonable model. Give your reasoning. [Here, P = death penalty, D = defendant's race, V = victim's race.]

d. Do the data in the table give evidence of statistical interaction? Why or why not?

e. Is it plausible that victim's race may be a suppressor variable? Why or why not?

16. Sociologist Gary T. Marx studied the relation between religiosity and "militance" among American blacks ("Religion: Opiate or Inspiration of Civil Rights Militancy Among Negroes," *American Sociological Review, 32*:64–72, 1967). He found that the more religious the respondents were, the less militant they were on social and political issues. He wrote, "Religiosity and militancy are also related to age, sex, education, . . . and region of country. . . . Thus it is possible that the relationship observed is simply the consequence of the fact that religiosity and militancy are related to some third variable."

a. What type of three-variable model is Marx suggesting?

b. Draw a figure to depict this model for the variables religiosity, militance, and education.

c. What does Marx need to do to test whether this model describes the data?

17. Refer to Problem 16. The accompanying tables reproduce some of Marx's results.

Bivariate Table

| | DEGREE OF RELIGIOSITY | | | |
	Very	*Somewhat*	*Not very*	*Not at all religious*
Nonmilitant	170	366	107	11
Militant	60	157	88	25

Kendall's tau-*b* = −.162, standard error = .030
Gamma = −.299, standard error = .054

Partial Tables (Controlling for Education)

Grammar School

| | RELIGIOSITY | | | |
	Very	*Somewhat*	*Not very*	*Not at all religious*
Sample size	108	201	42	2
Percent militant	17%	22%	31%	50%

Tau-*b* = −.101, standard error = .051
Gamma = −.226, standard error = .113

High School

Sample size	96	270	119	19
Percent militant	34%	32%	45%	58%

Tau-*b* = −.103, standard error = .043
Gamma = −.187, standard error = .077

College

Sample size	26	61	34	15
Percent militant	38%	48%	59%	87%

Tau-*b* = −.230, standard error = .074
Gamma = −.388, standard error = .120

a. Describe the relationship found in the partial tables and describe how education seems to be related to the original variables.

b. What conclusion can be made about the relationships, based on the partial tables? What can be said about Marx's hypothesized model described in the question in Problem 16?

18. The accompanying table is based on responses in the 1974 and 1975 General Social Surveys to the question "Do you believe that women should take care of running their homes and leave running the country up to men?"

EDUCATION	RESPONSE	SEX OF RESPONDENT	
		Male	*Female*
≤ 8 years	Agree	161 (64.1%)	169 (71.6%)
	Disagree	90 (35.9%)	67 (28.4%)
> 8 years	Agree	304 (28.8%)	386 (29.0%)
	Disagree	750 (71.2%)	944 (71.0%)

a. *Simpson's paradox* refers to the fact that in a three-way table, the associations in the partial tables can all have a different direction than the association in the corresponding bivariate table. Treating education as a control variable, show that these sample data satisfy Simpson's paradox.

b. Is there evidence of severe statistical interaction for these data? (The apparent difference in response between males and females for the ≤ 8 education group is not sufficient to imply a true difference in the population, since $\chi^2 = 3.1$ based on df = 1 for that 2×2 table.)

*19. Suppose we are interested in the association between two ordinal variables X and Y, controlling for a third categorical variable, Z. Let C_i and D_i denote the numbers of concordant and discordant pairs in the ith partial table. *Partial gamma* is a summary measure of partial association defined by

$$\hat{\gamma}_{XY \cdot Z} = \frac{\Sigma(C_i - D_i)}{\Sigma(C_i + D_i)}$$

The value of gamma in the ith partial table is

$$\hat{\gamma}_i = (C_i - D_i)/(C_i + D_i)$$

Show that partial gamma is the weighted average of the $\{\hat{\gamma}_i\}$ given by

$$\hat{\gamma}_{XY \cdot Z} = \Sigma w_i \hat{\gamma}_i$$

with weights $\{w_i = (C_i + D_i)/\Sigma(C_j + D_j)\}$.

Bibliography

Agresti, A. (1984). *Analysis of Ordinal Categorical Data*. New York: Wiley.
Hyman, H. (1955). *Survey Design and Analysis*. Princeton, N.J.: Princeton University Press.
McGaw, D. and G. Watson (1976). *Political and Social Inquiry*. New York: Wiley.
Rosenberg, M. (1968). *The Logic of Survey Analysis*. New York: Basic Books.

CHAPTER 11

Multiple Regression and Correlation Procedures

Contents

In Chapter 9, we introduced a linear model for relating two interval variables. More complex models are usually needed, however, to model social science relationships in a realistic manner. One reason for this is that there are usually several independent variables that have an effect on any dependent variable, and those variables are usually correlated among themselves. To get a good predictor of Y = college GPA, for example, it would probably be best to use several indices, among them perhaps X_1 = high school GPA, X_2 = college entrance exam math score, X_3 = college entrance exam verbal score, X_4 = IQ, X_5 = rating by high school guidance counselor, and X_6 = age. In modeling the variation in Y = voter registration rates among the precincts of a large city, we might want to consider several characteristics of the precincts, such as X_1 = percentage of families owning their homes, X_2 = percentage of nonwhite residents, X_3 = percentage of vote for Democratic candidate in last presidential election, X_4 = median family income, X_5 = median age of residents, and X_6 = median length of residence in the precinct for adults.

In this chapter, we will discuss methods for modeling the relationship between a dependent variable Y and a collection of independent variables. These methods enable us to develop a better predictor of a dependent variable than can be obtained by using only one independent variable. Also, these more complex models allow us to analyze *partial* relationships between two variables, controlling for other variables. This ability to describe partial relationships is important because many social science hypotheses are phrased in terms of the relationship between a dependent variable and an independent variable, controlling for other variables. In Chapter 10 we observed that partial associations, in which certain variables are controlled, can be quite different from the bivariate associations that are obtained when the other variables are ignored rather than controlled. Thus, the models presented in this chapter give us information that we cannot obtain by using simple models that are able to accommodate only two variables at a time.

In the first section of this chapter, we will see how to extend the simple linear regression model to incorporate any number of independent variables. This more general model is referred to as a *multiple regression model*. In Section 11.2, we introduce some data that will be used to illustrate the procedures described in this and the next chapter. In Section 11.3, some multivariate measures of association are defined. These include measures of *partial association* and a measure of *multiple correlation* that describes the degree of association between a dependent variable Y and a set of independent variables. The inference procedures for testing for statistical independence between a dependent variable and a collection of independent variables and between a dependent variable and a single independent variable, controlling for other variables, are illustrated in Section 11.4. Finally, in Section 11.5, standardized regression coefficients are introduced for describing the partial effect on the dependent variable of a standard deviation change in each independent variable. Throughout this chapter, we assume that the relationship between the dependent variable and each independent variable, controlling for other variables of interest, is linear in form.

11.1 The Multiple Regression Model

In Chapter 9, we modeled the relationship between the mean of the dependent variable Y and the independent variable X by the linear equation $E(Y \mid X) = \alpha + \beta X$. In this chapter, we will refer to this model containing a dependent variable and a *single* independent variable as the **bivariate linear model**. When there are k independent variables, denoted by $X_1, X_2, X_3, \ldots, X_k$, a natural way to generalize this model is to use the equation

The Basic Model

$$E(Y \mid X_1, \ldots, X_k) = \alpha + \beta_1 X_1 + \beta_2 X_2 + \cdots + \beta_k X_k$$

In this equation, $\alpha, \beta_1, \ldots, \beta_k$ are parameters (to be discussed below) and $E(Y \mid X_1, \ldots, X_k)$ denotes the mean of Y for particular values of $X_1, X_2, \ldots, X_k$. This equation is referred to as a **multiple regression model**. We will abbreviate the $E(Y \mid X_1, \ldots, X_k)$ symbol as $E(Y)$, unless we need to specify particular values of $X_1, \ldots, X_k$.

Unfortunately, the multiple regression model is more difficult to interpret graphically than was the bivariate linear model. For $k = 2$ independent variables, we could take the X_1 and X_2 axes to be perpendicular but lying in a horizontal plane, and then we could take the Y axis to be vertical and perpendicular to both the X_1 and X_2 axes (see Figure 11.1). The equation $E(Y) = \alpha + \beta_1 X_1 + \beta_2 X_2$ then traces out a plane cutting through three-dimensional space, when graphed as a function of the values of X_1 and X_2. More generally, if we have a separate axis for Y and for each of k independent variables, then the regression equation $E(Y) = \alpha + \beta_1 X_1 + \cdots + \beta_k X_k$ traces out a surface in $(k + 1)$-dimensional space. This makes mathematical sense for any value of k, but it is difficult to visualize for $k > 2$.

 **Fig. 11.1** Graphical Depiction of a Multiple Regression Equation

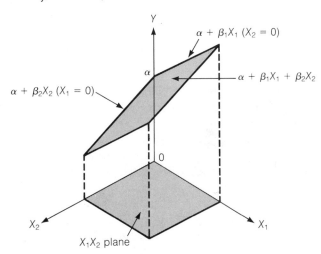

The easiest way to interpret the multiple regression model is to treat all but one of the independent variables as control variables and fix them at particular levels. Then, we are left with a linear equation describing the relationship between the mean of Y and the remaining independent variable, controlling for the other variables. To illustrate, let us consider the case in which there are $k = 2$ independent variables.

Treating the equation $E(Y) = \alpha + \beta_1 X_1 + \beta_2 X_2$ as a function of only the variable X_1 (by taking X_2 to be some constant), we have a linear equation with Y-intercept ($\alpha + \beta_2 X_2$) and with slope β_1. Thus, controlling for X_2, there is a linear relationship between $E(Y)$ and X_1 with slope β_1. The Y-intercept ($\alpha + \beta_2 X_2$) depends on the fixed value of X_2. When $X_2 = 0$, the Y-intercept is α; when $X_2 = 1$, it is $\alpha + \beta_2(1) = \alpha + \beta_2$; and so forth. However, for this model the slope β_1 of the controlled relationship between Y and X_1 is the same for each fixed value of X_2. Thus, if X_1 were increased 1 unit with X_2 held constant, the mean change in Y would be β_1. The parameter β_1 is a measure of the partial effect of X_1 on Y—that is, the effect on Y of a 1-unit increase in X_1 when X_2 is held constant. Similarly, we can consider the partial effect of X_2 on Y by holding constant the value of X_1. The partial relationship between Y and X_2 has slope β_2. More generally, for the multiple regression model with k independent variables, the coefficient β_i of X_i describes the change in the mean of Y when there is a 1-unit increase in X_i, controlling for the other ($k - 1$) variables.

The parameter α in the multiple regression equation is the conditional mean of Y when each of the independent variables equals 0. The parameters $\beta_1, \ldots, \beta_k$, which are the slopes of the partial relationships, are referred to as *partial regression coefficients*. We add the adjective *partial* here to distinguish these parameters from the corresponding regression coefficients for the *bivariate* relationships with Y for each of the independent variables. The coefficient β in the bivariate model $E(Y) = \alpha + \beta X$, discussed in Chapter 9, describes the slope of the linear relationship between Y and X, *ignoring* other independent variables, not *controlling* for their effects. Since other possible independent variables are omitted from the bivariate model, we cannot control their influences by fixing them at constant levels with that simple model.*

Example 11.1   To illustrate the multiple regression model, suppose that for students at a particular university, the relationship between Y = college GPA (with range 0–4.0), X_1 = high school GPA (range 0–4.0), and X_2 = college board score (range 200–800) has the form

$$E(Y) = .2 + .5X_1 + .002X_2$$

Then, the mean college GPA for the population of students having high school GPA (X_1) of 3.0 and college board score (X_2) of 500, for example, is $E(Y \mid X_1 = 3.0, X_2 = 500) = .2 + .5(3.0) + .002(500) = 2.7$. Similarly, the mean college GPA for the population having any particular values of X_1 and X_2 can be obtained by substituting those values into the regression equation.

*The partial regression coefficients are sometimes denoted differently from the bivariate coefficient to represent explicitly the controlled variables. For example, the symbol $\beta_{Y1 \cdot 23}$ is used to represent the partial slope of X_1 with Y, controlling for X_2 and X_3. The multiple regression model with three independent variables would then be expressed as $E(Y) = \alpha + \beta_{Y1 \cdot 23} X_1 + \beta_{Y2 \cdot 13} X_2 + \beta_{Y3 \cdot 12} X_3$. For simplicity, we have omitted these extra subscripts.

Let us consider the relationship between Y and X_1, controlling for X_2. The partial relationship between college GPA and high school GPA for those students with a college board score of $X_2 = 500$, for example, is given by

$$E(Y \mid X_1, X_2 = 500) = .2 + .5X_1 + .002(500)$$
$$= .2 + .5X_1 + 1 = 1.2 + .5X_1$$

This particular straight line is plotted in Figure 11.2.

Fig. 11.2 The Partial Relationship Between Y and X_1 for the Multiple Regression Equation $E(Y) = .2 + .5X_1 + .002X_2$

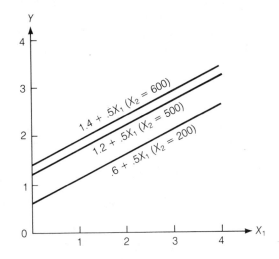

On the other hand, for those students with $X_2 = 600$, $E(Y \mid X_1, X_2 = 600) = 1.4 + .5X_1$. Thus, increasing X_2 by 100 units results in shifting the partial line relating Y to X_1 upward by $100\beta_2 = .2$ unit (see Figure 11.2). However, the slope of the relationship remains the same, so the line is parallel to the original one. By setting X_2 at a variety of values, we could generate a collection of parallel lines, each having slope $\beta_1 = .5$. Similarly, by setting X_1 at a variety of values, we could generate a collection of parallel lines, each having slope .002, that relate the mean of $\hat{Y}$ to X_2. In other words, controlling for high school GPA, the slope of the partial relationship between the mean college GPA and the college board score is $\beta_2 = .002$. Note that even though $\beta_1 = .5$ is the larger partial regression coefficient, this does not necessarily mean that X_1 has the greater partial effect on Y, since the two variables have different units of measurement. If X_2 had been scaled from 2 to 8 (instead of 200–800) for instance, then we would have $\beta_2 = .2$ (instead of .002). Section 11.5 will introduce *standardized* regression coefficients, whose values *can* be compared. ∎

The form of the multiple regression model introduced above is a relatively simple one, even though it allows for the introduction of any number of independent variables. To apply the model, we must assume that the slope of the partial relationship between Y and any particular X is identical for *all* combinations of values of the other independent variables. In essence, this means that this model is appropriate when there is no *statistical interaction*, as that term was introduced in Section 10.2. Thus, if the true partial slope between Y and X_1 were very different at $X_2 = 500$ than at $X_2 = 600$, for example, a more complex model would be needed.*

Also, we should realize that the partial relationship between Y and some independent variable X_i may be different from the bivariate relationship considered in Chapter 9. To illustrate, the slope in the bivariate relationship $E(Y) = \alpha + \beta X_1$ could be different in magnitude or in sign from the corresponding partial slope β_1 of X_1 in the multivariate model. In Example 11.1, it is possible that the relationship between Y and X_1, ignoring (not controlling for) the effects of other variables, is given by the equation $E(Y) = .5 + .7X_1$, for example. Figure 11.3 illustrates a situation in which the bivariate relationship between Y and a variable X_1 is positive, but at each of the five fixed levels of another variable X_2, the partial relationship is negative. This is an example of Simpson's paradox (see Problem 18 in Chapter 10). The partial slope for X_1 would be exactly the same as its bivariate slope if the correlation between X_1 and the control variable X_2 were 0. Thus, when X_1 and X_2 are independent causes of Y, the effect of X_1 on Y does not change when we control for X_2.

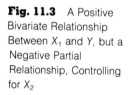 **Fig. 11.3** A Positive Bivariate Relationship Between X_1 and Y, but a Negative Partial Relationship, Controlling for X_2

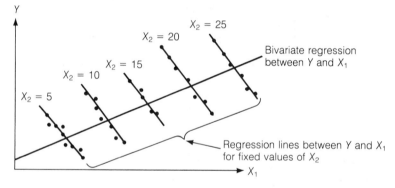

As with the bivariate model, the multiple regression model is probabilistic (as opposed to deterministic), since we model the *mean* of the dependent variable as a linear function of each of the independent variables. Any particular observation on Y can be modeled as the sum of this mean and some deviation ε from the mean. That is, $Y = \alpha + \beta_1 X_1 + \beta_2 X_2 + \cdots + \beta_k X_k + \varepsilon$, where ε represents the error that is unexplained by modeling Y as a linear function of these k independent variables. Further assumptions concerning this model will be introduced in Section 11.3 when we discuss confidence intervals and testing procedures.

Least Squares Equation

Once we propose the equation $E(Y) = \alpha + \beta_1 X_1 + \cdots + \beta_k X_k$ as a model for the multivariate relationship among a set of variables, the next step is to estimate the unknown parameters in that model based on the sample values for the variables.

*A model that incorporates terms for this type of situation is introduced in Section 12.2.

Notation

Let $\{a, b_1, b_2, \ldots, b_k\}$ denote point estimates of $\{\alpha, \beta_1, \beta_2, \ldots, \beta_k\}$, and let $\hat{Y} = a + b_1X_1 + \cdots + b_kX_k$ be the prediction equation that is used to estimate the multiple regression equation $E(Y) = \alpha + \beta_1X_1 + \cdots + \beta_kX_k$.

For any particular prediction equation, we can calculate predicted values $\{\hat{Y}_1, \hat{Y}_2, \ldots, \hat{Y}_n\}$ of the dependent variable for the n members in the sample by substituting the X-values for each into the equation. For example, we obtain $\hat{Y}_1$ (the predicted value of Y for the first member) by substituting the values for the independent variables $X_1, \ldots, X_k$ for the first member into the prediction equation $\hat{Y} = a + b_1X_1 + \cdots + b_kX_k$. The prediction error for that individual is the *residual* $Y_1 - \hat{Y}_1$, the difference between the actual and predicted values of the dependent variable. For each possible prediction equation, we could summarize the goodness of its fit by the *sum of squared errors*,

$$\text{SSE} = \sum_{i=1}^{n} (Y_i - \hat{Y}_i)^2$$

The formula for this summary measure of prediction errors is identical to the one in Chapter 9. The only difference is that several independent variables (instead of just one) are used simultaneously in obtaining the predictions on Y.

In this chapter, we will again use point estimates satisfying the least squares criterion. These estimates are the numbers $\{a, b_1, \ldots, b_k\}$ that yield the prediction equation $\hat{Y} = a + b_1X_1 + \cdots + b_kX_k$ having the *smallest* sum of squared errors (SSE) of all possible equations of this form. As we have seen in Section 9.2, the formula for obtaining these estimates requires a fair amount of arithmetic even when there is only one independent variable. When there are two or more independent variables in the model, the calculations become much more cumbersome and are most conveniently handled by using matrix algebra. In practice, the least squares estimates are most easily obtained by using a packaged computer program, rather than by hand calculation, and the formulas for their calculation are of little intuitive value. Therefore, we will not give explicit formulas for these estimates in this text.

**11.2
Example Based
on Computer
Analysis**

To illustrate the concepts presented in this and the next chapter, we shall refer to the data described in Example 11.2. As an aid to the analysis of these data, we present some figures that are typical of computer printouts for the regression models we have considered.

Example 11.2

A study is conducted in a southern county to investigate the relationship between certain mental health indices and several independent variables, including socioeconomic indices. Primary interest centers on a general index of mental health, which incorporates various dimensions of psychiatric symptoms, including aspects of anxiety and depression. This measure, which we treat as the dependent variable Y, ranges from 17 to 41 in the sample; higher scores indicate greater psychiatric impairment. We will consider two independent variables in relation to the mental health index, X_1 = life events score and X_2 = socioeconomic status (SES). The life events variable is a composite measure of both the number and severity of important life events that have occurred within the past 3 years. These events range from such severe personal disruptions as a death in the family, a jail sentence, or an extra-marital affair, to less severe events such as getting a new job, the birth of a child, moving within the same city, or having a child marry. The measure, which ranges from 3 to 97 in the sample, was introduced by Paykel et al. (1971). A high life events score represents a greater number and/or greater severity of these life events. The second independent variable, X_2 = SES, is measured on a standard scale based on occupation, income, and education. It ranges from 0 to 100; the higher the score, the higher the status. These indices are, at best, crude approximations for the under-lying concepts that are truly of interest. However, much of social science research deals with the construction, use, and improvement of such indices, and we shall treat them as interval variables in our analyses.

Table 11.1

Scores on Y = Mental Health Index, X_1 = Life Events Index, and X_2 = Socioeconomic Status

OBSERVATION NUMBER	Y	X_1	X_2	OBSERVATION NUMBER	Y	X_1	X_2
1	17	46	84	16	28	37	50
2	19	39	97	17	28	30	90
3	20	27	24	18	28	13	56
4	20	3	85	19	29	5	40
5	20	10	15	20	30	44	53
6	21	37	78	21	31	35	38
7	22	35	91	22	31	95	29
8	22	78	60	23	31	63	53
9	24	33	67	24	31	42	7
10	24	18	39	25	32	38	32
11	25	81	87	26	34	70	58
12	26	22	95	27	34	57	16
13	26	50	40	28	34	40	29
14	27	55	88	29	41	49	3
15	28	97	89	30	41	89	75

In Table 11.1, the scores on the three variables of interest are presented for a random sample of thirty adults in the county.* The marginal distributions of the three variables are summarized by their estimated means and standard deviations, as listed in Table 11.2. Figures 11.4 and 11.5, presented in the form of typical computer printouts for many regression packages, describe two *bivariate* relationships, one between Y and X_1, the other between Y and X_2. The separate prediction equations

*This example is based on a more general survey conducted for a much larger sample size, as reported by Holzer (1977). The authors thank Dr. Holzer for permission to use the study as the basis of this example.

Table 11.2

Estimated Means and
Standard Deviations of
Y = Mental Health Index,
X_1 = Life Events Score,
and X_2 = Socioeconomic
Status

VARIABLE	MEAN	STANDARD DEVIATION
Y	27.47	6.04
X_1	44.60	25.44
X_2	55.60	28.76

are $\hat{Y} = 23.4276 + .0906X_1$ and $\hat{Y} = 32.3506 - .0878X_2$. The mental health index is positively related to the life events score, since the coefficient of X_1 (.091) is positive. In other words, the greater the number and severity of life events in the previous 3 years, the higher the index of psychiatric symptoms (i.e., the poorer the mental health of the respondent) tends to be. Also, the mental health index is negatively related to socioeconomic status. The greater the SES level, the smaller the index of psychiatric symptoms tends to be. The Pearson correlations between the mental health index and each of the independent variables are $r_{YX_1} = .381$ and $r_{YX_2} = -.418$.

Fig. 11.4 Regression Analysis for Y = Mental Health Index and X_1 = Life Events Score

SOURCE	DF	SUM OF SQUARES	R-SQUARE		
REGRESSION	1	153.92	.145		
ERROR	28	905.55			
TOTAL	29	1059.47			
		T FOR H0:		STD ERR OF	
PARAMETER	ESTIMATE	PARAMETER = 0	PROB> |T|	ESTIMATE	CORRELATION
INTERCEPT	23.4276				
X1	.0906	2.1816	.0377	.0415	.3812

Fig. 11.5 Regression Analysis for Y = Mental Health Index and X_2 = Socioeconomic Status

SOURCE	DF	SUM OF SQUARES	R-SQUARE		
REGRESSION	1	185.12	.175		
ERROR	28	874.35			
TOTAL	29	1059.47			
		T FOR H0:		STD ERR OF	
PARAMETER	ESTIMATE	PARAMETER = 0	PROB> |T|	ESTIMATE	CORRELATION
INTERCEPT	32.3506				
X2	-.0878	-2.4348	.0215	.0361	-.4180

The computer printout corresponding to fitting the multiple regression model $E(Y) = \alpha + \beta_1 X_1 + \beta_2 X_2$ to the data is given in Figure 11.6 (next page). Much of what is listed on that printout will appear unfamiliar to you at this stage, but it will be explained in the next few sections of this chapter. From the column labeled ESTIMATE, we see that the least squares prediction equation is

$$\hat{Y} = a + b_1 X_1 + b_2 X_2 = 28.3240 + .1024X_1 - .0976X_2$$

Controlling for SES, there is a positive relationship between the mental health index and life events score, since the coefficient of the life events score ($b_1 = .102$) is positive. We would estimate that there is a .102-unit increase in the mean of the mental health index for every 1-unit increase in the life events score, controlling for SES. Since $b_2 = -.098$, there is a negative association between the mental health index and SES, controlling for life events. For example, over the 100-unit range of SES values (from a minimum value of 0 to a maximum value of 100), the mean mental health index is estimated to decrease by 100(.098) = 9.8. Since the mental health index ranges only from 17 to 41, a change of 9.8 points in the mean score can be considered fairly important.

Fig. 11.6 Multiple Regression Analysis for Y = Mental Health Index, X_1 = Life Events Score, and X_2 = Socioeconomic Status

SOURCE	DF	SUM OF SQUARES	MEAN SQUARE	F VALUE	PROB > F	R-SQUARE	ROOT MSE
REGRESSION	2	379.68	189.84	7.54	.0028	.358	5.018
ERROR	27	679.79	25.18				
TOTAL	29	1059.47					

PARAMETER	ESTIMATE	T FOR H0: PARAMETER = 0	PROB > |T|	STD ERR OF ESTIMATE	STANDARDIZED ESTIMATE
INTERCEPT	28.3240				
X1	.1024	2.7799	.0098	.0368	.4310
X2	-.0976	-2.9944	.0058	.0326	-.4643

OBS. NO.	OBSERVED VALUE	PREDICTED VALUE	RESIDUAL	OBS. NO.	OBSERVED VALUE	PREDICTED VALUE	RESIDUAL
1	17.0	24.839	-7.839	16	28.0	27.235	.765
2	19.0	22.854	-3.854	17	28.0	22.615	5.385
3	20.0	28.747	-8.747	18	28.0	24.191	3.809
4	20.0	20.338	- .338	19	29.0	24.933	4.067
5	20.0	27.885	-7.885	20	30.0	27.659	2.341
6	21.0	24.503	-3.503	21	31.0	28.201	2.799
7	22.0	23.030	-1.030	22	31.0	35.224	-4.224
8	22.0	30.458	-8.458	23	31.0	29.605	1.395
9	24.0	25.166	-1.166	24	31.0	31.942	- .942
10	24.0	26.362	-2.362	25	32.0	29.093	2.907
11	25.0	28.131	-3.131	26	34.0	29.834	4.166
12	26.0	21.308	4.692	27	34.0	32.600	1.400
13	26.0	29.542	-3.542	28	34.0	29.591	4.409
14	27.0	25.370	1.630	29	41.0	33.049	7.951
15	28.0	29.574	-1.574	30	41.0	30.121	10.879

CORRELATION MATRIX	Y	X1	X2
Y	1.000	.381	-.418
X1	.381	1.000	.107
X2	-.418	.107	1.000

Individual predictions for the dependent variable Y can be made as in the bivariate regression model presented in Chapter 9. The first individual in the sample had scores of $Y = 17$, $X_1 = 46$, and $X_2 = 84$ (see Table 11.1). The predicted mental health score for this individual is $\hat{Y} = 28.3240 + .1024(46) - .0976(84) = 24.84$. The prediction error or residual using this model is $Y - \hat{Y} = 17 - 24.84 = -7.84$. The predictions and residuals for all thirty individuals sampled are also listed in Figure 11.6. We observe from the SUM OF SQUARES column that the sum of squared errors (residuals) for this prediction equation is

$$\text{SSE} = \Sigma (Y_i - \hat{Y}_i)^2 = 679.79$$

According to the criterion underlying the method of least squares, any other estimates a, b_1, and b_2 in this model would have yielded a larger value for this term.

Figure 11.6 also contains a correlation matrix, which gives the sample Pearson correlation between each pair of variables. The correlations on the diagonal running from the upper-left corner to the lower-right corner of the table all equal 1.0, indicating simply that the correlation between a variable and itself is 1.0 (e.g., if we know the value of Y, then we can predict the value of Y perfectly). The correlation between each distinct pair of variables appears twice in the figure. The correlations r_{YX_1} and r_{YX_2} also appeared in Figure 11.4 and Figure 11.5, respectively.

Comparing Figure 11.6 to Figures 11.4 and 11.5, we see that the partial slopes for the data are quite similar to the uncontrolled slopes. The coefficient of $X_1 =$ life events score in the bivariate model (Figure 11.4) is .091, whereas in the multiple regression model it is .102 (controlling for SES). Likewise, with the addition of $X_1 =$ life events score as a control variable in the model of the relationship between mental health score and $X_2 =$ SES, the coefficient of X_2 changes only from $-.088$ in the bivariate model (Figure 11.5) to $-.098$ in the multiple regression model. Thus, in each case, the introduction of the second independent variable does little to alter the effect of the other independent variable, indicating that these variables are nearly independent in their sample effects on Y. In fact, the sample correlation between X_1 and X_2 is very weak ($r_{X_1 X_2} = .107$). We will next see how to measure the joint association of the independent variables with the dependent variable and the partial association between each independent variable and the dependent variable, controlling for the other variables in the model. ■

11.3 Multiple and Partial Correlations

Once we have obtained the least squares prediction equation, we might be interested in a measure of how good the predictions of the dependent variable are. In Section 9.3, we used the coefficient of determination r^2 to describe the goodness of predictions based on the bivariate prediction equation relative to the naive estimate $\bar{Y}$ in which the independent variable is ignored. We will now define an analogous measure, again based on the proportional reduction in error concept, that summarizes the relative improvement in predictions using the prediction equation instead of $\bar{Y}$. For the multiple regression model to be useful, we would hope that there would be a significant improvement in predictability relative not only to $\bar{Y}$ but also to the separate bivariate models for the dependent variable and each of the independent variables.

Coefficient of Multiple Determination

An analog of the coefficient of determination discussed in Section 9.3 that would be appropriate for the multiple regression model has the following elements.

Rule 1   The dependent variable is predicted without knowledge of $X_1, \ldots, X_k$. The best predictor for the members in the sample is then the sample mean, $\bar{Y}$.

Rule 2   To incorporate information on $X_1, \ldots, X_k$, we use the least squares prediction equation $\hat{Y} = a + b_1X_1 + b_2X_2 + \cdots + b_kX_k$ in making the predictions about the dependent variable. By substituting the observed values of $X_1, \ldots, X_k$ for the ith member into this equation, we get the predicted value, $\hat{Y}_i$, for that member.

Prediction Errors   The prediction error for the ith member is the difference between the observed and the predicted vaues of Y. Using Rule 1, the error is the difference $Y_i - \bar{Y}$; using Rule 2, it is the residual $Y_i - \hat{Y}_i$. In either case, the total prediction error for the entire sample is summarized by the sum of the squared prediction errors. For Rule 1, this is $TSS = \Sigma (Y_i - \bar{Y})^2$. This quantity is the same regardless of which regression equation is used, since it does not depend on the values of any independent variables. For Rule 2, the summary error quantity is $SSE = \Sigma (Y_i - \hat{Y}_i)^2$, the sum of squared errors in using the prediction equation.

Definition of Measure   The proportional reduction in error obtained by using the linear prediction equation $\hat{Y} = a + b_1X_1 + \cdots + b_kX_k$ instead of $\bar{Y}$ to obtain predictions on the dependent variable is

$$R^2 = \frac{TSS - SSE}{TSS}$$

This measure of association is referred to as the **coefficient of multiple determination** for the multiple regression model. It measures the proportion of the total variation in Y that is explained by the simultaneous predictive power of all k independent variables through the multiple regression model. We use the uppercase notation R^2 to distinguish this PRE measure from the corresponding PRE measure r^2 for the bivariate model. Their formulas are identical, in fact, and r^2 is the special case of the measure R^2 applied to a regression equation with $k = 1$ independent variable.

The properties of R^2 are similar to those of r^2. Predictions can be no worse overall using $\hat{Y}$ instead of $\bar{Y}$ as a predictor, since $\hat{Y}$ uses additional information (the values of $X_1, \ldots, X_k$). Therefore, SSE can be no larger than TSS, and since SSE is nonnegative, it follows that R^2 must fall between 0 and 1. The larger the value of R^2, the better is the set of independent variables $(X_1, \ldots, X_k)$ in collectively predicting Y. The value of $R^2 = 1$ occurs only when all of the residuals are 0 (i.e., when all $Y_i = \hat{Y}_i$, so that SSE $=0$). In that case, the regression equation passes through all of the observed points. An R^2 value of 0 occurs when the least squares predictions do not vary as any of the X-values vary. In that case, $b_1 = b_2 = \cdots = b_k = 0$, and $\hat{Y}$ is identical to $\bar{Y}$, since the independent variables do not add any predictive power. This happens when the Pearson correlation between Y and each of the independent variables is 0.

The numerator of R^2, TSS $-$ SSE, is interpreted as the amount of variation in Y that is explained through use of the multiple regression model. This difference, which can be shown to equal $\Sigma\,(\hat{Y}_i - \bar{Y})^2$, is often referred to as the *regression* (or *model*) *sum of squares*. Thus, the total sum of squares TSS of the Y-values about $\bar{Y}$ may be partitioned into the sum of the variation explained by the model (regression sum of squares) and the variation not explained by the model (sum of squared errors or residuals, SSE).

Multiple Correlation Coefficient

The positive square root of the coefficient of multiple determination, $R = +\sqrt{R^2}$, is called the *multiple correlation coefficient*. This quantity is also used as a measure of the linear association between Y and the independent variables $X_1, \ldots, X_k$. The relationship between this measure and R^2 is analogous to the relationship between the Pearson correlation r and r^2 for the bivariate linear model. In fact, the multiple correlation is identical to the bivariate Pearson correlation computed between the Y- and $\hat{Y}$-values. In other words, when for each member in the sample we combine the information on the independent variables $X_1, \ldots, X_k$ according to the combination $a + b_1 X_1 + \cdots + b_k X_k$, referred to as a *linear combination* of the independent variables, we form a new variable, denoted by $\hat{Y}$. For each of the sample members, there is a Y-value and a $\hat{Y}$-value. In Figure 11.6, for example, these are the values listed under the headings OBSERVED VALUE and PREDICTED VALUE. When the sample Pearson correlation between the Y- and $\hat{Y}$-values is computed, we obtain precisely the value R, the positive square root of R^2. It can be shown that no other linear combination of the independent variables would be more strongly correlated with Y than the least squares one. Thus, the least squares equation yields the best prediction of the dependent variable in this additional sense that it represents the linear reduction of $X_1, \ldots, X_k$ to the single variable that is most strongly related to Y. It can also be shown that $\hat{Y}$ cannot be negatively correlated with Y (otherwise $\bar{Y}$ would be a better predictor of Y), so R must always be between 0 and 1. In this respect, the multiple correlation is unlike the Pearson correlation, which can take on values between -1 and $+1$.

It is impossible to explain *less* variation in Y by adding independent variables to a regression model. For example, the worst that could happen when X_2 is added to a model already containing X_1 as an independent variable is that it would be useless for predictive purposes, in which case the least squares procedure would yield $b_2 = 0$. Then, the predictions would be the same as when X_1 alone was an independent variable, so that SSE would be unchanged. Therefore, SSE for the multiple regression model can be no larger than SSE for the bivariate regression model in which Y is modeled as a linear function of any one of the independent variables. Since TSS is the same regardless of the model, R^2 for the multiple regression model must be at least as large as $r^2_{YX_1}, r^2_{YX_2}, \ldots, r^2_{YX_k}$. That is, the proportional reduction in error for the multiple regression model with the k independent variables $X_1, \ldots, X_k$ is at least as large as the proportional reduction in error for each of the bivariate models, Y as a linear function of X_1, Y as a linear function of X_2, and so forth. Similarly, the multiple correlation R is at least as large as the absolute value of any of the bivariate Pearson correlations $r_{YX_1}, \ldots, r_{YX_k}$. More generally, if R_1 is the multiple correlation for a particular multiple regression model and R_2 is the corresponding coefficient for another model in which only a subset of the independent variables from the first model is used, then $R_1 \geq R_2$. For example, the multiple correlation for the model $E(Y) = \alpha + \beta_1 X_1 + \beta_2 X_2 + \beta_3 X_3$ must be at least as large as the multiple correlation for the model $E(Y) = \alpha + \beta_1 X_1 + \beta_3 X_3$.

Example 11.3   For the data on Y = mental health index, X_1 = life events score, and X_2 = SES introduced in Example 11.2, we obtained the least squares prediction equation $\hat{Y} = 28.324 + .102X_1 - .098X_2$. The computer output for this model was given in Figure 11.6. The total sum of squares of the dependent variable about its mean is TSS = $\Sigma (Y_i - \bar{Y})^2 = 1{,}059.47$. The sum of squared errors resulting from using the least squares equation to predict the dependent variable is SSE = $\Sigma (Y_i - \hat{Y}_i)^2 = 679.79$. The difference between the two, TSS − SSE = 379.68, is listed in Figure 11.6 as the regression sum of squares. The coefficient of multiple determination for this multiple regression model is

$$R^2 = \frac{\text{TSS} - \text{SSE}}{\text{TSS}} = \frac{379.68}{1{,}059.47} = .358$$

This statistic also appears in Figure 11.6 under R-SQUARE. We may conclude that by using the life events score and SES simultaneously to predict mental health scores, we obtain a 35.8% reduction in the prediction error relative to using only $\bar{Y}$. From Figures 11.4 and 11.5, we see that $r^2_{YX_1} = .145$ and $r^2_{YX_2} = .175$. Thus, the multiple regression model yields a substantially larger reduction in error than either of the bivariate models. It appears, therefore, that the multiple model is more useful and informative, at least for predictive purposes.

The multiple correlation between the mental health score and the two independent variables is $R = +\sqrt{.358} = .599$. This is precisely the value we would get for the Pearson correlation between the two sets of values labeled OBSERVED (i.e., Y) and PREDICTED (i.e., $\hat{Y}$) in Figure 11.6. Thus, the linear combination of the independent variables that gives a new variable as highly correlated as possible with the mental health score is $\hat{Y} = 28.324 + .102X_1 - .098X_2$; this variable has correlation $R = .599$ with Y. Any other linear combination, such as $\hat{Y} = 28 + .15X_1 - .20X_2$, would yield predicted values that are less strongly correlated with the actual values on the mental health index. Notice that $R > .381 = |r_{YX_1}|$ and $R > .418 = |r_{YX_2}|$, corresponding to the fact that SSE is smaller in Figure 11.6 (for the multiple regression model) than in Figure 11.4 or 11.5 (for the bivariate models).   ∎

Partial Correlation   The multiple regression model enables us to analyze the relationship between two variables, controlling for other variables of interest. To illustrate, in Example 11.2, $b_1 = .102$ is the slope of the relationship between Y and X_1, controlling for X_2, and $b_2 = -.098$ is the slope of the relationship between Y and X_2, controlling for X_1. It is often of interest to describe the strength of the association between two interval variables, controlling for one or more other variables. For example, we might want a measure of the association between the mental health index and the life events score, controlling for SES. We might ask, for instance, "Controlling for SES, what proportion of the variation in the mental health index can be explained by the life events score?"

As we observed in Section 9.3, slopes are inadequate for describing *strength* of association, since their values depend on the units of measurement of the variables and can therefore be any real numbers. We next introduce a set of measures that describe the partial association of Y with each of the independent variables, controlling for the others, and that are restricted in range between -1 and $+1$.

For interval variables, a summary partial measure can be computed directly from the bivariate Pearson correlations between each pair of variables. In the case of one control variable, this measure of association is defined as indicated in the box.

Partial Correlation Coefficient

The sample *partial correlation coefficient* between Y and X_2, controlling for X_1, is

$$r_{YX_2 \cdot X_1} = \frac{r_{YX_2} - r_{YX_1} r_{X_1 X_2}}{\sqrt{(1 - r_{YX_1}^2)(1 - r_{X_1 X_2}^2)}}$$

In the symbol $r_{YX_2 \cdot X_1}$ for the partial correlation, the variable to the right of the dot represents the controlled variable. Since one variable is being controlled, the partial correlations $r_{YX_1 \cdot X_2}$ and $r_{YX_2 \cdot X_1}$ are called *first-order partial correlations.* The analogous formula for $r_{YX_1 \cdot X_2}$ is

$$r_{YX_1 \cdot X_2} = \frac{r_{YX_1} - r_{YX_2} r_{X_1 X_2}}{\sqrt{(1 - r_{YX_2}^2)(1 - r_{X_1 X_2}^2)}}$$

Example 11.4 For a group of 100 children of ages varying from 3 to 15, the Pearson correlation between $Y =$ vocabulary score on an achievement test and $X_1 =$ height of child is $r_{YX_1} = .65$. We might expect that this correlation can be explained by the joint relationship of both of these variables with another variable, $X_2 =$ age. In other words, we would expect both $Y =$ vocabulary score and $X_1 =$ height to be strongly positively related to the children's ages, and we would expect only a weak, if any, association between vocabulary and height for children of equal age. To illustrate the formula for the partial correlation, let us suppose that the Pearson correlation between vocabulary score and age for this sample is $r_{YX_2} = .85$ and that the Pearson correlation between height and age is $r_{X_1 X_2} = .75$. Then, the partial correlation between vocabulary and height, controlling for age, is

$$r_{YX_1 \cdot X_2} = \frac{r_{YX_1} - r_{YX_2} r_{X_1 X_2}}{\sqrt{(1 - r_{YX_2}^2)(1 - r_{X_1 X_2}^2)}} = \frac{.65 - .85(.75)}{\sqrt{(1 - .85^2)(1 - .75^2)}} = .036$$

As expected, $r_{YX_1 \cdot X_2}$ is only a small fraction as large as r_{YX_1}, and it is not even significantly nonzero (see Problem 23 at the end of the chapter). The relationship between height and vocabulary thus appears to be spurious, in the sense that it is due to their joint dependence on age. ∎

Under certain assumptions that we make for conducting inference procedures in the next section, $r_{YX_2 \cdot X_1}$, can be interpreted as the Pearson correlation between Y and X_2 at every *fixed* value of X_1. If we could control X_1 by considering a subpopulation of members all having the same value on X_1, then $r_{YX_2 \cdot X_1}$ would be the correlation between Y and X_2 for that subpopulation. As with the bivariate Pearson correlation, $r_{YX_2 \cdot X_1}$ must fall between -1 and $+1$. It has the same sign as the partial slope (b_2) that describes the effect of X_2 in the prediction equation $\hat{Y} = a + b_1 X_1 + b_2 X_2$, just as the bivariate correlation has the same sign as the bivariate slope. The larger its absolute value, the stronger the association between Y and X_2, controlling for X_1. The partial correlation is symmetric, in the sense that $r_{YX_2 \cdot X_1} = r_{X_2 Y \cdot X_1}$. In other words, if X_2 is treated as the dependent variable and Y as the independent variable (with X_1 still the control variable), then the same partial correlation value occurs. In addition, the value of the partial correlation does not depend on the units of measurement of the variables.

Again, like the behavior of the Pearson correlation, the square of the partial correlation has a proportional reduction in error interpretation. In this interpretation, controlling for X_1 is equivalent to removing from consideration the portion of the total sum of squares (TSS) in Y that is explained by X_1, and then finding the proportion of the *remaining* variation in Y that can be explained by X_2. Now, $r_{YX_1}^2$ is the proportion of the variation in Y that is explained by X_1, and the remaining proportion $(1 - r_{YX_1}^2)$ represents the variation left unexplained. When X_2 is added to the model, an additional part of this unexplained variation is accounted for, resulting in the total proportion R^2 of the variation in Y being accounted for by X_1 and X_2 jointly. Here, R^2 refers to the coefficient of multiple determination for the multiple regression model with both X_1 and X_2 as independent variables. So, $R^2 - r_{YX_1}^2$ is the additional proportion of the variability in Y explained by X_2, after the effects of X_1 have been removed or controlled (see Figure 11.7). The maximum this difference could be is $1 - r_{YX_1}^2$, the proportion of variation yet to be explained after accounting for the influence of X_1. We divide $R^2 - r_{YX_1}^2$ by this maximum possible difference in order to get a measure that has a maximum possible value of 1. In fact, this ratio is the squared partial correlation between Y and X_2, controlling for X_1.

The square of the partial correlation $r_{YX_2 \cdot X_1}$ gives the proportion of the variation left unexplained by X_1 that is accounted for by X_2, or

$$r_{YX_2 \cdot X_1}^2 = \frac{R^2 - r_{YX_1}^2}{1 - r_{YX_1}^2} = \frac{\text{Partial proportion explained by } X_2 \text{ alone}}{\text{Proportion unexplained by } X_1}$$

In Figure 11.7, this relationship is represented by the ratio of the partial contribution of X_2 beyond that of X_1 (namely, $R^2 - r_{YX_1}^2$), divided by the proportion $(1 - r_{YX_1}^2)$ left unexplained by X_1. We can interpret $r_{YX_2 \cdot X_1}^2$ as the proportion of variation in Y that is

Fig. 11.7

Representation of $r^2_{YX_2 \cdot X_1}$ as the Proportion of Variability Unexplained by X_1 That Can Be Explained by X_2

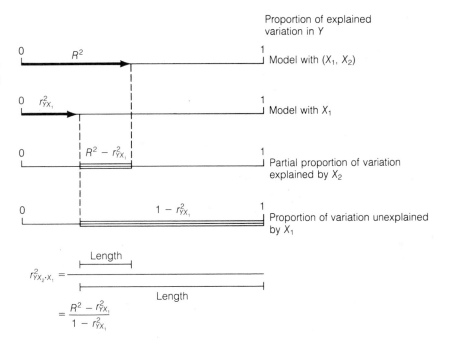

Proportion of explained variation in Y

explained by X_2, controlling for the effect of X_1. Similarly, the square of $r_{YX_1 \cdot X_2}$ can be expressed as

$$r^2_{YX_1 \cdot X_2} = \frac{R^2 - r^2_{YX_2}}{1 - r^2_{YX_2}}$$

the proportion of variation in Y that is explained by X_1, out of that part left unexplained by X_2.

Example 11.5

From Figure 11.6, $r_{YX_1} = .381$, $r_{YX_2} = -.418$, and $r_{X_1 X_2} = .107$. The partial correlation between the mental health index and life events score, controlling for SES, is therefore

$$r_{YX_1 \cdot X_2} = \frac{r_{YX_1} - r_{YX_2} r_{X_1 X_2}}{\sqrt{(1 - r^2_{YX_2})(1 - r^2_{X_1 X_2})}} = \frac{.381 - (-.418)(.107)}{\sqrt{[1 - (-.418)^2](1 - .107^2)}} = .471$$

Alternatively, from Figure 11.6, we know that $R^2 = .358$, so that

$$r^2_{YX_1 \cdot X_2} = \frac{R^2 - r^2_{YX_2}}{1 - r^2_{YX_2}} = \frac{.358 - (-.418)^2}{1 - (-.418)^2} = .222$$

Hence, controlling for SES, 22.2% of the variation in the mental health scores is explained by the life events score. Knowing that $r^2_{YX_1 \cdot X_2} = .222$, we can recover the partial correlation value of $r_{YX_1 \cdot X_2} = +\sqrt{.222} = .471$. We take the positive square root here, since $r_{YX_1 \cdot X_2}$ must have the same sign as the partial slope b_1 of X_1, controlling for X_2, in the prediction equation. ∎

Second-Order and Higher Partial Correlations*

Similar expressions can be given when the number of independent variables being controlled is greater than one. For example, the square of the partial correlation between Y and X_k, controlling for $X_1, X_2, \ldots, X_{k-1}$, is

$$r^2_{YX_k \cdot X_1, \ldots, X_{k-1}} = \frac{R^2_{Y(X_1, \ldots, X_k)} - R^2_{Y(X_1, \ldots, X_{k-1})}}{1 - R^2_{Y(X_1, \ldots, X_{k-1})}}$$

Here, $R^2_{Y(X_1, \ldots, X_k)}$ denotes the value of R^2 for the multiple regression model including all k independent variables, and $R^2_{Y(X_1, \ldots, X_{k-1})}$ is the value of R^2 for the model containing just the $(k - 1)$ control variables. The difference $R^2_{Y(X_1, \ldots, X_k)} - R^2_{Y(X_1, \ldots, X_{k-1})}$ represents the increase in the proportion of explained variance when X_k is added to the multiple regression model. The denominator $1 - R^2_{Y(X_1, \ldots, X_{k-1})}$ is the proportion of the variation left unexplained when just $X_1, \ldots, X_{k-1}$ are the independent variables in the model. To illustrate, the square of the *second-order partial correlation* between Y and X_3, controlling for X_1 and X_2, is

$$r^2_{YX_3 \cdot X_1, X_2} = \frac{R^2_{Y(X_1, X_2, X_3)} - R^2_{Y(X_1, X_2)}}{1 - R^2_{Y(X_1, X_2)}}$$

Multicollinearity

In this section we have seen that R^2 cannot decrease when independent variables are added to a multiple regression model. On the other hand, once certain important variables are in the model, the addition of other independent variables may result in only a small boost in R^2. In other words, these other variables may have small partial correlations with Y, given the variables already in the model. This often happens in social science research when the independent variables are highly correlated, no one having much unique explanatory power. This condition is referred to as *multicollinearity* and will be considered in more detail in Section 12.4.

For predictive purposes, not much is gained by adding to a model independent variables that are strongly correlated to ones already in the model, since R^2 usually does not increase much. Also, the standard errors of the estimated regression parameters tend to become larger when multicollinearity exists. Ideally, for prediction purposes, one should attempt to model Y as a function of independent variables that are relatively unrelated to each other but have strong correlations with Y. Unfortunately, this is not always possible, especially if there are certain variables that we want to include in the model for theoretical reasons.

11.4 Inferences for Partial Coefficients and Correlations

In order to make inferences about the parameters of the multiple regression equation, it is necessary to add additional elements to the basic model considered in Section 11.1. In the earlier discussion, we assumed that the relationship between the mean of the dependent variable and the independent variables $X_1, \ldots, X_k$ could be represented by the equation $E(Y) = \alpha + \beta_1 X_1 + \cdots + \beta_k X_k$. In other words, for particular values of $X_1, \ldots, X_k$, the value $\alpha + \beta_1 X_1 + \cdots + \beta_k X_k$ represents the mean of the scores on the dependent variable for the population having those values on $X_1, \ldots, X_k$. We shall now assume in addition that the population distribution of the scores on the dependent variable is normal about the mean $\alpha + \beta_1 X_1 + \cdots + \beta_k X_k$, for each combination of values of $X_1, \ldots, X_k$. The conditional standard deviation, σ, of these scores about the regression equation is also assumed to be constant over the entire range of values of the independent variables. As usual, the sample is assumed to be randomly selected. These assumptions, like those we encountered in Chapter 9, are necessary for the actual sampling distributions of the statistics studied to equal those quoted in this section. In practice, we do not expect the assumptions to be satisfied exactly. The better they are satisfied, however, the more likely our conclusions are to be correct.

There are two types of inferences that are of primary interest after the least squares equation $\hat{Y} = a + b_1X_1 + \cdots + b_kX_k$ has been obtained as an estimate of the regression equation $E(Y) = \alpha + \beta_1X_1 + \cdots + \beta_kX_k$. The first of these is a broad test used to investigate whether *any* of the independent variables are statistically related to the dependent variable. If the null hypothesis in this test is rejected, we then consider each of the partial regression coefficients individually. We do this in order to assess which of the independent variables have significant partial effects on the dependent variable and to estimate the sizes of these partial effects. Other inferences that are sometimes of interest include prediction intervals for values of the dependent variable, interval estimation of the regression function at particular values of the independent variables, and inferences about the difference between two partial slopes or between two partial correlations. We refer the reader to Neter and Wasserman (1974) and Younger (1979) for discussion of these latter procedures.

As in the bivariate regression model, the goodness of the least squares estimates is related to the size of the conditional standard deviation σ. The smaller the variability of the values of the dependent variable about the regression equation, the better are the estimates, in the sense that their standard errors become smaller. An unbiased estimate of σ^2 is given by

$$\hat{\sigma}^2 = \frac{\Sigma(Y_i - \hat{Y}_i)^2}{n - (k + 1)} = \frac{\text{SSE}}{\text{df}}$$

The degrees of freedom for the estimate equals the sample size n minus the number of parameters in the multiple regression equation. For this general model with k independent variables, there are $(k + 1)$ parameters—the k β-values and the α term. Therefore, $df = n - (k + 1)$. When there is only $k = 1$ independent variable, df reduces to the $n - 2$ term used in the denominator of $\hat{\sigma}^2$ in Section 9.2. For the data and printout in Figure 11.6 corresponding to the multiple regression model, we see that SSE = 679.79, $n = 30$, and $k = 2$, so df = $n - 3 = 27$ and

$$\hat{\sigma}^2 = \frac{\text{SSE}}{\text{df}} = \frac{679.79}{27} = 25.18$$

This estimate of the conditional variance is also referred to as the *mean square error*, abbreviated by MSE. The estimate of the conditional standard deviation is $\hat{\sigma} = \sqrt{25.18} = 5.02$, which appears under the heading ROOT MSE in the printout. To the extent that the conditional distributions are approximately bell-shaped, we would estimate that most mental health scores would fall within about ten units (two standard deviations) of the conditional mean given by the regression equation.

Collective Influence of the Independent Variables

The first question we consider is whether the k independent variables collectively have a statistically significant effect on the dependent variable Y. We do this by testing the null hypothesis

$$H_0: \quad \beta_1 = \beta_2 = \cdots = \beta_k = 0$$

which states that the mean of Y does not depend on the values of $X_1, \ldots, X_k$. That is, if all the regression coefficients were 0, our model would reflect the fact that Y is statistically independent of all k independent variables. The alternative hypothesis takes the general form

$$H_a: \quad \text{At least one } \beta_i \neq 0$$

So, if we reject H_0, we cannot necessarily conclude that *all* of the independent variables are related to Y, but we can feel confident that *at least one* of them is related to Y, controlling for the others. Acceptance of the alternative hypothesis corresponds to concluding that a better model is obtained by using $X_1, \ldots, X_k$ simultaneously to predict Y using the prediction equation $\hat{Y} = a + b_1X_1 + \cdots + b_kX_k$ than by using just $\bar{Y}$. Hence, these hypotheses are equivalent to

$$H_0: \quad \mathrm{P} = 0$$
$$H_a: \quad \mathrm{P} > 0$$

where P (uppercase rho) denotes the population value of the multiple correlation coefficient. The equivalence of the hypotheses corresponds to the fact that the multiple correlation coefficient is 0 only in those situations in which all of the regression coefficients are 0. Since the coefficient of multiple determination is 0 exactly when the multiple correlation is 0, the hypotheses are also equivalent to $H_0: \mathrm{P}^2 = 0$ and $H_a: \mathrm{P}^2 > 0$, where P^2 is the population analog of R^2.

F Distribution

The null hypotheses just presented can be tested with the test statistic

$$F = \frac{R^2/k}{(1 - R^2)/[n - (k + 1)]}$$

We use the symbol F here because the sampling distribution of this statistic is usually referred to as the **F distribution** (in honor of one of the most eminent statisticians of this century, R. A. Fisher). Like the chi-square distribution, the F distribution can assume only nonnegative values and it is somewhat skewed to the right (see Figure 11.8). Its exact shape is determined by two degrees of freedom terms, denoted by df_1 and df_2. The first of these, $df_1 = k$, appears as the divisor of the R^2 term in the F statistic. It is equal to the number of independent variables in the multiple regression model. The second term, $df_2 = n - (k + 1)$, appears as the divisor of the $1 - R^2$ term in the F statistic. It equals the number of parameters in the multiple regression model $(k + 1)$ subtracted from the sample size n. Hence, df_2 is the degrees of freedom associated with the estimate $\hat{\sigma}^2$ of the conditional variance. The mean of the F distribution equals $df_2/(df_2 - 2)$, which approaches 1.0 as n (and thus df_2) increases.

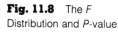

Fig. 11.8 The F
Distribution and P-value

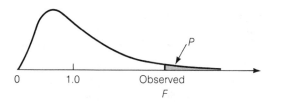

The larger the sample value of the coefficient of multiple determination R^2 (and hence the smaller the value of $1 - R^2$), the larger the ratio $R^2/(1 - R^2)$ becomes and the larger an F test statistic value is obtained. Thus, relatively large values of the F test statistic represent strong evidence against H_0. The P-value is taken to be the probability of obtaining an F-value at least as large as the observed one, if H_0 were true. This is the right-hand curve area under the F distribution with $df_1 = k$ and $df_2 = n - (k + 1)$, beyond the observed F-value (see Figure 11.8). Table D at the end of the text lists the F-values corresponding to P-values of .05, .01, and .001, for various combinations of df_1 and df_2. Using this table, we can observe whether $P > .05$, $.01 < P < .05$, $.001 < P < .01$, or $P < .001$. More complete tables are available (see Beyer, 1966), and many computer regression routines print out the exact P-value corresponding to the F statistic.

Example 11.6 For the data introduced in Example 11.2, there were $k = 2$ independent variables and $n = 30$ observations. The two degrees of freedom terms needed for use of the F distribution are $df_1 = k = 2$ and $df_2 = n - (k + 1) = 30 - 3 = 27$. From Table D, $F = 3.35$ and $F = 5.49$ correspond to right-hand tail probabilities of .05 and .01, respectively. In other words, an observed F-value of $F > 5.49$ corresponds to a P-value of $P < .01$, for these degrees of freedom. In this example, the null hypothesis H_0: $\beta_1 = \beta_2 = 0$, or H_0: P $= 0$, corresponds to the mental health score being statistically independent of the life events score and socioeconomic status.

In Example 11.3, we observed a coefficient of multiple determination of $R^2 = .358$. The F test statistic value is therefore

$$F = \frac{R^2/k}{(1 - R^2)/[n - (k + 1)]} = \frac{.358/2}{.642/27} = 7.54$$

Since $7.54 > 5.49$, the P-value is $P < .01$. From the computer printout (Figure 11.6), we see that the exact P-value is $P = .0028$. This value is listed under the heading PROB > F, which is next to F VALUE, where the F test statistic is given. We conclude that at least one of the independent variables is related to the mental health index. In other words, significantly better predictions of Y are obtained by using the prediction equation $\hat{Y} = 28.324 + .102X_1 - .098X_2$ than by using $\bar{Y}$. ∎

**Using Mean
Squares*** An equivalent way of obtaining the F-value for this test involves the sums of squares. We have remarked that $\hat{\sigma}^2 = SSE/[n - (k + 1)] = SSE/df_2$ is an unbiased estimate of the conditional variance. This term, also called the **mean square error**, appears in the computer printout in the MEAN SQUARE column, in the row labeled ERROR. It equals the ratio of the SUM OF SQUARES to DF terms listed in that row. Another

possible estimate of the conditional variance is given by the ratio of the regression sum of squares (TSS − SSE) to $df_1 = k$. This term, the **regression mean square**, tends to *overestimate* σ^2 when H_0 is false and tends to be an unbiased estimate only when H_0 is true. The F test statistic equals the ratio of these two estimates; that is, the F statistic equals the regression mean square divided by the error mean square. If H_0 is false, the F ratio tends to be relatively large, since the regression mean square tends to overestimate σ^2. On the printout (Figure 11.6) for our example, the error mean square is $\hat{\sigma}^2 = 25.18$, and the regression mean square is

$$\frac{\text{Regression SS}}{df_1} = \frac{379.68}{2} = 189.84$$

again leading to the test statistic value of

$$F = \frac{\text{Regression mean square}}{\text{Error mean square}} = \frac{189.84}{25.18} = 7.54$$

A statistical test such as this one, which is based on a comparison of variance estimates, is referred to as an **analysis of variance** procedure. We shall study the general principle underlying such tests in Chapter 13.

Inferences for Individual Regression Coefficients

In most practical situations, we would expect at least one of the independent variables to be related to the dependent variable, so we would not be surprised to get a small P-value in testing H_0: $\beta_1 = \beta_2 = \cdots = \beta_k = 0$. When we reject that null hypothesis, we may conclude only that at least one of the independent variables is related to the dependent variable, controlling for the other independent variables. More specific types of analysis are needed for judging *which* partial effects are nonzero and for estimating the sizes of those effects. Now, the test of H_0: $\beta = 0$ given in Section 9.4 was designed to evaluate whether the dependent variable and a particular independent variable are statistically dependent, *ignoring* other variables. The corresponding test for the partial regression coefficient of that independent variable is designed to detect dependence between the two variables, *controlling* for the other variables in the multiple regression model.

To test for the existence of a partial effect of an independent variable X_i on the dependent variable, we set up the null hypothesis H_0: $\beta_i = 0$, where β_i is the coefficient of X_i in the multiple regression model. If $\beta_i = 0$, then the mean of the dependent variable is identical for all values of X_i, controlling for the other independent variables. We could test H_0 against the general alternative H_a: $\beta_i \neq 0$ or the more specific alternatives H_a: $\beta_i > 0$ or H_a: $\beta_i < 0$, according to whether we wish to predict the direction of the partial relationship. The form of the test statistic is

$$t = \frac{b_i}{\hat{\sigma}_{b_i}}$$

where $\hat{\sigma}_{b_i}$ denotes the estimated standard error of the point estimate b_i of β_i. As usual, the t test statistic is formed by taking the best point estimate (b_i) of the parameter (β_i), subtracting the null hypothesis value of the parameter (0), and dividing by the estimated standard error $(\hat{\sigma}_{b_i})$ of the point estimate. If H_0 is true and if the assumptions for the model hold, the t statistic has the t distribution with df $= n - (k + 1)$. The degrees of freedom term for this test equals the degrees of freedom term for the point estimate $\hat{\sigma}^2$ of the conditional variance (upon which $\hat{\sigma}_{b_i}$ depends), which is also the same as df_2 in the test of H_0: $\beta_1 = \cdots = \beta_k = 0$ just considered. The formula for $\hat{\sigma}_{b_i}$ is rather complex, but fortunately this term is given on most outputs from computer multiple regression procedures.

As in other contexts, it is often more important to estimate the size of a partial regression coefficient than to test simply whether there is a nonzero partial association. A confidence interval for β_i has the form

$$b_i \pm t_{\alpha/2}\hat{\sigma}_{b_i}$$

where the $t_{\alpha/2}$-value also has df $= n - (k + 1)$ and is selected to give the desired confidence coefficient. We infer with $100(1 - \alpha)\%$ confidence that the interval contains the true value of the change in the mean of Y for a 1-unit increase in X_i, controlling for the other variables in the multiple regression model.

Example 11.7   Let us consider the parameter β_1 in the multiple regression model for $Y = $ mental health index, $X_1 = $ life events score, and $X_2 = $ SES. The null hypothesis H_0: $\beta_1 = 0$ states that, controlling for SES, the mental health index is statistically independent of the life events score; that is, the full multiple regression model $E(Y) = \alpha + \beta_1 X_1 + \beta_2 X_2$ reduces to the simple bivariate model $E(Y) = \alpha + \beta_2 X_2$. If H_0 is false, then $\beta_1 \neq 0$, so that the full model provides a better fit than the bivariate model that has X_2 alone as an independent variable.

The point estimate of β_1 is $b_1 = .1024$. The estimated standard error of b_1 is listed under the heading STD ERR OF ESTIMATE in Figure 11.6—namely, $\hat{\sigma}_{b_1} = .0368$. The test statistic value is

$$t = \frac{b_1}{\hat{\sigma}_{b_1}} = \frac{.1024}{.0368} = 2.78$$

which is listed under the heading T FOR H0: PARAMETER $= 0$. The statistic is based on df $= n - (k + 1) = 30 - 3 = 27$. The P-value is listed under PROB $> |T|$. For this example, it is $P = .0098$, the probability of getting a t statistic at least as large as 2.78 in absolute value if H_0 were true. The P-values are listed on most computer package printouts for the two-sided alternative hypothesis, H_a: $\beta_1 \neq 0$. If we had stated the one-sided alternative H_a: $\beta_1 > 0$, we would halve this value and obtain a P-value of $P = .0049$. In either case, we would reject H_0 at the $\alpha = .01$ or $\alpha = .05$ level and conclude that the mental health score is related to the life events score, controlling. for SES.

To form a 99% confidence interval for β_1, we would use $t_{.005} = 2.771$, the t-value for df $= 27$ corresponding to an area of $\alpha/2 = .01/2 = .005$ in each tail. We get the interval of numbers $b_1 \pm t_{.005}\,\hat{\sigma}_{b_1} = .1024 \pm 2.771(.0368) = .1024 \pm .1020$, or $(.0004, .2044)$. Controlling for SES, we are 99% confident that the change in the mean mental health score per 1-unit increase in the life events score is between

.0004 and .2044. The interval does not contain 0, in agreement with the fact that we rejected H_0: $\beta_1 = 0$ in favor of H_a: $\beta_1 \neq 0$ at the $\alpha = .01$ level. It contains only positive numbers, so we may infer that the relationship between the mental health index and the life events score is positive, controlling for SES. The interval is relatively wide, however, in the sense that an increase of 100 units in the life events score is inferred to correspond to anywhere from a $100(.0004) = .04$ to a $100(.2044) = 20.44$ unit increase in the mean mental health index. This is due primarily to the small sample size. ∎

A note of caution must be inserted here. When severe multicollinearity exists, it is possible that *none* of the individual partial effects will be judged to be significant, even if there is a large R^2 and large F statistic in the global test for the β's. When there are strong correlations among independent variables, any particular variable may explain *uniquely* very little of the variation in Y, even though together the variables explain a lot of the variation. Reasons for this behavior will be discussed in Section 12.4.

Inference for Partial Correlations*

Controlling for a certain set of variables, the slope β_i of the partial relationship between Y and X_i is 0 in exactly the same situations in which the partial correlation between Y and X_i is 0. Let us denote the population value of the partial correlation by $\rho_{YX_i \cdot —}$, where the horizontal bar after the dot indicates that *all* other independent variables in the model are being treated as control variables. For example, if there are five independent variables, then $\rho_{YX_2 \cdot —}$ represents $\rho_{YX_2 \cdot X_1, X_3, X_4, X_5}$. Now, the test of H_0: $\beta_i = 0$, which we have just considered for a set of variables, is equivalent to a test of H_0: $\rho_{YX_i \cdot —} = 0$. The equivalent t test statistic is given by

$$t = \frac{r_{YX_i \cdot —}}{\sqrt{\dfrac{1 - r_{YX_i \cdot —}^2}{n - (k + 1)}}}$$

where $r_{YX_i \cdot —}$ is the sample estimate of $\rho_{YX_i \cdot —}$. When H_0 is true, this statistic has the t distribution with df $= n - (k + 1)$. This yields the same t-value as $t = b_i / \hat{\sigma}_{b_i}$ and, hence, leads to the same P-value. When there are no variables controlled (i.e., the number of independent variables is $k = 1$), the t statistic reduces to

$$t = \frac{r}{\sqrt{\dfrac{1 - r^2}{n - 2}}}$$

the statistic we used for testing the hypothesis that the population Pearson correlation is 0 (see Section 9.4).

Example 11.8   In Example 11.5, we obtained $r_{YX_1 \cdot X_2} = .471$ for the sample partial correlation between the mental health and life events indices, controlling for SES. There are $k = 2$ independent variables and $n = 30$ observations. In order to test H_0: $\rho_{YX_1 \cdot X_2} = 0$ against H_a: $\rho_{YX_1 \cdot X_2} \neq 0$, we use the following test statistic:

$$t = \frac{r_{YX_1 \cdot X_2}}{\sqrt{\dfrac{1 - r^2_{YX_1 \cdot X_2}}{n - (k + 1)}}} = \frac{.471}{\sqrt{\dfrac{1 - (.471)^2}{27}}} = 2.78$$

This is precisely the same test statistic value as that obtained in testing H_0: $\beta_1 = 0$ against H_a: $\beta_1 \neq 0$ in Example 11.7. Thus, the P-value would also be the same, i.e., $P = .0098$. ∎

For large samples, a confidence interval for the population value $\rho_{YX_i \cdot}$ of a partial correlation can be obtained by using the transformation (given in Table E) that we studied in Section 9.4 for the Pearson correlation. The standard deviation of the transformed statistic must be modified, however, to $\sigma_T = 1/\sqrt{n - 3 - c}$, where c is the number of controlled variables. Using the sample partial correlation, we obtain the transformed statistic $T(r)$ from Table E and form the confidence interval $T(r) \pm z_{\alpha/2}\sigma_T$. We locate the endpoints of this interval in the body of Table E and observe which two numbers are transformed into those endpoints in order to get the corresponding endpoints of the confidence interval for $\rho_{YX_i \cdot}$.

Relationship Between F- and t-values*

On computer printouts for some regression packages (such as SPSS^X), F-values instead of t-values are given for the tests of the individual regression coefficients. The two statistics are related and lead to the same P-values. In fact, in the context of testing that a particular partial regression coefficient β_i equals 0, squaring the t test statistic yields a test statistic that has the F distribution with $df_1 = 1$ and $df_2 = n - (k + 1)$, when H_0 is true. To illustrate, in Example 11.8, a test of H_0: $\beta_1 = 0$ against H_a: $\beta_1 \neq 0$ can be conducted using $F = t^2 = 2.78^2 = 7.728$, which has the F distribution with $df_1 = 1$ and $df_2 = 27$ if H_0 is true. From Table D, the P-value is barely less than .01, and in fact the exact value would be $P = .0098$ if we had a more complete table. In general, if a statistic has the t distribution with ν degrees of freedom, then the square of that statistic has the F distribution with $df_1 = 1$ and $df_2 = \nu$. A disadvantage of the F approach is that it does not give information about the direction of the association, so it cannot be used for one-sided alternative hypotheses.

11.5 Standardized Regression Coefficients

If we wish to gauge the relative effects of different independent variables, comparing the sizes of their partial regression coefficients is not appropriate, since these coefficients depend on the units in which the variables were measured. As with the slopes in the bivariate models studied in Chapter 9, we must also *standardize* multiple regression coefficients in order to make meaningful comparisons.

Standardized Regression Coefficient

The *i*th *standardized regression coefficient*, denoted by β_i^*, represents the change in the mean of Y, in Y standard deviations, for a one standard deviation increase in X_i, controlling for the other independent variables.

The coefficient β_i^* can be interpreted as the value we would get for the partial slope (the coefficient of X_i) in the multiple regression equation if the units of measurement were such that Y and X_i had the same standard deviation.

The Standardization Mechanism

The estimated regression coefficients $\{b_1, b_2, \ldots, b_k\}$ can be standardized by adjusting for the fact that the standard deviation of X_i may be different from the standard deviation of Y. Let $\hat{\sigma}_Y$ be the estimated standard deviation of the marginal distribution of the dependent variable [i.e., $\hat{\sigma}_Y = \sqrt{\sum (Y_i - \bar{Y})^2 / (n - 1)}$], and let $\hat{\sigma}_{X_1}$, $\hat{\sigma}_{X_2}, \ldots, \hat{\sigma}_{X_k}$ denote the estimated standard deviations of the independent variables. The standardization of the regression coefficients is accomplished by multiplying b_i by the ratio of $\hat{\sigma}_{X_i}$ to $\hat{\sigma}_Y$.

> If b_i is the least squares estimate of the regression coefficient β_i in a multiple regression equation, then
>
> $$b_i^* = b_i(\hat{\sigma}_{X_i}/\hat{\sigma}_Y)$$
>
> is the estimate of the standardized regression coefficient, β_i^*.

The value b_i^* gives us an estimate of the partial effect of X_i in standard units. The standardized parameters $\beta_1^*, \ldots, \beta_k^*$ are referred to in some publications as **beta weights**,* or as **path coefficients** when used in a technique known as path analysis (see Chapter 16). In a sense, these coefficients measure the relative weights attached to the various independent variables in contributing to the mean of the dependent variable. The larger the absolute value of β_i^*, the greater is the effect on Y that is produced by a standard deviation change in X_i, controlling for the other variables. If $|\beta_2^*| > |\beta_1^*|$, for example, then a particular change in X_2 has a greater partial effect on Y than does a comparable change in X_1, measured in standard deviations.

Example 11.9

The estimated means and standard deviations of Y = mental health index, X_1 = life events score, and X_2 = SES were presented in Table 11.2 for the data set we have been analyzing. The standard deviations were listed as $\hat{\sigma}_Y = 6.04$, $\hat{\sigma}_{X_1} = 25.44$, and $\hat{\sigma}_{X_2} = 28.76$. The unstandardized partial slope of X_1 on Y is $b_1 = .1024$, so the estimated standardized regression coefficient is

$$b_1^* = b_1 \left(\frac{\hat{\sigma}_{X_1}}{\hat{\sigma}_Y}\right)$$

$$= .1024 \left(\frac{25.44}{6.04}\right) = .431$$

---

*On printouts from some computer package programs (such as SPSS^X), the estimated standardized regression coefficients are presented in a column labeled BETA. These should not be confused with the parameters $\beta_1 \ldots, \beta_k$ representing the *unstandardized* effects of the independent variables in the *population* multiple regression equation.

Similarly, $b_2 = -.0976$, so that

$$b_2^\star = b_2 \left(\frac{\hat{\sigma}_{X_2}}{\hat{\sigma}_Y} \right) = -.0976 \left(\frac{28.76}{6.04} \right) = -.464$$

So, the estimated change in the mean of Y for a one standard deviation increase in X_1, controlling for X_2, is of approximately the same magnitude as for a one standard deviation increase in X_2, controlling for X_1. However, the partial effect of X_1 is positive, whereas the partial effect of X_2 is negative. ■

Properties of Standardized Coefficients

For the bivariate regression model, we observed that standardizing the regression coefficient yields the Pearson correlation coefficient between the variables, which is a symmetric measure. For the multiple regression model, though, the standardized partial regression coefficient is not, in general, symmetric. If $\bar{b}_i^\star$ denotes the estimated standardized regression coefficient when X_i is treated as the *dependent* variable and Y as an *independent* variable (controlling for the same set of other variables), then $\bar{b}_i^\star$ need not equal $b_i^\star$. In other words, the standardized effect of Y on X_1, controlling for X_2, need not be the same as the standardized effect of X_1 on Y, controlling for X_2. The square of the partial correlation between Y and X_i, controlling for the other independent variables, *is* a symmetric measure that is related to these two nonsymmetric standardized coefficients by

$$r_{YX_i \cdot —}^2 = b_i^\star \bar{b}_i^\star$$

In the special case in which $b_i^\star = \bar{b}_i^\star$, $r_{YX_i \cdot —}$ is their common value. The partial correlation always falls between $b_i^\star$ and $\bar{b}_i^\star$, and it is said to be their **geometric average.** Unlike partial or Pearson correlation coefficients, $b_i^\star$ is not constrained to fall between -1 and $+1$, but the product $b_i^\star \bar{b}_i^\star$ cannot exceed 1.*

Standardized regression coefficients are often compared as a means of assessing which of the independent variables has the greatest impact on the dependent variable. Comparisons of this nature should be made with caution for several reasons. In some cases, the observed differences in the $b_i^\star$ may be no larger than what would be expected due to sampling error. Also, the effects we are considering are partial ones and are therefore specific to the variables in the model. An independent variable that appears to be relatively important in one system of variables may lose its importance when other variables are controlled. For example, it is possible that $|b_2^\star| > |b_1^\star|$ in a model with two independent variables, yet when a third independent variable is added to the model, $|b_2^\star| < |b_1^\star|$. Finally, if X_i is highly correlated with one or more other independent variables, it may be artificial to conceive of X_i changing and the other X-values remaining fixed in value. As an extreme example of this, suppose that for each person in a sample, we measure $Y =$ height, $X_1 =$ length of left foot, and $X_2 =$ length of right foot. Then the Pearson correlation between X_1 and X_2 would be very close to 1, and it would not make sense

*The occurrence of a $|b_i^\star| > 1$ is occasionally observed when X_i is highly correlated with another independent variable in the model.

to imagine how Y changes as X_1 changes while X_2 is controlled. In some situations, it might be of greater interest to compare uncontrolled effects of the X_i on Y, using Pearson correlations, than to compare partial effects.

It is unnecessary to standardize in order to compare the effect of the *same* variable for two groups, since the units of measurement are the same in each case. In fact, it is often unwise to standardize in this case, because the standardized coefficients are more susceptible than the unstandardized coefficients to differences in the standard deviations. Two groups that have the same regression coefficients will have different standardized coefficients if the ratio σ_X/σ_Y differs for the two groups.

Standardized Form of Equations*

Regression equations and prediction equations are often expressed in terms of the standardized regression coefficients and their estimates. When this is done, the dependent variable and independent variables must be expressed in standardized form.

Notation

Let z_Y, z_{X_1}, ..., z_{X_k} denote the standardized versions of the variables Y, X_1, ..., X_k. That is, the z-score z_Y denotes the number of standard deviations that an observation on Y is from its mean, and so forth for the other variables.

To illustrate, if $z_{X_1} = 2.0$ for a member of a sample, then that member falls two standard deviations (in X_1 units) above the mean $\bar{X}_1$ of that variable. That is, for that member, the score X_1 on the first variable is such that $z_{X_1} = (X_1 - \bar{X}_1)/\hat{\sigma}_{X_1} = 2.0$. For each member in a sample, the scores on Y, X_1, ..., X_k can be transformed to z-scores for the variables, given by z_Y, z_{X_1}, ..., z_{X_k}. In terms of these standardized variables and the estimated standardized coefficients, the prediction equation can be written as

$$\hat{z}_Y = b_1^* z_{X_1} + b_2^* z_{X_2} + \cdots + b_k^* z_{X_k}$$

where $\hat{z}_Y = (\hat{Y} - \bar{Y})/\hat{\sigma}_Y$ denotes the predicted z-score on the dependent variable.* This equation provides a way of predicting how far an observation on the dependent variable will fall from its mean, in standard deviation units, based on how far the values of the independent variables are from their means, in standard deviation units.

Example 11.10

The standardized prediction equation relating the z-score on mental health to the z-scores on the life events scale and SES is $\hat{z}_Y = .431 z_{X_1} - .464 z_{X_2}$, since $b_1^* = .431$

---

*No intercept term is needed. When the z-scores for all of the X-values are 0 (i.e., when we select X-values equal to their corresponding means), then $\hat{Y} = \bar{Y}$, so that

$$\hat{z}_Y = \frac{\hat{Y} - \bar{Y}}{\hat{\sigma}_Y} = 0$$

and $b_2^* = -.464$. Consider a person who scores two standard deviations above the mean on the life events index but two standard deviations below the mean on SES. Such a person would have a predicted z-score on the dependent variable of

$$\hat{z}_Y = .431(2) - .464(-2) = 1.790$$

In other words, that person would be predicted to score 1.79 standard deviations above the mean on the mental health index. Assuming a normal distribution of mental health scores, this person would be predicted to have some degree of mental health impairment, since only about 3.67% of the scores in a normal distribution are at least 1.79 standard deviations above their mean. ■

The reader should become familiar with both the standardized and unstandardized approaches to writing and interpreting regression equations, since they are both commonly used in social science literature. Since the standardized regression coefficients are just multiples of the unstandardized coefficients, the tests of hypotheses of H_0: $\beta_i^* = 0$ are equivalent to the tests we have considered in the previous section of H_0: $\beta_i = 0$. Thus, we shall not consider separate inference procedures for the standardized models.

Summary

In this chapter, we have generalized the bivariate regression equation to allow for the inclusion of additional independent variables. The partial effects of the independent variables, controlling for other variables, are described by the *partial regression coefficients* in a *multiple regression equation*. For comparison purposes, these may be *standardized* to remove the effects of the units of measurement. A standardized coefficient describes the change in Y (in Y standard deviation units) for a one standard deviation increase in a particular independent variable, controlling for the other independent variables. The *partial correlation coefficient* describes the degree of association between two variables, controlling for others. The squared partial correlation coefficient represents the proportion of that variation in the dependent variable left unexplained by a set of control variables that can be explained by another variable. The *multiple correlation coefficient* and its square, the *coefficient of multiple determination*, are used to represent the degree of predictability of the dependent variable by the collective set of independent variables. Some of the basic properties of these measures and those introduced in Chapter 9 are summarized in Table 11.3 on page 344.

The model considered in this chapter is still somewhat restrictive in the sense that the relationship between the dependent variable and each independent variable is assumed to be linear, and the slope of the relationship between two variables is assumed to be the same at each combination of values of the control variables. In Chapter 12, we will study how these and other assumptions can be relaxed by using the basic multiple regression structure as a foundation for building and evaluating more general types of models.

Table 11.3 Summary of Bivariate and Multiple Regression

	BIVARIATE REGRESSION	MULTIPLE REGRESSION	
		Simultaneous effect of $X_1, \ldots, X_k$	Partial effect of one X_i
Model	$E(Y) = \alpha + \beta X$	$E(Y) = \alpha + \beta_1 X_1 + \cdots + \beta_k X_k$	
Prediction equation	$\hat{Y} = a + bX$	$\hat{Y} = a + b_1 X_1 + \cdots + b_k X_k$	
Properties of measures	b = Slope r = Pearson correlation, standardized slope, $-1 \leq r \leq 1$, r has same sign as b r^2 = Coefficient of determination, PRE measure, $0 \leq r^2 \leq 1$	R = Multiple correlation, $0 \leq R \leq 1$ R^2 = Coefficient of multiple determination, PRE measure, $0 \leq R^2 \leq 1$	b_i = Partial slope b_i^* = Standardized regression coefficient $r_{YX_i \cdot}$ = Partial correlation, $-1 \leq r_{YX_i \cdot} \leq 1$, $r_{YX_i \cdot}$ has same sign as b_i and b_i^*, $r_{YX_i \cdot}^2$ is PRE measure, $r_{YX_i \cdot}^2 = b_i^* \bar{b}_i^*$
Tests of no association	$H_0\colon \beta = 0$ or $H_0\colon \rho = 0$, Y not associated with X	$H_0\colon \beta_1 = \cdots = \beta_k = 0$, or $H_0\colon \mathbf{P} = 0$, Y not associated with $X_1, \ldots, X_k$	$H_0\colon \beta_i = 0$, or $H_0\colon \rho_{YX_i \cdot} = 0$, Y not associated with X_i, controlling for other X variables
Test statistic	$t = \dfrac{b}{\hat{\sigma}_b} = \dfrac{r}{\sqrt{\dfrac{1 - r^2}{n - 2}}}$ $df = n - 2$	$F = \dfrac{\text{Regression mean square}}{\text{Error mean square}}$ $= \dfrac{R^2/k}{(1 - R^2)/[n - (k + 1)]}$ $df_1 = k,\ df_2 = n - (k + 1)$	$t = \dfrac{b_i}{\hat{\sigma}_{b_i}} = \dfrac{r_{YX_i \cdot}}{\sqrt{\dfrac{1 - r_{YX_i \cdot}^2}{n - (k + 1)}}}$ $df = n - (k + 1)$

Note

Section 11.3

1. The squared partial correlation $r^2_{YX_2 \cdot X_1} = (R^2 - r^2_{YX_1})/(1 - r^2_{YX_1})$ gives the proportion of variation accounted for by X_2, out of that left unexplained by X_1. The numerator $R^2 - r^2_{YX_1}$ gives the increase in the proportion of explained variation that is obtained by adding X_2 to the model. This increment, denoted by $r^2_{Y(X_2 \cdot X_1)}$, is referred to as the squared *semipartial* (or *part*) correlation. Squared semipartial correlations can be used to partition the variation in the dependent variable. For instance, for three independent variables,

$$R^2_{Y(X_1, X_2, X_3)} = r^2_{YX_1} + (R^2_{Y(X_1, X_2)} - r^2_{YX_1}) + (R^2_{Y(X_1, X_2, X_3)} - R^2_{Y(X_1, X_2)})$$
$$= r^2_{YX_1} + r^2_{Y(X_2 \cdot X_1)} + r^2_{Y(X_3 \cdot X_1, X_2)}.$$

In other words, the total variation in Y explained by X_1, X_2, and X_3 together can be partitioned into three parts: (a) the proportion explained by X_1 (i.e., $r^2_{YX_1}$), (b) the proportion explained by X_2 beyond that explained by X_1 (i.e., $r^2_{Y(X_2 \cdot X_1)}$, and (c) the proportion explained by X_3 beyond that explained by X_1 and X_2 (i.e., $r^2_{Y(X_3 \cdot X_1, X_2)}$).

To illustrate, in Example 11.3, $r^2_{YX_1} = .145$ and $R^2_{Y(X_1, X_2)} = .358$. Thus, the squared semipartial correlation $r^2_{Y(X_2 \cdot X_1)}$ equals $R^2 - r^2_{YX_1} = .358 - .145 = .213$. This means that 14.5% of the variation in Y is explained by X_1, and an additional 21.3% is explained by X_2 when it is added to the model as a second independent variable.

Problems

1. For a sample of twelve nations on Y = crude birth rate, X_1 = percentage of women employed, and X_2 = percentage of workers in agricultural jobs, the least squares equation is $\hat{Y} = 35 - .5X_1 + .3X_2$.
   a. Interpret the coefficient $-.5$ appearing in this equation.
   b. Interpret the coefficient .3 in this equation.
   c. Plot on the same graph the relationship between Y and X_1 when $X_2 = 20$, $X_2 = 50$, and $X_2 = 80$. Interpret the results.
   d. Plot on the same graph the relationship between Y and X_2 when $X_1 = 20$, $X_1 = 50$, and $X_1 = 80$. Interpret the results.

2. A printout is given at the top of the next page for the relationship between the dependent variable Y = number of children in family and the independent variables X_1 = mother's educational level (MEDUC) in years, and X_2 = father's socioeconomic status (FSES), for a random sample of forty-nine college students.

SOURCE	SUM OF SQUARES
REGRESSION	31.8
ERROR	199.3
TOTAL	231.1

PARAMETER	ESTIMATE
INTERCEPT	5.25
MEDUC	-.24
FSES	.02

a. Write the prediction equation. Can you tell from this equation which independent variable has the greatest partial effect on the dependent variable?

b. Consider the families in which the mother has had 8 years of education. Describe the relationship between Y and X_2. Do the same for the families in which the mother has had 16 years of education, and compare results.

c. For the first member in the sample, $X_1 = 12$, $X_2 = 61$, and $Y = 5$. Find the predicted value of Y and the residual for this member.

d. What is the value of SSE? How could it be calculated if you had all the data?

e. Find the multiple correlation coefficient. Is it possible that $r_{YX_2} = .40$? Why?

f. Can you tell from this printout whether r_{YX_1} is positive or negative? Why?

3. If $\hat{Y} = 2 + 3X_1 + 5X_2 - 8X_3$, then controlling for X_2 and X_3, the predicted mean change in Y when X_1 is increased from 10 to 20 is which of the following?

a. 3

b. 30

c. .3

d. Cannot be given—depends on specific values of X_2 and X_3.

4. For a linear model with two independent variables X_1 and X_2, which of the following must be incorrect? Why?

a. $r_{YX_1} = .01$, $r_{YX_2} = -.2$, $R = .75$

b. $r_{YX_1} = .01$, $r_{YX_2} = -.75$, $R = .2$

c. $r_{YX_1} = .4$, $r_{YX_2} = .4$, $R = .4$

d. The sum of squared errors for the model exceeds the sum of squared errors for the model with X_1 alone as the independent variable.

5. Explain the difference in the purposes of the Pearson correlation, the multiple correlation, and the partial correlation.

6. Give an example of three variables for which you would expect $\beta \neq 0$ in the model $E(Y) = \alpha + \beta X_1$ but $\beta_1 = 0$ in the model $E(Y) = \alpha + \beta_1 X_1 + \beta_2 X_2$.

7. Refer to Example 9.9 on Y = percentage of income taxed and X_1 = gross income and to Problem 9.20 on the second independent variable, X_2 = number of deductions claimed. The sample size is small, but for illustrative purposes use a computer package to do the following multiple regression analyses.

a. Find the prediction equation for the model $E(Y) = \alpha + \beta_1 X_1 + \beta_2 X_2$, and interpret the estimated regression coefficients.

b. Find the predicted values and residuals for the ten observations.

c. Obtain the matrix of Pearson correlations, and interpret.

d. Find R^2, and interpret its value.

8. The accompanying table gives the results of fitting various regression models to data on Y = college GPA, X_1 = high school GPA, X_2 = mathematics entrance exam score, and X_3 = verbal entrance exam score.

ESTIMATES	MODEL		
	$E(Y) = \alpha + \beta X_1$	$E(Y) = \alpha + \beta_1 X_1 + \beta_2 X_2$	$E(Y) = \alpha + \beta_1 X_1 + \beta_2 X_2 + \beta_3 X_3$
Coefficient of X_1	.450	.400	.340
Coefficient of X_2		.003	.002
Coefficient of X_3			.002
R^2	.25	.34	.38

Indicate which of the following statements are false. Give a reason for your answer.

a. The correlation between Y and X_1 is positive.

b. A 1-unit increase in X_1 corresponds to a predicted change of .45 in the mean of Y, controlling for X_2 and X_3.

c. The value of SSE increases as additional variables are added to the model.

d. It follows from the sizes of the estimates for the third model that X_1 has the strongest partial effect on Y.

e. The value of $r^2_{YX_3}$ is .40.

f. The partial correlation $r_{YX_1 \cdot X_2}$ is positive.

g. The partial correlation $r_{YX_1 \cdot X_3}$ could be negative.

h. Controlling for X_1, a 100-unit increase in X_2 is predicted to correspond to an increase of .3 in the mean of college GPA.

i. For the first model, the estimated standardized regression coefficient equals .450.

9. In the context of regression analysis, indicate which of the following statements must be false, and why.

a. For the model $E(Y) = \alpha + \beta_1 X_1$, Y is significantly related to X_1 at the .05 level, but when another variable is added to the model $[E(Y) = \alpha + \beta_1 X_1 + \beta_2 X_2]$, Y is not significantly related to X_1 at the .05 level.

b. The estimate of β_1 for the bivariate linear model is positive, but the estimate of β_1 for the multiple regression model is negative.

c. When the variable X_2 is replaced by a different variable $X_2' = X_2/2$, the estimate of β_2 is twice as large but the Pearson and partial correlations are the same as before.

d. $r_{YX_2 \cdot X_1}$ cannot exceed r_{YX_2}.

For Problems 10–12, select the correct answer and indicate why the other possible responses are inappropriate.

10. If $\hat{Y} = 2 + 3X_1 + 5X_2 - 8X_3$:

a. The strongest Pearson correlation is between Y and X_3.

b. The variable with the strongest partial influence on Y is X_2.

c. The variable with the strongest partial influence on Y is X_3, but one cannot tell which pair has the strongest Pearson correlation from this equation.

d. Insufficient information to answer.

11. If $\hat{Y} = 2 + 3X_1 + 5X_2 - 8X_3$:

a. $r_{YX_3} < 0$

b. $r_{YX_3 \cdot X_1} < 0$

c. $r_{YX_3 \cdot X_1, X_2} < 0$

d. Insufficient information to answer.

e. Answers **a**, **b**, and **c** are all correct.

12. If $\hat{Y} = 2 + 3X_1 + 5X_2 - 8X_3$, and $H_0: \beta_3 = 0$ is rejected at the .05 level, then:

a. $H_0: \rho_{YX_3 \cdot X_1, X_2} = 0$ is rejected at the .05 level.

b. $H_0: \rho_{YX_3} = 0$ is rejected at the .05 level.

c. $r_{YX_3 \cdot X_1, X_2} > 0$

13. The linear model $E(Y) = \alpha + \beta_1 X_1 + \beta_2 X_2 + \beta_3 X_3$ is used to represent the relationship in the precincts of a large city between Y = percentage of votes received by the Republican candidate in a presidential election and X_1 = mean income of voting-age residents (in thousands of dollars), X_2 = mean education of voting-age residents (years completed), and X_3 = percentage of voting-age residents in minority groups.

a. What does the value of β_2 represent?

b. What assumptions are made in order to conduct inferences using the least squares equation $\hat{Y} = a + b_1 X_1 + b_2 X_2 + b_3 X_3$?

c. Suppose that for a random sample of thirty-four precincts, $\hat{Y} = -10 + 2X_1 + 3X_2 - .5X_3$. What is the predicted percentage voting for the Republican candidate for a precinct with mean income $8,000, mean education 13 years, and 10% minority group residents?

d. The multiple correlation coefficient has a value of .5. Is there sufficient evidence to indicate that the three independent variables have collectively a significant effect on the vote for the Republican candidate? Report the P-value.

14. Refer to Figure 11.6.

a. Test the null hypothesis $H_0: \beta_2 = 0$ that the mental health index is independent of SES, controlling for the life events score. Report the P-value for the alternative H_a: $\beta_2 \neq 0$.

b. Report the P-value for $H_a: \beta_2 < 0$.

15. Refer to Problem 7.

a. Report the P-value for testing $H_0: \beta_1 = \beta_2 = 0$, and interpret the result of the test.

b. Test the significance of the partial effects, using $\alpha = .05$, and interpret.

c. Find the estimated standardized regression coefficients, and interpret their values.

16. Refer to Table 9.1 and Problem 9.19. When the model $E(Y) = \alpha + \beta_1 X_1 + \beta_2 X_2$ is fitted to these data on Y = crude birth rate, X_1 = percentage of women who are economically active, and X_2 = per capita GNP (in thousands of dollars), the results shown in the accompanying printout are obtained.

Computer Printout for Problem 16

SOURCE	DF	SUM OF SQUARES	MEAN SQUARE	F VALUE	PROB > F	R-SQUARE
REGRESSION	2	1432.80	716.40	20.27	.0005	.818
ERROR	9	318.11	35.35			
TOTAL	11	1750.92				ROOT MSE
						5.945

PARAMETER	ESTIMATE	T FOR HO: PARAMETER = 0	PR > | T |	STD ERROR OF ESTIMATE
INTERCEPT	45.350			
X1	-.568	-3.26	.0098	.174
X2	-1.794	-2.05	.0711	.877

CORRELATION MATRIX

	Y	X1	X2
Y	1.000	-.857	-.777
X1	-.857	1.000	.648
X2	-.777	.648	1.000

VARIABLE	MEAN	STANDARD DEVIATION
Y	26.58	12.616
X1	23.92	13.521
X2	2.88	2.684

a. Report the value of each of the following:
i. r_{YX_1} ii. r_{YX_2} iii. R^2
iv. TSS   v. SSE   vi. MSE
vii. $\hat{\sigma}$ viii. $\hat{\sigma}_Y$ ix. $\hat{\sigma}_{b_1}$
x. t for H_0: $\beta_1 = 0$
xi. P for H_0: $\beta_1 = 0$ against H_a: $\beta_1 \neq 0$
xii. P for H_0: $\beta_1 = 0$ against H_a: $\beta_1 < 0$
xiii. F for H_0: $\beta_1 = \beta_2 = 0$
xiv. P for H_0: $\beta_1 = \beta_2 = 0$
xv. df for $\hat{\sigma}$

b. Give the prediction equation, and carefully interpret the three estimated regression coefficients.

c. Interpret the Pearson correlations r_{YX_1} and r_{YX_2}.

d. Show how the coefficient of multiple determination is calculated, and interpret its value.

e. Calculate the multiple correlation and give its interpretation.

f. Find the partial correlation between Y and X_1, controlling for X_2. Interpret both the partial correlation and the value of its square.

g. Show how the estimate of the conditional standard deviation is calculated, and interpret its value.

h. Show how the F statistic for testing H_0: $\beta_1 = \beta_2 = 0$ is calculated, give its P-value, and interpret the result of that test.

i. Show how the t statistic for testing H_0: $\beta_1 = 0$ is calculated, give its P-value for H_a: $\beta_1 < 0$, and interpret the result of that test.

j. Calculate the estimates of the standardized regression coefficients, and interpret their values.

*k. Write the prediction equation using standardized variables.

17. Refer to Problem 13.

a. Indicate which of the following statements must be false, based on parts **c** and **d** of Problem 13.

    i. $r_{YX_1} = .6$

    ii. $r_{YX_1} = -.4$ and $r_{YX_2} = .4$

    iii. $r_{YX_1 \cdot X_2} \le 0$

    iv. $b_1^* = .6$, $b_2^* = .1$, and $b_3^* = -.1$

    v. If X_1 were measured in francs, b_1 would still equal 2.

    vi. $r_{YX_3 \cdot X_1, X_2} = .1$

b. If $\hat{\sigma}_{b_3} = .30$ for the sample of thirty-four precincts, test the hypothesis that the percentage vote for the Republican candidate is independent of the percentage of minority residents, controlling for income and education.

18. The data in the table on page 351 are taken from a study of the moral integration of American cities by Robert C. Angell. The first variable refers to moral integration and is based on a number of indices such as crime rates and welfare effort. The heterogeneity variable refers to population heterogeneity in terms of racial–ethnic groups. The mobility variable refers to the degree to which individuals move into the city or move out of the city. The printout is for the model $E(Y) = \alpha + \beta_1 X_1 + \beta_2 X_2$ fitted to these data, where Y = integration index, X_1 = heterogeneity index, and X_2 = mobility index.

Printout for Problem 18

				CORRELATION MATRIX		
SOURCE	DF	SUM OF SQUARES		Y	X1	X2
REGRESSION	2	93.97	Y	1.000	-.156	-.456
ERROR	26	132.29	X1	-.156	1.000	-.513
TOTAL	28	226.26	X2	-.456	-.513	1.000

		STD ERR	STANDARDIZED
PARAMETER	ESTIMATE	OF ESTIMATE	ESTIMATE
INTERCEPT	21.832		
X1	-.167	.055	-.530
X2	-.214	.051	-.728

a. Give the prediction equation for the multiple regression model. Find the predicted value and residual for the city of Rochester.

Data for Problem 18

CITY	INTEGRATION INDEX	HETEROGENEITY INDEX	MOBILITY INDEX	CITY	INTEGRATION INDEX	HETEROGENEITY INDEX	MOBILITY INDEX
Rochester	19.0	20.6	15.0	Grand Rapids	12.8	15.7	24.2
Syracuse	17.0	15.6	20.2	Toledo	12.7	19.2	21.0
Worcester	16.4	22.1	13.6	San Diego	12.5	15.9	49.8
Erie	16.2	14.0	14.8	Baltimore	12.0	45.8	12.1
Milwaukee	15.8	17.4	17.6	South Bend	11.8	17.9	27.4
Bridgeport	15.3	27.9	17.5	Akron	11.3	20.4	22.1
Buffalo	15.2	22.3	14.7	Detroit	11.1	38.3	19.5
Dayton	14.3	23.7	23.8	Tacoma	10.9	17.8	31.2
Reading	14.2	10.6	19.4	Flint	9.8	19.3	32.2
Des Moines	14.1	12.7	31.9	Spokane	9.6	12.3	38.9
Cleveland	14.0	39.7	18.6	Seattle	9.0	23.9	34.2
Denver	13.9	13.0	34.5	Indianapolis	8.8	29.2	23.1
Peoria	13.8	10.7	35.1	Columbus	8.0	27.4	25.0
Wichita	13.6	11.9	42.7	Portland (Ore.)	7.2	16.4	35.8
Trenton	13.0	32.5	15.8				

Source: Angell, R. C. "The Moral Integration of American Cities." *American Journal of Sociology*, 57 (July): 17, 1951. Reprinted by permission of The University of Chicago Press.

b. Find the coefficients of determination for the bivariate models $E(Y) = \alpha + \beta X_1$ and $E(Y) = \alpha + \beta X_2$. Find the coefficient of multiple determination for the multiple regression model. Compare the values.

c. Find the partial correlation between Y and X_1, controlling for X_2. Interpret the square of its value. How does this partial correlation compare to the Pearson correlation between Y and X_1?

d. Conduct a test of $H_0: \beta_1 = \beta_2 = 0$, report the P-value, and interpret.

e. Test $H_0: \beta_1 = 0$ against $H_a: \beta_1 \neq 0$ at the $\alpha = .01$ level. Interpret.

f. Find a 95% confidence interval for the difference in the mean of Y for cities that are 30 units apart on X_2, controlling for X_1.

*g. Write the prediction equation using standardized variables and the standardized regression coefficients. Find the predicted z-score on integration for a city that is two standard deviations above the mean on heterogeneity and one standard deviation below the mean on mobility.

h. Find the estimate of the conditional standard deviation of the values on the dependent variable about the regression equation.

19. For a random sample of sixty-six state precincts, data are available on

Y = Percentage of adult residents who are registered to vote

X_1 = Percentage of adult residents owning homes

X_2 = Percentage of adult residents who are nonwhite

X_3 = Median family income (thousands of dollars)

X_4 = Median age of residents

X_5 = Percentage of residents who have lived in the precinct at least 10 years

A portion of the printout used to analyze the data is shown on page 353.

a. Fill in all the missing values in the printout.

b. Give the prediction equation and interpret the coefficient of X_1.

c. Do you think that it is necessary to include all five independent variables in the model? Why?

d. Interpret the R-SQUARE value.

e. To what test does the F VALUE refer? Interpret the result of that test.

f. To what test does the t-value opposite X1 refer? What conclusion would be reached in that test if an $\alpha = .05$ significance level were used?

g. Give the interpretation of the value listed under ROOT MSE.

h. Find a 95% confidence interval for the change in the mean of Y for a 1-unit increase in the percentage of adults owning homes, controlling for the other variables.

i. Find a 95% confidence interval for the change in the mean of Y for a 50-unit increase in the percentage of adults owning homes, controlling for the other variables.

j. Interpret the estimated standardized regression coefficient for X_1.

k. For these data, which variable had the strongest partial effect on voter registration rates? In what sense was its effect the strongest?

Printout for Problem 19

SOURCE	DF	SUM OF SQUARES	MEAN SQUARE	F VALUE	PROB > F	R-SQUARE	ROOT MSE
REGRESSION	---	----	-----	-----	-----	-----	-----
ERROR	---	2940.0	-----				
TOTAL	---	3758.3					

PARAMETER	ESTIMATE	T FOR H0: PARAMETER = 0	PROB > $\lvert T \rvert$	STD ERR OF ESTIMATE	STANDARDIZED ESTIMATE
INTERCEPT	70.000	-----	-----		
X1	.100	-----	-----	.045	.150
X2	-.150	-----	-----	.075	-.110
X3	.100	-----	-----	.200	.020
X4	-.040	-----	-----	.050	-.010
X5	.120	-----	-----	.050	.100

OBS NO	X1	X2	X3	X4	X5	Y	PREDICTED VALUE	RESIDUAL
1	70	10	14	35	60	86	---	---
2	50	20	11	30	40	-	---	-6.7

20. A multiple regression model is used to model the relationship among a collection of cities between Y = murder rate (number of murders per 100,000 residents) and

X_1 = Number of police officers (per 100,000 residents)

X_2 = Mean length of prison sentence given to convicted murderers (in years)

X_3 = Mean income of residents of city (in thousands of dollars)

X_4 = Unemployment rate in city

These variables are measured for the year 1985 for a random sample of thirty cities with population size exceeding 35,000. For these cities, the least squares equation is $\hat{Y} = 30 - .02X_1 - .1X_2 - 1.2X_3 + .8X_4$. The basic descriptive statistics for these cities are $\bar{Y} = 15$, $\bar{X}_1 = 100$, $\bar{X}_2 = 15$, $\bar{X}_3 = 13$, $\bar{X}_4 = 7.8$, $\hat{\sigma}_Y = 8$, $\hat{\sigma}_{X_1} = 30$, $\hat{\sigma}_{X_2} = 10$, $\hat{\sigma}_{X_3} = 2$, $\hat{\sigma}_{X_4} = 2$.

a. Can you tell from the coefficients of the prediction equation which independent variable has the greatest partial effect on Y? Why?

b. Find the standardized regression coefficients and interpret their values.

*c. Write the prediction equation using standardized variables. Find the predicted z-score on murder rate for a city that is one standard deviation above the mean on X_1, X_2, and X_3, and one standard deviation below the mean on X_4. Interpret the value.

21. Suppose that the standardized regression coefficient is computed for a regression model containing only one independent variable. What measure does this yield?

*22. For the models $E(Y) = \alpha + \beta X$ and $E(Y) = \alpha + \beta_1 X_1 + \beta_2 X_2$, give the null hypotheses expressed in terms of correlations that correspond to the following:

a. $H_0: \beta = 0$

b. $H_0: \beta_1 = \beta_2 = 0$

c. $H_0: \beta_2 = 0$

*23. For 100 observations on the three variables Y = vocabulary score, X_1 = height, and X_2 = age, the pairwise Pearson correlations are $r_{YX_1} = .65$, $r_{YX_2} = .85$, and $r_{X_1X_2} = .75$. Test whether Y and X_1 are uncorrelated, controlling for X_2, using the $\alpha = .05$ level.

*24. If X_1 and X_2 are uncorrelated, and if R^2 denotes the coefficient of multiple determination for the model $E(Y) = \alpha + \beta_1 X_1 + \beta_2 X_2$, then $R^2 = r^2_{YX_1} + r^2_{YX_2}$. Interpret this result.

*25. Which of the following sets of correlations would you expect to yield the highest R^2 value? Why?

a. $r_{YX_1} = .4$, $r_{YX_2} = .3$, $r_{X_1X_2} = .2$

b. $r_{YX_1} = .4$, $r_{YX_2} = .4$, $r_{X_1X_2} = .2$

c. $r_{YX_1} = .4$, $r_{YX_2} = .4$, $r_{X_1X_2} = 0$

*26. Suppose that the Pearson correlation between Y and X_1 equals the multiple correlation between Y and X_1 and X_2. What does this imply about the partial correlation $r_{YX_2 \cdot X_1}$? Interpret this result.

*27. The correlation between the number of children in a family and the mother's education (number of years) is $-.50$. Controlling for mother's education, the first-order partial correlation between the number of children in a family and father's education is $-.20$. Find the multiple correlation between the dependent variable, the number of children in a family, and the independent variables, mother's education and father's education.

*28. Let SSE_1 represent the sum of squared errors for the bivariate model $E(Y) = \alpha + \beta X_1$, and let SSE_{12} represent the sum of squared errors for the multiple regression model $E(Y) = \alpha + \beta_1 X_1 + \beta_2 X_2$. Using a diagram similar to that used in Figure 11.7, except letting the scale take on a maximum value of TSS instead of 1, show that

$$r^2_{YX_2 \cdot X_1} = \frac{SSE_1 - SSE_{12}}{SSE_1}$$

The numerator in this ratio, $SSE_1 - SSE_{12}$, is referred to as the *partial sum of squares* for X_2 in the multiple regression model with independent variables X_1 and X_2. [*Hint:* SSE corresponds to unexplained variation, so SSE_1 and SSE_{12} correspond in length to $1 - r^2_{YX_1}$ and $1 - R^2$, respectively, in Figure 11.7.]

*29. Refer to Problem 28. Identify the partial sum of squares for X_1 and calculate $r^2_{YX_1 \cdot X_2}$ in Example 11.5 using the formula

$$r^2_{YX_1 \cdot X_2} = \frac{SSE_2 - SSE_{12}}{SSE_2}$$

*30. Refer to Example 11.5. Find a 95% confidence interval for $\rho_{YX_1 \cdot X_2}$, the population partial correlation between the mental health index and the life events score, controlling for SES.

*31. The sample value of R^2 tends to overestimate the population value P^2, especially when the sample size is relatively small. A somewhat better estimate of the population coefficient of multiple determination is given by the *adjusted R^2 value*,

$$R^2_{adj} = R^2 - \left(\frac{k-1}{n-k}\right)(1 - R^2)$$

a. Suppose that $R^2 = .358$ for a multiple regression model with $k = 2$ independent variables (such as in the example in the text relating to Figure 11.6). Calculate R^2_{adj} for the following sample sizes: 10, 30 (as in the text example), 50, 100, and 1000. Observe that R^2_{adj} approaches R^2 in value as n increases.

b. Show that R^2_{adj} is negative when $R^2 < (k-1)/(n-1)$. (R^2_{adj} is usually defined to be 0 in such cases.)

c. Show that R^2_{adj} could decrease when independent variables are added to a regression model.

*32. Refer to Problem 16.

a. Find and interpret the squared semipartial correlation $r^2_{Y(X_2 \cdot X_1)}$.

b. Find and interpret the squared semipartial correlation $r^2_{Y(X_1 \cdot X_2)}$.

*33. Show that the squared semipartial correlation $r^2_{Y(X_2 \cdot X_1)}$ cannot be larger than the squared partial correlation $r^2_{YX_2 \cdot X_1}$.

Bibliography

Afifi, A. A. and V. Clark (1984). *Computer-Aided Multivariate Analysis*. Belmont, Calif.: Lifetime Learning.

Beyer, W. H., ed. (1966). *Handbook of Tables for Probability and Statistics*. Cleveland: Chemical Rubber Co.

Draper, N. R. and H. Smith (1981). *Applied Regression Analysis,* 2nd ed. New York: Wiley.

Holzer, C. E., III (1977). *The Impact of Life Events on Psychiatric Symptomatology*. Ph.D. dissertation, University of Florida.

Neter, J. and W. Wasserman (1974). *Applied Linear Statistical Models*. Homewood, Ill.: Richard D. Irwin.

Paykel, E. S., B. A. Prusoff, and E. H. Uhlenhuth (1971). "Scaling of Life Events." *Archives of General Psychiatry, 75*: 340–347.

Pedhazur, E. (1982). *Multiple Regression in Behavioral Research,* 2nd ed. New York: Holt, Rinehart and Winston.

Younger, M. S. (1979). *Handbook for Linear Regression*. North Scituate, Mass.: Duxbury Press.

CHAPTER 12

Model Building with Multiple Regression

Contents

The purpose of this chapter is twofold. First, we examine methods for modeling systems of variables that do not satisfy the restrictions we made in Chapters 9 and 11. In particular, procedures are described for modeling nonlinear relationships and relationships in which interaction is present. Second, we introduce some of the basic tools for constructing and evaluating multiple regression models. Techniques for modeling nonlinear relationships are described in Section 12.1. In Section 12.2, we see how to introduce additional terms into the multiple regression equation as a means of modeling the effects on a dependent variable of statistical interaction between independent variables. Then, in Section 12.3 we consider criteria for building a good regression model by deciding which of a possibly large collection of variables should be included in the model. Finally, in the last section of the chapter, we discuss methods for evaluating a particular regression model, with regard to the appropriateness of the model and the validity of the assumptions required for its use.

12.1 Modeling a Nonlinear Response

In modeling the relationship between the mean of Y and an independent variable X in Chapter 9, we assumed that the form of the relationship was linear. In Chapter 11, we assumed that the partial relationship between the mean of Y and each independent variable was linear in form, controlling for other independent variables. Although most social science relationships are not *exactly* linear in form, the degree of non-linearity is often so minor that they can be reasonably well approximated with linear equations. Occasionally, though, the simple linear model is inadequate, even for approximation. Evidence of this fact may be indicated by a scatter diagram that reveals a highly nonlinear relationship between two variables. Another possible reason for wanting to use a nonlinear model is that one's theoretical formulation of expected relationships might indicate a nonlinear relationship.

There are many situations in which we would expect to find a curvilinear relationship between two variables. For example, we would expect medical expenses to tend to be relatively high for the very young and the very old, but lower for older children and young adults (see Figure 12.1a). Relationships are also encountered in which the mean of Y increases (or decreases) approximately linearly over a limited range of X-values, but then levels off for very large X-values. As an illustration, the relationship between X = number of hours studied and the mean of Y = grade on an exam for a homogeneous group of students would perhaps be approximately a

 **Fig. 12.1** Two Nonlinear Relationships

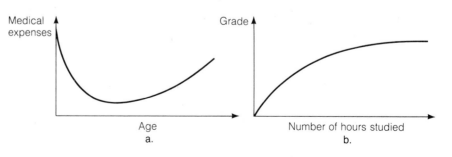

linearly increasing one, up to a certain point. However, beyond a certain number of hours studied, additional time would probably result in little, if any, improvement in the mean exam grade (see Figure 12.1b).

We have already seen some of the consequences of using linear models to describe relationships that are curvilinear in form. One of the main problems is that the measures of association we have introduced tend to underestimate the true degree of association. Measures such as the Pearson correlation are not designed to detect curvilinear patterns of bivariate association. In addition, estimates of the mean of Y at various X-values may be badly biased if the relationship is highly curvilinear, since the prediction line may not be a very good approximation to the true regression curve. In this section, we will illustrate some approaches for modeling nonlinear relationships.

There are two types of nonlinear models that are most frequently used. In the first of these, the regression function takes the form of a *polynomial*. The class of polynomial functions contains a very broad set of functional patterns, including linear functions as a special case. The multiple regression model can be adapted to incorporate such functions. The second approach to modeling nonlinear relationships involves finding a mathematical transformation of one or both variables such that the transformed variables are linearly related. For example, for certain forms of curvilinear relationships, the logarithm of the dependent variable yields a new variable that is linearly related to the independent variable.

Polynomial Models

A *polynomial regression function* has the form

$$E(Y) = \alpha + \beta_1 X + \beta_2 X^2 + \cdots + \beta_k X^k$$

In this model, the independent variable X occurs in powers from the first $(X = X^1)$ to some integer k. In Chapter 9 we considered the case $k = 1$, for which this formula reduces to the linear function $E(Y) = \alpha + \beta_1 X$. The index k (the highest power) in the polynomial equation is called the **degree** of the equation. The polynomial function that is most commonly used for nonlinear relationships is the second-degree polynomial $E(Y) = \alpha + \beta_1 X + \beta_2 X^2$, sometimes referred to as a **quadratic function**. The graph of a function in this class is parabolic in form and is symmetric about a vertical axis (see Figure 12.2). In other words, a second-degree polynomial is a particular curvilinear function having one bend.

Fig. 12.2 Graphs of Some Second-Degree Polynomials

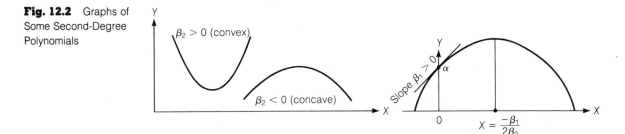

If a scatter diagram reveals an overall pattern of points with one bend, then a second-degree polynomial is a natural choice for improving upon the linear fit. A third-degree polynomial $E(Y) = \alpha + \beta_1 X + \beta_2 X^2 + \beta_3 X^3$, called a *cubic function*, is a curvilinear function having two bends. In general, a kth degree polynomial is a curvilinear function having $(k - 1)$ bends; the straight line corresponding to degree $k = 1$ has $k - 1 = 0$ bends.

Figure 12.3 is a scatter diagram for the twelve observations on Y = crude birth rate and X = percentage of women who are economically active, analyzed in Chapter 9. We observed there that a linear model provided a relatively good fit, resulting in a high r^2 value. We might expect, however, that as the percentage of economically active women increases above a certain level, the rate of decrease in the crude birth rate would diminish, and the regression curve would level off. Also, the linear prediction equation $\hat{Y} = 45.7 - .8X$ for these data gives absurd predictions for very large X-values ($\hat{Y}$ is negative for $X > 57$). Of course, a parabola would not provide a good fit for *all* possible X-values, because it would curve upward after a certain point (see Figure 12.3). However, it might be very adequate over the range of X-values that are usually observed and of greatest interest.

Fig. 12.3 Scatter Diagram and Best-Fitting Second-Degree Polynomial for Data on Y = Crude Birth Rate and X = Percentage of Women Who Are Economically Active

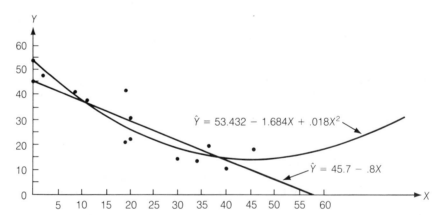

By considering the collection of possible values for the parameters α, β_1, and β_2 in the second-degree polynomial $E(Y) = \alpha + \beta_1 X + \beta_2 X^2$, we can generate a large class of parabolic functions having a variety of shapes and locations. Unlike linear functions, for which the slope of the line remains constant over all X-values, the mean change in Y for a 1-unit increase in X *depends on the value of X*. For example, a straight line drawn tangent to the rightmost parabola given in Figure 12.2 would have positive slope for relatively small values of X, zero slope where the parabola achieves its maximum value, and negative slope for relatively large values of X. The rate of change of the line varies to produce a curve having a smooth bend.

The sign of the coefficient β_2 of the X^2 term in the second-degree polynomial function determines whether the function is convex (bowl-shaped) or concave (mound-shaped). A positive β_2 coefficient corresponds to a convex function and a negative coefficient corresponds to a concave function (see Figure 12.2). Of course, if $\beta_2 = 0$, the function reduces to a linear function. The coefficient α represents the Y-intercept. The coefficient β_1 of X can be interpreted as the slope of the line that is tangent to the parabola as it crosses the Y axis. If $\beta_1 > 0$, for example, then the parabola is sloping upward at $X = 0$ (see Figure 12.2).

The point at which the relationship changes directions is $X = -\beta_1/2\beta_2$. If the parabola is concave, this is the point at which the mean of Y is at a maximum; if it is convex, this is the point at which the mean of Y is at its minimum. This information would not be of interest if $X = -\beta_1/2\beta_2$ were out of the range of sampled X-values, since we would not be justified in extrapolating the function over those values.

We can estimate the parameters of the quadratic model $E(Y) = \alpha + \beta_1 X + \beta_2 X^2$ by treating it as a special case of the multiple regression model $E(Y) = \alpha + \beta_1 X_1 + \beta_2 X_2$. In the multiple regression model with two independent variables, we identify X_1 with the independent variable X of interest, and we identify X_2 with its square, X^2. The data input for the computer regression procedure consists of the Y-values for the members in the sample, the corresponding X-values (called X_1), and an artificial variable (X_2) consisting of the squares of the X-values. The computer program then uses the least squares approach for a multiple regression model to find the best-fitting quadratic function out of the class of all second-degree polynomials.

The assumptions needed for applying the standard inference procedures to curvilinear models are the same as for the linear regression model. For the quadratic model, for example, we interpret $E(Y) = \alpha + \beta_1 X + \beta_2 X^2$ as representing the mean of the conditional distribution of the dependent variable for each fixed value of the independent variable X. The conditional distribution of Y-values is assumed to be normal about the mean, with constant conditional standard deviation σ at all X-values.

For a polynomial model of a particular degree k, the coefficient of multiple determination R^2 as defined in Section 11.3 for the multiple regression model can be used to describe the strength of the association for that nonlinear model. In this context, it describes the proportional reduction in error obtained from using the polynomial model, instead of $\bar{Y}$, to predict Y. This measure can be compared to the coefficient of determination r^2 for the bivariate linear model to determine how much better a fit is provided by the curvilinear model than by the linear model. Since the polynomial model has additional terms besides the X term, R^2 will always be at least as large as r^2. The difference $R^2 - r^2$ measures the additional reduction in prediction error obtained by using the second-degree polynomial instead of the straight line.

Example 12.1 To find the best-fitting quadratic equation for the data on the twelve nations on $Y =$ crude birth rate and $X =$ percentage of women who are economically active, we use the independent variables $X_1 = X$ and $X_2 = X^2$ in a computer multiple regression procedure. The values of Y, X_1, and X_2 were given in the first three columns of Table 9.2. The printout for the model $E(Y) = \alpha + \beta_1 X + \beta_2 X^2$ is shown in Figure 12.4 (page 362). The least squares estimates of α, β_1, and β_2 are $a = 53.432$, $b_1 = -1.684$, and $b_2 = .018$. The quadratic prediction equation $\hat{Y} = 53.432 - 1.684X + .018X^2$ is plotted over the scatter diagram in Figure 12.3. Notice that the residuals are all quite

Fig. 12.4　Computer Printout for Second-Degree Polynomial Model

SOURCE	DF	SUM OF SQUARES	MEAN SQUARE	F VALUE	PROB>F	R-SQUARE	ROOT MSE
REGRESSION	2	1391.56	695.78	17.425	.0011	.795	6.319
ERROR	9	359.36	39.93				
TOTAL	11	1750.92					

PARAMETER	ESTIMATE	T FOR H0: PARAMETER=0	PROB>!T!	STD ERR OF ESTIMATE
INTERCEPT	53.432			
X	-1.684	-3.0111	.0147	.5592
X SQUARED	.018	1.6345	.1366	.0111

OBSERVATION	OBSERVED VALUE	PREDICTED VALUE	RESIDUAL
ALGERIA	48.0	50.137	-2.137
ARGENTINA	21.0	27.991	-6.991
DENMARK	14.0	17.162	-3.162
E. GERMANY	11.0	15.118	-4.118
GUATEMALA	41.0	41.123	-.123
INDIA	37.0	35.839	1.161
IRELAND	22.0	27.015	-5.015
JAMAICA	31.0	27.015	3.985
JAPAN	19.0	15.977	3.023
PHILIPPINES	42.0	27.991	14.009
U.S.	15.0	19.252	-4.252
U.S.S.R.	18.0	14.380	3.620

small except for the one corresponding to the Philippines. Since $b_2 > 0$, the graph of the prediction equation is convex in form. Also, since $b_1 < 0$, the curve is decreasing as it crosses the Y axis.

The best-fitting *linear* prediction equation was seen in Chapter 9 to be $\hat{Y} = 45.7 - .8X$. This equation, which has an r^2 value of .734, is also plotted in Figure 12.3. From Figure 12.4, the coefficient of multiple determination for the second-degree polynomial prediction equation is $R^2 = .795$. The best second-degree polynomial, in other words, explains about 6% more of the variability in Y than does the best-fitting linear equation.

If $\beta_2 = 0$, the quadratic regression equation $E(Y) = \alpha + \beta_1 X + \beta_2 X^2$ reduces to the linear regression equation $E(Y) = \alpha + \beta_1 X$. Therefore, to test the null hypothesis that the relationship is linear against the alternative hypothesis that it is quadratic, we test the hypothesis H_0: $\beta_2 = 0$; i.e., that the regression coefficient of the X^2 term equals 0. For the sample of size $n = 12$ in this example, the P-value for testing H_0: $\beta_2 = 0$ against H_a: $\beta_2 \neq 0$ is seen on the printout to be $P = .1366$. Thus, the quadratic prediction equation does not result in a significantly better fit than is obtained with the linear equation. To reject H_0 for such a small sample size, we would need to obtain a rather substantial increase in the coefficient of multiple determination by including the X^2 term in the model (see Problem 32 at the end of the chapter). ∎

The regression coefficients for a polynomial regression model do not have the partial slope interpretation that we provided for the coefficients of the multiple regression model. For example, it does not make sense to refer to the change in the mean of Y when X^2 is increased one unit and X is held constant. One cannot control X and vary X^2, or vice versa, since X^2 is a deterministic function of X. Similarly, it would not make sense to interpret the partial correlations $r_{YX^2 \cdot X}$ or $r_{YX \cdot X^2}$ as measures of association, controlling for X or X^2. However, the coefficient $r^2_{YX^2 \cdot X}$ may be of interest as a measure of the proportion of the variation unaccounted for by the linear model that is explained by the quadratic model. In Example 12.1, applying the formula for $r^2_{YX_2 \cdot X_1}$ from Section 11.3 yields

$$r^2_{YX^2 \cdot X} = \frac{R^2 - r^2_{YX}}{1 - r^2_{YX}} = \frac{.795 - .734}{1 - .734} = .229$$

Of the variation in Y unexplained by the linear model, about 23% is explained by the introduction of the quadratic term into the model.

Of all the polynomial models, the linear and quadratic equations are by far the most useful in social science research. Rarely is it necessary to use higher than a second-degree polynomial to describe the general trend in the mean of Y as a function of X. We should be cautious in examining scatter diagrams, lest we read too much into the data. There is sometimes a tendency to let one or two points (whose deviation from a general trend could be due to sampling error) suggest another bend in the trend curve. In fact, if there are n observations, there always exists a polynomial of degree $n - 1$ that passes through *all* the points. We would be foolish to expect all future observations on the same phenomena to fall exactly on the same curve, however, so this model would be inappropriate. Good model-building follows the principle of parsimony, whereby no more parameters are introduced than are necessary to represent adequately the basic form of the relationship. One reason for this is that simple and compact models are easier to understand and interpret than complex ones containing large numbers of variables. Another reason is that when unnecessary variables are added to a model, the standard errors of the estimates of the regression coefficients tend to inflate in value, thus hindering efforts at making inferences.

Log Transformation for Exponential Functions

Although polynomial models provide a diverse collection of functions, there are occasions in which other mathematical functions are more appropriate. Perhaps the most important case of this is when the dependent variable is an *exponential* function of the independent variable.

Exponential Regression Function

An exponential regression function is a function of the form $E(Y) = \alpha\beta^X$.

In this equation, the independent variable appears as the exponent of a parameter. An exponential function increases (if $\beta > 1$) or decreases (if $\beta < 1$) at a faster rate than any polynomial of finite degree k. Example 12.2 illustrates this functional form.

Example 12.2

Exponential functions are often used to model population growth. If a population is growing and if the *rate* of growth remains constant, then the size of that population grows exponentially fast. Suppose, for example, that the population size at some fixed time is denoted by α, and suppose that the growth rate is 2% per year. After 1 year, the population is 2% larger than it was at the beginning of the year. Then, the population size grows by a multiplicative factor of 1.02 each year. Thus, the population size in this hypothetical population after 1 year is $\alpha(1.02)$. Similarly, the population size after 2 years would be

(Population size at end of 1 year)(1.02) = $[\alpha(1.02)]1.02 = \alpha(1.02)^2$

After 3 years, the population size would be $\alpha(1.02)^3$, and in general, after X years, the population size would be $\alpha(1.02)^X$. Thus, the population size after X years is an exponential function $\alpha\beta^X$ with parameters given by the initial population size α and the rate of growth factor $\beta = 1.02$.

Letting $X = 35$ in this example, we would have $\alpha\beta^X = \alpha(1.02)^{35} = 2\alpha$. That is, after 35 years the population size would have doubled from its original size of α. If the rate of growth remained constant at 2% per year, the population would continue to double in size every 35 years. After 70 years, the population size would be 4α; after 105 years it would be 8α; after 140 years it would be 16 times its original size; and so forth. In general, the exponentially increasing function has the property that its doubling time is a constant. As can be seen by considering the sequence of population sizes at 35-year intervals, this is an extremely fast increase even though the yearly rate of growth (2%) seems relatively small. It is interesting to note that the world population has been following an exponential growth pattern, with recent rate of growth at about 1.6% per year.* ▪

Exponentially increasing or decreasing functions appear in many other contexts. For example, if we were to invest α dollars in a savings account that has interest compounded annually at 6%, after X years we would have $\alpha(1.06)^X$ dollars. Here, $\beta = 1.06$ is the growth factor of the savings, and the doubling time is only about 12 years. Also, the death rate among adults is approximately an exponentially increasing function of age (see Montroll and Badger, 1974, p. 47).

In general, the parameter α in the model $E(Y) = \alpha\beta^X$ represents the value of the mean of Y when $X = 0$. The parameter β represents the exponential increase factor. It gives the *multiplicative* change in the mean of Y for a 1-unit increase in X. For example, the mean of Y at $X = 10$ equals β *multiplied* by the mean of Y at $X = 9$. By contrast, the parameter β in the linear model $E(Y) = \alpha + \beta X$ represents the *additive* change in the mean of Y for a 1-unit increase in X. In the linear model, the mean of Y at $X = 10$ equals β *plus* the mean of Y at $X = 9$.

If the mean of a dependent variable is approximately an exponential function of an independent variable, then regression procedures can be applied by *transforming* the dependent variable so that it is linearly related to the independent variable. This can be done by creating an artificial dependent variable by taking the logarithms of the observations on the dependent variable. The log scores (to any base) of the dependent variable will be approximately linearly related to the independent variable X. More precisely, if the dependent variable Y behaves approximately like the exponential function $\alpha\beta^X$ (for some parameters α and β) when viewed as a function of X, then the variable log Y behaves approximately like log α + (log β)X. This latter function has the form of a straight line with intercept log α and slope log β. A model for the relationship would be

$$E(\log Y) = \log \alpha + (\log \beta)X$$

where log Y is a transformed variable created by taking the logarithm of the dependent variable. An estimate $\hat{Y} = ab^X$ of the exponential relationship can be obtained by using bivariate regression methods to get an estimate $\widehat{\log Y} = \log a +$ (log b)X of the transformed relationship, and by then taking antilogarithms.

Example 12.3   Table 12.1 (page 366) shows the population size of the United States at 10-year intervals beginning in 1890. Figure 12.5 is a plot of these values over time. The logarithms (to the base-10)[†] of the population values are also given in Table 12.1. These transformed values are plotted in Figure 12.6. The log population sizes appear to grow approximately linearly over time, suggesting that population growth

---

*An exponential population increase is called *Malthusian growth*, named for the English clergyman and political economist Thomas Malthus (1766–1834). He predicted that the world population size would outgrow the food supply, which does not increase exponentially.

[†]By log Y (to the base-10) we mean the following: $u = \log Y$ is the number such that $Y = 10^u$. For example, since $10^1 = 10$, we have log 10 = 1; since $10^2 = 100$, then log 100 = 2. The log of the population size in 1890 is log 62.95 = 1.799. This means that $62.95 = 10^{1.799}$.

Table 12.1
Population Sizes and
$\log_{10}$ Population Sizes by
Decade from 1890 to
1970

YEAR	NUMBER OF DECADES SINCE 1890 X	POPULATION SIZE (MILLIONS) Y	$\log_{10} Y$	$\widehat{\log_{10} Y}$	$\hat{Y}$
1890	0	62.95	1.7990	1.8242	66.7
1900	1	75.99	1.8808	1.8851	76.8
1910	2	91.97	1.9636	1.9460	88.3
1920	3	105.71	2.0241	2.0069	101.6
1930	4	122.78	2.0891	2.0676	116.8
1940	5	131.67	2.1195	2.1285	134.4
1950	6	150.70	2.1781	2.1896	154.7
1960	7	179.32	2.2536	2.2505	178.0
1970	8	200.25	2.3016	2.3112	204.7

Source: U.S. Bureau of the Census.

Fig. 12.5 U.S. Population Size Since 1890

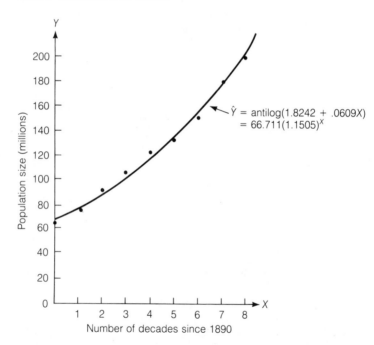

over this period has been exponential with a relatively constant growth rate. We shall now estimate the regression curve, treating time as the independent variable X. For convenience, we identify the time points 1890, 1900, . . . , 1970 as times 0, 1, . . . , 8; that is, X represents the time in decades after 1890. Our approach will be to estimate the linear model $E(\log Y) = \log \alpha + (\log \beta)X$. Applying the formulas from Section 9.2 to the times {0, 1, . . . , 8} and the log population values (the X and $\log_{10} Y$ columns in Table 12.1), we get the least squares prediction equation $\widehat{\log Y} = 1.8242 + .0609X$. By substituting $X = 0, 1, 2, . . . , 8$ into this equation, we get the predicted values for log population size, which are also given in Table 12.1 under the heading $\widehat{\log_{10} Y}$.

The prediction equation is plotted in Figure 12.6. The strength of the linear association for the variables X = time and log Y = log population size is described by the Pearson correlation between the two, which equals $r_{X,\log Y}$ = .9954.

Fig. 12.6 Log Population Sizes Since 1890

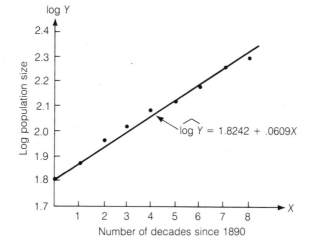

log $\hat{Y}$ = 1.8242 + .0609X

Number of decades since 1890

Predictions on the original dependent variable, Y = population size (untransformed), are given in a column next to the $\widehat{\log Y}$ predictions in Table 12.1. We can get these $\hat{Y}$ predicted values by taking the antilogs of the $\widehat{\log Y}$ values predicted from the model using the transformed variable. The plot of the exponential prediction equation for population size, $\hat{Y} = ab^X$ = antilog(1.8242 + .0609X), is shown in Figure 12.5. Since we used logarithms to the base-10 in transforming the population sizes, the values a and b in the prediction equation $\hat{Y} = ab^X$ satisfy $\log_{10} a$ = 1.8242 and $\log_{10} b$ = .0609. Therefore, a = antilog(1.8242) = $10^{1.8242}$ = 66.711, and b = antilog(.0609) = $10^{.0609}$ = 1.1505. We predict the population size X decades after 1890 to be $\hat{Y} = ab^X$ = 66.711$(1.1505)^X$. Since b = 1.1505, this equation corresponds to a predicted 15.05% growth per decade. Equivalently, this is a 1.4% predicted growth *per year*, since $(1.014)^{10}$ = 1.15. In other words, a 1.4% growth per year (a multiplicative growth factor of 1.014) corresponds to a growth of 15% per decade. So the predicted U.S. population size (in millions) X *years* after 1890 is 66.711$(1.014)^X$. ∎

Other Nonlinear Models

Other transformations of the independent or dependent variables are useful in some situations. For example, suppose that the dependent variable tends to increase or decrease over a certain range of X-values, but once a certain X-value has been reached, further increases in X have less effect on Y, as in Figure 12.1b. Then the trend may often be linearized by taking the logarithms of the X-values or by inverting the X-values (i.e., using $1/X$ as the independent variable).

One other use of transforming a variable is to obtain data that more nearly satisfy assumptions that are required for regression inferences. This is discussed at the end of the chapter. Of course, one problem with creating transformed variables is that they may not be as easy to interpret as the original variables. Similarly, summary statistics such as means, standard deviations, and correlation coefficients may not have as clear or important meanings when calculated for models containing transformed variables as when they are obtained for untransformed variables.

Nonlinear relationships can also be modeled with the multiple regression equation when there are several independent variables. For example, the model $E(Y) = \alpha + \beta_1 X_1 + \beta_2 X_2 + \beta_3 X_2^2$ is a special case of the multiple regression model with three independent variables. Here, we are identifying the third independent variable, X_3, with the square of X_2. The interpretation of this model would be that for fixed X_2, the mean of Y is a linear function of X_1 with slope β_1; for fixed X_1, the mean of Y is a quadratic function of X_2.

12.2 Modeling Interaction Among Interval Variables

The multiple regression model

$$E(Y) = \alpha + \beta_1 X_1 + \beta_2 X_2 + \cdots + \beta_k X_k$$

which we studied in Chapter 11, is actually the simplest one we can use for a collection of interval variables. In that model, the partial relationship between Y and each X_i is treated as a linear one. Also, the slope β_i of the partial relationship between Y and X_i is assumed to be identical for *all* values of the other independent variables. That is, this model is such that the change in the mean of Y for a 1-unit increase in X_i, controlling for the other independent variables, equals β_i no matter what the fixed values of those other variables.

In some situations, such a simplified model would be inappropriate. In the previous section, we considered ways of modeling departures from linearity. Another type of deviation often encountered in practice is that of *statistical interaction*. We first used this term in Section 10.2, in the discussion of issues that are important to the subject of statistical control. There, we applied the term loosely to represent situations in which the basic nature of the relationship between two variables changes according to the values of the control variables. A linear relationship between two interval variables can be described by the slope of the regression line. Thus, in terms of the effects of interval variables $X_1, \ldots, X_k$ on Y, there is *no* interaction if the partial slope of the relationship between Y and each X_i is the same at all combinations of levels of the other X's. Otherwise, there *is* interaction.

Statistical Interaction

For interval variables, *statistical interaction* exists when the slope of the relationship between the dependent variable and one of the independent variables changes as the levels of the other variables are varied.

For example, if the relationship between X_1 and the mean of Y is given by the equation $E(Y) = 4 + 2X_1$ when $X_2 = 1$ and by $E(Y) = 4 + 10X_1$ when $X_2 = 2$, then X_1 and X_2 *interact* in their effect on Y.

Cross-Product Terms The simplest and most commonly used method for modeling interaction is to introduce *cross-product terms* of the independent variables into the basic multiple regression model. To illustrate what we mean by this, let us first consider the case in which there are only two independent variables. A multiple regression model designed to allow for interaction has the form

$$E(Y) = \alpha + \beta_1 X_1 + \beta_2 X_2 + \beta_3 X_1 X_2$$

This is a special case of the basic multiple regression model with three independent variables, in which X_3 is an artificial variable created as the cross-product $X_3 = X_1 X_2$ of the two primary independent variables. To see how Y is related to X_1, controlling for X_2, in this model, we rewrite the equation as

$$E(Y) = (\alpha + \beta_2 X_2) + (\beta_1 + \beta_3 X_2)X_1 = \alpha' + \beta' X_1$$

where

$$\alpha' = \alpha + \beta_2 X_2 \quad \text{and} \quad \beta' = \beta_1 + \beta_3 X_2$$

So, treated as a function of X_1, the mean of Y changes linearly. The Y-intercept of the relationship (for fixed X_2) is $\alpha' = \alpha + \beta_2 X_2$, which depends on the value of the controlled variable. The slope of the relationship is $\beta' = \beta_1 + \beta_3 X_2$, which also depends on the value of X_2. According to this multiple regression model, the mean of Y is a linear function of X_1 but the slope of the function depends on X_2. Similarly, this interactive model implies that the mean of Y is a linear function of X_2, controlling for X_1, but that the slope $(\beta_2 + \beta_3 X_1)$ of the relationship varies according to the value of X_1.

Example 12.4 The model $E(Y) = \alpha + \beta_1 X_1 + \beta_2 X_2 + \beta_3 X_1 X_2$ can be applied to the data considered in Example 11.2 on Y = mental health index, X_1 = life events score, and X_2 = SES, by creating a third independent variable X_3 that is the cross-product of X_1 and X_2 for the thirty individuals. For example, the X_3 scores entered into the data set are 46(84) = 3,864 for the first individual, 39(97) = 3,783 for the second, 27(24) = 648 for the third, and so forth. Part of the printout that would be given for this model is shown in Figure 12.7 (page 370). The least squares prediction equation takes the form

$$\hat{Y} = 25.866 + .161X_1 - .056X_2 - .00097X_1 X_2$$

The relationship between the mental health score and the life events measure is graphed for a few distinct SES values in Figure 12.8. For an SES score of $X_2 = 0$, the estimated relationship between Y and X_1 takes the form $\hat{Y} = 25.866 + .161X_1$. When $X_2 = 50$, the relationship is

$$\hat{Y} = 25.866 + .161X_1 - .056(50) - .00097(50)X_1 = 23.066 + .112X_1$$

Fig. 12.7   Interaction Model for Y = Mental Health Index, X_1 = Life Events Score, and X_2 = SES

SOURCE	DF	SUM OF SQUARES	MEAN SQUARE	F VALUE	PROB>F	R-SQUARE	ROOT MSE
REGRESSION	3	391.27	130.42	5.07	.0069	.369	5.070
ERROR	26	668.20	25.70				
TOTAL	29	1059.47					

PARAMETER	ESTIMATE	T FOR H0: PARAMETER=0	PROB>|T|	STD ERR OF ESTIMATE
INTERCEPT	25.86616			
X1	.16130	1.693	.1024	.09527
X2	-.05607	-.801	.4306	.07003
X1·X2	-.00097	-.672	.5078	.00144

Fig. 12.8   The Relationship Between Y and X_1, Controlling for X_2

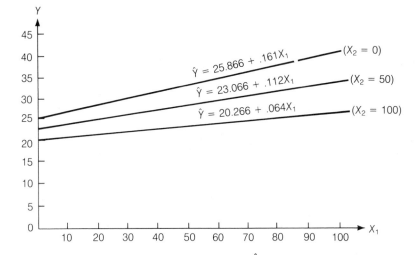

When $X_2 = 100$, the prediction equation is $\hat{Y} = 20.266 + .064X_1$. Notice that the higher the value of X_2 = SES, the smaller the slope becomes between the mental health index and the life events score. The higher the SES value, the smaller is the impact of an increase in life events on the mental health index. The interpretation suggested by this model is that a person who possesses greater resources (in the form of higher SES) is better able to withstand the mental stress of potentially traumatic life events. For individuals possessing fewer resources, there is a larger slope between mental health and life events than for individuals with greater resources.

We can test the necessity of including the interaction term by testing the null hypothesis H_0: $\beta_3 = 0$. If the coefficient of the cross-product term is 0, then there is no interaction and the model reduces to the one considered in Chapter 11. From the printout in Figure 12.7, we see that the P-value for testing H_0: $\beta_3 = 0$ against H_a: $\beta_3 \neq 0$ equals $P = .5078$. Thus, there is not enough evidence to conclude that the interaction term is needed. The variation in the slope of the relationship between the mental health index and the life events score for various SES levels could be due to sampling variability. Studies (e.g., Holzer, 1977) based on much larger sample sizes have shown that interaction of the type seen in this example does in fact exist for these variables. ■

It is interesting to observe that, in Example 12.4, none of the tests of H_0: $\beta_1 = 0$, H_0: $\beta_2 = 0$, or H_0: $\beta_3 = 0$ yields small P-values (see Figure 12.7). On the other hand, the tests of both H_0: $\beta_1 = 0$ and H_0: $\beta_2 = 0$ were highly significant for the model $E(Y) = \alpha + \beta_1 X_1 + \beta_2 X_2$ (see Figure 12.9).* The reason for the loss of significance is that $X_3 = X_1 X_2$ is highly correlated with X_1 and X_2. It can be shown that $r_{X_1 X_3} = .771$ and $r_{X_2 X_3} = .642$. These strong correlations are not surprising, since $X_3 = X_1 X_2$ is completely determined by X_1 and X_2. Since there is considerable overlap in the variation in Y that is explained by X_1 and by $X_1 X_2$, and also by X_2 and $X_1 X_2$, the *partial* variability explained by each is relatively small. For example, much of the predictive power contained in X_1 is also contained in X_2 and $X_1 X_2$. When X_1 is the only independent variable in the model, it is significantly related to Y at the $P = .0377$ level (see Figure 11.4). However, the *unique* contribution of X_1 (or X_2) to the model is relatively small (and nonsignificant), when X_2 (or X_1) and $X_1 X_2$ are in the model.

Fig. 12.9 Model for Y = Mental Health Index, X_1 = Life Events Score, and X_2 = SES, Without Interaction Term

SOURCE	DF	SUM OF SQUARES	MEAN SQUARE	F VALUE	PROB>F	R-SQUARE	ROOT MSE
REGRESSION	2	379.68	189.84	7.54	.0028	.358	5.018
ERROR	27	679.79	25.18				
TOTAL	29	1059.47					

PARAMETER	ESTIMATE	T FOR H0: PARAMETER=0	PROB>¦T¦	STD ERR OF ESTIMATE
INTERCEPT	28.324			
X1	.102	2.780	.0098	.037
X2	-.098	-2.994	.0058	.033

Generally, if there is not strong evidence of interaction, it is best to drop the interaction term from the model before testing hypotheses such as H_0: $\beta_1 = 0$ or H_0: $\beta_2 = 0$ about partial effects. On the other hand, if there *is* strong evidence of interaction, then it no longer makes sense to test these other hypotheses, since one has already concluded that the effect of each variable exists and differs according to the level of the other variable.

Generalizations and Limitations

Interaction can be modeled when there are more than two independent variables by introducing cross-products for each pair of independent variables. For example, if there are three independent variables, we could use the model

$$E(Y) = \alpha + \beta_1 X_1 + \beta_2 X_2 + \beta_3 X_3 + \beta_4 X_1 X_2 + \beta_5 X_1 X_3 + \beta_6 X_2 X_3$$

*The printout in Figure 12.9 is a portion of the one presented in Figure 11.6.

Again, this is a special case of a multiple regression model in which we identify X_4 with $X_1 X_2$, X_5 with $X_1 X_3$, and X_6 with $X_2 X_3$. In general, if there are k primary independent variables, there will be $k(k - 1)/2$ artificial variables formed from cross-products of the pairs of those variables. Significance tests can be used to judge which, if any, of the cross-product terms are needed in the model.

Whenever interaction exists and cross-product terms are included in the final model for a relationship, one should keep in mind that summary measures for linear partial relationships, such as the partial correlations and standardized regression coefficients, do not make sense. If the strength of the relationship between Y and X_1 varies according to the value of X_2, then a summary partial measure obscures this fact. It is perhaps best in such situations to sketch a collection of lines or curves such as those in Figure 12.8 to describe just how the relationship between two variables changes according to the values of the control variables. Alternatively, one could divide the data into groups according to the value on the control variable (e.g., high on X_2, medium high on X_2, medium low on X_2, and low on X_2) and compute the correlation or slope between Y and X_1 within each subset as a means of describing the nature of the interaction.

12.3 Comparison of Regression Models

We often have a large collection of independent variables in social science research, any number of which could potentially be included in a multiple regression model for some dependent variable. For example, in developing a model for predicting the mental health index of a population, we might also (in addition to SES and the life events variable) want to consider the effects of age, number of times married, number of children, number of jobs held in the previous 5 years, age at which individual left parents' home, distance lived from close relatives, number of close friends, frequency of church attendance, and so forth. Usually, there will be some independent variables that we will want to include in the model for theoretical reasons. Others we may wish to include strictly for exploratory purposes, perhaps to see if they explain much of the variation in the dependent variable. We might also wish to include square terms and cross-product terms to allow for nonlinearity and interaction. In such situations, it can be very difficult to decide which variables to use and which to omit in the final model.

We might be tempted to formulate a model with every potentially useful independent variable included, find the corresponding least squares equation, and then drop out those terms for which the partial contributions are not significant. We might consider dropping those variables X_i, for example, for which $H_0: \beta_i = 0$ is not rejected at a preassigned α-level. The problem with this procedure is that many of the independent variables are likely to be highly correlated with at least one of the other independent variables (or with linear combinations of those variables) when the number included is large. It is conceivable that few, if any, of the independent variables would make significant *partial* contributions, given that all of the other independent variables are in the model. In Example 12.4, we observed that X_1, X_2, and X_1X_2 did not generate a small P-value in the tests for the partial effects, even though X_1 and X_2 were highly significant when X_1X_2 was not included in the model. Thus, we need a different procedure for deciding which independent variables to include in the model. In the first part of this section, we will introduce a general test for comparing two models for which the terms in one of the models are a subset of the terms in the other model. Then, as an application of this test, we will describe a sequential procedure for selecting independent variables for a regression model.

Comparing Complete and Reduced Models

Suppose we are considering using the multiple regression model

$$E(Y) = \alpha + \beta_1 X_1 + \cdots + \beta_k X_k$$

for a particular research problem, but we wonder whether it is necessary to include all k independent variables. Some of the k independent variables might represent powers or cross-products of other independent variables. We will now consider a test of whether this model, which we refer to as the *complete model*, gives a significantly better fit than another model that contains only a subset of these k independent variables. The second model, which we call the *reduced model*, can be represented as

$$E(Y) = \alpha + \beta_1 X_1 + \cdots + \beta_g X_g$$

where $g < k$. The complete model contains all g of these variables besides an additional $(k - g)$ independent variables. For convenience, we shall suppose that the independent variables have been labeled so that the first g variables ($X_1, \ldots, X_g$) are identical in both models, and that the extra variables in the complete model are $X_{g+1}, \ldots, X_k$. The complete and reduced models are identical if the regression coefficients $\beta_{g+1}, \beta_{g+2}, \ldots, \beta_k$ for the extra variables are all 0. In that case, none of the extra independent variables contributes toward an increase in the explained variability in Y, in the population of interest. Thus, testing whether the complete model is identical to the reduced model is equivalent to testing the null hypothesis $H_0: \beta_{g+1} = \cdots = \beta_k = 0$. The alternative hypothesis is that at least one of these regression coefficients is not 0, in which case the complete model is better than the reduced model, in the sense of explaining more variation.

Example 12.5

A model with three independent variables that allows for all possible second-order interactions has the form

$$E(Y) = \alpha + \beta_1 X_1 + \beta_2 X_2 + \beta_3 X_3 + \beta_4 X_1 X_2 + \beta_5 X_1 X_3 + \beta_6 X_2 X_3$$

To test the hypothesis of no second-order interaction, we compare this complete model to the reduced model

$$E(Y) = \alpha + \beta_1 X_1 + \beta_2 X_2 + \beta_3 X_3$$

by testing $H_0: \beta_4 = \beta_5 = \beta_6 = 0$. Here there are $k = 6$ independent variables in the complete model and $g = 3$ independent variables in the reduced model. ∎

A relatively simple test of this type of null hypothesis involves a comparison of the sums of squared errors for the two models, complete and reduced. We shall denote $SSE = \Sigma(Y_i - \hat{Y}_i)^2$ for the reduced model by SSE_r and for the complete model by SSE_c. When we obtain the least squares prediction equations corresponding to the two models, we know that SSE_r will be at least as large as SSE_c, since the reduced model has only a subset of the terms appearing in the complete model. Of course, even if the null hypothesis were true, the estimated values of $\beta_{g+1}, \ldots, \beta_k$ would likely not be 0. That is, a certain reduction in error from fitting the extra $(k - g)$ terms is expected due to sampling variability. We will be able to reject H_0 at a particular α-level if the reduction is *larger* than would be expected if H_0 were true.

Now, the complete model has k independent variables, so that for a sample of size n there are $n - (k + 1)$ degrees of freedom corresponding to SSE_c. Similarly, the sum of squared errors SSE_r for the reduced model, which contains g independent variables, is based on df $= n - (g + 1)$. The addition of the extra $(k - g)$ terms in the complete model, in other words, leads to a further reduction of $(k - g)$ in the degrees of freedom. The reduction in error, $SSE_r - SSE_c$, that results from adding the extra independent variables to the model is said to be based on $(k - g)$ degrees of freedom. The test statistic for testing H_0: $\beta_{g+1} = \cdots = \beta_k = 0$ is based on a comparison of this reduction to the sum of squared errors for the complete model. This statistic, which has the F distribution when H_0 is true, has the form

$$F = \frac{(SSE_r - SSE_c)/(k - g)}{SSE_c/[n - (k + 1)]}$$

In the numerator, we divide the reduction in error by its degrees of freedom; in the denominator, we divide the sum of squared errors for the complete model by its degrees of freedom. A relatively large reduction in error yields a large F statistic. The F sampling distribution for this test is the one identified by the two sets of degrees of freedom, $df_1 = k - g$ and $df_2 = n - (k + 1)$. The P-value is the right-hand tail probability, i.e., the probability of getting an F-value at least as large as the observed F-value if H_0 were true. The test statistic for this procedure can also be expressed in terms of a comparison of the R^2-values for the two models (see Problem 31 at the end of the chapter).

Example 12.6 We could compare the complete model

$$E(Y) = \alpha + \beta_1 X_1 + \beta_2 X_2 + \beta_3 X_1 X_2$$

to the reduced model

$$E(Y) = \alpha + \beta_1 X_1 + \beta_2 X_2$$

for the data considered in Chapter 11 in order to test whether statistical interaction exists. The complete model has just one additional term, and the null hypothesis takes the form H_0: $\beta_3 = 0$. We know from Section 11.4 that the t test based on the statistic $t = b_3/\hat{\sigma}_{b_3}$ with df $= n - (k + 1)$ can be used to test a hypothesis about a single regression coefficient in a multiple regression model. From the printout in Figure 12.7, the t value

$$t = b_3/\hat{\sigma}_{b_3} = -.00097/.00144 = -.67$$

has P-value $P = .5078$ for H_a: $\beta_3 \neq 0$. Equivalently, we can get this result with the F test for complete and reduced models. The sum of squared errors for the complete model is $SSE_c = 668.20$ (see Figure 12.7), while for the reduced model it is $SSE_r = 679.79$ (see Figure 12.9). The difference of $SSE_r - SSE_c = 679.79 - 668.20 = 11.59$ is based on $df_1 = 1$, since there are $k = 3$ independent variables in the complete model, $g = 2$ independent variables in the reduced model, and $k - g = 1$. Since the sample size is $n = 30$, $df_2 = n - (k + 1) = 30 - 4 = 26$. The F test statistic value is therefore

$$F = \frac{(SSE_r - SSE_c)/(k - g)}{SSE_c/[n - (k + 1)]} = \frac{11.59/1}{668.20/26} = .45$$

A complete F table for $df_1 = 1$ and $df_2 = 26$ would yield $P = .5078$ for this F-value. So we get the same result as in the t test;* there is not enough evidence to conclude that the interaction term in needed. Of course, the t test method can be used to test only one term at a time, while the complete versus reduced model F test can be used to test a number of regression parameters simultaneously in order to see if any of them are nonzero. ∎

Forward Selection of Independent Variables

We now return to the question of which independent variables to include in a regression model. There are two basic guidelines that are usually followed in the construction of regression models. First, it is desirable to include sufficiently many variables to make the model useful for predictive, explanatory, or theoretical purposes. Thus, we would want to include those variables that are of theoretical importance to us. We would also like to obtain a model that has good predictive power as measured by a reasonably high R^2-value. As a counterbalance to this goal, it is desirable to keep the model as simple as possible. The presence of unnecessary or redundant variables makes the model more difficult to interpret, presents more parameters to be estimated, may result in an inflation in the standard errors of the estimates of these parameters, and hence may make it impossible to assess the partial contributions of variables that are important theoretically. To avoid multicollinearity, it is helpful to have independent variables that are correlated with the dependent variable but are not highly correlated among themselves. Also, it is not a good idea to build complex models if the data set is small. Usually the number of

---

*In fact, the F test statistic is simply the square of the t statistic. Refer to the final subsection in Section 11.4.

independent variables in the model should not exceed about one-tenth of the sample size.

Keeping these thoughts in mind, there is still no unique or optimal approach for selecting the independent variables for a model. Since each of the k variables can be either included or omitted from the final model (two possibilities for each variable), there are 2^k potential subsets of variables that could be selected. For example, if there are $k = 2$ independent variables, there are $2^k = 2^2 = 4$ possible models: one with both X_1 and X_2, one with X_1 alone, one with X_2 alone, and one with neither variable. In the general case, the potential models range from the trivial model in which none of the independent variables is included, to the most complete model in which all k of them are included. The collection of corresponding models is too large to evaluate practically if k is even of moderate size. For example, if $k = 7$, there are $2^7 = 128$ potential models.

Several computerized search procedures have been proposed that scan a set of independent variables to choose a subset for inclusion in the model. For any particular sample and set of variables, however, different procedures may yield different subsets of variables for the final model. Most of these routines share the basic idea of sequentially building a model by entering or removing variables from the model, one at a time according to some criterion, until a final model is reached. These procedures take much less time than fitting and comparing *all* possible regression models consisting of some subset of the k independent variables under consideration. Among the most popular sequential methods for selecting the subset of independent variables are those referred to as the *forward selection* procedure, *stepwise regression* procedure, and *backward elimination* procedure. We will now consider in detail the forward selection procedure. The other two procedures will be discussed briefly at the end of the section.

The **forward selection procedure** begins with none of the k potential independent variables in the model. It adds one variable at a time to the model until it reaches a point where none of the remaining variables makes a significant partial contribution to the prediction of Y. At each step, the variable that is added is the one that is most highly correlated with Y, controlling for the independent variables already in the model. The contribution of the variable must be significant at some preassigned α-level (e.g., $\alpha = .05$ or $\alpha = .10$) in order to be admitted into the model. The sequence of steps in building a regression model according to the forward selection procedure may be outlined as follows:

1.   Consider the set of Pearson correlations r_{YX_j} between the dependent variable and each of the independent variables. The first independent variable entered into the model is the one most highly correlated with Y. In the event that the correlation is not significantly nonzero at the preassigned α-level, however, none of the independent variables is chosen. That is, the variable X_j (say) is the first independent variable entered into the model if the absolute value of the Pearson correlation between Y and X_j is larger than the absolute value of the Pearson correlation between Y and each other independent variable, and if $|t|$ is sufficiently large,* where

$$t = \frac{r_{YX_j}}{\sqrt{\dfrac{1 - r_{YX_j}^2}{n - 2}}}$$

2. If X_j denotes the variable first entered into the model, we next consider the partial correlations $r_{YX_i \cdot X_j}$ between Y and each of the remaining independent variables X_i, controlling for the variable already in the model. We select the variable (call it X_l) having the highest (in absolute value) partial correlation with Y, if it is significantly nonzero. This variable is the one explaining the greatest partial variability in Y, controlling for X_j. If it is not significant, the process stops with X_j as the only independent variable.

3. Letting X_j and X_l denote the first two variables entered into the model, we next consider all second-order partial correlations $r_{YX_i \cdot X_j X_l}$, controlling for the two variables already in the model. The third independent variable selected is the one having the highest of these partial correlations in absolute value, if it is significant. If not significant, the process terminates with only two independent variables, X_j and X_l.

4. We continue in this manner, at each stage admitting the independent variable making the greatest contribution to explaining the remaining variability in Y, controlling for the variables previously admitted into the model. When we reach the point at which none of the remaining independent variables makes a significant partial contribution to the model, the process stops and the variables previously chosen constitute the final model. If a variable X_i is not in the final model, then the partial correlation between Y and X_i, controlling for the independent variables in the model, is not significantly nonzero.

At each step, the t test for significance of a Pearson or partial correlation is equivalent to the F test we considered earlier in this section for comparing complete and reduced models. In this context, the reduced model contains the independent variables previously entered, and the complete model contains those variables plus the one most highly correlated with Y, controlling for the others. At each stage, the variable with the highest absolute partial correlation with Y (i.e., the highest squared partial correlation) is also the variable having the highest F test statistic value in the test comparing the model thus far generated to a new one containing an additional variable.

*The sampling distribution of the *maximum* of a set of correlations is somewhat different from the sampling distribution (given here) for the correlation of a pair of variables selected a priori. As a result, the probability is actually larger than α that at least one of the correlations would be declared significant, even if all of the true correlations were 0.

Example 12.7   Using the thirty observations on Y = mental health index, X_1 = life events score, and X_2 = SES, we now consider the forward selection process with the collection of independent variables X_1, X_2, $X_3 = X_1X_2$, $X_4 = X_1^2$, and $X_5 = X_2^2$. We require a variable to reach significance at the α = .10 level to be included in the model. The r^2-values between Y and each of the independent variables are shown in the first row of Table 12.2. Variable X_2 is most highly correlated with Y. Also, it is significant at the P = .0215 level [verify in Figure 11.5 for the corresponding test of H_0: β = 0 in the model $E(Y) = \alpha + \beta X_2$], so X_2 is the first independent variable added to the model. Next, the $r^2_{YX_i \cdot X_2}$ values are given in the second row of Table 12.2. Controlling for X_2, the variable X_1 explains the greatest amount of the remaining variability in Y. Also, $r^2_{YX_1 \cdot X_2}$ = .2225 is significantly nonzero at the P = .0098 level [verify from Figure 12.9 for the corresponding test of H_0: β_1 = 0 in the model $E(Y) = \alpha + \beta_1 X_1 + \beta_2 X_2$], so X_1 is added to the model. The $r^2_{YX_i \cdot X_1, X_2}$ values are listed in the last row of Table 12.2. The largest of these, $r^2_{YX_3 \cdot X_1, X_2}$ = .0170, is *not* significant at the .10 level [verify that P = .5078 from Figure 12.7 for the corresponding test of H_0: β_3 = 0 in the model $E(Y) = \alpha + \beta_1 X_1 + \beta_2 X_2 + \beta_3 X_1 X_2$]. Thus, the iterative search procedure ends with only X_1 and X_2 in the model as independent variables. According to the forward selection procedure, the best prediction equation based on the five independent variables is $\hat{Y}$ = 28.32 + .102X_1 − .098X_2, the one given in Figure 12.9 for the model containing only X_1 and X_2 as independent variables.   ■

Table 12.2

Squared Correlations and Partial Correlations Used in the Forward Selection Procedure

$r^2_{YX_i}$:	$r^2_{YX_1}$	$r^2_{YX_2}$	$r^2_{YX_3}$	$r^2_{YX_4}$	$r^2_{YX_5}$
	.1453	.1747	.0000	.1683	.1177
$r^2_{YX_i \cdot X_2}$:	$r^2_{YX_1 \cdot X_2}$		$r^2_{YX_3 \cdot X_2}$	$r^2_{YX_4 \cdot X_2}$	$r^2_{YX_5 \cdot X_2}$
	.2225		.1515	.0003	.1961
$r^2_{YX_i \cdot X_1, X_2}$:			$r^2_{YX_3 \cdot X_1, X_2}$	$r^2_{YX_4 \cdot X_1, X_2}$	$r^2_{YX_5 \cdot X_1, X_2}$
			.0170	.0000	.0018

Stepwise Regression and Backward Elimination

Once we obtain the final model according to the forward selection process, not all of the independent variables appearing in it need necessarily be significantly related to Y. The variability in Y explained by a variable that is entered at an early stage may overlap with the variability explained by other variables added later. For example, suppose that X_1 is the first variable added to the model, but that X_2 and X_3 are later added to the model and together explain most of the same variability originally explained by X_1 (see Figure 12.10). In other words, X_1 is highly correlated with X_2 and with X_3, and when these variables are controlled, X_1 is no longer strongly correlated with Y. Then X_1 would be in the final model but might not be significantly related to Y, controlling for the other independent variables. The *stepwise regression procedure* is a modification of the forward selection procedure that drops variables from the model if they lose their significance as other variables are added. The general approach is the same as in the forward selection procedure except that at each step, after entering the new variable, we drop from the model any variables

Fig. 12.10 Variability in Y Explained by X_1, X_2, and X_3 [*Note:* Shaded portion is amount explained by X_1 that is also explained by X_2 and X_3]

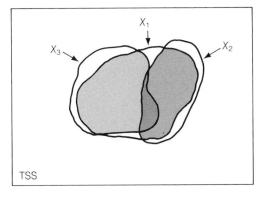

whose partial contributions are no longer significant. With this procedure, a variable entered into the model at a particular stage may eventually be eliminated because of its strong relationship to other variables entered at later stages.

The *backward elimination procedure* works in the reverse direction from the forward selection method. In backward elimination, we begin by placing all of the independent variables under consideration in the model. If they all make significant partial contributions, then that model is the final one. Otherwise, the independent variable having the least absolute partial correlation with Y, controlling for the other independent variables, is removed from the model. Next, for the model with that variable removed, the partial correlations with Y and each X_i (controlling for the other variables still in the model) are recomputed. If they are all significant, that model is the final model. Otherwise, the variable with the smallest absolute partial correlation is removed. The process continues until each remaining independent variable makes a significant partial contribution to explaining the variability in Y.

Modifications of these basic routines are sometimes useful. For example, for theoretical considerations it might be important to include a certain set of independent variables in the model, regardless of whether they make significant partial contributions to the dependent variable. Subject to this constraint, we might want to conduct the forward selection procedure on another large set of variables. We can thereby ensure that the final model includes the variables of primary interest to us as well as other variables that are useful for predictive purposes. This type of option is available in many computer regression packages. See Hocking (1976) for a critical survey of many procedures for selecting subsets of independent variables.

A warning should be added here. There is a basic difference between *explanatory* and *exploratory* approaches in variable selection. In **explanatory research**, one should have a theoretical model worked out that one then tests by multiple regression. We might want to test whether a hypothesized spurious association disappears when other variables are controlled, for example. In such research, computerized search procedures are usually not appropriate, because the theory determines which variables should be in the model. This means that for most scientific research, we should be wary of variable selection procedures.

In *exploratory research*, on the other hand, the goal is not to *explain* relationships among variables so much as it is to find a good set of predictors. Here we want to maximize R^2, and we do not worry so much about theoretical explanations. Thus, educational researchers might like to find a set of test scores and other factors that would give a good prediction of how a student would perform in college. A variable selection procedure could be used for this purpose, but we must then be very cautious in giving causal interpretations to the relative effects of the different variables. For example, it is quite possible that the "best" predictor of your income at age 25 might be the number of major appliances your parents had when you were in high school. Also, when a large number of independent variables are scanned for potential inclusion in a model, a few variables that are not really important may look impressive simply due to chance (random sampling error). In summary, these computerized variable selection procedures are no substitute for careful theory construction in guiding the formulation of models.

12.4 Evaluating the Model

We conclude this chapter by discussing in greater detail some important topics in regression analysis that have been only briefly mentioned previously. First, we consider some of the effects of multicollinearity, the existence of highly intercorrelated independent variables, on inference procedures. Then we discuss some ways in which the residuals may be analyzed as a means of checking for gross violations of assumptions. Finally, we mention some alternative methods of applying regression analysis to adjust for departures from the basic assumptions.

Effects of Multicollinearity

We have used the term *multicollinearity* to refer to the situation in which there are strong intercorrelations among the independent variables. To illustrate the effect of multicollinearity on the sampling error of the least squares estimates, we shall consider in detail the case in which there are only two independent variables. When the dependent variable is modeled as a linear function of only X_1 according to the bivariate regression equation $E(Y) = \alpha + \beta X_1$, we know from Section 9.4 that the standard error of the least squares estimate b of β is $\hat{\sigma}_b = \hat{\sigma}/\sqrt{\Sigma (X_1 - \bar{X}_1)^2}$, where $\hat{\sigma} = \sqrt{SSE/(n - 2)}$ and $\Sigma (X_1 - \bar{X}_1)^2$ denotes the sum of squares of the deviations of the X_1-values about their mean $\bar{X}_1$. Now, for the multiple regression model $E(Y) = \alpha + \beta_1 X_1 + \beta_2 X_2$, the coefficient of X_1 is β_1, and the least squares estimate is b_1. The standard error of b_1 for this model is

$$\hat{\sigma}_{b_1} = \frac{1}{\sqrt{1 - r_{X_1 X_2}^2}} \left(\frac{\hat{\sigma}}{\sqrt{\Sigma (X_1 - \bar{X}_1)^2}} \right)$$

In this formula, the term $\Sigma (X_1 - \bar{X}_1)^2$ is the same as in the previous formula, since the sum of squares of the deviations of the X_1-values about their mean does not depend on what other independent variables are in the model. The term $\hat{\sigma}$ for the model with two independent variables (and hence three unknown parameters) has the form $\hat{\sigma} = \sqrt{SSE/(n - 3)}$. The effect of the correlation of the independent variables enters through the term $\sqrt{1 - r_{X_1 X_2}^2}$ in the denominator. Other things being equal, the stronger the correlation between the independent variables, the smaller the difference $1 - r_{X_1 X_2}^2$, the larger the ratio $1/\sqrt{1 - r_{X_1 X_2}^2}$, and hence the larger the standard error of b_1. A similar formula applies to the standard error of b_2, so it also has a larger standard error, the larger the value of $r_{X_1 X_2}^2$. In general, a primary effect of multicollinearity is that the estimated regression coefficients tend to have large standard errors. As a result, the corresponding tests of H_0: $\beta_i = 0$ tend to have relatively large P-values unless the sample size is very large.

Multicollinearity between two independent variables X_1 and X_2 is often indicated when the partial regression coefficient for the variable already in the model (say, X_1) changes substantially when the other variable is introduced. For example, the first step in a forward selection procedure could bring in X_1 with a partial regression coefficient of .4, but when X_2 is added in the second step, the coefficient of X_1 could change to .9. Such a pattern would possibly indicate a high correlation between X_1 and X_2.

Another type of evidence of multicollinearity exists when there is a highly significant R^2 between Y and the set of independent variables, but individually each partial regression coefficient is not significant. In other words, H_0: $\beta_1 = \cdots = \beta_k = 0$ is rejected, but H_0: $\beta_1 = 0$, H_0: $\beta_2 = 0$, and so forth, are not rejected. An example of this type of behavior was seen in Example 12.4 (see the printout in Figure 12.7) for the model $E(Y) = \alpha + \beta_1 X_1 + \beta_2 X_2 + \beta_3 X_1 X_2$. Thus, it is very difficult to assess individual partial effects when there is a severe case of multicollinearity.

The remarks we have just made about estimating partial regression coefficients also apply to partial correlation coefficients. To illustrate, suppose that X_1 and X_2 are identically correlated with Y (say, $\rho_{YX_1} = \rho_{YX_2} = .65$), and suppose that they are also highly correlated with each other (say, $\rho_{X_1 X_2} = .85$). Then it can be shown that the two partial correlations $\rho_{YX_1 \cdot X_2}$ and $\rho_{YX_2 \cdot X_1}$ are both .244 (see Problem 21c at the end of the chapter). Now, suppose that a sample is selected and we observe the sample correlations $r_{YX_1} = .70$, $r_{YX_2} = .60$, and $r_{X_1 X_2} = .90$. Unless the sample is very large, these values are well within the limits of sampling error for the true population values given above. Based on this relatively small observed difference between the two bivariate correlations r_{YX_1} and r_{YX_2}, we obtain $r_{YX_1 \cdot X_2} = .46$ and $r_{YX_2 \cdot X_1} = -.10$ (see Problem 21b). Thus, relatively small differences in r_{YX_1} and r_{YX_2} yield relatively substantial differences in $r_{YX_1 \cdot X_2}$ and $r_{YX_2 \cdot X_1}$ when the independent variables are highly correlated. If the difference between r_{YX_1} and r_{YX_2} could be due to sampling error, then so could the difference between $r_{YX_1 \cdot X_2}$ and $r_{YX_2 \cdot X_1}$. So, $r_{YX_1 \cdot X_2} = .46$ and $r_{YX_2 \cdot X_1} = -.10$ would not be especially unusual sample results for this example, even though $\rho_{YX_1 \cdot X_2} = \rho_{YX_2 \cdot X_1}$. This illustrates the fact that partial correlations also have large standard errors when multicollinearity exists. Someone who is unaware of this fact might make erroneous conclusions based on observing a seemingly large difference between the sample partial correlations. For example, for the values just obtained, an unwary observer might conclude that the partial effects of X_1 and X_2 have opposite signs and that the partial effect of X_1 is much stronger, when in fact they are identical in the population of interest.

Since a regression coefficient in a multiple regression model represents the effect of an independent variable when other variables are held constant, it tends to lose its meaning when multicollinearity exists. If $|r_{X_1 X_2}|$ is quite high, then as X_1 changes, X_2 also tends to change in a linear manner, and it may be somewhat artificial to envision X_1 or X_2 as being held constant. Thus, the coefficients of a multiple regression equation have dubious interpretations when multicollinearity exists.

Although multicollinearity makes it difficult to assess *partial* effects of independent variables, it does not hinder the assessment of their *joint* effects. If newly added variables are highly correlated with those variables already in the model, then SSE will not decrease very much, but the fit will not be poorer. So, the presence of multicollinearity does not diminish the goodness of the fit of the equation to the observed points.

There are several remedial measures to reduce the effects of multicollinearity. A procedure called **ridge regression** produces estimates of regression coefficients that are slightly biased but which have smaller standard errors than the ordinary least squares estimates. Alternatively, we could use a procedure such as forward selection for choosing a subset of the independent variables and omitting those that explain an insignificant portion of the variation in Y. Or, since it may not make sense to study partial effects if the independent variables are highly correlated, we could use simple bivariate regression models to analyze the relationship between Y and each X_i separately. Alternatively, we might create an index by combining sets of highly correlated variables into one variable. For example, we use SES to represent the joint effects of education, income, and occupational prestige. Also, there are other procedures, such as **factor analysis** (to be treated briefly in Chapter 16), for creating artificial variables based on linear combinations of the original ones in such a way that the new variables are uncorrelated. For further discussion of the effects of multicollinearity and methods for dealing with it, see Blalock (1963) and Neter and Wasserman (1974, pp. 339–347).

Examination of the Residuals

The use of inference procedures with the bivariate or multiple regression model is founded on several assumptions. The basic ones are as follows:

1. The true regression function has the form used in the model (e.g., linear, quadratic).
2. The conditional distribution of Y is normal.
3. The conditional distribution of Y has constant standard deviation throughout the range of values of the independent variables (a condition referred to as *homoscedasticity*).
4. The observations on the dependent variable are statistically independent (as would occur in random sampling).

There are statistical tests for checking these assumptions (see, e.g., Neter and Wasserman, 1974, p. 112). However, a particular regression model may be useful even if these assumptions are not strictly fulfilled, so it is usually adequate to check that none of them is grossly violated. This can be done informally through a visual examination of the observed residuals. The residuals represent the deviations of the observations from the prediction equation values. If the observations are in fact normally distributed about the unknown population regression equation with constant conditional standard deviation σ, then the residuals should be approximately normally distributed. To check this, we can plot the residuals about their mean value 0. They should occur approximately symmetrically about 0, and if the sample size is large, about 68% of them should be between $-\hat{\sigma}$ and $\hat{\sigma}$, and about 95% of them should be between $-2\hat{\sigma}$ and $+2\hat{\sigma}$. Figure 12.11 is a plot of the residuals as given in the printout of Figure 11.6 for the model $E(Y) = \alpha + \beta_1 X_1 + \beta_2 X_2$ applied to the data on Y = mental health index, X_1 = life events score, and X_2 = SES. No severe nonnormality seems to be indicated for the data, since the residuals are roughly symmetric about 0 with 76.7% (23 out of 30) within $\hat{\sigma}$ of 0 and 96.7% (29 out of 30) within $2\hat{\sigma}$ of 0.

Fig. 12.11 Residuals (e) for the Model $E(Y) = \alpha + \beta_1 X_1 + \beta_2 X_2$ for Y = Mental Health Index, X_1 = Life Events Score, and X_2 = SES

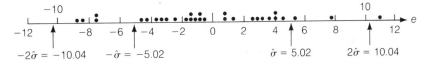

If a particular residual for a set of data occurs several $\hat{\sigma}$ below or above 0, the corresponding observation should be checked to make sure it has not been recorded improperly. Such extreme observations are called *outliers*. If an outlier represents an error in measurement, it could cause a major bias in the least squares equation. Even if it is not an error, it should be investigated because it represents an observation that is not typical of the sample data. It is often of interest to study outliers carefully to try to ascertain reasons for their peculiarity.

It is also useful to plot the residuals against each of the independent variables to check for other deviations from the assumptions. If the residuals appear to fluctuate randomly about 0 with no particular trend or change in dispersion as the values of a particular X_i increase, then no abnormality is indicated. The pattern should be roughly as that in Figure 12.12a. If the residuals tend to become more (or less) disperse as X_i increases, then the conditional standard deviation of Y is not constant over all X_i-values (see Figure 12.12b). If the model used was a linear function of X_i, a scattering of the residuals as in Figure 12.12c indicates that Y is nonlinearly related to X_i, since Y tends to be below $\hat{Y}$ for very small and very large X_i-values (giving negative residuals) and above $\hat{Y}$ for medium-sized X_i-values (giving positive residuals). This particular pattern would suggest the addition of an X_i^2 term. A scatter

Fig. 12.12 Possible Patterns for Residuals (e), Plotted Against an Independent Variable X

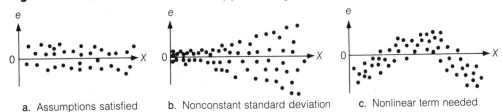

a. Assumptions satisfied   b. Nonconstant standard deviation   c. Nonlinear term needed

diagram of observations such as the one in Figure 12.13 would yield a pattern of residuals such as the one in Figure 12.12c for the bivariate regression model. For *multiple* regression models, it is not possible to use scatter diagrams such as Figure 12.13 to plot all the variables simultaneously. Simple two-dimensional scatter diagrams can be inadequate for detecting ways that multivariate models fit poorly, and residual plots are especially useful in that case.

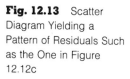

Fig. 12.13 Scatter Diagram Yielding a Pattern of Residuals Such as the One in Figure 12.12c

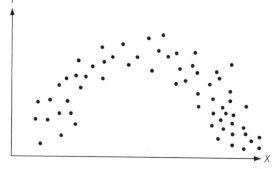

In many social science studies, the observations are obtained sequentially over time. For economic variables, in particular, we might naturally obtain observations daily, monthly, or yearly. We might then question whether we have independent observations. By sampling individuals randomly from some population, we can ensure that one observation is not statistically dependent on another. However, we would often expect neighboring observations obtained in a time sequence to be related in some way. For example, if nationwide unemployment is relatively high in February 1986, it is probably also relatively high in March 1986. The residuals can be plotted over time to check for this type of dependence. Ideally, they should fluctuate in a random pattern about 0 as time changes, as shown in Figure 12.14a. In Figure 12.14b, the standard deviation of the observations seems to be increasing with time. Figure 12.14c reflects the presence of a positive time effect (i.e., the residuals are positively linearly related to time) that is not accounted for by the independent variables included in the model. A cyclical pattern of residuals over time, such as that shown in Figure 12.14d, reflects a cycle of values in the dependent variable about the regression equation such that observations close together in time tend to be similar in value. The residuals are then said to be **autocorrelated**. The procedures given in this text are based on random sampling and are inappropriate in such situations. For example, the formula given in Section 9.4 for obtaining a confidence interval for a slope would not be applicable to the time series data in Example 12.2 relating the log of population size to time. Methods of analysis of time series data reflecting severe dependence are discussed in most econometrics textbooks, such as Wonnacott and Wonnacott (1970).

The graphical techniques discussed in this section are meant to illustrate some general considerations in the analysis of residuals. In practice, of course, the patterns are rarely as neat as these. One should be careful not to read a pattern into an

Fig. 12.14 Possible Patterns for Residuals Plotted Against Time

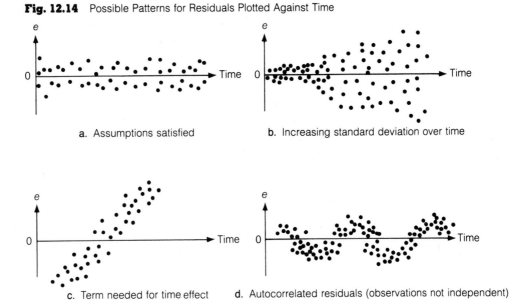

a. Assumptions satisfied

b. Increasing standard deviation over time

c. Term needed for time effect

d. Autocorrelated residuals (observations not independent)

array of points that could be due just to sampling error. For a more detailed treatment of how to analyze residuals, see Draper and Smith (1981) and Neter and Wasserman (1974).

Transformation of Data*

If the multiple linear regression model does not appear to be adequate for a particular set of variables, we have seen ways of improving the model through the use of nonlinear functional forms, interaction terms, or the sequential selection of other possibly important independent variables. However, when assumptions such as those of constant standard deviation or normality appear to be badly violated, we have not considered what alternative we have to the models studied in this chapter. Let us first discuss the problem of *heteroscedasticity*, or nonconstancy of the conditional standard deviation. In terms of getting the best estimate of the regression equation, we would expect the observations occurring in the range of X-values where the standard deviation in Y is smaller to give relatively more information. An adjusted type of least squares analysis (referred to as *weighted least squares*) can be used to get least squares estimates of regression coefficients that have smaller standard errors than those we get in using the standard approach. In the weighted analysis, more influence is given to these observations where the dispersion in Y is smaller.

A different approach to the problem of heteroscedasticity is to make some mathematical transformation of the observations that yields new data satisfying the usual assumptions. For example, depending on the way in which the standard deviation of Y changes according to the value of X, one of the transformed variables $\log Y$, $\sqrt{Y}$, or

$1/Y$ may be approximately linearly related to X with constant standard deviation. If the standard deviation of Y is proportional to the value of X, for example, then the transformations $1/X$ and Y/X yield a relationship in which the standard deviation is constant. This last transformation is equivalent to a weighted least squares approach. If the assumptions are fulfilled for the transformed data, then the standard inference procedures are conducted with these data. For example, suppose that the variability of the Y-values tends to increase as X increases, so that inference procedures are suspect. Suppose, however, that $\sqrt{Y}$ is linearly related to X, with a homogeneous variability of $\sqrt{Y}$-values about the least squares line relating $\sqrt{Y}$ to X. Then, we can test the hypothesis $H_0: \beta = 0$ that the slope of the regression equation relating $\sqrt{Y}$ to X equals 0, using standard procedures with the data on X and $\sqrt{Y}$. Now, if the mean of $\sqrt{Y}$ does not tend to vary as X varies, then neither does the mean of Y. Hence, this test also gives us a way of testing whether the slope of the regression equation relating Y and X equals 0.

Many transformations that reduce the degree of heteroscedasticity simultaneously improve the normality of the conditional distributions. Thus, many of the same transformations are useful for this deficiency as well. The inverse transformation is used to express the results in terms of the original variables, since the transformed data may be difficult to interpret. There are detailed discussions of various types of transformations in Neter and Wasserman (1974, pp. 123–126).

Summary

In this chapter, we have been concerned with several important topics in building regression models. We have seen how some of the restrictions of the models studied in Chapter 11 can be eased. For example, the basic multiple regression structure was altered to model *nonlinear* relationships through the use of *polynomial* (particularly *quadratic*) functions. In order to allow for the possibility of *interaction, cross-product terms* were added to the model. Since a large number of terms might be suggested as independent variables in order to attain a precise model, the *forward selection* procedure was presented as a method of deciding through an iterative process which variables to include in the final model. The statistical test upon which this process is based is a special case of a procedure for comparing a *complete model* to a *reduced model*. This test will also be valuable in other contexts in Chapters 13 and 14. We have seen some of the effects of *multicollinearity*, a condition of highly correlated independent variables that often appears in social science research. We have also briefly discussed how the *residuals* may be used to check whether the model is adequate and whether the assumptions made for conducting inferences are reasonable.

In Chapter 13, we will return to the problem of comparing several groups on some characteristic. We first encountered this problem in Chapter 7 for the case of two groups. We will see that the *analysis of variance* procedure for interval response variables is a special case of a multiple regression analysis.

Problems

1. Give an example of two social science variables that you would not expect to be linearly related. Describe the pattern you would expect for the form of their relationship, and explain how you would model that pattern.

2. Draw rough sketches of the following mathematical functions on the same set of axes, for values of X between 0 and 5.
a. $\hat{Y} = 10 + 4X$
b. $\hat{Y} = 10 + 4X + X^2$
c. $\hat{Y} = 10 + 4X - X^2$
d. $\hat{Y} = 10 - 4X$
e. $\hat{Y} = 10 - 4X + X^2$
f. $\hat{Y} = 10 - 4X - X^2$

3. Draw rough sketches of the following mathematical functions on the same set of axes, for values of X between 0 and 35.
a. $\hat{Y} = 4(1.02)^X$ ($\hat{Y}$ = world population size in billions, X years from now if there is a 2% rate of growth every year)
b. $\hat{Y} = 4(1.04)^X$ (What does this represent?)

4. Consider the formula $\hat{Y} = 4(2)^X$.
a. Calculate the $\hat{Y}$-values for integer values of X between 0 and 7, and sketch the graph of the function.
b. Obtain the logarithms (to the base-10) of the $\hat{Y}$-values calculated in part **a**, and plot log $\hat{Y}$ against X. What is the intercept and what is the slope of this line?

5. Draw a sketch of the relationship between Y and X if:
a. log Y is linearly related to X.
b. The model $E(Y) = \alpha + \beta_1 X + \beta_2 X^2$ applies with $\beta_1 < 0$ and $\beta_2 > 0$.
c. The model $E(Y) = \alpha + \beta_1 X + \beta_2 X^2$ applies with $\beta_1 > 0$ and $\beta_2 < 0$.

6. A planner in a Florida city is quoted as saying, "This city has been growing at the rate of 4.2% per year. That's not slow growth by any means. It corresponds to 42% growth per decade." Explain what is incorrect about this statement. If, in fact, the present population size of the city is 100,000 and in each of the next 10 years the city increases in size by 4.2% relative to the previous year, then what would be the population size after a decade?

7. Refer to Problem 18 in Chapter 11, and consider the bivariate relationship between Y = integration index and X = mobility index. When the model $E(Y) = \alpha + \beta X$ is used, we obtain the prediction equation $\hat{Y} = 16.27 - .13X$, with a resulting sum of squared prediction errors of SSE = 179.13. When the model $E(Y) = \alpha + \beta_1 X + \beta_2 X^2$ is used, we obtain the printout shown at the top of the next page.
a. Draw a scatter diagram for integration and mobility. Plot the linear prediction equation over it, and plot the quadratic prediction equation over it.

Computer Printout for Problem 7

SOURCE	DF	SUM OF SQUARES
REGRESSION	2	74.44
ERROR	26	151.82
TOTAL	28	226.26

PARAMETER	ESTIMATE	T FOR HO: PARAMETER = 0	PROB > | T |	STD ERR OF ESTIMATE
INTERCEPT	23.23252	6.70		
X	-.69138	-2.64	.0138	.26185
X-SQUARED	.00976	2.16	.0399	.00451

b. Find the coefficient of determination for the linear model, and find the coefficient of multiple determination for the quadratic model. How much increase is there in the proportion of explained variation when the quadratic term is added to the model?

c. Out of the portion of the variability in integration scores left unexplained by the linear model, what proportion is explained by the introduction of the quadratic term? What measure does this represent?

d. Using the information in the printout, show all steps of a test of the null hypothesis that the quadratic effect is 0. What conclusion would be reached at the $\alpha = .05$ level?

8. The accompanying table presents, for white men in the United States, the number of deaths per thousand individuals of a fixed age within a period of a year.

AGE	DEATH RATE (PER THOUSAND)
30	3
40	6
50	14
60	27
70	60
80	125

Let X denote age and Y denote death rate.

a. Plot X against Y, and indicate whether a linear model would be reasonable for the relationship.

b. Plot X against $\log_{10} Y$. What does this plot indicate about the relationship between death rate and age? [*Note:* Do not round much, or the answers in part **d** will be greatly affected.]

c. Find the least squares line for the model $E(\log Y) = \log \alpha + (\log \beta)X$. Find the six predicted values for $\log Y$ and plot the least squares line on the graph in part **b**.

d. Find the estimates a and b for the prediction equation $\hat{Y} = ab^X$. Obtain the six predicted values for Y and plot this prediction equation on the graph in part **a**.

9. Plot the prediction equation $\hat{Y} = 10 + 4X_1 - X_1^2 - 2X_2$ in the following cases:

a. Between $\hat{Y}$ and X_1, for values of X_1 between 0 and 5, when X_2 is fixed at $X_2 = 2$.

b. Between $\hat{Y}$ and X_1, for values of X_1 between 0 and 5, when X_2 is fixed at $X_2 = 5$. (Use the same axes as in part **a.**)

c. Between $\hat{Y}$ and X_2, for values of X_2 between 0 and 5, when X_1 is fixed at $X_1 = 2$.

d. Between $\hat{Y}$ and X_2, for values of X_2 between 0 and 5, when X_1 is fixed at $X_1 = 5$. (Use the same axes as in part **c.**)

10. Give an example of a situation in which you would expect to find interaction between two interval variables in their effects on a dependent variable. Describe the likely nature of the interaction; for example, as X_2 increases, would the slope of the relationship between Y and X_1 tend to increase, or decrease?

11. A study is conducted in which the relationships are analyzed among the variables $Y =$ percentage vote for Democratic candidate, $X_1 =$ percentage of registered voters who are Democrats, and $X_2 =$ percentage of registered voters who vote in the election, for several congressional elections in 1984. The researchers hypothesize the existence of interaction, since they believe that there will be a higher slope between Y and X_1 for larger values of X_2 than for smaller values of X_2. The prediction equation they obtain is $\hat{Y} = 20 + .30X_1 + .05X_2 + .005X_1X_2$.

a. Plot the prediction equation relating Y to X_1 for the fixed values of $X_2 = 20$, $X_2 = 50$, and $X_2 = 80$. Interpret the results.

b. Plot the prediction equation relating Y to X_2 for the fixed values of $X_1 = 20$, $X_1 = 50$, and $X_1 = 80$. Interpret.

12. Refer to Problem 18 in Chapter 11. When the model $E(Y) = \alpha + \beta_1 X_1 + \beta_2 X_2 + \beta_3 X_1 X_2$ is used, the accompanying computer printout would result.

Computer Printout for Problem 12

SOURCE	DF	SUM OF SQUARES
REGRESSION	3	115.16
ERROR	25	111.10
TOTAL	28	226.26

PARAMETER	ESTIMATE	T FOR H0: PARAMETER = 0	PROB > | T |	STD ERR OF ESTIMATE
INTERCEPT	17.2977			
X1	.1058	.78	.442	.1353
X2	.0257	.21	.832	.1200
X1·X2	- .0149	-2.18	.039	.0068

a. Draw a scatter diagram for $Y =$ integration and $X_2 =$ mobility. Identify the points corresponding to the ten largest X_1-values, and the points corresponding to the ten smallest X_1-values. As investigated in this rather crude manner, does there appear to be interaction?

b. Give the prediction equation for the above model, and plot the estimated relationship between Y and X_2, for $X_1 = 10, 20, 30, 40$, and 50.

c. Find the coefficient of multiple determination for this model, and compare it to the corresponding value for the model without the interaction term.

d. Show all steps of a t test of the null hypothesis that the interaction effect is 0, report the P-value, and interpret.

13. Refer to Problem 12. Using the F test for complete and reduced models, test whether the model

$$E(Y) = \alpha + \beta_1X_1 + \beta_2X_2 + \beta_3X_1X_2$$

is significantly better than the model $E(Y) = \alpha + \beta_1X_1 + \beta_2X_2$. Compare the P-value to the one for the t test in Problem 12d.

14. The accompanying table gives the results of fitting models to 54 observations on Y = mental health score, X_1 = degree of social interaction, and X_2 = SES (socioeconomic status). The variables X_1 and X_2 are measured on scales of 0–100, and larger Y-scores represent better mental health. The variable symbol X1**2 represents X_1^2, and X1*X2 represents X_1X_2.

MODEL	VARIABLE	PARAMETER ESTIMATE	SSE FOR MODEL
1.	Intercept	20	400
	X1	.09	
2.	Intercept	15	350
	X1	.200	
	X1**2	−.001	
3.	Intercept	18	208
	X1	.06	
	X2	.05	
4.	Intercept	16	200
	X1	.07	
	X2	.04	
	X1*X2	−.0006	

a. When model 2 is fitted, which best describes the result over the range 0–100 of X_1-values?

i. $\hat{Y}$ is a convex function of X_1, first decreasing and then increasing.

ii. $\hat{Y}$ is an increasing convex function of X_1.

iii. $\hat{Y}$ is a concave function of X_1, first increasing and then decreasing.

iv. $\hat{Y}$ is an increasing concave function of X_1.

b. When model 4 is fitted, which best describes the result over the observed ranges?

i. $\hat{Y}$ is a linear function of X_1 with positive slope that is the same for all X_2.

ii. $\hat{Y}$ is a linear function of X_1 with positive slope for some values of X_2 and negative slope for others.

iii. $\hat{Y}$ is a linear function of X_1 with positive slope, but the magnitude of that slope is smaller for larger values of X_2.

iv. $\hat{Y}$ is a quadratic function of X_1 and X_2.

c. Give all steps of the test of whether the model with interaction term is significantly better than the multiple regression model omitting it. Interpret the P-value.

15. A multiple regression analysis is conducted to investigate the relationship between Y = college GPA and several independent variables. The variables are measured for a random sample of 200 students at a large state university. The total sum of squares on the dependent variable for these students is TSS = 32. First, five independent variables having to do with the students' performance in high school courses and on college entrance exams are entered into the regression model. The sum of squared errors for this model is SSE = 20. Next, four variables having to do with parents' education and income are simultaneously added to the model in order to determine if they have an effect on the students' college GPA, controlling for the student high school performance variables. The sum of squared errors for this expanded model is SSE = 19. Test at the α = .01 level whether this model is significantly better than the one containing only the student high school performance independent variables.

16.

a. Describe carefully the steps that are conducted in a forward selection procedure.

*b. Suppose a forward selection procedure is to be used, subject to the condition that X_2 and X_6 are already in the model (as the first two variables). Describe the steps of the procedure.

17. Using a regression computer package that has selection procedures as options, conduct the forward selection analysis described in Example 12.7.

18. Give an example of a dependent variable and a pair of independent variables for which you would expect the forward selection procedure to produce a model containing only one independent variable. Explain your reasoning.

19. A sociologist's first reaction upon studying selection methods such as the forward selection procedure was that they had the danger of leading to crass empiricism in theory-building. From a theoretical perspective, describe the dangers in such methods. What guidelines could be developed for avoiding these problems?

20. Suppose that Y = height, X_1 = length of left leg, and X_2 = length of right leg are measured for a sample of 100 adults in some society. The model $E(Y) = \alpha + \beta_1 X_1 + \beta_2 X_2$ is fitted to the data, and neither H_0: $\beta_1 = 0$ nor H_0: $\beta_2 = 0$ is rejected.

a. Does this imply that length of leg is not a good predictor of height? Why?

b. Does this imply that $H_0: \beta_1 = \beta_2 = 0$ would not be rejected? Why?

21.

a. If $\rho_{YX_1} = \rho_{YX_2}$, show that $\rho_{YX_1 \cdot X_2} = \rho_{YX_2 \cdot X_1}$ for the multiple linear regression model.

b. Suppose that in a sample, X_1 and X_2 are highly correlated ($r_{X_1 X_2} = .9$), and that the correlations between X_1 and Y and between X_2 and Y are of approximately the same magnitude ($r_{YX_1} = .7$ and $r_{YX_2} = .6$). Calculate $r_{YX_1 \cdot X_2}$ and $r_{YX_2 \cdot X_1}$, and note how small differences in Pearson correlations generate large differences in partial correlations when multicollinearity exists.

c. Suppose that the true correlations are $\rho_{X_1 X_2} = .85$, $\rho_{YX_1} = .65$, and $\rho_{YX_2} = .65$. Then find the true values of $\rho_{YX_1 \cdot X_2}$ and $\rho_{YX_2 \cdot X_1}$. What does this imply about making inferences about the partial effects of independent variables when multicollinearity is present?

d. As a comparison, compute the partial correlations in part b when $r_{YX_1} = .7$ and $r_{YX_2} = .6$, but $r_{X_1 X_2} = 0$; $r_{X_1 X_2} = .3$; and $r_{X_1 X_2} = .6$.

22. Refer to Problem 18 in Chapter 11. When the model $E(Y) = \alpha + \beta X$ is used for the relationship between $Y =$ integration index and $X =$ mobility index, we obtain the prediction equation $\hat{Y} = 16.265 - .1344X$. Find the predicted values and residuals for the twenty-nine cities and plot the residuals against X. What type of lack of fit is indicated? (Note the results in Problem 7.)

For multiple choice Problems 23–28, select the correct response(s).

23. In the model $E(Y) = \alpha + \beta_1 X + \beta_2 X^2$, the coefficient β_2:

a. Is the mean change in Y as X^2 is increased 1 unit with X held constant.

b. Is a curvature coefficient that describes whether the regression equation is convex or concave.

c. Equals 0 if the relationship between Y and X is linear.

d. Equals 0 if the population value of R^2 for this model equals ρ_{YX}^2.

24. The log transformation of the dependent variable in a regression analysis can be useful when:

a. Y is approximately a logarithmic function of X.

b. Y is approximately an exponential function of X.

c. $\log Y$ is approximately a linear function of X.

d. Unit changes in X are expected to have a multiplicative (rather than additive) effect on the mean of Y.

25. In the multiple regression model $E(Y) = \alpha + \beta_1 X_1 + \beta_2 X_2 + \beta_3 X_1 X_2$:

a. There is interaction.

b. The slope between Y and X_2 has different values depending on the value of X_1.

c. Y is a linear function of X_2, for fixed X_1.

d. Y is a quadratic function of X_2, for fixed X_1.

26. The F test for comparing a complete model to a reduced model:

a. Can be used to test the significance of a single regression parameter in a multiple regression model.

b. Can be used to test $H_0: \beta_1 = \cdots = \beta_k = 0$ in a multiple regression equation.

c. Can be used to test H_0: No interaction in the model

$$E(Y) = \alpha + \beta_1 X_1 + \beta_2 X_2 + \beta_3 X_3 + \beta_4 X_1 X_2 + \beta_5 X_1 X_3 + \beta_6 X_2 X_3$$

d. Can be used to test whether the quadratic model $E(Y) = \alpha + \beta_1 X_1 + \beta_2 X_1^2$ gives a significantly better fit than the interaction model $E(Y) = \alpha + \beta_1 X_1 + \beta_2 X_2 + \beta_3 X_1 X_2$.

27. Forward selection and stepwise regression are similar in the sense that, if they have the same α-level for entry:

a. They always select the same final regression model.

b. They always select the same initial regression model (when they enter the first independent variable).

c. Any variable that is not in the final model does not have a significant partial association with Y, controlling for the variables that are in the final model.

d. It is impossible that all the variables listed for potential inclusion are in the final model.

28. There is evidence of multicollinearity in a multiple regression model when:

a. There are strong intercorrelations among independent variables.

b. The R^2-value is very small.

c. The partial association between Y and X_1 is the same as the bivariate association between Y and X_1.

d. The F test of $H_0: \beta_1 = \cdots = \beta_k = 0$ is highly significant but the individual tests of $H_0: \beta_1 = 0, \ldots, H_0: \beta_k = 0$ are not significant.

29. Select the best response for each of the following terms (not every response will be used):

Heteroscedasticity   _____

Multicollinearity   _____

Forward selection   _____

Interaction   _____

Exponential model   _____

Ridge regression   _____

Stepwise regression   _____

a. The mean of Y is multiplied by β for each unit increase in X.

b. The log of Y is linearly related to the log of X.

c. A residual plot indicates that the residuals are much more spread out at large values of X than at small values of X.

d. The bivariate association between Y and X_1 is different from the partial association between Y and X_1 controlling for X_2.

e. Strong intercorrelations among independent variables.

f. May be used to get regression parameter estimates with smaller standard errors when there is multicollinearity.

g. At each stage the variable considered for entry into the model is the one explaining the greatest portion of the remaining unexplained variability in Y.

h. At each stage after a new variable is entered, all variables previously entered are retested to see if they still have a significant partial effect on Y.

i. The slope between Y and X_1 has different values depending on the value of X_2.

*30. Suppose that the variables in Problem 20 are measured for a sample of 100 adults in some society. Suppose that $r_{YX_1} = .80$, $r_{YX_2} = .81$, and $r_{X_1X_2} = .99$. Apply the forward selection procedure to the variables X_1 and X_2 and indicate which variable(s) would be in the final model, using the $\alpha = .05$ level for entrance.

*31. Show that the F test statistic considered in Section 12.3 for comparing a complete model to a reduced model can be expressed in terms of the coefficients of multiple determination of the two models by

$$F = \frac{(R_c^2 - R_r^2)/(k - g)}{(1 - R_c^2)/[n - (k + 1)]}$$

In this form of the test statistic, R_c^2 is the coefficient of multiple determination for the complete model, and R_r^2 is the corresponding coefficient for the reduced model. Again $df_1 = k - g$ and $df_2 = n - (k + 1)$, where k and g are the numbers of independent variables in the complete and reduced models, respectively.

*32. Refer to Problem 31 and to Example 12.1.

a. Show that we would need $R^2 = .878$ for the quadratic model in order to achieve $P = .01$ in testing $H_0: \beta_2 = 0$ against $H_a: \beta_2 \neq 0$.

b. Show that if $r^2 = .734$ for the linear model had been based on $n = 30$ measurements, then the observed value $R^2 = .795$ for the quadratic model would have been a significant improvement at the $\alpha = .01$ level for this test.

*33. Consider the data shown in the accompanying table.

X	1	1	1	2	2	2	3	3	3	4	4	4
Y	0	1	2	1	3	5	2	5	9	5	10	14

a. Draw a scatter diagram for the twelve observations on X and Y. Does the pattern of points tend to indicate a homoscedastic or heteroscedastic relationship between X and Y?

b. Make the transformation $Z = \sqrt{Y}$ and draw a scatter diagram for the twelve observations on X and Z. Observe how the transformation stabilizes the variability.

c. Assuming that these data are a random sample from some population of interest, test the null hypothesis that the conditional mean of Y is the same for all X-values (i.e., that the slope of the relationship between the mean of Y and X equals 0).

*34. Show that when we use a cross-product term to model interaction, we are implicitly assuming that the slope of the relationship between Y and X_1 changes linearly as X_2 changes. How would you suggest modeling interaction if, instead, you expect the slope of the linear relationship between Y and X_1 first to increase as X_2 changes from low to moderate values and then to decrease as X_2 changes from moderate to high values?

Bibliography   Afifi, A. A. and V. Clark (1984). *Computer-Aided Multivariate Analysis*. Belmont, Calif.: Lifetime Learning.

Blalock, H. M. (1963). "Correlated Independent Variables: The Problem of Multicollinearity." *Social Forces, 62*: 233–238.

Draper, N. R. and H. Smith (1981). *Applied Regression Analysis*, 2nd ed. New York: Wiley. Chaps. 3–7.

Hocking, R. R. (1976). "The Analysis and Selection of Variables in Linear Regression." *Biometrics, 32* (March): 1–49.

Holzer, C. E., III (1977). *The Impact of Life Events on Psychiatric Symptomatology*. Ph.D. dissertation, University of Florida.

Montroll, E. W. and W. W. Badger (1974). *Introduction to Quantitative Aspects of Social Phenomena*. New York: Gordon and Breach Science Publishers.

Neter, J. and W. Wasserman (1974). *Applied Linear Statistical Models*. Homewood, Ill.: Richard D. Irwin.

Pedhazur, E. J. (1982). *Multiple Regression in Behavioral Research,* 2nd ed. New York: Holt, Rinehart and Winston.

Wonnacott, R. J. and T. H. Wonnacott (1970). *Econometrics*. New York: Wiley. Chaps. 1–6.

Younger, M. S. (1979). *Handbook for Linear Regression*. North Scituate, Mass.: Duxbury Press.

CHAPTER 13

Comparison of Several Groups

Contents

In Chapter 8 we considered methods of testing for and describing the strength of association between two nominal or ordinal variables. In Chapters 9, 11, and 12, we used various models to investigate relationships between interval variables. In this chapter, we will consider bivariate analyses in which one of the variables is a categorical one. The categories of this variable, which is treated as nominal in level, represent different groups that are compared on another variable. This second variable is treated as the response (i.e., dependent) variable on which the groups are to be compared. The procedures presented in this chapter are generalizations of those studied in Chapter 7 for comparing *two* groups on a response variable. As in that chapter, we have organized the procedures by the measurement level of the response variable.

For each measurement level, the primary method presented will be a test of whether there are differences among the various groups on some characteristic of the response variable. If there is evidence of such differences, a secondary analysis involves finding just which groups are different and the degree to which they differ. The first five sections of the chapter contain procedures appropriate for interval response variables. In that case, we compare the means of the various groups by using a technique known as the *analysis of variance*. For estimation purposes, we construct confidence intervals for differences between pairs of group means. In Section 13.3, we see that the procedure for comparing means can be treated as a special case of a multiple regression analysis. We introduce the concept of a *dummy variable* as a way of including categorical variables as independent variables in a multiple regression model. For nominal response variables, the analysis in Section 13.6 is another application of the chi-square test and nominal measures of association. For ordinal response variables, in Section 13.7 we introduce the *Kruskal–Wallis test*, a generalization of the Wilcoxon test for comparing the groups on a mean rank criterion.

13.1 Interval Scales: One-Way Analysis of Variance

Groups measured on an interval response variable are usually compared according to their means. For example, the income distributions of men and women having a particular occupation can be compared by considering the difference in mean incomes for the two groups. The productivity of assembly-line workers organized into four different types of work groups can be analyzed by comparing the mean number of jobs completed per week for each of the four groups.

In Section 7.2 we studied a small-samples procedure for comparing the means of an interval variable for *two* groups. In this section, we introduce an analogous procedure for simultaneously comparing means of *several* groups. This procedure, referred to as an **analysis of variance,** is an exploratory test designed to detect evidence of any difference among a set of group means. If there is sufficient evidence, we then estimate the sizes of the differences between various pairs of means.

Assumptions and Notation

In the following formulas, we let m represent the number of groups to be compared. The means of the distributions of the interval response variable for the m populations are denoted by $\mu_1, \mu_2, \ldots, \mu_m$. The analysis of variance test is an F test of the null hypothesis H_0: $\mu_1 = \mu_2 = \cdots = \mu_m$ against the general alternative hypothesis H_a: at least two of the means are unequal. The assumptions upon which the test is based are as follows:

1. The population distributions on the response variable for the m groups are normal in form.
2. The standard deviations of the population distributions for the m groups are equal (see Figure 13.1). We denote this common value by σ.
3. Independent random samples are selected from the m populations.

Fig. 13.1 Assumptions About Population Distributions: Normal with Equal Standard Deviations, σ

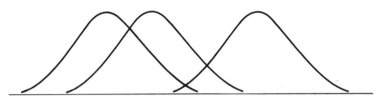

The sample sizes are denoted by $n_1, n_2, \ldots, n_m$, and the total sample size is denoted by $N = n_1 + n_2 + \cdots + n_m$.

In the formulas that follow, we let Y_{ij} denote the jth sample observation from the ith group. The n_1 observations on the response variable for the first group are represented by $Y_{11}, Y_{12}, Y_{13}, \ldots, Y_{1n_1}$. The n_2 observations for the second group are $Y_{21}, Y_{22}, \ldots, Y_{2n_2}$, and so forth. The first subscript denotes the group number, and the second subscript denotes the observation number within the group. The sample mean for the observations in the first sample is $\bar{Y}_1 = \sum_{j=1}^{n_1} Y_{1j}/n_1$; the sample mean for the second sample is $\bar{Y}_2 = \sum_j Y_{2j}/n_2$; and so forth.* The overall mean for the combined sample of size $N = n_1 + n_2 + \cdots + n_m$ is denoted by $\bar{Y} = \sum_i \sum_j Y_{ij}/N$. The double summation notation $\sum_i \sum_j$ is used to indicate summation over both subscripts i and j. In this context, the double sum $\sum_i \sum_j Y_{ij}$ represents the sum over all the samples ($i = 1, \ldots, m$) and over all observations in each of the samples ($j = 1, 2, \ldots, n_i$ for the ith group), that is, the sum of all the observations in the combined sample, or the sum of the group sums. This general notation for a data set is summarized in Table 13.1 at the top of the next page.

The analysis of variance procedure for testing equality of means is based on a comparison of the variability of the sample means $\bar{Y}_i$ about the overall mean $\bar{Y}$, relative to the variability of the sample observations Y_{ij} about their $\bar{Y}_i$ means—the Y_{1j}-values about $\bar{Y}_1$, the Y_{2j}-values about $\bar{Y}_2$, and so forth. To illustrate, if the sample

*We shall frequently write a summation such as $\sum_{j=1}^{n_2} Y_{2j}$ in the abbreviated form $\sum_j Y_{2j}$; it is then implied that the index j ranges from 1 to its maximum value (n_2 in this case).

Table 13.1

Notation for Observations
on an Interval Variable for
Samples from m Groups

SAMPLE	OBSERVATION NUMBER			SAMPLE SUM	SAMPLE SIZE	SAMPLE MEAN
	1	2	$3 \ldots n_1$			
1	Y_{11}	Y_{12}	$Y_{13} \ldots Y_{1n_1}$	$\Sigma_j \, Y_{1j}$	n_1	$\bar{Y}_1 = \Sigma \, Y_{1j}/n_1$
2	Y_{21}	Y_{22}	$Y_{23} \ldots Y_{2n_2}$	$\Sigma_j \, Y_{2j}$	n_2	$\bar{Y}_2 = \Sigma \, Y_{2j}/n_2$
3	Y_{31}	Y_{32}	$Y_{33} \ldots Y_{3n_3}$	$\Sigma_j \, Y_{3j}$	n_3	$\bar{Y}_3 = \Sigma \, Y_{3j}/n_3$
$\vdots$	$\vdots$	$\vdots$	$\vdots \qquad \vdots$	$\vdots$	$\vdots$	$\vdots$
m	Y_{m1}	Y_{m2}	$Y_{m3} \ldots Y_{mn_m}$	$\Sigma_j \, Y_{mj}$	n_m	$\bar{Y}_m = \Sigma \, Y_{mj}/n_m$
Overall sample				$\Sigma_i \, \Sigma_j \, Y_{ij}$	N	$\bar{Y} = \Sigma_i \, \Sigma_j \, Y_{ij}/N$

Fig. 13.2 Two Sets of
Samples; Variability Within
Groups Is Larger in
Second Set

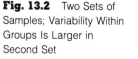

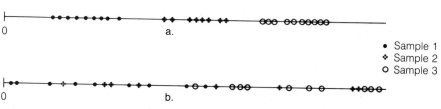

• Sample 1
❖ Sample 2
○ Sample 3

observations from three groups are as illustrated in Figure 13.2a, then it is relatively clear that the means of the populations represented by these samples are unequal. The basis for this conclusion is that the variability *between* each pair of sample means is large relative to the variability of the observations *within* each of the samples. In Figure 13.2b, however, the variability *within* the groups is also relatively large, and it is not clear whether the groups are significantly different, even though the sample means are the same as in Figure 13.2a. Roughly speaking, the greater the variability between sample means relative to the variability within each set of sample observations, the more sure we can be that the null hypothesis of equal means is false.

The F test statistic in the procedure involves two statistically independent estimates of the population variance, σ^2, of the measurements in the groups. The first of these is based on the variability of the observations within each of the samples. This estimate is referred to as the **within (groups) estimate** of the variance. It has good properties as an estimate, regardless of whether H_0: $\mu_1 = \mu_2 = \cdots = \mu_m$ is true or false. The other estimate is based on the variability between each of the sample means $\bar{Y}_i$ and the overall sample mean $\bar{Y}$. We refer to it as the **between (groups) estimate** of the variance. If H_0 is true, the between estimate tends to be good, about the same value as the within estimate, apart from sampling error. If H_0 is false, however, the between estimate tends to overestimate σ^2. The F test statistic is the ratio of the between estimate to the within estimate. When H_0 is false, the between estimate (since it then tends to overestimate σ^2) tends to be larger than the within estimate and the ratio of the two tends to be considerably larger than 1.0. Hence, large F-values lead to small P-values in the test.

Example 13.1   Suppose we are interested in studying the degree of residential segregation between blacks and whites in cities in different regions of the country. As a measure of
segregation, we can compute the *index of dissimilarity* (see Taeuber and Taeuber,
1965) in each of a random sample of cities from the various regions of the country.
This index, which is referred to as the *segregation index* in this context, can assume
values ranging from 0 to 100, with higher values indicating greater segregation of
black from white residences. The index is interpreted as the percentage of nonwhites who would have to change the block on which they live in order to produce a
nonsegregated city—one in which the percentage of nonwhites living in each block
is the same for all blocks in the city.

Suppose that, in order to compare the regions on the degree of segregation in
1960, we take a random sample of cities from the 1960 U.S. census and calculate
their segregation indices.* The cities and their segregation indices are given in Table
13.2, along with the estimated means and standard deviations for each region. The
analysis of variance will be used to test whether the population of all cities shows
regional differences in residential segregation, based on the data in these samples.
The null hypothesis for that test is $H_0: \mu_1 = \mu_2 = \mu_3 = \mu_4$, where μ_i is the mean
segregation index for all cities in region i. ∎

Table 13.2 Segregation Indices, by Region (1960)

NORTHEAST		NORTH CENTRAL		SOUTH		WEST	
Bridgeport, Conn.	70	Battle Creek, Mich.	80	Amarillo, Tex.	89	Stockton, Ca.	71
Erie, Pa.	87	Chicago, Ill.	93	Durham, N.C.	93	Phoenix, Ariz.	86
Jersey City, N.J.	78	Lansing, Mich.	89	Houston, Tex.	94	Richmond, Ca.	77
Passaic, N.J.	72	St. Paul, Minn.	87	Miami, Fla.	98	Spokane, Wash.	80
Providence, R.I.	77	Waterloo, Iowa	89	Mobile, Ala.	92	Las Vegas, Nev.	92
White Plains, N.Y.	78	Youngstown, Ohio	78	Orlando, Fla.	98	Denver, Colo.	86
						Bakersfield, Ca.	87
						Portland, Ore.	77
Mean: $\bar{Y}_1 = 77$		Mean: $\bar{Y}_2 = 86$		Mean: $\bar{Y}_3 = 94$		Mean: $\bar{Y}_4 = 82$	
St. dev.: $\hat{\sigma}_1 = 5.9$		St. dev.: $\hat{\sigma}_2 = 5.8$		St. dev.: $\hat{\sigma}_3 = 3.5$		St. dev.: $\hat{\sigma}_4 = 6.9$	

Source: K. E. Taeuber and A. F. Taeuber, *Negroes in Cities* (Chicago: Aldine, 1965), pp. 32–34.

Within Estimate of Variance   The within estimate of the variance is based on pooling together the sums of squares
of the observations about their respective means and dividing by a degrees of
freedom term. Now, $\Sigma_{j=1}^{n_1} (Y_{1j} - \bar{Y}_1)^2$ is the sum of squares of the measurements in the
first sample about their mean. This sum of squares is based on $n_1 - 1$ degrees of
freedom, since one parameter is estimated (μ_1, by $\bar{Y}_1$) before the sum of squares is
computed. Similarly, $\Sigma_{j=1}^{n_2} (Y_{2j} - \bar{Y}_2)^2$ is the sum of squares of the measurements in
the second sample about their sample mean, and is based on $n_2 - 1$ degrees of

*Actually, we took the cities and index values from Taeuber and Taeuber (1965, pp. 32–34).

freedom. The sum of these sum of squares terms for the m samples is referred to as the *within sum of squares,* since it is based on sums of squares calculated within each sample. Denoting this sum by WSS, we have*

$$\text{WSS} = \sum_{j=1}^{n_1} (Y_{1j} - \bar{Y}_1)^2 + \sum_{j=1}^{n_2} (Y_{2j} - \bar{Y}_2)^2 + \cdots + \sum_{j=1}^{n_m} (Y_{mj} - \bar{Y}_m)^2$$

This sum has degrees of freedom equal to the sum of the degrees of freedom of the component parts: $(n_1 - 1) + (n_2 - 1) + \cdots + (n_m - 1) = (n_1 + n_2 + \cdots + n_m) - m = N - m$. the ratio

$$\hat{\sigma}^2 = \frac{\text{WSS}}{\text{df}} = \frac{\text{WSS}}{N - m}$$

is the within estimate of the population variance σ^2 of the m groups.

The form of the within estimate may seem rather strange at first glance. The best point estimate of σ^2 based only on the first sample is $\sum_{j=1}^{n_1} (Y_{1j} - \bar{Y}_1)^2/(n_1 - 1)$. In Table 13.2, for example, this is just the square of the reported estimated standard deviation, $\hat{\sigma}_1 = 5.9$. Similarly, the best point estimate based only on the second sample would be $\sum_{j=1}^{n_2} (Y_{2j} - \bar{Y}_2)^2/(n_2 - 1)$, and so forth for the remaining samples. Under the assumption that the population variances of the m groups are identical, these terms are all estimates of the same parameter, σ^2. Now, the numerator and denominator of the within estimate $\hat{\sigma}^2$ are obtained by pooling the information from these m estimates by adding their numerators and also adding their denominators. The resulting estimate can be interpreted as a weighted average of the estimates from the m separate samples, with relatively more weight given to the samples having larger sample sizes (see Problem 38). This within estimate has good properties (e.g., unbiasedness, small standard error) relative to other potential estimates, regardless of the values of $\mu_1, \mu_2, \ldots, \mu_m$.

Example 13.2   For the data presented in Table 13.2, the sample means are $\bar{Y}_1 = 77$, $\bar{Y}_2 = 86$, $\bar{Y}_3 = 94$, and $\bar{Y}_4 = 82$. These are based on sample sizes of $n_1 = n_2 = n_3 = 6$, and $n_4 = 8$, for a total sample size of $N = 26$. The sum of squares of the segregation scores for the six cities in the Northeast about their mean of 77 is

$$\sum_{j=1}^{n_1} (Y_{1j} - \bar{Y}_1)^2 = \sum_{j=1}^{6} (Y_{1j} - 77)^2$$

$$= (70 - 77)^2 + (87 - 77)^2 + (78 - 77)^2$$
$$+ (72 - 77)^2 + (77 - 77)^2 + (78 - 77)^2$$

$$= 176$$

Similarly, the sums of squares of the segregation scores for the cities in the other regions about their means are

---

*Using double summation notation to represent summation over the samples as well as within each sample, we can abbreviate this term by $\text{WSS} = \sum_i \sum_j (Y_{ij} - \bar{Y}_i)^2$.

$$\sum_{j=1}^{n_2} (Y_{2j} - \bar{Y}_2)^2 = \sum_{j=1}^{6} (Y_{2j} - 86)^2 = 168 \quad \text{(North central)}$$

$$\sum_{j=1}^{n_3} (Y_{3j} - \bar{Y}_3)^2 = \sum_{j=1}^{6} (Y_{3j} - 94)^2 = 62 \quad \text{(South)}$$

$$\sum_{j=1}^{n_4} (Y_{4j} - \bar{Y}_4)^2 = \sum_{j=1}^{8} (Y_{4j} - 82)^2 = 332 \quad \text{(West)}$$

The within sum of squares is the sum of these terms, or

$$\text{WSS} = 176 + 168 + 62 + 332 = 738$$

The degrees of freedom on which the sum is based is $N - m = $ (Total sample size $-$ Number of groups) $= 26 - 4 = 22$. The within estimate of the variance is therefore

$$\hat{\sigma}^2 = \frac{\text{WSS}}{N - m} = \frac{738}{22} = 33.55$$

The corresponding within estimate of the standard deviation of the segregation values in each of the four regions is $\hat{\sigma} = 5.79$, a value that summarizes the four separate estimated standard deviations given in Table 13.2. ∎

Between Estimate of Variance

In order to understand the between estimate of the variance, suppose for a moment that the sample sizes of the m groups are all equal to some number n, and that the population means all equal some number μ. The sampling distribution of each $\bar{Y}_i$ is centered about μ with variance σ^2/n. We could therefore treat each of the $\bar{Y}_i$-values as an observation from a population having mean μ and variance σ^2/n. The sample mean of the $\bar{Y}_i$-values, when the sample sizes are equal, is just $\bar{Y}$, the mean of the combined set of observations from all the samples. This sample mean serves as an estimate of μ based on the overall sample. Treating $\bar{Y}_1, \bar{Y}_2, \ldots, \bar{Y}_m$ as m observations having the sample mean $\bar{Y}$, the term $\sum_{i=1}^{m} (\bar{Y}_i - \bar{Y})^2/(m - 1)$ is a point estimate of the variance σ^2/n of the distribution of the $\bar{Y}_i$-values. But if $\sum_{i=1}^{m} (\bar{Y}_i - \bar{Y})^2/(m - 1)$ estimates $\sigma_{\bar{Y}_i}^2 = \sigma^2/n$, we can multiply it by n to get an estimate of σ^2. Hence,

$$n \left[\sum_{i=1}^{m} (\bar{Y}_i - \bar{Y})^2/(m - 1) \right] = \sum_{i=1}^{m} n(\bar{Y}_i - \bar{Y})^2/(m - 1)$$

is an estimate of σ^2. If the null hypothesis $H_0: \mu_1 = \cdots = \mu_m = \mu$ is true, in other words, $\sum_{i=1}^{m} n(\bar{Y}_i - \bar{Y})^2/(m - 1)$ is a point estimate of σ^2 based on variability between the $\bar{Y}_i$-values and the overall mean $\bar{Y}$, for the case in which all sample sizes are equal. We could replace n by n_i to get the analogous estimate

$$\frac{\sum_{i=1}^{m} n_i(\bar{Y}_i - \bar{Y})^2}{m - 1}$$

for the case in which the sample sizes are unequal.

The numerator of this estimate is called the *between sum of squares,* and is denoted by BSS. It represents the sum of squares of the differences between each $\bar{Y}_i$ and the overall $\bar{Y}$, where each squared difference is weighted by the sample size upon which it is based. The ratio of BSS to its degrees of freedom, $m - 1$, gives us the between estimate of the variance σ^2. It is an unbiased estimate only if H_0 is true. If the population means are unequal, then the $\bar{Y}_i$-values will tend to be more disperse than if the population means are equal. Thus, when H_0: $\mu_1 = \cdots = \mu_m$ is false, the between sum of squares will tend to be inflated and the between estimate will tend to be considerably larger than the true value of σ^2. Hence, the ratio

$$F = \frac{\text{Between estimate}}{\text{Within estimate}} = \frac{\text{BSS}/(m - 1)}{\text{WSS}/(N - m)}$$

will tend to be relatively large when H_0 is false. When H_0 is true, this F test statistic has the F sampling distribution with $\text{df}_1 = m - 1$ and $\text{df}_2 = N - m$. This sampling distribution was introduced in Section 11.4. The two degrees of freedom terms are just the denominator of the between estimate ($\text{df}_1 = m - 1$) and the denominator of the within estimate ($\text{df}_2 = N - m$). As in the F test for the parameters of a multiple regression model, the P-value is the probability of obtaining an F-value at least as large as the observed one, if H_0 were true.

Example 13.3 The between sum of squares for the data in Table 13.2 is

$$\text{BSS} = \sum_{i=1}^{4} n_i(\bar{Y}_i - \bar{Y})^2$$

$$= n_1(\bar{Y}_1 - \bar{Y})^2 + n_2(\bar{Y}_2 - \bar{Y})^2 + n_3(\bar{Y}_3 - \bar{Y})^2 + n_4(\bar{Y}_4 - \bar{Y})^2$$

The overall mean $\bar{Y}$ is the mean of the combined sample of $N = 26$ measurements, which is

$$\bar{Y} = \frac{\sum_i \sum_j Y_{ij}}{N} = \frac{(70 + 87 + \cdots + 77)}{26} = \frac{2{,}198}{26} = 84.538$$

Therefore, since $\bar{Y}_1 = 77$, $\bar{Y}_2 = 86$, $\bar{Y}_3 = 94$, and $\bar{Y}_4 = 82$,

$$\text{BSS} = 6(77 - 84.538)^2 + 6(86 - 84.538)^2 + 6(94 - 84.538)^2$$
$$+ 8(82 - 84.538)^2 = 942.46$$

This sum of squares is based on degrees of freedom $m - 1 = $ Number of groups $- 1$ $= 4 - 1 = 3$, so that the between estimate of the variance is

$$\frac{\text{BSS}}{m - 1} = \frac{942.46}{3} = 314.15$$

We previously obtained a within estimate of the variance of $\hat{\sigma}^2 = \text{WSS}/(N - m) = 33.55$, so the F test statistic equals

$$F = \frac{\text{BSS}/(m - 1)}{\text{WSS}/(N - m)} = \frac{314.15}{33.55} = 9.36$$

In other words, the between estimate of σ^2 is over nine times as large as the within estimate. This statistic is based on the degrees of freedom values $df_1 = m - 1 = 3$ and $df_2 = N - m = 22$. From Table D, $F = 7.80$ corresponds to $P = .001$, so the P-value is $P < .001$. Hence, there is strong evidence against H_0: $\mu_1 = \mu_2 = \mu_3 = \mu_4$, and we can conclude that there is a difference among the mean segregation indices for the populations of all cities in the four regions. ∎

A table similar to the one used to summarize the various sums of squares in a regression analysis is frequently used to record the computations and results of an analysis of variance test. This table is usually referred to as an *ANOVA table.* The basic format is indicated in Table 13.3 for the test just conducted. The sums of squares divided by their corresponding degrees of freedom are referred to as *mean squares.* The two mean squares are the between and within estimates of the population variances σ^2, which are themselves mean squares—precisely, the mean of the squared differences between the population measurements and their mean for each group. In the BETWEEN row of the ANOVA table, BSS divided by df_1 gives the between mean square $BSS/df_1 = 942.46/3 = 314.15$. In the WITHIN row, WSS divided by df_2 gives the within mean square $WSS/df_2 = 738.00/22 = 33.55$. The ratio of the two mean squares gives the F test statistic, $F = 314.15/33.55 = 9.36$, which has P-value $P < .001$.

Table 13.3
ANOVA Table

SOURCE	SUM OF SQUARES	DF	MEAN SQUARE	F	PROB > F
Between	942.46	3	314.15	9.36	P < .001
Within	738.00	22	33.55		
Total	1,680.46	25			

The sum of BSS and WSS is referred to as the *total sum of squares,* denoted by TSS. In fact, TSS can be shown to equal $TSS = \Sigma_i \Sigma_j (Y_{ij} - \bar{Y})^2$, which is the sum of squares of the combined sample of N observations about the overall mean, $\bar{Y}$. The analysis of variance procedure involves partitioning this measure of the total variability of the observations about the overall mean into two independent parts. One of these, BSS, is the portion of the total that is *explained* by the differences among the sample means. The other part, WSS, is the portion of the total that cannot be explained by these differences. It represents the fact that there is still variability among the measurements when we classify them into separate groups. The analogy between these sums of squares and the regression and error sums of squares calculated in regression analysis will be discussed in Section 13.3.

A Further Note on Assumptions

The assumption that the population distributions must be normal with identical standard deviations is a rather stringent one that would not be satisfied for many variables in social science research. Moderate departures from normality of the populations and equality of the standard deviations can be tolerated, in the sense that the F sampling distribution still provides a good approximation to the actual sampling distribution of the ratio of the variance estimates. In the special case in which the sample sizes are all equal, the F test is particularly robust to violations of the assumption of equal standard deviations. That is, if $n_1 = n_2 = \cdots = n_m$, the F test works well in practice even if the population standard deviations are very different.

Histograms can be constructed for each of the sample distributions to check for extreme deviations from normality, when the sample sizes are moderate. Misleading results may occur in the F test if the population distributions are highly skewed or if there are relatively large differences among the population standard deviations (say, the largest sample standard deviation is several times as large as the smallest one) and the sample sizes are unequal. In such cases, the analysis is sometimes performed by first applying a transformation to the data that preserves the orderings of the observations and their means, such as a logarithmic or square root transformation, so that the transformed data better fit the assumption. If the ratios of each pair of population variances are known (or estimated precisely), we can perform a weighted analysis by giving relatively more weight to observations from populations having smaller variances (see Neter and Wasserman, 1974, pp. 506–515; Scheffé, 1959, Chap. 10). As usual, errors in interpretation may occur if the observations are not independent (e.g., as in nonrandom sampling); the procedure is not robust to violations of this assumption.

For the data in Table 13.2, the estimated standard deviations of all regions except the South are approximately equal. The ratio of the largest to the smallest standard deviation is about 2, which would not be especially unusual even if the population standard deviations were all equal, given the small sample sizes. Also, the values given in Table 13.2 show no strong evidence of extreme skewness of the distributions since, in each sample, about half of the observations occur on each side of the sample mean.

An alternative procedure for comparing the groups without such restrictive assumptions is to treat the response variable as ordinal and use the Kruskal–Wallis test, to be introduced in Section 13.7. In fact, even if the assumptions of normal population distributions with identical standard deviations are fulfilled, the Kruskal–Wallis test is very nearly as powerful as the F test in detecting false null hypotheses. The Kruskal–Wallis test is almost as efficient as the analysis of variance procedure for detecting differences among a number of groups, even when the assumptions for which that F test is designed are exactly fulfilled. For testing purposes, then, there is usually little sacrifice in using only the ordinal characteristics of the data.

**13.2
Interval Scales:
Multiple
Comparison of
Means**
━━━━━━━━━━━

The analysis of variance test of $H_0: \mu_1 = \mu_2 = \cdots = \mu_m$ is merely an exploratory technique, just like the test of $H_0: \beta_1 = \cdots = \beta_k = 0$ considered for the multiple regression model in Chapter 11. The conclusion of the test does not result in a specification of *which* means are different or *how* different they are. Therefore, more detailed inferences are often conducted when H_0 is rejected. Also, in many applications there would be greater interest in estimating the means than in merely testing

Preplanned
Comparisons

whether they are all equal. We may be especially interested, for example, in confidence intervals for each of the means $\mu_1, \mu_2, \ldots, \mu_m$, or in confidence intervals for the differences between each pair of means, $\mu_i - \mu_j$. Using the same notation as that in the previous section, the following formulas apply for these purposes:

1. A $100(1 - \alpha)\%$ confidence interval for μ_i is

$$\bar{Y}_i \pm t_{\alpha/2} \frac{\hat{\sigma}}{\sqrt{n_i}}$$

In this formula, $\hat{\sigma} = \sqrt{\text{WSS}/(N - m)}$ is the square root of the within estimate of σ^2 used in the denominator of the F test statistic, and the t-value, $t_{\alpha/2}$, is based on the degrees of freedom of that estimate, df $= N - m$.

2. A $100(1 - \alpha)\%$ confidence interval for $\mu_i - \mu_j$ is

$$(\bar{Y}_i - \bar{Y}_j) \pm t_{\alpha/2} \hat{\sigma} \sqrt{\frac{1}{n_i} + \frac{1}{n_j}}$$

In this formula, as in the previous one, df $= N - m$ for the t-value. The difference between μ_i and μ_j is judged to be significant at the α-level if the interval does not contain 0. If the interval contains only positive numbers, we would conclude that μ_i exceeds μ_j. Similarly, we would conclude that μ_j exceeds μ_i if the interval contains only negative numbers.

For the special case of $m = 2$ groups, the confidence interval given here for $\mu_i - \mu_j$ is identical to the one given at the end of Section 7.2 for $\mu_2 - \mu_1$. For large samples, we might prefer to use the confidence interval formula from the beginning of Section 7.2, since it is not based on the assumption of equal standard deviations or normal population distributions.

Example 13.4

Suppose we were particularly interested in the difference in the mean segregation index between cities in the Northeast and cities in the South. In Table 13.2, we observed $\bar{Y}_1 = 77$ for $n_1 = 6$ cities in the Northeast and $\bar{Y}_3 = 94$ for $n_3 = 6$ cities in the South. Also, the within estimate of the standard deviation was $\hat{\sigma} = 5.79$, based on df $= N - m = 26 - 4 = 22$. For a 95% confidence interval with df $= 22$, $t_{\alpha/2} = t_{.025} = 2.074$. A 95% confidence interval for $\mu_3 - \mu_1$ is

$$(\bar{Y}_3 - \bar{Y}_1) \pm t_{.025} \, \hat{\sigma} \sqrt{\frac{1}{n_1} + \frac{1}{n_3}} = (94 - 77) \pm 2.074(5.79) \sqrt{\frac{1}{6} + \frac{1}{6}}$$

$$= 17 \pm 6.9 \quad \text{or} \quad (10.1, 23.9)$$

We can be 95% confident that the mean of the segregation indices for all southern cities in 1960 was between 10.1 and 23.9 units higher than the mean of the segregation indices for all northeastern cities in 1960. ■

The confidence intervals just described are appropriate only for comparisons that are planned *before observing the data*. It is not proper to scan the data to decide which means appear to be different and then to form confidence intervals for those differences. If the number of groups m is relatively large, the number of different possible pairwise comparisons [$m(m - 1)/2$] can be very large, and we might expect some of the differences to appear to be different *even if all of the population means were equal.* When there are $m = 10$ groups, for example, there are $m(m - 1)/2 = 45$ pairs of means to be compared; we would expect that, on the average, $45(.05) = 2.25$ of the confidence intervals would not contain the true differences, if there is a 5% error rate (a 95% confidence coefficient) for each comparison. When there are ten groups that all have equal means, for example, it can be shown that the probability is .60 that at least one of the pairs of means would be judged to be unequal.

We must keep in mind that .05 is the a priori probability that *any particular one* of the confidence intervals does not contain the true difference. When *several* confidence intervals are formed, the probability that *at least one* of the confidence intervals is in error is considerably larger than the error rate for any particular interval. The larger the number of groups being compared, the greater is the chance of making at least one incorrect inference. In particular, if we simply scan the sample means and select the largest and smallest means for a confidence interval, the probability will be quite large that the interval will not contain 0, even if $\mu_1 = \cdots = \mu_m$. When we construct confidence intervals for all possible comparisons of means, we will refer to the probability that at least one of the intervals is in error (i.e., does not contain the *true* difference in means) as the **multiple comparison error rate**. We next consider how to control this error rate at an admissibly small level.

Scheffé Multiple Comparisons   The a priori probability that the $100(1 - \alpha)$% confidence interval for $\mu_i - \mu_j$ does not contain the actual value of $\mu_i - \mu_j$ is α. If several such confidence intervals are formed for pairwise differences in means, the probability is considerably larger than α that at least one of them is in error. For this reason, these intervals are typically used (if at all) for only a few preplanned comparisons. When we wish to make a large number of comparisons, other approaches are available in which the probability that *all* intervals contain the true differences can be controlled at a precise level. Such a set of intervals is referred to as a set of **simultaneous confidence intervals,** since all intervals are known to contain the true parameters *simultaneously* with fixed probability. For example, if there are $m = 10$ means, the set of 95% simultaneous confidence intervals is such that the a priori probability that *all* 45 (not any particular *one* of the 45) of these intervals contain the corresponding pairwise differences $\mu_i - \mu_j$ is .95. In other words, the probability that *at least one* of the intervals is in error is controlled at the level .05. Procedures yielding several intervals that apply simultaneously at a fixed confidence level are referred to as **multiple comparison techniques.** The multiple comparison error rate is the probability that at least one of the intervals is in error, which equals 1 minus the simultaneous confidence coefficient. In the context of testing for differences between pairs of means, this error rate is the probability that at least one of the differences is judged to be significantly nonzero when actually all the means are equal. It is the probability of making at least one Type I error.

Several multiple comparison techniques have been proposed for obtaining simultaneous confidence intervals. Among these are the approaches referred to as *Scheffé's method, Tukey's method, Duncan's method,* and the *Bonferroni method.*

We shall discuss the Scheffé approach, which enables us to obtain confidence intervals for a wide variety of comparisons. We can use this approach even to consider comparisons suggested by the data, often referred to as *post hoc comparisons.*

In Scheffé's method, the interval for $\mu_i - \mu_j$ is given by

$$(\bar{Y}_i - \bar{Y}_j) \pm \hat{\sigma}\sqrt{(m-1)F_\alpha\left(\frac{1}{n_i} + \frac{1}{n_j}\right)}$$

where F_α denotes the value from the F distribution with $df_1 = m - 1$ and $df_2 = N - m$ having right-tail area α. In other words, F_α is the value that the F test statistic in the analysis of variance test must exceed in order to reject H_0 at the α-level. The means μ_i and μ_j are judged to be unequal if this interval does not contain 0. The selected level α is the multiple comparison error rate—the probability that *at least one* of the $m(m-1)/2$ intervals does not contain the actual difference of means. Equivalently, the simultaneous confidence coefficient that applies to the entire set of intervals is $1 - \alpha$.[*]

Example 13.5 We refer again to the data in Table 13.2, for which $\hat{\sigma} = 5.79$. There are $m = 4$ groups, so we have $m(m-1)/2 = 4(3)/2 = 6$ pairs of means to be compared. To obtain 95% simultaneous confidence intervals, we use the $F_{.05}$ value based on $df_1 = m - 1 = 3$ and $df_2 = N - m = 22$, which is $F_{.05} = 3.05$. The interval for $\mu_2 - \mu_1$, the difference between the north central and northeast regions in the mean segregation index, is

$$(\bar{Y}_2 - \bar{Y}_1) \pm \hat{\sigma}\sqrt{(m-1)F_{.05}\left(\frac{1}{n_1} + \frac{1}{n_2}\right)}$$

$$= (86 - 77) \pm 5.79\sqrt{3(3.05)\left(\frac{1}{6} + \frac{1}{6}\right)}$$

$$= 9 \pm 10.1 \quad \text{or} \quad (-1.1, 19.1)$$

The intervals for each of the other five pairs of means are obtained in a similar way and are given in Table 13.4 (page 410). All six of the confidence intervals hold simultaneously with confidence coefficient .95. The a priori probability that one or more of them does not contain the true difference is only .05.

We see that the differences between the means for the South and the Northeast and for the West and South are judged to be significant, since the confidence intervals for $\mu_3 - \mu_1$ and $\mu_4 - \mu_3$ do not contain 0. The six pairwise comparisons can be summarized by the diagram

NE   W   NC   S
_____
      _____

---

[*]In fact, the set of comparisons that hold simultaneously with confidence coefficient $1 - \alpha$ includes a large class of comparisons of a nature we have not discussed, such as differences between averages of two groups of the means. See Neter and Wasserman (1974, p. 477) for details. Other multiple comparison procedures typically yield slightly narrower intervals if one is interested only in pairwise comparisons.

where we have ordered the regions according to the sizes of their sample mean segregation indices. The South and the Northeast, and the South and the West are not connected by a line, indicating that there is sufficient evidence that these regions differ in their mean segregation levels, as measured by the segregation index.

Table 13.4

Scheffé Multiple Comparison Procedure for Pairwise Comparisons of Mean Segregation Indices by Region

REGIONS	DIFFERENCE OF MEANS $\mu_i - \mu_j$	ESTIMATED DIFFERENCE $\bar{Y}_i - \bar{Y}_j$	95% SIMULTANEOUS CONFIDENCE INTERVAL
(North central, Northeast)	$\mu_2 - \mu_1$	9	$(-1.1, 19.1)$
(South, Northeast)	$\mu_3 - \mu_1$	17	$(6.9, 27.1)^*$
(West, Northeast)	$\mu_4 - \mu_1$	5	$(-4.5, 14.5)$
(South, North central)	$\mu_3 - \mu_2$	8	$(-2.1, 18.1)$
(West, North central)	$\mu_4 - \mu_2$	-4	$(-13.5, 5.5)$
(West, South)	$\mu_4 - \mu_3$	-12	$(-21.5, -2.5)^*$

Note: An asterisk * indicates a significant difference.

Notice that the comparison of groups just described is not transitive. In other words, if NE and NC are not significantly different, and if NC and S are not significantly different, it is not necessarily true that NE and S are not significantly different. It may be that the difference between the means for NE and NC is not quite large enough to be significant at the chosen α-level, and similarly for the means for NC and S, yet the difference between the means for NE and S may well be large enough to be significant at the chosen α-level. ■

The Scheffé intervals tend to be wider than the corresponding intervals using the t distribution described earlier in this section. For example, we added and subtracted 6.9 from $\bar{Y}_3 - \bar{Y}_1$ to get a 95% confidence interval for $\mu_3 - \mu_1$ in Example 13.4. However, we added and subtracted 10.1 from $\bar{Y}_3 - \bar{Y}_1$ to get the interval for $\mu_3 - \mu_1$ in the simultaneous set just obtained. The reason for the difference in widths is that each of the intervals $(\bar{Y}_i - \bar{Y}_j) \pm t_{\alpha/2}\hat{\sigma}\sqrt{(1/n_i) + (1/n_j)}$ holds a priori with probability $1 - \alpha$; the entire set holds simultaneously with probability considerably less than $1 - \alpha$.* For that interval, the error rate is α for each comparison, not for the entire set of pairwise comparisons. Thus, although each of the t intervals appears to be more precise, this precision is gained at the sacrifice of overall confidence.

The interval $(\bar{Y}_i - \bar{Y}_j) \pm \hat{\sigma}\sqrt{(m - 1)F_\alpha[(1/n_i) + (1/n_j)]}$ that we use for the Scheffé method may appear somewhat different in form from other confidence intervals presented in this text. For $m = 2$ groups, though, it reduces to the standard form. When $m = 2$, $df_1 = m - 1 = 1$ for the F distribution, and $F_\alpha = t^2_{\alpha/2}$, the square of the

*In general, the exact level at which they hold simultaneously cannot be specified. The Bonferroni multiple comparison procedure uses the t intervals but sets a very high level of confidence for each interval, so that the entire set applies simultaneously with at least the desired confidence. See Neter and Wasserman (1974, p. 480) for details.

t-value used for the t confidence interval. Thus, in that case, the Scheffé interval reduces to

$$(\bar{Y}_i - \bar{Y}_j) \pm \hat{\sigma} \sqrt{(2 - 1)t_{\alpha/2}^2 \left(\frac{1}{n_i} + \frac{1}{n_j}\right)} = (\bar{Y}_i - \bar{Y}_j) \pm t_{\alpha/2}\,\hat{\sigma} \sqrt{\frac{1}{n_i} + \frac{1}{n_j}}$$

the same formula as introduced earlier in this section.

13.3 ANOVA and Regression

In Chapters 11 and 12, we used the multiple regression model to describe the relationship between the mean of an interval variable and a collection of independent variables also of interval scale. The analysis of variance procedure introduced in Section 13.1 is used to study the relationship between the mean of an interval variable and the levels of a categorical variable that is of nominal measurement (or at least treated as nominal). We shall now see that the analysis of variance can also be viewed as a special case of a multiple regression analysis. In this case, artificial independent variables are introduced into the regression model to represent the different levels of the categorical variable.

Dummy Variables

As before, suppose that we wish to compare the mean of some interval variable Y across m levels of a categorical variable. We will set up a collection of variables, each designed to represent by its value whether an observation occurs in a particular category. To begin, suppose that $m = 4$. Let the variable denoted by Z_1 take on value 1 when observations are taken from the first of the four levels, and value 0 otherwise. Let the variable Z_2 take on value 1 when observations are taken from the second of the four levels, and value 0 otherwise. Similarly, let the variable Z_3 equal 1 when observations are taken from level 3 of the categorical variable, and 0 otherwise. That is, when $Z_1 = 1$, $Z_2 = 0$, and $Z_3 = 0$, the observation is from the first level. When $Z_1 = 0$, $Z_2 = 1$, and $Z_3 = 0$, the observation is from the second level. When $Z_1 = 0$, $Z_2 = 0$, and $Z_3 = 1$, the observation is from the third level. Finally, when $Z_1 = 0$, $Z_2 = 0$, and $Z_3 = 0$, the observation is from the fourth level. It is not possible for more than one of the Z variables to be nonzero for a particular observation. Table 13.5 summarizes the coding of these artificially defined variables for the four levels.

Table 13.5

Interpretation of Parameters and Dummy Variables in Model $E(Y) = \alpha + \beta_1 Z_1 + \beta_2 Z_2 + \beta_3 Z_3$

LEVEL	Z_1	Z_2	Z_3	MEAN OF Y	INTERPRETATION OF β
1	1	0	0	$\mu_1 = \alpha + \beta_1$	$\beta_1 = \mu_1 - \mu_4$
2	0	1	0	$\mu_2 = \alpha + \beta_2$	$\beta_2 = \mu_2 - \mu_4$
3	0	0	1	$\mu_3 = \alpha + \beta_3$	$\beta_3 = \mu_3 - \mu_4$
4	0	0	0	$\mu_4 = \alpha$	

We can determine from the values of Z_1, Z_2, and Z_3 which level an observation represents. For example, the combination ($Y = 36$, $Z_1 = 0$, $Z_2 = 0$, $Z_3 = 0$) implies that an observation of 36 is made on the interval response variable for a member in the fourth level. The artificial variables Z_1, Z_2, and Z_3 are called *dummy variables.* The dummy variables are used simply to denote the classification (not magnitude) of an observation on the independent variable. It is not necessary to set up a dummy variable for observations from the last (fourth) level of the classification, since those observations can be represented by values of 0 for the other three Z variables. Thus, it would be redundant to add a Z_4 dummy variable. Whereas it takes only one term to represent the linear effect of an interval variable in a regression model, $m - 1$ terms are needed to represent the m levels of a categorical variable.

Now, using the dummy variables just defined, let us consider the equation

$$E(Y) = \alpha + \beta_1 Z_1 + \beta_2 Z_2 + \beta_3 Z_3$$

For observations from the fourth level, $Z_1 = Z_2 = Z_3 = 0$, and the equation reduces to $E(Y) = \alpha + \beta_1(0) + \beta_2(0) + \beta_3(0) = \alpha$. The parameter α therefore represents the mean of the dependent variable for the fourth level. For observations from the first level, $Z_1 = 1$, $Z_2 = 0$, and $Z_3 = 0$, so $E(Y) = \alpha + \beta_1(1) + \beta_2(0) + \beta_3(0) = \alpha + \beta_1$ represents the mean for that level. Similarly, $\alpha + \beta_2$ represents the mean for the second level (let $Z_1 = 0$, $Z_2 = 1$, $Z_3 = 0$) and $\alpha + \beta_3$ represents the mean for the third level (let $Z_1 = Z_2 = 0$, $Z_3 = 1$). Since $\alpha + \beta_1$ is the mean for level 1 and α is the mean for level 4, the parameter β_1 represents the *difference between the means* of levels 1 and 4 on the dependent variable. Similarly, β_2 is the difference between the mean for level 2 and the mean for level 4, and β_3 is the difference between the mean for level 3 and the mean for level 4. So, the β-values represent differences between the means of the first three levels and the mean of the last level. The parameters of the regression model and their correspondence with the four means are summarized in Table 13.5.

This coding of dummy variables works because it allows the population means to take arbitrary values, with no assumed distances between groups. A coding such as $Z = 1$ for level 1, $Z = 2$ for level 2, $Z = 3$ for level 3, and $Z = 4$ for level 4 would not work, because the model $E(Y) = \alpha + \beta Z$ would then assume an ordering as well as equal distances between levels, and hence it would treat the nominal variable as if it were interval.

Regression for Comparing Means

The null hypothesis in the analysis of variance F test is H_0: $\mu_1 = \mu_2 = \mu_3 = \mu_4$ for the case of $m = 4$ levels. Now, if H_0 is true, then $\mu_1 - \mu_4 = 0$, $\mu_2 - \mu_4 = 0$, and $\mu_3 - \mu_4 = 0$. Since $\mu_1 - \mu_4 = \beta_1$, $\mu_2 - \mu_4 = \beta_2$, and $\mu_3 - \mu_4 = \beta_3$, the null hypothesis H_0: $\mu_1 = \mu_2 = \mu_3 = \mu_4$ is equivalent to H_0: $\beta_1 = \beta_2 = \beta_3 = 0$ in the regression model $E(Y) = \alpha + \beta_1 Z_1 + \beta_2 Z_2 + \beta_3 Z_3$. If all of the β-values in that model equal 0, then the mean of the interval variable equals α for each of the four levels. By setting up the dummy variables as we have, then, we can perform the analysis of variance test by conducting the F test of H_0: $\beta_1 = \beta_2 = \beta_3 = 0$ for this multiple regression model. Also, the sample means can be determined from the terms a, b_1, b_2, and b_3 in the prediction equation $\hat{Y} = a + b_1 Z_1 + b_2 Z_2 + b_3 Z_3$ that is obtained from using the least squares method to estimate the regression equation. Just as $\alpha = \mu_4$, so does $a = \bar{Y}_4$. Similarly, $b_1 = \bar{Y}_1 - \bar{Y}_4$, so $\bar{Y}_1 = a + b_1$; $b_2 = \bar{Y}_2 - \bar{Y}_4$, so $\bar{Y}_2 = a + b_2$; and $b_3 = \bar{Y}_3 - \bar{Y}_4$, so $\bar{Y}_3 = a + b_3$.

The assumption from regression analysis that the conditional distributions on Y about the regression equation are normal with constant standard deviation corresponds here to the assumption that the population distributions for the levels are normal, with the same standard deviation for each level. These are precisely the assumptions that were made in Section 13.1 for conducting the ANOVA F test.

In the general case in which there are m levels in the classification scheme, we can set up dummy variables for the first $(m - 1)$ levels and use the model $E(Y) = \alpha + \beta_1 Z_1 + \beta_2 Z_2 + \cdots + \beta_{m-1} Z_{m-1}$. For observations from level 1, $Z_1 = 1$ and the other Z-values are 0; for observations from level 2, $Z_2 = 1$ and the other Z-values are 0; and so forth for the other levels. For observations from the last level (level m), all Z-values equal 0. The parameter α represents the mean for level m, whereas the β-values represent the differences between the other means and the mean for level m. The null hypothesis H_0: $\mu_1 = \mu_2 = \cdots = \mu_m$ of identical means is equivalent to H_0: $\beta_1 = \cdots = \beta_{m-1} = 0$ in terms of the parameters of the regression model. In Section 11.4, we saw that the F statistic for that test is based on degrees of freedom terms $df_1 = k$ and $df_2 = N - (k + 1)$, where k is the number of independent variables in the regression model. For this model, there are $k = m - 1$ independent variables, namely, the $m - 1$ dummy variables. Hence, $df_1 = m - 1$ and $df_2 = N - m$, the values we used for the ANOVA F test in Section 13.1. In fact, the F statistic for the regression model test of H_0: $\beta_1 = \cdots = \beta_{m-1} = 0$ is identical in value to the F statistic given for the ANOVA test in Section 13.1.

Example 13.6   For the data in Table 13.4, there are $m = 4$ levels of the nominal variable, region. The regression model for the analysis of variance procedure is

$$E(Y) = \alpha + \beta_1 Z_1 + \beta_2 Z_2 + \beta_3 Z_3$$

We artificially set the values of the dummy variables so that only $Z_1 = 1$ for observations from the Northeast, only $Z_2 = 1$ for observations from the North central region, only $Z_3 = 1$ for observations from the South, and $Z_1 = Z_2 = Z_3 = 0$ for observations from the West. A portion of the printout that we might obtain with this regression model is shown in Figure 13.3.

The least squares equation is $\hat{Y} = 82.0 - 5.0Z_1 + 4.0Z_2 + 12.0Z_3$. Therefore, the estimated mean segregation index for the West is $a = 82.0$ ($Z_1 = Z_2 = Z_3 = 0$). The

Fig. 13.3   Printout for Regression Model $E(Y) = \alpha + \beta_1 Z_1 + \beta_2 Z_2 + \beta_3 Z_3$

SOURCE	DF	SUM OF SQUARES	MEAN SQUARE	F VALUE	PROB > F	ROOT MSE
REGRESSION	3	942.46	314.15	9.36	.0006	5.792
ERROR	22	738.00	33.55			
TOTAL	25	1680.46				

PARAMETER	ESTIMATE
INTERCEPT	82.0
Z1	-5.0
Z2	4.0
Z3	12.0

estimated mean for the Northeast is $a + b_1 = 82.0 - 5.0 = 77.0$, that for the North central is $a + b_2 = 82.0 + 4.0 = 86.0$, and that for the South is $a + b_3 = 82.0 + 12.0 = 94.0$.

Notice next the similarity between the top part of Figure 13.3 and the ANOVA table given in Table 13.3. What we have referred to as the between sum of squares in ANOVA is simply the regression sum of squares in the regression model, or the variability explained by the differences between the means. The within sum of squares is the sum of squared errors (SSE), the variability within the categories that is unexplained by including parameters in the model to account for the differences between the means. The sum of squared errors divided by its degrees of freedom gives the error mean square, which is identical to the within estimate $\hat{\sigma}^2 = 33.55$ of the variance of the measurements within the regions. Similarly, the regression mean square is the between estimate. The ratio of the regression mean square to the error mean square gives the F-value based on $df_1 = 3$ and $df_2 = 22$ for testing $H_0: \beta_1 = \beta_2 = \beta_3 = 0$. This hypothesis is equivalent to the hypothesis that the population means for the four regions are identical. Using this approach, we obtain exactly the same F-value as in Example 13.3. The P-value is printed out by the program as $P = .0006$.

■

One of the main reasons for showing how the analysis of variance procedure can be treated as a special case of a multiple regression analysis is the following. Many times the populations that we would like to compare are obtained as the cells of a cross-classification of two or more nominal variables. For example, the levels (white men, white women, black men, and black women) are obtained by the cross-classification of the variables race and sex. The procedure for comparing the mean of an interval variable across the levels of one of the categorical variables while controlling for another categorical variable is referred to as a *two-way analysis of variance.* In this chapter, we have so far considered only the one-way analysis, that is, a comparison across the levels of one nominal variable (ignoring other variables). The corresponding computations for the two-way (or higher-order) analysis are much more complicated, especially when the sample sizes are unequal. It is often easier to define dummy variables and to use a computer regression package for the analysis, unless a special package is available for the analysis of variance procedure. The next two sections of this chapter deal with these more complex methods, with special emphasis on the two-way analysis.

13.4 Two-Way Analysis of Variance

The one-way analysis of variance procedure presented earlier in this chapter is used to analyze the relationship between the mean of an interval variable and the levels of a single categorical variable. It is frequently of interest to perform this type of analysis while simultaneously controlling for one or more other variables. For example, we might be interested in comparing the mean segregation index for various regions of the country, controlling for size of city or type of economic base. In this section, we will consider such analyses for the case in which the control variable is categorical.

In Chapter 14, we will study an analogous procedure for the case in which the control variable is of interval level.

When two or more categorical variables are chosen as independent variables, the mean of the interval response variable can be compared over the levels of any one of these variables, controlling for the other(s). If there are k categorical variables, then the different groups to be compared arise from the k-dimensional cross-classification of levels of those variables. For example, if the segregation index is considered for all cities classified according to both region of country (Northeast, North central, South, West) and population size of city (over 150,000, under 150,000),* we would get the eight populations defined by the $2(4) = 8$ combinations of the levels shown in Table 13.6.

Table 13.6

A Two-Way Classification of the Mean Segregation Index by Region and Size of City

SIZE OF CITY	NORTHEAST	NORTH CENTRAL	SOUTH	WEST
Over 150,000	μ_{11}	μ_{12}	μ_{13}	μ_{14}
Under 150,000	μ_{21}	μ_{22}	μ_{23}	μ_{24}

We will use the notation μ_{ij} to represent the mean segregation index for all cities in the cell occurring in row i and column j of Table 13.6. For example, μ_{23} is the mean segregation index for cities in row 2 and column 3 (cities having a population of less than 150,000 that are in the South). For the two-way classification of means in Table 13.6, we could compare the segregation index across the four regions, controlling for size of city. That is, we could compare the regional means $\mu_{11}, \mu_{12}, \mu_{13}$, and μ_{14} on the segregation index for large cities; and we could compare the corresponding regional means $\mu_{21}, \mu_{22}, \mu_{23}$, and μ_{24} for small cities. Alternatively, we could compare the segregation index for the two sizes of cities, controlling for region, by comparing means within each column of the table.

Interaction   In our study of the relationships among three or more categorical variables in Section 10.2, and three or more interval variables in Section 12.2, we observed that the concept of *interaction* was important. In each case, the absence of interaction refers to the situation in which the nature of the relationship between the dependent variable and an independent variable does not change for different levels of the control variable(s). When there is no interaction, the summary of the relationships is much simpler than when it is present. The same remarks apply to the relationship between an interval response variable and a collection of categorical independent variables.

In order to understand the idea of interaction in the context of a two-way classification of means, consider the following illustrations. Suppose, first, that there is no interaction between size of city and region in their effects on the segregation index. Then, the difference in the population mean segregation index between each pair of regions is the same for both sizes of city. Also, the difference in the population mean

*For simplicity of illustration, we are dichotomizing the variable size of city. We could measure it more finely at an interval level, using the exact population size of the city; then we would use *analysis of covariance*, to be discussed in Chapter 14.

segregation index between the two city sizes is the same for each region of the country. Table 13.7 shows a set of means that illustrate no interaction. The difference in the mean segregation index between cities with population under 150,000 and cities with population over 150,000 is 5 for each region considered. Similarly, the difference in the mean segregation index between each pair of regions is the same for each size of city. The difference in the mean segregation index between the South and the West, for example, is 12 for cities of both sizes. We see, therefore, that the absence of interaction allows us to summarize by one number the difference in the means of the response variable between a particular pair of levels of one of the categorical variables, controlling for the other categorical variable.

Table 13.7

Means for a Two-Way
Classification with No
Interaction

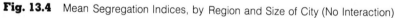

SIZE OF CITY	NORTHEAST	NORTH CENTRAL	SOUTH	WEST
Over 150,000	75	83	91	79
Under 150,000	80	88	96	84

In Figure 13.4, we have plotted the mean segregation scores from Table 13.7 for the levels of each of the categorical variables, within each level of the other categorical variable. The ordering of the levels on the horizontal axis is unimportant, since we are treating the categorical variables as nominal in scale. The absence of interaction is indicated by the parallel sequences of points for the various groups.

Fig. 13.4   Mean Segregation Indices, by Region and Size of City (No Interaction)

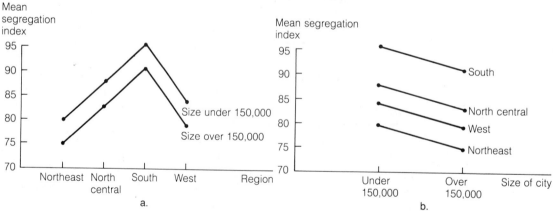

Table 13.8 and Figure 13.5 show a set of means for which there is interaction. The difference in the mean segregation index between cities with population sizes under 150,000 and over 150,000 is 10 for the Northeast, −10 for the North central, and 0 for the South and West. In this case, the difference in means could not be summarized by one number without obscuring the effect of the control variable region, since the difference depends on the region considered. If the sample sizes upon which the cell means are based happen to be equal, then the overall mean segregation index

Table 13.8
Means for a Two-Way Classification for Which Interaction Exists

SIZE OF CITY	NORTHEAST	NORTH CENTRAL	SOUTH	WEST
Over 150,000	75	85	95	90
Under 150,000	85	75	95	90

Fig. 13.5 Mean Segregation Indices, by Region and Size of City (With Interaction)

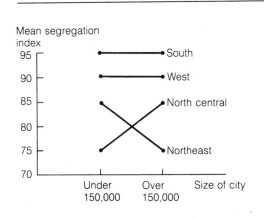

(ignoring region) is 86.25 for both sizes of city, leading to an overall difference in means of 0. In other words, a one-way analysis of the mean segregation index across the two levels of city size would very likely result in a conclusion that size of city has no effect. However, a two-way analysis treating region as a control variable would probably detect an effect of the size of the city within two of the regions, but having opposite directions.

General Hypotheses

In a one-way analysis of variance, the general hypothesis considered is that the population means on the response variable are identical in each of the categories of the independent variable. In a two-way analysis, there are three primary hypotheses. We can test the hypothesis that the population means are identical across the levels of the first categorical variable, controlling for the second categorical variable. For example, we could test that the mean segregation index is identical for each of the four regions, controlling for size of city. Table 13.9 contains a set of population means satisfying this null hypothesis.

Table 13.9
Mean Segregation Indices Identical Across Regions, Controlling for Size of City

SIZE OF CITY	NORTHEAST	NORTH CENTRAL	SOUTH	WEST
Over 150,000	80	80	80	80
Under 150,000	90	90	90	90

We can similarly test the null hypothesis that the population means are identical across the levels of the second categorical variable, controlling for the first. In terms of our example, this would be a test of whether the mean segregation index is identical for the two sizes of cities, controlling for region. Table 13.10 (page 418) gives a set of means satisfying this null hypothesis. If both of these hypotheses are true, then all of the cell means are equal.

Table 13.10

Mean Segregation Indices Identical Across Size of City, Controlling for Region

SIZE OF CITY	NORTHEAST	NORTH CENTRAL	SOUTH	WEST
Over 150,000	75	85	90	85
Under 150,000	75	85	90	85

It is not meaningful to consider a summary difference in means between two levels of one categorical variable, if that difference *varies* according to the level of the other categorical variable. For that reason, the usual approach in a two-way analysis of variance is to first test the hypothesis of no interaction, the third primary hypothesis. If that hypothesis is not rejected, we can then test the other two hypotheses. On the other hand, if there is evidence of important interaction, the means across one of the classifications should be compared by the level of the other classification. For instance, within each row we could compare the means for the levels of the column variable using a one-way analysis of variance.

The tests of the three primary hypotheses in a two-way analysis of variance are based on the assumptions that the distributions of scores in the populations corresponding to each cell of the cross-classification are normal, and that the standard deviations of the scores are identical for each cell. The formulas for the test statistics are very complicated except in the special case in which the sample sizes in all cells are equal. Since this is rarely the case for nonexperimental research, we shall omit the computational details for the two-way analysis of variance procedure. Instead, we shall see how a multi-way analysis can be conducted through the use of a multiple regression model incorporating dummy variables.

13.5 Two-Way ANOVA and Regression

A comparison of means over a two-way classification can be conducted by using a multiple regression model through the creation of dummy variables for the levels of the categorical variables. As an illustration, we will consider the relationship between the mean segregation index and the cross-classification of region of country and size of city. We will refer to the regions Northeast, North central, South, and West as levels 1, 2, 3, and 4, respectively, of the variable region, and we will refer to the city sizes over 150,000 and under 150,000 as levels 1 and 2, respectively, of the variable size of city. We use the symbol Z as a dummy variable to represent a level of region and the symbol U as a dummy variable to represent a level of size of city; that is,

$$Z_1 = \begin{cases} 1 \text{ if city is in Northeast} \\ 0 \text{ otherwise} \end{cases}$$

$$Z_2 = \begin{cases} 1 \text{ if city is in North central} \\ 0 \text{ otherwise} \end{cases}$$

$$Z_3 = \begin{cases} 1 \text{ if city is in South} \\ 0 \text{ otherwise} \end{cases}$$

All three Z-values equal 0 when the city is in the West. Also,

$$U_1 = \begin{cases} 1 \text{ if the city has more than 150,000 residents} \\ 0 \text{ if the city has less than 150,000 residents} \end{cases}$$

As in the one-way analysis, it would be redundant to include dummy variables for the last levels of the categorical variables.

Model Without Interaction

We can model the situation in which no interaction exists by the formula

$$E(Y) = \alpha + \beta_1 Z_1 + \beta_2 Z_2 + \beta_3 Z_3 + \delta_1 U_1$$

We are using the symbol δ_1 (delta) instead of β_4 for the regression coefficient of U_1. This is strictly for convenience so that the index of the coefficient agrees with the number of the level, the β-values for the first three levels of region, and δ_1 for the first level of city size.

To note the correspondence between the means μ_{ij} and the regression parameters, we substitute the various combinations of values for the dummy variables. To illustrate, for cities with population over 150,000 ($U_1 = 1$) in the South ($Z_1 = Z_2 = 0$, $Z_3 = 1$), the mean segregation index is

$$\mu_{13} = \alpha + \beta_1(0) + \beta_2(0) + \beta_3(1) + \delta_1(1) = \alpha + \beta_3 + \delta_1$$

The means for all eight combinations of region and size of city are shown in Tables 13.11 and 13.12. Notice that the difference in means between the first and second rows in Table 13.12 is δ_1 in each of the four columns. That is, δ_1 represents the difference in the mean segregation index between large cities and small cities, controlling for region. Hence, the null hypothesis that there is no difference between the two sizes of city in the mean segregation index, controlling for region, is just H_0: $\delta_1 = 0$.

Table 13.11 Cell Means for a Two-Way Classification with No Interaction

| SIZE OF CITY | REGION | DUMMY VARIABLES | | | | MEAN OF Y |
		Z_1	Z_2	Z_3	U_1	$\alpha + \beta_1 Z_1 + \beta_2 Z_2 + \beta_3 Z_3 + \delta_1 U_1$
Over 150,000	Northeast	1	0	0	1	$\mu_{11} = \alpha + \beta_1 + \delta_1$
Over 150,000	North central	0	1	0	1	$\mu_{12} = \alpha + \beta_2 + \delta_1$
Over 150,000	South	0	0	1	1	$\mu_{13} = \alpha + \beta_3 + \delta_1$
Over 150,000	West	0	0	0	1	$\mu_{14} = \alpha + \delta_1$
Under 150,000	Northeast	1	0	0	0	$\mu_{21} = \alpha + \beta_1$
Under 150,000	North central	0	1	0	0	$\mu_{22} = \alpha + \beta_2$
Under 150,000	South	0	0	1	0	$\mu_{23} = \alpha + \beta_3$
Under 150,000	West	0	0	0	0	$\mu_{24} = \alpha$

Table 13.12

Cell Means from Table 13.11

SIZE OF CITY	NORTHEAST	NORTH CENTRAL	SOUTH	WEST
Over 150,000	$\alpha + \beta_1 + \delta_1$	$\alpha + \beta_2 + \delta_1$	$\alpha + \beta_3 + \delta_1$	$\alpha + \delta_1$
Under 150,000	$\alpha + \beta_1$	$\alpha + \beta_2$	$\alpha + \beta_3$	α

The β terms represent the differences in the means between each of the first three regions and the last region (the West), controlling for size of city. For example, for each city size, the difference in the mean segregation index between the Northeast and the West is β_1, between the North central and the West is β_2, and between the

South and the West is β_3 (see Table 13.12). The β-values, then, are similar in their interpretations to the β-values we defined for the regression model for a one-way classification, except that the differences between the regions are given here controlling for size of city. Hence, the null hypothesis that there are no differences among the regions in the mean segregation index, controlling for size of city, can be expressed as $H_0: \beta_1 = \beta_2 = \beta_3 = 0$. If both $H_0: \beta_1 = \beta_2 = \beta_3 = 0$ and $H_0: \delta_1 = 0$ are true, then all eight of the cell means are equal, and their common value is α.

The two hypotheses of interest when there is no interaction could be tested with the F test studied in Section 12.3 for complete and reduced regression models. For example, the test of the hypothesis $H_0: \beta_1 = \beta_2 = \beta_3 = 0$ of no regional differences in the segregation index, controlling for city size, is identical to the procedure for comparing the models

$$E(Y) = \alpha + \beta_1 Z_1 + \beta_2 Z_2 + \beta_3 Z_3 + \delta_1 U_1$$

and

$$E(Y) = \alpha + \delta_1 U_1.$$

Example 13.7　In Section 13.1, we compared the four regions with respect to the segregation index, using a sample of $n = 26$ cities. In Table 13.13, we have also classified the cities according to population size. The sample means of the segregation index for the eight combinations of region and size of city are shown in that table. The data do not provide strong evidence of the existence of interaction, since the difference in the sample mean segregation index between each pair of regions is approximately equal for the two city sizes. A formal test of no interaction is given in the next subsection.

Table 13.13
Sample Means on
Segregation Index, by
Region and Size of City

SIZE OF CITY	NORTHEAST	NORTH CENTRAL	SOUTH	WEST
Over 150,000	Bridgeport Jersey City Providence	Chicago St. Paul Youngstown	Houston Miami Mobile	Denver Phoenix Portland Spokane
	$\bar{Y}_{11} = 75.0$	$\bar{Y}_{12} = 86.0$	$\bar{Y}_{13} = 94.67$	$\bar{Y}_{14} = 82.25$
Under 150,000	Erie Passaic White Plains	Battle Creek Lansing Waterloo	Amarillo Durham Orlando	Bakersfield Las Vegas Richmond Stockton
	$\bar{Y}_{21} = 79.0$	$\bar{Y}_{22} = 86.0$	$\bar{Y}_{23} = 93.33$	$\bar{Y}_{24} = 81.75$

Most analysis of variance or multiple regression computer programs will print out an ANOVA table similar to Table 13.14 for describing the results of the tests of the hypotheses

$$H_0: \beta_1 = \beta_2 = \beta_3 = 0 \quad \text{and} \quad H_0: \delta_1 = 0$$

Table 13.14
ANOVA Table for Two-Way Analysis of Segregation Index, by Region and Size of City, Assuming No Interaction

SOURCE	SUM OF SQUARES	DF	MEAN SQUARE	F-VALUE	PROB > F
Regions	942.462	3	314.154	8.96	.0005
Sizes	1.385	1	1.385	.04	.8444
Error	736.615	21	35.077		
Total	1,680.462	25			

The various sums of squares in the ANOVA table describe how much of the variability in the segregation scores is explained by each set of terms in the regression model. For example, the regions sum of squares is the amount of the variation accounted for by introducing the terms $\beta_1 Z_1 + \beta_2 Z_2 + \beta_3 Z_3$ into the model, once the other terms are already there. It represents the difference between the sum of squared errors when these terms are omitted and the sum of squared errors when these terms are included. There is a difference of three parameters in the size of the model in these two cases, so this sum of squares is based on three degrees of freedom. The variability not accounted for by the region and size of city terms is the sum of squared errors for the model, which has the same interpretation as SSE for a regression model. As usual, its number of degrees of freedom equals the total sample size minus the number of parameters in the regression model. In this case, this is $26 - 5 = 21$.

The mean square error, which is the sum of squared errors divided by its degrees of freedom, gives the best estimate of the variance of the population scores within each of the cells. In this case, it is

$$\hat{\sigma}^2 = \frac{SSE}{df} = \frac{736.615}{21} = 35.077$$

Each null hypothesis is tested by finding another estimate of the variance that is inflated if H_0 is not true. These estimates, listed in Table 13.14 under MEAN SQUARE, are obtained by dividing each sum of squares by its corresponding degrees of freedom. The F test statistics are obtained by taking the ratios of these estimates to $\hat{\sigma}^2$. The degrees of freedom for the F statistics are $df_1 =$ degrees of freedom for the numerator estimate, and $df_2 =$ degrees of freedom upon which $\hat{\sigma}^2$ is based (21, in this case). The P-value is the probability of getting at least as large an F-value as the observed one if H_0 were true.

The null hypothesis that there is no difference in the mean segregation index by region, controlling for city size, is H_0: $\mu_{11} = \mu_{12} = \mu_{13} = \mu_{14}$ and $\mu_{21} = \mu_{22} = \mu_{23} = \mu_{24}$ (see Table 13.11). In terms of the regression model, this is equivalent to H_0: $\beta_1 = \beta_2 = \beta_3 = 0$. The F test statistic is the ratio

$$F = \frac{\text{Regions mean square}}{\text{Error mean square}} = \frac{314.154}{35.077} = 8.96$$

based on $df_1 = 3$ and $df_2 = 21$, for which the P-value is $P = .0005$. There is strong evidence of a difference among the four regions on the mean segregation index, when controlling for population size of city.

Also, we could consider the null hypothesis that there is no difference in the mean segregation index between the two sizes of city, controlling for region. This hypothesis is H_0: $\mu_{11} = \mu_{21}$, $\mu_{12} = \mu_{22}$, $\mu_{13} = \mu_{23}$, and $\mu_{14} = \mu_{24}$, or in terms of the regression model, H_0: $\delta_1 = 0$. The F test statistic based on $df_1 = 1$ and $df_2 = 21$ is

$$F = \frac{\text{Sizes mean square}}{\text{Error mean square}} = \frac{1.385}{35.077} = .04$$

This gives $P = .8444$, so there is negligible evidence of a difference in the mean segregation index between city sizes, within each region.

The prediction equation for the no interaction model is $\hat{Y} = 82.23 - 5.0Z_1 + 4.0Z_2 + 12.0Z_3 - .46U_1$. The coefficient of U_1, $-.46$, is the estimated difference in the mean segregation index between large cities and small cities, for each region. The test of H_0: $\delta_1 = 0$ indicated that this difference is not statistically significant. The coefficient of Z_1, -5.0, is the estimated difference in the mean segregation index between the Northeast and the West, for each size of city. The coefficients of Z_2 and Z_3 give comparisons of North central and Southern regions to the West, respectively. These can be used to obtain differences for other pairs of regions. For instance, the estimated difference between the Northeast and Southern regions is $(-5.0) - (12.0) = -17.0$, for each size of city. Predicted means that satisfy the no interaction model can also be obtained for the various cells. For instance, for small cities in the South, $Z_1 = Z_2 = 0$, $Z_3 = 1$, $U_1 = 0$, so $\hat{Y} = 82.23 - 5.0(0) + 4.0(0) + 12.0(1) - .46(0) = 94.23$. ∎

Model with Interaction

The model we have considered thus far is not adequate when there is interaction. In Section 12.2, we noted that cross-product terms could be added to the multiple regression model to represent interaction. Here, as well, we can take cross-products of dummy variables to obtain a regression model that includes the effects of interaction. The appropriate model for a two-way classification of variables with four and two levels is

$$E(Y) = \alpha + \beta_1 Z_1 + \beta_2 Z_2 + \beta_3 Z_3 + \delta_1 U_1 + \gamma_1 (U_1 Z_1) + \gamma_2 (U_1 Z_2) + \gamma_3 (U_1 Z_3)$$

The γ (gamma) parameters are the regression coefficients of the cross-product terms that represent the degree of interaction. It is not necessary to take cross-products of dummy variables from levels of the same categorical variable, such as $Z_1 Z_2$, $Z_2 Z_3$, and $Z_1 Z_3$. This is because no more than one Z can be nonzero for any observation, since an observation cannot be in more than one level of the categorical variable. Hence, all such cross-products would equal 0. The null hypothesis of no interaction for this example is H_0: $\gamma_1 = \gamma_2 = \gamma_3 = 0$. If this hypothesis is not rejected, then we can proceed to the tests of H_0: $\beta_1 = \beta_2 = \beta_3 = 0$ and H_0: $\delta_1 = 0$ discussed previously for the model that assumes no interaction.

Table 13.15 is an ANOVA table for the model that allows interaction in the effects of region and size of city on the segregation index. The interaction mean square is an estimate of σ^2 based on

$$\frac{\text{Interaction SS}}{\text{df}} = \frac{25.782}{3} = 8.594$$

The hypothesis of no interaction (H_0: $\gamma_1 = \gamma_2 = \gamma_3 = 0$) is tested using

$$F = \frac{\text{Interaction mean square}}{\text{Error mean square}} = \frac{8.594}{39.491} = .218$$

From the F distribution with $df_1 = 3$ and $df_2 = 18$, this gives $P = .883$, as listed under PROB $> F$ in Table 13.15. There is not strong evidence of interaction, and this test suggests that we can delete the cross-product terms from the model. Hence, we can feel justified in using the simpler model summarized in Table 13.14. In particular, since we can assume an absence of interaction, it makes sense to conduct the tests presented in Table 13.14 for the effects of region and size of city on the segregation index.

Table 13.15

ANOVA Table for Two-Way Analysis of Segregation Index, by Region and Size of City

SOURCE	SUM OF SQUARES	DF	MEAN SQUARE	F-VALUE	PROB > F
Regions	942.462	3	314.154	7.955	.0017
Sizes	1.385	1	1.385	.035	.8536
Interaction	25.782	3	8.594	.218	.8830
Error	710.833	18	39.491		
Total	1,680.462	25			

Comments   If any of the three null hypotheses are rejected, we next investigate what differences are responsible for the rejection. Usually, the greatest interest focuses on estimating differences between pairs of means—either between various cell means or between means of various pairs of levels of one of the categorical variables, controlling for the other one. If there appears to be a practically significant degree of interaction, then we cannot make summary comparisons between the levels of one of the categorical variables, controlling for the other. Instead, we could compare each pair of cell means. In practice, it is usually sufficient to compare all pairs of rows, within each column, or else all pairs of columns, within each row.

If the null hypothesis of no interaction is not rejected, it is not necessary to compare each pair of cell means. In Example 13.7, we would probably be interested only in estimating simultaneously the differences in the mean segregation index between each pair of regions, controlling for city size—a total of six comparisons. Multiple comparison procedures such as the Scheffé method for several-way analyses of variance are discussed by Neter and Wasserman (1974) and Scheffé (1959).

The analysis of variance examples we have given in this chapter use *fixed effects* models. By this term, we mean that we consider *all* the levels of certain categorical variables and test for differences among those levels. In some situations, we will have only a *sampling* of the levels. For example, in comparing different teaching methods for a sample of students, we might be interested in comparing mean scores across the levels of the variable, teacher. If we select a random sample of the available teachers from the population of interest in the experiment, we could call the factor teacher a *random effect,* since the differences among the levels of that variable on the response variable depend on which random sample of teachers is chosen. If the classification variables are a mixture of random and fixed effects, then the model used in conducting the analysis is called a *mixed* model. For the types of procedures studied in this chapter, the computations of sums of squares and degrees of freedom for the random and mixed models are identical to those given for fixed effects models. However, the construction of the test statistics differs for some of the tests. The reader is referred to Neter and Wasserman (1974, p. 616) for further details on these models.

When the data are obtained from an experiment, the type of analysis conducted depends on the design of that experiment. Experiments in which independent random samples are selected from each of the levels or combinations of levels of the classification variables are said to be based on a *completely randomized experimental design.* This design is commonly used for one-way analyses. Two-way analyses of variance often arise from what is referred to as a *randomized block design.* In that case, the researcher is primarily interested in differences among levels of one of the classification variables. The other classification is used as a control variable for improving precision by eliminating extraneous and possibly confounding variation. The levels of that control variable are referred to as *blocks.* For a detailed exposition of the linkage of analysis of variance procedures with experimental designs, see Kirk (1968) and Winer (1971).

13.6 Nominal Scales: Chi-Square as a Test of Homogeneity

Often we are interested in comparing several groups on a variable that is only nominal in level. For example, we might want to compare Puerto Ricans, Italian-Americans, Irish-Americans, and Mexican-Americans with respect to political party preference. Or we might be interested in comparing the counties of a state with respect to the representations of the major ethnic groups.

When the response variable is nominal, we can use a cross-classification table to compare the groups by contrasting the proportions of observations at the various levels of the response variable. The null hypothesis that the groups are identical in the proportional distributions on the dependent variable is equivalent to the null hypothesis that the response variable is statistically independent of the classification variable. Thus, to test whether several groups have identical distributions on a response variable having unordered categories, we can use the chi-square test of independence studied in Section 8.2. Since that test has already been discussed in detail, we will not review it here. When used to compare several groups on a nominal response variable, the chi-square test is referred to as a *test of homogeneity.*

If the null hypothesis in the chi-square test is rejected, we conclude that at least two of the groups differ in their distributions on the response variable. Further analysis could take several forms. We could use a nominal measure of association such as Goodman and Kruskal's tau (see Section 8.4) to describe the degree to which the response on the dependent variable is associated with the group membership of the individual. Alternatively, we could select a particular level of the response variable and compare the proportions of the various groups classified at that level. We might, for example, compare the proportions of Puerto Ricans, Italian-Americans, Irish-Americans, and Mexican-Americans who are Democrats. We could make the comparisons by obtaining confidence intervals for the differences in these proportions for each pair of groups. This procedure was discussed in Section 7.1 for the special case in which there were only two groups and the response variable was dichotomous. A somewhat modified procedure for making these many comparisons that takes into account the overall probability of making at least one incorrect inference is discussed by Goodman (1965). The idea behind that approach is very similar to the one introduced in Section 13.2 for comparing several means.

13.7
Ordinal Scales: Kruskal–Wallis Test

In this section, we introduce a procedure designed to detect differences among several groups on an ordinal response variable. This procedure could be used to test for differences among members of various religious denominations in their response to the question, "How important do you feel your religious faith is in your daily life?" The possible responses might be very important, somewhat important, not very important, and not at all important. Or, it could be used to compare adults classified by region of the country on the rating of the president's performance in office, with levels excellent, very good, good, fair, and poor. The procedure that will be applied to these problems is a generalization of the Wilcoxon test for comparing *two* groups on an ordinal characteristic. Before reading this section, you may wish to review the Wilcoxon test (Section 7.3), since the ideas and notation used here are very similar. In social science research, ordinal variables are usually categorical, so we will mainly discuss that case.

Ordinal Categorical Response

Suppose that we want to compare m groups on a response variable with levels consisting of c ordered categories. We will assume that we have independent random samples from each of the m groups. The sample sizes are denoted by n_1, n_2, ..., n_m. The most basic null hypothesis is that the response variable is independent of the group, in the sense that the m groups have identical distributions on the response variable. That is, this null hypothesis states that the population proportion making the first response is identical for all m groups, the population proportion making the second response is identical for all m groups, and so forth. The alternative hypothesis for the test is that at least two of the groups differ in the distribution of the response variable. The most commonly used procedure for testing these hypotheses is the *Kruskal–Wallis test.* The test statistic in that test is designed to detect differences among the groups as measured by the mean ranks. In other words, the Kruskal–Wallis test results in a rejection of H_0 if the differences among the sample mean ranks are sufficiently large.

As in Section 7.3 we will use transformations of the ranks, called *ridit scores,* which fall between 0 and 1 and are simpler to interpret. The ridits are calculated using the marginal distribution of the response variable (as shown in Section 7.3), and then the sample mean ridit $\bar{r}_i$ is calculated for each group, $i = 1, \ldots, m$. The null hypothesis implies that the population mean ridits are all equal.

The variability of the mean ridits $\{\bar{r}_1, \ldots, \bar{r}_m\}$ about the overall mean ridit of .5 can be summarized by the sum of squares $\sum_{i=1}^m n_i(\bar{r}_i - .5)^2$, where each squared deviation is weighted by the sample size upon which it is based. Let $N = n_1 + n_2 + \cdots + n_m$ denote the total sample size. The Kruskal–Wallis test statistic has the form

$$W = \frac{12N}{(N+1)T} \sum n_i(\bar{r}_i - .5)^2$$

In this formula, T denotes a correction factor for ties that equals

$$T = 1 - \frac{\sum_{i=1}^{c}(t_i^3 - t_i)}{N^3 - N}$$

where t_i is the number of observations tied at the ith level of the response variable. The factor T is usually close to 1.0 unless a large proportion of the observations occur in just one or two of the response categories. As long as none of the sample sizes $(n_1, \ldots, n_m)$ is especially small, the sampling distribution of the statistic W can be approximated by the chi-square distribution with $(m - 1)$ degrees of freedom (number of groups being compared, minus one), when H_0 is true. Relatively large values of W occur when there is more variation in the mean ridits than would be expected due to sampling error if the m population distributions were actually identical. The P-value is the probability of getting a value of W at least as large as the observed one, if H_0 were true. In other words, P equals the right-hand tail probability for the chi-square distribution with df $= m - 1$.

Example 13.8 A study is conducted to compare selected characteristics of high school graduates in Orange County, California, grouped according to the type of high school attended (public, private nondenominational, private religious affiliated). One of the response variables measured is the frequency of reading a daily newspaper, with categories of every day, most days, at least once a week, hardly ever, and never. A random sample of 200 high school graduates is divided into three groups according to type of high school attended, yielding three independent samples. The response distributions of the three groups are summarized in Table 13.16.

Table 13.16
Data for Example 13.8

TYPE OF HIGH SCHOOL	FREQUENCY OF READING A DAILY NEWSPAPER					
	Never	Hardly ever	At least once a week	Most days	Every day	Sample size
Public	34	30	17	29	40	150
Private, non-denominational	2	2	2	4	10	20
Private, religious affiliated	5	7	4	4	10	30
Total	41	39	23	37	60	200

One way of testing for a difference among the three types of high schools would be to use the chi-square test of independence, as discussed in Section 8.2. If the groups tend to differ in location on the response variable, however, that chi-square test is not the optimal one to use, since it treats *both* variables as nominal. There are more powerful procedures that use the ordering of the categories of the response variable. For example, if there are differences in location, the Kruskal–Wallis test is more likely than the chi-square test to result in rejection of the null hypothesis (see, e.g., Problem 33).

As in Section 7.3, let $\hat{\pi}_i$ denote the proportion of the sample that is in the ith response category of the ordinal variable. The ridit scores are

$$\hat{r}_1 = \frac{\hat{\pi}_1}{2} = \frac{1}{2}\left(\frac{41}{200}\right) = .1025$$

$$\hat{r}_2 = \hat{\pi}_1 + \frac{\hat{\pi}_2}{2} = \frac{41}{200} + \frac{1}{2}\left(\frac{39}{200}\right) = .3025$$

$$\hat{r}_3 = \hat{\pi}_1 + \hat{\pi}_2 + \frac{\hat{\pi}_3}{2} = \frac{41 + 39}{200} + \frac{1}{2}\left(\frac{23}{200}\right) = .4575$$

$$\hat{r}_4 = \hat{\pi}_1 + \hat{\pi}_2 + \hat{\pi}_3 + \frac{\hat{\pi}_4}{2} = \frac{41 + 39 + 23}{200} + \frac{1}{2}\left(\frac{37}{200}\right) = .6075$$

$$\hat{r}_5 = \hat{\pi}_1 + \hat{\pi}_2 + \hat{\pi}_3 + \hat{\pi}_4 + \frac{\hat{\pi}_5}{2} = \frac{41 + 39 + 23 + 37}{200} + \frac{1}{2}\left(\frac{60}{200}\right) = .8500$$

The mean ridit score for the 150 public high school graduates is

$$\bar{r}_1 = \frac{34(.1025) + 30(.3025) + 17(.4575) + 29(.6075) + 40(.8500)}{150} = .4797$$

Similarly, the other mean ridits are $\bar{r}_2 = .6328$ and $\bar{r}_3 = .5130$. The mean ridits indicate that individuals in the second sample (private nondenominational) tend to read the newspaper more frequently than others, since larger ridits correspond to higher levels on the ordinal variable.

Using these values, we can compute

$$\sum n_i(\bar{r}_i - .5)^2 = 150(.4797 - .5)^2 + 20(.6328 - .5)^2 + 30(.5130 - .5)^2 = .4193$$

The numbers of ties at the five levels of the response variable are $t_1 = 41$, $t_2 = 39$, $t_3 = 23$, $t_4 = 37$, and $t_5 = 60$, so

$$\sum_{i=1}^{5} (t_i^3 - t_i)$$

$$= (41^3 - 41) + (39^3 - 39) + (23^3 - 23) + (37^3 - 37) + (60^3 - 60)$$

$$= 406,860$$

The correction factor for ties is

$$T = 1 - \frac{\sum_{i=1}^{5} (t_i^3 - t_i)}{N^3 - N} = 1 - \frac{406,860}{200^3 - 200} = 1 - \frac{406,860}{7,999,800} = .949$$

Finally, the value of the Kruskal–Wallis test statistic is

$$W = \frac{12N}{(N+1)T} \sum n_i(\bar{r}_i - .5)^2$$

$$= \frac{12(200)}{(201)(.949)}(.4193) = 5.28$$

The number of degrees of freedom for the chi-square sampling distribution is $m - 1 = 3 - 1 = 2$. From Table C, $W = 5.28$ corresponds to $P < .10$ but $P > .05$. There is not enough evidence at the $\alpha = .05$ level to refute the null hypothesis that graduates of the three types of high schools have identical distributions on frequency of reading daily newspapers. ∎

Ungrouped Response Data

If the response variable is measured more finely than by ordered categories, the test statistic W defined above can still be used to test the null hypothesis that the m distributions are identical. If there are no ties, then the correction factor T reduces to 1.0. If the number of ties is very small relative to the sample size, then the value of T tends to be very close to 1.0. For cases (rare in the social sciences) in which there are no ties, the sample sizes are all less than or equal to 5, and the number of groups is $m = 3$, exact P-values have been tabulated for the W statistic. In other cases, the chi-square distribution with df $= m - 1$ is used as an approximation for the sampling distribution of W. The larger the sample size, the better the approximation tends to be. Details are provided in most nonparametric statistics books, including Lehmann (1975) and Siegel (1956).

Pairwise Comparisons of Groups

When we reject the null hypothesis in a Kruskal–Wallis test, we are concluding that at least two of the populations have different distributions on the response variable. In many studies, we would want to know, in addition, which groups are different from which other groups, and by how much. The sample mean ridits can be used to describe differences among the groups, as discussed in Section 7.3. For instance, $\bar{r}_3 - \bar{r}_1 + .5$ approximates the probability that a randomly selected individual from group 3 ranks higher than a randomly selected individual from group 1, for an underlying continuous response distribution.

If there are m groups, we could conduct a Wilcoxon test at a particular α-level for each of the $m(m - 1)/2$ pairs of groups in order to judge the significance of the mean ridit differences. In fact, the Wilcoxon test is simply the special case of the Kruskal–Wallis test applied to two groups. The W test statistic (with df $= 2 - 1 = 1$) equals the square of the z test statistic that we introduced in Section 7.3 for comparing two groups.*

If a Wilcoxon test for comparing two groups is conducted at a particular α-level, then there is a probability equal to α of rejecting the null hypothesis H_0 of identical

---

*In general, if a statistic z has the standard normal sampling distribution, then the square of that statistic, $W = z^2$, has the chi-square sampling distribution with df $= 1$.

distributions, if H_0 is in fact true. If the number of groups m is even of moderate size, there may be a very large number of pairwise comparisons to be made, in which case it would also be important to control the probability of making one or more Type I errors in all of these comparisons. For a complete treatment of pairwise multiple comparisons for these tests, see Lehmann (1975, pp. 238–247).

Summary

In this chapter, we have studied methods for comparing several groups according to their distributions on dependent variables of various levels of measurement. When the dependent variable is nominal, the *chi-square test of independence* can be used to test for differences among the groups. The *Kruskal–Wallis test* is designed to detect differences among group distributions on an ordinal variable. For interval dependent variables, the *analysis of variance* is used to test for differences among the group means. In addition, the analysis of variance technique can be extended to test for differences among groups that arise from the cross-classification of two or more categorical variables. The analysis of variance procedure was seen to be a special case of multiple regression analysis, with *dummy variables* as independent variables representing levels of the categorical variables. We have also seen in this chapter that *multiple comparisons* of the groups can be made to see *which* groups differ and the *extent* to which they differ. The statistical tests discussed in Sections 13.1, 13.6, and 13.7 for comparing several groups on a response variable are summarized in Table 13.17 (page 430).

In Chapters 9, 11, and 12, we discussed ways of modeling an interval dependent variable when the independent variables are interval in scale. This chapter has introduced the modeling of an interval dependent variable as a function of categorical independent variables through the use of dummy variables. In Chapter 14, we will introduce equations that include both categorical and interval independent variables in modeling an interval dependent variable.

Note

1. In Chapter 7 and in this chapter, most methods we have considered for comparing groups are based on *independent* random samples from those groups. Often, observations in the various samples are not independent, but rather statistically matched. For example, in a repeated measures study, the samples could consist of the same individuals considered at different times (such as before and after some experiment). Another example is a matched-pairs experiment. Different statistical procedures from the ones we have studied for independent samples must be used in those situations. For nominal and ordinal response variables, Cochran's Q test and Friedman's test, respectively, are designed to make comparisons for several dependent samples. These procedures are discussed by Siegel (1956). Analysis of variance methods for interval-scale repeated measures are discussed in detail in Winer (1971).

Table 13.17   Statistical Tests for Comparing Several Groups on a Response Variable

ELEMENT OF TEST	MEASUREMENT LEVEL OF RESPONSE VARIABLE		
	Nominal (Chi-square)	Ordinal (Kruskal–Wallis)	Interval (Analysis of variance)
1. Assumptions	Independent random samples	Independent random samples	Independent random samples, normal population distributions, equal population standard deviations
2. Hypotheses	H_0: Identical distributions (response independent of group) H_a: At least two distributions not identical	H_0: Identical distributions (mean ridits equal) H_a: At least two distributions not identical	H_0: Identical distributions (means equal: $\mu_1 = \mu_2 = \cdots = \mu_m$) H_a: At least two distributions not identical
3. Test statistic	$\chi^2 = \sum \dfrac{(f_o - f_e)^2}{f_e}$ Chi-square distribution, with df $= (r - 1)(c - 1)$ if at least 75% of $f_e \geq 5$, other $f_e \geq 1$.	$W = \dfrac{12N}{(N+1)T} \sum n_i(\bar{r}_i - .5)^2$ Chi-square distribution, with df $= m - 1$ if all $n_i > 5$.	$F = \dfrac{\text{Between estimate}}{\text{Within estimate}}$ Between estimate $= \dfrac{\text{BSS}}{m-1}$ Within estimate $= \dfrac{\text{WSS}}{N-m}$ F distribution, with $df_1 = m - 1$, $df_2 = N - m$
4. P-value	Right-hand tail area	Right-hand tail area	Right-hand tail area

Problems

1. The data in the table represent scores on the first quiz in a beginning French course (maximum score 10 points) for the following three groups of students:

Group A: Never studied foreign language before, but have good English skills
Group B: Never studied foreign language before; have poor English skills
Group C: Studied other foreign language

A	B	C
4	1	9
6	5	10
8		5

Assuming that the students in this course are a random sample of all ninth-grade students taking this beginning course, conduct a statistical test that can be used to investigate whether the three populations represented would have different means on this quiz.

2. Set up the ANOVA table for the results in Problem 1, and interpret the results.

3. A psychologist wants to compare the mean amount of time of REM sleep for subjects under three conditions. She uses three groups of subjects, with four subjects in each group. Partial results of the analysis are given in the accompanying table.

$N = 12$
$m = 3$

SOURCE	SUM OF SQUARES	DF	MEAN SQUARE	F	PROB > F
Between	72	2	36	4	2.95
Within	81	9	9		
Total	153	11			

a. Fill in the blanks in the ANOVA table.
b. Interpret the result of the F test. CAN not reject at $\alpha = .05$
c. Set up dummy variables that could be incorporated into a regression model so that the F test could be performed using regression techniques.
d. Refer to part c and give the prediction equation that would be obtained in fitting this regression equation, if $\bar{Y}_1 = 12$, $\bar{Y}_2 = 15$, $\bar{Y}_3 = 18$.

4. In a study of attitudes of Protestant clergy on various matters, one of the variables is an index of political conservatism, which is developed from responses to a series of questions. The scores for random samples of six clergy from three of those denominations are given in the table at the top of the next page.

LUTHERAN	METHODIST	PRESBYTERIAN
10	5	0
40	20	15
41	43	37
53	50	38
62	75	65
88	80	70

a. Use a computer package for one-way analysis of variance to analyze whether there are differences among the denominations in the mean value of this index.
b. Interpret the result of the test, if $\alpha = .05$.

5. A geographer wants to compare residential lot sizes in four quadrants of a city. To do this, a random sample of 300 records is taken from a city file on home residences, and the lot sizes (in thousands of square feet) are recorded by quadrant. The ANOVA table is for a comparison of mean lot sizes for the northeast (NE), northwest (NW), southwest (SW), and southeast (SE) quadrants of the city.

SOURCE	SUM OF SQUARES	DF	MEAN SQUARE	F	PROB > F
Between	2,700	3	——	——	——
Within	1,480	296	——		
Total	4,180	299			

a. Find the F test statistic for testing $H_0: \mu_1 = \mu_2 = \mu_3 = \mu_4$, and report the P-value. Interpret the result of the test.
b. Suppose that the mean lot sizes (in thousands of square feet) for the NE, NW, SW, and SE quadrants are 8, 15, 11, and 9, respectively, based on sample sizes of $n_1 = 100$, $n_2 = 100$, $n_3 = 50$, and $n_4 = 50$. Find the overall mean $\bar{Y}$, and verify the value given for the between sum of squares in the ANOVA table.
c. Find the square root of the mean square in the WITHIN row of the table, and interpret its value.

6. Refer to Problem 5. Find simultaneous 95% confidence intervals for the pairwise differences in means, using the sample mean values given in part **b.** Interpret the intervals.

7. A consumer protection group decides to compare three different types of front bumpers that have been developed for a particular model of automobile. A test is conducted by driving an automobile of that model into a brick wall at 10 miles per hour. Due to the potentially large costs involved, only two tests are run with each bumper type so that only six vehicles need to be used. The results of the test are expressed in terms of the amount of damage to the car, as measured by the repair costs (in hundreds of dollars).

BUMPER A	BUMPER B	BUMPER C
1	2	11
3	4	15

Conduct a test of the hypothesis that the mean repair costs are the same for the three types of bumpers. Report the P-value.

8. Set up the ANOVA table for the results in Problem 7.

9. Refer to Problem 7. Obtain simultaneous confidence intervals for the differences in mean repair costs for each pair of bumpers, using a .95 confidence coefficient. Interpret the results, and give a diagram that indicates which types of bumpers (if any) are judged to be different in mean repair cost.

10. Refer to Problem 7.
a. Set up the regression model with dummy variables that corresponds to that analysis.
b. Show the regression printout (including the estimated regression parameters) that would be obtained from fitting this model.

11. A research project involves the study of several aspects of family life in a Latin American country. For the random sample of 43 families studied, 22 families lived in large cities, 8 lived in small towns, and 13 were rural. The mean family sizes for each of these groups were 5.3, 5.0, and 7.5, respectively. The estimated common standard deviation of family size for the three groups was 3.0.
a. Use the Scheffé method to obtain 95% simultaneous confidence intervals for the differences between the mean family sizes for each pair of residential groups.
b. Suppose that we obtained *separate* 95% confidence intervals for the differences between each pair of means. Would these be wider or narrower than the intervals obtained in part **a**? Why would they not be identical to those intervals?
c. Draw a diagram indicating which pairs of residential types (if any) are significantly different in mean family size, according to the results in part **a**.

12. Explain carefully the difference between the following:
a. A probability of Type I error of .05 for a single comparison of two means
b. A multiple comparison error rate of .05 for comparing all pairs of means

13. Suppose that four randomly selected groups of five individuals each were used in an experiment. Furthermore, imagine that the overall sample mean was 60.
a. What would the data be like if the F test resulted in $F = 0$?
b. What would the data be like if $F = \infty$?

14. A comparison is made of the mean level of contributions to political campaigns made by registered Democrats and registered Republicans in a particular state.
a. Write a regression equation that can be used for this purpose, and interpret the parameters in the model.
b. Explain how, in the context of regression analysis, one can test the null hypothesis of equal mean contributions for Democrats and Republicans.

15. Refer to Problem 5.

a. Set up dummy variables that could be incorporated into a regression model so that the *F* test could be performed using regression techniques.

b. State the regression model that incorporates the dummy variables in part **a**, and interpret the parameters of that model.

c. Give the prediction equation that would be obtained in fitting this regression equation to the data.

d. Give the regression printout that would be obtained in the above analysis.

16. Use a computer package to produce the one-way ANOVA results reported in Example 13.3.

17. A census survey reported the accompanying estimates of mean personal income in the United States in 1981, classified by race and sex. Do you think the two-way ANOVA model that assumes no interaction could adequately describe these data? Why or why not?

		RACE		
		White	*Black*	*Spanish Origin*
SEX	*Men*	$17,195	$10,531	$12,324
	Women	$7,519	$6,728	$6,389

Source: *Statistical Abstract of the United States 1984,* Table 773.

18. Construct a numerical example of the means of an interval variable for a two-way classification under the following conditions:

a. Row effects only are present.

b. Row and column effects, but no interaction effects, are present.

c. Row, column, and interaction effects are all present.

d. Row, column, and interaction effects are all absent.

19. Suppose that the null hypothesis of equality of means across the categories of one of the variables in a two-way classification were rejected in a two-way analysis of variance. Does this imply that the corresponding hypothesis would be rejected in a one-way analysis of variance *F* test, if the data were collapsed over the levels of the second variable? Why?

20. Suppose that the means were equal across the categories of a variable in a one-way analysis of variance. Does this imply that they are equal across those categories, *within* each level of another classification in a two-way analysis of variance? Why?

21. Write the regression model corresponding to a comparison of means over a two-way classification with three levels for each variable under the following conditions:

a. There is no interaction.

b. There is interaction.

22. Consider the regression model $E(Y) = \alpha + \beta Z + \delta U + \gamma(UZ)$, where Y = income (thousands of dollars), $Z = 1$ for men and 0 for women, $U = 1$ for whites and 0 for blacks.

a. Suppose that, in the population, $\gamma = 0$. Interpret β and δ in the regression equation.

b. The prediction equation for a certain sample is $\hat{Y} = 10 + 2Z + 3U + 4UZ$. Find the predicted mean income for each of the four sex–race combinations.

23. Use a computer package to fit the no interaction model to the data discussed in Section 13.5, and verify the results given there.

24. Use a computer package to fit the interaction model to the data discussed in Section 13.5. Find the eight estimated cell means, and compare them to the actual sample means.

25. Consider the accompanying table showing the results for an analysis of variance conducted on the response variable depression index and the categorical variables sex and marital status (married, never married, divorced).

SOURCE	SUM OF SQUARES	DF	MEAN SQUARE	F-VALUE	PROB > F
Sex	100	1	100	5.56	p < .05
Marital status	200	2	100	5.56	p < .01
Interaction	100	2	.50	2.78	p > .05
Error	3,600	200	18		
Total	4,000	205			

$$n = 206$$

a. Give the regression model corresponding to this analysis.
b. Give the sample size for the study and fill in the blanks in the ANOVA table.
c. Interpret the result of the F test for no interaction.

26. Refer to Problem 10 in Chapter 7. Suppose further investigation reveals that the 25 women who are in the humanities and social science division of the college have a mean salary of $26,600, whereas the other five who are in the mathematics and natural science division have a mean salary of $29,000. On the other hand, the 20 men who are in the humanities and social science division have a mean salary of $26,400, and the 30 men in the mathematics and natural science division have a mean salary of $28,733.

a. Construct a table of sample mean incomes for the 2×2 cross-classification of sex and division of college. Show that the cell means are consistent with the overall means for men and women presented in Problem 7.10.

b. Discuss how the results of a one-way (descriptive) comparison of mean incomes by sex would differ from the results of a two-way comparison of mean incomes by sex, controlling for division of college. [*Note:* This reversal with respect to which sex has the higher mean salary, according to whether division of college is controlled, is an example of *Simpson's paradox*. See Section 10.3 and Problem 10.18.]

27. A random sample of 26 female students at a major university were surveyed about their attitudes toward abortion. Each received a score on abortion attitude according to how many from a list of eight possible reasons for abortion she would accept as a legitimate reason for a woman to seek abortion. Thus, the higher the score, the more favorable the person was toward abortion as an option in a variety of circumstances. The students were classified as "fundamentalist" or "non-fundamentalist" in their religious beliefs. They were also classified according to their church attendance frequency, "frequent" (more than once a month) or "infrequent." The 26 abortion attitude scores, classified by religion and frequency of church attendance, are given in the accompanying table. Using a computer package, analyze the data. Give your findings in the form of a short report, indicating the models fitted, hypotheses tested, and interpretations that follow from your inferences.

| | | RELIGION | |
		Fundamentalist	Nonfundamentalist
CHURCH ATTENDANCE	Frequent	0, 3, 4, 0, 3 2, 0, 1, 1	2, 5, 1, 2 3, 3
	Infrequent	4, 3, 4	6, 8, 6, 4 6, 3, 7, 4

Select the best response(s) in Problems 28–32.

28. The Wilcoxon test is to the Kruskal–Wallis test as the two-sample test for comparing means is to:
a. The regression test that a partial correlation is 0.
b. The one-way ANOVA F test.
c. Three-way ANOVA.
d. The chi-square test.

29. Analysis of variance and regression are similar in the sense that:
a. They both assume an interval dependent variable.
b. They both have F tests for testing that the dependent variable is statistically independent of the independent variable(s).
c. For inferential purposes, they both assume that the dependent variable Y is normally distributed with the same standard deviation at all combinations of levels of the independent variable(s).
d. They both can be regarded as ways of partitioning the variation in Y into "explained" and "unexplained" components.

30. In one-way ANOVA, we have relatively more evidence that $H_0: \mu_1 = \cdots = \mu_m$ is false:
a. The smaller the "between" variation and the larger the "within" variation.
b. The smaller the "between" variation and the smaller the "within" variation.
c. The larger the "between" variation and the smaller the "within" variation.
d. The larger the "between" variation and the larger the "within" variation.

31. After the rejection of H_0: $\mu_1 = \mu_2 = \mu_3 = \mu_4$ in a one-way ANOVA, the Scheffé multiple comparison method is used to obtain simultaneous 95% confidence intervals for the differences between the six pairs of means. Then:
a. For each confidence interval, there is a .95 chance that it contains the true difference.
b. The probability that all six confidence intervals are correct is .70.
c. The probability that all six confidence intervals are correct is .95.
d. The probability that all six confidence intervals are correct is $(.95)^6$.
e. The probability is .05 that at least one of the confidence intervals does not contain the true difference.
f. The Scheffé confidence intervals are wider than the ones obtained by calculating a separate 95% confidence interval for each difference.

32. Interaction terms are needed in a two-way ANOVA model when:
a. Each pair of variables is associated.
b. Both independent variables have significant effects in the model without interaction terms.
c. The difference in means between two levels of one independent variable varies greatly among the levels of the other independent variable.
d. The mean square for interaction is huge compared to the mean square error.

33. The accompanying data represent observations on the degree of participation in school sports for random samples of 30 boys and 30 girls in middle schools.

| | PARTICIPATION | | |
	Low	Moderate	High
Boys	7	10	13
Girls	13	10	7

a. Test for a difference between boys and girls in participation, using the chi-square test (Section 8.2) to test whether participation is independent of sex (use the $\alpha = .10$ level).
b. Now test for a difference using the Kruskal–Wallis test, which is designed to exploit the ordering of the participation levels (use the $\alpha = .10$ level).
c. Compare the results of parts **a** and **b**, and discuss why it is generally inappropriate to use the chi-square test of independence if one or both variables are ordinal.
d. Give the median response for each group. Why is the median insufficient here as a summary measure?

34. A random sample of 100 adults is selected in California, in order to survey opinion about whether the amount of state funding of higher education should change. The respondents are also classified according to their political party affiliations. The frequencies are given in the table at the top of the next page.
a. Find the median response for each political party affiliation.
b. Test the null hypothesis of no difference in opinion distributions among the three political party affiliations, and report the P-value.

| | OPINION ON STATE FUNDING OF HIGHER EDUCATION | | | | | TOTAL |
	Greatly decrease	Slightly decrease	Remain same	Slightly increase	Greatly increase	
POLITICAL Republican	5	8	5	2	0	20
PARTY Democrat	2	7	10	14	7	40
AFFILIATION Independent	4	8	14	10	4	40
TOTAL	11	23	29	26	11	100

c. Use the sample mean ridits to help interpret the differences among the political parties in their opinion distributions.

35. Refer to Example 13.8. Use the Kruskal–Wallis test to compare graduates of public schools with graduates of private, nondenominational schools, in terms of frequency of reading a daily newspaper. (Note that the ridits and their means must be recomputed for the 2 × 5 table, and that this test is equivalent to the Wilcoxon test, since there are only two groups.)

*36. As part of a statewide analysis of job earnings in California, an analysis of variance is conducted to compare mean personal annual earnings in ten counties of the state and for four types of jobs.

a. How many pairs of means are there to be compared in a one-way analysis of earnings across counties?

b. How many pairs of means are there to be compared in a one-way analysis of earnings across types of jobs?

c. Suppose that there is interaction between county and type of job with respect to earnings. Then, for the two-way classification of mean income by county and type of job, how many pairs of (cell) means are there to be compared?

*37. Refer to Problem 34. Using the $\alpha = .01$ level, compare each pair of political parties using the Wilcoxon test. Use a connecting line diagram of the groups ordered according to their mean ridits to indicate which (if any) pairs are not significantly different.

*38. Show that the within estimate $\hat{\sigma}^2$ of the variance for a one-way classification may be expressed as

$$\hat{\sigma}^2 = \left(\frac{n_1 - 1}{N - m}\right)\hat{\sigma}_1^2 + \left(\frac{n_2 - 1}{N - m}\right)\hat{\sigma}_2^2 + \cdots + \left(\frac{n_m - 1}{N - m}\right)\hat{\sigma}_m^2$$

where $\hat{\sigma}_1^2, \hat{\sigma}_2^2, \ldots, \hat{\sigma}_m^2$ are the point estimates from the separate samples. Based on this formula, show that $\hat{\sigma}^2$ can be interpreted as a weighted average of these separate estimates, with weights depending on the separate sample sizes.

*39. Suppose you were given the estimated mean and standard deviation and the sample size for each of five groups. Could you carry out an analysis of variance F test for these five groups, or would you need more information?

*40. Suppose that 95% confidence intervals are formed in five different situations.

   a. Assuming that the results of the intervals are statistically independent, find the (a priori) probability that *all* five intervals contain the parameters they are designed to estimate. What is the probability that at least one of the intervals is in error? [*Hint:* Use the binomial distribution, discussed in Section 6.5.]

   b. What confidence coefficient must be used for each interval so that the probability that all five of the intervals contain the parameters equals .95?

*41. Show how a regression model could be set up for the analysis of mean income in a factory over a three-way classification of sex (male, female), race (white, black), and type of job (assembly-line worker, janitorial). Interpret the parameters in the model. Assume that there is no interaction.

Bibliography

Goodman, L. A. (1965). "On Simultaneous Confidence Intervals for Multinomial Proportions." *Technometrics*, 7: 247–254.

Kirk, R. E. (1968). *Experimental Design: Procedures for the Behavioral Sciences.* Belmont, Calif.: Brooks/Cole. Chaps. 1–5.

Lehmann, E. L. (1975). *Nonparametrics: Statistical Methods Based on Ranks.* San Francisco: Holden-Day. Chap. 5.

Neter, J. and W. Wasserman (1974). *Applied Linear Statistical Models.* Homewood, Ill.: Richard D. Irwin.

Scheffé, H. (1959). *The Analysis of Variance.* New York: Wiley. Chap. 10.

Siegel, S. (1956). *Nonparametric Statistics for the Behavioral Sciences.* New York: McGraw-Hill. Chap. 8.

Taeuber, K. E. and A. F. Taeuber (1965). *Negroes in Cities.* Chicago: Aldine.

Winer, B. J. (1971). *Statistical Principles in Experimental Design.* New York: McGraw-Hill.

CHAPTER 14

Comparison of Several Groups While Controlling for a Covariate

Contents

We introduced regression analysis in Chapters 9, 11, and 12 as a technique for describing the relationship between an interval dependent variable and one or more interval independent variables. In Chapter 13, we observed that regression techniques could be used to model the relationship between an interval dependent variable and one or more categorical independent variables in the analysis of variance procedure. In this chapter, we will introduce a procedure that can be viewed as a combination of analysis of variance (where the independent variable is categorical) and standard regression analysis (where the independent variable is interval). This method, which is often referred to as *analysis of covariance*, is used for modeling an interval dependent variable in terms of both interval level *and* categorical independent variables.

A covariance analysis would be appropriate, for example, in modeling a mental health index as a function of a life events index, socioeconomic status, age (interval variables), race, and sex (nominal variables). Covariance analyses are especially useful when we wish to compare several groups (treated as levels of a categorical variable) on some interval dependent variable Y, while simultaneously controlling for an interval variable, which is referred to as the *covariate*. For example, in comparing income by sex in some society, we might wish to control for the effects of differing levels of education or job experience between men and women. Or, in comparing grade point average by race for students completing their first year in a particular university, it might be important to control for their college entrance exam scores or their high school grade point averages. In one-way ANOVA, interval-scale covariates are ignored, rather than controlled. If a covariate is correlated with Y and if some groups have higher values than others on the covariate, then the results of the covariance analysis will differ from the results of the analysis of variance procedure. For instance, job experience is usually correlated with income, so if men tend to have higher levels of experience than women at a particular job, the results of a comparison of income by sex will depend on whether we control for experience.

In our treatment of the analysis of covariance, for simplicity we deal with the case in which there are only two independent variables, one categorical and one interval. In addition, we consider only the case in which the relationship between the interval variables is linear. In the first section, we describe the two different emphases that the analysis may take—one in which the interval variable is treated as a control variable, and the other in which the categorical variable is treated as a control variable. In Sections 14.2 and 14.3, we see that a regression model with dummy variables can be used to represent the system of variables, with the exact form of the model depending on whether there is interaction. In Section 14.4, the two primary tests in an analysis of covariance are introduced in the context of testing hypotheses about the parameters of regression models. In Section 14.5, the interval variable is treated as the control variable, and we obtain adjusted means on the dependent variable for the various levels of the categorical variable, adjusted to remove or control the effects of the interval variable. In Section 14.6, the categorical variable is treated as the control variable. There, we describe the degree of association between the interval variables, controlling for the categorical variable.

14.1 Comparing Adjusted Means and Comparing Regression Lines

The primary emphasis in an analysis of covariance can be in either of two directions. In the first of these, the emphasis is on a regression-type analysis. We consider the form of the regression equation between interval variables Y and X within each of the levels of the categorical variable, with the categorical variable in effect being treated as a control variable. In the second type of analysis, the emphasis is more like that of analysis of variance. Here, the main interest is in comparing the means of the dependent variable for the groups defined by the various levels of the categorical variable. In this approach, the interval independent variable is the control variable. Before introducing the technical details (which are the same in either case), we will discuss further the two types of emphases and the types of results that could occur.

Comparing Regression Lines

To illustrate the analysis of covariance with a regression emphasis, we will refer again to the relationship between the interval variables Y = segregation index and X = population size of city and the categorical variable region. In Sections 13.4 and 13.5, we artificially treated X as a categorical variable by dichotomizing it. With the analysis of covariance procedure, however, we can fully utilize the interval measurement of this variable. Now, suppose that we want to treat region as a control variable in analyzing the relationship between the segregation index and city population size. This is equivalent to looking at the relationship between X and Y within each region. Based on independent random samples of cities from each region, we could find the best-fitting straight line for each of the four separate sets of points, assuming linear relationships. We could then compare the relationships between the segregation index and city size for the four regions by comparing characteristics of the four lines.

Whenever we have considered systems of three or more variables in this text, we have seen that the notion of interaction plays a central role. In this context, no interaction means that the slope of the relationship between X and the mean of Y is the same for each level of the categorical variable. Equality of slopes implies that the regression lines are parallel (see Figure 14.1a). In the special case in which the Y-intercepts are also equal, each category can be represented by the same regression line (see Figure 14.1b).

Fig. 14.1 Regression Lines Between Interval Variables Y and X

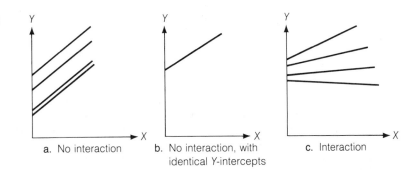

a. No interaction　　b. No interaction, with identical Y-intercepts　　c. Interaction

If the slopes of the regression lines are not the same for each level of the categorical variable, then there is interaction. If the rate of change of the mean segregation index as a function of population size varied according to region, for example, then the four regression lines would not be parallel (see Figure 14.1c). The analysis for comparing the regression equations first involves a check for interaction by testing whether the best-fitting straight lines for the observations from the various groups have significantly different slopes. If interaction exists, then we need to use separate lines with different slopes to best describe the system. If we find that the hypothesis of no interaction seems reasonable, then we can fit a collection of lines having identical slopes. In that case, the next step in the analysis is to check for equality of intercepts. In other words, we test to see whether all levels of the categorical variable can be represented by the same regression line between Y and X. Occasionally, it is also of interest to test whether X and Y are independent, controlling for the categorical variable. This corresponds to a test of whether the slopes of the regression lines are 0 for all categories.

As with other trivariate systems, the relationship between X and Y while controlling for a categorical variable may be different in substantial ways from the relationship in the absence of control. For instance, the association between X and Y could be spurious, in which case the association disappears when we control for the categorical variable. To illustrate, Figure 14.2 displays a set of points for which there is an overall positive relationship between Y and X when the control variable is ignored. Within each level of the control variable, however, the regression line relating Y to X is horizontal. The overall positive trend is due to the tendency for the levels with relatively high (low) scores on Y to have relatively high (low) scores on X also.

Fig. 14.2 A Spurious Relationship Between X and Y, Controlling for a Categorical Variable

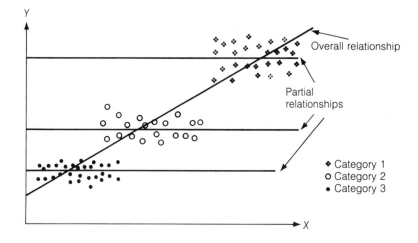

Comparing Means on Y, Controlling for X

Now, suppose that our primary goal is to compare the mean of Y across the levels of the categorical variable. If the interval variable X were ignored, we could do this by conducting a one-way analysis of variance. Instead of ignoring X, however, we can treat it as a control variable. As an illustration of this type of analysis, let us consider the relationship between yearly income (Y) and sex, controlling for years of experience (X) for individuals in a particular occupation. Based on a two-sample comparison of men and women in that occupation, suppose we conclude that the mean yearly income is higher for men than for women. If the occupation is such that yearly income tends to increase with experience, and if women have only recently begun to enter that occupation in any substantial numbers, we might study whether the observed difference in incomes can be explained by differences in experience. Hence, we might compare mean incomes for men and women having equal levels of experience. This analysis involves adjusting the sample mean incomes so that they reflect the expected differences if the men and women had the same average experience. That is, controlling for experience corresponds to making an adjustment in the observed mean incomes so that we obtain values that reflect what we would expect if both sexes were equal, on the average, in experience.

If there is no interaction, then the regression line between income and experience for the male employees is parallel to that for the female employees. In that case, the difference between mean incomes for men and women is identical for all fixed values of X = number of years of experience. Therefore, the difference in the means, controlling for experience, can be summarized by one number. This is illustrated in Figure 14.3a, where the mean income for men is the same amount higher than the mean income for women at every experience level X. If the *same* regression line applies to both sexes, as shown in Figure 14.3b, the mean income for the two sexes is identical at each level of experience. In that case, there would be no difference in male and female incomes, controlling for experience.

Fig. 14.3 Y = Income by X = Number of Years Experience, and Sex

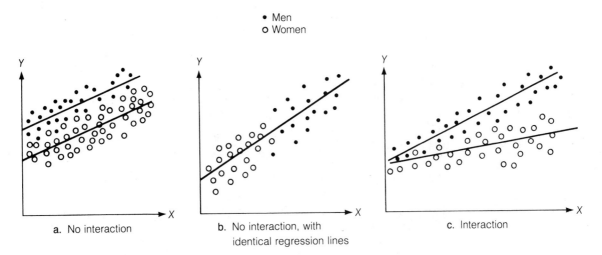

a. No interaction

b. No interaction, with identical regression lines

c. Interaction

If interaction exists, then the regression line for men would not be parallel to the regression line for women. In that case, the difference between the mean incomes of men and women varies according to the level of experience. For example, for the lines depicted in Figure 14.3c, the mean income for men is larger than the mean income for women at all experience levels, but the difference between the means increases as X increases. Thus, the discrepancy in mean incomes is relatively larger for individuals with more experience. When interaction is present, it is not possible to report one number for the difference in the mean incomes, controlling for experience. Instead, we must describe how the difference varies according to the value of the control variable.

The steps in the analysis parallel those described earlier, when the primary concern was to describe the regression line, controlling for the categorical variable. We first test for interaction. If the differences between the group means can be assumed to be the same at all X-values, then we can test whether these differences all equal 0. Also, to describe the effect of controlling X, we can calculate the adjusted means. These represent the means of Y for the various groups, adjusted or controlled for differing distributions of those groups on the X variable.

If the groups have considerably different distributions on X, then the results of the analysis of covariance procedure may differ considerably from the results of the corresponding analysis of variance in which X is ignored rather than controlled. For example, Figure 14.3b depicts a situation in which the overall mean income for men is greater than that for women. Hence, $H_0: \mu_1 = \mu_2$ would probably be rejected in a two-sample comparison of means. However, the reason for the difference in this case is that men have more experience. In fact, the same regression line fits the relationship between income and experience for both sexes. It appears that the mean incomes are equal, therefore, controlling for experience. Figure 14.3a, on the other hand, depicts a situation in which men have higher mean incomes, both ignoring *and* controlling for experience. Another possible occurrence is no difference in the overall means, but a difference when X is controlled.

The analysis of covariance is a useful technique for comparing the means of several groups by adjusting for differences in the distribution of a covariate X. However, it must be used with caution when those distributions on X are *substantially* different. The control process that we have been describing is a hypothetical one that infers what would happen *if* all groups had the same mean for the control variable X. If there is a great deal of difference among the groups in their distributions on X, the results of this control may be purely speculative. For example, suppose that the relationship between income and sex and experience is as shown in Figure 14.3b, where nearly all of the women have less experience than the men. In concluding that the means are equal, controlling for experience, we are assuming that the particular regression line shown also applies to women with more experience than those in the sample and to men with less experience. If it does not, then our conclusions are incorrect.

14.2 Analysis of Covariance Model Without Interaction Terms

We now consider how to use one regression model to represent simultaneously the linear relationship between interval variables Y and X within the m levels of a categorical variable. In this section, we discuss the special case in which there is no interaction, so that the regression lines are parallel. The model includes parameters for representing the (possibly) different Y-intercepts and the common slope of those parallel lines.

Quantitative and Dummy Independent Variables

If we were ignoring the interval variable X, the model relating Y to a categorical variable with m levels is simply the model corresponding to an analysis of variance. From Section 13.3, that model is expressed as

$$E(Y) = \alpha + \delta_1 Z_1 + \delta_2 Z_2 + \cdots + \delta_{m-1} Z_{m-1}$$

where $Z_1, \ldots, Z_{m-1}$ are dummy variables representing the first $(m - 1)$ levels and the δ-values represent differences in means between the various levels and the last (mth) one.* Now, in order to include the covariate X in the model, we adjust that formula slightly to get the analysis of covariance model

$$E(Y) = \alpha + \beta X + \delta_1 Z_1 + \cdots + \delta_{m-1} Z_{m-1}$$

where β describes the partial effect of X on the mean of Y for the m groups. The dummy variables are defined as in Chapter 13: $Z_1 = 1$ for observations from the first level of the categorical variable and $Z_1 = 0$ otherwise; $Z_2 = 1$ for observations from the second level and $Z_2 = 0$ otherwise; and so forth. For observations from the mth level, all $(m - 1)$ dummy variables equal 0. Thus, $Z_1, \ldots, Z_{m-1}$ are used in the regression equation to indicate the level into which an observation is classified.

When we successively set each Z equal to 1 with the other Z-values equal to 0, we generate the formulas for the m regression lines that relate X to the mean of Y within each of the m levels of the categorical variable. For example, letting $Z_1 = 1$ with the other Z-values equal to 0, we see that the relationship between X and the mean of Y within the first level is

$$E(Y) = \alpha + \beta X + \delta_1(1) + \delta_2(0) + \delta_3(0) + \cdots + \delta_{m-1}(0)$$
$$= (\alpha + \delta_1) + \beta X$$

In the first level, in other words, the mean of Y is linearly related to X with slope β and Y-intercept $\alpha + \delta_1$. Similarly, in the second level of the categorical variable, we get

$$E(Y) = \alpha + \beta X + \delta_1(0) + \delta_2(1) + \delta_3(0) + \cdots + \delta_{m-1}(0)$$
$$= (\alpha + \delta_2) + \beta X$$

---

*We use the symbol δ for the regression parameters here instead of β, since we will reserve the symbol β for the coefficient of the covariate X.

In general, in the ith level, the relationship between X and the mean of Y is a straight line with slope β and Y-intercept $\alpha + \delta_i$. All of the Z_i-values equal 0 in level m, and the regression equation in that level reduces to

$$E(Y) = \alpha + \beta X + \delta_1(0) + \cdots + \delta_{m-1}(0)$$
$$= \alpha + \beta X$$

Interpretation of Parameters

From the representation $E(Y) = \alpha + \beta X$ for the mth level, we see that α is the Y-intercept of the relationship between X and the mean of Y within that level. Since $\alpha + \delta_1$ is the corresponding Y-intercept for the first level, we see that δ_1 represents the difference in the Y-intercept between the first and the mth levels. In fact, since the regression lines are parallel, δ_1 is the vertical distance between those two regression lines *at any fixed value of X*. That is, controlling for X, δ_1 is the difference between the means of Y for the first and last levels. Similarly, δ_2 represents the difference between the means of Y in the second and the last levels, controlling for X, and so forth. Table 14.1 lists the separate equations and the parameter interpretations for the case of $m = 3$ levels.

Table 14.1

Summary of Equations and Parameters for Analysis of Covariance Model with No Interaction, When Categorical Variable Has $m = 3$ Levels

LEVEL	Y-INTERCEPT	SLOPE	MEAN AT FIXED X, $E(Y)$	DIFFERENCE FROM MEAN OF LEVEL 3, CONTROLLING FOR X
1	$\alpha + \delta_1$	β	$(\alpha + \delta_1) + \beta X$	δ_1
2	$\alpha + \delta_2$	β	$(\alpha + \delta_2) + \beta X$	δ_2
3	α	β	$\alpha + \beta X$	0

Figure 14.4 is a graphical display of the case in which $m = 3$ with $\delta_1 > 0$ and $\delta_2 < 0$, so that the first level has the highest mean and the second has the lowest mean, controlling for X. We need only one slope parameter, β, since the slope is the same for all levels of the categorical variable, for the model with no interaction.

Fig. 14.4 A Model with No Interaction, When the Categorical Variable Has $m = 3$ Levels

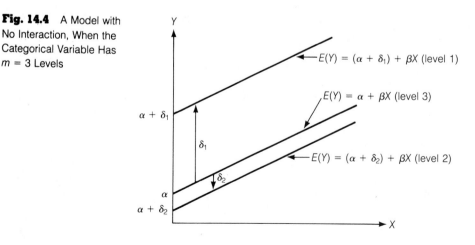

$E(Y) = (\alpha + \delta_1) + \beta X$ (level 1)

$E(Y) = \alpha + \beta X$ (level 3)

$E(Y) = (\alpha + \delta_2) + \beta X$ (level 2)

To summarize, in the linear model assuming no interaction, β is the slope of the regression lines between Y and X for all m levels. The δ-values represent the differences in the mean of Y between each level and the mth level, controlling for X. Hence, if all the lines are in fact identical, the δ parameters all equal 0, yielding the line $E(Y) = \alpha + \beta X$ for each of the m levels. The δ-values describe differences only between each level and the suppressed (mth) level, but it is also possible to describe differences between any two levels. To illustrate, the difference between the means of Y in the first and second levels, at a fixed X-value, is

$$[(\alpha + \delta_1) + \beta X] - [(\alpha + \delta_2) + \beta X] = \delta_1 - \delta_2$$

Hence, the differences in the regression coefficients of the dummy variables represent differences in the corresponding means, controlling for X. Again, since the lines are parallel, these differences are equal for all X-values.

Example 14.1 illustrates fitting this regression model to a set of data and the interpretations of the parameters. The data in the example will also be used to illustrate the analyses to be introduced later in the chapter.

Example 14.1   A researcher is interested in factors associated with fertility in a large Latin American city. Of particular interest is whether migrants from other cities or migrants from rural areas differ from natives of the city in their completed family sizes. The specific groups to be compared are (a) urban natives, those born in the city in which they now reside; (b) urban migrants, those born in other cities, but who moved to the present city after age 15; and (c) rural migrants, those born in rural areas who moved to the city after age 15. Since the fertility of women is known to be negatively related to educational level, and since educational level might differ among the three groups, it is decided to control that variable. Thus, the model to be tested uses migrant status (a categorical variable) and education (in years, an interval variable) to predict the interval dependent variable, fertility. In order to ensure comparability of the groups on fertility, only married women above age 45 are sampled, and their fertility is defined to be their total number of live births.

The set of observations in Table 14.2 (page 450) corresponds to a random sample of married women over age 45 who are classified by migrant status. There are $n_1 = 16$ urban natives, $n_2 = 18$ urban migrants, and $n_3 = 21$ rural migrants, for a total sample size of $N = n_1 + n_2 + n_3 = 55$. The mean fertility and education values for those observations are given in Table 14.3. As can be seen there, rural migrants had less education and more children, on the average, than either urban migrants or natives. It is possible, though, that the observed differences in fertility arise from the different educational levels of the groups.

Let us consider the regression model

$$E(Y) = \alpha + \beta X + \delta_1 Z_1 + \delta_2 Z_2$$

which is appropriate for these data if there is no interaction. In this equation, X is the number of years of education for the respondent, $Z_1 = 1$ if the respondent is an urban native, $Z_1 = 0$ otherwise; $Z_2 = 1$ if the respondent is an urban migrant, $Z_2 = 0$

Table 14.2

Observations on Y = Fertility (Number of Children) and X = Number of Years of Education, for Three Levels of Migrant Status

URBAN NATIVES $(Z_1 = 1, Z_2 = 0)$		URBAN MIGRANTS $(Z_1 = 0, Z_2 = 1)$		RURAL MIGRANTS $(Z_1 = Z_2 = 0)$	
X	Y	X	Y	X	Y
0	7	0	7	0	4
0	5	0	6	0	6
1	5	0	7	0	10
1	4	1	5	0	8
2	7	2	2	1	7
4	4	2	6	2	8
5	4	3	3	3	5
7	3	4	6	3	6
8	5	7	4	4	7
8	2	7	4	5	7
8	3	8	4	6	8
9	3	11	3	6	6
10	4	11	3	7	4
11	3	11	4	7	5
11	2	12	2	8	4
12	3	12	4	8	4
		12	2	8	6
		13	3	8	5
				9	3
				9	7
				10	4

Table 14.3 Mean Fertility and Education, by Migrant Status

	URBAN NATIVES	URBAN MIGRANTS	RURAL MIGRANTS	TOTAL SAMPLE
Mean fertility	$\bar{Y}_1 = 4.000$	$\bar{Y}_2 = 4.167$	$\bar{Y}_3 = 5.905$	$\bar{Y} = 4.782$
Mean education	$\bar{X}_1 = 6.062$	$\bar{X}_2 = 6.444$	$\bar{X}_3 = 4.952$	$\bar{X} = 5.764$
Sample size	$n_1 = 16$	$n_2 = 18$	$n_3 = 21$	$N = 55$

otherwise; and $Z_1 = Z_2 = 0$ if the respondent is a rural migrant. Fitting the model using least squares techniques, we get a prediction equation $\hat{Y} = a + bX + d_1Z_1 + d_2Z_2$, where a, b, d_1, and d_2 denote the point estimates of the regression parameters α, β, δ_1, and δ_2, respectively. Figure 14.5 shows part of the printout that would be obtained from using a computer regression package to fit the model to the data on fertility, educational level, and migrant status. The prediction equation takes the form

$$\hat{Y} = a + bX + d_1Z_1 + d_2Z_2$$
$$= 7.161 - .254X - 1.623Z_1 - 1.360Z_2$$

Fig. 14.5 Printout for Fitting Model $E(Y) = \alpha + \beta X + \delta_1 Z_1 + \delta_2 Z_2$, Assuming No Interaction, to Data on Y = Fertility, X = Education, and Migrant Status

SOURCE	DF	SUM OF SQUARES	MEAN SQUARE	R-SQUARE	PARAMETER	ESTIMATE
REGRESSION	3	102.028	34.009	.544	INTERCEPT	7.161
ERROR	51	85.354	1.674		X(EDUCATION)	-.254
TOTAL	54	187.382			Z1(URB-NAT)	-1.623
					Z2(URB-MIG)	-1.360

Hence, the lines relating $\hat{Y}$ = predicted fertility to X = education for urban natives, urban migrants, and rural migrants each have a slope of $b = -.254$, since we are assuming no interaction. The Y-intercept of the line for the rural migrants is $a = 7.161$, the predicted number of children for a rural migrant with no education. The Y-intercept for urban natives is

$$a + d_1 = 7.161 - 1.623 = 5.538$$

and the Y-intercept for urban migrants is

$$a + d_2 = 7.161 - 1.360 = 5.801$$

A scatter diagram showing the observed relationship between Y and X for the three groups is shown in Figure 14.6. On that diagram, we have plotted the parallel prediction equations based on the assumption of no interaction:

$$\hat{Y} = (a + d_1) + bX = 5.538 - .254X \quad \text{(Urban natives)}$$
$$\hat{Y} = (a + d_2) + bX = 5.801 - .254X \quad \text{(Urban migrants)}$$
$$\hat{Y} = a + bX = 7.161 - .254X \qquad \text{(Rural migrants)}$$

Fig. 14.6 Plot of Prediction Equation for Model Assuming No Interaction

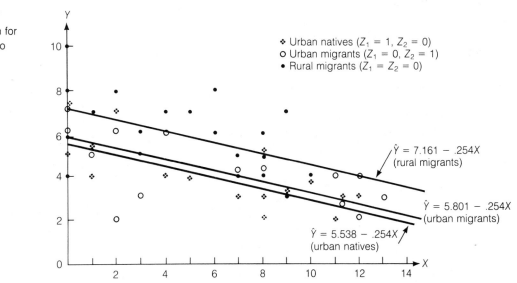

The vertical distance between the lines for urban natives and rural migrants is $d_1 = -1.623$. Thus, the estimated mean number of children for urban natives is 1.623 lower than the estimated mean number of children for rural migrants, at each fixed level of education. Similarly, $d_2 = -1.360$ represents the estimated difference between the mean number of children for urban migrants and rural migrants, controlling for education. The estimated difference between the mean number of children for urban natives and urban migrants (i.e., levels 1 and 2 of the categorical variable) is given by

$$d_1 - d_2 = -1.623 - (-1.360) = -.263$$

The coefficient of multiple determination R^2 has the usual interpretation; namely, it is the proportional reduction in error from using the prediction equation

$$\hat{Y} = 7.161 - .254X - 1.623Z_1 - 1.360Z_2$$

to predict fertility instead of using the overall mean $\bar{Y}$. That is,

$$R^2 = \frac{\text{TSS} - \text{SSE}}{\text{TSS}} = .544$$

where $\text{TSS} = \Sigma_{i=1}^{55} (Y_i - \bar{Y})^2 = 187.382$, and $\text{SSE} = 85.354$ is the sum of squared errors in predicting observations for urban natives using the prediction line $\hat{Y} = 5.538 - .254X$, for urban migrants using the prediction line $\hat{Y} = 5.801 - .254X$, and for rural migrants using the prediction line $\hat{Y} = 7.161 - .254X$. ■

14.3 Analysis of Covariance Model with Interaction Terms

To model interaction, we must introduce terms into the regression model to account for the different slopes of the m regression lines. This is accomplished, as usual, by taking cross-products of the independent variables. The cross-products of the interval variable X with the dummy variables $Z_1, Z_2, \ldots, Z_{m-1}$ representing the levels of the categorical variable yield the artificial variables $XZ_1, XZ_2, \ldots, XZ_{m-1}$. It is not necessary to take cross-products of the Z-values (such as $Z_1 Z_2$), since only one Z can be nonzero at once, and the products would always equal 0.

Model with Cross-Product Terms

We shall use the symbol γ (gamma) for the coefficients of the cross-product terms to distinguish them from the parameters introduced in the previous section for the slope (β) and the differences in Y-intercepts (the δ terms). For the case in which there are $m = 3$ levels of the categorical variable, we express the analysis of covariance model with interaction terms as

$$E(Y) = \alpha + \beta X + \delta_1 Z_1 + \delta_2 Z_2 + \gamma_1(XZ_1) + \gamma_2(XZ_2)$$

For the third level, $Z_1 = Z_2 = 0$ and we have the regression equation $E(Y) = \alpha + \beta X$ for the relationship between Y and X. If there is interaction, the regression line in the first level may have a different slope and intercept. For observations in the first level, $Z_1 = 1$ and $Z_2 = 0$, and we get the regression line

$$E(Y) = \alpha + \beta X + \delta_1(1) + \delta_2(0) + \gamma_1(X \cdot 1) + \gamma_2(X \cdot 0)$$
$$= \alpha + \beta X + \delta_1 + \gamma_1 X$$
$$= (\alpha + \delta_1) + (\beta + \gamma_1)X$$

This regression line has Y-intercept $(\alpha + \delta_1)$ and slope $(\beta + \gamma_1)$. Hence, δ_1 again describes the difference in the Y-intercepts between the first and the last level. However, this is the difference between the levels *only* at $X = 0$, since this equation has a different slope $(\beta + \gamma_1)$ from the slope for the last level. Since β represents the slope for the last (third) level, γ_1 represents the *difference in slopes* between the first and last levels. The two lines are parallel only when $\gamma_1 = 0$.

Similarly, we can see by substituting $Z_1 = 0$ and $Z_2 = 1$ that

$$E(Y) = (\alpha + \delta_2) + (\beta + \gamma_2)X$$

for the second level. Hence, δ_2 is the difference in the Y-intercepts between the second and the last level, and γ_2 is the difference in the slopes for those two levels. Table 14.4 summarizes the interpretations of the parameters in the model for this case of $m = 3$ levels.

Table 14.4

Summary of Equations and Parameters for Analysis of Covariance Model with Interaction Terms, When Categorical Variable Has $m = 3$ Levels

LEVEL	Y-INTERCEPT	SLOPE	MEAN AT FIXED X, $E(Y)$	DIFFERENCE FROM LEVEL 3 OF	
				Y-intercept	*Slope*
1	$\alpha + \delta_1$	$\beta + \gamma_1$	$(\alpha + \delta_1) + (\beta + \gamma_1)X$	δ_1	γ_1
2	$\alpha + \delta_2$	$\beta + \gamma_2$	$(\alpha + \delta_2) + (\beta + \gamma_2)X$	δ_2	γ_2
3	α	β	$\alpha + \beta X$	0	0

Figure 14.7 depicts three regression lines for which interaction is present. In that diagram $\delta_1 > 0$ and $\delta_2 < 0$, because the first level has the largest Y-intercept and the second level has the smallest Y-intercept. Also, $\gamma_1 < 0$, since the first level has a smaller slope than the third level (in numerical value, not necessarily absolute value), whereas $\gamma_2 > 0$, since the second level has a larger slope.

Fig. 14.7 A Model with Interaction Terms

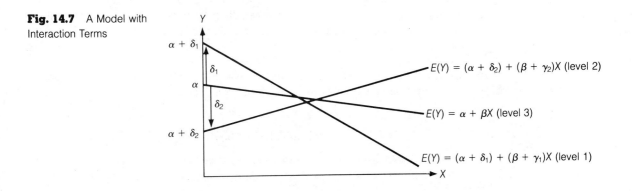

We now illustrate the analysis of covariance model with interaction terms, using the data presented in Table 14.2.

Example 14.2   To allow for the possibility of interaction in the relationship between fertility and education for the three levels of migrant status, we use the model

$$E(Y) = \alpha + \beta X + \delta_1 Z_1 + \delta_2 Z_2 + \gamma_1(XZ_1) + \gamma_2(XZ_2)$$

The least squares method yields the results shown in Figure 14.8.

Fig. 14.8   Printout for Fitting Model $E(Y) = \alpha + \beta X + \delta_1 Z_1 + \delta_2 Z_2 + \gamma_1(XZ_1) + \gamma_2(XZ_2)$, with Interaction Terms, to Data on Y = Fertility, X = Education, and Migrant Status

SOURCE	DF	SUM OF SQUARES	MEAN SQUARE	R-SQUARE	PARAMETER	ESTIMATE
REGRESSION	5	102.365	20.473	.546	INTERCEPT	7.286
ERROR	49	85.016	1.735		X(EDUCATION)	-.279
TOTAL	54	187.382			Z1(URB-NAT)	-1.696
					Z2(URB-MIG)	-1.614
					XZ1	.017
					XZ2	.045

The overall model is estimated by the equation

$$\hat{Y} = 7.286 - .279X - 1.696Z_1 - 1.614Z_2 + .017(XZ_1) + .045(XZ_2)$$

In essence, this model corresponds to fitting three separate lines, each of which minimizes the sum of squared errors for a particular level of migrant status. For the urban natives ($Z_1 = 1$, $Z_2 = 0$), the best-fitting prediction equation is

$$\hat{Y} = 7.286 - .279X - 1.696(1) - 1.614(0) + .017(X \cdot 1) + .045(X \cdot 0)$$
$$= (7.286 - 1.696) + (-.279 + .017)X = 5.590 - .262X$$

For the urban migrants ($Z_1 = 0$, $Z_2 = 1$),

$$\hat{Y} = (7.286 - 1.614) + (-.279 + .045)X = 5.672 - .234X$$

For rural migrants ($Z_1 = Z_2 = 0$), $\hat{Y} = 7.286 - .279X$. These three prediction equations are plotted in Figure 14.9. As can be readily seen, the slopes are very similar. In fact, these three lines are not much different from those obtained in Example 14.1, where we assumed no interaction. Over the range of education values measured, rural migrants always have the highest predicted fertility, and urban natives have the lowest.   ■

Model for m Categories   Generally, for an arbitrary number m of levels for the categorical variable, the analysis of covariance model allowing for interaction can be written as

$$E(Y) = \alpha + \beta X + [\delta_1 Z_1 + \delta_2 Z_2 + \cdots + \delta_{m-1} Z_{m-1}]$$
$$+ [\gamma_1(XZ_1) + \gamma_2(XZ_2) + \cdots + \gamma_{m-1}(XZ_{m-1})]$$

Dummy variables are included for all except the last level of the categorical variable. Cross-products of X with each of the dummy variables are also included. The γ_i

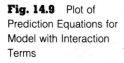

Fig. 14.9 Plot of Prediction Equations for Model with Interaction Terms

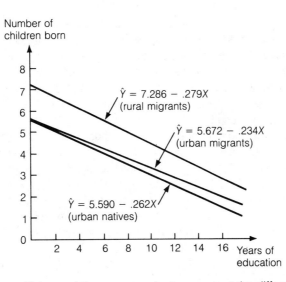

coefficients of the cross-products represent the differences between the slopes for the various levels and the slope for the *m*th level. In the special case in which all the γ-values equal 0, the *m* slopes are all equal so that the model reduces to the model without interaction, which was considered in the previous section. The δ_i coefficients represent the differences between the *Y*-intercepts for the various levels and the *Y*-intercept for the *m*th level.

It is important to note that, when the lines are not parallel, the δ_i values are the vertical distances between the various lines and the line for the last level *only* at $X = 0$. When interaction exists, therefore, it would usually not make sense to calculate a summary difference between categories in terms of their means on *Y*, controlling for *X*, since the difference in means varies as a function of *X*. For example, the difference in the mean of *Y* between the first and last categories at a particular *X*-value is

$$[(\alpha + \delta_1) + (\beta + \gamma_1)X] - (\alpha + \beta X) = \delta_1 + \gamma_1 X$$

which depends on the value of *X* when $\gamma_1 \neq 0$. As *X* changes, the difference in the means changes as a linear function of *X*, with the nature of the change depending on the values of the parameters δ_1 and γ_1.

14.4 Tests for Interaction and for Equivalence of Regression Lines

There are two primary tests in an analysis of covariance. The first of these is a test of the hypothesis of no interaction. In a regression context, where we treat the categorical variable as a control variable, the null hypothesis of no interaction corresponds to the null hypothesis that the *m* regression lines between *Y* and *X* for the *m* levels of the categorical variable are parallel. In the analysis of variance context, where we treat the interval variable as a control variable, it corresponds to the hypothesis that the difference between means for each pair of levels of the categorical variable is the same at each X-value. If the null hypothesis of no interaction is not rejected, then in futher analyses we assume that the m regression lines are parallel. The next hypothesis that is typically of interest is that the m regression lines are in fact identical; that is, they have not only the same slope, but also the same Y-intercept. Equivalently, this hypothesis states that the mean of Y, controlling for X, is the same for each level of the categorical variable.

Both of these hypotheses can be tested using the F test for the comparison of a complete and a reduced regression model, as introduced in Section 12.3. In the test of no interaction, we compare the complete model containing the interaction terms to the reduced model omitting those terms. Assuming no interaction, we can then conduct the test of identical regression lines by comparing the complete model containing a single slope but terms for differences in intercepts (the reduced model for the test of no interaction) to the reduced model in which a single line applies to each of the levels. The form of the test statistic for comparing the complete and reduced models in these tests is

$$F = \frac{(\text{SSE}_r - \text{SSE}_c)/(k - g)}{\text{SSE}_c/[N - (k + 1)]}$$

where k and g are the numbers of independent variables in the two models (including artificial dummy variables and cross-product terms), SSE_r and SSE_c are the sums of squared errors for the reduced and complete models, and $df_1 = k - g$ and $df_2 = N - (k + 1)$. As in other regression tests, we must assume that the conditional distribution of Y at each fixed X-value is normal for each of the categories, and that the standard deviation of Y is constant over all levels of the independent variables.

Test of No Interaction

We will consider the general situation in which the categorical variable has an arbitrary number m of levels. The complete model, including interaction terms, is

$$E(Y) = \alpha + \beta X + [\delta_1 Z_1 + \cdots + \delta_{m-1} Z_{m-1}] + [\gamma_1(XZ_1) + \cdots + \gamma_{m-1}(XZ_{m-1})]$$

If there is no interaction, the γ_i difference in slope parameters all equal 0. Hence, the null hypothesis of no interaction is equivalent to

$$H_0: \quad \gamma_1 = \gamma_2 = \cdots = \gamma_{m-1} = 0$$

namely, that the difference between the slope for each level and that for the mth level is 0. The model corresponding to the null hypothesis being true is the reduced model

$$E(Y) = \alpha + \beta X + \delta_1 Z_1 + \delta_2 Z_2 + \cdots + \delta_{m-1} Z_{m-1}$$

We reject H_0, in favor of H_a: at least one $\gamma_i \neq 0$, if the addition of the interaction terms $\gamma_1(XZ_1) + \cdots + \gamma_{m-1}(XZ_{m-1})$ gives a significant improvement in the fit. The difference $df_1 = k - g$ in the number of terms in the two models equals $m - 1$, the number of interaction terms in the complete model. The two hypotheses for this test are depicted in Figure 14.10.

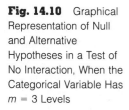

Fig. 14.10 Graphical Representation of Null and Alternative Hypotheses in a Test of No Interaction, When the Categorical Variable Has $m = 3$ Levels

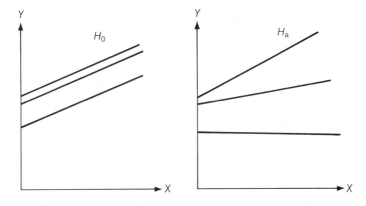

Example 14.3   The complete model containing interaction terms for the relationship between fertility, education, and migrant status is

$$E(Y) = \alpha + \beta X + \delta_1 Z_1 + \delta_2 Z_2 + \gamma_1(XZ_1) + \gamma_2(XZ_2)$$

The null hypothesis that there is no interaction is H_0: $\gamma_1 = \gamma_2 = 0$. In Figure 14.8, we observed a sum of squared errors of $SSE_c = 85.016$ when this complete model with $k = 5$ independent variables (X, Z_1, Z_2, XZ_1, and XZ_2) was fitted to the $N = 55$ observations. The sum of squares was based on $df_2 = N - (k + 1) = 55 - (5 + 1) = 49$, the sample size minus the number of parameters for that model. The reduced model that corresponds to H_0 being true is $E(Y) = \alpha + \beta X + \delta_1 Z_1 + \delta_2 Z_2$. In Figure 14.5, the sum of squared errors for this model, with $g = 3$ independent variables, was $SSE_r = 85.354$, barely larger than when the interaction terms are included in the model. The difference in the number of independent variables in the two models is $df_1 = k - g = 5 - 3 = 2$, precisely the number of γ terms appearing in H_0.

The F test statistic for testing H_0: $\gamma_1 = \gamma_2 = 0$, based on $df_1 = 2$ and $df_2 = 49$, is

$$F = \frac{(SSE_r - SSE_c)/df_1}{SSE_c/df_2} = \frac{(85.354 - 85.016)/2}{85.016/49}$$

$$= \frac{.169}{1.735} = .097$$

a relatively small and nonsignificant value. Hence, in the remainder of the chapter, we are justified in making the assumption that there is no interaction among these variables. ∎

Test for Equivalence of Regression Lines (Equality of Means, Controlling for X)   Assuming failure to reject the null hypothesis of no interaction, further analysis is considerably simplified since the interaction terms can be omitted from the model, leaving

$$E(Y) = \alpha + \beta X + \delta_1 Z_1 + \delta_2 Z_2 + \cdots + \delta_{m-1} Z_{m-1}$$

The m regression lines are then assumed to be parallel, with δ_i being the difference between the ith and the last (mth) line at each fixed X-value. The procedures considered in the remainder of this chapter are appropriate when this assumption is valid.

We next test whether the model can be even further reduced. In the regression context, we might test whether the m categories can all be represented by the same regression line. In the analysis of variance context, we might test the hypothesis that the mean of the dependent variable is the same for all m groups, controlling for X. In either case, the null hypothesis is equivalent to H_0: $\delta_1 = \delta_2 = \cdots = \delta_{m-1} = 0$. This hypothesis states that the difference δ in the mean of Y (or equivalently, the vertical difference in the regression lines) between each level and the last level of the categorical variable is 0, controlling for X. This implies that the corresponding difference between *any two* of the levels is 0.

The model corresponding to H_0: $\delta_1 = \delta_2 = \cdots = \delta_{m-1} = 0$ being true is the reduced one, $E(Y) = \alpha + \beta X$, representing the fact that the same regression line $\alpha + \beta X$ can be used for all m levels. Hence, testing H_0: $\delta_1 = \cdots = \delta_{m-1} = 0$ corresponds to comparing the complete model

$$E(Y) = \alpha + \beta X + \delta_1 Z_1 + \cdots + \delta_{m-1} Z_{m-1}$$

to the reduced model $E(Y) = \alpha + \beta X$ (see Figure 14.11). We reject H_0 if the complete model gives a significantly better fit to the data than the reduced model.

Fig. 14.11 Graphical Representation of Null and Alternative Hypotheses in a Test of Equivalence of Regression Lines, When the Categorical Variable Has $m = 3$ Levels (Test Assumes No Interaction)

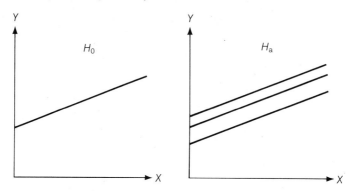

Example 14.4   The null hypothesis that mean fertility is the same for each of the three levels of migrant status, controlling for X = education, can be expressed as H_0: $\delta_1 = \delta_2 = 0$. For this test, the complete model is

$$E(Y) = \alpha + \beta X + \delta_1 Z_1 + \delta_2 Z_2$$

representing three different but parallel regression equations between fertility and education. From Figure 14.5, we see that $SSE_c = 85.354$, based on $df_2 = N - (k + 1) = 55 - (3 + 1) = 51$. Since the complete model here was the reduced model in the test of no interaction, SSE_c is precisely the sum of squared errors that was identified as SSE_r in the previous test.

If H_0: $\delta_1 = \delta_2 = 0$ is true, the reduced model

$$E(Y) = \alpha + \beta X$$

is appropriate, meaning that all three migrant status groups can be represented by the same equation for the relationship between fertility and education. The computer printout for this model is shown in Figure 14.12. The prediction equation for all three groups according to that model is $\hat{Y} = 6.394 - .280X$, and the sum of squared errors is $SSE_r = 113.884$. The difference in the number of independent variables between the complete and reduced models is $df_1 = k - g = 3 - 1 = 2$. Hence, the F statistic for testing H_0: $\delta_1 = \delta_2 = 0$ is

$$F = \frac{(SSE_r - SSE_c)/df_1}{SSE_c/df_2} = \frac{(113.884 - 85.354)/2}{85.354/51} = \frac{14.265}{1.674} = 8.522$$

based on $df_1 = 2$ and $df_2 = 51$. From Table D, the P-value is $P < .001$. We would probably conclude, therefore, that the regressions of Y on X are different for at least two of the levels of migrant status. ∎

Fig. 14.12 Printout for Fitting Model $E(Y) = \alpha + \beta X$ to Data on Y = Fertility and X = Education

SOURCE	DF	SUM OF SQUARES	MEAN SQUARE	R-SQUARE	PARAMETER	ESTIMATE
REGRESSION	1	73.498	73.498	.392	INTERCEPT	6.394
ERROR	53	113.884	2.149		X(EDUCATION)	-.280
TOTAL	54	187.382				

In Table 14.5, we have summarized the models and corresponding sums of squared errors for the tests considered in this section. We see that there is a substantial reduction in error from using three parallel lines, instead of one, to obtain predictions on fertility. However, there is a small and insignificant reduction by allowing for different slopes for the three lines.

Table 14.5 Results of Comparisons of Three Models in Examples 14.3 and 14.4

	INTERACTION, $E(Y) = \alpha + \beta X + \delta_1 Z_1 + \delta_2 Z_2 + \gamma_1(XZ_1) + \gamma_2(XZ_2)$	NO INTERACTION, UNEQUAL MEANS CONTROLLING FOR X, $E(Y) = \alpha + \beta X + \delta_1 Z_1 + \delta_2 Z_2$	NO INTERACTION, EQUAL MEANS CONTROLLING FOR X, $E(Y) = \alpha + \beta X$
SSE	85.016	85.354	113.884
R^2	.546	.544	.392
H_0: $\gamma_1 = \gamma_2 = 0$ (No interaction)	Complete model	Reduced model	—
H_0: $\delta_1 = \delta_2 = 0$ (Equal means, controlling for X)	—	Complete model	Reduced model

14.5 Comparing Adjusted Means

If neither of the null hypotheses considered in the previous section is rejected, then the model $E(Y) = \alpha + \beta X$ can be regarded as a reasonable one. The implication is then that the same regression equation can be used for each level of the categorical variable, or equivalently, that the mean of Y at a fixed level of X is given by $\alpha + \beta X$ within each level. On the other hand, if H_0: no interaction is rejected in the first test of the previous section, then lines with different Y-intercepts and different slopes must be used for those levels, and estimates of the differences in the mean of Y between any two levels vary as a function of X. In the final two sections, we will examine additional analyses that can be conducted under the third possibility, in which H_0: no interaction is not rejected but H_0: $\delta_1 = \delta_2 = \cdots = \delta_{m-1} = 0$ is rejected.* In this section, we consider the case in which the interval variable is treated as the control variable, so that the rejected null hypothesis is that of equal means on Y, controlling for X.

Adjusted Means

In an analysis of an interval variable Y for several groups, we have used the means as summary descriptive measures. To control for the effects on Y of another interval variable X, we use as measures *the values we would have expected to obtain for the means on Y if those groups all had the same mean on X*. These values are referred to as the *adjusted means* on the dependent variable, since they are adjusted for the fact that different groups had different means on the covariate X.

Adjusted Mean

The (population) *adjusted mean* on Y for a particular group is its conditional mean on Y at the X-value equal to the mean of X for the combined population of m groups.

In other words, the regression function for a particular group evaluated at the overall mean of the X-values gives the adjusted mean for that group. It may help in understanding the concept of the adjusted means to refer to Figure 14.13, which illustrates the case where $m = 3$. Let μ_X refer to the mean of X for the combined population of the three separate groups. Then, the adjusted mean of Y for a particular group is just the value of the regression function for that group evaluated at μ_X. The adjusted mean for the mth group is $\alpha + \beta\mu_X$; for the first group, it is $(\alpha + \delta_1) + \beta\mu_X$; and so forth. To estimate these adjusted means, we calculate their sample analogs.

Notation

Denote the sample adjusted means for m groups on a dependent variable Y by $\bar{Y}_1', \bar{Y}_2', \ldots, \bar{Y}_m'$. In other words, $\bar{Y}_1'$ is the sample mean of Y for the first group, controlling for the interval variable X, and so forth.

---

*If interaction exists but the differences in the slopes are so small as to be judged practically insignificant, these types of analyses might also be used.

Fig. 14.13 Population Adjusted Means, When the Categorical Variable Has $m = 3$ Levels

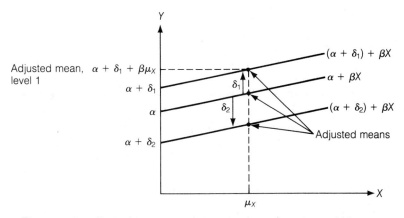

The sample adjusted means are interpreted as what we would have expected for the sample means of Y for the various groups if the sample mean on the covariate X for each group had equaled the overall sample mean $\bar{X}$. The sample adjusted means are obtained by substituting the overall sample mean $\bar{X}$ into the prediction equations for the various groups. For example, the prediction equation for the first level, in which $Z_1 = 1$, is

$$\hat{Y} = (a + d_1) + bX$$

and the corresponding sample adjusted mean is

$$\bar{Y}'_1 = (a + d_1) + b\bar{X}$$

Similarly, the sample adjusted mean for the second level is $\bar{Y}'_2 = (a + d_2) + b\bar{X}$. For the last level, all Z-values are 0, and the sample adjusted mean is $\bar{Y}'_m = a + b\bar{X}$.

The differences between the true adjusted means can be expressed in terms of the δ parameters. For example, δ_1 is the difference between the adjusted mean for the first group $(\alpha + \delta_1 + \beta\mu_X)$ and the adjusted mean for the mth group $(\alpha + \beta\mu_X)$. Inferences about the differences in the true adjusted means can be based on the d estimates of the δ parameters. These estimates are simply the differences in the *sample* adjusted means. In other words, $d_1 = \bar{Y}'_1 - \bar{Y}'_m$, $d_2 = \bar{Y}'_2 - \bar{Y}'_m$, $d_3 = \bar{Y}'_3 - \bar{Y}'_m$, and so forth.

Example 14.5 From Table 14.3, the overall mean education for the combined sample of 55 observations is $\bar{X} = 5.764$. Table 14.6 (page 462) lists the three separate prediction equations for the three levels of migrant status, for the model assuming no interaction. For urban natives, the prediction equation between fertility and education is $\hat{Y} = 5.538 - .254X$. Hence, the sample adjusted mean fertility for that group, controlling for education, is $\bar{Y}'_1 = 5.538 - .254\bar{X} = 5.538 - .254(5.764) = 4.074$. This value is larger than the unadjusted mean fertility of $\bar{Y}_1 = 4.000$. The reason for this is that the mean education for urban natives ($\bar{X}_1 = 6.062$) is larger than the mean education for the combined sample. Since there is a negative relationship between fertility and education, we are predicting that urban natives would have a slightly higher fertility rate if their mean education were slightly lower (equal to $\bar{X} = 5.764$).

Table 14.6 Summary Unadjusted Means, Adjusted Means, and Prediction Equations for Model Assuming No Interaction

GROUP	PREDICTION EQUATION	MEAN ON X, $\bar{X}_i$	MEAN ON Y, $\bar{Y}_i$	ADJUSTED MEAN, $\bar{Y}'_i$	DIFFERENCE IN ADJUSTED MEANS, $d_i = \bar{Y}'_i - \bar{Y}'_3$
Urban natives	$\hat{Y} = 5.538 - .254X$	6.062	4.000	4.074	−1.623
Urban migrants	$\hat{Y} = 5.801 - .254X$	6.444	4.167	4.337	−1.360
Rural migrants	$\hat{Y} = 7.161 - .254X$	4.952	5.905	5.697	

Similarly, the sample adjusted means for urban migrants and rural migrants are

$$\bar{Y}'_2 = 5.801 - .254(5.764) = 4.337$$
$$\bar{Y}'_3 = 7.161 - .254(5.764) = 5.697$$

Figure 14.14 depicts the sample adjusted means, which are tabulated together with the unadjusted means in Table 14.6. Notice that $d_1 = -1.623 = \bar{Y}'_1 - \bar{Y}'_3$ is the estimated difference in adjusted mean fertility between urban natives and rural migrants, whereas $d_2 = -1.360 = \bar{Y}'_2 - \bar{Y}'_3$ is the estimated difference in the adjusted means between urban migrants and rural migrants. Since the groups had different means on the covariate education, the adjusted means and their differences are not the same as the unadjusted means and differences. For example, from Table 14.6, $\bar{Y}_1 - \bar{Y}_3 = 4.000 - 5.905 = -1.905$ is the unadjusted difference in mean fertility between urban natives and rural migrants. ∎

Fig. 14.14 Sample Adjusted Means for Data on Y = Fertility and Migrant Status, Controlling for X = Education

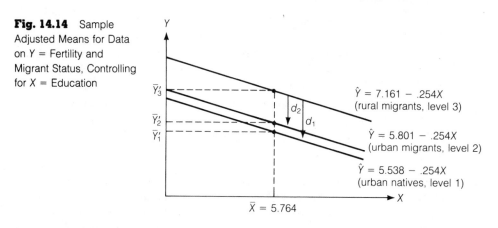

Graphical Interpretation*   The relationship between the adjusted means $\bar{Y}'_i$ and the unadjusted means $\bar{Y}_i$ can be illustrated by the following argument. We shall state the argument in terms of the first level and refer to Figure 14.15 showing a hypothetical prediction line for that level, although the same reasoning applies to any of the levels. Now, it can be shown that the least squares prediction equation

$$\hat{Y} = a + bX + d_1Z_1 + \cdots + d_{m-1}Z_{m-1}$$

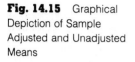

Fig. 14.15 Graphical Depiction of Sample Adjusted and Unadjusted Means

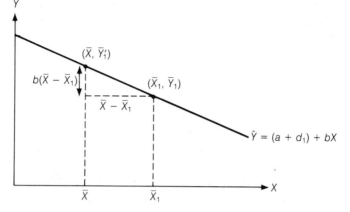

predicts a value of $\bar{Y}_i$ at the X-value of $X = \bar{X}_i$ for the ith level. In particular, the prediction line $\hat{Y} = (a + d_1) + bX$ for the first level passes through the point $(\bar{X}_1, \bar{Y}_1)$ in the (X, Y) coordinate system. In other words, the *unadjusted mean* $\bar{Y}_1$ for the first level is the value $\bar{Y}_1 = (a + d_1) + b\bar{X}_1$ of the prediction equation for that level evaluated at the X-value of $\bar{X}_1$, the mean of the X-values *for that level alone* [see the point $(\bar{X}_1, \bar{Y}_1)$ in Figure 14.15].

Now, the *adjusted mean* $\bar{Y}'_1$ for the first level is the value of that prediction equation evaluated at the X-value given by the *overall mean* $\bar{X}$ for the combined sample. That is, by definition, $\bar{Y}'_1 = (a + d_1) + b\bar{X}$. Hence, the prediction line for that level also passes through the point $(\bar{X}, \bar{Y}'_1)$, as shown in Figure 14.15. The difference in the X coordinates between the points $(\bar{X}, \bar{Y}'_1)$ and $(\bar{X}_1, \bar{Y}_1)$ is the horizontal distance $\bar{X} - \bar{X}_1$, indicated in Figure 14.15. Since the slope of the prediction equation is b, the vertical change in the line over the X distance of $\bar{X} - \bar{X}_1$ is just $b(\bar{X} - \bar{X}_1)$. That is, the change in the Y direction for a $(\bar{X} - \bar{X}_1)$ unit change in the X direction is $b(\bar{X} - \bar{X}_1)$ for a line with slope b. This vertical change is precisely the difference $\bar{Y}'_1 - \bar{Y}_1$ between the Y coordinates of the points $(\bar{X}, \bar{Y}'_1)$ and $(\bar{X}_1, \bar{Y}_1)$.

Thus, we have reasoned that the difference between the adjusted mean and unadjusted mean for the first group is given by

$$\bar{Y}'_1 - \bar{Y}_1 = b(\bar{X} - \bar{X}_1)$$

In other words, the difference between the adjusted and unadjusted means depends directly on the difference between the X distribution for the combined sample and the X distribution for that particular group (as described by the difference in their means). Rearranging the formula, we can express the adjusted mean for the first group in terms of the unadjusted mean as

$$\bar{Y}'_1 = \bar{Y}_1 + b(\bar{X} - \bar{X}_1)$$

In controlling for X, we are in essence taking the sample mean on Y and adjusting it by multiplying the difference $(\bar{X} - \bar{X}_1)$ in the means on X by the slope b of the prediction equation. This produces an estimate of what the value of $\bar{Y}$ would be for the first group *if* that group had the same mean on X as does the combined sample, *assuming* that the mean would change according to the regression of Y on X for that group.

Similar reasoning applies to other groups. For the ith group, the difference between the adjusted and unadjusted means is

$$\bar{Y}_i' - \bar{Y}_i = b(\bar{X} - \bar{X}_i)$$

If there is a negative slope ($b < 0$) between X and Y for those groups, then the sample mean $\bar{Y}_i$ is adjusted upward if $\bar{X}_i > \bar{X}$ (i.e., if $\bar{X} - \bar{X}_i < 0$). This reflects the argument that the mean on Y would have been larger had the distribution of X-values for that group had as small a mean as the combined samples (as in Figure 14.15). If the ith group is below average in the mean of X (i.e., $\bar{X}_i < \bar{X}$), then $b(\bar{X} - \bar{X}_i)$ is negative when $b < 0$, so the mean is adjusted downward. The reverse adjustments apply when the slope of the prediction equation is positive. Figure 14.16 depicts the adjustment process on fertility for the three migrant status groups.

Fig. 14.16 Adjustment Process for Fertility by Migrant Status, Controlling for Education

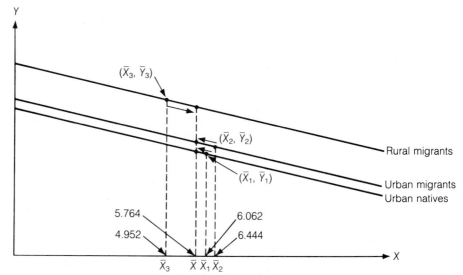

Multiple Comparisons of Adjusted Means

After presenting the F test for the one-way analysis of variance in Chapter 13, we introduced the Scheffé procedure for comparing all pairs of sample means simultaneously with a fixed confidence coefficient. Control variables were omitted in that analysis, so the means that we compared there were the *unadjusted means*. The Scheffé multiple comparison procedure can be generalized to the consideration of all pairwise comparisons of *adjusted means*.

We first set a multiple comparison error rate α for the set of comparisons. The Scheffé interval for the difference in adjusted means in the two categories numbered i and j has the formula

$$(\bar{Y}_i' - \bar{Y}_j') \pm \hat{\sigma} \sqrt{(m-1)F_\alpha \left[\frac{1}{n_i} + \frac{1}{n_j} + \frac{(\bar{X}_i - \bar{X}_j)^2}{\text{WSS}_X} \right]}$$

The set of all $m(m - 1)/2$ intervals for differences in adjusted means simultaneously contains the true differences with (a priori) probability $1 - \alpha$. In each formula, $\hat{\sigma}$ is the estimate of the standard deviation of the conditional distribution of Y at a fixed value of X for the regression model without interaction terms. This estimate, the root mean square error, is the square root of $\hat{\sigma}^2 = \text{SSE}/[N - (m + 1)]$, where SSE is the sum of squared errors for that regression model, and $N - (m + 1)$ is the total sample size minus the number of parameters in the model.* The value F_α is the number from the F table corresponding to the right-hand tail area α, for $df_1 = m - 1$, $df_2 = N - (m + 1)$. This is the number that must be exceeded by the F test statistic in order to reject the null hypothesis $H_0: \delta_1 = \delta_2 = \cdots = \delta_{m-1} = 0$ at the α-level in the test for equality of the adjusted means. The term WSS_X is the within sum of squares of the X-values; that is,

$$\text{WSS}_X = \sum_{j=1}^{n_1} (X_{1j} - \bar{X}_1)^2 + \sum_{j=1}^{n_2} (X_{2j} - \bar{X}_2)^2 + \cdots + \sum_{j=1}^{n_m} (X_{mj} - \bar{X}_m)^2$$

the sum (over all m samples) of the sums of squares of the X observations in each group about their means within those groups. The formula for this term is the same one that we used in computing the within sum of squares in the one-way analysis of variance in Section 13.1, except that here it is computed on the X-values instead of the Y-values.

If two groups being compared have the same mean for X (i.e., if $\bar{X}_i = \bar{X}_j$), then the last term under the square root sign in the formula for the confidence interval drops out. In that case, the difference in the sample adjusted means is identical to the difference in the sample unadjusted means on Y, and the interval has a form similar to the Scheffé interval introduced in Section 13.2. Generally, the sample adjusted means are not very different from the sample unadjusted means if the $\bar{X}_i$-values are relatively close to the overall $\bar{X}$, or if the slope b of the prediction equations is relatively small.

Example 14.6 The results of fitting the model assuming no interaction to the variables fertility, education, and migrant status were given in Figure 14.5. The estimate of the conditional variance of Y at a fixed value of X for each of the $m = 3$ regression equations is

$$\hat{\sigma}^2 = \frac{\text{SSE}}{N - (m + 1)} = \frac{85.354}{55 - 4} = 1.674$$

the mean square error in that table. The corresponding estimate of the conditional standard deviation is $\hat{\sigma} = \sqrt{1.674} = 1.294$. The term WSS_X is the sum of squares of the 55 X-values about their category means,

$$[(0 - 6.062)^2 + \cdots + (12 - 6.062)^2] + [(0 - 6.444)^2 + \cdots + (13 - 6.444)^2]$$
$$+ [(0 - 4.952)^2 + \cdots + (10 - 4.952)^2] = 916.334$$

That is, we take the sum of squares of the education values about their group means: 6.062 for the urban natives, 6.444 for the urban migrants, and 4.952 for the rural

*In the regression model with no interaction, there are $(m - 1)$ coefficients of dummy variables, an α term, and a β term, for a total of $(m + 1)$ parameters.

migrants. If we wish to apply a .95 simultaneous confidence coefficient to the set of intervals for the pairwise differences in adjusted means, the value $F_\alpha = F_{.05} = 3.19$, corresponding to $df_1 = m - 1 = 2$ and $df_2 = N - (m + 1) = 51$, is inserted into the formula.

To illustrate, let us consider the difference in adjusted mean fertility between urban natives and rural migrants. The estimated difference is $d_1 = \bar{Y}'_1 - \bar{Y}'_3 = -1.623$, based on the sample sizes $n_1 = 16$ and $n_3 = 21$. Hence, the Scheffé confidence interval is

$$(\bar{Y}'_1 - \bar{Y}'_3) \pm \hat{\sigma} \sqrt{(m-1)F_\alpha \left[\frac{1}{n_1} + \frac{1}{n_3} + \frac{(\bar{X}_1 - \bar{X}_3)^2}{\text{WSS}_X}\right]}$$

$$= -1.623 \pm 1.294 \sqrt{2(3.19)\left[\frac{1}{16} + \frac{1}{21} + \frac{(6.062 - 4.952)^2}{916.334}\right]}$$

$$= -1.623 \pm 1.091 \quad \text{or} \quad (-2.714, -.532)$$

Since the interval consists entirely of negative numbers, we can conclude that the adjusted mean fertility for urban natives is smaller than the adjusted mean fertility for rural migrants.

The intervals for the other two pairwise differences are calculated in a similar manner. The comparisons are summarized in Table 14.7. We can be 95% confident that all three of these intervals simultaneously contain the true differences in adjusted means. The only two groups for which there is insufficient evidence to indicate a difference in adjusted mean fertility are urban natives and urban migrants. Both of these groups seem to differ from rural migrants, though, in the adjusted means. ∎

Table 14.7

Scheffé Multiple Comparisons of Difference in Mean Fertility by Migrant Status, Controlling for Education

MIGRANT STATUS	ESTIMATED DIFFERENCE, $\bar{Y}'_i - \bar{Y}'_j$	SIMULTANEOUS 95% CONFIDENCE INTERVALS
Urban natives, rural migrants	$d_1 = \bar{Y}'_1 - \bar{Y}'_3 = -1.623$	$(-2.714, -.532)^*$
Urban migrants, rural migrants	$d_2 = \bar{Y}'_2 - \bar{Y}'_3 = -1.360$	$(-2.422, -.298)^*$
Urban natives, urban migrants	$d_1 - d_2 = \bar{Y}'_1 - \bar{Y}'_2 = -.263$	$(-1.387, .861)$

Note: An asterisk (*) indicates significant difference.

Caution Before leaving the topic of comparing means on a dependent variable Y while controlling for a covariate X, we should reemphasize the tentative nature of the inferences described in this section. The adjusted means refer to the expected values on the dependent variable *if all groups had the same mean on the control variable X*. If the distribution on the covariate is quite different for the various groups, this may be a large *if*. We must assume (a) that it makes sense to conceive of the groups as being adjusted on this covariate, and (b) that the relationship between Y and X would continue to have the same linear form within each level as the X distribution is shifted for each level.

To illustrate the potential difficulties, Figure 14.17 displays data points for two groups such that the same line would fit the relationship between Y and X for each group. For these data, the null hypothesis H_0: $\delta = 0$ of no difference in the two adjusted means would not be rejected. However, if the relationship for each group between Y and X over the X region not observed is as illustrated by the dotted lines, then there would in fact be a difference between the means of Y at a fixed X value. Whenever this analysis of covariance procedure is used, we should check the degree to which the distributions differ on the mean of X. Excessively large differences may mean that the conclusions need to be qualified. On the other hand, if there are no differences or relatively small differences in the $\bar{X}_i$, then controlling for X will have very little effect, and the results of the comparisons of adjusted means will be nearly identical to the results of the comparisons of unadjusted means in an analysis of variance.

Fig. 14.17 A Situation in Which an Analysis of Covariance Would Yield Misleading Results

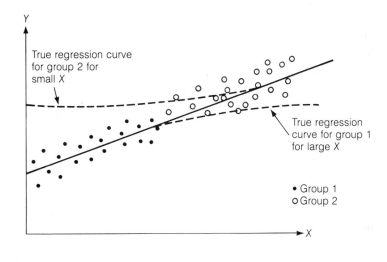

14.6 Comparing Regression Lines

In the analysis of adjusted means considered in the previous section, we treated the interval variable X as a control variable. In this section, we consider the situation in which it is more natural to treat the categorical variable as the control variable and devote primary attention to the nature of the relationship between Y and X within each category. In this case, we would be less interested in calculating the adjusted means than in describing the form of the regression and the strength of the association between Y and X, controlling for the categorical variable. The analyses we consider are again based on the assumption of no interaction.

We have seen that the test of H_0: $\delta_1 = \delta_2 = \cdots = \delta_{m-1} = 0$ corresponds to testing whether the regression lines are identical for the m levels. Now, two parallel lines are identical if their corresponding adjusted means are equal. Therefore, just as the Scheffé multiple comparison intervals reveal which pairs of adjusted means are significantly different, so do they reveal which pairs of lines are significantly different.

For example, if the interval for the difference between the ith and the jth adjusted means does not contain 0 (i.e., if the two population adjusted means are judged to be unequal), then the regression lines between Y and X for those two levels are judged to have different intercepts. The set of all such pairwise comparisons of the regression lines holds simultaneously with confidence coefficient $1 - \alpha$. From Example 14.6, we see that the regression equations for urban natives and rural migrants are significantly different, as well as the regression equations for urban migrants and rural migrants.

A Partial Correlation Measure

If the assumption of no interaction appears to be justified by the failure to reject the hypothesis H_0: $\gamma_1 = \cdots = \gamma_{m-1} = 0$ considered in Section 14.4, then the m regression lines can be estimated by m parallel lines. The slopes of the relationships can be summarized by the common slope b of these lines in that case. Since the value of the slope depends on the units of measurement of X and Y, it is sometimes of interest to pool together the results from the m levels in order to calculate a summary partial correlation between X and Y, controlling for the categorical variable. Letting Z denote the categorical variable, we use the symbol $r_{YX \cdot Z}$ to represent this measure. In a crude sense, we can conceive of $r_{YX \cdot Z}$ as being a weighted average of the m Pearson correlations between X and Y within the m levels of the categorical variable. It need not be the same as or even close to the *overall* Pearson correlation between X and Y, *ignoring* Z (recall Figure 14.2).

The interpretation of the squared partial correlation $r_{YX \cdot Z}^2$ is the same as was given in Section 11.3 for the general case. We consider all of the variability in Y that remains after first introducing the categorical variable as an independent variable. Then, $r_{YX \cdot Z}^2$ is the proportion of that unexplained variation that can be explained by next adding X as an independent variable into the equation.

The variability in Y that remains after the categorical variable alone (via the dummy variables $Z_1, Z_2, \ldots, Z_{m-1}$) is used as a predictor is simply the sum of squared errors for the model $E(Y) = \alpha + \delta_1 Z_1 + \cdots + \delta_{m-1} Z_{m-1}$ corresponding to the one-way analysis of variance. That is, it is the error from predicting Y in the first category by $\bar{Y}_1$, in the second category by $\bar{Y}_2$, and so forth. In Section 13.3, we saw that the sum of squared errors for the regression model corresponding to the analysis of variance procedure is precisely the within sum of squares

$$\text{WSS} = \sum_{j=1}^{n_1} (Y_{1j} - \bar{Y}_1)^2 + \sum_{j=1}^{n_2} (Y_{2j} - \bar{Y}_2)^2 + \cdots + \sum_{j=1}^{n_m} (Y_{mj} - \bar{Y}_m)^2$$

for the F test in that procedure. We denote this term by SSE(Z), since it represents the sum of squared errors when the categorical variable Z alone is used as a predictor. After next adding X to the linear model, the remaining error is the value of SSE for the model

$$E(Y) = \alpha + \beta X + \delta_1 Z_1 + \cdots + \delta_{m-1} Z_{m-1}$$

which incorporates both the interval and categorical variables, assuming no interaction. We denote this error value by SSE(X, Z). Now, SSE(X, Z) cannot be any larger than SSE(Z), since the sum of squared errors cannot increase when an independent variable (X) is added to the model. The difference $SSE(Z) - SSE(X, Z)$ represents the partial reduction in error that occurs from adding X to the model, *beyond* the variability explained by the categorical variable. Hence, the proportion of the variability in Y explained by X out of that left unexplained by the categorical variable is

$$r^2_{YX \cdot Z} = \frac{SSE(Z) - SSE(X, Z)}{SSE(Z)} = \frac{WSS - SSE(X, Z)}{WSS}$$

This measure can be interpreted as the proportional reduction in error obtained by fitting m separate but parallel lines as predictors of Y for the m levels instead of predicting Y by using $\bar{Y}_i$ for observations in the ith level, $i = 1, 2, \ldots, m$. The interpretation of $r^2_{YX \cdot Z}$ is depicted in Figure 14.18. The sum of squared errors about the group $\bar{Y}_i$-values shown in Figure 14.18a yields $WSS = SSE(Z)$. The sum of squared errors about the separate (but parallel) prediction lines shown in Figure 14.18b yields $SSE(X, Z)$. The partial correlation $r_{YX \cdot Z}$ is taken to be the square root of the measure $r^2_{YX \cdot Z}$, with the same sign as the sign of the slope b of the estimated regression lines.

Fig. 14.18 Depiction of Errors That Are Squared to Obtain $r^2_{YX \cdot Z}$

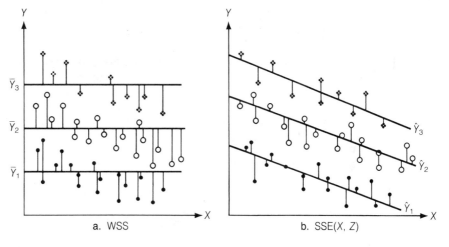

a. WSS   b. SSE(X, Z)

Example 14.7   From Figure 14.5, when both education and migrant status appear as independent variables in the regression model with no interaction, the sum of squared errors is $SSE(X, Z) = 85.354$. Figure 14.19 is the ANOVA table corresponding to the analysis of variance of the fertility scores among the migrant statuses. That is, Figure 14.19 represents the results of fitting the model $E(Y) = \alpha + \delta_1 Z_1 + \delta_2 Z_2$, which ignores the effect of education. In that case, the estimated regression coefficients d_1 and d_2 are

Fig. 14.19   ANOVA Printout for Fitting Model $E(Y) = \alpha + \delta_1 Z_1 + \delta_2 Z_2$ for Analyzing Fertility by Migrant Status

SOURCE	DF	SUM OF SQUARES	MEAN SQUARE	R-SQUARE	PARAMETER	ESTIMATE
REGRESSION	2	43.072	21.536	.230	INTERCEPT	5.905
ERROR	52	144.310	2.775		Z1 (URB-NAT)	-1.905
TOTAL	54	187.382			Z2 (URB-MIG)	-1.738

precisely the differences in the *unadjusted* fertility means between urban natives and rural migrants, and between urban migrants and rural migrants. The within sum of squares for that analysis is WSS = SSE(Z) = 144.310. It follows that the squared partial correlation between fertility and education, controlling for migrant status, is

$$r^2_{YX \cdot Z} = \frac{SSE(Z) - SSE(X, Z)}{SSE(Z)} = \frac{144.31 - 85.35}{144.31} = .409$$

Of the variability in fertility not explained by the differences in migrant status, 40.9% is explained by education. The partial correlation $r_{YX \cdot Z}$ must be negative, since the slope $b = -.254$ of the three fitted regression lines is negative. Hence, $r_{YX \cdot Z} = -\sqrt{.409} = -.639$.

For this example, the partial correlation $r_{YX \cdot Z}$ is very similar to the bivariate Pearson correlation r_{YX}, ignoring migrant status. If a single straight line were fit to the $N = 55$ observations on fertility and education, without regard to migrant status, we would get the prediction equation, $\hat{Y} = 6.394 - .280X$, with corresponding Pearson correlation $r_{YX} = -\sqrt{.392} = -.626$ (see Figure 14.12). ∎

Occasionally, it may be of interest to test the hypothesis H_0: $\rho_{YX \cdot Z} = 0$ that the partial correlation between Y and X is 0 within each of the levels of the categorical variable. This can be done using the standard t test described in Section 11.4 for a partial correlation. Since there are $(m + 1)$ parameters in the model $E(Y) = \alpha + \beta X + \delta_1 Z_1 + \cdots + \delta_{m-1} Z_{m-1}$, the test statistic is

$$t = \frac{r_{YX \cdot Z}}{\sqrt{\dfrac{1 - r^2_{YX \cdot Z}}{N - (m + 1)}}}$$

and has the t distribution with df $= N - (m + 1)$ if H_0 is true. Now, $\rho_{YX \cdot Z} = 0$ precisely when the slope of the regression equation between Y and X is 0 within each of the levels of the categorical variable. Therefore, the test of H_0: $\rho_{YX \cdot Z} = 0$ is equivalent to a test of H_0: $\beta = 0$ for this model. That is, the t statistic $t = b/\hat{\sigma}_b$, where $\hat{\sigma}_b$ denotes the estimated standard error of b, yields exactly the same t-value based on df $= N - (m + 1)$.

Example 14.8 To test the hypothesis H_0: $\rho_{YX \cdot Z} = 0$ that fertility and education are independent, controlling for migrant status, we form the test statistic

$$t = \frac{r_{YX \cdot Z}}{\sqrt{\dfrac{1 - r^2_{YX \cdot Z}}{N - (m + 1)}}} = \frac{-.639}{\sqrt{\dfrac{1 - .409}{55 - 4}}} = -5.93$$

based on df $= N - (m + 1) = 51$. The corresponding P-value is $P = .0001$ for the alternative hypothesis H_a: $\rho_{YX \cdot Z} \neq 0$.* Hence, we would conclude that there is an association between fertility and education, controlling for migrant status. ∎

*From Figure 14.5, $b = -.254$; if we had shown the entire printout for that model, we would have noted that $\hat{\sigma}_b = .043$, $t = b/\hat{\sigma}_b = -5.935$, and $P = .0001$.

Some Final Comments

In Chapter 13, we observed that the analysis of variance procedure may be viewed as a method whereby the total sum of squares TSS $= \sum_{i=1}^{m} \sum_{j=1}^{n_i} (Y_{ij} - \bar{Y})^2$ about the overall sample mean of Y is partitioned into component parts. In this chapter, we have added an interval variable X to the basic model. The analysis of covariance procedure can be viewed as a method whereby the term $\sum_{i=1}^{m} \sum_{j=1}^{n_i} (X_{ij} - \bar{X})(Y_{ij} - \bar{Y})$ is partitioned into several component parts (see Snedecor and Cochran, 1967). This term is a measure of the *covariation* between X and Y. That is, it is a measure of the way in which X and Y vary jointly around their means $\bar{X}$ and $\bar{Y}$. The cross-product $(X_{ij} - \bar{X})(Y_{ij} - \bar{Y})$ for the jth observation on X and Y in the ith sample summarizes the amount by which those observations are both above or both below their means (in which case it is positive), or one above and the other below their means (in which case the cross-product is negative). It is from such a representation of the method that the name *analysis of covariance* originates.

Although for simplicity we have considered only the case of one interval scale and one nominal scale independent variable in this chapter, similar approaches can be used when there are additional independent variables. For example, the model

$$E(Y) = \alpha + \beta_1 X_1 + \cdots + \beta_k X_k + \delta_1 Z_1 + \cdots + \delta_{m-1} Z_{m-1}$$

could be used to compare the means in m levels of a categorical variable controlling for the effects of k interval variables $X_1, \ldots, X_k$ and assuming no interaction. Similarly, the model

$$E(Y) = \alpha + \beta X + \delta_1 Z_1 + \cdots + \delta_{m-1} Z_{m-1} + \lambda_1 U_1 + \cdots + \lambda_{l-1} U_{l-1}$$

can be used to conduct a two-way analysis of means over an $l \times m$ cross-classification of two categorical variables, controlling for X and assuming no interaction. The U dummy variables in this model represent the levels of the second categorical variable. The reader is referred to Mendenhall (1970) and Neter and Wasserman (1974) for details on these more general analyses.

Summary

In this chapter we have seen how the general regression model can be used to describe the relationship between an interval dependent variable and both interval and categorical independent variables. Using this procedure, called **analysis of covariance**, we can compare the mean on the dependent variable among the various groups defined by the categories of the categorical variable, while controlling for an interval variable. Alternatively, we can compare the groups on the relationship between two interval variables by comparing their regression lines.

To compare the means across the levels of the categorical variable while controlling for the interval variable, we compute **adjusted means** that take into account the different distributions on the interval variable for those groups. Simultaneous comparisons of all pairs of adjusted means can be made by using the **Scheffé multiple comparison procedure**. A **partial correlation measure** can be computed to describe the degree of association between the interval variables, controlling for a categorical variable. The adjusted means and the partial correlation can be meaningfully interpreted only when there is no interaction. The hypothesis of no interaction, as well as the hypothesis of equal adjusted means or identical regression lines, can be tested using an F test corresponding to the comparison of a complete and a reduced regression model.

Note

Section 14.5

1. In the SAS System computer package, adjusted means are referred to as *least squares means*.

Problems

1. The regression equation relating Y = education of respondent (number of years completed) to race ($Z = 1$ for whites, $Z = 0$ for blacks) in a certain society is $E(Y) = 10 + 3Z$. The regression equation relating education of respondent to race and to father's education (X) is $E(Y) = 3 + .8X - .6Z$.
   a. Give the difference between the mean education of whites and blacks.
   b. Plot the relationship between X and the mean of Y for whites and for blacks.
   c. Give the difference between the mean education of whites and blacks, controlling for father's education.

2. Let Y = death rate and X = average age of residents, measured for each county in Massachusetts and in Florida. Draw a scatter diagram, identifying points for each state, for each of the following situations:
   a. The mean death rate is higher in Florida than in Massachusetts when X is ignored, but not when it is controlled.
   b. The mean death rate is higher in Florida than in Massachusetts both when X is ignored and when it is controlled.

3. Draw a scatter diagram of X and Y with two sets of points (representing two groups) such that H_0: equal means on Y would be rejected in a one-way ANOVA, but would not be rejected in an analysis of covariance (i.e., when X is controlled rather than ignored).

4.
   a. Give a linear regression equation that could be used to model the proportion of a nation's married population using modern birth control methods as a function of the proportion of the population living in urban areas and of the predominant form of religion for the nation (one of four categories). Identify all parameters in the model and indicate what assumptions are made in fitting the model and making inferences with it.

b. Give the null hypothesis that is tested to check for the presence of interaction.

c. Assuming no interaction, and controlling for urban proportion, how would you test for differences in the use of modern birth control methods for the four religion types?

5. Give an example of a situation in which you would expect there to be interaction between an interval variable and a categorical variable in their effects on an interval dependent variable.

In Problems 6–7, select the correct response(s).

6. In the United States, the mean annual income for blacks (μ_1) is smaller than for whites (μ_2), the mean number of years of education is smaller for blacks than for whites, and annual income is positively related to number of years of education. Assuming that there is no interaction, the difference in the mean annual income between whites and blacks, controlling for education, is:

a. Less than $\mu_2 - \mu_1$.
b. Greater than $\mu_2 - \mu_1$.
c. Possibly equal to $\mu_2 - \mu_1$.

7. In the model $E(Y) = \alpha + \beta X + \delta Z$, where Z is a dummy variable,

a. The categorical variable has two levels.
b. One line has slope β and the other has slope δ.
c. δ is the difference between the mean of Y for the second and first levels of the categorical variable.
d. δ is the difference between the adjusted mean of Y (controlling for X) for the second and first levels of the categorical variable.

8. Consider the model

$$E(Y) = \alpha + \beta X + \delta_1 Z_1 + \delta_2 Z_2 + \gamma_1(XZ_1) + \gamma_2(XZ_2)$$

where Z_1 and Z_2 are dummy variables.

a. Identify what each parameter represents in terms of the dependent variable $Y =$ annual income (thousands of dollars), the independent variable $X =$ age (years), and the nominal variable marital status (three categories—married, divorced, single).

b. Suppose that 30 individuals are randomly sampled from each category. When the above model is fitted, SSE = 820. When the interaction terms are omitted, SSE = 860. Test H_0: $\gamma_1 = \gamma_2 = 0$ at the .05 α-level.

c. For the model $E(Y) = \alpha + \beta X + \delta_1 Z_1 + \delta_2 Z_2$, the prediction equation is $\hat{Y} = 8.0 + .3X + 1.0Z_1 - 1.0Z_2$. Give the equations for the three separate lines fitted under the assumption of no interaction. Give an estimate of the income of an individual who is 30 years old, for each of the marital status levels.

d. For the model $E(Y) = \alpha + \beta X$, SSE = 1,200. Can we conclude at the .05 α-level that there is a difference in mean income for different marital status groups, controlling for age? Estimate the difference for each pair of marital statuses.

e. If the sample means for X are as listed in the table, then find the unadjusted and adjusted means for Y. [*Hint:* The unadjusted means are the values of the separate prediction equations evaluated at the $\bar{X}_i$.] Why are the adjusted means so different from the unadjusted means?

MARITAL STATUS	$\bar{X}_i$
Married	43
Divorced	36
Single	26

For Problems 9–23, a study is conducted of the relationship between Y = percentage of adults voting, X = percentage of adults registered to vote, and racial-ethnic representation, for precincts in the state of Texas for a gubernatorial election. Racial-ethnic representation is defined to be the group (Anglo, black, or Mexican-American) having the strongest representation in a precinct. A random sample of 40 precincts is selected after a particular election and classified by racial-ethnic representation. The values on Y and X for those precincts are given in the table. The accompanying printouts A–D give the results of fitting four different models to the data.

Primary Racial-Ethnic Representation of Precinct

ANGLO		BLACK		MEXICAN-AMERICAN	
Y	X	Y	X	Y	X
55	80	30	50	28	40
60	85	40	62	36	52
45	62	30	39	30	35
55	91	34	53	5	15
40	78	26	44	31	48
51	73	15	28	50	63
48	69	30	46	20	38
58	85	36	62	18	30
40	66	33	51	28	43
72	94	36	60	20	33
53	81				
54	76				
50	75				
57	78				
47	74				
61	82				
43	65				
42	58				
60	80				
55	72				

Printout A Model $E(Y) = \alpha + \beta X$

SOURCE	DF	SUM OF SQUARES	R-SQUARE	PARAMETER	ESTIMATE
REGRESSION	1	7896.65	.917	INTERCEPT	-3.72
ERROR	38	713.25		% REGISTERED	.73
TOTAL	39	8609.90			

Printout B Model $E(Y) = \alpha + \delta_1 Z_1 + \delta_2 Z_2$

SOURCE	DF	SUM OF SQUARES	MEAN SQUARE	PARAMETER	ESTIMATE
REGRESSION	2	5619.30	2809.65	INTERCEPT	26.6
ERROR	37	2990.60	80.83	Z1 (ANGLO)	25.7
TOTAL	39	8609.90		Z2 (BLACK)	4.4

Printout C Model $E(Y) = \alpha + \beta X + \delta_1 Z_1 + \delta_2 Z_2$

SOURCE	DF	SUM OF SQUARES	MEAN SQUARE	PARAMETER	ESTIMATE
REGRESSION	3	7936.73	2645.58	INTERCEPT	-2.78
ERROR	36	673.17	18.70	% REGISTERED	.74
TOTAL	39	8609.90		Z1 (ANGLO)	-1.31
				Z2 (BLACK)	-2.85

Printout D Model $E(Y) = \alpha + \beta X + \delta_1 Z_1 + \delta_2 Z_2 + \gamma_1(XZ_1) + \gamma_2(XZ_2)$

SOURCE	DF	SUM OF SQUARES	MEAN SQUARE	PARAMETER	ESTIMATE
REGRESSION	5	7990.52	1598.10	INTERCEPT	-8.25
ERROR	34	619.38	18.22	% REGISTERED	.88
TOTAL	39	8609.90		Z1 (ANGLO)	6.97
				Z2 (BLACK)	9.80
				XZ1	-.17
				XZ2	-.28

9. Draw a scatter diagram for the relationship between percentage voting and percentage registered, identifying the points by racial-ethnic representation of precinct.

10. Give the least squares estimate of the analysis of covariance model assuming no interaction. Interpret the estimates in that equation. Give the three best lines by level of racial-ethnic representation, and plot them on the scatter diagram.

11. Give the least squares estimate of the analysis of covariance model allowing for interaction. Interpret the estimates in that equation. Give the three best lines by level of racial-ethnic representation for this model, and compare them to the corresponding lines obtained under the assumption of no interaction.

12. Give the least squares line between Y and X, ignoring racial-ethnic representation, and compare it to the lines obtained in Problem 10.

13. Using the $\alpha = .05$ level, test whether the interaction terms can be omitted from the model.

14. Using the $\alpha = .05$ level, test whether the regression lines between Y and X for the three levels have the same slope.

15. Using the $\alpha = .05$ level, test whether the regression lines between Y and X for the three levels are identical.

16. Using the $\alpha = .05$ level, test whether the mean voting percentages are equal for the three levels of racial-ethnic representation, controlling for percentage registered.

17. The means of percentage registered for the three levels are $\bar{X}_1 = 76.2$, $\bar{X}_2 = 49.5$, $\bar{X}_3 = 39.7$, with an overall mean of $\bar{X} = 60.4$. Find the adjusted means on percentage voting for the three levels, and compare their values to the unadjusted means. [*Note:* The unadjusted means $\bar{Y}_1$, $\bar{Y}_2$, and $\bar{Y}_3$ can be determined from Printout B (review Section 13.3). They also can be obtained using the prediction equation in Printout C and the information given on the $\bar{X}_i$-values, or by direct calculation from the table of data values.]

18. The sum of squared registration percentages for the three levels about their respective means are 1,631.2, 1,052.5, and 1,548.1. Find 95% simultaneous confidence intervals for the differences in the true adjusted means. Interpret the intervals.

19. Calculate the partial correlation between percentage voting and percentage registered, controlling for ethnic representation. Compare its value to the Pearson correlation between percentage voting and percentage registered, ignoring racial-ethnic representation.

20. Give the *P*-value for testing the null hypothesis that percentage voting and percentage registered are independent, controlling for racial-ethnic representation. Use the alternative hypothesis that there is a positive relationship under that control.

21. Using the results of the appropriate model, test at the $\alpha = .05$ level the null hypothesis that the *unadjusted* means on percentage voting are equal. Compare the result of this test to the one in Problem 16.

***22.** Describe how the model assuming no interaction could be expanded to include the additional categorical variable, location of precinct, with levels urban, suburban, small town, and rural.

***23.** Describe how the model assuming no interaction could be expanded to include the additional interval independent variable, percentage of residents in precinct who are homeowners.

24. Refer to Problem 1. Suppose that the mean of father's education is 12 years. Find the adjusted mean educational levels for whites and blacks, controlling for father's education, and compare them to the unadjusted means.

25. Use a computer package to analyze the accompanying data on Y = income (thousands of dollars), X = education (number of years), and Z = race ($Z = 1$, white; $Z = 0$, black), for a sample of adult males.

WHITES						BLACKS	
Y	X	Y	X	Y	X	Y	X
16	12	12	10	9	12	6	10
19	18	20	16	7	8	8	5
16	7	12	7	25	13	10	9
37	18	28	13	25	16	6	11
20	10	10	6	14	10	15	14
15	12	35	16	20	13	8	12
12	12	18	18	13	10	16	16
30	12	20	16	13	16	16	18
16	16	20	14	20	18		
14	11	12	11	10	12		
16	9	14	12	9	14		
18	12	18	16	7	13		

Note: These values have means similar to ones reported for adult males in the United States in 1981. According to the *Statistical Abstract of the United States, 1984*, $\bar{Y} = 17.2$ and $\bar{X} = 12.7$ for whites, and $\bar{Y} = 10.5$ and $\bar{X} = 12.2$ for blacks.

a. Fit the one-way ANOVA model $E(Y) = \alpha + \delta Z$, and interpret the parameter estimates.

b. Test the hypothesis of equal mean incomes for whites and blacks, using $\alpha = .05$. Interpret.

c. Fit the covariance model $E(Y) = \alpha + \beta X + \delta Z$, and interpret the parameter estimates.

d. Fit the covariance model that allows for interaction. Find the predicted difference between the mean incomes of whites and blacks at $X = 8$, and also at $X = 16$. Interpret the nature of the predicted interaction.

e. Test, using $\alpha = .05$, whether the interaction model in part **d** gives a better fit than the model with no interaction in part **c**. Interpret.

f. Find the sample adjusted mean incomes for whites and blacks. Compare their differences to the difference in unadjusted means, and interpret.

g. Construct a 95% confidence interval for the difference in population adjusted means.

h. Construct a graph of the model with no interaction for these data, and identify on it the unadjusted and adjusted means.

i. Fit the model $E(Y) = \alpha + \beta X$, and compare it to the model with no interaction in order to test (using $\alpha = .05$) that the population adjusted means are equal.

j. Redo all the steps of an analysis of covariance, if the sample also includes six males of Spanish origin (treated as the third category of race), whose (X, Y)-values are (11, 12), (8, 9), (14, 15), (13, 11), (9, 11), and (14, 16). [*Note:* In 1981, X and Y were actually estimated to average 11.5 and 12.3, respectively, for this group.]

*26. The model $E(Y) = \alpha + \beta_1 X_1 + \beta_2 X_2 + \beta_3 X_3 + \beta_4 X_4$ is used to describe the relationship between Y = college GPA, X_1 = high school GPA, X_2 = verbal plus mathematics SAT score (in hundreds, 0–16 range), X_3 = sex (1 = female, 0 = male), and X_4 = race (1 = black, 0 = white). For a sample of 100 college seniors, the accompanying results are obtained.

Computer Printout for Problem 26

PARAMETER	ESTIMATE	STANDARD ERROR	SUM OF SQUARED RESIDUALS
INTERCEPT	.700		95.0
X1	.400	.150	
X2	.150	.060	
X3	-.050	.070	
X4	.090	.080	

a. Interpret each of the estimates in the prediction equation.
b. Based on the reported standard errors, comment on the effects of the independent variables.
c. For the simpler model $E(Y) = \alpha + \beta_1 X_1 + \beta_2 X_2$, the sum of squared residuals equals 98.0. Test the null hypothesis that mean college GPA is independent of sex and race, controlling for college GPA and total SAT score.
d. For the model $E(Y) = \alpha + \beta_1 X_3 + \beta_2 X_4$, the estimated regression coefficient for the effect of race is $-.100$. Explain the difference in the interpretation of this estimate and the one given in the printout for the more complex model.
e. Give the model that has interaction terms for each pair of independent variables.
f. If the sum of squared residuals equals 86.0 for the model in part **e**, test the null hypothesis of no interaction.

*27. The figure at the top of page 479 is an example of a computer printout for a multiple regression analysis using SPSS^X. The analysis refers to General Social Survey data combined for the years 1977, 1978, and 1980. The dependent variable is an index of attitudes toward premarital, extramarital, and homosexual sex. Higher scores represent more permissive attitudes. The categorical independent variables are race (0 for whites, 1 for blacks), sex (0 for males, 1 for females), region (0 for South, 1 for non-South), and religion (R_1 = 1 for liberal Protestant sect, R_2 = 1 for conservative Protestant, R_3 = 1 for fundamentalist Protestant sect, R_4 = 1 for Catholic, R_5 = 1 for Jewish; no religious affiliation when $R_1 = \cdots = R_5 = 0$). The quantitative independent variables are age, education (number of years), attendance at church (higher values represent more frequent attendance), and a variable for which higher values represent greater intolerance of freedom of speech for atheists and communists. On the SPSS^X printout, BETA denotes the standardized regression coefficient, the column of F values are the squares of the t statistics for testing partial effects, STANDARD ERROR is the root mean square error, and (CONSTANT) is the Y-intercept.

a. Write the regression model for this analysis, and give the prediction equation.
b. Which variable seems to be the best predictor of sexual attitudes?
c. For each independent variable, describe its effect on the dependent variable.
d. For which sex, which race, and which religion is attitude most permissive?
e. Based on the regression parameter estimates, give a profile of a person you would expect to be least permissive with respect to sexual attitudes.

Computer Printout for Problem 27

ANALYSIS OF VARIANCE	DF	SUM OF SQUARES	MEAN SQUARE	F
REGRESSION	12.	2583.32552	215.27713	54.09752
RESIDUAL	1092.	4345.53420	3.97943	

MULTIPLE R	0.61060
R SQUARE	0.37284
ADJUSTED R SQUARE	0.36594
STANDARD ERROR	1.99485

VARIABLES IN THE EQUATION

VARIABLE	B	BETA	STD ERROR B	F
RACE	0.9931678	0.12474	0.20397	23.708
AGE	-0.2900217D-01	-0.18939	0.00417	48.405
SEX	-0.2894541	-0.05766	0.12301	5.537
EDUC	0.7316427D-01	0.09178	0.02230	10.768
REGION	0.6169766	0.11488	0.14012	19.387
ATTEND	-0.2857745	-0.30388	0.02548	125.832
R1	-0.2962109	-0.04942	0.28257	1.099
R2	-0.6048863	-0.11345	0.27823	4.727
R3	-1.187424	-0.12838	0.34375	11.932
R4	-0.1274659	-0.02276	0.28561	0.199
R5	0.5209279	0.03381	0.44174	1.391
FREESPCH	-0.4654554	-0.22707	0.05810	64.174
(CONSTANT)	9.372561			

*28. A sample is taken to study the relationship between yearly wage (thousands of dollars) and years experience for a particular type of job in a large industry. The relationship is considered for three ethnic groups, which we shall refer to as A, B, and C. An analysis of covariance is conducted, assuming no interaction, in which the results in the accompanying table are obtained. When the least squares line is calculated, ignoring ethnic group, SSE = 315. When the covariance model is fit, SSE = 152.5 (assuming no interaction). The within sum of squares for the experience values is $WSS_x = 200$. For the wage values, the total sum of squares is TSS = 362.7, and the within sum of squares is WSS = 250.

ETHNIC GROUP	SAMPLE SIZE	MEAN EXPERIENCE	MEAN WAGE	MEAN WAGE ADJUSTED FOR EXPERIENCE
A	20	7	8.5	8.176
B	30	5	5.8	5.876
C	15	4	5.4	5.676

a. Give the analysis of covariance model for this problem, identifying the meaning of all parameters and stating all assumptions.

b. Give the estimates of all the parameters in this model.

c. Test whether the adjusted means are all equal, using the .05 α-level.

d. Controlling for experience, find simultaneous 95% confidence intervals for the differences between each pair of means for yearly wage.

e. Calculate the Pearson correlation between wage and experience. Calculate the partial correlation between wage and experience, controlling for ethnic group. Give an interpretation to the square of each of the values.

29. Summarize the differences in purpose of the following:

a. A regression analysis for two interval variables

b. A one-way analysis of variance

c. A two-way analysis of variance

d. An analysis of covariance

Bibliography

Blalock, H. M. (1979). *Social Statistics*. Revised 2nd ed. New York: McGraw-Hill. Chap. 20.

Mendenhall, W. (1970). *An Introduction to Linear Models and the Design and Analysis of Experiments*. Belmont, Calif.: Wadsworth.

Neter, J. and W. Wasserman (1974). *Applied Linear Statistical Models*. Homewood, Ill.: Richard D. Irwin. Chap. 22.

Pedhazur, E. J. (1982). *Multiple Regression in Behavioral Research*, 2nd ed. New York: Holt, Rinehart and Winston. Chaps. 12 and 13.

Snedecor, G. W. and W. G. Cochran (1967). *Statistical Methods*. 6th ed. Ames: Iowa State University Press. Chap. 14.

CHAPTER 15

Models for Categorical Variables

Contents

The regression models we have studied so far assume that the dependent variable is of interval scale. This chapter considers the case in which the dependent variable is instead categorical.

Section 15.1 introduces the *logistic regression model,* formulated for interval-scale independent variables. A related *logit model* for categorical independent variables is presented in Section 15.2. For simplicity in these sections, we present the models for the case in which the dependent variable is a simple dichotomy. For instance, the response could be a person's choice in a presidential election (Democrat or Republican), modeled with the predictor variables annual income, education level, religious affiliation, and sex. Or, we might model how the choice regarding early retirement (yes or no) depends on savings, annual income, job satisfaction, and various health and family characteristics. Whether a subject has symptoms of a certain form of mental illness (yes or no) might be modeled in terms of factors such as socioeconomic status and a life events index.

Loglinear models, discussed in Section 15.3, are more general than logit models. They can be used to model association patterns among a set of categorical variables, even when none of the variables is treated as a dependent variable. In Section 15.4 we discuss the *odds ratio,* a measure that is helpful for summarizing associations in logit and loglinear models. The final section illustrates how ordinal variables can be treated differently from nominal variables in these models.

15.1 Logistic Regression

Suppose that the dependent variable Y is dichotomous. We shall score the responses on Y using 0 and 1. For instance, if the possible responses on Y are "yes" and "no," we could let 0 denote no and 1 denote yes. The sum of the scores in the sample is then the number of "yes" responses. The mean of the 0 and 1 scores, which is the sum divided by the total sample size, is simply the proportion of "yes" responses. In other words, a proportion is the special case of a mean calculated for a dichotomous variable having a (0, 1) scoring (see also Note 5.5).

In standard regression analysis, we model the mean of the dependent variable. For dichotomous dependent variables, we therefore model how the proportion of responses in one of the two categories depends on independent variables. Let $\pi = E(Y)$ denote the proportion of "1" responses in the population. Now π also represents the probability that a randomly selected subject makes the response "1," and this probability may vary according to the values of the independent variables. For a single independent variable, X, the simple model $\pi = \alpha + \beta X$ implies that the probability of a "1" response is a linear function of X. Unfortunately, this is usually not a valid model. Figure 15.1 shows that this model implies probabilities below 0 or above 1 for sufficiently small or large X-values, whereas probabilities must fall between 0 and 1. Inference assumptions also break down in this case, since the dichotomous response distributions are drastically different from normal distributions with constant standard deviation.

More realistic response curves, having an S-shape, are also shown in Figure 15.1. With these curves, the predicted probability of a "1" response falls between 0 and 1 for all possible X-values. In addition, for substantive reasons these curves are often more appropriate than straight lines. A fixed change in X often has a smaller impact on π when π is near 0 or near 1 than when π is near the middle of its range. For instance, consider the decision to rent or to buy housing. An increase of $1,000 in X = annual income may have less effect when X = $5,000 (for which π is near 0) or when X = $75,000 (for which π is near 1) than when X = $20,000.

Fig. 15.1 Linear and Logistic Regression Models for a (0, 1) Response

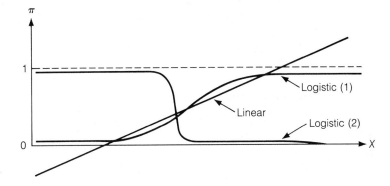

Logistic Regression Model

The curvilinear relationships shown in Figure 15.1 are usually well described by the formula

$$\log\left(\frac{\pi}{1-\pi}\right) = \alpha + \beta X$$

The function $\log[\pi/(1-\pi)]$ is called the *logistic transformation* (or *logit*), and this model is referred to as a *logistic regression model*. It is standard to use natural logs (base e) in logistic models. As π increases from 0 to 1, the logit increases from $-\infty$ to ∞. The probability $\pi = 1/2$ corresponds to a logit of 0, and π-values above (below) 1/2 correspond to positive (negative) logits.

If $\beta = 0$ in the logistic model, the logit (and hence π) does not change as X changes, so the curve flattens to a horizontal straight line. For positive β, π increases as X increases, as in logistic curve (1) in Figure 15.1. For negative β, π decreases as X increases; in other words, the probability of a "1" response tends toward 0 for larger values of X, as in logistic curve (2) in Figure 15.1. Sometimes it is useful to know the X-value at which $\pi = 1/2$. This occurs when $\log[\pi/(1-\pi)] = 0 = \alpha + \beta X$; that is, when $X = -\alpha/\beta$. The steepness of the curve at that point increases as $|\beta|$ increases. For instance, $|\beta|$ for curve (2) is greater than β for curve (1). To interpret the magnitude of β, one can use the fact that $1/|\beta|$ is the approximate distance between the X-values at which $\pi = 1/4$ (or $\pi = 3/4$) and at which $\pi = 1/2$. Notice that β cannot be interpreted as a simple slope (as it can in the model $\pi = \alpha + \beta X$), because the rate at which the curve climbs or descends changes* according to the value of X.

*The greatest rate of change is at the point where $\pi = 1/2$. A line drawn tangent to the curve at that point has slope $\beta/4$, where β is the logistic regression coefficient.

Logistic regression models can be fitted using computer packages such as PROC LOGIST in the SAS System, and the LOGLINEAR and PROBIT routines in SPSS[X]. The hypothesis H_0: $\beta = 0$ that X has no effect on the dichotomous response can be tested using $z = b/\hat{\sigma}_b$, where b is the estimate of β and $\hat{\sigma}_b$ is the standard error of b.

Example 15.1   A sample of 54 elderly men are given a psychiatric examination to determine whether symptoms of senility are present. A subtest of the Wechsler Adult Intelligence Scale (WAIS) is used as the independent variable. The data are shown in Table 15.1. The WAIS scores in the sample range from 4 to 20, with a mean of 11.6. Higher values indicate more effective intellectual functioning.

Table 15.1
Data on X = WAIS Score and Y = Senility (1 = symptoms present)

X	Y	X	Y	X	Y	X	Y	X	Y
9	1	7	1	7	0	17	0	13	0
13	1	5	1	16	0	14	0	13	0
6	1	14	1	9	0	19	0	9	0
8	1	13	0	9	0	9	0	15	0
10	1	16	0	11	0	11	0	10	0
4	1	10	0	13	0	14	0	11	0
14	1	12	0	15	0	10	0	12	0
8	1	11	0	13	0	16	0	4	0
11	1	14	0	10	0	10	0	14	0
7	1	15	0	11	0	16	0	20	0
9	1	18	0	6	0	14	0		

Fitting the logistic regression model (using a computer routine that does a *maximum likelihood* fit) gives us the prediction equation

$$\log\left(\frac{\hat{\pi}}{1 - \hat{\pi}}\right) = a + bX = 2.404 - .324X$$

with $a = 2.404$ and $b = -.324$. Since the estimate b of β is negative, this sample suggests that the likelihood of senility symptoms decreases at higher levels of the WAIS. The prediction curve is shown in Figure 15.2. It takes the value $\hat{\pi} = 1/2$ at $X = -a/b = (-2.404)/(-.324) = 7.4$, and the predicted probability of senility is below 1/2 for WAIS scores above 7.4.

Fig. 15.2 Prediction Curve for Example 15.1

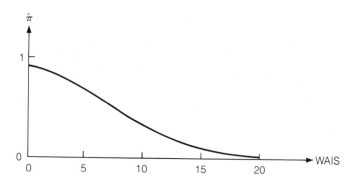

The null hypothesis H_0: $\beta = 0$ states that the probability of senility is the same at all levels of the WAIS score. The estimated standard error of b is $\hat{\sigma}_b = .114$. To test H_0: $\beta = 0$, we form the test statistic $z = b/\hat{\sigma}_b = -.324/.114 = -2.84$. This results in a P-value of $P = .0046$ for H_a: $\beta \neq 0$ and $P = .0023$ for H_a: $\beta < 0$. Hence, there is strong evidence of a negative association between the presence of senility and the WAIS score.

It is interesting to note that a least squares fit of the simple linear model $\pi = \alpha + \beta X$ gives $\hat{\pi} = .847 - .051X$. This gives quite different $\hat{\pi}$ predictions at the low end and at the high end of the WAIS scale. For instance, we get the prediction $\hat{\pi} < 0$ when $X > 16.6$.   ■

Equations for Probabilities and Odds

Solving the logistic regression equation for π, we can express the model directly in terms of π as

$$\pi = e^{\alpha + \beta X}/[1 + e^{\alpha + \beta X}]$$

Here e raised to some power represents the antilog of that number when natural logs are used.* In Example 15.1, for instance, the predicted proportion of elderly men who have symptoms of senility is

$$\hat{\pi} = e^{2.404 - .324X}/[1 + e^{2.404 - .324X}]$$

For men who score 4 on the WAIS (the lower limit for this sample), the predicted proportion is

$$\hat{\pi} = e^{2.404 - .324(4)}/[1 + e^{2.404 - .324(4)}]$$

$$= e^{1.11}/(1 + e^{1.11}) = 3.03/4.03 = .75$$

For WAIS = 20 (the upper limit for this sample), the predicted proportion is only .02. At the mean WAIS score of 11.6, the predicted proportion is .21.

The ratio $\pi/(1 - \pi)$ that appears in the logit transformation is referred to as the *odds*. For instance, when $\pi = .75$, the odds equals $.75/.25 = 3.0$, meaning that a response of "1" is three times as likely as a response of "0." An important way of interpreting the logistic regression coefficient β is as an effect on the odds. Specifically, taking antilogs of both sides of the logistic equation $\log[\pi/(1 - \pi)] = \alpha + \beta X$, we obtain

$$\frac{\pi}{1 - \pi} = e^{\alpha + \beta X} = e^\alpha (e^\beta)^X$$

The right-hand side of this equation has the *exponential* form studied in Section 12.1. This exponential relationship implies that every unit increase in X produces a multiplicative effect of e^β on the odds.

In Example 15.1, the antilog of β is estimated to be $e^b = e^{-.324} = .723$. Hence, when WAIS increases by one unit, the estimated odds in favor of senility are multiplied by .723. When WAIS = 20, for example, the odds for senility are estimated to be .723 times what they are when WAIS = 19. When WAIS = 20, the odds for senility

*Many pocket calculators can calculate powers of e.

are only $(.723)^{10} = .04$ times as high as when WAIS = 10. For instance, when WAIS = 10,

$$\frac{\hat{\pi}}{1 - \hat{\pi}} = e^{2.404 - .324(10)} = .433$$

whereas when WAIS = 20,

$$\frac{\hat{\pi}}{1 - \hat{\pi}} = e^{2.404 - .324(20)} = .017$$

which is only 4% of the value of .433 obtained when WAIS = 10.

Generalizations   A multiple logistic regression model can be used when there are several independent variables. This has the form

$$\log\left(\frac{\pi}{1 - \pi}\right) = \alpha + \beta_1 X_1 + \cdots + \beta_k X_k$$

Alternatively, the equation can be expressed as

$$\pi = e^{\alpha + \beta_1 X_1 + \cdots + \beta_k X_k} / [1 + e^{\alpha + \beta_1 X_1 + \cdots + \beta_k X_k}]$$

Cross-product terms can be introduced to allow for interactions among the independent variables in their effects on the response. If some of the independent variables are categorical, then dummy variables can be used as they were in the analysis of covariance models of Chapter 14. Models for categorical independent variables are discussed in the next section.

15.2 Logit Models for Categorical Variables

In the previous section we introduced the logistic transformation (or logit) as a device for modeling a dichotomous dependent variable in terms of quantitative independent variables. The same transformation can be used when the independent variables are categorical. Again, an important reason for modeling the logit instead of π itself is that linear models produce predicted values in the $(-\infty, \infty)$ range rather than the restricted $(0, 1)$ range.

Logits for Categorical Data   Logit models can be formulated for categorical independent variables by introducing dummy variables, as was done in analysis of variance and analysis of covariance models. We shall introduce here a somewhat different coding, one that is more commonly used in computer packages for logit and loglinear models. Instead of comparing each category to the last category, we give an effect for each category that compares it to an overall average effect.

To illustrate, suppose there are two categorical independent variables, denoted by A and B. Then the data are cell counts in a three-dimensional cross-classification table, where the third dimension is the dichotomous dependent variable. Let π_{ij} denote the probability of response "1" on the dependent variable when A is at level i and B is at level j. A basic logit model is

$$\log \left(\frac{\pi_{ij}}{1 - \pi_{ij}} \right) = \mu + \lambda_i^A + \lambda_j^B$$

In this model, μ represents an overall average of the logits for all the combinations of A and B. The parameter λ_i^A represents the effect of being classified in level i of variable A, and λ_j^B represents the effect of being classified in level j of variable B. These are usually scaled so that $\Sigma_i \lambda_i^A = 0$ and $\Sigma_j \lambda_j^B = 0$. For instance, if variable A has two categories and if $\lambda_1^A = 1.5$, then $\lambda_2^A = -1.5$. For these values, classification in the first category of A has a positive effect on the logit. Since higher logits correspond to higher π-values, being classified in the first category of A increases the chance that a subject makes response "1" on the dependent variable.

If an independent variable has *no* effect on the dichotomous dependent variable, then all of its lambda parameters are 0. For instance, if all $\lambda_j^B = 0$, the logit model simplifies to

$$\log \left(\frac{\pi_{ij}}{1 - \pi_{ij}} \right) = \mu + \lambda_i^A$$

The interpretation of this model is that the dependent variable is statistically independent of variable B, controlling for variable A. An even simpler model is

$$\log \left(\frac{\pi_{ij}}{1 - \pi_{ij}} \right) = \mu$$

which assumes that classification on the dependent variable does not depend on variable B or variable A.

When all the variables are interval scale, a regression model that is analogous to the logit model $\log[\pi_{ij}/(1 - \pi_{ij})] = \mu + \lambda_i^A + \lambda_j^B$ is

$$E(Y) = \alpha + \beta_1 X_1 + \beta_2 X_2$$

Obtaining all $\lambda_j^B = 0$ in the logit model is analogous to having $\beta_2 = 0$ for the regression model. As with the regression model, the logit model implies that both independent variables may have an effect on the dependent variable, but it also assumes that there is no interaction. That is, this logit model assumes that the effect of A on the dependent variable is the same at all levels of B, and the effect of B on the dependent variable is the same at all levels of A. For a three-dimensional cross-classification table, this condition is referred to as *no three-factor interaction*. This implies that the association between any two of the variables has the same form at all levels of the third variable.

Logit models for categorical independent variables can be fitted using computer routines such as LOGLINEAR in SPSS[X] and PROC CATMOD in the SAS System.

Example 15.2

Table 15.2, based on data presented by Radelet (1981), is an example of a three-dimensional cross-classification table. Radelet's article concerns the effects of racial characteristics on the decision regarding whether to impose the death penalty after an individual is convicted of a homicide. The variables considered in Table 15.2 are "death penalty verdict," having categories (yes, no), "race of defendant," having categories (white, black), and "race of victim," having categories (white, black).

Table 15.2

Death Penalty Verdict by Defendant's Race and Victim's Race

DEFENDANT'S RACE	VICTIM'S RACE	DEATH PENALTY		PROPORTION YES
		Yes	*No*	
White	White	19	132	0.126
	Black	0	9	0.000
Black	White	11	52	0.175
	Black	6	97	0.058

Source: Radelet (1981). Reprinted by permission.

For each of the four combinations of defendant's race and victim's race, Table 15.2 lists the proportion of subjects who received the death penalty. For white defendants, the death penalty was imposed over 12 percentage points more often when the victim was white than when the victim was black. (In fact, the death penalty was never imposed in this sample when a white killed a black.) Similarly, for black defendants, the death penalty was imposed about 12 percentage points more often when the victim was white than when the victim was black. Controlling for defendant's race, therefore, the death penalty verdict seems to be more likely when a white is killed than when a black is killed.

Now, consider the association between defendant's race and the death penalty verdict, controlling for victim's race. When the victim was white, the death penalty was imposed about 5 percentage points more often when the defendant was black than when the defendant was white. When the victim was black, the death penalty was imposed over 5 percentage points more often when the defendant was black than when the defendant was white. In summary, controlling for victim's race, black defendants were somewhat more likely to be given the death penalty than were white defendants.

These data can be summarized well by a logit model. Arbitrarily, we take yes = 1 and no = 0 in scoring the dependent variable, death penalty verdict. Then, π_{ij} denotes the probability of a "yes" death penalty verdict when the defendant's race is i ($i = 1$, white; $i = 2$, black) and the victim's race is j ($j = 1$, white; $j = 2$, black). In the logit model

$$\log\left(\frac{\pi_{ij}}{1 - \pi_{ij}}\right) = \mu + \lambda_i^D + \lambda_j^V,$$

λ_i^D represents the effect on the logit of defendant's race being i, and λ_j^V represents the effect of victim's race being j, where $\lambda_1^D + \lambda_2^D = 0$ and $\lambda_1^V + \lambda_2^V = 0$.

Figure 15.3 is an example of a computer printout for the parameter estimates when this model is fitted using a *maximum likelihood* solution. The estimate $\hat{\mu} = -2.40$ represents an estimated mean of the logits. The negative value reflects the fact that most defendants do not receive the death penalty. That is, estimates of π are well below 1/2 (so estimated logits are negative) for all four combinations of defendant's race and victim's race. For the effect of defendant's race on death penalty verdict, we obtain $\hat{\lambda}_1^D = -.220$. The value of $\hat{\lambda}_2^D$ is not reported, but it is $\hat{\lambda}_2^D = .220$, since $\hat{\lambda}_1^D + \hat{\lambda}_2^D = 0$. Thus, defendant classification as white (category 1) has a negative effect on the logit, meaning that it lowers the chance of a "yes" death penalty verdict. Similarly, the chance of a "yes" death penalty verdict is higher when the defendant is black, since $\hat{\lambda}_2^D > 0$. For the effect of victim's race on death penalty verdict, Figure 15.3 shows $\hat{\lambda}_1^V = .662$, so that $\hat{\lambda}_2^V = -.662$. Hence, the odds of the death penalty verdict "yes" increases when the victim was white (category 1), whereas the odds decreases when the victim was black. ∎

Fig. 15.3 Parameter Estimates for Logit Model for Death Penalty Data

PARAMETER	COEFF	STD.ERR.	Z-VALUE	P-VALUE
INTERCEPT	-2.400	.240		
DEFENDANT 1	-.220	.200	-1.098	.272
VICTIM 1	.662	.260	2.550	.011

ESTIMATES FOR PARAMETERS

Effects on Odds

The logit model is formulated in terms of the log of the odds, and the parameter estimates refer to that log scale. It is easier to understand numbers expressed as odds or probabilities than numbers expressed as log odds. As with the logistic regression model, antilogs of the parameter estimates are multiplicative effects on the odds scale.

In Example 15.2, for instance, the average logit of $\hat{\mu} = -2.40$ corresponds to an odds of $e^{\hat{\mu}} = e^{-2.40} = .091$. An odds of .091 means that the chance of the death penalty verdict "yes" is only 9.1% as large as the chance of the "no" verdict. The effect of victim's race being white is to multiply the odds of a "yes" death penalty verdict by $e^{\hat{\lambda}_1^V} = e^{.662} = 1.939$ (i.e., to increase the odds). The effect of victim's race being black is to multiply the odds by $e^{\hat{\lambda}_2^V} = e^{-.662} = .516 = 1/1.939$ (i.e., to decrease the odds of a "yes" verdict). Hence, when the victim was white the odds of the "yes" death penalty verdict are $1.939/.516 = (1.939)^2 = 3.76$ times higher than when the victim was black. The actual values of the odds depend as well on defendant's race, but this *ratio* of the odds is the same at each level of defendant's race.

The expression for the log odds is *additive*, but in taking antilogs, we are utilizing a *multiplicative* expression for the estimated odds,

$$\frac{\hat{\pi}_{ij}}{1 - \hat{\pi}_{ij}} = e^{\hat{\mu}} e^{\hat{\lambda}_i^D} e^{\hat{\lambda}_j^V}$$

In other words, the antilogs of the parameter estimates are *multiplied* to obtain the estimated odds. We can use this expression to calculate odds estimates for specific combinations of defendant's race and victim's race. For instance, when the defendant is black (category 2 of D) and the victim is white (category 1 of V), the estimated odds are

$$\frac{\hat{\pi}_{21}}{1 - \hat{\pi}_{21}} = e^{\hat{\mu}} e^{\hat{\lambda}_2^D} e^{\hat{\lambda}_1^V} = e^{-2.40} e^{.220} e^{.662}$$
$$= (.091)(1.246)(1.939) = .219$$

Thus, a predicted logit L can be transformed to the odds scale by

odds = antilog(L) = e^L

It can also be transformed to the (0, 1) probability scale using

$$\hat{\pi} = e^L/(1 + e^L) = \text{odds}/(1 + \text{odds})$$

For instance, when the defendant is black and the victim is white, the estimated odds just calculated of $\hat{\pi}_{21}/(1 - \hat{\pi}_{21}) = .219$ corresponds to an estimated death penalty probability of $\hat{\pi}_{21} = \text{odds}/(1 + \text{odds}) = .219/1.219 = .180$, which is close to the actual sample proportion of .175 reported in Table 15.2.

Inference for Logit Models

In Section 8.2 we studied the chi-square test of independence for two-dimensional tables. That test can be regarded as a goodness-of-fit test for the model which states that the two categorical variables are statistically independent. The chi-square statistic compares the observed frequencies to *expected frequencies*, which are numbers that have the same row and column totals but that satisfy the independence model. Similarly, for multidimensional tables there are also chi-square tests that check the adequacy of models which specify certain independence patterns or association linkages among the variables. Each model has a set of cell expected frequencies, numbers that perfectly satisfy the model. The mechanism for obtaining the expected frequencies is too complex to discuss here, but the values are easily calculated using computer packages for logit and loglinear models. The goodness-of-fit of a model is tested by comparing the expected frequencies, denoted by $\{f_e\}$, to the actual observed frequencies $\{f_o\}$. The discrepancies are summarized by a chi-square statistic, with larger differences between the observed and expected frequencies leading to larger values of the statistic and more evidence that the model is inadequate.

Two chi-square statistics are commonly used to compare the $\{f_o\}$ to the $\{f_e\}$. The *Pearson statistic*

$$\chi^2 = \sum \frac{(f_o - f_e)^2}{f_e}$$

was the one presented in Section 8.2 for testing independence. Another statistic, called the *likelihood-ratio statistic*, is

$$G^2 = 2 \sum f_o \log (f_o/f_e)$$

If the model for which the expected frequencies are calculated truly holds, both these statistics have approximate chi-square distributions. The approximation is better for larger sample sizes. The Pearson statistic is generally preferred when the sample size is rather small. The likelihood-ratio statistic is useful for comparing fits of various models, as will be shown in Section 15.3.

The number of degrees of freedom (df) for the chi-square statistics depends on the model fitted. The df value equals the number of logits minus the number of distinct parameters in the model. The number of logits is simply the number of combinations of levels of independent variables, since there is one logit for each combination. In counting parameters, we exclude redundant ones. For instance, if there are r levels for variable A, there are $r-1$ distinct $\{\lambda_i^A\}$ parameters, since λ_r^A is determined from the others by the constraint $\Sigma \lambda_i^A = 0$. When $r = 2$, for example, $\lambda_1^A + \lambda_2^A = 0$, so λ_2^A is determined from λ_1^A by $\lambda_2^A = -\lambda_1^A$.

Example 15.3 We again consider the logit model

$$\log \left(\frac{\pi_{ij}}{1 - \pi_{ij}} \right) = \mu + \lambda_i^D + \lambda_j^V$$

for the death penalty data. This model permits both defendant's race (D) and victim's race (V) to affect the death penalty verdict, but it assumes no three-factor interaction. In other words, the effects of D on the logit are assumed to be the same at both levels of V, and vice versa. Figure 15.4 is an example of part of an SPSS^X printout of observed and expected frequencies for this model. For each of the eight cells in the table, f_e is quite close to f_o.

Fig. 15.4 Expected Frequencies and Adjusted Residuals for Death Penalty Data

FACTOR	CODE	OBS. COUNT	EXP. COUNT	ADJ.RESID.
PENALTY	YES			
DEFEND	WHITE			
VICTIM	WHITE	19.00	18.67	.6128
VICTIM	BLACK	.00	.33	-.6128
DEFEND	BLACK			
VICTIM	WHITE	11.00	11.33	-.6128
VICTIM	BLACK	6.00	5.67	.6128
PENALTY	NO			
DEFEND	WHITE			
VICTIM	WHITE	132.00	132.33	-.6128
VICTIM	BLACK	9.00	8.67	.6128
DEFEND	BLACK			
VICTIM	WHITE	52.00	51.67	.6128
VICTIM	BLACK	97.00	97.33	-.6128

GOODNESS-OF-FIT TEST STATISTICS

LIKELIHOOD RATIO CHI SQUARE = .701   DF = 1   P = .403
PEARSON CHI SQUARE = .376   DF = 1   P = .540

The good fit of the model is summarized by the small values of the chi-square statistics, with Pearson $\chi^2 = .38$ and likelihood-ratio $G^2 = .70$. There are four combinations of levels of D and V (W–W, W–B, B–W, B–B), and thus four logits. There are three distinct parameters: μ, λ_1^D, λ_1^V; the parameters λ_2^D and λ_2^V are determined by λ_1^D and λ_1^V. Hence, both statistics are based on

df = Number of logits − Number of parameters = 4 − 3 = 1

For testing the null hypothesis that the model truly holds (i.e., that there is no three-factor interaction), the G^2 test statistic has a P-value of $P = .403$. This is the right-hand tail probability above the observed value of $G^2 = .70$. Hence, the data do not contradict the model, and it seems reasonable to assume that the effect of defendant's race on the death penalty verdict is the same for each victim's race. Other models for these data will be considered in Section 15.3.   ∎

Many computer packages report *adjusted residuals*, which make a cell-by-cell comparison of f_o and f_e. These adjusted residuals behave like standard normal variables when the model truly holds. Hence, a large adjusted residual (say, exceeding 2 or 3 in absolute value) gives evidence of some lack of fit in that cell. The adjusted residuals reported in Figure 15.4 are quite small and give no evidence of lack of fit for the model we applied to the death penalty data. Some computer packages also report for each cell a *residual*, which equals $f_o - f_e$, and a *standardized residual*, which equals $(f_o - f_e)/\sqrt{f_e}$. These are more difficult to interpret inferentially than adjusted residuals, because their sampling distributions are not standard normal.

More complex models containing interaction terms (denoted by $\{\lambda_{ij}^{AB}\}$) may be necessary if the models that assume no three-factor interaction fit poorly. Generally, more complex models require more parameters. Since the degrees of freedom is equal to the number of logits minus the number of parameters, the more complex the model, the smaller the degrees of freedom. In the next section we shall see how to compare the fits given by various models.

15.3 Loglinear Models for Categorical Variables

Logit models are similar to regression models, in the sense that both types express a dependent variable in terms of independent variables. By contrast, with loglinear models it is not necessary to select a dependent variable. These models express the logs of the cell expected frequencies in terms of partial associations among all the variables. The actual model formulas are rather complex, and in this section we will instead use a symbolic approach that indicates which variables are assumed to be associated. Problem 15.12 shows why the models are referred to as "loglinear" models.

A Hierarchy of Models for Three Variables

Suppose we have a cross-classification of three categorical variables, A, B, and C. A pair of variables could be statistically independent at each level of the third variable, in which case the pair is said to be *conditionally independent*. Or, there might be associations in some or all of the partial tables. If all pairs of variables have partial associations, there is still some simplification of structure if we can assume no three-factor interaction. We now consider a hierarchy of five loglinear models, ordered in terms of the extent of association and three-factor interaction:

1. All three pairs of variables are conditionally independent. That is,

A is independent of B, controlling for C;

A is independent of C, controlling for B;

B is independent of C, controlling for A.

2. Two of the pairs of variables are conditionally independent. For example,

A is independent of C, controlling for B;

B is independent of C, controlling for A;

A and B are associated, controlling for C.

Similarly, the sole associated pair could be A and C, or it could be B and C.

3. One of the pairs of variables is conditionally independent. For example,

A is independent of C, controlling for B;

A and B are associated, controlling for C;

B and C are associated, controlling for A.

Similarly, the sole conditionally independent pair could be A and B, or it could be B and C.

4. None of the pairs of variables is conditionally independent, but there is no three-factor interaction.
5. There is three-factor interaction. Hence, all pairs of variables are associated, but the association between each pair varies according to the level of the third variable.

Each model can be represented by a symbol that indicates the pairs of variables that are conditionally independent. Associated variables appear joined together in the symbol, with no comma between them. For instance, (AB, C) denotes the model in which A and B have a partial association but the other pairs are conditionally independent. Table 15.3 (page 494) lists the symbols corresponding to the models just described. All the models provide some structure to the pattern of association except for the last one, (ABC). This model, which allows for three-factor interaction, fits *any* sample three-way table perfectly. It is referred to as the *saturated model*. This means that the model has so many parameters that it forces all $f_e = f_o$, and consequently, $\chi^2 = G^2 = 0$ based on df = 0.

Table 15.3
Some Loglinear Models
for Three-Dimensional
Tables

MODEL SYMBOL	INTERPRETATION
(A, B, C)	All pairs are conditionally independent.
(AB, C)	A and B is the only associated pair.
(AB, BC)	A and C is the only conditionally independent pair.
(AB, BC, AC)	Each pair associated, controlling for the other variable. No three-factor interaction.
(ABC)	All pairs associated. Three-factor interaction.

The simpler the model (in the sense that it has fewer associations), the larger the number of degrees of freedom. It is usually preferable to represent the data by the simplest model that gives a good fit to the data. Expected values, chi-square statistics, and df values for loglinear models can be obtained using computer routines such as LOGLINEAR in SPSS^X and 4F in BMDP.

Example 15.4   Table 15.4 contains the G^2 chi-square statistic and df values for the results of fitting several loglinear models to the death penalty data of Table 15.2. The smaller G^2 is, the better the fit. The table gives P-values for testing goodness of fit of the models. Small P-values contradict the null hypothesis that the model is appropriate. In viewing the G^2-values, recall that the chi-square distribution is concentrated on the positive part of the line with mean equal to df. Hence, a value such as $G^2 = 137.9$ based on df = 4 is far out in the right-hand tail, has a tiny P-value, and indicates a poor fit. The only unsaturated models that pass the goodness-of-fit test are (VP, DV) and (DP, VP, DV). The models that do not contain the DV term fit terribly, indicating that it is important to allow an association between defendant's race and victim's race. The model (VP, DV) assumes that death penalty verdict (P) is independent of defendant's race (D) controlling for victim's race (V), but permits associations for the other two pairs of variables. A slightly better fit is provided by the model (DP, VP, DV), which allows association between all pairs of variables but still assumes no three-factor interaction. ■

Table 15.4
Goodness-of-Fit Tests for
Loglinear Models Relating
Death Penalty Verdict (P),
Defendant's Race (D),
and Victim's Race (V)

MODEL	G^2	df	P-VALUE
(D, V, P)	137.93	4	0.000
(VP, D)	131.68	3	0.000
(DP, V)	137.71	3	0.000
(DV, P)	8.13	3	0.043
(DP, VP)	131.46	2	0.000
(DP, DV)	7.91	2	0.019
(VP, DV)	1.88	2	0.390
(DP, VP, DV)	0.70	1	0.402
(DVP)	0	0	—

Source: Data from Radelet (1981). See Table 15.2.

Comparing
G^2-Values

Table 15.4 can be used to illustrate some important properties of the likelihood-ratio G^2 statistic. First, G^2 is similar to the SSE measure calculated in fitting regression models, in the sense that it cannot increase as the model becomes more complex.* For instance, (DV, P) is a more complex model than (D, V, P), since it allows one association. Hence, it gives a better fit (i.e., the $\{f_e\}$ tend to be closer to $\{f_o\}$), and its G^2-value [denote it by $G^2(DV, P)$] is smaller. Similarly,

$$0 = G^2(DVP) \le G^2(DP, VP, DV) \le G^2(VP, DV) \le G^2(DV, P) \le G^2(D, V, P)$$

A pair of models such as (DV, P) and (DP, VP) cannot be compared in this way. Neither is a special case of the other, since each allows association that the other excludes.

In Section 12.3 we gave a test for comparing two regression models when one is a special case of the other, based on the reduction in SSE. There is a similar test for comparing loglinear models based on the reduction in G^2-values. To test the null hypothesis that a model truly holds, versus the alternative hypothesis that a more complex model gives a better fit, the test statistic is the difference in G^2-values. This difference can be treated as a chi-square statistic with degrees of freedom equal to the difference in df values for the two models.

For instance, suppose that we compare models (VP, DV) and (DP, VP, DV). The test statistic is $G^2(VP, DV) - G^2(DP, VP, DV) = 1.88 - .70 = 1.18$ based on df $= 2 - 1 = 1$. This chi-square statistic has a right-hand tail probability of $P > .20$, so model (DP, VP, DV) does not give a significantly better fit than (VP, DV). Next, let us check whether an even simpler model than (VP, DV) fits adequately. The model (DV, P) is the best-fitting model having only one of these two associations. However, the increase in G^2-values is $8.13 - 1.88 = 6.25$ based on df $= 3 - 2 = 1$, which gives $P < .02$. Hence, (VP, DV) gives a better fit, and it does seem important to allow for a VP association.

Connection
Between Logit and
Loglinear Models

Notice that the G^2-value of .70 reported in Table 15.4 for model (DP, VP, DV) is exactly the same as the G^2-value reported in Example 15.3 for the logit model discussed there. In fact, any logit model for categorical data is equivalent to a corresponding loglinear model. That loglinear model contains the same associations as the logit model does between the dependent variable and the independent variables, and it contains the most general term for describing relationships among the independent variables. Table 15.5 (page 496) illustrates the correspondence between loglinear and logit models for three-dimensional tables, when A and B are independent variables and C is a dichotomous dependent variable. Since A and B are the potential predictors in each logit model, the loglinear model contains the AB association term plus associations between C and any independent variable actually appearing in the logit model. In the first logit model, for example, neither A nor B has an effect on C, so the corresponding loglinear model (AB, C) is the one in which the AC and BC associations are omitted.

---

*The Pearson χ^2 statistic does not have this property.

Table 15.5
Correspondence Between
Logit and Loglinear
Models, When C Is a
Dichotomous Dependent
Variable

LOGIT MODEL	LOGLINEAR MODEL
$\log\left(\dfrac{\pi_{ij}}{1-\pi_{ij}}\right) = \mu$	$(AB,\, C)$
$\log\left(\dfrac{\pi_{ij}}{1-\pi_{ij}}\right) = \mu + \lambda_i^A$	$(AB,\, AC)$
$\log\left(\dfrac{\pi_{ij}}{1-\pi_{ij}}\right) = \mu + \lambda_j^B$	$(AB,\, BC)$
$\log\left(\dfrac{\pi_{ij}}{1-\pi_{ij}}\right) = \mu + \lambda_i^A + \lambda_j^B$	$(AB,\, AC,\, BC)$

For a more complex example, consider a four-dimensional table having a dichotomous response variable D. The logit model

$$\log\left(\frac{\pi_{ijk}}{1-\pi_{ijk}}\right) = \mu + \lambda_i^A + \lambda_j^B + \lambda_k^C$$

assumes that D is associated with each of A, B, and C, but that the effects of each independent variable on D are the same at each level of the other variables. The corresponding loglinear model is symbolized by (AD, BD, CD, ABC). Again, we include the most general term (ABC) for the possible interaction among the independent variables, since nothing is assumed about the structure of their relationships in the logit model.

Example 15.5   We have seen that the loglinear model (DP, VP, DV) gives a good fit to the death penalty data, with $G^2 = .70$. If we treat death penalty verdict P as a dependent variable, this loglinear model is exactly equivalent to the logit model

$$\log\left(\frac{\pi_{ij}}{1-\pi_{ij}}\right) = \mu + \lambda_i^D + \lambda_j^V$$

Hence, the G^2-value and expected frequencies for fitting (DP, VP, DV) are exactly the same as those given in Example 15.3 for this logit model.

We have seen that the loglinear model (VP, DV) also gives a good fit, not significantly worse than (DP, VP, DV). This simpler loglinear model is equivalent to the logit model

$$\log\left(\frac{\pi_{ij}}{1-\pi_{ij}}\right) = \mu + \lambda_j^V$$

in which D has no effect on P (i.e., the $\lambda_i^D = 0$), controlling for V. Hence, if we were to fit this logit model, we would get the G^2-value of 1.88 reported in Table 15.4 for the corresponding loglinear model. ∎

In summary, logit models require a dependent variable, whereas loglinear models do not. Though designed for this different purpose, logit models do imply association patterns among variables that are equivalent to ones expressed by corresponding loglinear models.

15.4
Odds Ratios

In the previous section, we introduced loglinear model symbols to represent the possible patterns of association, and chi-square tests enabled us to determine which patterns fit the data well. In this section we consider ways of interpreting the models and describing the strengths of the associations that seem to be present. A measure of association that helps us with these tasks is the *odds ratio*.

Definition and Interpretation of Odds Ratios

Consider a 2 × 2 table having frequencies denoted as follows:

a	b
c	d

The odds of being classified in column 1 instead of column 2 equals a/b for the first row, and c/d for the second row. The ratio of these two odds is referred to as the *odds ratio*. Denoting this measure by $\hat{\theta}$, we have

$$\hat{\theta} = \frac{a/b}{c/d} = \frac{ad}{bc}$$

An alternative name for it is the **cross-product ratio**, since $\hat{\theta}$ equals the ratio of the products ad and bc of entries from cells that are diagonally opposite.

When the odds ratio is smaller (larger) than 1.0, subjects in the first row are less (more) likely to be classified in column 1 than are subjects in the second row. Independence of row and column variables corresponds to a population value of $\theta = 1$. The odds ratio falls between 0 and ∞, with the extreme values occurring if any of the cell entries is 0. Sample estimates of $\hat{\theta} = 0$ or $\hat{\theta} = \infty$ are undesirable when it is believed that the population cell proportions are all nonzero. A less biased estimator is obtained by calculating $\hat{\theta}$ for an adjusted table in which .5 is added to each cell count.

If the rows (or the columns) of the table are interchanged, the new table has the inverse (i.e., $1/\hat{\theta}$) of the original odds ratio value $\hat{\theta}$. Hence, for any positive number x, $\hat{\theta} = x$ represents the same strength of association as $\hat{\theta} = 1/x$, but in opposite directions. For instance, $\hat{\theta} = 3$ means that the odds of classification in column 1 is three times as high in row 1 as in row 2, whereas $\hat{\theta} = 1/3$ means that the odds of classification in column 1 is three times as high in row 2 as in row 1.

Example 15.6

We now show how the odds ratio can be used to describe the partial associations for the death penalty data of Table 15.2. Consider the association between death penalty verdict and victim's race, controlling for defendant's race. For white defendants, the *VP* partial table has the entries shown in the following table:

		P	
		Yes	No
V	White	19	132
	Black	0	9

The odds ratio is

$$\hat{\theta} = \frac{19/132}{0/9} = \frac{19 \times 9}{132 \times 0} = \infty$$

since one of the cell counts in the denominator is 0. A more stable estimate of θ is $\hat{\theta} =$ $(19.5 \times 9.5)/(132.5 \times .5) = 2.80$, in which .5 is added to each cell count before $\hat{\theta}$ is calculated. This latter value means that the odds of a "yes" death penalty verdict are estimated to be 2.80 times higher when the victim is white than when the victim is black. For black defendants, the *VP* partial table has the following entries:

		P	
		Yes	No
V	White	11	52
	Black	6	97

The odds ratio is $(11 \times 97)/(52 \times 6) = 3.42$ for these counts, and 3.29 when .5 is first added to each cell. Hence, for black defendants we also estimate that the odds for the death penalty are much higher when the victim is white than when the victim is black.

Marginal frequencies are obtained when we sum the cell counts over the levels of a variable (or variables), so that the variable is ignored rather than controlled in the analysis. Adding the partial tables corresponding to the two levels of defendant's race, for instance, we obtain the following marginal *VP* table:

		P	
		Yes	No
V	White	30	184
	Black	6	106

This table has an odds ratio of 2.88. Hence, ignoring defendant's race, we observe that the marginal *VP* table also suggests that the death penalty is more likely to be given when the victim is white.   ∎

For $r \times c$ tables, odds ratios can be calculated for the rectangular pattern of cells formed using each pair of rows in combination with each pair of columns. For instance, refer to Table 15.6. Independence corresponds to the situation in which all of these odds ratios equal 1.0 in the population.

Table 15.6

A Typical Odds Ratio
ad/bc for an $r \times c$ Table

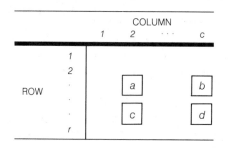

Odds Ratios of Expected Frequencies

The odds ratio is the most appropriate measure of association for interpreting logit and loglinear models. Notions of conditional independence and higher-order interaction can be defined using odds ratios. For example, *conditional independence* between A and B means that all the population odds ratios in the AB partial tables equal 1.0. *No three-factor interaction* means that the population odds ratios in the AB partial tables are identical at each level of C. For instance, for a $2 \times 2 \times 3$ table, if the odds ratio for the AB partial association is $\theta = 2.2$ at the first level of C, $\theta = 2.2$ at the second level of C, and $\theta = 2.2$ at the third level of C, then there is no three-factor interaction. When the AB odds ratios are the same at all levels of C, it is necessarily true that the AC odds ratios are the same at all levels of B, and the BC odds ratios are the same at all levels of A.

Even if there is no three-factor interaction, the common partial association for A and B may differ from the marginal AB association for the two-way table in which C is ignored rather than controlled. In Chapter 10, we discussed factors that cause partial and marginal associations to be different. The result stated in the box gives conditions under which these associations, as measured by the odds ratio, must necessarily be the same.

Conditions for Equivalence of Partial and Marginal Associations

In terms of the odds ratio, the partial association between A and B (controlling for C) is identical to the marginal association between A and B (ignoring C) if either or both of the following conditions hold:

1. C and A are conditionally independent, given B.
2. C and B are conditionally independent, given A.

To illustrate this important result, suppose that the loglinear model (AC, BC) perfectly fits a population table. This model implies that A and B are conditionally independent, so the AB partial odds ratios equal 1.0 at each level of C. However, neither condition 1 nor condition 2 given in the box holds, since for model (AC, BC) variable C has a partial association with A and with B. Hence, the AB marginal table may have odds ratios unequal to 1.0. In summary, for model (AC, BC), A and B are independent when C is controlled, but they may be associated when C is ignored. Notice that the AC partial odds ratios at each level of B *are* identical to the corresponding odds ratios for the AC marginal table, because the model (AC, BC) implies that B is conditionally independent of A. That is, the AC partial association is the same as the AC marginal association, because the partialed-out variable (B) is conditionally independent of one of these two variables. The same remark applies to the BC partial and marginal odds ratios. The model (AC, BC) is an important one. A noticeable association between A and B may be spurious or it may be part of a chain relationship (see Sections 10.2 and 10.3), if the researcher finds a third variable C such that the AB association disappears when C is controlled.

When a loglinear model is fitted to a data set, the expected frequencies have odds ratios that perfectly satisfy the assumptions of the model. If the model fits well, these odds ratios can be used to interpret the nature of the associations that are implied by the model.

Example 15.7　　Table 15.7 contains expected frequencies for five loglinear models fitted to the death penalty data. As an illustration of the different association patterns implied by the models, Table 15.8 presents marginal and partial odds ratios for these expected frequencies. For example, the entry 1.0 for the partial association for model (VP, DV) is the common value of the DP partial odds ratios of expected frequencies at the two levels of V; that is,

$$1.0 = \frac{21.17 \times 54.17}{129.83 \times 8.83} = \frac{0.48 \times 97.48}{8.52 \times 5.52}$$

Table 15.7　Expected Frequencies for Five Loglinear Models Fitted to the Death Penalty Data

DEFENDANT'S RACE	VICTIM'S RACE	DEATH PENALTY	MODEL				
			(D, V, P)	(P, DV)	(VP, DV)	(DP, VP, DV)	(DVP)
White	White	Yes	11.60	16.68	21.17	18.67	19
		No	93.43	134.32	129.83	132.32	132
	Black	Yes	6.07	0.99	0.48	0.33	0
		No	48.90	8.01	8.52	8.68	9
Black	White	Yes	12.03	6.96	8.83	11.32	11
		No	96.94	56.04	54.17	51.70	52
	Black	Yes	6.30	11.37	5.52	5.68	6
		No	50.73	91.63	97.48	97.30	97
	G^2		137.9	8.1	1.9	0.7	0
	df		4	3	2	1	0
	P-value		0.00	0.04	0.39	0.40	—

The entry of 1.65 for the marginal DP association for that same model is the corresponding odds ratio of expected frequencies for the marginal DP table (which is the sum of the two DP partial tables); that is,

$$1.65 = \frac{(21.17 + 0.48)(54.17 + 97.48)}{(129.83 + 8.52)(8.83 + 5.52)}$$

The odds ratios for the observed data are those reported for model (DVP), since there the model gives a perfect fit.

For each model, the odds ratios satisfy properties of the model and also reflect the conditions for equivalence of marginal and partial associations.

Table 15.8

Summary of Estimated Odds Ratios

MODEL	PARTIAL ASSOCIATIONS			MARGINAL ASSOCIATIONS		
	DP	VP	DV	DP	VP	DV
(D, V, P)	1.0	1.0	1.0	1.0	1.0	1.0
(P, DV)	1.0	1.0	27.4	1.0	1.0	27.4
(VP, DV)	1.0	2.9	27.4	1.65	2.9	27.4
(DP, VP, DV)	0.6	3.7	28.7	1.2	2.9	27.4
(DVP) Level 1	0.68	∞	∞	1.2	2.9	27.4
	(0.67)	(2.80)	(22.04)			
Level 2	0	3.42	27.36			
	(0.79)	(3.29)	(25.90)			

Note: Values in parentheses for model (DVP) are obtained after adding .5 to each cell.

Model (D, V, P)   This model implies that each pair of variables is conditionally independent, so its expected frequencies have all partial odds ratios equal to 1.0. Also, each marginal association is necessarily the same as the corresponding partial association (i.e., equal to 1.0), since the equivalence conditions are satisfied. For instance, the DP marginal association must be the same as the DP partial associations (controlling for V) because, for this model, V and D are conditionally independent given P (or because V and P are conditionally independent, given D).

Model (P, DV)   This model permits only a DV partial association, so only the DV odds ratios do not equal 1.0. All partial odds ratios are necessarily the same as the corresponding marginal odds ratios, since an equivalence condition is satisfied for each association. For instance, the DV partial odds ratios are

$$\frac{16.68 \times 11.37}{.99 \times 6.96} = \frac{134.32 \times 91.63}{8.01 \times 56.04} = 27.4$$

whereas the DV marginal odds ratio is

$$\frac{(16.68 + 134.32)(11.37 + 91.63)}{(.99 + 8.01)(6.96 + 56.04)} = 27.4$$

These are the same, since for this model P is independent of V (given D), or because P is independent of D (given V).

Model (VP, DV)   For this model only the DP partial odds ratios equal 1.0. However, notice that the DP *marginal* odds ratio is different (1.65), since in this model V is not conditionally independent of P or D. The partial DV odds ratios are the same as the marginal DV odds ratio (27.4), since P is conditionally independent of D. Similarly, the VP partial and marginal odds ratios are the same.

Model (*DP*, *VP*, *DV*)   For this model all pairs of variables are conditionally dependent. Thus, none of the partial odds ratios equal 1.0, and none of the partial odds ratios need be the same as the corresponding marginal odds ratios. With this model and all the others considered here except (*DVP*), there is assumed to be no three-factor interaction. Hence, for each association the two partial odds ratios are identical. This model fits very well, so we can use these odds ratios to interpret the data. The partial odds ratios tell us that (**a**) the odds for the death penalty is estimated to be .6 times as high for a white defendant as for a black defendant (controlling for *V*), (**b**) the odds for the death penalty is estimated to be 3.7 times higher when the victim is white than when the victim is black (controlling for *D*), (**c**) the odds that the victim is white is estimated to be 28.7 times higher when the defendant is white than when the defendant is black (controlling for *P*).

Model (*DVP*)   Since this model allows three-factor interaction, the two partial odds ratios for a given pair of variables are no longer equal. They *are* close (after .5 is added to each cell), however, which explains why the model (*DP*, *VP*, *DV*) fits so well.

For the (*DVP*) and (*DP*, *VP*, *DV*) models, it is interesting to observe the reversal in the *DP* partial and marginal associations. For each model, the marginal odds ratio indicates that when the effects of victim's race are ignored, white defendants are more likely than black defendants to receive the death penalty. On the other hand, the partial odds ratios indicate that when we control for victim's race, black defendants are more likely to receive the death penalty. This reversal is due to the nature of the association of *V* with *P* and *V* with *D*. Specifically, the death penalty tends to be more likely when the victim is white, and white victims tend to be more likely when the defendant is white. The reversal in the nature of the *DP* partial and marginal associations is an example of Simpson's paradox (see Problems 15 and 18 in Chapter 10).

Finally, observe that the marginal odds ratios for the data [model (*DVP*)] are identical to the marginal odds ratios of expected frequencies for some of the models. Loglinear models have the property that the expected frequencies match the observed data in the marginal tables for those pairs of variables that are modeled as being associated. For instance, all the two-way marginal tables of the expected frequencies for the (*DP*, *VP*, *DV*) model must be the same as the corresponding two-way marginal tables for the actual data. Hence, the marginal odds ratios are also the same.   ∎

15.5 Modeling Ordinal Variables

Our presentation of logit and loglinear models in this chapter has made no distinction between treatment of nominal and ordinal variables. In fact, the standard models discussed in Sections 15.2 and 15.3 can be used for variables of either scale, but they treat all variables as nominal. Models can be formulated that more efficiently use information on orderings of categories.

For instance, consider a three-way table in which C is a dichotomous dependent variable, and A and B are independent variables with A nominal and B ordinal. The logit model

$$\log\left(\frac{\pi_{ij}}{1 - \pi_{ij}}\right) = \mu + \lambda_i^A + \lambda_j^B$$

treats both independent variables as nominal. If the effects of B have the same ordering as its categories, then the $\{\lambda_j^B\}$ follow a linear trend for some set of scores. Hence, we could simplify this model by assigning an ordered set of scores $\{x_1 < x_2 < \cdots < x_c\}$ to the levels of B and assuming

$$\log\left(\frac{\pi_{ij}}{1 - \pi_{ij}}\right) = \mu + \lambda_i^A + \beta x_j$$

The assignment of scores to B means that it is treated more like an interval variable than a nominal one. The right-hand side of the equation has a term (λ_i^A) of the type used in Section 15.2 for nominal independent variables, and it has a term (βx_j) of the type used in Section 15.1 for interval independent variables. Hence, this model is analogous to the analysis of covariance model for interval dependent variables.

In this model the parameter β represents a linear effect of B on the logit for C, and the model is referred to as a ***linear logit model***. Suppose it is reasonable to use the equal-interval scores $\{x_1 = 1, x_2 = 2, \ldots\}$. Then the antilog of β can be interpreted as the effect on the odds of a single category change in B. If $\beta = .5$, for instance, then the odds of making response "1" on C is multiplied by $e^{.5} = 1.65$ for every change of one category for B, controlling for A.

Models in which ordinal variables are treated in a quantitative manner can be fitted using computer packages, for example, by using the CONTRAST command in the LOGLINEAR program in SPSS^X. There are many advantages to be gained from using ordinal models instead of (or in addition to) the standard nominal ones. In summary, they include the following:

1. Ordinal models can have greater power for detecting important alternatives to null hypotheses such as the hypothesis of independence.
2. Ordinal data description is based on measures that are similar to those (such as correlations, slopes, means) used in ordinary regression and analysis of variance for continuous variables.
3. Ordinal analyses can use a greater variety of models, most of which are more parsimonious and have simpler interpretations than the standard models for nominal variables.
4. Interesting ordinal models can be applied in settings in which the standard nominal models are trivial or else have too many parameters to be tested for goodness of fit.

There is not space to discuss models for ordinal variables further in this book, but they are discussed in detail in the survey article and book by Agresti (1983, 1984).

Chapters 1–4 and 6 of that book also give a more thorough introduction to loglinear and logit models.

Notes

Section 15.2

1. Some computer routines (such as CATMOD in the SAS System) report chi-square values for testing significance of parameters. When df = 1 for the chi-square value, that statistic is simply the square of the z statistic we have used.

2. The parameter estimates given by the LOGLINEAR program in SPSS^X refer to the loglinear model corresponding to the fitted logit model. These estimates must be doubled for them to match the ones we have introduced here for logit models.

Sections 15.1–15.3

3. The article by Swafford (1980) examines the relative merits of linear, loglinear, and logit models for the probability π. Occasionally the simpler linear model is adequate, but it should be fitted using *weighted* least squares (as is done by PROC CATMOD in the SAS System).

4. Karl Pearson suggested the chi-square test for bivariate tables in 1900. However, loglinear methods for multidimensional tables were not well developed until the 1970's. The statistician and sociologist Leo Goodman is responsible for many of the recent developments in this area (see Goodman, 1978).

Problems

1. A logistic model is used to describe how the probability π of voting for the Republican candidate in a presidential election depends on X, the voter's total family income (in thousands of dollars) in the previous year. The prediction equation obtained using a particular sample is

$$\log\left(\frac{\hat{\pi}}{1 - \hat{\pi}}\right) = -1.4 + .05X$$

a. At what income is the estimated probability of voting for the Republican candidate equal to .5?

b. Over what region of income values is the voter predicted to be more likely to vote Republican than Democrat?

c. What is the estimated probability of voting for the Republican candidate when:
i. Income = $10,000? ii. Income = $20,000? iii. Income = $50,000?

d. Use the prediction equation to obtain an interpretation of how the odds of voting Republican depends on family income.

2. Refer to Problem 1. The estimated standard error of b = .05 is $\hat{\sigma}_b$ = .018. Assuming the sample was randomly selected, test the hypothesis that the probability of voting for the Republican candidate is independent of family income. Use the alternative hypothesis of a positive association.

3. Refer to Problems 1 and 2. When the independent variables are X_1 = family income, X_2 = number of years of education, and X_3 = sex (1 = male, 0 = female), the logistic prediction equation is

$$\log\left(\frac{\hat{\pi}}{1 - \hat{\pi}}\right) = -2.0 + .03X_1 + .08X_2 + .20X_3$$

For this sample, X_1 ranges from 5 to 70 with a standard deviation of 12.4, and X_2 ranges from 7 to 20 with a standard deviation of 2.8.

a. Give the estimated effect of a standard deviation change in X_1 on the odds for voting Republican, controlling for X_2 and X_3.

b. Give the estimated effect of a standard deviation change in X_2 on the odds for voting Republican, controlling for X_1 and X_3.

c. *Fill in the blank:* Controlling for income and education, the odds of voting for the Republican candidate is estimated to be _____ times higher when the voter is male than when the voter is female.

4. Let π_{ijk} denote the probability that a randomly selected respondent supports current laws legalizing abortion, for sex i of respondent (i = 1, male; i = 2, female), religious affiliation j (j = 1, Protestant; j = 2, Catholic; j = 3, Jewish), and political party affiliation k (k = 1, Democrat; k = 2, Republican; k = 3, Independent). The logit model

$$\log\left(\frac{\pi_{ijk}}{1 - \pi_{ijk}}\right) = \mu + \lambda_i^S + \lambda_j^R + \lambda_k^P$$

is fitted to a sample of data. The parameter estimates are $\hat{\mu} = .62$, $\hat{\lambda}_1^S = -.08$, $\hat{\lambda}_2^S = .08$, $\hat{\lambda}_1^R = -.16$, $\hat{\lambda}_2^R = -.25$, $\hat{\lambda}_3^R = .41$, $\hat{\lambda}_1^P = .87$, $\hat{\lambda}_2^P = -1.27$, $\hat{\lambda}_3^P = .40$,

a. Give the effect on the odds for supporting legalized abortion of being classified:
   i. Male   ii. Female   iii. Protestant   iv. Democrat

b. Find the estimated probability of supporting legalized abortion, for:
   i. Female Jewish Democrats
   ii. Male Protestant Independents
   iii. Male Catholic Republicans

c. Give the df value for fitting this model. If $G^2 = 10.4$, test the goodness of fit of the model.

d. Give the symbol for the loglinear model that is equivalent to this logit model.

e. Give the logit model corresponding to the loglinear model (*AR, AP, SRP*), where A denotes the dependent variable (opinion on current laws legalizing abortion).

f. Refer to parts **c** and **e**. If $G^2 = 11.6$ for the model in part **e**, determine whether sex is a significant predictor of opinion on abortion, controlling for R and P.

5. Consider a four-dimensional cross-classification of variables A, B, C, and D.

a. Give the symbol for the loglinear model in which:
   i. All pairs of variables are independent.

ii. *A* and *B* are associated but other pairs of variables are independent.

iii. All pairs of variables are associated, but there is no three-factor interaction.

b. Suppose *D* is a dichotomous dependent variable. Write down the logit model that is equivalent to the loglinear model symbolized by (*ABC*, *AD*, *BD*).

6. The hypothetical population cell proportions in the accompanying table describe the relationship among income, sex, and college of employment within the university.

COLLEGE	SEX	INCOME	
		Low	High
Liberal Arts	Women	.18	.12
	Men	.12	.08
Professional	Women	.02	.08
	Men	.08	.32

a. Calculate the partial odds ratios for each pair of variables, and interpret them.

b. Which loglinear model do these cell proportions satisfy?

c. If income is a dependent variable, which logit model do these cell proportions satisfy?

d. Construct the marginal income–sex table, and calculate the odds ratio. Why is it so different from the partial odds ratios for these two variables?

The following data for Problems 7–10 refer to individuals who applied for admission into graduate school at the University of California in Berkeley, for the fall 1973 session. Data are presented for five of the six largest graduate departments at the university. The variables for the 2 × 2 × 5 table are denoted by:

A: Whether admitted (yes, no)

S: Sex of applicant (male, female)

D: Department to which application was sent (D_1, D_2, D_3, D_4, D_5)

DEPARTMENT	SEX	ADMITTED	
		Yes	No
D_1	M	353	207
	F	17	8
D_2	M	120	205
	F	202	391
D_3	M	138	279
	F	131	244
D_4	M	53	138
	F	94	299
D_5	M	22	351
	F	24	317

Source: Data from Freedman et al. (1978, p. 14).

7.

a. Construct the marginal table for sex and whether admitted.

b. Find the odds ratio for the table in part **a**, and interpret its value. Based on your interpretation, for which sex is the likelihood of admission higher?

8. Using a computer routine, fit the loglinear model for which A is independent of S and D, but S and D are associated.

a. Test the goodness of fit of the model, and interpret the result.

b. If A is treated as the dependent variable, give the logit model that is equivalent to this loglinear model.

9. Using a computer routine, fit the loglinear model for which A is conditionally independent of S, controlling for D, but the other pairs of variables are associated.

a. Test the goodness of fit of the model, and interpret the result.

b. If A is treated as the dependent variable, give the logit model that is equivalent to this loglinear model.

c. For the $\{f_e\}$ for this model, what is the value of the odds ratio between whether admitted and sex, controlling for department? Would you get the same value if you ignored (rather than controlled) department? Why?

10. Consider the model corresponding to dependence for all pairs of variables, but no three-factor interaction.

a. Fit this model and test its goodness of fit.

b. Test whether this model gives a better fit than the model (AD, SD). Interpret the result of the test.

c. In summary, how would you interpret these data? In your explanation, be sure to describe why the observed marginal association described in Problem **7b** is so different from the corresponding partial association for the loglinear models that fit well.

11. Give the symbols for the loglinear models for categorical variables that are implied by the following causal diagrams.

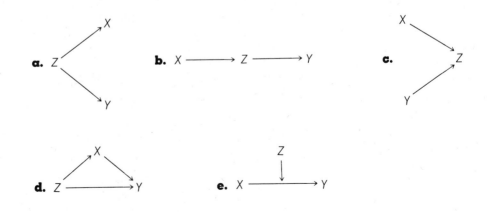

*12. For a two-way table, let r_i denote the ith row total, let c_j denote the jth column total, and let n denote the total sample size. From Section 8.2, recall that the expected frequency in the cell in row i and column j for the independence model can be expressed as $f_e = r_i c_j / n$. Show that the log of the expected frequency can be modeled by an additive formula with terms representing the influence of the ith row total, the jth column total, and the sample size. This formula is the loglinear model for independence in a two-way table.

*13. A sample odds ratio $\hat{\theta}$ can be used to obtain a confidence interval for a population odds ratio θ. For a 2×2 table with cell counts a, b, c, d, the statistic $\log \hat{\theta}$ has approximately a normal sampling distribution with estimated standard error

$$\hat{\sigma}(\log \hat{\theta}) = \sqrt{\frac{1}{a + .5} + \frac{1}{b + .5} + \frac{1}{c + .5} + \frac{1}{d + .5}}$$

A $100(1 - \alpha)\%$ confidence interval for $\log \theta$ is given by

$$\log \hat{\theta} \pm z_{\alpha/2} \, \hat{\sigma}(\log \hat{\theta})$$

The antilogs of the endpoints for this interval are the endpoints of the corresponding confidence interval for θ. Use this approach to obtain a 95% confidence interval for the odds ratio for the marginal *VP* table for the death penalty data.

*14. Explain what is meant by the absence of statistical interaction in modeling the relationship among a dependent variable Y and two independent variables X_1 and X_2 in each of the following cases. Use graphs or tables to illustrate.
a. Y, X_1, and X_2 are of interval scale.
b. Y and X_1 are interval; X_2 is categorical.
c. Y is interval; X_1 and X_2 are categorical.
d. Y, X_1, and X_2 are categorical.

Bibliography

Agresti, A. (1983). "A Survey of Strategies for Modeling Cross-Classifications Having Ordinal Variables." *Journal of the American Statistical Association, 78:* 184–198.

Agresti, A. (1984). *Analysis of Ordinal Categorical Data.* New York: Wiley.

Fienberg, S. E. (1980). *The Analysis of Cross-Classified Categorical Data,* 2nd ed. Cambridge, Mass.: MIT Press.

Freedman, D., R. Pisani, and R. Purves (1978). *Statistics.* New York: W. W. Norton.

Gilbert, G. N. (1981). *Modelling Society.* London: Allen & Unwin.

Goodman, L. A. (1978). *Analyzing Qualitative/Categorical Data: Log-Linear Analysis and Latent Structure Analysis.* Cambridge, Mass.: Abt.

Radelet, M. (1981). "Racial Characteristics and the Imposition of the Death Penalty." *American Sociological Review, 46:* 918–927.

Reynolds, H. T. (1977). *The Analysis of Cross-Classifications.* Riverside, N.J.: Free Press.

Swafford, M. (1980). "Three Parametric Techniques for Contingency Table Analysis: A Nontechnical Commentary." *American Sociological Review, 45:* 664–690.

Theil, H. (1970). "On the Estimation of Relationships Involving Qualitative Variables." *American Journal of Sociology, 76:* 103–154.

Upton, G. J. G. (1978). *The Analysis of Cross-Tabulated Data.* New York: Wiley.

CHAPTER 16

An Introduction to Advanced Methodology

Contents

The purpose of this chapter is to introduce briefly a few statistical procedures that are somewhat more complex than those already discussed. In an introductory text such as this one, there is not enough space to consider them in detail. However, a social science researcher is likely to encounter reference to these methods in journal articles, and it is helpful to have at least a rudimentary understanding of their nature and purposes.

Our emphasis here will not be the same as in earlier chapters. We will not go into technical details about how to use the procedures or how to conduct inferences. Instead, we give a relatively brief explanation for each method of (a) what it is used for, and (b) the types of results that may occur and interpretations that can be made. The specific procedures to be described are *path analysis, factor analysis, LISREL,* and *Markov chain modeling*.

16.1 Path Analysis

Path analysis is a technique that uses the linear regression models studied in Chapters 9 and 11 to test specific theories of causal relationships among a set of variables. Statistically, it is usually nothing more than a series of multiple regression analyses, but there are certain advantages to conducting the analyses within the path analytic framework. The primary advantage is that the path technique forces the researcher to specify very explicitly the presumed causal relationships among the variables. This can help the researcher to work more efficiently in the data analysis, while contributing to logically clear explanations of variable relationships.

Thus, path analysis involves looking not only for relationships among variables, but also for causal relationships. Statistical association is one characteristic of a cause–effect relationship, but as we observed in Section 10.1, it is not sufficient to show causation. Two variables that are both causally dependent on a third one will themselves be associated, for example. Neither is a cause of the other, however, and the association disappears when the third variable is controlled. Thus, it is important in causal modeling to develop theories that include the proper control variables. In general, we consider an independent variable X to be a possible cause of a dependent variable Y if changes in X give rise to changes in Y, even when all relevant variables are controlled, and if there is the proper time order.

If the association between two variables disappears under a control, we can conclude that there is not a direct causal relationship between them. If the association does not disappear, though, we cannot necessarily conclude that the relationship is causal, since the relationship could disappear when other variables (perhaps unknown to us) are controlled. Thus, we can prove noncausality but we can never prove causality. A hypothesis of a causal relationship is bolstered, though, if the association remains even after we control what we believe to be the relevant variables.

Path Diagrams

In developing theoretical explanations of cause–effect relationships, we might hypothesize a system of relationships in which some variables believed to be caused by others may in turn have effects on other variables. Thus, a single multiple regression model may be insufficient for that system, since it can handle only one dependent variable. Path analysis utilizes the number of regression models necessary to include all proposed relationships in the theoretical explanation.

For example, suppose our theory specified that one's educational attainment depends on several factors, in particular upon one's parent's income level and one's own motivation to achieve. We might hypothesize, in addition, that one's motivation to achieve depends on several other (prior) factors—among them, the parent's educational level and one's general intelligence level; that the income of the parent depends in part on the parent's educational level; and that educational attainment may also depend directly on one's intelligence. Figure 16.1 shows a graphic summary of the theory just outlined, in the form of a *path diagram*. These diagrams are generalizations of the causal diagrams used in Chapter 10.

Fig. 16.1 Example of Preliminary Path Diagram

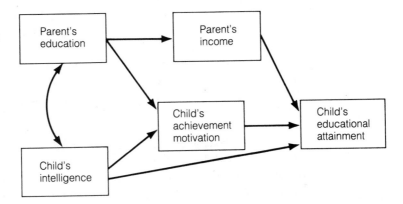

In looking at the diagram, we can see some basic conventions of path diagrams. First, a cause–effect relationship is represented by a straight arrow pointing toward the effect (dependent) variable and leading from the causal (independent) variable. In other words, the dependent variables of the regression equations are the variables to which the arrows point, whereas the independent variables for an equation with a particular dependent variable are those variables with arrows pointing toward that dependent variable. Thus, parent's income is modeled as depending on parent's education; child's educational attainment as depending on parent's income, child's intelligence, and child's achievement motivation; and, finally, child's achievement motivation as depending on parent's education and child's intelligence. The curved line between parent's education and child's intelligence, with arrows in both directions, simply means that, although the two variables may be associated, no causal relationship is presumed by the theory.

Path Coefficients Ordinarily in a path diagram, each arrow (including the curved line) would have a number written over it. These numbers, called *path coefficients*, are simply standardized regression coefficients for the regression equation for the dependent variable to which the arrows point. In Figure 16.1, there are three sets of coefficients that must be estimated, since there are three different dependent variables. For example, the coefficient of the path leading from parent's education to child's achievement motivation is the standardized regression coefficient from the multiple regression model, with child's achievement motivation as the dependent variable and parent's education and child's intelligence as the independent variables. Parent's income, in this model, depends only on parent's education, and so the path coefficient for that arrow would be the standardized bivariate regression coefficient, which is simply the Pearson correlation. Finally, the three path coefficients for paths leading directly to the dependent variable, child's educational attainment, are estimated from another regression equation with the three independent variables, parent's income, child's achievement motivation, and child's intelligence.

The path coefficients show both the relative strength of association between variables, controlling for other variables in the sequence, and the sign of the influence. Their interpretation is simply that of multiple regression b^* coefficients (see Section 11.5): A one standard deviation increase in the independent variable corresponds to a b^* standard deviation change in the dependent variable, controlling for the other independent variables in that particular regression equation.

An unmeasured *residual variable path* is usually attached to each dependent variable in the path diagram to account for the variation unexplained by its independent variables. Each residual variable represents the remaining portion $(1 - R^2)$ of the unexplained variation in its corresponding dependent variable, where R^2 is the coefficient of multiple determination for the regression equation with that dependent variable. Its path coefficient equals $\sqrt{1 - R^2}$. Every dependent variable will have a residual path associated with it. It is assumed that the residual factors are uncorrelated with the other independent variables in the system and with other residual variables associated with other dependent variables in the system.

Most path models will have variables that are dependent on some other variables but are, in turn, causes of other dependent variables. These variables are sometimes labeled *intervening variables* (see Section 10.3) since they occur in sequence between other variables. Thus, in our example, the child's achievement motivation intervenes between child's educational attainment and child's intelligence. This means that, if the theory is correct, the child's intelligence affects his or her educational attainment in part through its effect on achievement motivation. Thus, its effect in this sense is *indirect*. However, the model also proposes that the child's intelligence has a *direct* effect on his or her educational attainment, over and above its effect through achievement motivation. By performing the regression analyses, we can test whether this is true. For example, if intelligence affects educational attainment *only* through its effect on motivation, then the direct path (controlling for motivation) will have a nonsignificant path coefficient. However, if intelligence works both directly and indirectly, then all three coefficients of parts of paths leading from intelligence to educational attainment should be significant. If we do find a nonsignificant path, then we can erase that path from the diagram and perform the appropriate analyses again to reestimate the coefficients of the remaining paths. An important reason for using path analysis is that it enables one to partition the effect of a variable on another into its direct and indirect components.

Figure 16.2 shows the original path diagram from Figure 16.1 with the path coefficients added. It is in this form that the path diagram is typically seen in research literature. The residual variables for the three dependent variables are denoted by R_1, R_2, and R_3. If 28% of the child's educational attainment were explained by its three predictors, for example, then the path coefficient of the residual variable R_1 for the child's educational attainment would be $\sqrt{1 - R^2} = \sqrt{1 - .28} = .85$. It seems from Figure 16.2 that of the three direct predictors, the achievement motivation of the child had the strongest partial effect on his or her educational attainment (controlling for the child's intelligence and the parent's income). The child's intelligence has a moderate indirect effect, through increasing achievement motivation, as well as a direct effect on educational attainment. The parent's income is not as important as the child's achievement motivation or intelligence in determining the child's educational attainment, but the parent's educational level has an important effect on the child's achievement motivation. Of course, such conclusions would have to be weakened or modified if there were substantial sampling error for the path coefficients.

Fig. 16.2 Path Diagram with Path Coefficients Added

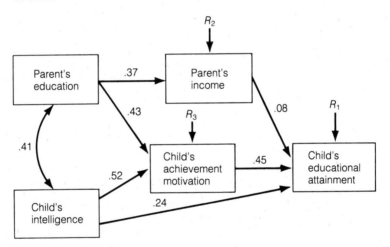

In summary, the basic steps in a path analysis are as follows:

1. Set up a preliminary theory to be tested, drawing the path diagram without the path coefficients.
2. Do the necessary regression modeling to estimate the path coefficients and the residual coefficients.
3. Evaluate the model, perhaps erasing nonsignificant paths and recalculating path coefficients for the new model.

16.2
Factor Analysis

Factor analysis is a statistical technique that is used for a wide variety of purposes (see Rummel, 1970; Afifi and Clark, 1984, Chap. 14). These include:

1. Revealing patterns of interrelationships among variables.
2. Detecting clusters of variables, each of which contains variables that are strongly intercorrelated and hence somewhat redundant.
3. Reducing a large number of variables to a smaller number of statistically independent variables (called *factors*) that are each linearly related to the original variables.

The third of these uses is particularly helpful when we are confronted with a large number of variables, many of which are highly intercorrelated. For example, when we encounter multicollinearity in multiple regression modeling, we can use factor analysis to transform the independent variables to a smaller set of factors that have nearly as large an R^2 (when used to predict the dependent variable) but that are uncorrelated among themselves.

Factor Model

The model upon which the basic factor analysis procedure is based is summarized as follows. Suppose that there are k variables $X_1, \ldots, X_k$ on which we measure the sample. The factor analytic model expresses the mean of each of these k variables in terms of a linear function of m statistically independent artificial variables, called *factors*. The number of factors m is specified by the researcher and must be less than the number of variables k. The model consists of a set of k equations, one for each of the original variables. The same m factors appear in each of the equations. Roughly speaking, the model corresponds to condensing the k variables to just m statistically independent factors.

The Pearson correlation of the ith variable ($i = 1, \ldots, k$) with the jth factor ($j = 1, \ldots, m$) is referred to as the *loading* of the ith variable on the jth factor. A matrix with k rows (one for each variable) and m columns (one for each factor) can be used to summarize these loadings. The sum of squares of the m loadings for the ith variable is called the *communality* for that variable. It represents the proportion of the variance of the variable that is explained by the m factors.

The factor loadings are unknown parameters that must be estimated using a data set. Unlike regression analysis, in which the independent variables are observable, the factors in the factor analysis model are hypothetical constructs whose values can only be estimated from the observed data. The factors in general are merely convenient descriptive summarizations of the observed data. Equations can also be estimated for expressing the factors as linear functions of the original variables. For example, the first factor constructed, denoted by f_1, might be obtained by multiplying X_1 by .9, X_2 by $-.1, \ldots, X_k$ by 1.3, and adding (i.e., $f_1 = .9X_1 - .1X_2 + \cdots + 1.3X_k$). The formulas for the coefficients of the variables in such equations are based on the sample correlations between the variables. Using the factor equations, values on the k variables for each member sampled can be converted (and condensed) to scores on the m factors.

The existence of m factors is a hypothesis that can be tested, under certain assumptions, using a chi-square test. The researcher can often form a good estimate for the number of factors that should be used by inspecting the table of correlation coefficients between pairs of variables. If different sets of variables cluster together, in the sense that there are strong correlations between each pair of variables in each set but small correlations between variables occurring in different sets, then we might try using as many factors as there are clusters.

There is no unique solution to the problem of obtaining estimates of the factors. Most factor analytic procedures obtain estimates of the factor loadings from the correlations between variables and initial guesses of the sizes of the communalities. Each row of m factor loadings is treated as a point in m-dimensional space, and the estimates are rotated in order to obtain more meaningful factors with the simplest possible factor structure. The purpose of the rotation is to bring most of the loadings of a variable close to 0, so that each variable is highly correlated with only one or two factors. This makes it easier to interpret each factor as representing the effects of a particular subset of variables. There often is one general factor that is strongly related to all of the variables. Ideally, after rotation, the structure of the factor loadings might appear as listed in the following table:

| | | FACTOR | | |
		1	2	3
	1	*	*	0
	2	*	.*	0
	3	*	*	0
VARIABLE	4	*	0	*
	5	*	0	*
	6	*	0	*
	7	*	0	0

*Denotes a significantly nonzero loading.

The factor analysis procedure is most easily understood at this level by considering examples of its use. The correlations in Table 16.1 (page 516) are from an example given by Harman (1967, pp. 165–166). The correlations refer to the following eight variables, which were measured in an election for 147 districts in Chicago:

1. Percentage vote for Lewis (Democratic candidate in mayoral election)
2. Percentage vote for Roosevelt (Democratic candidate in presidential election)
3. Percentage of straight party votes
4. Median rental cost
5. Percentage homeownership
6. Percentage unemployed
7. Percentage moved in last year
8. Percentage completed more than 10 years school

Table 16.1   Correlation Matrix for Eight Variables Measured for 147 Districts in Chicago Election

					VARIABLE NUMBER				
		1	2	3	4	5	6	7	8
	1	1.0							
	2	.84	1.0						
	3	.62	.84	1.0					
VARIABLE	4	−.53	−.68	−.76	1.0				
NUMBER	5	.03	−.05	.08	−.25	1.0			
	6	.57	.76	.81	−.80	.25	1.0		
	7	−.33	−.35	−.51	.62	−.72	−.58	1.0	
	8	−.66	−.73	−.81	.88	−.36	−.84	.68	1.0

Reprinted from Harman (1967, pp. 165–166) by permission of The University of Chicago Press.

From Table 16.1, we see that variables 1, 2, 3, and 6 are highly positively cor-related, as are variables 4, 7, and 8. Hence, we might hypothesize that this system of eight variables can be reasonably well represented by two factors. When that factor model is fitted to the data using the *principal factor* solution, we get the factor loadings shown in Table 16.2. There are $m = 2$ columns and $k = 8$ rows in that table, containing estimates of the true factor loadings. The first factor is referred to as *bipolar*, since it contains high positive and high negative loadings. Since the positive correlations are with variables 1, 2, 3, and 6, and since these variables tend to have high scores in districts where the vote is heavily Democratic, this factor is interpreted as a measure of the traditional Democratic vote. Factor 2, which is highly positively correlated with variable 5 and negatively correlated with variable 7, is interpreted as a measure of home permanency. In other words, the higher the score on factor 2 for a district, the higher the percentage of homeownership tends to be and the lower the percentage of those who have moved in the previous year tends to be.

Table 16.2

Factor Loadings for a
Two-Factor Solution for
the Correlations in Table
16.1

		LOADINGS		COMMUNALITY
		Factor 1	Factor 2	
	1	.69	−.28	.55
	2	.88	−.48	1.00
	3	.87	−.17	.79
VARIABLE	4	−.88	−.09	.78
NUMBER	5	.28	.65	.50
	6	.89	.01	.79
	7	−.66	−.56	.75
	8	−.96	−.15	.94

Figure 16.3 is a plot of the loadings of the variables on the two factors. Each point in Figure 16.3 represents a particular variable. For example, the point labeled 4 has as X coordinate the loading of variable 4 on factor 1 (−.88) and as Y coordinate the loading of variable 4 on factor 2 (−.09). We see from this plot that variables 1, 2, 3, and 6 cluster together, in the sense that they are all very similar in their two loadings. Also, variables 4, 7, and 8 cluster together.

Fig. 16.3 Loadings of the Eight Variables on the Two Factors

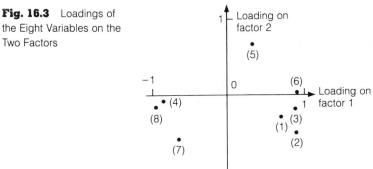

In further analyses of these data, we might consider replacing the eight variables with these two artificial factors. They seem to have a relatively clear interpretation. They are statistically independent, so there are no redundancies when both are used in regression analyses. Also, the communalities are relatively large, implying that the factors explain most of the variation in the original variables. Equations could be obtained for expressing each of the factors in terms of the eight variables, so that scores on the two factors can be obtained for the 147 districts.

16.3 LISREL

LISREL is the name given to a specialized computer program that implements methodology developed since 1970 by K. Jöreskog and others. The program can fit a very general collection of models that combine elements of path analysis and factor analysis. The name LISREL is an acronym for *li*near *s*tructural *rel*ationships. The model is also referred to as a *covariance structure model*, because it attempts to explain the variances and correlations among a set of observed variables in terms of a causal system of unobserved factors. In its general form, LISREL is a quite complex and powerful tool, one that requires much study to use properly. In this section, we hope simply to explain to the reader some reasons for using LISREL. The references at the end of the chapter provide much more detailed explanation as well as illustrative examples.

A covariance structure model consists of two parts. The first part is called the *measurement model*. It resembles a factor analysis, a set of factors being derived from the observed variables. The second part is called the *structural equation model*. It resembles a path analysis in which the regression models are specified for the factors derived in the measurement model.

Measurement Model

The measurement model specifies how the observed variables are related to a set of hypothetical factors, called *latent variables*. This part of the analysis is similar to factor analysis, except that there is more structured modeling in the sense that the latent variables are assigned, a priori, to specific sets of variables. This is accomplished by forcing certain factor loadings to equal 0.

The measurement model explicitly represents the researcher's admission that the observed variables, being subject to measurement error and problems with validity and reliability, are imperfect indicators of the concepts of true interest. For instance, a battery of IQ tests might be treated as crude indicators of intelligence that can be factor analyzed, producing a single latent variable that is a better measure of intelligence than any one of the IQ tests. Thus, the latent variables are constructed to better operationalize characteristics that are difficult to measure well in social science research, such as motivation, mental health, prejudice, anxiety, and conservatism.

Structural Equation Model

The second part of a covariance structure model is the structural equation model. This part of the model resembles a path analysis for the latent variables. In other words, the structural equation model uses linear regression models to specify causal relationships among the latent variables. One or more of the latent variables are identified as dependent variables, and the other latent variables are identified as independent variables. The dependent latent variables can be regressed on themselves as well as on the independent latent variables. LISREL uses the maximum likelihood estimation technique to obtain standardized or unstandardized estimates of regression parameters. Unlike the least squares method used in ordinary path analysis, this approach allows the fitting of models that have two-way causation, in which latent variables may be regressed on each other.

We will use Figure 16.4, based on an example given in Pedhazur (1982, p. 670), to illustrate an application of the covariance structure model. The purpose of the modeling is to analyze the effects of intelligence and socioeconomic status on achievement. The observed variables are the indicators of intelligence, X_1 = Wechsler score and X_2 = Stanford-Binet IQ score; the indicators of socioeconomic status, X_3 = father's education, X_4 = mother's education, and X_5 = parents' total

Fig. 16.4 A Covariance Structure Model for Achievement, Intelligence, and Socioeconomic Status Latent Variables

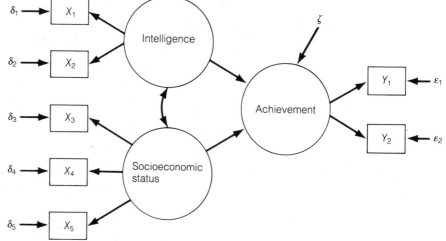

income; and the indicators of achievement, Y_1 = verbal score and Y_2 = quantitative score on an achievement test. The achievement indicators are regarded as dependent variables.

In Figure 16.4, squares are used to represent observed variables and circles are used to represent latent variables. Thus, an intelligence latent variable is derived from X_1 and X_2, a socioeconomic status latent variable is derived from X_3, X_4, and X_5, and an achievement latent variable is derived from Y_1 and Y_2. The observed variables are represented as being dependent on the latent variables. The paths among the latent variables indicate that achievement is directly dependent on intelligence and socioeconomic status, and that there is an association between intelligence and socioeconomic status. LISREL uses the sample covariation among the observed variables to estimate parameters in the measurement model and in the structural equation model. For instance, parameters in the structural equation model include the regression coefficients of the intelligence and socioeconomic status latent variables on the achievement latent variable.

As in any regression analysis, one does not assume that one variable is completely determined by the others in the system. The δ's and ε's pointing to the observed variables are errors, representing the fact that the variation in these variables is not completely explained by the latent variables. In other words, the δ's and ε's represent unexplained variation in the measurement error model. The ζ symbol refers to unexplained variation in the structural equation model, representing the fact that the achievement latent variable is not completely determined by the intelligence and socioeconomic status latent variables.

Comments   An attractive feature of LISREL is its flexibility. A regression parameter can be forced to equal another in the system (it is then referred to as a *constrained* parameter), or it can be forced to assume a fixed value, such as 0 (it is then referred to as a *fixed* parameter), or it can be completely unknown (a *free* parameter). In Figure 16.4, for instance, the factor loadings of X_1 and X_2 on the socioeconomic status latent variable equal 0, so they are fixed parameters, whereas the regression coefficients of intelligence and socioeconomic status on achievement are free parameters. LISREL allows errors affecting different variables to be correlated, a real advantage for longitudinal data. If desired, we can treat an observed variable as if it were perfectly measured, in which case the corresponding latent variable is forced to be identical to the observed variable. In doing this, we are assuming that there is no error in that part of the measurement model. All the observed variables can be treated as dependent variables, in which case LISREL simplifies to factor analysis. This type of factor analysis is referred to as *confirmatory*, meaning that the analysis is designed to confirm a hypothesized factor-loading pattern for prespecified latent variables. This contrasts with the *exploratory* factor analysis described in Section 16.2, in which researchers do not judge the number of important factors and their relationships with the observed variables until they view the matrix of factor loadings. With exploratory factor analysis, there is greater danger of going on a fishing expedition that produces results that seem interesting but may be due mainly to random sampling error.

Good features of using LISREL are that (**a**) it forces researchers to provide theoretical underpinnings to their analyses, and (**b**) the fit of the data to the theoretical model can be tested with a chi-square test.

In summary, LISREL gives a very versatile format for carrying out a variety of analyses that are of importance in social science research. The frequency of its use by social scientists is likely to increase dramatically in the near future.

16.4 Markov Chains

The examples we have considered in this text have referred primarily to static situations—in other words, to data on one or more variables measured for some sample at a fixed time. Researchers are often interested, however, in the *changes* in the distributions of variables over time. In studying nationwide migration patterns, we might be interested in the proportions of Americans living in each of four regions of the country at the beginning of each decade during the last 200 years. In studying presidential elections, we might be interested in the change in the distribution of the vote between the Democratic and Republican candidates over several decades.

A sequence of observations that varies randomly in some way is referred to as a *stochastic process*. The possible values for the process at each step are referred to as *states* of the process. For example, the possible states for the social class of a family considered over a span of several generations might be upper, middle, and lower. Many types of stochastic models have been developed for describing sequences of observations on a variable. One of the simplest of these, and probably the most commonly used, is the *Markov chain model*.* This model is appropriate if, given the behavior of the process at times $t, t - 1, t - 2, \ldots, 1$, the probability distribution of the outcome at time $t + 1$ can be specified entirely by the outcome at just time t. In other words, given the outcome at time t, the outcome at time $t + 1$ is statistically independent of the outcome at all times previous to time t.

Transition Probabilities

To illustrate the Markov structure, suppose we were considering social class mobility over a three-generation period, which we label by grandfather, father, and son. We could follow a particular family line by considering the sequence of firstborn sons as they reach a specified age, say, 40 years. In each generation, the possible states of the process are upper, middle, and lower. Now, suppose this process behaves like a Markov chain. This implies, for example, that for all fathers in the upper class, the social class of the son is statistically independent of the social class of the grandfather. Similarly, for all fathers in the middle (or lower class), the social class of the son is statistically independent of the social class of the grandfather. Using the vertical slash | to represent *given* or *conditioned on*, the following four probabilities would be identical, for example:

Pr(son in M | father in U, grandfather in L)

Pr(son in M | father in U, grandfather in M)

Pr(son in M | father in U, grandfather in U)

Pr(son in M | father in U)

*This model was first introduced by the Russian probabilist, A. A. Markov, in 1907.

The common probability is called the *transition probability* of moving from the upper class to the middle class in one generation, and is denoted by P_{UM}.

It should be emphasized here that the Markov property is *not* that the state at time $t + 1$ is independent of the state at time $t - 1$, $t - 2$, and so on; rather only that for a *fixed* value of the process at time t, they are independent. Letting X_1, X_2, . . . denote the successive states of the chain, this is like saying that X_{t+1} is associated with X_{t-1}, X_{t-2}, . . . but that, conditioned on X_t, X_{t+1} is statistically independent of X_{t-1}, X_{t-2}, ... Basically, the zero-order associations are nonzero, but the partial associations (e.g., between X_{t+1} and X_{t-1}, controlling for X_t) are 0.

In using the Markov chain model, we are usually interested in answering questions such as the following:

1. What is the probability of moving from one given state to another in a particular amount of time?
2. How long, on the average, does it take to move from one particular state to another?
3. In the long run, what is the probability of being in each of the states?
4. Are the transition probabilities between each pair of states constant over time? (If they are, the process is said to have *stationary* transition probabilities.)
5. Does the process evolve according to the Markov property, or is there a more complex dependence structure?

All of the properties concerning the probabilistic behavior of a Markov chain are based on the transition probabilities. These are usually studied through the transition probability matrix, denoted by **P**. For an s-state chain, this matarix is an $s \times s$ table such that the entry in the cell in the ith row and the jth column is the probability that, given that the chain is presently in state i, at the next time period it will be in state j. Table 16.3 gives the format for such a matrix for the social mobility example, with a set of potential transition probabilities. The row labels show the father's class, and the column labels give the son's class. In the table, $P_{UM} = .48$ means that if the father is in the upper class, then the probability is .48 that the son is in the middle class. Similarly, if the father is in the upper class, the probability that the son is in the upper class is $P_{UU} = .45$, whereas the probability that the son is in the lower class is $P_{UL} = .07$. The sum of the probabilities within each row of the matrix is 1.0. The true transition probabilities can be estimated in practice by calculating the proportion of the transitions from each state into each of the other states. For example, if there are 100 father–son pairs such that the father is in the upper class, and if out of these pairs 45 of the sons are classified in the upper class, then we would estimate $\hat{P}_{UU} = 45/100 = .45$.

Table 16.3
Sample Format for Matrix
P of Transition
Probabilities

Time $t + 1$

$$
\text{Time } t \quad
\begin{array}{c}
U \\ M \\ L
\end{array}
\begin{bmatrix}
P_{UU} & P_{UM} & P_{UL} \\
P_{MU} & P_{MM} & P_{ML} \\
P_{LU} & P_{LM} & P_{LL}
\end{bmatrix}
=
\begin{array}{c}
U \\ M \\ L
\end{array}
\begin{bmatrix}
.45 & .48 & .07 \\
.05 & .70 & .25 \\
.01 & .50 & .49
\end{bmatrix}
$$

Matrix
Multiplication

Let $P^{(n)}$ denote the matrix of transition probabilities for transitions over a time period of length n. In other words, the entry in the ith row and the jth column of $P^{(n)}$ is the probability that the chain is in state j at time $(t + n)$, given that the chain is in state i at time t; that is,

$$\Pr(X_{t+n} = j \mid X_t = i)$$

Now, $P^{(n)}$ can be obtained by taking the nth power of the (one-step) transition probability matrix, P. That is, $P^{(1)} = P$, $P^{(2)} = P \cdot P$, $P^{(3)} = P \cdot P \cdot P$, and so forth. To obtain these products, we use matrix multiplication. The general rule in multiplying two square matrices of the same dimensions is as follows: To obtain the element in the ith row and the jth column of the product of two matrices A and B, multiply each term in the ith row of A (left to right) by the corresponding term in the jth column of B (top to bottom), and sum the results.

To illustrate this rule, let us consider the product

$$P^{(2)} = P^2 = P \cdot P = \begin{bmatrix} .45 & .48 & .07 \\ .05 & .70 & .25 \\ .01 & .50 & .49 \end{bmatrix} \begin{bmatrix} .45 & .48 & .07 \\ .05 & .70 & .25 \\ .01 & .50 & .49 \end{bmatrix}$$

$$= \begin{bmatrix} P^{(2)}_{UU} & P^{(2)}_{UM} & P^{(2)}_{UL} \\ P^{(2)}_{MU} & P^{(2)}_{MM} & P^{(2)}_{ML} \\ P^{(2)}_{LU} & P^{(2)}_{LM} & P^{(2)}_{LL} \end{bmatrix} = \begin{bmatrix} .23 & .59 & .19 \\ .06 & .64 & .30 \\ .03 & .60 & .37 \end{bmatrix}$$

The term $P^{(2)}_{UM}$ represents the probability that, if the grandfather is in the upper class, the son is in the middle class. Here, we are considering a time difference of $n = 2$ generations. To calculate $P^{(2)}_{UM}$, we multiply the first row of P (since U is the first state) by the second column of P (since M is the second state) and add the terms, yielding

$$P^{(2)}_{UM} = .45(.48) + .48(.70) + .07(.50) = .59$$

Similarly,

$$P^{(2)}_{UU} = .45(.45) + .48(.05) + .07(.01) = .23$$

$$P^{(2)}_{UL} = .45(.07) + .48(.25) + .07(.49) = .19$$

The set of two-step transition probabilities is given above. To get the three-generation transition probabilities, we would calculate $P^{(3)} = P^3 = P \cdot P \cdot P = P \cdot P^2$. That is, we could multiply P by P^2.

An interesting property of Markov chains is that, in a broad class of situations, they tend toward a *probabilistic equilibrium*. This means that the n-step transition probabilities $P^{(n)}_{ij}$ stabilize as n increases so that they cease to depend on the initial state i or the length of time that the process has been operating. To illustrate, for the social mobility matrix P, the six-step transition matrix and higher-step matrices equal

$$P^{(6)} = \begin{array}{c} \\ U \\ M \\ L \end{array} \begin{array}{ccc} U & M & L \\ \begin{bmatrix} .06 & .63 & .31 \\ .06 & .63 & .31 \\ .06 & .63 & .31 \end{bmatrix} \end{array}$$

In other words, the son's class is independent of the great-great-great-great-grand-father's class (six generations earlier). In the long run, about 6% of the descendants of the upper class, middle class, and lower class in this model are in the upper class; about 63% are in the middle class; and about 31% are in the lower class. Of course, the long-run behavior assumes that the one-step transition probabilities in *P* remain constant over time.

The number of time units that it takes to get from one particular state to another is called the *first-passage time* for that pair of states. The *recurrence time* is the first-passage time from a state to itself. Formulas exist for calculating the mean of the distribution for each first-passage time. For example, the mean amount of time that it takes to return to a state equals the inverse of the long-run probability of being in that state. To illustrate, in the social mobility example, the long-run probability of being in the lower class is .31. Hence, given that a person is presently in the lower class, the expected (mean) number of generations until that family line is again in the lower class is $1/.31 = 3.2$ generations.

The types of results we have been quoting apply to Markov chains with stationary transition probabilities. If this model is applied to real data, it is important to test the adequacy of these assumptions. Chi-square tests are available for testing the null hypothesis of stationary transition probabilities and the null hypothesis of Markov dependence (see Goodman, 1962). Standard measures of association can be applied to the tables upon which these tests are based in order to describe the degree to which these assumptions are violated, if at all.

Bibliography ## Path Analysis

Duncan, O. D. (1966). "Path Analysis: Sociological Examples." *American Journal of Sociology, 72* (July): 1–16.
Land, K. (1969). "Principles of Path Analysis." In *Sociological Methodology 1969*, ed. E. Borgatta. San Francisco: Jossey–Bass.
Pedhazur, E. J. (1982). *Multiple Regression in Behavioral Research*, 2nd ed. New York: Holt, Rinehart and Winston. Chap. 15.

Factor Analysis

Afifi, A. A. and V. Clark (1984). *Computer-Aided Multivariate Analysis*. Belmont, Calif.: Lifetime Learning. Chap. 14.
Harman, H. (1967). *Modern Factor Analysis*, 2nd ed. Chicago: University of Chicago Press.
Rummel, R. J. (1970). *Applied Factor Analysis*. Evanston, Ill.: Northwestern University Press.

LISREL

Bentler, P. M. (1980). "Multivariate Analysis with Latent Variables: Causal Modelling." *Annual Review of Psychology, 31*:419–456.
Everitt, B. S. (1984). *An Introduction to Latent Variable Models*. London: Chapman and Hall. Chap. 3.

Jöreskog, K. G. and D. Sorbom (1981). *LISREL V Manual*. Chicago: National Educational Resources.

Long, J. S. (1983). *Confirmatory Factor Analysis* and *Covariance Structure Models, An Introduction to LISREL*, Sage University Paper Series on Quantitative Applications in the Social Sciences, series no. 07-033, 034. Beverly Hills and London: Sage Publications.

Pedhazur, E. J. (1982). *Multiple Regression in Behavioral Research*, 2nd ed. New York: Holt, Rinehart and Winston. Chap. 16.

Markov Chains

Bartholomew, D. J. (1982). *Stochastic Models for Social Processes*, 3rd ed. New York: Wiley.

Derman, C., L. J. Gleser, and I. Olkin (1973). *A Guide to Probability Theory and Application*. New York: Holt, Rinehart and Winston. Chaps. 11 and 12.

Goodman, L. A. (1962). "Statistical Methods for Analyzing Processes of Change." *American Journal of Sociology, 68* (July): 57–78.

TABLES

Contents

Table A Normal curve areas

Standard normal probability in right-hand tail (for negative values of z, areas are found by symmetry)

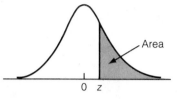

Area

0 z

z	SECOND DECIMAL PLACE OF z									
	.00	.01	.02	.03	.04	.05	.06	.07	.08	.09
0.0	.5000	.4960	.4920	.4880	.4840	.4801	.4761	.4721	.4681	.4641
0.1	.4602	.4562	.4522	.4483	.4443	.4404	.4364	.4325	.4286	.4247
0.2	.4207	.4168	.4129	.4090	.4052	.4013	.3974	.3936	.3897	.3859
0.3	.3821	.3783	.3745	.3707	.3669	.3632	.3594	.3557	.3520	.3483
0.4	.3446	.3409	.3372	.3336	.3300	.3264	.3228	.3192	.3156	.3121
0.5	.3085	.3050	.3015	.2981	.2946	.2912	.2877	.2843	.2810	.2776
0.6	.2743	.2709	.2676	.2643	.2611	.2578	.2546	.2514	.2483	.2451
0.7	.2420	.2389	.2358	.2327	.2296	.2266	.2236	.2206	.2177	.2148
0.8	.2119	.2090	.2061	.2033	.2005	.1977	.1949	.1922	.1894	.1867
0.9	.1841	.1814	.1788	.1762	.1736	.1711	.1685	.1660	.1635	.1611
1.0	.1587	.1562	.1539	.1515	.1492	.1469	.1446	.1423	.1401	.1379
1.1	.1357	.1335	.1314	.1292	.1271	.1251	.1230	.1210	.1190	.1170
1.2	.1151	.1131	.1112	.1093	.1075	.1056	.1038	.1020	.1003	.0985
1.3	.0968	.0951	.0934	.0918	.0901	.0885	.0869	.0853	.0838	.0823
1.4	.0808	.0793	.0778	.0764	.0749	.0735	.0722	.0708	.0694	.0681
1.5	.0668	.0655	.0643	.0630	.0618	.0606	.0594	.0582	.0571	.0559
1.6	.0548	.0537	.0526	.0516	.0505	.0495	.0485	.0475	.0465	.0455
1.7	.0446	.0436	.0427	.0418	.0409	.0401	.0392	.0384	.0375	.0367
1.8	.0359	.0352	.0344	.0336	.0329	.0322	.0314	.0307	.0301	.0294
1.9	.0287	.0281	.0274	.0268	.0262	.0256	.0250	.0244	.0239	.0233
2.0	.0228	.0222	.0217	.0212	.0207	.0202	.0197	.0192	.0188	.0183
2.1	.0179	.0174	.0170	.0166	.0162	.0158	.0154	.0150	.0146	.0143
2.2	.0139	.0136	.0132	.0129	.0125	.0122	.0119	.0116	.0113	.0110
2.3	.0107	.0104	.0102	.0099	.0096	.0094	.0091	.0089	.0087	.0084
2.4	.0082	.0080	.0078	.0075	.0073	.0071	.0069	.0068	.0066	.0064
2.5	.0062	.0060	.0059	.0057	.0055	.0054	.0052	.0051	.0049	.0048
2.6	.0047	.0045	.0044	.0043	.0041	.0040	.0039	.0038	.0037	.0036
2.7	.0035	.0034	.0033	.0032	.0031	.0030	.0029	.0028	.0027	.0026
2.8	.0026	.0025	.0024	.0023	.0023	.0022	.0021	.0021	.0020	.0019
2.9	.0019	.0018	.0017	.0017	.0016	.0016	.0015	.0015	.0014	.0014
3.0	.00135									
3.5	.000233									
4.0	.0000317									
4.5	.00000340									
5.0	.000000287									

$$\frac{1}{\sqrt{2\pi}} \int_{z}^{\infty} e^{-\frac{x^2}{2}} dx$$

Source: R. E. Walpole, *Introduction to Statistics* (New York: Macmillan, 1968).

Table B

t Distribution

Values corresponding to various right-hand tail areas

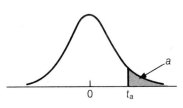

df	$t_{.100}$	$t_{.050}$	$t_{.025}$	$t_{.010}$	$t_{.005}$
1	3.078	6.314	12.706	31.821	63.657
2	1.886	2.920	4.303	6.965	9.925
3	1.638	2.353	3.182	4.541	5.841
4	1.533	2.132	2.776	3.747	4.604
5	1.476	2.015	2.571	3.365	4.032
6	1.440	1.943	2.447	3.143	3.707
7	1.415	1.895	2.365	2.998	3.499
8	1.397	1.860	2.306	2.896	3.355
9	1.383	1.833	2.262	2.821	3.250
10	1.372	1.812	2.228	2.764	3.169
11	1.363	1.796	2.201	2.718	3.106
12	1.356	1.782	2.179	2.681	3.055
13	1.350	1.771	2.160	2.650	3.012
14	1.345	1.761	2.145	2.624	2.977
15	1.341	1.753	2.131	2.602	2.947
16	1.337	1.746	2.120	2.583	2.921
17	1.333	1.740	2.110	2.567	2.898
18	1.330	1.734	2.101	2.552	2.878
19	1.328	1.729	2.093	2.539	2.861
20	1.325	1.725	2.086	2.528	2.845
21	1.323	1.721	2.080	2.518	2.831
22	1.321	1.717	2.074	2.508	2.819
23	1.319	1.714	2.069	2.500	2.807
24	1.318	1.711	2.064	2.492	2.797
25	1.316	1.708	2.060	2.485	2.787
26	1.315	1.706	2.056	2.479	2.779
27	1.314	1.703	2.052	2.473	2.771
28	1.313	1.701	2.048	2.467	2.763
29	1.311	1.699	2.045	2.462	2.756
∞	1.282	1.645	1.960	2.326	2.576

Source: "Table of Percentage Points of the *t*-Distribution." Computed by Maxine Merrington, *Biometrika, 32* (1941): 300. Reproduced by permission of the *Biometrika* trustees.

Table C χ^2 Distribution

Values for various right-hand tail probabilities

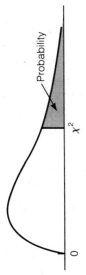

df	.99	.98	.95	.90	.80	.70	.50	.30	.20	.10	.05	.02	.01	.001
1	0³157	0³628	00393	0158	0642	.148	.455	1.074	1.642	2.706	3.841	5.412	6.635	10.827
2	.0201	.0404	.103	.211	.446	.713	1.386	2.408	3.219	4.605	5.991	7.824	9.210	13.815
3	.115	.185	.352	.584	1.005	1.424	2.366	3.665	4.642	6.251	7.815	9.837	11.345	16.268
4	.297	.429	.711	1.064	1.649	2.195	3.357	4.878	5.989	7.779	9.488	11.668	13.277	18.465
5	.554	.752	1.145	1.610	2.343	3.000	4.351	6.064	7.289	9.236	11.070	13.388	15.086	20.517
6	.872	1.134	1.635	2.204	3.070	3.828	5.348	7.231	8.558	10.645	12.592	15.033	16.812	22.457
7	1.239	1.564	2.167	2.833	3.822	4.671	6.346	8.383	9.803	12.017	14.067	16.622	18.475	24.322
8	1.646	2.032	2.733	3.490	4.594	5.527	7.344	9.524	11.030	13.362	15.507	18.168	20.090	26.125
9	2.088	2.532	3.325	4.168	5.380	6.393	8.343	10.656	12.242	14.684	16.919	19.679	21.666	27.877
10	2.558	3.059	3.940	4.865	6.179	7.267	9.342	11.781	13.442	15.987	18.307	21.161	23.209	29.588
11	3.053	3.609	4.575	5.578	6.989	8.148	10.341	12.899	14.631	17.275	19.675	22.618	24.725	31.264
12	3.571	4.178	5.226	6.304	7.807	9.034	11.340	14.011	15.812	18.549	21.026	24.054	26.217	32.909
13	4.107	4.765	5.892	7.042	8.634	9.926	12.340	15.119	16.985	19.812	22.362	25.472	27.688	34.528
14	4.660	5.368	6.571	7.790	9.467	10.821	13.339	16.222	18.151	21.064	23.685	26.873	29.141	36.123
15	5.229	5.985	7.261	8.547	10.307	11.721	14.339	17.322	19.311	22.307	24.996	28.259	30.578	37.697
16	5.812	6.614	7.962	9.312	11.152	12.624	15.338	18.418	20.465	23.542	26.296	29.633	32.000	39.252
17	6.408	7.255	8.672	10.085	12.002	13.531	16.338	19.511	21.615	24.769	27.587	30.995	33.409	40.790
18	7.015	7.906	9.390	10.865	12.857	14.440	17.338	20.601	22.760	25.989	28.869	32.346	34.805	42.312
19	7.633	8.567	10.117	11.651	13.716	15.352	18.338	21.689	23.900	27.204	30.144	33.687	36.191	43.820
20	8.260	9.237	10.851	12.443	14.578	16.266	19.337	22.775	25.038	28.412	31.410	35.020	37.566	45.315
21	8.897	9.915	11.591	13.240	15.445	17.182	20.337	23.858	26.171	29.615	32.671	36.343	38.932	46.797
22	9.542	10.600	12.338	14.041	16.314	18.101	21.337	24.939	27.301	30.813	33.924	37.659	40.289	48.268
23	10.196	11.293	13.091	14.848	17.187	19.021	22.337	26.018	28.429	32.007	35.172	38.968	41.638	49.728
24	10.856	11.992	13.848	15.659	18.062	19.943	23.337	27.096	29.553	33.196	36.415	40.270	42.980	51.179
25	11.524	12.697	14.611	16.473	18.940	20.867	24.337	28.172	30.675	34.382	37.652	41.566	44.314	52.620
26	12.198	13.409	15.379	17.292	19.820	21.792	25.336	29.246	31.795	35.563	38.885	42.856	45.642	54.052
27	12.879	14.125	16.151	18.114	20.703	22.719	26.336	30.319	32.912	36.741	40.113	44.140	46.963	55.476
28	13.565	14.847	16.928	18.939	21.588	23.647	27.336	31.391	34.027	37.916	41.337	45.419	48.278	56.893
29	14.256	15.574	17.708	19.768	22.475	24.577	28.336	32.461	35.139	39.087	42.557	46.693	49.588	58.302
30	14.953	16.306	18.493	20.599	23.364	25.508	29.336	33.530	36.250	40.256	43.773	47.962	50.892	59.703

Source: From Table IV of R. A. Fisher and F. Yates, *Statistical Tables for Biological, Agricultural and Medical Research*, published by Longman Group Ltd., London, 1974. (Previously published by Oliver & Boyd, Edinburgh.) Reprinted by permission of the authors and publishers.

Table D   F Distribution

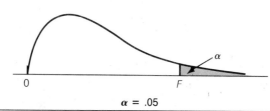

$\alpha = .05$

df$_1$ df$_2$	1	2	3	4	5	6	8	12	24	∞
1	161.4	199.5	215.7	224.6	230.2	234.0	238.9	243.9	249.0	254.3
2	18.51	19.00	19.16	19.25	19.30	19.33	19.37	19.41	19.45	19.50
3	10.13	9.55	9.28	9.12	9.01	8.94	8.84	8.74	8.64	8.53
4	7.71	6.94	6.59	6.39	6.26	6.16	6.04	5.91	5.77	5.63
5	6.61	5.79	5.41	5.19	5.05	4.95	4.82	4.68	4.53	4.36
6	5.99	5.14	4.76	4.53	4.39	4.28	4.15	4.00	3.84	3.67
7	5.59	4.74	4.35	4.12	3.97	3.87	3.73	3.57	3.41	3.23
8	5.32	4.46	4.07	3.84	3.69	3.58	3.44	3.28	3.12	2.93
9	5.12	4.26	3.86	3.63	3.48	3.37	3.23	3.07	2.90	2.71
10	4.96	4.10	3.71	3.48	3.33	3.22	3.07	2.91	2.74	2.54
11	4.84	3.98	3.59	3.36	3.20	3.09	2.95	2.79	2.61	2.40
12	4.75	3.88	3.49	3.26	3.11	3.00	2.85	2.69	2.50	2.30
13	4.67	3.80	3.41	3.18	3.02	2.92	2.77	2.60	2.42	2.21
14	4.60	3.74	3.34	3.11	2.96	2.85	2.70	2.53	2.35	2.13
15	4.54	3.68	3.29	3.06	2.90	2.79	2.64	2.48	2.29	2.07
16	4.49	3.63	3.24	3.01	2.85	2.74	2.59	2.42	2.24	.201
17	4.45	3.59	3.20	2.96	2.81	2.70	2.55	2.38	2.19	1.96
18	4.41	3.55	3.16	2.93	2.77	2.66	2.51	2.34	2.15	1.92
19	4.38	3.52	3.13	2.90	2.74	2.63	2.48	2.31	2.11	1.88
20	4.35	3.49	3.10	2.87	2.71	2.60	2.45	2.28	2.08	1.84
21	4.32	3.47	3.07	2.84	2.68	2.57	2.42	2.25	2.05	1.81
22	4.30	3.44	3.05	2.82	2.66	2.55	2.40	2.23	2.03	1.78
23	4.28	3.42	3.03	2.80	2.64	2.53	2.38	2.20	2.00	1.76
24	4.26	3.40	3.01	2.78	2.62	2.51	2.36	2.18	1.98	1.73
25	4.24	3.38	2.99	2.76	2.60	2.49	2.34	2.16	1.96	1.71
26	4.22	3.37	2.98	2.74	2.59	2.47	2.32	2.15	1.95	1.69
27	4.21	3.35	2.96	2.73	2.57	2.46	2.30	2.13	1.93	1.67
28	4.20	3.34	2.95	2.71	2.56	2.44	2.29	2.12	1.91	1.65
29	4.18	3.33	2.93	2.70	2.54	2.43	2.28	2.10	1.90	1.64
30	4.17	3.32	2.92	2.69	2.53	2.42	2.27	2.09	1.89	1.62
40	4.08	3.23	2.84	2.61	2.45	2.34	2.18	2.00	1.79	1.51
60	4.00	3.15	2.76	2.52	2.37	2.25	2.10	1.92	1.70	1.39
120	3.92	3.07	2.68	2.45	2.29	2.17	2.02	1.83	1.61	1.25
∞	3.84	2.99	2.60	2.37	2.21	2.09	1.94	1.75	1.52	1.00

Source: From Table V of R. A. Fisher and F. Yates, *Statistical Tables for Biological, Agricultural and Medical Research,* published by Longman Group Ltd., London, 1974. (Previously published by Oliver & Boyd, Edinburgh.) Reprinted by permission of the authors and publishers.

$\alpha = .01$

df₂ \ df₁	1	2	3	4	5	6	8	12	24	∞
1	4052	4999	5403	5625	5764	5859	5981	6106	6234	6366
2	98.49	99.01	99.17	99.25	99.30	99.33	99.36	99.42	99.46	99.50
3	34.12	30.81	29.46	28.71	28.24	27.91	27.49	27.05	26.60	26.12
4	21.20	18.00	16.69	15.98	15.52	15.21	14.80	14.37	13.93	13.46
5	16.26	13.27	12.06	11.39	10.97	10.67	10.27	9.89	9.47	9.02
6	13.74	10.92	9.78	9.15	8.75	8.47	8.10	7.72	7.31	6.88
7	12.25	9.55	8.45	7.85	7.46	7.19	6.84	6.47	6.07	5.65
8	11.26	8.65	7.59	7.01	6.63	6.37	6.03	5.67	5.28	4.86
9	10.56	8.02	6.99	6.42	6.06	5.80	5.47	5.11	4.73	4.31
10	10.04	7.56	6.55	5.99	5.64	5.39	5.06	4.71	4.33	3.91
11	9.65	7.20	6.22	5.67	5.32	5.07	4.74	4.40	4.02	3.60
12	9.33	6.93	5.95	5.41	5.06	4.82	4.50	4.16	3.78	3.36
13	9.07	6.70	5.74	5.20	4.86	4.62	4.30	3.96	3.59	3.16
14	8.86	6.51	5.56	5.03	4.69	4.46	4.14	3.80	3.43	3.00
15	8.68	6.36	5.42	4.89	4.56	4.32	4.00	3.67	3.29	2.87
16	8.53	6.23	5.29	4.77	4.44	4.20	3.89	3.55	3.18	2.75
17	8.40	6.11	5.18	4.67	4.34	4.10	3.79	3.45	3.08	2.65
18	8.28	6.01	5.09	4.58	4.25	4.01	3.71	3.37	3.00	2.57
19	8.18	5.93	5.01	4.50	4.17	3.94	3.63	3.30	2.92	2.49
20	8.10	5.85	4.94	4.43	4.10	3.87	3.56	3.23	2.86	2.42
21	8.02	5.78	4.87	4.37	4.04	3.81	3.51	3.17	2.80	2.36
22	7.94	5.72	4.82	4.31	3.99	3.76	3.45	3.12	2.75	2.31
23	7.88	5.66	4.76	4.26	3.94	3.71	3.41	3.07	2.70	2.26
24	7.82	5.61	4.72	4.22	3.90	3.67	3.36	3.03	2.66	2.21
25	7.77	5.57	4.68	4.18	3.86	3.63	3.32	2.99	2.62	2.17
26	7.72	5.53	4.64	4.14	3.82	3.59	3.29	2.96	2.58	2.13
27	7.68	5.49	4.60	4.11	3.78	3.56	3.26	2.93	2.55	2.10
28	7.64	5.45	4.57	4.07	3.75	3.53	3.23	2.90	2.52	2.06
29	7.60	5.42	4.54	4.04	3.73	3.50	3.20	2.87	2.49	2.03
30	7.56	5.39	4.51	4.02	3.70	3.47	3.17	2.84	2.47	2.01
40	7.31	5.18	4.31	3.83	3.51	3.29	2.99	2.66	2.29	1.80
60	7.08	4.98	4.13	3.65	3.34	3.12	2.82	2.50	2.12	1.60
120	6.85	4.79	3.95	3.48	3.17	2.96	2.66	2.34	1.95	1.38
∞	6.64	4.60	3.78	3.32	3.02	2.80	2.51	2.18	1.79	1.00

Table D   (continued)

α = .001

df₂ \ df₁	1	2	3	4	5	6	8	12	24	∞
1	405284	500000	540379	562500	576405	585937	598144	610667	623497	636619
2	998.5	999.0	999.2	999.2	999.3	999.3	999.4	999.4	999.5	999.5
3	167.5	148.5	141.1	137.1	134.6	132.8	130.6	128.3	125.9	123.5
4	74.14	61.25	56.18	53.44	51.71	50.53	49.00	47.41	45.77	44.05
5	47.04	36.61	33.20	31.09	29.75	28.84	27.64	26.42	25.14	23.78
6	35.51	27.00	23.70	21.90	20.81	20.03	19.03	17.99	16.89	15.75
7	29.22	21.69	18.77	17.19	16.21	15.52	14.63	13.71	12.73	11.69
8	25.42	18.49	15.83	14.39	13.49	12.86	12.04	11.19	10.30	9.34
9	22.86	16.39	13.90	12.56	11.71	11.13	10.37	9.57	8.72	7.81
10	21.04	14.91	12.55	11.28	10.48	9.92	9.20	8.45	7.64	6.76
11	19.69	13.81	11.56	10.35	9.58	9.05	8.35	7.63	6.85	6.00
12	18.64	12.97	10.80	9.63	8.89	8.38	7.71	7.00	6.25	5.42
13	17.81	12.31	10.21	9.07	8.35	7.86	7.21	6.52	5.78	4.97
14	17.14	11.78	9.73	8.62	7.92	7.43	6.80	6.13	5.41	4.60
15	16.59	11.34	9.34	8.25	7.57	7.09	6.47	5.81	5.10	4.31
16	16.12	10.97	9.00	7.94	7.27	6.81	6.19	5.55	4.85	4.06
17	15.72	10.66	8.73	7.68	7.02	6.56	5.96	5.32	4.63	3.85
18	15.38	10.39	8.49	7.46	6.81	6.35	5.76	5.13	4.45	3.67
19	15.08	10.16	8.28	7.26	6.61	6.18	5.59	4.97	4.29	3.52
20	14.82	9.95	8.10	7.10	6.46	6.02	5.44	4.82	4.15	3.38
21	14.59	9.77	7.94	6.95	6.32	5.88	5.31	4.70	4.03	3.26
22	14.38	9.61	7.80	6.81	6.19	5.76	5.19	4.58	3.92	3.15
23	14.19	9.47	7.67	6.69	6.08	5.65	5.09	4.48	3.82	3.05
24	14.03	9.34	7.55	6.59	5.98	5.55	4.99	4.39	3.74	2.97
25	13.88	9.22	7.45	6.49	5.88	5.46	4.91	4.31	3.66	2.89
26	13.74	9.12	7.36	6.41	5.80	5.38	4.83	4.24	3.59	2.82
27	13.61	9.02	7.27	6.33	5.73	5.31	4.76	4.17	3.52	2.75
28	13.50	8.93	7.19	6.25	5.66	5.24	4.69	4.11	3.46	2.70
29	13.39	8.85	7.12	6.19	5.59	5.18	4.64	4.05	3.41	2.64
30	13.29	8.77	7.05	6.12	5.53	5.12	4.58	4.00	3.36	2.59
40	12.61	8.25	6.60	5.70	5.13	4.73	4.21	3.64	3.01	2.23
60	11.97	7.76	6.17	5.31	4.76	4.37	3.87	3.31	2.69	1.90
120	11.38	7.31	5.79	4.95	4.42	4.04	3.55	3.02	2.40	1.56
∞	10.83	6.91	5.42	4.62	4.10	3.74	3.27	2.74	2.13	1.00

Table E Values of $T(r) = 1.151 \log\left(\dfrac{1+r}{1-r}\right)$

r	.000	.001	.002	.003	.004	.005	.006	.007	.008	.009
.000	.0000	.0010	.0020	.0030	.0040	.0050	.0060	.0070	.0080	.0090
.010	.0100	.0110	.0120	.0130	.0140	.0150	.0160	.0170	.0180	.0190
.020	.0200	.0210	.0220	.0230	.0240	.0250	.0260	.0270	.0280	.0290
.030	.0300	.0310	.0320	.0330	.0340	.0350	.0360	.0370	.0380	.0390
.040	.0400	.0410	.0420	.0430	.0440	.0450	.0460	.0470	.0480	.0490
.050	.0501	.0511	.0521	.0531	.0541	.0551	.0561	.0571	.0581	.0591
.060	.0601	.0611	.0621	.0631	.0641	.0651	.0661	.0671	.0681	.0691
.070	.0701	.0711	.0721	.0731	.0741	.0751	.0761	.0771	.0782	.0792
.080	.0802	.0812	.0822	.0832	.0842	.0852	.0862	.0872	.0882	.0892
.090	.0902	.0912	.0922	.0933	.0943	.0953	.0963	.0973	.0983	.0993
.100	.1003	.1013	.1024	.1034	.1044	.1054	.1064	.1074	.1084	.1094
.110	.1105	.1115	.1125	.1135	.1145	.1155	.1165	.1175	.1185	.1195
.120	.1206	.1216	.1226	.1236	.1246	.1257	.1267	.1277	.1287	.1297
.130	.1308	.1318	.1328	.1338	.1348	.1358	.1368	.1379	.1389	.1399
.140	.1409	.1419	.1430	.1440	.1450	.1460	.1470	.1481	.1491	.1501
.150	.1511	.1522	.1532	.1542	.1552	.1563	.1573	.1583	.1593	.1604
.160	.1614	.1624	.1634	.1644	.1655	.1665	.1676	.1686	.1696	.1706
.170	.1717	.1727	.1737	.1748	.1758	.1768	.1779	.1789	.1799	.1810
.180	.1820	.1830	.1841	.1851	.1861	.1872	.1882	.1892	.1903	.1913
.190	.1923	.1934	.1944	.1954	.1965	.1975	.1986	.1996	.2007	.2017
.200	.2027	.2038	.2048	.2059	.2069	.2079	.2090	.2100	.2111	.2121
.210	.2132	.2142	.2153	.2163	.2174	.2184	.2194	.2205	.2215	.2226
.220	.2237	.2247	.2258	.2268	.2279	.2289	.2300	.2310	.2321	.2331
.230	.2342	.2353	.2363	.2374	.2384	.2395	.2405	.2416	.2427	.2437
.240	.2448	.2458	.2469	.2480	.2490	.2501	.2511	.2522	.2533	.2543
.250	.2554	.2565	.2575	.2586	.2597	.2608	.2618	.2629	.2640	.2650
.260	.2661	.2672	.2682	.2693	.2704	.2715	.2726	.2736	.2747	.2758
.270	.2769	.2779	.2790	.2801	.2812	.2823	.2833	.2844	.2855	.2866
.280	.2877	.2888	.2898	.2909	.2920	.2931	.2942	.2953	.2964	.2975
.290	.2986	.2997	.3008	.3019	.3029	.3040	.3051	.3062	.3073	.3084
.300	.3095	.3106	.3117	.3128	.3139	.3150	.3161	.3172	.3183	.3195
.310	.3206	.3217	.3228	.3239	.3250	.3261	.3272	.3283	.3294	.3305
.320	.3317	.3328	.3339	.3350	.3361	.3372	.3384	.3395	.3406	.3417
.330	.3428	.3439	.3451	.3462	.3473	.3484	.3496	.3507	.3518	.3530
.340	.3541	.3552	.3564	.3575	.3586	.3597	.3609	.3620	.3632	.3643
.350	.3654	.3666	.3677	.3689	.3700	.3712	.3723	.3734	.3746	.3757
.360	.3769	.3780	.3792	.3803	.3815	.3826	.3838	.3850	.3861	.3873
.370	.3884	.3896	.3907	.3919	.3931	.3942	.3954	.3966	.3977	.3989
.380	.4001	.4012	.4024	.4036	.4047	.4059	.4071	.4083	.4094	.4106
.390	.4118	.4130	.4142	.4153	.4165	.4177	.4189	.4201	.4213	.4225
.400	.4236	.4248	.4260	.4272	.4284	.4296	.4308	.4320	.4332	.4344
.410	.4356	.4368	.4380	.4392	.4404	.4416	.4429	.4441	.4453	.4465
.420	.4477	.4489	.4501	.4513	.4526	.4538	.4550	.4562	.4574	.4587
.430	.4599	.4611	.4623	.4636	.4648	.4660	.4673	.4685	.4697	.4710
.440	.4722	.4735	.4747	.4760	.4772	.4784	.4797	.4809	.4822	.4835
.450	.4847	.4860	.4872	.4885	.4897	.4910	.4923	.4935	.4948	.4961
.460	.4973	.4986	.4999	.5011	.5024	.5037	.5049	.5062	.5075	.5088
.470	.5101	.5114	.5126	.5139	.5152	.5165	.5178	.5191	.5204	.5217
.480	.5230	.5243	.5256	.5279	.5282	.5295	.5308	.5321	.5334	.5347
.490	.5361	.5374	.5387	.5400	.5413	.5427	.5440	.5453	.5466	.5480

Source: Albert E. Waugh, *Statistical Tables and Problems* (New York: McGraw-Hill, 1952), Table A11, pp. 40–41, with the kind permission of the author and publisher.

Table E (continued)

r	.000	.001	.002	.003	.004	.005	.006	.007	.008	.009
.500	.5493	.5506	.5520	.5533	.5547	.5560	.5573	.5587	.5600	.5614
.510	.5627	.5641	.5654	.5668	.5681	.5695	.5709	.5722	.5736	.5750
.520	.5763	.5777	.5791	.5805	.5818	.5832	.5846	.5860	.5874	.5888
.530	.5901	.5915	.5929	.5943	.5957	.5971	.5985	.5999	.6013	.6027
.540	.6042	.6056	.6070	.6084	.6098	.6112	.6127	.6141	.6155	.6170
.550	.6184	.6198	.6213	.6227	.6241	.6256	.6270	.6285	.6299	.6314
.560	.6328	.6343	.6358	.6372	.6387	.6401	.6416	.6431	.6446	.6460
.570	.6475	.6490	.6505	.6520	.6535	.6550	.6565	.6579	.6594	.6610
.580	.6625	.6640	.6655	.6670	.6685	.6700	.6715	.6731	.6746	.6761
.590	.6777	.6792	.6807	.6823	.6838	.6854	.6869	.6885	.6900	.6916
.600	.6931	.6947	.6963	.6978	.6994	.7010	.7026	.7042	.7057	.7073
.610	.7089	.7105	.7121	.7137	.7153	.7169	.7185	.7201	.7218	.7234
.620	.7250	.7266	.7283	.7299	.7315	.7332	.7348	.7364	.7381	.7398
.630	.7414	.7431	.7447	.7464	.7481	.7497	.7514	.7531	.7548	.7565
.640	.7582	.7599	.7616	.7633	.7650	.7667	.7684	.7701	.7718	.7736
.650	.7753	.7770	.7788	.7805	.7823	.7840	.7858	.7875	.7893	.7910
.660	.7928	.7946	.7964	.7981	.7999	.8017	.8035	.8053	.8071	.8089
.670	.8107	.8126	.8144	.8162	.8180	.8199	.8217	.8236	.8254	.8273
.680	.8291	.8310	.8328	.8347	.8366	.8385	.8404	.8423	.8442	.8461
.690	.8480	.8499	.8518	.8537	.8556	.8576	.8595	.8614	.8634	.8653
.700	.8673	.8693	.8712	.8732	.8752	.8772	.8792	.8812	.8832	.8852
.710	.8872	.8892	.8912	.8933	.8953	.8973	.8994	.9014	.9035	.9056
.720	.9076	.9097	.9118	.9139	.9160	.9181	.9202	.9223	.9245	.9266
.730	.9287	.9309	.9330	.9352	.9373	.9395	.9417	.9439	.9461	.9483
.740	.9505	.9527	.9549	.9571	.9594	.9616	.9639	.9661	.9684	.9707
.750	.9730	.9752	.9775	.9799	.9822	.9845	.9868	.9892	.9915	.9939
.760	.9962	.9986	1.0010	1.0034	1.0058	1.0082	1.0106	1.0130	1.0154	1.0179
.770	1.0203	1.0228	1.0253	1.0277	1.0302	1.0327	1.0352	1.0378	1.0403	1.0428
.780	1.0454	1.0479	1.0505	1.0531	1.0557	1.0583	1.0609	1.0635	1.0661	1.0688
.790	1.0714	1.0741	1.0768	1.0795	1.0822	1.0849	1.0876	1.0903	1.0931	1.0958
.800	1.0986	1.1014	1.1041	1.1070	1.1098	1.1127	1.1155	1.1184	1.1212	1.1241
.810	1.1270	1.1299	1.1329	1.1358	1.1388	1.1417	1.1447	1.1477	1.1507	1.1538
.820	1.1568	1.1599	1.1630	1.1660	1.1692	1.1723	1.1754	1.1786	1.1817	1.1849
.830	1.1870	1.1913	1.1946	1.1979	1.2011	1.2044	1.2077	1.2111	1.2144	1.2178
.840	1.2212	1.2246	1.2280	1.2315	1.2349	1.2384	1.2419	1.2454	1.2490	1.2526
.850	1.2561	1.2598	1.2634	1.2670	1.2708	1.2744	1.2782	1.2819	1.2857	1.2895
.860	1.2934	1.2972	1.3011	1.3050	1.3089	1.3129	1.3168	1.3209	1.3249	1.3290
.870	1.3331	1.3372	1.3414	1.3456	1.3498	1.3540	1.3583	1.3626	1.3670	1.3714
.880	1.3758	1.3802	1.3847	1.3892	1.3938	1.3984	1.4030	1.4077	1.4124	1.4171
.890	1.4219	1.4268	1.4316	1.4366	1.4415	1.4465	1.4516	1.4566	1.4618	1.4670
.900	1.4722	1.4775	1.4828	1.4883	1.4937	1.4992	1.5047	1.5103	1.5160	1.5217
.910	1.5275	1.5334	1.5393	1.5453	1.5513	1.5574	1.5636	1.5698	1.5762	1.5825
.920	1.5890	1.5956	1.6022	1.6089	1.6157	1.6226	1.6296	1.6366	1.6438	1.6510
.930	1.6584	1.6659	1.6734	1.6811	1.6888	1.6967	1.7047	1.7129	1.7211	1.7295
.940	1.7380	1.7467	1.7555	1.7645	1.7736	1.7828	1.7923	1.8019	1.8117	1.8216
.950	1.8318	1.8421	1.8527	1.8635	1.8745	1.8857	1.8972	1.9090	1.9210	1.9333
.960	1.9459	1.9588	1.9721	1.9857	1.9996	2.0140	2.0287	2.0439	2.0595	2.0756
.970	2.0923	2.1095	2.1273	2.1457	2.1649	2.1847	2.2054	2.2269	2.2494	2.2729
.980	2.2976	2.3223	2.3507	2.3796	2.4101	2.4426	2.4774	2.5147	2.5550	2.5988
.990	2.6467	2.6996	2.7587	2.8257	2.9031	2.9945	3.1063	3.2504	3.4534	3.8002

r	T(r)
.9999	4.95172
.99999	6.10303

ANSWERS TO SELECTED PROBLEMS

Chapter 1

3a. A *statistic* is a characteristic of a sample, whereas a *parameter* is a characteristic of a population.   **b.** A statistic, since it would almost surely be based on a sample and not the population of all graduating seniors

4a. All students at the University of Wisconsin   **b.** The most common response for the 100 students in the sample

6a. Everyone in Massachusetts who voted in the presidential contest   **b.** The percentage of votes cast in Massachusetts for the Democratic candidate in the presidential election   **c.** The sample percentage of votes cast for the Democratic candidate in Massachusetts (i.e., 53%)   **d.** No. The first 1,000 votes reported may come from a precinct that has a tendency to be more (or less) Democratic than the state as a whole.

Chapter 2

2a. Ordinal   **b.** Nominal   **c.** Interval   **d.** Nominal   **e.** Nominal   **f.** Ordinal   **g.** Interval   **h.** Ordinal
i. Nominal   **j.** Interval   **k.** Nominal
3a. Nominal   **b.** Nominal   **c.** Ordinal   **d.** Interval   **e.** Interval   **f.** Interval   **g.** Ordinal   **h.** Interval
4a. Interval   **b.** Ordinal   **c.** Nominal   **6.** Ordinal
7. Age, latitude and longitude, distance of residence from place of employment
8. Length of residence, task completion time, intelligence, authoritarianism, alienation
9. Students numbered 10, 22, 24   **10.** b
11a. 15011, 06907, 14342, 12765, 21382, 32363, 27001, 33062, 01536, 25595
13. Cluster sampling, systematic random sampling, and simple random sampling (each nursing home is a cluster)

Chapter 3

1a.

INTERVAL	FREQUENCY
.00– 3.00	0
3.01– 6.00	1
6.01– 9.00	4
9.01–12.00	7
12.01–15.00	8
15.01–18.00	10
18.01–21.00	8
21.01–24.00	6
24.01–27.00	4
27.01–30.00	2
Total	50

b.

RELATIVE FREQUENCY
0
.02
.08
.14
.16
.20
.16
.12
.08
.04
1.00

c. Relative frequency

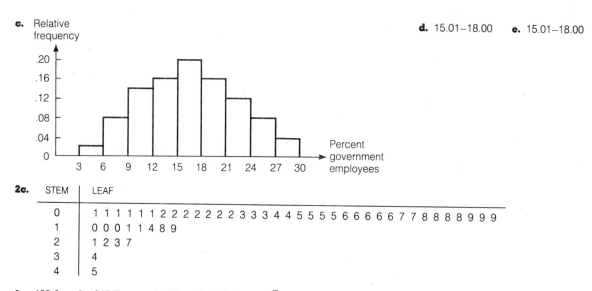

d. 15.01–18.00   **e.** 15.01–18.00

2c.

STEM	LEAF
0	1 1 1 1 1 1 2 2 2 2 2 2 2 3 3 3 4 4 5 5 5 5 6 6 6 6 6 7 7 8 8 8 8 9 9 9
1	0 0 0 1 1 4 8 9
2	1 2 3 7
3	4
4	5

4a. 439.8   **b.** 218.5   **c.** 1,760   **d.** 608.3   **5.** $\bar{Y}$ = $1,082.50; median =$1,025; range = $1,280; s = $465.82
6. $\bar{Y}$ = 50; median = 48.5; s = 9.53   **8.** Any nominal variable   **10a.** (i)   **b.** Mean: (i), (ii), (v); median: (iii), (iv)
11. Skewed left: a, d; skewed right: c, f, g; bell-shaped: b; U-shaped: e
12a. Grade point averages; IQ scores; proportion of registered voters (by county)   **b.** Income; age at first marriage;
number of children in family   **c.** Exam scores; age of individual in retirement community; age at death   **d.** Number of
years of education completed (peaks at 12 and at 16)   **e.** Number of times arrested for drug use; number of courses failed
in college; number of times hospitalized in previous year
13. $20,200   **14.** $\bar{Y}$ = 2; median = 0; mode = 0; range = 10, s^2 = 12.44; s = 3.5   **16.** 12   **17.** $160 to $640
18. Approximately 68% between $56,000 and $108,000; approximately 95% between $30,000 and $134,000; $\bar{Y}$ + .5s =
$95,000   **19a.** 60%   **b.** 100%   **c.** 100%   **d.** 20%   **20.** .33
21. No, because the lowest possible value of 0 is less than one standard deviation below $\bar{Y}$ = 2. If the distribution were
approximately bell-shaped, we could expect the lowest possible value to be about two or three standard deviations below
the mean. The distribution is probably highly skewed to the right, some observations being many standard deviations
above the mean.   ***23.** $\bar{Y}$ = 77; s = 20   ***24.** $\bar{Y}$ = 53; s = 20   ***25.** $\bar{Y}$ = 3.2; s = 5.6
*31a. 1/4, 1/9, 1/100   **b.** Tchebysheff: no more than 25%; Empirical Rule: about 5%. The Tchebysheff result is an
upper bound that holds for *any* distribution, whereas the Empirical Rule gives only an *approximation* and holds only for
approximately *bell-shaped* distributions.

Chapter 4

1. $P(0)$ = .1; $P(1)$ = .6; $P(2)$ = .3   **2.** $P(0)$ = $P(1)$ = $P(2)$ = $\cdots$ = $P(9)$ = .10
3a. .1587   **b.** .1587   **c.** .2514   **d.** .0505   **4a.** 2.33   **b.** 1.96   **c.** 1.645   **d.** 1.28   **e.** .67   **f.** 0.00
5. 1.65, 1.96, 2.33, 2.58   **6.** 1.28, 1.65, 2.05, 2.33   **7.** .2611, .7389   **8a.** .0179   **b.** .0179   **c.** .9821
9. z = 2.33   **10a.** .1056   **b.** .8413   **c.** 137   **11a.** .2119   **b.** 12.65, 19.35   **c.** 11.8
12. Yes, a murder rate of 30 is z = (30 − 10.5)/3.8 = 5.13 standard deviations above the mean, which would be an
extremely rare event for a normal distribution.   **13.** .0475, .1335   **14a.** .50   **b.** .3085   **15a.** .3783   **b.** .0062
16. Approximately normal with mean 13.0 and standard error .50
17a. Approximately normal with mean 5.2 and standard error .50   **b.** .6826   **c.** .905   **d.** Yes, because z = −4.0
18a. .50   **b.** .4207   **c.** .1586   **d.** z = −.67; no   **e.** The standard normal distribution (mean = 0, standard
deviation = 1)

19a. By the Central Limit Theorem, the distribution is normal with $\mu = 100$ and $\sigma_{\bar{Y}} = 1$.   **b.** .00135   **c.** .9973
d. $z = -10$; yes   **e.** The sampling distribution of mean anxiety is much less spread out ($\sigma_{\bar{Y}} = 1$) than the distribution of anxiety scores ($\sigma = 15$). Thus, a relatively small proportion (.1586) of the anxiety scores are between 97 and 103, yet the probability is very large (.9973) that the mean of 225 anxiety scores falls between 97 and 103. Similarly, an anxiety score of 90 would not be unusual, but it would be extremely unusual to take a random sample of size 225 and get a *mean* anxiety score of 90.   **f.a.** Normal, $\mu = 100$, $\sigma_{\bar{Y}} = 3$ **b.** .1587   **c.** .6826   **d.** $z = -3.33$; somewhat, though not exceptionally, unusual

21. $\sigma_{\bar{Y}} = 5$, $z = 6/5 = 1.2$; probability within 1.2 standard deviations of μ equals $2(.3849) = .7698$
22a. $\sigma_{\bar{Y}} = 40$, $z = 1.25$; probability more than 1.25 standard deviations from μ equals $2(.1056) = .2112$
b. .0950   **c.** .0124   **23a.** .8164   **b.** Larger (.9544)   **24.** c   **25.** b   ***28.** .8
*30a. (1, 1), (1, 2), (1, 3), (1, 4), (1, 5), (1, 6)
      (2, 1), (2, 2), (2, 3), (2, 4), (2, 5), (2, 6)
      (3, 1), (3, 2), (3, 3), (3, 4), (3, 5), (3, 6)
      (4, 1), (4, 2), (4, 3), (4, 4), (4, 5), (4, 6)
      (5, 1), (5, 2), (5, 3), (5, 4), (5, 5), (5, 6)
      (6, 1), (6, 2), (6, 3), (6, 4), (6, 5), (6, 6)

b.

$\bar{Y}$	FREQUENCY	PROBABILITY
1.0	1	1/36
1.5	2	2/36
2.0	3	3/36
2.5	4	4/36
3.0	5	5/36
3.5	6	6/36
4.0	5	5/36
4.5	4	4/36
5.0	3	3/36
5.5	2	2/36
6.0	1	1/36

c. Population distribution (probabilities uniformly spread over integers 1 through 6):

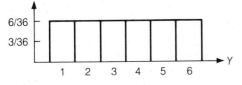

Sampling distribution of $\bar{Y}$ for $n = 2$ (starting to approach bell shape):

*31c. $\mu = 47.18$ **d.** $\sigma_{\bar{Y}} = 14.74/\sqrt{9} = 4.91$ [$\sigma_{\bar{Y}} = .91(4.91) = 4.47$ using finite population correction]

Chapter 5

1. $\bar{Y} = 3.0$; $\hat{\sigma} = 3.10$ **4a.** $\bar{Y} = 2.0$ **b.** $\hat{\sigma} = 1.05$ **5a.** (1.71, 2.29) **b.** (1.62, 2.38)
6a. $\bar{Y} = 60.0$; $\hat{\sigma} = 20.67$ **b.** $60.0 \pm 1.96(20.67)/\sqrt{30} = 60.0 \pm 7.4$, or (52.6, 67.4) **c.** 60.0 ± 9.7, or (50.3, 69.7)
7. (4.8, 5.8) **8a.** ($24,616, $26,184) **b.** ($19,414, $20,786)
9a. $\bar{Y} = 20$; $\hat{\sigma} = \sqrt{5,040/35} = 12$ **b.** $20 \pm 1.96(12)/\sqrt{36} = 20 \pm 3.92$, or (16.08, 23.92) **c.** $20 \pm 2.58(12)/\sqrt{36} =$
20 ± 5.16, or (14.84, 25.16). The interval is wider since the confidence coefficient is greater. We can be 99%
confident that the mean number of days absent in the previous year for all assembly-line employees in this company is
between 14.84 and 25.16.
10a. $340 \pm 2.58(40)/\sqrt{30} = 340 \pm 18.84$, or (321.2, 358.8) **b.** 340 ± 37.68, or (302.3, 377.7). Twice as wide.
c. 340 ± 9.42. Half as wide, since the sample is four times larger.
11. $16 \pm 2.33(6)/\sqrt{100} = 16 \pm 1.4$, or (14.6, 17.4)
12. $6.3 \pm 1.645(4.0)/\sqrt{100} = 6.3 \pm .7$, or (5.6, 7.0)
13. a **14.** b **15.** b, e **16a.** 2.33 **b.** .67 **c.** 3.00
19a. $\hat{\pi} = .76$ **b.** (.72, .80); yes **20.** (.320, .368) **21.** (.35, .39) **22.** (.17, .43)
23a. $\hat{\pi} = .333$ **b.** (.309, .357) **c.** yes
24a. $.34 \pm 2.58\sqrt{(.34)(.66)/50} = .34 \pm .17$, or (.17, .51) **b.** $.34 \pm .12$, or (.22, .46) **c.** $.34 \pm .06$, or (.28, .40); half as wide
as in part **b,** since the sample size is four times as large.
25. $\hat{\pi} = 160/400 = .40$; $.40 \pm 2.58\sqrt{(.40)(.60)/400} = .40 \pm .06$, or (.34, .46); yes, because the interval consists entirely of
numbers below .50, corresponding to Jones receiving a minority of the vote.
26. $\hat{\pi} = 16/40 = .40$ (same as in Problem 25); $.40 \pm 2.58\sqrt{(.40)(.60)/40} = .40 \pm .20$, or (.20, .60). We would not predict a
winner, since the interval contains numbers both below and above .50. The point estimate of π is the same (.40) as in
Problem 25, but the confidence interval is much wider because the sample size is so much smaller.
27. $\hat{\pi} = 230/400 = .575$; $.575 \pm 2.33\sqrt{(.575)(.425)/400} = .575 \pm .058$, or (.517, .633). The mayor should not veto
the decision. **28a.** (.134, .266) **c.** 400 **29.** 196 **30.** 188
31a. $B = .10$, $\alpha = .05$, $z_{\alpha/2} = 1.96$; $n = .25(1.96/.1)^2 = 96$ **b.** 384 **c.** 666 **d.** 16,641
32a. $n = (1.96)^2(.1)(.9)/(.01)^2 = 3,457$ **b.** $n = 9,604$ **33.** 246 **34.** $n = (50)^2(1.96/5)^2 = 384$
35. $\bar{Y} \pm 1.96(100)/\sqrt{384} = \bar{Y} \pm 10.0$ ***38.** $\bar{Y} = 5.0$; $\hat{\sigma} = 4.59$ ***41.** $n = \sigma^2(1.96/B)^2$

Chapter 6

1a. .0359 **b.** .0718 **c.** .9641 (*the probability of getting z < 1.8 when H_0 is true; P-values are left-hand curve areas
for this alternative*) **2a.** 1.28 **b.** ± 1.645 **c.** -1.28
3. H_0: $\mu = 3.1$, H_a: $\mu < 3.1$; $z = (2.9 - 3.1)/.167 = -1.20$; $P = .1151$
4. $z = (106 - 100)/2 = 3.0$; $P = 2(.00135) = .0027$ **5.** $z = -1.33$; $P = 2(.0918) = .1836$
6. H_0: $\mu = 600$, H_a: $\mu > 600$; $z = 8.0$; reject H_0 and conclude that the limit is being exceeded, on the average.
7a. H_0: $\mu = 80,000$, H_a: $\mu \neq 80,000$ **b.** $z = -5.0$, $P = .000000574$; very strong evidence that mean is different in
Dayton
9. If H_0 were true, the probability would have been .057 of getting a z test statistic at least as large as the observed z, in
absolute value (i.e., if $\mu = 100$, the probability of getting $\bar{Y}$ at least 20 units from 100 equals .057).
10a. H_0: $\pi = .5$, H_a: $\pi > .5$ **b.** $z = -5.0$; $P = .999999713$ **c.** The evidence does not contradict H_0 in favor of H_a:
$\pi > .5$, but rather in favor of H_a: $\pi < .5$.
11a. H_0: $\pi = .25$, H_a: $\pi > .25$, where π is the population proportion correctly answering the question.
b. $z = (.3125 - .25)/.022 = 2.84$, $P = .0023$; very strong evidence against H_0
12a. H_0: $\pi = .5$, H_a: $\pi > .5$, where π is the population proportion desiring a larger portion spent on mass transit.
b. $z = (.6 - .5)/.05 = 2.0$; $P = .0228$
13a. $z = (.575 - .5)/.025 = 3.0$; $P = .0027$ **b.** *Yes, since the P-value is so small* **c.** $\hat{\pi} = .575$ again, but now $z =$
$(.575 - .5)/.07 = .95$, so $P = .3422$. We would not predict a winner, since there is a moderate probability (.342) of one or
the other of the candidates having at least 23 supporters out of a sample of size 40 when $\pi = .5$.

14. $z = (.22 - .20)/.040 = .50$, $P = .3085$; do not reject H_0

15. $z = (0 - .05)/.0126 = -3.97$; reject H_0, and conclude that she is not the author. We assume that the sentences beginning with *whereas* are randomly dispersed through that author's writings.

16a. $t = 1.761$ **b.** $|t| = 2.145$ **c.** $t = -1.761$

17. $t = (270 - 300)/9 = -3.33$, $P < .005$; strong evidence that women's mean income is smaller

18. $8 \pm 2.064(1)$, or $(5.94, 10.06)$. We assume that the distribution of absenteeism rates is approximately normal.

19. $\bar{Y} = 7$, $\hat{\sigma} = 2.83$; $t = (7 - 3)/1.07 = 3.74$ (df = 6); $P < .005$

20a. H_0: $\mu = 16$, H_a: $\mu \neq 16$ **b.** $t = (14.5 - 16)/1.2 = -1.25$ (df = 24); $P > 2(.100) = .200$, so there is not strong evidence of a change.   **c.** $14.5 \pm 2.064(1.2) = 14.5 \pm 2.5$, or $(12, 17)$ **21.** $t = 4.0$, df = 3, $P < .025$

22a. $P(0) = [10!/(0!10!)](.01)^0(.99)^{10} = (.99)^{10} = .904$ **b.** $P(0) + P(1) = .904 + .091 = .995$

23a.

X	0	1	2	3	4	5	6
P(X)	.0156	.0938	.2344	.3124	.2344	.0938	.0156

b. .1094   **c.** .8906   **24.** $P(5) = P(0) = [5!/(5!0!)](.5)^5(.5)^0 = (.5)^5 = .031$; $P = P(0) + P(5) = .062$

25a. $P(0) = (.20)^4 = .0016$ **b.** $P = .0016$ in testing H_0: $\pi = .8$ against H_a: $\pi < .8$ **26a.** .0024   **b.** $P = .0024$

27a. (i) Reject H_0 (ii) Do not reject H_0 **28.** Reject H_0 for H_a: $\mu > \mu_0$

29a. Do not reject H_0 **b.** Do not reject H_0 **c.** Reject H_0 **30.** Reject H_0 and conclude that $\mu \neq 100$.

31a. Do not reject H_0 **b.** No   **32.** All of them   **33.** $X = 6$ **35.** a, c   **36.** b, d   **37.** d   **38.** a   **39.** a

41b. Greater than .10

42. .36, .009, 0; They are smaller than when $\hat{\sigma}_{\bar{Y}} = 2.0$. For a fixed α-level, increasing the sample size tends to decrease the probability of Type II error.

44. No   ***45.** Yes

*47a. $P(7) = [7!/(7!0!)](.5)^7(.5)^0 = (.5)^7 = .0078$ **b.** $P = P(0) + P(7) = 2(.0078) = .0156$; do not reject H_0 at $\alpha = .01$ level. (In Example 6.7, H_0 was rejected at nearly any level.) The sign test requires fewer assumptions than the t test, but it tends to be less powerful.   ***48a.** $P(20) = [20!/(20!0!)](.95)^{20}(.05)^0 = (.95)^{20} = .358$ **b.** $1 - .358 = .642$ ***49.** b, d

Chapter 7

1. $.040 \pm 1.96 \sqrt{\dfrac{(.41)(.59)}{1,600} + \dfrac{(.45)(.55)}{1,800}} = .040 \pm .033$, or $(.007, .073)$. We infer that there has been an increase in support. This interval is narrower (leading to a different conclusion) than the 99% confidence interval, since the confidence coefficient is smaller.

2. $-.04 \pm 2.58 \sqrt{\dfrac{(.59)(.41)}{1,600} + \dfrac{(.55)(.45)}{1,800}} = -.04 \pm .044$, or $(-.084, .004)$

3. $-.049 \pm .048$, or $(-.097, -.001)$. We can be 95% confident that the proportion of men favoring abolition is between .097 and .001 lower than the proportion of women favoring abolition.   **4.** $.20 \pm .056$, or $(.144, .256)$

5a. Yes   **b.** $.30 \pm .345$, or $(-.045, .645)$ **c.** Not at this confidence level, since 0 is contained in the interval

d. $.30 \pm .11$, or $(.19, .41)$. We conclude that there is a difference.

6. $(-.033, .037)$ **7.** $(.460, .556)$ **8.** Educational level   **9a.** $(.04, .14)$ **b.** Yes

10. We can be 95% confident that the mean salary for male assistant professors is between $272 and $1,328 higher than the mean salary for female assistant professors.   **11a.** $(4.2, 19.8)$ **b.** $z = 3.0$, $P = .00135$; yes

12. $\hat{\sigma}_{\bar{Y}_2 - \bar{Y}_1} = \sqrt{\dfrac{3^2}{255} + \dfrac{4^2}{45}} = .625$, $z = (12.5 - 13.2)/.625 = -1.12$; $P = 2(.1314) = .2628$, do not reject H_0

13. $-.7 \pm 1.96(.625) = -.7 \pm 1.2$, or $(-1.9, .5)$. The 95% confidence interval contains 0; this corresponds to not rejecting H_0 at the $\alpha = .05$ level in Problem 12.   **14.** $z = (75 - 81)/2.50 = -2.40$, $P = .0082$; yes, reject H_0

15a. $H_0: \mu_1 = \mu_2$, $H_a: \mu_1 \neq \mu_2$ **b.** $z = 2.0$ **c.** $P = .0456$ **16.** Do not reject H_0 **17.** Reject H_0
18a. $\bar{Y}_1 = 2.0$; $\bar{Y}_2 = 6.0$ **b.** 1.0   **c.** (.6, 7.4)   **d.** $t = 4.0$; $P < .01$ **19.** Reject H_0; drug B is better
20a. (45.2, 94.8)   **b.** $t = 6.6$, df = 3; $P < .01$ **21a.** $(-1.2, 41.2)$ **b.** (7.6, 32.4)
22a. $\bar{D} = 7.0$, $\hat{\sigma} = 5.25$; $t = 4.22$, df = 9; $P < .01$ **b.** (4.0, 10.0)
24a. $t = -1.17$, df = 4; $P > .10$ **b.** $(-67.4, 27.4)$ **d.** $R_1 = 13$; $P = .20$
25a. .1289, .4437, .8148   **b.** $\bar{r}_1 = .424$, $\bar{r}_2 = .642$; Republicans   **c.** .72   **d.** $T = .8806$; $z = 9.5$; $P = 0$ **e.** Yes
26a. $z = 3.3$; $P < .0027$ **b.** Republicans: remain same; Democrats: less severe
27a. .398, .602   **b.** $z = 3.23$; $P < .00135$ **28a.** .594, .406   **b.** $z = -2.35$; $P = .0188$ **29.** b   **30.** a, c
31. a, c, d   **32.** b, d   ***33a.** $\bar{Y}_A = 4.83$; $\bar{Y}_B = 6.00$ **b.** $\bar{Y}_A = 8.70$; $\bar{Y}_B = 7.07$ ***34a.** (.021, .059)   **b.** Yes

Chapter 8

1a.

		GRAY HAIR	
		Yes	No
CHILDREN	Yes	0	5
	No	4	0

b.

		GRAY HAIR	
		Yes	No
CHILDREN	Yes	0%	100%
	No	100%	0%
	TOTAL	100%	100%

2a, b.

		AFFILIATION		
		D	R	I
INTENDED	D	12 (60%)	1 (6.7%)	7 (46.7%)
VOTE	R	4 (20%)	12 (80%)	4 (26.7%)
	U	4 (20%)	2 (13.3%)	4 (26.7%)

c. $\chi^2 = 15.67$, df = 4, $P < .01$; reject H_0

3a, b.

	D	R	I
Y	12 (60%)	10 (66.7%)	8 (53.3%)
N	8 (40%)	5 (33.3%)	7 (46.7%)

c. $\chi^2 = .56$, df = 2; do not reject H_0 **7a.** 3.84   **b.** 9.49   **c.** 26.30   **d.** 26.30

8.

10	20	30
30	40	30
10	20	10

9. $\chi^2 = 3.61$, df = 4, $P < .50$ **10.** $\chi^2 = 12.0$, df = 2, $P < .01$ **11.** $\chi^2 = 5.01$, df = 1, $P < .05$, but $P > .02$; reject H_0

12a. $\chi^2 = 3.125$, df = 1, $P < .10$, but $P > .05$; do not reject H_0 **b.** $(.65 - .50) \pm 1.96\sqrt{\dfrac{(.5)(.5)}{50} + \dfrac{(.65)(.35)}{100}} =$

$.15 \pm .167$, or $(-.017, .317)$; interval containing 0 corresponds to not rejecting H_0

13. c   **15a.** $\hat{\tau} = .40$ **b.** $\hat{\tau} = .12$ **16.** $E_1 = 32.0$, $E_2 = 25.87$; $\hat{\tau} = .19$

17. $E_1 = 178.5$, $E_2 = 177.62$; $\hat{\tau} = .0049$. There is only a 0.49% reduction in error in predicting the preferred brand when one is given the market location. Thus, there is a very weak association between preferred brand and market location.

18a.

10	0	0
0	10	0
0	0	10

b.

10	0	0
0	10	10
0	0	0

c.

10	5	5
10	5	5
10	5	5

19. .65, .35

20a. $C = 1,630$ **b.** $D = 492$ **c.** $\hat{\gamma} = .536$ **d.** X = political philosophy, Y = opinion; $T_x = 1,850$, $T_y = 1,633$
e. $\hat{\tau}_b = .355$. The more conservative a person, the greater the tendency to favor an increase in the defense budget. If we could measure the variables more finely so that there were no ties, we would expect a difference of about .355 between the proportions of concordant and discordant pairs.

21a. 91.5 in each cell **b.** $\chi^2 = 13.4$, df = 1, $P < .001$ **c.** $\hat{\tau}_b = -.191$ **22b.** (see Table 8.16) **23.** Part 1: b;
part 2: a, b, c, d

24. $C = 1,225$, $D = 2,425$, $T_x = 2,340$, $T_y = 1,740$; $\hat{\tau}_b = -.236$. The greater the age, the less favorable opinion toward gambling tends to be. **25.** $-.329$

26. $C = 6,400$, $D = 14,400$, $T_x = T_y = 39,800$; $\hat{\tau}_b = -.20$ **27.** $\hat{\gamma} = -.385$

28a. Very weak, since the three conditional distributions are nearly identical **b.** $C = 16$, $D = 0$; $\hat{\tau}_b = .118$
c. $\hat{\gamma} = 1.0$

29. $\sigma_{C-D} = 287.5$, $z = (1,630 - 492)/287.5 = 3.96$; reject H_0

30a. $\Sigma t_i^3 = 192,000$, $\Sigma u_i^3 = 108,000$, $\sigma_{C-D}^2 = 160,000$, $z = (1,225 - 2,425)/400 = -3.0$, $P = 2(.00135) = .0027$
b. $\chi^2 = 10.0$ (df = 6), $P < .20$, but $P > .10$ **c.** Reject H_0: $\tau_b = 0$, but do not reject H_0: Independence.
d. The z test of H_0: $\tau_b = 0$ is more powerful, since it utilizes the ordinal nature of the variables.

*31a. $\hat{\lambda} = 0$ **b.** $\hat{\tau} = .044$ ***33a.** $-.001$ **b.** 3.0

*34a.

	LOW	MEDIUM	HIGH
HIGH	0	0	10
MEDIUM	0	10	0
LOW	10	0	0

b.

	LOW	MEDIUM	HIGH
HIGH	10	0	0
MEDIUM	0	10	0
LOW	0	0	10

c.

	LOW	MEDIUM	HIGH
HIGH	10	10	10
MEDIUM	5	15	5
LOW	10	5	10

*36. $-.250$ ***39b.** $\hat{\tau} = .556$ ***40a.**

1	4
4	1

b. $C = 16$, $D = 1$, $T_x = T_y = 20$, $\hat{\tau}_b = .60$ **c.** $\hat{\gamma} = .882$. $\hat{\tau}_b$ is much closer than $\hat{\gamma}$ to the value ($\hat{\tau} = .556$) obtained in Problem 39 when there are no ties. This illustrates that gamma tends to be inflated in value above the corresponding value for no ties (where $\hat{\gamma} = \hat{\tau}_b = \hat{\tau}$). ***41b.** $H = .036$ **c.** $H = 1$

Chapter 9

2a. For each increase of 1% in residents voting, we predict an increase of .1 in the percentage of vote for the Democratic candidate. **b.** No, since $X = 0$ corresponds to nobody voting. **3c.** 80 **d.** 45 **5b.** $a = 0, b = 1$
6b. $\hat{Y} = .87$. For a nation in which half the labor force is in agricultural occupations, we predict that the proportion of households with nuclear family members only is .87. **c.** It is negative, since the slope ($b = -.20$) is negative.
7a. .50 **9b.** The line $\hat{Y} = 5 - .4X$ perfectly fits the data. **c.** $r = -1$ **10c.** Average annual income
11a. $r = .50$ **b.** $\hat{Y} = 1.0 + 1.5X$; $r = .50$ **c.** No; yes, the slopes are the same only if $\hat{\sigma}_X = \hat{\sigma}_Y$.
12a. True **b.** False **c.** True **d.** True **e.** False **f.** True **g.** True **h.** True **i.** False **j.** False
k. True **13.** b **14.** b **15.** c, f **16b.** $\hat{Y} = -2.49 + .17X$ **c.** $r = .86$ **d.** $r^2 = .73$
17a. $\bar{X} = 9.88$, $\hat{\sigma}_X = 3.77$; $\bar{Y} = 3.35$, $\hat{\sigma}_Y = 2.19$ **b.** $\hat{Y} = 5.40 - .207X$; $a = 5.40$: We predict that the mean number of children for women with no formal education is 5.40; $b = -.207$: We predict that the mean number of children decreases by .207 for each increase of one year in mother's education. **c.** 3.7; 2.9; 2.1 **d.** $r = -.356$. For a one standard deviation increase in education, there is predicted to be a .356 standard deviation decrease in the number of children. **e.** $r^2 = .127$. There is 12.7% reduction in error in using X to predict Y (through the prediction equation) instead of using $\bar{Y}$ to predict Y. **f.** $\hat{\sigma}_b = 2.07/\sqrt{681.27} = .079$, $t = -.207/.079 = -2.62$ (df = 47), P is about .01 **g.** $-.207 \pm 1.96(.079) = -.207 \pm .155$, or $(-.362, -.052)$ **h.** $8(-.207) \pm 1.96(8)(.079) = -1.66 \pm 1.24$, or $(-2.90, -.42)$
18b. $\hat{Y} = 1.05 + .337X$ **c.** The mean college GPA is estimated to increase .337 for a 100-unit increase in score on the SAT (a 1-unit increase in X). **d.** $\hat{Y} = 2.67$, $Y - \hat{Y} = -.27$ **e.** $r = .832$ **f.** $r^2 = .694$ **g.** $\hat{\sigma}_b = .079$, $t = .337/.079 = 4.26$ (df = 8); reject H_0 and conclude that there is a positive association. **h.** $.337 \pm 2.306(.079) = .337 \pm .182$, or (.155, .519) **i.** No, because there are no observed values on SAT that large.
19b. $\hat{Y} = 37.10624 - .00365X$ **c.** $r = -.7767$; $r^2 = .603$
20a. $\hat{Y} = 16.26 - 1.69X$ **b.** SSE = 234.49 **c.** $r = -.444$ **d.** $r^2 = .197$ **e.** $t = -1.40$, df = 8, $P = .099$
f. $(-4.48, 1.10)$ **g.** $(-22.4, 5.5)$ **h.** $(-.26, .84)$
21a. $n = 50$, since TOTAL DF (49) $= n - 1$ **b.** ERROR DF = 48; REGRESSION SUM OF SQUARES = TSS $-$ SSE = 100,000; R-SQUARE = 100,000/500,000 = .20; ROOT MSE = $\sqrt{400,000/48}$ = 91.29; CORRELATION = $-\sqrt{.20}$ = $-.447$; SUM OF SQUARED RESIDUALS = SSE = 400,000; T FOR H0: PARAMETER = 0 is $-5/1.443 = -3.465$; PROB > |T| is $P < .01$.
*25a. $b = .60(120)/80 = .90$, $a = 500 - .9(480) = 68$; $\hat{Y} = 68 + .90X$ **b.** 428; 608
*26. $\hat{Y} = 4.77 - .129X$; $r = -.227$. With the addition of this one observation, b changes from $-.40$ to $-.129$, and r changes from -1 to $-.227$. Thus, an observation that is far removed from a general linear trend can have a drastic effect on the slope and correlation. This is one problem with using the least squares criterion for fitting a straight line.
*28. $r = -.356$, $T(r) = -.3723$, $\sigma_T = 1/\sqrt{46} = .1474$. Confidence interval $-.3723 \pm 1.96(.1474)$ for $T(\rho)$ corresponds to confidence interval $(-.579, -.083)$ for ρ.
*29a. $r = .833$, $T(r) = 1.1979$, (.2227, 2.1731) for $T(\rho)$, (.220, .975) for ρ **b.** $(.220^2, .975^2) = (.048, .951)$
*30. $T_1 = .2132$, $T_2 = .1206$, $\sigma_{T_2 - T_1} = .428$, $z = .22$, $P = .8258$ ***31a.** (5.0, 19.1) **b.** (9.8, 14.3)

Chapter 10

8. b **9a.**

	PLAN ON VOTING				DO NOT PLAN ON VOTING		
	D	R	I		D	R	I
D	9	0	5	D	3	1	2
R	2	10	2	R	2	2	2
U	1	0	1	U	3	2	3

c. Yes

11a. Yes **b.** No **d.** No **e.** $O \to I \to P$ **f.** $I \nearrow^{O}_{\searrow P}$ **g.** Chain

12. Statistical interaction   **13b.** Statistical interaction

14a. Dependent: salary; Control: experience, field   **f.**

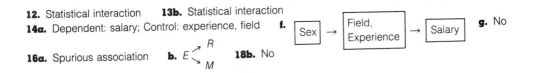

$Sex \rightarrow$ Field, Experience $\rightarrow$ Salary   **g.** No

16a. Spurious association   **b.** $E \nearrow^R_\searrow M$ **18b.** No

Chapter 11

1a. We estimate that the mean crude birth rate decreases by .5 for an increase of 1 in the percentage women employed, controlling for the percentage of workers in agricultural jobs.   **b.** We estimate that the mean crude birth rate increases by .3 for an increase of 1 in the percentage of workers in agricultural jobs, controlling for the percentage of women employed.

2a. $\hat{Y} = 5.25 - .24X_1 + .02X_2$; no   **b.** $\hat{Y} = 3.33 + .02X_2$; $\hat{Y} = 1.41 + .02X_2$ **c.** $\hat{Y} = 3.59$; $Y - \hat{Y} = 1.41$

d. SSE = 199.3   **e.** $R^2 = .1376$, $R = .371$; No, since R must be at least as large as $|r_{YX_1}|$ and $|r_{YX_2}|$ **f.** No; r_{YX_1} has the same sign as the slope of the *bivariate* equation relating Y to X_1.   **3.** b

4b. R cannot be smaller than $|r_{YX_2}|$.   **d.** SSE cannot increase when a variable is added to a model.

7a. $\hat{Y} = 5.01 + .38X_1 - .72X_2$ **c.**

	Y	X_1	X_2
Y	1.000	.880	−.444
X_1	.880	1.000	−.310
X_2	−.444	−.310	1.000

d. $R^2 = .806$ **8.** b, c, d, e, i are necessarily false   **9.** d   **10.** d   **11.** c   **12.** a

13c. $\hat{Y} = -10 + 2(8) + 3(13) - .5(10) = 40$ **d.** $H_0: P = 0$, $H_a: P > 0$, $F = 3.33$, $df_1 = 3$, $df_2 = 30$, $P < .05$

14a. $t = -2.99$, $P = .0058$ **b.** $P = .0029$

15a. $F = 14.53$, $df_1 = 2$, $df_2 = 7$, $P = .0032$ **b.** For $H_0: \beta_1 = 0$, $t = 4.69$ (df = 7), $P = .0022$ for $H_a: \beta_1 \neq 0$; for $H_0: \beta_2 = 0$, $t = -1.08$ (df = 7), $P = .3161$ for $H_a: \beta_2 \neq 0$ **c.** $b_1^* = .821$, $b_2^* = -.189$

16a. i. −.857   **ii.** −.777   **iii.** .818   **iv.** 1,750.92   **v.** 318.11   **vi.** 35.35   **vii.** 5.945   **viii.** 12.616

ix. .174   **x.** −3.26   **xi.** .0098   **xii.** .0049   **xiii.** 20.27   **xiv.** .0005   **xv.** 9

b. $\hat{Y} = 45.350 - .568X_1 - 1.794X_2$ **c.** X_1 and X_2 have strong negative linear associations with Y.   **d.** There is an 81.8% reduction in error when we use X_1 and X_2 simultaneously to predict Y (through the prediction equation) instead of using $\bar{Y}$ to predict Y.

e. $R = .90$ = correlation between Y and $\hat{Y}$ for this model   **f.** $r_{YX_1 \cdot X_2} = -.74$, $r^2_{YX_1 \cdot X_2} = .54$ = proportion of variation in Y explained by X_1, out of that part left unexplained by X_2.   **g.** For fixed X_1 and X_2, the standard deviation of the conditional distribution of Y is estimated to be $\hat{\sigma} = \sqrt{318.11/9} = 5.945$.   **h.** $F = \dfrac{.818/2}{(1 - .818)/9} = 20.27$, $P = .0005$; strong evidence that at least one of β_1 and β_2 is nonzero   **i.** $t = -.568/.174 = -3.26$, $P = .0049$; strong evidence that X_1 has a negative association with Y, controlling for X_2 **j.** $b_1^* = -.61$; $b_2^* = -.38$ ***k.** $\hat{z}_Y = -.61z_{X_1} - .38z_{X_2}$

17a. i. r_{YX_1} cannot exceed $R = .5$.   **v.** b_1 depends on the units of measurement of X_1.   **vi.** $r_{YX_3 \cdot X_1, X_2}$ must have the same sign as $b_3 = -.5$, and hence must be negative.   **b.** $t = -.5/.30 = -1.67$ (df = 30); do not reject $H_0: \beta_3 = 0$ in favor of $H_a: \beta_3 \neq 0$ at the $\alpha = .05$ level

18a. $\hat{Y} = 21.832 - .167X_1 - .214X_2$; $\hat{Y} = 15.2$ for Rochester; $Y - \hat{Y} = 3.8$ **b.** $r^2_{YX_1} = .024$; $r^2_{YX_2} = .208$; $R^2 = .415$

c. $r_{YX_1 \cdot X_2} = -.510$; $r^2_{YX_1 \cdot X_2} = .26$ means that X_1 explains 26% of the variation in Y that is unexplained by X_2; $r_{YX_1} = -.156$, so the association between integration and heterogeneity is much stronger when mobility is controlled than when it is ignored.   **d.** $F = 9.22$, $df_1 = 2$, $df_2 = 26$, $P < .001$ **e.** $t = -.167/.055 = -3.04$ (df = 26); reject H_0

f. $30(-.214) \pm 2.056(30)(.051) = -6.42 \pm 3.15$, or (−9.57, −3.27)   ***g.** $\hat{z}_Y = -.530z_{X_1} - .728z_{X_2}$, $\hat{z}_Y = -.332$

h. $\hat{\sigma} = \sqrt{132.29/26} = 2.256$

19a. TOTAL DF $= n - 1 = 65$; REGRESSION DF $= k = 5$; ERROR DF $= n - (k + 1) = 60$; REGRESSION SUM OF SQUARES $= 818.3$; REGRESSION MEAN SQUARE $= 163.66$; ERROR MEAN SQUARE $= 49.0$; ROOT MSE $= 7.0$; R-SQUARE $= .218$; F VALUE $= 3.34$; PROB $>$ F: $P = .010$ (df$_1 = 5$, df$_2 = 60$); T VALUES: 2.22, -2.00, .50, $-.80$, 2.40; PROB $> |T|$: .0264, .0456, .6170, .4238, .0164; OBS 1: PREDICTED VALUE $= 82.7$, RESIDUAL $= 3.3$; OBS 2: Y $= 70$, PREDICTED VALUE $= 76.7$ **b.** $\hat{Y} = 70.0 + .1X_1 - .15X_2 + .1X_3 - .04X_4 + .12X_5$ **c.** No, since the P-values for the coefficients of X_3 and X_4 are relatively large.   **d.** There is a 21.8% reduction in error obtained by predicting Y using $X_1, ..., X_5$ instead of using $\overline{Y}$.   **e.** Reject H_0: P $= 0$ (H_0: $\beta_1 = \cdots = \beta_5 = 0$) at $\alpha = .01$ level.   **f.** Test of H_0: $\beta_1 = 0$. We would reject H_0 at the $\alpha = .05$ level.
h. $.100 \pm 1.96(.045) = .100 \pm .088$, or $(.012, .188)$ **i.** $50(.100) \pm 1.96(50)(.045) = 5 \pm 4.41$, or $(.59, 9.41)$ **k.** X_1, since it has the greatest (in magnitude) standardized regression coefficient ($b_1^* = .150$).
20a. No, because the variables are unstandardized   **b.** $b_1^* = -.075$, $b_2^* = -.125$, $b_3^* = -.3$, $b_4^* = .2$ ***c.** $\hat{z}_Y = -.075z_{X_1} - .125z_{X_2} - .3z_{X_3} + .2z_{X_4}$. $\hat{z}_Y = -.7$: A city that is one standard deviation above the mean on number of police officers, mean length of prison sentence, and mean income of residents, and one standard deviation below the mean on unemployment, is predicted to be .7 standard deviation below the mean on murder rate.
21. Pearson correlation   ***22a.** H_0: $\rho = 0$ **b.** H_0: P $= 0$ **c.** H_0: $\rho_{YX_2 \cdot X_1} = 0$
*23. $r_{YX_1 \cdot X_2} = .036$, $t = .355$ (df $= 97$); do not reject H_0: $\rho_{YX_1 \cdot X_2} = 0$ ***25.** c
*26. $r_{YX_2 \cdot X_1} = 0$; X_2 adds nothing to the prediction of Y once X_1 is in the model.   ***27.** .529
*29. SSE$_2 = 874.35$, SSE$_{12} = 679.79$, $r_{YX_1 \cdot X_2}^2 = .222$
*30. $T(r) = .5114$, $\sigma_T = 1/\sqrt{26} = .1961$; interval $.5114 \pm 1.96(.1961)$ for $T(\rho)$ corresponds to $(.126, .714)$ for $\rho_{YX_1 \cdot X_2}$.
*31a. .278, .335, .345, .351, .357
*32a. .084   **b.** .214

Chapter 12

3b. $\hat{Y} =$ world population size, in billions, X years from now if there is a 4% rate of growth every year
4b. Intercept $= .602$; slope $= .301$
6. $(1.042)^{10}(100,000) = 150,896$
7b. $r^2 = .208$, $R^2 = .329$; increase of .121   **c.** $r_{YX^2 \cdot X}^2 = .153$ **d.** $t = .00976/.00451 = 2.16$ (df $= 26$), $P = .0399$; reject H_0: $\beta_2 = 0$
8c. $\widehat{\log Y} = -.50465 + .03253X$; predicted $\log Y$ values .4712, .7966, 1.1218, 1.4472, 1.7724, 2.0978   **d.** $a = .3129$, $b = 1.07778$; $\hat{Y}$-values 2.96, 6.26, 13.24, 28.00, 59.21, 125.26
12a. Yes, the slope between Y and X_2 seems to be larger in magnitude for the ten largest X_1-values than for the ten smallest X_1-values.   **b.** $\hat{Y} = 17.2977 + .1058X_1 + .1257X_2 - .0149X_1X_2$; $X_1 = 10$: $\hat{Y} = 18.36 - .12X_2$; $X_1 = 50$: $\hat{Y} = 22.59 - .72X_2$ **c.** $R^2 = .509$ ($R^2 = .415$ without the interaction term)   **d.** H_0: $\beta_3 = 0$, H_a: $\beta_3 \neq 0$; $t = -.0149/.0068 = -2.18$ (df $= 25$), $P = .039$
13. SSE$_c = 111.10$, SSE$_r = 132.29$; $F = 4.77$ (df$_1 = 1$, df$_2 = 25$); $P < .05$ but $P > .01$ (The exact level $P = .039$ matches Problem **12d**. In fact, $F = t^2$ when df$_1 = 1$.)   **14a.** iv   **b.** iii   **c.** $F = 2.0$, df$_1 = 1$, df$_2 = 50$, $P > .05$
15. $F = 2.50$ (df$_1 = 4$, df$_2 = 190$); do not reject H_0; the complete model is not significantly better at the $\alpha = .01$ level.
20a. No. It simply means that neither variable makes a significant partial contribution to predicting Y, when the other variable is also in the model. Any one of the variables may be a good predictor of Y by itself (when the other variable is ignored), and both of them together may yield good predictions of Y (as measured by a large R^2).   **b.** No. In fact, $R^2 = .656$, which is highly significant. When multicollinearity exists, it is not surprising to reject H_0: $\beta_1 = \cdots = \beta_k = 0$ but not to reject the hypotheses H_0: $\beta_i = 0$.
21b. $r_{YX_1 \cdot X_2} = .459$; $r_{YX_2 \cdot X_1} = -.096$ **c.** .244; the sampling error in the partial correlations may be substantial.
d. $r_{YX_1 \cdot X_2} = .875$; $r_{YX_2 \cdot X_1} = .840$; .681, .572; .531, .315   **23.** b, c, d   **24.** b, c, d   **25.** a, b, c
26. a, b, c   **27.** b, c   **28.** a, d   **29.** In order: c, e, g, i, a, f, h
*30. X_2 first entered ($t = 13.67$ significant); $r_{YX_1 \cdot X_2} = -.023$ not significant ($t = -.23$), so X_2 is the only independent variable in the final model.   ***32b.** $F = 8.034$ (df$_1 = 1$, df$_2 = 27$); $F > 7.68$, so reject H_0 at $\alpha = .01$ level.

*33a. Heteroscedastic   **c.** $r = .806$ between X and Z ($b = .729$), $t = 4.306$ (df $= 10$), so $P < .01$; conclude that there is a relationship between X and Z, and hence also between X and $Z^2 = Y$.

Chapter 13

1. $\bar{Y}_1 = 6$, $\bar{Y}_2 = 3$, $\bar{Y}_3 = 8$, $\bar{Y} = 6$; BSS $= 30$, $df_1 = 2$; WSS $= 30$, $df_2 = 5$; $F = 2.5$, $P > .05$ for testing $H_0: \mu_1 = \mu_2 = \mu_3$

2.

SOURCE	SUM OF SQUARES	DF	MEAN SQUARE	F	PROB > F
Between	30	2	15	2.5	> .05
Within	30	5	6		
Total	60	7			

3a.

SOURCE	SUM OF SQUARES	DF	MEAN SQUARE	F	PROB > F
Between	72	2	36	4.0	P > .05
Within	81	9	9		
Total	153	11			

b. Insufficient evidence to reject H_0 at $\alpha = .05$ level; it is plausible that $\mu_1 = \mu_2 = \mu_3$.

c.

CONDITION	Z_1	Z_2
1	1	0
2	0	1
3	0	0

d. $\hat{Y} = 18 - 6Z_1 - 3Z_2$

4a. $F = .27$, $df_1 = 2$, $df_2 = 15$, $P > .05$ **b.** Do not reject H_0; it is plausible that the mean level of political conservatism is the same for clergy of the three denominations.
5a. Between mean square $= 900$, within mean square $= 5$, $F = 180$ ($df_1 = 3$, $df_2 = 296$), $P < .01$; we conclude that at least two of the quadrants differ in mean lot size.   **b.** $\bar{Y} = 11$ **c.** $\hat{\sigma} = 2.24$ is the estimated standard deviation of the lot sizes within each of the quadrants.
6. NW − NE (6.12, 7.88); SW − SE: (.75, 3.25); NW − SW: (2.92, 5.08); NW − SE: (4.92, 7.08); SW − NE: (1.92, 4.08); SE − NE (−.08, 2.08)
7. $F = 18.5$ ($df_1 = 2$, $df_2 = 3$), $P < .05$ but $P > .01$

8.

SOURCE	SUM OF SQUARES	DF	MEAN SQUARE	F	PROB > F
Between	148	2	74	18.5	< .05
Within	12	3	4		
Total	160	5			

9. B − A: (−7.74, 9.74); C − A: (2.26, 19.74); C − B: (1.26, 18.74); <u>A B</u> C
10a. $E(Y) = \alpha + \beta_1 Z_1 + \beta_2 Z_2$, where $Z_1 = 1$ for Bumper A and $Z_1 = 0$ otherwise; and $Z_2 = 1$ for Bumper B and $Z_2 = 0$ otherwise

b.

SOURCE	DF	SUM OF SQUARES	MEAN SQUARE	F VALUE	PROB > F	ROOT MSE
REGRESSION	2	148	74	18.5	P < .05	2.0
ERROR	3	12	4			
TOTAL	5	160				

PARAMETER	ESTIMATE
INTERCEPT	13
Z1	-11
Z2	-10

11a. Large urban − Small urban: (−2.85, 3.45); Rural − Small urban: (−.93, 5.93); Rural − Large urban: (−.47, 4.87)
b. Narrower; *each* holds with 95% confidence. The confidence level for the entire set is less than 95% whereas it equals 95% in part **a.**
13a. $\bar{Y}_1 = \bar{Y}_2 = \bar{Y}_3 = \bar{Y}_4 = 60$ **b.** WSS = 0, all observations in a particular group equal the same number.
14a. $E(Y) = \alpha + \beta Z$, where $Z = 1$ if Democrat and $Z = 0$ if Republican; $\alpha = \mu_R$, $\beta = \mu_D - \mu_R$ **b.** Test $H_0: \beta = 0$
15a. $Z_1 = 1$ if NE and $Z_1 = 0$ otherwise; $Z_2 = 1$ if NW and $Z_2 = 0$ otherwise; $Z_3 = 1$ if SW and $Z_3 = 0$ otherwise
b. $E(Y) = \alpha + \beta_1 Z_1 + \beta_2 Z_2 + \beta_3 Z_3$; α = Mean lot size in SE; β_1 = Difference in mean lot size between NE and SE; β_2 = Difference in mean lot size between NW and SE; β_3 = Difference in mean lot size between SW and SE
c. $\hat{Y} = 9 - Z_1 + 6Z_2 + 2Z_3$

d.

SOURCE	DF	SUM OF SQUARES	MEAN SQUARE	F VALUE	PROB > F	ROOT MSE
REGRESSION	3	2700	900	180	P < .001	2.24
ERROR	296	1480	5			
TOTAL	299	4180				

PARAMETER	ESTIMATE
INTERCEPT	9
Z1	-1
Z2	6
Z3	2

18a.

10	10	10
20	20	20
5	5	5

b.

10	15	25
5	10	20
30	35	45

c.

10	15	25
5	20	10
20	10	30

d.

22	22	22
22	22	22
22	22	22

19. No   **20.** No
21a. $E(Y) = \alpha + \beta_1 Z_1 + \beta_2 Z_2 + \delta_1 U_1 + \delta_2 U_2$ **b.** $E(Y) = \alpha + \beta_1 Z_1 + \beta_2 Z_2 + \delta_1 U_1 + \delta_2 U_2 + \gamma_1(U_1 Z_1) + \gamma_2(U_1 Z_2) + \gamma_3(U_2 Z_1) + \gamma_4(U_2 Z_2)$
22b.

SEX	RACE	$\hat{Y}$
M	W	19
M	B	12
W	W	13
W	B	10

25a. $E(Y) = \alpha + \beta_1 Z_1 + \delta_1 U_1 + \delta_2 U_2 + \gamma_1(U_1 Z_1) + \gamma_2(U_2 Z_1)$, where $Z_1 = 1$ if male and $Z_1 = 0$ if female; $U_1 = 1$ if married and $U_1 = 0$ otherwise; $U_2 = 1$ if never married and $U_2 = 0$ otherwise **b.** Sample size = 206

26a.

DIVISION	MEN	WOMEN
Humanities	26,400	26,600
Natural science	28,733	29,000
Overall	27,800	27,000

for instance, for men, $\dfrac{20(26,400) + 30(28,733)}{50} = 27,800$

28. b **29.** a, b, c, d **30.** c **31.** c, e, f **32.** c, d
33a. $\chi^2 = 3.6$ (df = 2); do not reject H_0 **b.** $W = 3.54$ (df = 1); reject H_0 **d.** Moderate
34a. Republican: slightly decrease; Democrat: slightly increase; Independent: remain same
b. $T = .943$, $W = 14.5$ (df = 2), $P < .001$
35. $W = 5.2$, df = 1, $P < .05$ ***36a.** 45 **b.** 6 **c.** 780
*37. Republican − Democrat: $z = -3.69$, reject H_0; Republican − Independent: $z = -2.73$, reject H_0;
Democrat − Independent: $z = 1.49$, do not reject H_0; R $\underline{\text{I}}$ D ***39.** Yes, there would be enough information.
*40a. $1 - (.95)^5 = .226$ **b.** .9898

Chapter 14

1a. $13 - 10 = 3$ **c.** $-.6$ **6.** a **7.** a, d
8b. $SSE_c = 820$, $SSE_r = 860$, $F = 2.05$ (df$_1$ = 2, df$_2$ = 84); do not reject H_0 **c.** Single: $\hat{Y} = 8 + .3X$, $\hat{Y} = 17.0$ at $X = 30$; married: $\hat{Y} = 9 + .3X$, $\hat{Y} = 18.0$; divorced: $\hat{Y} = 7 + .3X$, $\hat{Y} = 16.0$ **d.** $SSE_c = 860$, $SSE_r = 1,200$, $F = 17$ (df$_1$ = 2, df$_2$ = 86); reject H_0 and conclude that at least one difference exists. Married − single: $d_1 = 1.0$ ($1,000); divorced − single: $d_2 = -1.0$; married − divorced: $d_1 - d_2 = 2.0$;

LEVEL	UNADJUSTED MEANS	ADJUSTED MEANS
Single	15.8	18.5
Married	21.9	19.5
Divorced	17.8	17.5

10. $\hat{Y} = 2.78 + .74X - 1.31Z_1 - 2.85Z_2$; Anglo: $-4.09 + .74X$; Black: $5.63 + .74X$; Mexican-American: $-2.78 + .74X$
11. $\hat{Y} = -8.25 + .88X + 6.97Z_1 + 9.80Z_2 - .17(XZ_1) - .28(XZ_2)$; Anglo: $\hat{Y} = -1.28 + .71X$; Black: $\hat{Y} = 1.55 + .60X$; Mexican-American: $\hat{Y} = -8.25 + .88X$ **12.** $\hat{Y} = -3.72 + .73X$
13. $SSE_c = 619.38$, $SSE_r = 673.17$, $F = 1.48$ (df$_1$ = 2, df$_2$ = 34); do not reject H_0 **14.** Same as Problem 13
15. $SSE_c = 673.17$, $SSE_r = 713.25$, $F = 1.07$ (df$_1$ = 2, df$_2$ = 36); do not reject H_0 **16.** Same as Problem 15
17.

LEVEL	ADJUSTED MEANS	UNADJUSTED MEANS
Anglo	40.6	52.3
Black	39.1	31.0
Mexican-American	41.9	26.6

18. Anglo − Black: $(-4.8, 7.8)$; Mexican − Anglo: $(-6.3, 8.9)$; Mexican-American − Black: $(-2.4, 8.0)$
19. $r^2_{YX \cdot Z} = \dfrac{2,990.60 - 673.17}{2,990.60} = .775$; $r_{YX \cdot Z} = .880$; $r_{YX} = .958$ **20.** $t = 11.1$ (df = 36), $P < .005$
21. $F = 34.76$ (df$_1$ = 2, df$_2$ = 37); reject H_0
*22. $E(Y) = \alpha + \beta X + \delta_1 Z_1 + \delta_2 Z_2 + \lambda_1 U_1 + \lambda_2 U_2 + \lambda_3 U_3$, where $U_1 = 1$ (urban), $U_1 = 0$ (otherwise); $U_2 = 1$ (suburban), $U_2 = 0$ (otherwise); $U_3 = 1$ (small town), $U_3 = 0$ (otherwise)

*23. $E(Y) = \alpha + \beta_1 X_1 + \beta_2 X_2 + \delta_1 Z_1 + \delta_2 Z_2$, where X_2 = percentage of residents owning home
24. Whites: 12.0; Blacks: 12.6
25a. $\hat{Y} = 10.625 + 6.597Z$ **b.** $F = 6.21$ ($df_1 = 1$, $df_2 = 42$), $P = .0168$ **c.** $\hat{Y} = -1.394 + 1.012X + 5.712Z$
d. $\hat{Y} = .973 + .813X + 2.544Z + .262(XZ)$; 4.6 at $X = 8$, 6.7 at $X = 16$; difference increases as X increases
e. $F = .18$ ($df_1 = 1$, $df_2 = 40$), $P = .6774$ (or $t = .42$)   **f.** $\bar{Y}'_W = 17.06$, $\bar{Y}'_B = 11.35$; the difference of 5.71 is slightly
smaller than the difference of 6.6 obtained when education is ignored instead of controlled.   **g.** (1.2, 10.2)
i. $F = 6.10$ ($df_1 = 1$, $df_2 = 41$), $P = .0178$ (or $t = 2.47$)
*26c. $F = 1.50$ ($df_1 = 2$, $df_2 = 95$), $P > .05$ **f.** $F = 1.55$ ($df_1 = 6$, $df_2 = 89$), $P > .05$
*27b. Church attendance   **d.** Male sex, black race, Jewish religion   **e.** A white, old female who is low in education,
lives in the South, attends church frequently, is a member of a fundamentalist Protestant sect, and is intolerant of free
speech
*28b. $\hat{Y} = 4.6 + .2X + 2.5Z_1 + .2Z_2$ **c.** $SSE_c = 152.5$, $SSE_r = 315$, $F = 32.5$ ($df_1 = 2$, $df_2 = 61$); reject H_0
d. A − B: (1.0, 3.6); A − C: (.9, 4.1); B − C: (−1.1, 1.5)   **e.** $r_{YX} = .363$; $r_{YX \cdot Z} = .624$

Chapter 15

1a. $X = 28$ **b.** Above $28,000   **c. i.** .29   **ii.** .40   **iii.** .75   **d.** The estimated odds of voting Republican is
multiplied by 1.05 for every $1,000 increase in income.
2. $z = 2.78$, $P = .0027$. There is strong evidence that the probability of voting for the Republican candidate increases as
family income increases.   **3a.** The odds is multiplied by 1.45.   **b.** The odds is multiplied by 1.25.   **c.** 1.22
4a. The estimated odds are multiplied by: **i.** .92   **ii.** 1.08   **iii.** .85   **iv.** 2.39   **b. i.** .88   **ii.** .69   **iii.** .27
c. df = 12; model fits adequately   **d.** (AS, AR, AP, SRP)   **e.** $\log\left(\dfrac{\pi_{ijk}}{1 - \pi_{ijk}}\right) = \mu + \lambda_j^R + \lambda_k^P$
f. Difference in G^2 is 1.2, df = 1; sex does not have a significant effect.
5a. i. (A, B, C, D)   **ii.** (AB, C, D)   **iii.** (AB, AC, AD, BC, BD, CD)   **b.** $\log\left(\dfrac{\pi_{ijk}}{1 - \pi_{ijk}}\right) = \mu + \lambda_i^A + \lambda_j^B$
6a. Income–Sex: $\theta = 1.0$ each table; Income–College: $\theta = 6.0$ each table; Sex–College: $\theta = 6.0$ each table
b. (IC, SC)   **c.** $\log\left(\dfrac{\pi_{ij}}{1 - \pi_{ij}}\right) = \mu + \lambda_j^C$ **d.** $\theta = 2.0$
7a.

686	1,180
468	1,259

b. $\hat{\theta} = 1.56$; males

8a. $G^2 = 539.46$ for model (A, SD), df = 9; poor fit   **b.** $\log\left(\dfrac{\pi_{ij}}{1 - \pi_{ij}}\right) = \mu$, where π_{ij} is probability of being
admitted for sex i and department j
9a. $G^2 = 2.68$ for (AD, SD), df = 5; good fit   **b.** $\log\left(\dfrac{\pi_{ij}}{1 - \pi_{ij}}\right) = \mu + \lambda_j^D$ **c.** 1.0; no
10a. $G^2 = 2.55$ for (AD, SD, AS), df = 4; good fit   **b.** Difference in G^2 is .13, df = 5 − 4 = 1; model (AD, SD) is
adequate   **c.** The causal diagram $S \rightarrow D \rightarrow A$ is consistent with the data.
11a. (XZ, YZ)   **b.** (XZ, YZ)   **c.** (XZ, YZ)   **d.** (XY, XZ, YZ)   **e.** (XYZ)
*13. (1.19, 6.94)

INDEX

Text designer: Janet Bollow
Cover designer: John Williams
Technical artists: Ben Turner Graphics
Editor and production coordinator: Susan Reiland
Typesetter: Typeset in 9/12 Helvetica Light
          by Jonathan Peck Typographers, Ltd.